EVERYTHING
YOU KNOW
ABOUT **GOD**
IS **WRONG**

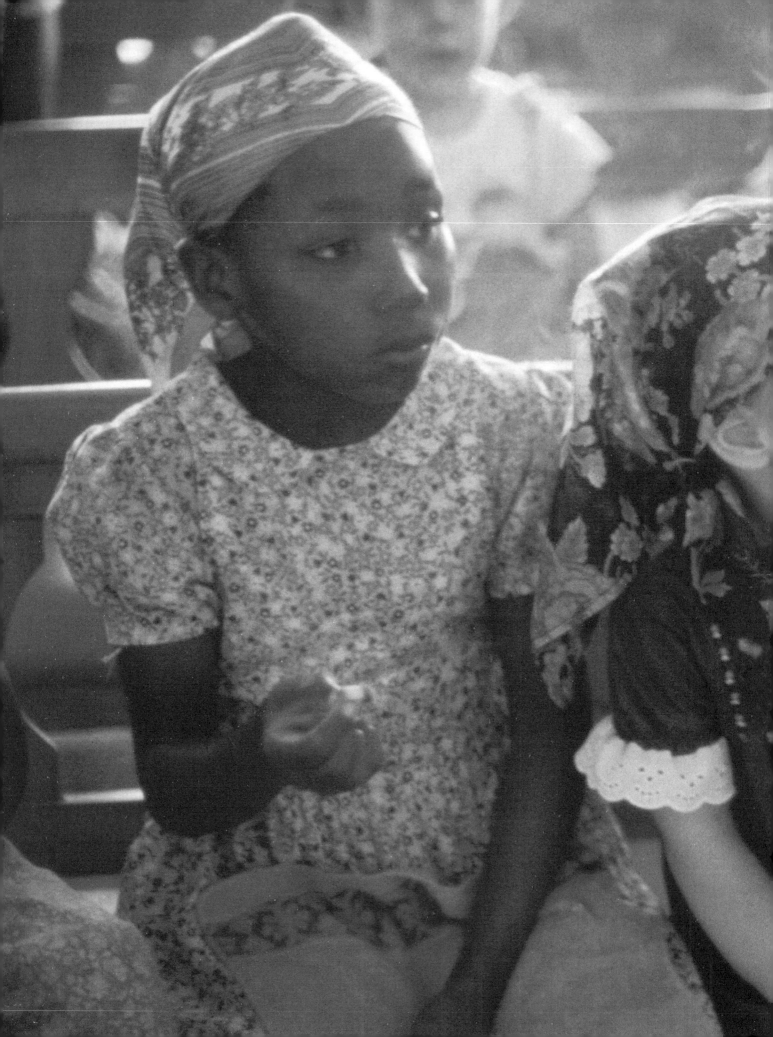

Service being held at the Ethiopian Zion Coptic Church near Kingston, Jamaica. The church is a Christian sect. Its sacrament is marijuana ("the weed of wisdom, angel's food, the tree of life"), which, when smoked, is a burning "sacrifice" to Jesus. Credit: Daniel Laine, Cosmos Photo Press Agency.

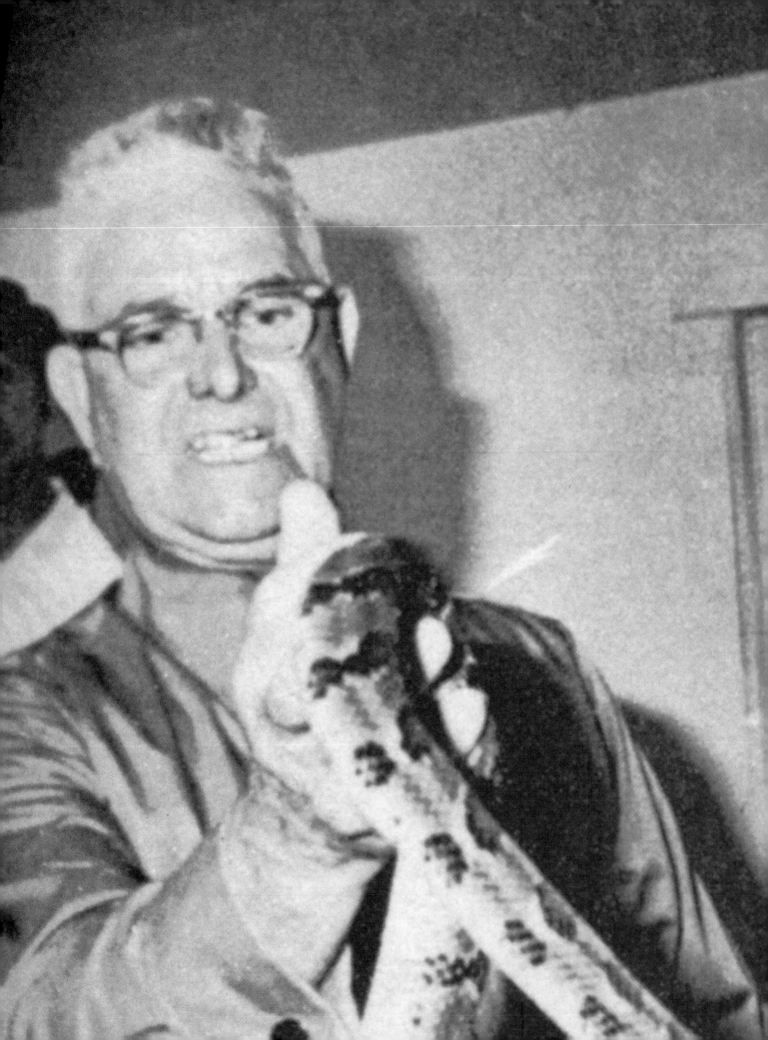

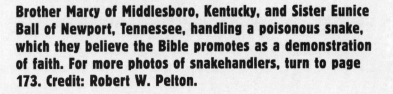

Brother Marcy of Middlesboro, Kentucky, and Sister Eunice Ball of Newport, Tennessee, handling a poisonous snake, which they believe the Bible promotes as a demonstration of faith. For more photos of snakehandlers, turn to page 173. Credit: Robert W. Pelton.

Published by The Disinformation Company Ltd.
163 Third Avenue, Suite 108
New York, NY 10003
Tel.: +1.212.691.1605
Fax: +1.212.691.1606
www.disinfo.com

Cover: Chika Azuma
Layout: Hedi El Kholti

Library of Congress Control Number: 2007930618

ISBN-10: 1-932857-59-1
ISBN-13: 978-1932857-59-7

Printed in USA

10 9 8 7 6 5 4 3 2 1

Distributed in the USA and Canada by:
Consortium Book Sales and Distribution
Toll Free: +1.800.283.3572 Local: +1.651.221.9035
Fax: +1.651.221.0124
www.cbsd.com

Distributed in the United Kingdom and Eire by: Virgin Books
Tel.: +44.(0)20.7386.3300 Fax: +44.(0)20.7386.3360
E-Mail: sales@virgin-books.co.uk

Distributed in Australia by: Tower Books
Tel.: +61.2.9975.5566 Fax: +61.2.9975.5599
E-Mail: info@towerbooks.com.au

Attention colleges and universities, corporations and other organizations: Quantity discounts are available on bulk purchases of this book for educational training purposes, fund-raising, or gift-giving. Special books, booklets, or book excerpts can also be created to fit your specific needs. For information contact Marketing Department of The Disinformation Company Ltd.

Disinformation is a registered trademark of The Disinformation Company Ltd.

The opinions and statements made in this book are those of the authors concerned. The Disinformation Company Ltd. has not verified and neither confirms nor denies any of the foregoing and no warranty or fitness is implied. The reader is encouraged to keep an open mind and to independently judge the contents.

EVERYTHING YOU KNOW ABOUT GOD IS WRONG

Edited by Russ Kick

disinformation®

CONTENTS

INTRODUCTION

SO WHAT WILL YOU FIND when I assemble and Disinformation publishes one of our patented huge anthologies, with the theme being religion? The proceedings open with a trinity of articles—from Richard Dawkins, James A. Haught, and Douglas Rushkoff—looking at the general problems inherent in religious belief. From this foundation, we jump right into several of the ways in which religion is presently grating its nails down society's chalkboard—from posting an old list of rules for late-Bronze-Age Israelites in public places to the decades-long cover-up of priests who rape children. The Buckners, a father-son team, demonstrate that the US simply was not founded on Christianity, and Douglas Rushkoff gives first-hand accounts of institutionalized Judaism's attempts to smother itself. Nasrin Alavi sounds a note of some hope regarding a possible Islamic Reformation beginning in Iran.

Next up, four steely-eyed looks at the Bible. Ruth Hurmence Green's long article irreparably destroys the lovely image of Jesus by doing the most straightforward thing imaginable: reading the New Testament, particularly the Gospels, and relaying what they say. And if you've wondered who actually wrote the Gospels traditionally accorded to Matthew, Mark, Luke, and John, Gary Greenberg's article will be, shall we say, a revelation. Bobbie Kirkhart examines the pretzels peo-

ple make of themselves while trying to take the Bible literally (except when they don't want to). And what would a look at "the good book" be without an illustrated story from it? You know, the kind you find in dentists' offices. Except that they never contain the gang rape, murder, and dismemberment of the Book of Judges chapter 19, presented by none other than Neil Gaiman and Steve Gibson.

The next section, bearing the pulpesque title "I Was There!," presents spine-tingling, nail-biting accounts of a jihad-oriented Muslim students' conference, a blood-thirsty Christian church, a new religious movement's weekend retreat, and a Macumba ceremony, complete with animal sacrifice. Two photo essays present startling images of religious relics, places, and rituals.

After that, Dianna Narciso, Greta Christina, and Paul Krassner discuss their nonbelief in a supreme being, which segues nicely into the following section, which looks at a few things that people have done in the name of God and prophecy, from cursing enemies to enslaving attractive women.

Because I'm constitutionally incapable of editing an anthology that doesn't deal to some degree with sex, prepare yourself for four articles on "The Most Popular Sin." The first two give us Eastern approaches, with a literal look at the explicit statues on Hindu temples and a sampling of the erotic verses crafted by one of the Dalai Lamas. In the second set, Christianity gets exposed when Jack Murnighan unearths a surprising medieval poem and Kristan Lawson finds something very peculiar on Christianity's most sacred altar.

From there, we turn to music and books. In the anthology's longest article, Dan Barker provides an epic look at the nonbelievers who gave us much of the world's greatest music through classical compositions and the Great American Songbook. You'll find some *very* familiar names. Then David V. Barrett and Michael Standaert read between the lines of two of the all-time most successful religious publishing phenomena: *The Da Vinci Code* and the *Left Behind* series.

Our history lessons open with Bill Brent's breezy look at the surprising nexus of religion and bowling, then becomes deadly serious when Michael Parenti strips away the romance and sugar-coating from Tibet's theocratic history.

Robert Damon Schneck entertains us with the true tale of a nineteenth-century man who took it upon himself to *build* a messiah, and Erik Davis brings us up to recent times by examining California's role as religious Petri dish.

We conclude with an unthemed collection of odds and ends, including H.G. Wells' surprising conversation with Jesus, an examination of the underappreciated roles of feces and urine in religious worship, Bejamin Radford's drubbing of exorcisms, and a collection of religion-related notes found by everyday folks. At the very end, I offer up mini-essays on a number of topics—from the long-running theological debate about exactly *how* the Virgin Mary got pregnant to the movie that triggered a major, though largely forgotten terrorist incident in the US—and book reviews covering, among other things, Jesus' penis in Renaissance art, Mark Twain's takedown of Christianity, the Islamic slave trade, the myth of Confucius, and the real creator of the word *scientology*.

The beliefs (or lack thereof) of any contributor cannot be assumed simply because he or she appears in this anthology. If a contributor reveals his or her beliefs in the course of an article, that's obviously a different matter, but simply appearing here is not an indication of affiliation.

Similarly, bear in mind that no contributor necessarily agrees with the other contributors. In fact, I'm sure some would get into arguments if invited to the same dinner party. So, inclusion is not an indication of collusion.

1

IN THE BEGINNING

Richard Dawkins

GERIN OIL

GERIN OIL (or Geriniol, to give it its scientific name) is a powerful drug which acts directly on the central nervous system to produce a range of symptoms, often of an anti-social or self-damaging nature. It can permanently modify the child brain to produce adult disorders, including dangerous delusions which are hard to treat. The four doomed flights of September 11, 2001, were Gerin Oil trips: All nineteen of the hijackers were high on the drug at the time. Historically, Geriniolism was responsible for atrocities such as the Salem witch hunts and the massacres of Native South Americans by conquistadores. Gerin Oil fueled most of the wars of the European Middle Ages and, in more recent times, the carnage that attended the partitioning of the Indian subcontinent and of Ireland.

Gerin Oil intoxication can drive previously sane individuals to run away from a normally fulfilled human life and retreat to closed communities of confirmed addicts. These communities are usually limited to one sex only, and they vigorously, often obsessively, forbid sexual activity. Indeed, a tendency towards agonized sexual prohibition emerges as a drably recurring theme amid all the colorful variations of Gerin Oil symptomatology. Gerin Oil does not seem to reduce the libido per se, but it frequently leads to a preoccupation with reducing the sexual pleasure of others. A current example is the prurience with which many habitual "Oilers" condemn homosexuality.

As with other drugs, refined Gerin Oil in low doses is largely harmless and can serve as a lubricant on social occasions, such as marriages, funerals, and state ceremonies. Experts differ over whether such social tripping, though harmless in itself, is a risk factor for upgrading to harder and more addictive forms of the drug.

> **Oil-heads can be heard talking to thin air or muttering to themselves, apparently in the belief that private wishes so expressed will come true, even at the cost of other people's welfare and the mild violation of the laws of physics.**

Medium doses of Gerin Oil, though not in themselves dangerous, can distort perceptions of reality. Beliefs that have no basis in fact are immunized, by the drug's direct effects on the nervous system, against evidence from the real world. Oil-heads can be heard talking to thin air or muttering to themselves, apparently in the belief that private wishes so expressed will come true, even at the cost of other people's welfare and the mild violation of the laws of physics. This autolocutory disorder is often accompanied by weird tics and hand gestures,

Chronic abuse of Geriniol can lead to "bad trips" in which the user suffers terrifying delusions, including fears of being tortured, not in the real world but in a postmortem fantasy world.

manic stereotypes such as rhythmic head-nodding toward a wall, or "Obsessive Compulsive Orientation Syndrome" (OCOS: facing towards the east five times a day).

Gerin Oil in strong doses is hallucinogenic. Hardcore mainliners may hear voices in the head or experience visual illusions which seem to the sufferers so real that they often succeed in persuading others of their reality. An individual who convincingly reports high-grade hallucinations may be venerated, even followed as some kind of leader, by others who regard themselves as less fortunate. Such follower-pathology can long postdate the original leader's death and may expand into bizarre psychedelia, such as the cannibalistic fantasy of "drinking the blood and eating the flesh" of the leader.

Chronic abuse of Geriniol can lead to "bad trips" in which the user suffers terrifying delusions, including fears of being tortured, not in the real world but in a postmortem fantasy world. Bad trips of this kind are bound up with a morbid punishment-lore, which is as characteristic of this drug as the obsessive fear of sexuality already noted. The punishment-culture fostered by Gerin Oil ranges from "smack" through "lash" to getting "stoned" (especially adulteresses and rape victims), and "demanifestation" (amputation of one hand), up to the sinister fantasy of allo-punishment or "cross-topping," the execution of one individual for the sins of others.

You might think that such a potentially dangerous and addictive drug would head the list of proscribed intoxicants, with exemplary sentences handed out for pushing it. But no, it is readily obtainable anywhere in the world, and you don't even need a prescription. Professional traffickers are numerous and organized in hierarchical cartels, openly trading on street corners and in purpose-made buildings. Some of these cartels are adept at fleecing poor people desperate to feed their habit. "Godfathers" occupy influ-

ential positions in high places, and they have the ear of royalty, of presidents and prime ministers. Governments don't just turn a blind eye to the trade; they grant it tax-exempt status. Worse, they subsidize schools founded with the specific intention of getting children hooked.

I WAS PROMPTED to write this article by the smiling face of a happy man in Bali. He was ecstatically greeting his death sentence for the brutal murder of large numbers of innocent holidaymakers whom he had never met and against whom he bore no personal grudge. Some people in the court were shocked at his lack of remorse. Far from remorse, his response was one of obvious exhilaration. He punched the air, delirious with joy that he was to be "martyred," to use the jargon of his group of abusers. Make no mistake about it, that beatific smile, looking forward with unalloyed pleasure to the firing squad, is the smile of a junkie. Here we have the archetypal mainliner, doped up with hard, unrefined, unadulterated, high-octane Gerin Oil.

Governments don't just turn a blind eye to the trade; they grant it tax-exempt status.

Whatever your view of the vengeance and deterrence theories of capital punishment, it should be obvious that this case is special. Martyrdom is a strange revenge against those who crave it, and, far from deterring, it always recruits more martyrs than it kills. The important point is that the problem would not arise in the first place if children were protected from getting hooked on a drug with such a bad prognosis for their adult minds.

James A. Haught

EVERYONE'S A SKEPTIC—ABOUT OTHER RELIGIONS

RELIGION IS AN EXTREMELY touchy topic. Church members often become angry if anyone questions their supernatural dogmas. (Bertrand Russell said this is because they subconsciously sense that their beliefs are irrational.) So I try to avoid confrontations that can hurt feelings. Nearly everyone wants to be courteous.

But sometimes disputes can't be avoided. If you think the spirit realm is imaginary, and if honesty makes you say so, you may find yourself under attack. It has happened to many doubters: Thomas Jefferson was called a "howling atheist." Leo Tolstoy was labeled an "impious infidel."

Well, if you wind up in a debate, my advice is: Try to be polite. Don't let tempers flare, if you can help it. Appeal to your accuser's intelligence.

I've hatched some questions you may find useful. They're designed to show that church members, even the most ardent worshipers, are skeptics, too—because they doubt every magical system except their own. If a churchman berates you, perhaps you could reply like this:

You're an unbeliever, just like me. You doubt many sacred dogmas. Let me show you:

• Millions of Hindus pray over statues of Shiva's penis. Do you think there's an invisible Shiva who wants his penis prayed over—or are you a skeptic?

• Mormons say that Jesus came to America after his resurrection. Do you agree—or are you a doubter?

• Santería worshipers sacrifice dogs, goats, chickens, etc., and toss their bodies into waterways. Do you think Santería gods want animals killed—or are you skeptical?

• Muslim suicide bombers who blow themselves up are taught that "martyrs" instantly go to a paradise full of lovely female *houri* nymphs. Do you think the bombers now are in heaven with *houri*—or are you a doubter?

You're an unbeliever, just like me. You doubt many sacred dogmas.

• Unification Church members think that Jesus visited Rev. Sun Myung Moon and told him to convert all people as "Moonies." Do you believe this sacred tenet of the Unification Church?

• Jehovah's Witnesses say that, any day now, exactly 144,000 of them will be physically lifted to heaven, where they will reign with Jesus Christ. Do you believe this solemn teaching of their church?

• Aztecs skinned maidens and cut out human hearts for a feathered serpent-god. What's your stand on invisible, feathered serpents? Aha!—just as I suspected, you don't believe.

• Catholics are taught that the Communion wafer and wine magically become the actual, literal body and blood of Jesus during chants and bell-ringing. Do you believe in the "real presence"—or are you a disbeliever?

• Faith-healer Ernest Angley says he has the power, described in the Bible, to "discern spirits," which enables him to see demons inside sick people and to see angels hovering at his revivals. Do you believe this religious assertion?

• The Bible says that people who work on the Sabbath must be killed: "Whosoever doeth any work in the sabbath day, he shall surely be put to death" (Exodus 31:15). Should we execute Sunday-workers—or do you doubt this scripture?

• At a golden temple in West Virginia, saffron-robed worshipers think they'll become one with Lord Krishna if they chant "Hare Krishna" enough. Do you agree—or do you doubt it?

• Members of the Heaven's Gate commune said they could "shed their containers" (i.e., their bodies) and be transported to a UFO behind the Hale-Bopp comet. Do you think they're now on that UFO—or are you a skeptic?

• During the witch hunts, inquisitor priests tortured thousands of women into confessing that they blighted crops, had sex with Satan, etc.—then executed them for it. Do you think the Church was right to enforce the Bible's command, "Thou shalt not suffer a witch to live" (Exodus 22:18)—or do you doubt this scripture?

• Members of Spiritualist churches say they talk with the dead during their worship services. Do you think they actually communicate with spirits of deceased people?

• Millions of American Pentecostals spout "the unknown tongue," a spontaneous outpouring of sounds. They say it's the Holy Ghost, the third part of the Trinity, speaking through them. Do you believe this sacred tenet of many Americans?

• Scientologists say each human has something akin to a soul, which is a "Thetan" that came from another planet. Do you believe their doctrine—or doubt it?

• Ancient Greeks thought a multitude of gods lived on Mt. Olympus—and some of today's New Agers think invisible Lemurians live inside Mt. Shasta. What's your position on mountain gods—belief or disbelief?

• In the mountains of West Virginia, some people obey Christ's farewell command that true believers "shall take up serpents" (Mark 16:18). They pick up rattlesnakes at church services. Do you believe this scripture, or not?

• India's Thugs thought the many-armed goddess Kali wanted them to strangle human sacrifices. Do you think there's an invisible goddess who wants people strangled—or are you a disbeliever?

• Tibet's Buddhists say that when an old Lama dies, his spirit enters a baby boy who's just being born somewhere. So they remain leaderless for a dozen years or more, then they find a boy who seems to have knowledge of the old Lama's private life, and they anoint the boy as the new Lama (actually the old Lama in a new body). Do you think that dying Lamas fly into new babies, or not?

What's your stand on invisible, feathered serpents?

• In China in the mid-1800s, a Christian convert said God appeared to him, told him he was Jesus' younger brother, and commanded him to "destroy demons." He raised an army of believers who waged the Taiping Rebellion that killed as many as 20 million people. Do you think he was Christ's brother—or do you doubt it?

Etc., etc. You get the picture.

I'll bet there isn't a church member anywhere who doesn't think that all those supernatural beliefs are goofy—except for the one he believes.

You see, by going through a laundry list of theologies, I think you can establish that the average Christian doubts 99 percent of the world's holy dogmas. But the 1 percent he believes is really no different than the rest. It's a system of miraculous claims without any reliable evidence to support it.

So, if we can show people that some sacred "truths" are nutty, maybe subconscious logic will seep through, and they'll realize that if some magical beliefs are irrational, all may be.

This progression is rather like a scene in the poignant Peter de Vries novel *The Blood of the Lamb*. A gushy woman compliments a Jew because "your people" reduced the many gods of polytheism to just one god. The man dourly replies: "Which is just a step from the truth."

Meanwhile, it's encouraging to realize that almost everyone in the world is a skeptic—at least about other people's religion.

Douglas Rushkoff

FAITH = ILLNESS

WHY I'VE HAD IT WITH RELIGIOUS TOLERANCE

OKAY, SO LET'S GET INTO this God game.

I think it's time to get serious about the role God plays in human affairs and evaluate whether it's appropriate to let everyone in on the bad news: God doesn't exist, never did, and the closest thing we'll ever see to God will emerge from our own collective efforts at making meaning.

Maybe I'm just getting old, but I no longer see the real value in being tolerant of other people's beliefs. Sure, when beliefs are relegated to the realm of pure entertainment, they pose no real danger. So, a kid believes U2 is really a supergroup on par with the Beatles or the Who. That's *his* problem, and it doesn't really do a lot of harm to anyone except those of us who still stop by MTV occasionally to see what might be playing.

When religions are practiced, as they are by a majority of those in most developed nations today, as a kind of nostalgic little ritual—a community event or an excuse to get together and not work—it doesn't really screw anything up too badly. But when they radically alter our ability to contend with reality, cope with difference, or implement the most basic ethical provisions, they must be stopped.

Like any other public health crisis, the belief in religion must now be treated as a sickness. It is an epidemic, paralyzing our nation's ability to behave in a rational way, and—given our weapons capabil-ities—posing an increasingly grave threat to the rest of the world.

Just look at the numbers. A Fox News poll (no doubt inflating these figures) claims that 92 percent of Americans say they believe in God, 85 percent believe in heaven, and 71 percent believe in the devil. (That's right—the guy with horns and a tail who presides over hell. The DeNiro character in *Angel Heart*, Pacino in *The Devil's Advocate*, and the one who tricks people into signing contracts on *The Twilight Zone*.) Given Fox News'

> **They've taken the metaphors of the Bible or Dante's *Inferno* and gone ahead and decided that these images and allegories are *real*.**

accuracy, we can cut these numbers in half yet still be confronted with a deeply frightening prospect: Half the people amongst whom we walk and work everyday believe some really fucked-up shit. They've taken the metaphors of the Bible or Dante's *Inferno* and gone ahead and decided that these images and allegories are *real*.

Add to that the more reliable polls finding that 35 percent of Americans say they are "born again"—a particularly modern phenomenon that came only after the charlatan rabble-rousers during the Great Depression—and you get a picture of a nation hoodwinked into a passive, childlike, yet dogmatic relationship to the myths that were originally written to sustain them, spur their motivation to social justice, and encourage continuing evolution.

As I've always understood them, and as I try to convey them in my comic book, *Testament* (published by DC Comics/Vertigo), the stories in the Bible are less significant because they happened at some moment in history than because their underlying dynamics seem to be happening in all moments. We are all Cain, struggling with our feelings about a sibling who seems to be more blessed than we are. We are always escaping the enslaved mentality of Egypt and the idolatry we practiced there. We are all Mordechai, bristling against the pressure to bow in subservience to our bosses.

But true believers don't have this freedom. Whether it's because they need the Bible to prove a real-estate claim in the Middle East, because they don't know how to relate to something that didn't really happen, or because they require the threat of an angry super-being who sees all in order to behave like good children, true believers— what we now call fundamentalists—are not in a position to appreciate the truth and beauty of the holy scriptures. No, the multidimensional document we call the Bible is not available to them because, for them, all those stories have to be accepted as historical truth.

Forget the fact that this is pretty much impossible to do. The Bible contradicts itself all over the place. There are even two different creation stories![1] And they're less than a page apart. Forget that the myths of the Bible had already been understood as mythology by the pre-biblical cultures from which many of them came. And forget that the Bible comments on its own stories, as stories, directly![2] On numerous occasions, the narration asks its hearers whether they get the joke.[3]

That's because, for the Torah's first hearers (Torah is the first five books of the Bible), all those jokes really were jokes. They understood that Jacob's sons weren't really the fathers of the Twelve Tribes of Israel, but parodies—racist parodies, at that—of the qualities that had come to be associated with each of these existing groups. They understood that the "plagues" against Egypt were literary desecrations of the Egyptian gods. (Blood desecrates the Nile, which was a god. Locusts desecrate the corn, a god, and so on.)

That the Bible could be understood metaphorically helped people relate to its "God" metaphorically, as well. It's not that God is some character who really exists but, rather, a way of relating the events in the world as they unfold. No one can grasp this, however, if they're stuck believing.

So I think it's time for those of us who have transcended this primitive approach to collective storytelling to speak up. This liberation from belief systems is precisely what the Bible is about. A people liberate from the death of a creationist model of reality and go out into the desert to write their own laws.

It's analogous to the story of America, in fact, where a bunch of people leave religious oppression in order to write a Constitution as an evolutionary document—something that, instead of being believed in forever, is understood to be an ongoing process. A participatory event.

Right now, America's true believers are locking down its laws along with its Bible. They are fighting the science of evolution because it accepts that things change over time—and such change is incompatible with static, everlasting truths. They are doing to today's progressives the very same thing that the Bible's Egyptians were doing to the Israelites. And they're doing it in the name of a God whom they believe they'll meet when they die. This is the very mindset and behavior that the Bible was written to stop.

Perhaps the best way to kill their God, in fact, is to take charge of the Bible. It is—in my own opinion as a media theorist—the greatest story ever told, and deserving of our continued support and analysis. For my part, I'm writing *Testament*, which I hope will bring these stories—told both in their biblical context and as a near-future sci-fi fable—to people who might never before have stumbled across them.

For others—especially our friends involved in the occult arts—I'd hope they consider using some Bible imagery and characters in their work and rituals. They're just as potent as anything in the Mahabharata and far more resonant with the Western popular culture in which most of us actually grew up. For those of you looking for an authentic tradition in which to base your art, music, or fiction, consider the themes of revolution, universal justice, and mind expansion as they're depicted in allegories from Eden to Babel and characters from Joseph to Jesus.

By appropriating these characters and metaphors as our own, we instill them with the power they require to release the stranglehold that true believers have over the myths built to help us face the truth. Their success in making

Perhaps the best way to kill their God, in fact, is to take charge of the Bible.

the Bible seem like a sanctimonious tome is just another testament to the deleterious effect of surrendering one of the best books ever written about sacred magick to people whose lives depend on ignoring the possibility of escape from the nightmare of eternal bondage to a vengeful deity.

The more we can make its mythology relevant to our present, the more easily we'll bring those who believe in it out of the past.

---

1. One in which Eve is created at the same time as Adam [Genesis 1:27], and another where she is grown from his rib [Genesis 2:22].

2. The laws against incest, for example, steal words and phrasing from the story of Lot's incest with his daughters—just to be sure we know that the two sections of text refer to each other.

3. The names of cities are often followed by the then-contemporary name of the same place—just so the audience knows what's being referred to. "Now it's called so and so." Clearly, Moses, the supposed writer of this, was not aware of what cities would be called hundreds of years after his death and would not write of their names in the present tense. Another example is found in the names of characters in the book of Ruth—each based on puns of words contemporary to the hearers, but having nothing to do with the language of those being stereotyped and dissed by these plays on words.

2

CURRENT EVENTS & CONTROVERSIES

Michael E. Buckner and **Edward M. Buckner**

THE US IS A FREE COUNTRY, *NOT* A CHRISTIAN NATION

THE BASIC ARGUMENT

THE UNITED STATES IS and ought to be a free country, *not* a Christian nation. Whatever anyone says or thinks, it cannot be both. Nations, including the US, have to choose either to endorse and support a religion or to be free. We're going to explain here exactly why the choice is necessary and why the only defensible choice is to be free. Everyone, including deeply religious Christians, should agree with us. And that's not arrogance on our part, nor is it foolish one-sidedness—so let us first explain our optimism: Why should readers—some of you are probably Christians, maybe even fundamentalists—why should you listen to a pair of secular humanists (we're son and father, by the way), much less decide that we're right? (After all, there are far more Christians in the US than there are secular humanists.) You should agree with us on this for two reasons: First, you rightly pride yourselves, we bet, on being bright and open-minded, sincere searchers for the truth, as well as strong, freedom-loving, patriotic Americans (readers from elsewhere are hereby invited to be patriotic to their own nation); and second, we really are right about this.

American history supports this view, showing conclusively that we are not a Christian nation. And, as many well-documented quotations demonstrate, America's founders supported religious liberty and

understood that the government's support of any religion undermines religious freedom.

There are many "myths"—false things that many people think they know about separation of religion and government—that need to be countered. But anyone who wants to claim that our government should support Christianity (or any other religion) must explain away American history, contradict our decidedly unchristian form of government, and, finally and most crucially, demonstrate that separation of church and state is not in everyone's best interest.

THE HISTORY PART OF OUR ARGUMENT

You might think that a country can be a "Christian nation," that it can do without "separation of church and state," and still be free, even for non-Christians. After all, some European states have vestigial establishments of religion, but no one is persecuted in England, for example, for not supporting the Church of England. But the actual history of the entanglement of religion and the state should disabuse anyone of that view. It was less than eighty years from the Emperor Constantine's proclamation that Christians were to have freedom of worship in the Roman Empire to Emperor Theodosius' proclamation that no one else did. Thereafter, for 1,300 years, Christian rulers engaged in crusades against

An infamous example of Protestant evil, an example given by Thomas Jefferson, is the execution of Michael Servetus.

"heathens," heretics, and most notoriously, Muslims; carried out forced conversions of entire populations; sought to control the Church or were controlled by it; tortured and executed "witches"; and set up special courts to hunt down religious dissenters (the notorious "inquisitions"). When major theological divisions among Christians appeared, persecution turned into war and massacre, from the bloody thirteenth-century Albigensian Crusade against the Cathars of southern France, to the French Wars of Religion in the sixteenth century and the infamous St. Bartholomew's Day Massacre of the French Protestants by French Catholics, to the Thirty Years' War between Catholic and Protestant princes that practically depopulated large areas of Germany in the seventeenth century.

The Catholic Inquisition is well-known for its persecutions, but the Protestants were no better. An infamous example of Protestant evil, an example given by Thomas Jefferson, is the execution of Michael Servetus. A Spanish physician, Servetus wrote that the doctrine of the Trinity makes no sense, that it contradicts the idea that there is only one God. Servetus was condemned to die by the Catholic Inquisition, but he wasn't present, so they couldn't kill him. He had fled to Protestant Switzerland, expecting to be protected there. Instead, the city leaders in Geneva, with the approval of John Calvin (one of the great fathers of Protestant thought) and other Protestant leaders across Europe, had Servetus burned alive (with green wood to give him longer to repent) in 1553.

When not persecuting their fellow Christians for practicing the wrong kind of Christianity, Christians would often turn against the adherents of Christianity's parent religion, Judaism. In 1290 Edward I of England decreed that every Jew in England be expelled from the kingdom (they weren't officially allowed to return for over 360 years). In 1306 King Philip "the Fair" followed suit in France. In 1492 Ferdinand and Isabella did the same for Spain. European Christians sometimes did worse than merely forcing their Jewish brethren from their homes; during the Crusades, Christians massacred Jews by the thousands, incited by the "blood libel"—false stories that the Jews were carrying out sacrifices of Christian infants—and by rumors that the Jews had secret rites in which they ritually desecrated the sacred objects of the Christian religion.

The American colonies did not escape this terrible history of religious persecution. The Puritans came to America to have freedom to practice their religion, then persecuted Quakers. Nineteen "witches" were hanged (in Salem); other people had holes bored in their tongues for "blasphemy" in colonial Massachusetts. In Virginia just before the Revolution, Episcopalians (who were then in charge) threw Baptist preachers in jail for the "crime" of telling people to read the Bible for themselves. There were bright spots, though. The Baptist preacher Roger Williams led the colony of Rhode

The Puritans came to America to have freedom to practice their religion, then persecuted Quakers.

Island to champion religious freedom for all—and called for separation of church and state. Quaker Pennsylvania was also an early champion of religious tolerance. Intended as a haven for Catholics (persecuted in Protestant England), Maryland allowed for at least a limited form of religious toleration. By the eve of the American Revolution, many in the thirteen colonies were ready to reject not only European views on government but also views on the relationship of Christianity to the state, which had existed for centuries in Christian Europe. Angered and horrified by the legal persecution of Baptist preachers in his native Virginia, James Madison, the "father of the Constitution," wrote in 1774: "Religious bondage shackles and debilitates the mind and unfits it for every noble enterprise, every expanded prospect."

As for those vestigial establishments in Europe, that's what they are: the last vestiges of a dying past of religious persecution. After the Reformation, Catholics and Protestants in England alternated in martyring each other for practicing their respective forms of Christianity; even as late as the nineteenth century, Britain discriminated against both Catholics and Protestant "dissenters" from the Established Church, who couldn't be elected to Parliament and weren't permitted to attend the great universities in Oxford and Cambridge. Although the nineteenth century saw an end to such practices, centuries of British religious policy in Ireland helped lay the foundation for the sectarian violence that plagued that country for much of the twentieth century. The last remnants of religious establishmentarianism no longer lead to violence or injustice in Britain only because Britain's Jews, Catholics, and dissenting Protestants have struggled for generations to render establishment a quaint and toothless relic. Britain's example hardly recommends religious establishment as a path to civic peace.

With these words, the founders of the US swept away nearly 1,500 years of European Christian political thought.

Because the Declaration of Independence does refer to God (albeit with the term "Creator"), the religious right loves to quote from it, but we can't be blind to the fact that the Declaration was a radical document. In fact, its theory of government, though not atheistic or *secular* humanist, was literally revolutionary:

> We hold these truths to be self-evident, that all men are created equal, that they are endowed by their Creator with certain unalienable Rights, that among these are Life, Liberty and the pursuit of Happiness.
> — That to secure these rights, Governments are instituted among Men, deriving their just powers from the consent of the governed,
> — That whenever any Form of Government becomes destructive of these ends, it is the Right of the People to alter or to abolish it, and to institute new Government, laying its foundation on such principles and organizing its powers in such form, as to them shall seem most likely to effect their Safety and Happiness.

The Constitution, invoking the authority of "We the people," doesn't even pay lip service to any divine authority.

With these words, the founders of the US swept away nearly 1,500 years of European Christian political thought: ideas of aristocracy, that some tiny segment of the people should be specially privileged above the rest; the "Divine Right of Kings," that some men are anointed by God to rule; and that the sole duty of the people is to obey their betters.

Unlike the Declaration of Independence, the Constitution of the United States *is* godless: the word "God" (like the words "Jesus," "Christ," "Christianity," "Bible," or even "Creator") simply does not appear anywhere in our country's fundamental legal document. The Constitution, invoking the authority of "We the people," doesn't even pay lip service to any divine authority. The only mention of religion in the original seven articles of the Constitution is to proclaim, in Article VI, that "no religious Test shall ever be required as a Qualification to any Office or public Trust under the United States."

The date of the Constitution at its end includes a standard Christian dating convention used on all formal documents at the time, and there is a reference to Sunday not counting as a workday for some purposes, and affirmations are declared to be acceptable substitutes for swearing, but nowhere in the body of the Constitution is there anything substantial based on any religious beliefs.

Benjamin Franklin suggested to the delegates at the Constitutional Convention that they bring in clergy to help get them past some hard disagreements, but the delegates tabled Franklin's motion and never voted on it. And this was the same Benjamin Franklin, by the way, who wrote in a letter to Richard Price, on October 9, 1780: "When a Religion is good, I conceive it will support itself; and when it does not support itself, and God does not take care to support it so that its Professors are obliged to call for help of the Civil Power, it is a sign, I apprehend, of its being a bad one."

When the Bill of Rights was added to the Constitution, it went even further: Congress was forbidden to pass any laws prohibiting the free exercise of *any* religion. Earlier colonial charters, such as Maryland's 1649 Toleration Act, had provided that anyone "professing to believe in Jesus Christ" was to be permitted to freely exercise his or her religion—but anyone denying the Christian religion was to be put to death. The Founders realized that toleration is not good enough; what they rightly demanded was religious *liberty*. As George Washington said, in a 1790 letter to the Jews of Newport, Rhode Island:

> It is now no more that toleration is spoken of as if it was by the indulgence of one class of the people that another enjoyed the exercise of their inherent natural rights. For happily the Government of the United States, which gives to bigotry no sanction, to persecution no assistance, requires only that those who live under its protection should demean themselves as good citizens in giving it, on all occasions, their effectual support.

Earlier colonial charters, such as Maryland's 1649 Toleration Act, had provided that anyone "professing to believe in Jesus Christ" was to be permitted to freely exercise his or her religion—but anyone denying the Christian religion was to be put to death.

Although most Americans unquestioningly accept the First Amendment's protection for the *free exercise* of religion, the other half of the First Amendment's edict on religion and government, the establishment clause or "separation of church and state," is more controversial. Despite what some would have you believe, there is no question that the authors of the Constitution and the Bill of Rights were unhesitatingly in favor of keeping government and religion separate. As Thomas Jefferson wrote in his 1782 book, *Notes on the State of Virginia*: "The legitimate powers of government extend to such acts only as are injurious to others. But it does me no injury for my neighbor to say there are twenty gods, or no god. It neither picks my pocket nor breaks my leg." In his 1787 work, *Defence of the Constitutions of Government of the United States of America*, John Adams declared:

Although the detail of the formation of the American governments is at present little known or regarded either in Europe or America, it may hereafter become an object of curiosity. It will never be pretended that any persons employed in that service had interviews with the gods, or were in any degree under the influence of Heaven, more than those at work upon ships or houses, or laboring in merchandise or agriculture; it will forever be acknowledged that these governments were contrived merely by the use of reason and the senses.

And James Madison, in an 1822 letter, plainly called not merely for refraining from establishing any particular denomination but for separating religion and government entirely: "And I have no doubt that every new example will succeed, as every past one has done, in shewing that religion & Gov't will both exist in greater purity, the less they are mixed together."

To sum up the history of all this and add one more telling bit of historical evidence, remember this sequence, ending in 1797: In 1776 the Declaration of Independence was issued and the Revolutionary War officially began. Eleven years later, after mounting frustration with the weak alliance of states under the Articles of Confederation, the delegates to the Constitutional Convention agreed on the US Constitution, which was then ratified in 1789.

"And I have no doubt that every new example will succeed, as every past one has done, in shewing that religion & Gov't will both exist in greater purity, the less they are mixed together." —James Madison

By November 1796, the US was near the end of George Washington's second term, and America was having problems with Muslim terrorists—seriously. These terrorists were attacking American ships in the Mediterranean, killing sailors, and stealing cargo. George Washington sent a diplomat, Joel Barlow, to see if he could appease the leaders and pirates of several Muslim countries. The leader of one of these nations, Jussof Bashaw Mahomet, the Bey of Tripoli—then a nation where Libya is now—signed a short treaty with Barlow on November 4, 1796.

The First Amendment—which says you may worship whatever God or gods you choose, in whatever manner your conscience demands, or believe in and worship no gods of any sort if that's where your reason guides you—stands in contrast to the First Commandment's dictate: "No other gods before me."

It took months to get the document back to the US, and by the time it arrived, John Adams was *President*. Adams sent the treaty to the Senate for consideration in May 1797, well over 200 years ago. The treaty was read aloud in the Senate, English copies of the treaty were printed and distributed to all Senators, and in a few weeks a committee recommended ratification.

In a rare unanimous vote, every member of the Senate who was present voted to approve it, and the Senate sent the treaty to the President. None of the careers of any of the men who voted in favor of that treaty was hurt by his support. (Many were re-elected, some became state governors, and one became Speaker of the House.) On June 10, 1797, Adams signed the treaty and declared it to be the official law of the land. Several major newspapers of the time carried the full text of the treaty, sometimes on the front page. You can hold one of those newspapers in your hands at the Library of Congress and see microfilm of several others.

It was a weak treaty, one in which the US tried to buy off the Muslims with tribute, rope, tar, money, and so on—and the treaty didn't succeed in stopping the terrorism, even temporarily. There is no record that the treaty stirred up controversy in its day, though Thomas Jefferson, who had recently been the Secretary of State, reportedly objected to the appeasement. President Jefferson, only about four years later, had to send the US Navy and Marines to the Mediterranean and wage war to get the terrorism stopped.

But what does all that have to do with this essay? The eleventh article of that treaty, written (very likely) by John Barlow, a former chaplain, is profoundly interesting. It says (emphasis added):

As the government of the United States is not in any sense founded on the Christian religion,… it is

declared by the parties that no pretext arising from religious opinion shall ever produce an interruption of harmony existing between the two countries.

The treaty, superseded a few years later, is of no lasting importance to our history, laws, nor, obviously, to our relationship with Muslim countries. It isn't needed to demonstrate that the framers of the Constitution did not set up a Christian government or intend to—the Constitution itself does that clearly. But the language of the treaty demonstrates beyond any reasonable doubt that in the years soon after the US was officially started, *everyone* understood that "the government of the United States is not in any sense founded on the Christian religion."

THE "NOT CHRISTIAN" PART OF THE ARGUMENT

Our history and the documented words of the founders and of the governing documents clearly show that American government was not designed to be Christian. But perhaps even more difficult for those who claim that the US is a Christian nation is the severe conflict between biblical Christianity and American government and society as it is now organized.

Not only was the Declaration of Independence politically radical, it was radical in religious terms, as well. We've already discussed how the Declaration explicitly denied the old doctrines of aristocracy and the "Divine Right of Kings":

That to secure these rights, Governments are instituted among Men, deriving their just powers from the consent of the governed, — That whenever any Form of Government becomes destructive of these ends, it is the Right of the People to alter or to abolish it, and to institute new Government, laying its foundation on such principles and organizing its powers in such form, as to them shall seem most likely to effect their Safety and Happiness.

These words weren't just a challenge to the power of kings; they also went against the plain text of the Bible:

Everyone must submit himself to the governing authorities, for there is no authority except that which God has established. The authorities that exist have been established by God. Consequently, he who rebels against the authority is rebelling against what God has instituted, and those who do so will bring judgment on themselves. For rulers hold no terror for those who do right, but for those who do wrong. Do you want to be free from fear of the one in authority? Then do what is right and he will commend you. For he is God's servant to do you good. But if you do wrong, be afraid, for he does not bear the sword for nothing. He is God's servant, an agent of wrath to bring punishment on the wrongdoer. Therefore, it is necessary to submit to the authorities, not only because of possible punishment but also because of conscience. This is also why you pay taxes, for the authorities are God's servants, who give their full time to governing. Give everyone what you owe him: If you owe taxes, pay taxes; if revenue, then revenue; if respect, then respect; if honor, then honor.
[Romans 13:1–7, New International Version—the version of the Bible used for all quotations in this essay.]

And the First Amendment's proclamation that there be no law abridging the free exercise of religion is a far cry from the demands of biblical law:

If your very own brother, or your son or daughter, or the wife you love, or your closest friend secretly entices you, saying, "Let us go and worship other gods" (gods that neither you nor your fathers have known, gods of the peoples around you, whether near or far, from one end of the land to the other), do not yield to him or listen to him. Show him no pity. Do not spare him or shield him. You must certainly put him to death. Your hand must be the first in putting him to death, and then the hands of all the people. Stone him to death, because he tried to turn you away from the LORD your God, who brought you out of Egypt, out of the land of slavery.

Then all Israel will hear and be afraid, and no one among you will do such an evil thing again.
[Deuteronomy 13:6–11]

The First Amendment—which says you may worship whatever God or gods you choose, in whatever manner your conscience demands, or believe in and worship no gods of any sort if that's where your reason guides you—stands in contrast to the First Commandment's dictate: "No other gods before me." Of course, Christians (and Jews) are still free to follow the First Commandment as a matter of individual conscience, but biblical laws (or Koranic ones) that would enforce one view of God over all others on pain of death can never be implemented in the United States—as long as we safeguard the unbiblical heritage of liberty bequeathed by the Founding Fathers.

The United States, with its refusal to have an official religion or national God, didn't start out very biblical, and it's gotten less biblical as time has gone on—which is a good thing in the view of nearly all Americans. One of the greatest blots on our history was the shameful legacy of some 250 years of treating other human beings as property, from colonial Jamestown right up until our bloodiest war, the Civil War. But after four years of bloodshed, the nation finally proclaimed in the Thirteenth Amendment: "Neither slavery nor involuntary servitude, except as a punishment for crime whereof the party shall have been duly convicted, shall exist within the United States, or any place subject to their jurisdiction." More generations of struggle allowed us to finally make good on the promises of equal rights for all Americans that were made after the Civil War. But ending slavery certainly wasn't the biblical thing to do. The Bible never condemns slavery, in either the Old Testament or the New; at most, the Bible calls for masters to treat their slaves kindly (Ephesians 6:9)—while calling for slaves to humbly obey their masters, as they would God himself (Ephesians 6:5–8). As for actually *freeing* all the slaves:

Your male and female slaves are to come from the nations around you; from them you may buy slaves. You may also buy some of the temporary residents living among you and members of their clans born in your country, and they will become your property. You can will them to your children as inherited property and can make them slaves for life, but you must not rule over your fellow Israelites ruthlessly. [Leviticus 25:44–46]

By the twentieth century, America had finally become a nation that acknowledged, in the Nineteenth Amendment, that men and women should be equal citizens: "the right of citizens of the United States to vote shall not be denied or abridged by the United States or by any State on account of sex." We have women as governors, as senators and representatives, as secretaries of state and ambassadors, and as corporate executives. Most Americans probably accept as a matter of course that someday the President will be a woman. But the Bible says: "A woman should learn in quietness and full submission. I do not permit a woman to teach or to have authority over a man; she must be silent" (1 Timothy 2:11–12). So much for Madeleine Albright, Condoleezza Rice—and Ann Coulter!

THE "MYTHS' THAT NEED CORRECTING" PART OF THE ARGUMENT

There are many half-truths or outright falsehoods about separation of church and state and about America's Constitution, symbols, and history that get repeated frequently.

1. Some say that church-state separation is anti-religious or anti-Christian, either by design or in effect. This is almost the direct opposite of the truth: The secular, nonreligious government of the US has stood the test of time, protecting religious liberty and the freely chosen religious beliefs of all Americans specifically by keeping the government out of the business of making religious decisions for any of America's citizens. The framers of the Constitution slammed the door on mixing government and religion not because they hated religion or Christianity (though some of them may have). They didn't slam that door only because they feared that strife over religious differences could destroy the nation (though many did have such fears, and the fears were well-founded, historically). What they most feared, because history repeatedly demonstrated to them the sound basis for fearing it, was that *liberty would be lost*, that power would become concentrated and individual liberty lost, that both the national government and religion would be

corrupted, if the two were entangled. (Some states did have, until 1833, established churches and no separation. Massachusetts was the last such state. The Fourteenth Amendment of 1868 makes the rights of US citizens more important and prohibits any future religious establishment by a state.) The framers were *not* anti-Christian or anti-religious, and they did not produce an anti-Christian or anti-religious Constitution—they were pro-freedom. And therefore this is a free country, for Christians and everyone else—and *not* a Christian nation!

Some religious leaders, today and in the earliest days of the American republic, spoke out in favor of separation. The Baptists in colonial America, who were certainly deeply religious Christians—led by men like John Leland and Isaac Backus—were strong *supporters* of separation of church and state. The Baptists of today, including the Southern Baptists, whom you might think oppose separation of church and state, are also officially very much on the side of religious liberty and the need for separation. The "Baptist Faith and Message," the official statement of the Southern Baptist Convention, is primarily a declaration of Christian, biblical principles. But it includes, in a section called "Religious Liberty," these sentences (emphasis added):

Church and state should be separate. The state owes to every church protection and full freedom in the pursuit of its spiritual ends. In providing for such freedom no ecclesiastical group or denomination should be favored by the state more than others. Civil government being ordained of God, it is the duty of Christians to render loyal obedience thereto in all things not contrary to the revealed will of God. *The church should not resort to the civil power to carry on its work.* The gospel of Christ contemplates spiritual means alone for the pursuit of its ends. *The state has no right to impose penalties for religious opinions of any kind. The state has no right to impose taxes for the support of any form of religion.*

2. Some say that, in public schools, separation means keeping Christian students from praying or saying grace before their lunches or from reading their Bibles in school. This is completely false. As the bumper sticker says, "As long as there are algebra tests, there will be prayer in schools." Sincere

believers in prayer—all of them that we know, at least—deny that anyone can keep anyone else from praying, especially if they pray in the way that Matthew 6:5–6 reports that Jesus told followers to pray: privately. All that is prohibited by separation is *forced* government-sponsored prayer. The First Amendment means that a Catholic or Muslim teacher cannot decide how or when or whether a Baptist or a Methodist student should pray—but there is and should be no restriction put on a student other than the obvious one that he cannot disrupt teaching or force other students to pray. If any teacher or principal has ever punished a student for praying before her lunch, the teacher or principal is the one who violated the First Amendment, not the student. (By the way, most, if not all, of the stories circulating about such incidents are fabrications.)

The great American hero, civil rights martyr, and Protestant minister Rev. Martin Luther King, Jr., as he knelt in prayer awaiting arrest during a protest in 1962, said of the Supreme Court school prayer decision (rendered a few weeks earlier): "Its prayer decision was sound and good, reaffirming something that is basic in our Constitution, namely separation of church and state."

3. Many claim that the words of the Ten Commandments are posted in the US Supreme Court Building and that it is therefore hypocritical for the Court not to allow them to be posted in schools or other courtrooms. Though often repeated, this is a false claim. We've been in the Supreme Court chambers ourselves and walked, carefully, all around the outside of the building, too. There are sculptural allusions, several of them, to Moses, just as there are to Confucius and Hammurabi and Napoleon and Muhammad and many others—but in every case these figures are presented as *lawgivers*—some religious, some not. In no case are the words of the Ten Commandments presented in English (there are a few Hebrew-looking fragments and some Roman numerals that could be interpreted as referring to the Ten Commandments or, more likely, to the Bill of Rights).

If government buildings—courtrooms or classrooms—did post and endorse the Ten Commandments, the very first one would directly oppose the First Amendment. "Thou shalt have no other gods before me" is a clear religious rule for Christians and Jews to follow, but if government is allowed to endorse *or* oppose it, *government* becomes the authority on religious truth, instead of each American citizen.

4. According to some people, the fact that our official national motto and all our money declare, "In God We Trust," is proof that the US is an official Christian nation. This is not true, and it's not what the founders wanted, either. The phrase didn't appear on coins until 1864 (due to religious fervor triggered by the Civil War) or on paper currency until 1957 (due to religious fervor triggered by the Cold War). The courts have ruled that the motto is constitutional only because, they say, it does *not* refer to Christianity or any specific religion.

The founders had a chance to choose a religious motto as our national motto, and they rejected it. They chose instead the motto that was our exclusive motto until 1956: "*E Pluribus Unum*," or, "Out of the Many, One."

The Baptists in colonial America, who were certainly deeply religious Christians—led by men like John Leland and Isaac Backus—were strong *supporters* of separation of church and state.

5. There are many "Christian" quotations that claim to demonstrate that the founders intended to establish a Christian government. The gross insult to the founders that this suggests is usually overlooked—that they wanted to create a Christian government but were too stupid or careless to remember to actually provide for this in the documents they wrote and approved. What matters is not whether these founders or leaders were Christian, as indeed many were, but whether they wanted to create a Christian government. Some historical Americans really did want that—but they lost the fight, and for very good reasons.

When someone shows you quotations in support of any idea, read carefully—if the point of a quotation offered is that some former leader is religious or specifically a strong Christian, it will *not* be relevant to this dispute. Some of the quotations from those who claim this is a Christian nation are suspect (fabricated or quoted out of context), but what matters is what we, as Americans, must do to protect religious liberty, *not* just what one of the framers said or wrote.

As one example—of many—of a phony quotation from a key founder, consider the claim that James Madison said or wrote, "We have staked the whole future of American civilization not upon the power of government, far from it. We have staked the future of all our political institutions upon the capacity of mankind for self-government, upon the capacity of each and all of us to govern ourselves, to control ourselves, to sustain ourselves according to the Ten Commandments." This bogus quotation appeared in David Barton's 1989 book *The Myth of Separation*.

If a nationwide vote were taken this fall, and 99 percent of US voters disagreed with you on a religious matter, would that change your mind?

Barton gave, in a footnote, two sources for the quotation: Harold K. Lane's *Liberty! Cry Liberty!* (Boston: Lamb and Lamb Tractarian Society, 1939) and Fredrick Nyneyer's *First Principles in Morality and Economics: Neighborly Love and Ricardo's Law of Association* (South Holland Libertarian Press, 1958). Both are obscure, twentieth-century publications from tiny Christian publishers. The latter publication got the quote off a Christian calendar. It's impossible to determine where Lane got the quote because no copies of *Liberty! Cry Liberty!* can be found. [Editor's note: The WorldCat database, which lists the holdings of over 10,000 libraries around the world—more than one billion items in all—doesn't show a single copy. A specific search of the Library of Congress' holdings also yields a goose egg. Nor is a used copy available via Amazon or the giant ABE Books website, in which 13,500 used/antiquarian booksellers from around the world list their inventories.]

Madison almost certainly never wrote or said that, regardless of how many alleged sources are cited. We have to ask questions like, Is it consistent with other things we know that he wrote or said? Is there any specific written evidence from a primary source for the quotation? If so, is the context in which it is found consistent with the apparent meaning of the quotation? No such quotation has ever been found among any of James Madison's writings. None of the biographers of Madison, past or present, has ever run across such a quotation, and most if not all would love to know where this false quotation originated. Despite the detective work of fundamentalist Christians, nonbelievers, and others, no one has been able to trace the quote back to any source earlier than Lane's unobtainable 1939 book. Apparently, David Barton did not check the work of the secondary sources he quoted, and he now admits that the quotation is "unconfirmed." The late Robert S. Alley, who was a distinguished historian at the University of Richmond, wrote of his unsuccessful attempt to track down the origin of the Madison quotation and about the implausibility of it as a Madison statement. (See "Public Education and the Public Good," *William and Mary Bill of Rights Journal*, Summer 1995, pages 316–18.)

Similar things can be said of another widely circulated quotation: "It is impossible to rightly govern the world without God and the Bible."—George Washington (according, at one time, to David Barton). But no one can find this quotation in Washington's papers, nor is it consistent with everything else we know about Washington. Be on guard against false quotations, no matter which side of an argument they support.

There's also the old saw that "separation of church and state" only appears in the *Soviet* Constitution, not in the US Constitution—another form of "misquoting." Separation of church and state *did* appear in the various constitutions of the USSR—so did freedom of speech, freedom of the press, and freedom of assembly. Too bad the Communists didn't actually live up to their constitution. The government persecuting religious believers has no more to do with *true* separation of church and state than one of those banana republic "elections," where the president is re-elected with 99.9 percent of the vote, has to do with free elections in a true democracy. The *words* are in some US state constitutions, but the *concept* was originally developed in the First Amendment.

THE "OUGHT TO BE FREE" PART OF THE ARGUMENT

History makes clear that there are many false claims related to separation of church and state. The documents and quotations from the founders of American government support this, as well. But whatever the history or opinions of the framers, why should anyone support freedom instead of their own religious beliefs? Were the founders right to create a free country instead of a Christian nation?

Anyone who wants to claim that our government should support any religion must show you why any of four very basic points don't stand. If he defeats *any* of these four closely related claims, convinces you that any of the four does not hold up, then and only then can he begin to build a case that this ought to be a Christian nation.

First: Not all American citizens hold the same opinions on religion.

Second: *Human* judgment is imperfect.

Third: Religious truth cannot be determined by votes or by force.

And fourth and finally: Freedom, especially religious liberty, is worth having and protecting.

Not all American citizens hold the same opinions on religion and on important matters related to religion (like whether or not there is a God and, if so, what its nature is, or how or when or whether to worship God, or what God says to us about how to live). This is not related to the question of whether you think your own religious ideas are the right ones—probably everyone thinks that he or she is right when it comes to religion. But clearly not all citizens have the *same* beliefs on important religious matters.

Human judgment is imperfect. For Catholics, the Pope is sometimes an exception, with regards to official matters of doctrine, but even Catholics, like all the rest of us, *don't* believe that human voters and human legislators always know what God wants us to do. The Bible is quite clear on this point: "Judge not, that ye be not judged," as it says in the beginning of Matthew, chapter 7, and dozens of other biblical passages make it clear that human judgment is not always reliable. Please keep in mind, whether you believe in God or not, this is not a declaration about whether *God's judgment* is perfect—only whether humanity's is.

Religious truth cannot be determined by votes or by force. In America, as in other genuinely free nations, neither a majority of citizens nor the government acting on the majority's behalf can make religious decisions for individuals. If you think you might disagree with idea #3, ask yourself: If a nationwide vote were taken this fall, and 99 percent of US voters disagreed with you on a religious matter, would that change your mind? If 99 percent of the citizens wanted this country to adopt Catholicism or Methodism or Islam or atheism as the "right" religious point of view, would you accept their decision?

Would that convince you? And it's not just voting, it's the law itself, the power of government, that we're talking about here. Remember Abdul Rahman, the poor citizen in Afghanistan who was arrested, faced the danger of being executed, and finally had to flee to another country in early 2006, all for the crime of changing his religious beliefs? Would you change your beliefs *or* be kept from changing them—could you even change what you really believe—if the law required you to?

There really is no middle ground here: Either governments have the power to make religious decisions for citizens, or governments lack that power. In 1785 James Madison wrote a petition against using Virginia taxpayer money to support Christians of all denominations. In that petition—signed by enough Virginians to get the legislation killed—Madison wrote:

> Who does not see that the same authority which can establish Christianity in exclusion of all other religions may establish, with the same ease, any particular sect of Christians in exclusion of all other sects? That the same authority which can force a citizen to contribute threepence only of his property for the support of any one establishment may force him to conform to any other establishment in all cases whatsoever?

Freedom, especially religious liberty, is worth having and protecting. This seems self-evident to most of us, regardless of which religious beliefs we hold. As Thomas Jefferson wrote to Benjamin Rush in 1803: "It behooves every man who values liberty of conscience for himself, to resist invasions of it in the case of others; or their case may, by change of circumstances, become his own."

That's it—that's really our whole argument. If all four of these ideas are correct, there is no doubt that we need to keep church and state separate, that we have to insist, as the framers of the Constitution did, that religion is far too important to mix it up with governmental power. If governments, any governments, get to control religious decisions for any of us, religious liberty cannot be guaranteed for anyone.

If you thought that America is or ought to be a Christian nation, what you thought was wrong. The reason it is not and ought not, can be summed up in one sentence: To guarantee your own religious liberty, you have to help protect everyone else's, too.

Peter Eckstein

POSTING THE TEN COMMANDMENTS

SINCE ROY MOORE, Chief Justice of the Alabama Supreme Court, took the first steps toward his eventual campaign for governor by erecting a gigantic Ten Commandments monument in the state's Supreme Court building, officials in other states have jumped on the bandwagon. In December 2005, Senator Tom Coburn of Oklahoma told a crowd rallying at a Ten Commandments monument outside a county courthouse that such monuments should be on every courthouse lawn. "We need more of this," he said, "not less."

In my own state, the Michigan House of Representatives passed a resolution in 2005 seeking to have the Commandments displayed in or around the state capitol building. The advocates depicted the Commandments as an infallible guide to morality and as an historical foundation of American law. State Representative Tom Casperson described posting them as an important way to restore "a moral compass to our society." He claimed that the founders used the Commandments to help draft the federal Constitution and that they "were part of the foundation of the judicial system." Rep. Robert Gosselin called the Commandments the "bedrock of Michigan law," while Rep. Jack Hoogendyk—then running for governor himself—called them "the foundation for the freedoms we hold dear."[1] Are any of these assertions anything more than legislative blather? Is governmental posting of the Commandments sound public policy?

The first problem is the version to be displayed. My own discussion will be largely based on the traditional King James Version. But there are currently well over a dozen other Protestant translations on the mass market,[2] as well as several Catholic, Orthodox, and Jewish translations. Should a state legislature choose one translation favored by just one segment of the Judeo-Christian tradition while excluding those favored by all the others?

> **Should a state legislature choose one translation favored by just one segment of the Judeo-Christian tradition while excluding those favored by all the others?**

Most public displays—including Justice Moore's version—are not the full Ten Commandments. They are abridgments of the originals—*Reader's Digest* versions—that exclude many of the thornier passages. The King James Version contains 334 words, but Moore has taken it upon himself to whittle them down to a mere 75.

The First Commandment begins, "I am the Lord thy God, which have brought thee out of the land of Egypt." An increasing number of Americans are Muslims, Hindus, Sikhs, Buddhists, Jains, Shintoists, Taoists, Confucians, adherents of Native American religions, animists, agnostics, and atheists—few of whom claim descent from the Israelite tribes who fled Egypt. Should a state government be in the business of declaring to all its citizens that they shall "have no other gods" above the God of the Israelites?

> **Most public displays—including Justice Moore's version—are not the full Ten Commandments. They are abridgments of the originals—*Reader's Digest* versions—that exclude many of the thornier passages.**

The Second Commandment forbids making any "graven," or carved, image[3]—and bowing down to one. This warning also ignores the wide range of religious practice. Some Hindus bow before graven images of their gods, and some Catholics genuflect before graven images of their saints. The Vatican is filled with graven images of Christ, saints, and popes. Nor are most state governments innocent of this practice. In Michigan the capitol lawn holds at least six graven images—a stone eagle atop a war memorial, two stags on the state seal, a wolverine on an historical marker, two soldiers, and an imposing statue of the state's Civil War governor. Should these statues display a warning from the legislature that God forbids the making of graven images?

The Second Commandment also threatens to visit "the iniquity of the fathers upon the children unto the third and fourth generation." Should a child visiting the capitol start to worry that she may be punished because decades ago a great-grandfather she never knew may have hit his thumb with a hammer and impulsively used the name of the Lord in vain? Does any American law seek to punish children, let alone grandchildren and great-grandchildren, for the transgressions of their fathers?

If the founders used the Ten Commandments in drafting the federal Constitution, they did a masterful job of disguising that fact. Not one key word from the Commandments appears in the text.[4] The only allusion to them is to the Second Commandment, and it is a decidedly negative one—

an absolute rejection of "Corruption of Blood," the philosophy of punishing children for the crimes of their parents. Chief Justice Charles Evans Hughes wrote, "It is the essence of the institutions of liberty that it be recognized that guilt is personal." Isn't such recognition a sounder foundation for our laws than the intergenerational vengeance propounded by the Second Commandment?[5]

The Fourth Commandment forbids any work on the Sabbath. Do the legislatures wish to reinstate "blue laws" that forbid working on Sunday (and presumably on Friday for Muslims and Saturday for Jews)? Do they wish to ban all shopping malls, golf courses, television stations, restaurants, backyard gardeners, and food harvesters from operating on the Sabbath? In Michigan, the legislature overwhelmingly voted a million-dollar subsidy for the 2006 Super Bowl in Detroit, even though the NFL championship is always held on a Sunday. The subsidy was opposed by only nine of the seventy-four legislators who had a few months earlier voted to post the Commandments—and none recorded a reason for that opposition. Why did none of the seventy-four legislators protest the fact that the football players, coaches, officials, cheerleaders, announcers, camera crews, food vendors, security guards, and others would all be working on the Christian Sabbath?

> **Should a state government be in the business of declaring to all its citizens that they shall "have no other gods" above the God of the Israelites?**

The Fourth Commandment justifies itself by asserting that "in six days the Lord made the heaven and earth" and "rested on the seventh day." Some legislators may actually believe this, but they should understand that there isn't a single shred of geological or paleontological evidence for this assertion. Geologists currently estimate that the earth is 4.5 billion years old and that it has taken nearly all that time—some 1.6 trillion days—to reach its present form.[6] This estimate may change, but can anyone imagine some new discovery that will suddenly compel geologists to compress their estimate of 1.6 trillion days to the six days stated as historical fact in the Fourth Commandment?

The great antiquity of the earth isn't disputed in most religious or in any truly scientific circles. In 1996 Pope John Paul II noted the "increasing precision" with which scientists were describing "the multiple manifestations of life" and correlating them with a "time line."[7] Even the proponents of "intelligent design" don't dispute this basic timeline for the emergence of different species. Their principal textbook points out that "the vast majority" of the known groupings of organisms appeared within a range of "10 to 40 million years"—a far cry from the six days described in Genesis and reaffirmed in the Fourth Commandment.[8]

Several other Commandments express commonly-held moral values but are not foundations of state law.

Violation of at least eight of the Ten Commandments is subject to the death penalty—typically by stoning.

The Third Commandment forbids taking "the name of the Lord thy God in vain." Important or not, its observance cannot be legally required, as courts have held that the First Amendment's guarantee of free speech protects even blasphemy.

The Fifth Commandment enjoins us to "honor thy father and thy mother." Most parents deserve to be honored, though no law requires it. In 2003 some 725,000 American children were victims of abuse or neglect perpetrated by a parent.[9] Should all these children be required to honor their parents? Should we condemn Joseph Stalin's daughter Svetlana for defecting from the Soviet Union in 1967 and denouncing her father's regime? As for the Commandment's injunction to observe it so that "thy days may be long," has any medical study verified that filial piety is statistically correlated with longevity? Svetlana, as least, made it to 80 years of age in 2006 without being struck down for her transgression. As of this writing, she's still very much alive.

The Seventh Commandment says, "Thou shalt not commit adultery." This was the foundation for some laws in the past, but, like many other states, Michigan has had no prosecutions for adultery for several decades. Has the practice just disap-

peared? If so, could this have happened even without the Seventh Commandment being posted in the state capitol? Or, as seems more likely, have the laws against it simply become a dead letter? In 2005 a Michigan public official called a press conference to admit that he had committed adultery, but neither the state Attorney General's office nor any county prosecutor has pressed charges.

The Tenth Commandment forbids coveting not only "thy neighbor's house" but also his wife, servants, ass, and "anything that is thy neighbor's." Half a century ago Frank Loesser articulated a clear principle of American law—"Brother, you can't go to jail for what you're thinking." More important, doesn't it seem just a little quaint today to be listing a wife as among a man's possessions? Consider, too, that the "maid servant" referred to in the Commandment was commonly a concubine or sex slave—often purchased from her own father.[10] Indeed, several of the additional laws Moses is said to have received from God seek to regulate slavery, not at all to forbid it.[11] How reliable is a "moral compass" that permits one man to purchase a sex slave but sees sin only when another man covets her?

So none of these seven Commandments can be seen in any way as part of the "bedrock" of law today. Only three enjoin behavior for which most states currently punish people: the Sixth forbids killing, the Eighth forbids stealing, and the Ninth forbids bearing false witness.[12] But these have been criminal offenses in many societies the world over that were quite innocent of the Ten Commandments. They were part of criminal law in ancient Babylon and Egypt centuries before the time of Moses. The Romans included them as early as the fifth century B.C.E., when they were still worshipping a whole stable of morally flawed gods, led by the lecherous Jupiter.[13] Many indigenous peoples of North America, Africa, and the South Pacific islands had comparable taboos.[14]

"Thou shalt not kill" is a powerful statement, but anyone who reads further in the texts will find its force vitiated. Violation of at least eight of the Ten Commandments is subject to the death penalty—typically by stoning. One such violation is murder, still subject to the death penalty in many states. But other execution-worthy violations are cursing one's parent, sacrificing to the wrong god, idolatry, adultery, blasphemy, working on the Sabbath, and bearing false witness.[15] Would legislatures ask us to emulate these archaic and brutal standards?

The judicial processes are illustrated in the case of observing the Sabbath. The Book of Numbers (15:32–36) recounts how the Israelites found a man who "gathered sticks" on a Saturday. They brought the man to Moses and Aaron, and "the Lord said unto Moses, The man shall surely be put to death," so the congregation "stoned him with stones, and he died; as the Lord commanded Moses."

How does any of this lay the foundation for the Bill of Rights in our Constitution? How can this be "part of the foundation" of our judicial system? Is there any allowance for "free exercise" of religion, any right to have charges presented only by a grand jury, any "due process of law" before being deprived of life itself, any jury trial, or any evidence of "assistance of Counsel" for the defense? Was there any concern over "cruel and unusual punishment"? Stoning to death for picking up stray sticks may not have been statistically "unusual" by the standards of the day, but would it not be considered "cruel" by any standard short of barbarism?

Proponents may call the Commandments "the foundation of the freedoms we hold dear," but the Commandments grant no freedoms except the choice of obeying or being killed. The US Constitution enumerates at least twenty-five non-economic rights.[16] Not one of them—from habeas corpus through the ban on slavery to the right of women to vote—is anticipated in any way by the Ten Commandments.

James Madison, the father of our Bill of Rights, advocated "total separation of the church from the state." He considered that separation a standard for political health and for a limited government that abstains from actions properly reserved for the domain of personal beliefs and personal religious practices.[17] We should not reject his wisdom. It is the modern embodiment of the line drawn by Jesus: "Render therefore unto Caesar the things which are Caesar's; and unto God the things that are God's."[18]

---

1. Coburn quoted in the *Ann Arbor News* (10 Dec 2005). Michigan legislator quotes are found in: Michigan House floor debate, 24 Mar 2005, taped by Michigan Government Television; Bailey, Amy F., and Chong W. Pyen. "Ten Commandments Bill OK'd." *Ann Arbor News* (25 Mar 2005): A8; Christoff, Chris. "Thou Shalt Study Thy Ten Commandments' Context." *Detroit Free Press* (14 Mar 2005); Bailey, Amy F. "Alabama Commandments Visit Capitol." *Lansing State Journal* (17 Mar 2005).

2. These include the New King James Version, the New International Version, the National Equivalent Translation, Today's New International Version, the New Reader's International Version, the American Standard Version, the New American Standard Version, the New Century Version, the Revised Standard Version, the New Revised Standard Version, the Holman Christian Standard Version, the English Standard Version, *The Message: The Bible in Contemporary Language*, the Good News Translation, the New Jerusalem Bible, the New American Bible, and the New Living Translation.

3. Pfeifer, Charles F. *The New Combined Bible Dictionary and Concordance*. Grand Rapids, MI: Baker Book House, 1961; paperback edition, 1999: 204.

4. Among the key words from the Commandments that don't appear in the body of the Constitution: *God, Lord, bondage, graven, image, bow, commandments, vain, Sabbath, holy, heaven, hallow, father, mother, kill* (or *murder*), *adultery, steal* (or *theft, thief*, or *robbery*), *false witness* (or *perjury, libel*, or *slander*), *covet, neighbor, maid-servant, man-servant, wife*, or *ass* (or *donkey*). The word *Lord* does appear in the signature portion of the document, where the date is expressed as "in the year of our Lord" 1787, a common way of expressing dates in documents of the era. In this case, of course, the Lord is Jesus, not the God of the Ten Commandments. Nor did the authors of the Federalist Papers, the classic explanation of the Constitution, anywhere use the terms *Bible, scripture*, or *Ten Commandments*. (The word search of the Federalist Papers is reported in: Finkelman, Paul. "The Ten Commandments on the Courthouse Lawn and Elsewhere." *Fordham Law Review*, Vol. 73 (2005): 1513.)

5. Quoted, for example, by Justice Hugo Black in his dissenting opinion in *American Communications Assn. v. Douds*, 339 U.S. 382, 8 May 1950, footnote 10. Legal scholar and historian Paul Finkelman makes clear: "The founding generation…was influenced by many English sources of law, such as the Magna Carta and the English Bill of Rights, as well as non-legal sources like the works of…Enlightenment thinkers…. Other sources of American law include Roman law, the civil law of continental Europe in the post-Roman period, private international law, biblical law, and Germanic tribal law. While English law had some biblical roots, by the time of…the Revolution, the Bible and religious issues had long been surpassed by more practical concerns, especially in the American colonies." See Finkelman: 1500–1.

6. Smithsonian Institution. *Earth*. James F. Luhr, ed. New York: DK Publishing, 2003: 22, 107, 161.

7. At the same time John Paul insisted that "the moment of transition into the spiritual cannot be the object of this kind of observation." From the "Message to Pontifical Academy of Science," 22 Oct 1996, Catholic Information Network website <cin.org>.

8. This, the authors point out, is "a geologically 'brief' period," given the vastly longer early age of the earth and the 500 million years that have followed. They list a dozen "living fossils"—organisms with very long histories on earth—as having originated in a range between 1,900 million years ago (for a particular protozoan) to 20 million years ago (for aardvarks). See: Davis, Percival, and Dean H. Kenyon. *Of Pandas and People*. Dallas: Haughton Publishing Co., 1989: 92, 95, 99.

9. Website of the Administration for Children and Families, US Department of Health and Human Services. "Summary: Child Maltreatment 2003." Updated on 24 Feb 2006. The number is based on approximately 906,000 children abused or neglected and approximately 80 percent of the perpetrators being parents.

10. *Servant* is often used as a euphemism for *slave* in the King James Version (Pfeiffer: 377). For example, in the version of the Ten Commandments in Exodus (20:2), the Lord tells the Israelites that he has "brought thee out of the land of Egypt, out of the house of bondage." The version in Deuteronomy (5:15) says, "thou was a servant in the land of Egypt." Psalm 105:17 refers to Joseph as having been "sold for a servant." Leviticus 25:6 distinguishes between "thy hired servant" and "thy servant," the latter presumably a slave. Several other translations of the Tenth Commandment use the term *slave* rather than *servant* (e.g., the Natural Equivalent Translation and the New Century Version).

11. For example, a newly bought slave may not eat a Passover meal until he has been circumcised. Someone buying a Hebrew slave must emancipate him after six years, but not any wife the master may have given the slave nor any children they may have had together. If a man sells his daughter into slavery, she need not be freed as the male slaves are. (Exodus 12:44, 21:2,4,7.) The Natural Equivalent Translation makes clear that all these references are to slaves.

12. Editor's note: And even then, lying is a criminal offense only when done in certain narrow circumstances, such as while testifying in court or filling out your income tax return. It's not against the law, for example, to lie to your spouse about how much you spent on a new jacket, or to your boss about why you missed work yesterday.

13. Finkelman: 1505–6, footnote 153. Murder, robbery, theft, fraud, libel, and false witness were all crimes in ancient Rome, and under some circumstances all but theft were subject to the death penalty. (Morey, William C. *Outlines of Roman Law*, second edition. New York: G.P. Putnam's Sons, 1914: 25, 41–2.) The Babylonian Code of Hammurabi (1728–1686 B.C.E.) had groupings that included false accusations, theft, burglary, robbery, embezzlement, and slander. (Van Den Ploeg, J. "Law, Ancient Near Eastern." In *New Catholic Encyclopedia*, Volume 8. Detroit: Thomson-Gale, 2003: 393–4.) During Egypt's Middle Kingdom (2040–1650 B.C.E.), the list of Judgments of the Dead included "murder and manslaughter, robbery, theft, perjury" and blasphemy. (Assmann, Jan. *The Mind of Egypt*. New York: Metropolitan Books, 2002: 165–6.)

14. Homicide, a noted anthropologist tells us, "is, under one set of conditions or another, legally prohibited everywhere." A century ago the Ashanti chiefs in present-day Ghana sat on their sacred stools and conducted trials for a variety of crimes and violations of taboos, including murder, theft, and slander. As for false witness, priests would require someone believed to have committed perjury to refund all the expenses of the party wrongly found guilty and to sacrifice a sheep to one of the local gods. See, for example: Hoebel, E. Adamson. *The Law of Primitive Man*. Cambridge: Harvard University Press, 1954: 286; Rattray, R.S. *Ashanti Law and Constitution*. Oxford: Clarendon Press, 1929: 295, 324–7, 384–7. Many forms of adultery were also punished under Ashanti law; blasphemy against the king was a capital offense, and in some areas farm work was forbidden on Wednesdays. (Rattray: 138, 163, 304, 317–8, 375.)

15. Murder: Exodus 21:12; dishonoring parents: Exodus 21:17; worshipping other gods: Exodus 22:20 and Deuteronomy 17:2–5; idolatry: Exodus 32:28; adultery: Leviticus 20:10; blasphemy: Leviticus 24:16; working on the Sabbath: Exodus 31:15 and 35:2 and Numbers 15:32–36; false witness: Proverbs 19:9 and 21:28.

16. These are contained in Article I, Section 9; Amendments I-VIII; and Amendments XIII, XV, and XIX. The only reference to religion in the body of the original Constitution is not a requirement that all Americans act in accordance with God's wishes but rather an explicit ban on religious tests for public officials.

17. Madison, letter to Robert Walsh, 2 Mar 1819, and letter to F.L. Schaeffer, 3 Dec 1821, in: Padover, Saul K. *The Complete Madison: His Basic Writings*. New York: Harper & Brothers, 1953.

18. Matthew 22:21.

PHILADELPHIA GRAND JURY REPORT

ON ABUSIVE PRIESTS AND THE CARDINALS

WHO ENABLED THEM

Editor's Note: In September 2005, a Philadelphia grand jury concluded the longest probe of sexually abusive priests ever undertaken by a grand jury or district attorney. During the course of three years, the jurors documented abuse by over sixty priests, involving hundreds of minors, with continuous cover-ups by the Philly Archdiocese. The resulting 423-page report, with another 309 pages of appendices, is an amazing document both for the way it refuses to shy away from detailed descriptions of the priests' crimes and for the barely contained anger and disgust that its authors obviously felt after years of examining secret documents and interviewing victims, perpetrators, and others.

When reading the excerpts below, keep in mind that it was written, not by people who view organized religion with suspicion, but by a group of ordinary citizens, including some Catholics, plucked from the jury pool—the very salt of the earth.

The entire report is available at the Philadelphia D.A.'s website [www.philadelphiadistrictattorney.com].

INTRODUCTION TO THE GRAND JURY REPORT

This report contains the findings of the Grand Jury: how dozens of priests sexually abused hundreds of children; how Philadelphia Archdiocese officials—including Cardinal Bevilacqua and Cardinal Krol—excused and enabled the abuse; and how the law must be changed so that it doesn't happen again. Some may be tempted to describe these events as tragic. Tragedies such as tidal waves, however, are outside human control. What we found were not acts of God, but of men who acted in His name and defiled it.

But the biggest crime of all is this: it worked. The abuser priests, by choosing children as targets and trafficking on their trust, were able to

> **The abuser priests, by choosing children as targets and trafficking on their trust, were able to prevent or delay reports of their sexual assaults, to the point where applicable statutes of limitations expired.**

prevent or delay reports of their sexual assaults, to the point where applicable statutes of limitations expired. And Archdiocese officials, by burying those reports they did receive and covering up the conduct, similarly managed to outlast any statutes of limitation. As a result, these priests and officials will necessarily escape criminal prosecution. We surely would have charged them if we could have done so.

But the consequences are even worse than the avoidance of criminal penalties. Sexually abusive priests were either left quietly in place or "recycled" to unsuspecting new parishes—vastly expanding the number of children who were abused. It didn't have to be this way. Prompt action and a climate of compassion for the child victims could have significantly limited the damage done. But the Archdiocese chose a different path. Those choices went all the way up to the top—to Cardinal Bevilacqua and Cardinal Krol personally.

Despite the dimensions and depth of the sex abuse scandal, this Grand Jury was not conducting an investigation of the Catholic religion or the Catholic Church. Many of us are Catholic. We have the greatest respect for the faith, and for the good works of the Church. But the moral principles on which it is based, as well as the rules of civil law under which we operate, demanded that the truth be told.

Here is a short description of each of the sections that follow this introduction.

SECTION II—OVERVIEW OF THE SEXUAL ABUSE BY ARCHDIOCESE PRIESTS

The Grand Jury was able to document child sexual abuse by at least **63 different priests** in the Archdiocese of Philadelphia. We have no doubt that there were many more. The evidence also revealed **hundreds of child victims** of these sexual offenders. Again, we have no doubt that there were many more. Because much of the abuse goes back several decades, however, and because many victims were unnamed, unavailable or unable to come forward, we could not present a comprehensive history of all sexual abuse that may have occurred in the Philadelphia Archdiocese. What we did learn was enough to convey the nature of the abuse that took place and was tolerated here.

We should begin by making one thing clear. When we say abuse, we don't just mean "inappropriate touching" (as the Archdiocese often chose to refer to it). We mean rape. Boys who were raped orally, boys who were raped anally, girls who were raped vaginally. But even those victims whose physical abuse did not include actual rape—those who were subjected to fondling, to masturbation, to pornography—suffered psychological abuse that scarred their lives and sapped the faith in which they had been raised.

These are the kinds of things that Archdiocese priests did to children:

—A girl, **11 years old**, was **raped** by her priest and became **pregnant**. The Father took her in for an **abortion**.

—A 5th-grader was molested by her priest **inside the confessional booth**.

—A teenage girl was groped by her priest while she lay **immobilized in traction in a hospital bed**. The priest stopped only when the girl was able to ring for a nurse.

—A boy was repeatedly molested in his own **school auditorium**, where his priest/teacher **bent the boy over and rubbed** his genitals against the boy until the priest **ejaculated**.

—A priest, no longer satisfied with mere pederasty, regularly began forcing sex on **two boys at once** in his bed.

—A boy woke up intoxicated in a priest's bed to find the Father sucking on his penis **while three other priests watched** and masturbated themselves.

—A priest offered money to boys in exchange for **sadomasochism**—directing them to place him in **bondage**, to "break" him, to make him their "**slave**," and to defecate so that he could lick excrement from them.

—A 12-year-old, who was raped and sodomized by his priest, **tried to commit suicide**, and remains **institutionalized in a mental hospital** as an adult.

—A priest told a 12-year-old boy that his **mother** knew of and **had agreed** to the priest's **repeated rape** of her son.

—A boy who told his father about the abuse his younger brother was suffering was **beaten** to the point of unconsciousness. "**Priests don't do that**," said the father as he punished his son for what he thought was a vicious lie against the clergy.

SECTION III—OVERVIEW OF THE COVER-UP BY ARCHDIOCESE OFFICIALS

The behavior of Archdiocese officials was perhaps not so lurid as that of the individual priest sex abusers. But in its callous, calculating manner, the Archdiocese's "handling" of the abuse scandal was at least as immoral as the abuse itself. The evidence before us established that Archdiocese officials at the highest levels received reports of abuse; that they chose not to conduct any meaningful investigation of those reports; that they left dangerous priests in place or transferred them to different parishes as a means of concealment; that they never alerted parents of the dangers posed by these offenders (who typically went out of their way to be friendly and helpful, especially with children); that they intimidated and retaliated against victims and witnesses who came forward about abuse; that they manipulated "treatment" efforts in order to create a false impression of action; and that they did many of these things in a conscious effort simply to avoid civil liability.

In short, as abuse reports grew, the Archdiocese chose to call in the lawyers rather than confront the abusers. Indeed Cardinal Bevilacqua himself was a lawyer, with degrees from both a canon law school and an American law school. Documents and testimony left us with no doubt that he and Cardinal Krol were personally informed of almost all of the allegations of sexual abuse by priests, and personally decided or approved of how to handle those allegations.

Here are some incidents that exemplify the manner in which the Archdiocese responded to the sexual abuse of its most vulnerable parishioners:

—The Archdiocese official in charge of abuse investigations described one abusive priest as **"one of the sickest people I ever knew."** Yet Cardinal Bevilacqua allowed him to continue in ministry, with full access to children—until the priest scandal broke in 2002.

—One abusive priest was **transferred so many times** that, according to the Archdiocese's own records, they were **running out of places to send him** where he would not already be known.

—On at least one occasion Cardinal Bevilacqua agreed to harbor a known abuser from another diocese, giving him a cover story and a neighborhood parish here because the priest's arrest for child abuse had aroused too much controversy there. Officials referred to this sort of practice as **"bishops helping bishops."**

—A **nun who complained** about a priest who was still ministering to children—even after he was convicted of receiving child pornography—**was fired** from her position as director of religious education.

—A **seminarian** studying for the priesthood **who revealed that he himself had been abused** as an altar boy was accused of homosexuality—and **was dismissed from the diocese**. He was able to become a priest only by relocating to another area.

—When the Archdiocese did purport to seek psychological evaluation of a priest, the **primary tool for diagnosis was "self reporting"**—in other words, whether the abuser was willing to admit that he was a pedophile. Absent such a "diagnosis," the Archdiocese declined to treat any priest as a pedophile, no matter how compelling the evidence.

—Even when admitted, the abuse was excused: an Archdiocese official comforted one sexually abusive priest by **suggesting that the priest had been "seduced" by his 11-year-old victim**.

—An Archdiocese official explained that the church could not discipline one especially egregious abuser because, as the official put it, he was **not a "pure pedophile"**—that is, he not only abused little boys; he also slept with women.

—When one priest showed signs of seeking penance from his victims, the church-run "treatment" facility urged Archdiocese officials to move him to another assignment away from the victims—in other words, transfer him before he apologizes again.

Such cynicism toward priest sexual abuse may not have started in Philadelphia; indeed media reports have revealed strikingly similar tactics throughout the country. Bishops in other dioceses also shuttled abusive priests from parish to parish, until there was no place left to go, ignored repeated reports of abuse, absent a direct confession or "diagnosis" of pedophilia, and looked to legalisms, at the expense of decency. But these parallels, far from excusing Philadelphia church officials, serve only to underscore that their actions were no accident. They knew what they were doing.

SECTION IV—LEGAL ANALYSIS AND RECOMMENDATIONS

The notion of prosecuting a priest—let alone a high Church official or even the Archdiocese itself—may seem shocking to some. But our oath required us to explore any criminal statute whose terms might fit the conduct we discovered. By the same token, we were obligated not to recommend criminal charges against priests or church leaders merely because of our moral outrage at what they did, over and over again. What we found was that many offenses applied to the evidence before us, but were barred by statutes of limitation, while many others narrowly failed to apply because of what we believe are unintended or unwise limitations in the law.

With regard to the priest offenders, any number of sexual offenses were readily made out by the evidence: rape, involuntary deviate sexual intercourse, statutory sexual assault, indecent assault, endangering welfare of children, corruption of minors. In every case, however, our information was simply too old. As we learned from experts in the field, it takes many years—often decades—before most victims of child sexual abuse are able to come forward. By then it is simply too late to prosecute, at least under current Pennsylvania law. We are convinced that more recent victims exist, and perhaps in the future they will be able to give

testimony. For now we were able to document many assaults, but none still prosecutable.

With regard to the leaders of the Archdiocese, we explored a variety of possible charges. These included endangering the welfare of children, corruption of minors, victim/witness intimidation, hindering apprehension, and obstruction of justice. All, however, are currently defined in ways that would allow church supervisors to escape criminal sanction, or have relatively short statutes of limitation that would bar prosecution in any event.

With regard to the Archdiocese itself, Pennsylvania law does establish the possibility of corporate criminal liability for the kind of ongoing, institutional misconduct that we discovered here. The Archdiocese, however, has chosen not to organize itself as a legal corporation, thus immunizing itself from such liability. Current Pennsylvania law concerning criminal conduct by unincorporated associations like the Archdiocese is much more limited, and cannot form the basis of a prosecution against the Archdiocese as an entity.

We are left, then, with what we consider a travesty of justice: a multitude of crimes for which no one can be held criminally accountable. We cannot issue the presentments we would otherwise have returned. If nothing else, however, it is our hope that this report can help ensure that nothing like this happens in the future. We therefore make the following recommendations concerning Pennsylvania law:

—**abolish the statute of limitations for sexual offenses against children**, as several other states have already done.

—**expand the offense of endangering welfare of children**, to ensure that it covers reckless conduct and the conduct of those who directly employ or supervise caretakers of children.

—**increase the penalty for indecent assault** where there is a pattern of abuse against a child.

—**tighten** the Pennsylvania Child Protective Services Law, to make clear that the **obligation to report child abuse to authorities** applies to those who learn of abuse even if not directly from the child, and even if the child is no longer in the abuser's control. Other children may be.

—amend the Child Protective Services Law to **require background checks** not just on school employees, but for employees of any organization that supervises children.

—**hold unincorporated associations to the same standards** as corporations for crimes concerning the sexual assault of children.

—**enlarge or eliminate statutes of limitation on civil suits** involving child sexual assault, in order to ensure not just a criminal penalty but a continuing financial disincentive to engage in abuse.

OVERVIEW OF THE SEXUAL ABUSE BY ARCHDIOCESE PRIESTS

It is hard to think of a crime more heinous, or more deserving of strict penalties and an unlimited statute of limitations, than the sexual abuse of children. This is especially so when the perpetrators are priests—men who exploit the clergy's authority and access to minors, as well as the trust of faithful families, to prey on children in order to gratify perverted urges. After reviewing thousands of documents from Archdiocese files and hearing statements and testimony from over a hundred witnesses—including Archdiocese managers, priests, abuse victims, and experts on the Church and child abuse—we, the Grand Jurors, were taken aback by the extent of sexual exploitation within the Philadelphia Archdiocese. We were saddened to discover the magnitude of the calamity in terms of the abuse itself, the suffering it has caused, and the numbers of victims and priests involved.

The Jurors heard testimony that will stay with us for a very long time, probably forever. We heard of Philadelphia-area priests committing countless acts of sexual depravity against children entrusted to their care through the Archdiocese's parishes and schools. The abuses ranged from glancing touches of genitals under the guise of innocent wrestling to sadomasochistic rituals and relentless anal, oral, and vaginal rapes. We found that no matter what physical form the abuse took, or how often it was repeated, the damage to these children's psyches was devastating. Not only were the victims betrayed by a loved and revered father figure, but they also faced lifelong guilt and shame, isolation from family and peers, and torments that typically included alcoholism, addictions, marital difficulties, and sometimes thoughts of suicide. In many cases, we discovered, the victims believed God had abandoned them.

For any who might want to believe that the abuse problem in the Philadelphia area was limited in scope, this Report will disabuse them of that impression. The Jurors heard from some victims who were sexually abused once or twice, and from many more who were abused week after week for years. Many of the priests whose cases we examined had more than 10 victims; some abused multiple victims simultaneously. Indeed, the evidence arising from the Philadelphia Archdiocese reveals criminality against minors on a widespread scale—sparing no geographic sector, no income level, no ethnic group. We heard testimony about priests molesting and raping children in rectory bedrooms, in church sacristies, in parked cars, in swimming pools, at Saint Charles Borromeo Seminary, at the priests' vacation houses in the Poconos and the Jersey Shore, in the children's schools and even in their own homes.

> **We heard testimony about priests molesting and raping children in rectory bedrooms, in church sacristies, in parked cars, in swimming pools, at Saint Charles Borromeo Seminary, at the priests' vacation houses in the Poconos and the Jersey Shore, in the children's schools and even in their own homes.**

From all the documents and testimony put before us, we have received a tragic education—about the nature of child abuse, for example: how predators manipulate their prey, why the abuse so often goes unreported, how its impact on victims and their families remains lifelong. Even so, we find it hard to comprehend or absorb the full extent of the malevolence and suffering visited on this community, under cover of the clerical collar, by powerful, respected, and rapacious priests.

A. THE EVIDENCE REVEALS THAT CHILD SEXUAL ABUSE FOLLOWS REGULAR PATTERNS.

When we gathered, many of the Jurors did not understand the dynamics of clergy members' sexual abuse of minors. We could not understand how children who were so awfully abused could fail to tell anyone or, worse, would return to their abuser again and again. We learned from one of the leading American experts in the field, Kenneth Lanning, formerly of the Federal Bureau of Investigation, that the answer lies in the twisted relationship that acquaintance molesters initiate with their victims.

Those who prey on children first are careful in selecting their victims. They seek out vulnerable children who are needy for attention, often because of difficulties at home, because vulnerable children are easiest to mold to the abuser's desires. They then achieve power over their victims in a process that the experts call "grooming." Child molesters have enormous patience, identifying and pursuing victims sometimes for months before initiating the abuse. One might take a child to the beach, the cinema, or the local ice cream parlor, showering his prey with toys and treats. He will give his victim what the child believes is benign attention and "love." Abusers also often befriend the families of their victims, visiting their homes, becoming dinner guests, exploiting parishioners' reverence for the priesthood. The parents are pleased and flattered by a priest's attentions to their children.

What surprised the Jurors most in Lanning's lengthy testimony was that so many of these men come across as "nice guys," that they can be so outwardly likeable. Mothers and fathers like them. The children who are their targets often love them. These are not "Stranger Danger" predators who look shady or menacing; they are the pillars of the Catholic community, respected and admired by all. Meanwhile, many of the targeted children do not understand sex in the first instance, so that when the priest reaches the point where he begins to act out sexually, the victims are utterly defenseless. As the abuse continues, their initial confusion turns to guilt and shame over what they believe they have allowed to happen. Many victims continue to think that priests can do no wrong or feel responsible for making a "good" priest go bad.

For the vulnerable child who craves love and security, and the devout child raised never to question the clergy's authority, it becomes nearly impossible to break free from the abusive priest, even after the sexual abuse begins. Experts refer to this phenomenon as the "trauma bond." Even though the abusive relationship is terribly damaging to the victim, he finds it difficult to remove himself from it because of the priest's power over him and the psychological and emotional bond that has resulted.

1. Sexually abused children rarely report their abuse.

Related to the question of why victims seem unable to break free of their abusers is the question of why it takes some victims decades to report priest sexual abuse. We learned there are many reasons for delayed reporting. Most of the victims are devout and/or come from devout families. Therefore, many of them regard priests as God's representatives on Earth. The well-educated priests, for their part, know very well the esteem in which trusting children and their parents hold them, and they manipulate that trust to ensure the victims' silence. Some of the priests whose cases we examined told their victims that God had sanctioned the sexual relationship and would punish them if they revealed it. Others told children that they loved them, and that the sexual abuse should be their little secret. Still others told their prey that they, the victims, were responsible for the abuse, and that no one would believe them if they told.

Psychological denial is not an unusual response to trauma, confusion, shame, and despair. And there are other, powerful disincentives to report a priest's abuse. Some victims fear damaging the Church's reputation. Others fear their parents' disbelief or anger—not toward the priest, but toward them. Some worry that such a horrific revelation could destroy their parents' sustaining faith in the Church. Many adolescent boys fear that revealing sexual contact with a man would call into question whether they are heterosexual.

2. The lifelong impact extends from isolation to "soul murder."

The priests' manipulation of their victims, we found, can be as cunning as it is cruel. Often the offenders isolate their victims from others, dominating their time, criticizing their parents and friends, and discouraging activities outside of the church and the priests' presence. The victims come to believe that the abusive relationship is the only one they have. This strategy of isolating victims not only deprives them of someone in whom they might confide; it also serves the priest's purpose—to continue the abusive relationship. Subsequently, the isolation often becomes one of the cruelest consequences of abuse, destroying families and lasting decades.

We saw victims who had been told by their abuser that their parents had sanctioned the priest's actions. In two cases, the victims discovered only recently, as they prepared to testify before the Grand Jury, that what the priest had told them was not true. For 20 years they had been estranged from their parents, sometimes hating them, because they believed that their parents had knowingly allowed their abuse. If a priest and God could betray them, how could they know that their parents had not as well? Parents, for their part, cannot understand their abused children, who for no apparent reason have turned their backs on school, church, friends, and family. Who suddenly are not funloving and happy, but sullen and withdrawn. Who are abusing alcohol and drugs and acting out in other ways. The parents blame their children.

Meanwhile, if other children suspect a boy is being abused, they often ridicule the victim, suggesting he is homosexual. And not just children do this. We heard testimony about a nun, the teacher of one victim, who—after the boy reported his abuse to police—began calling him by a girl's name in class, eliciting giggles from his fellow students. Most devastating of all, we saw firsthand what Father Thomas Doyle calls "soul murder." As Father Doyle, a conscientious Dominican priest who has assisted clergy-abuse victims around the world, points out, these children suffer from the abuse not just physically and psychologically, but spiritually. The faith they need to cope with the tragedies of life is for them forever defiled. In order for a priest to satisfy his sexual impulses, these children lose their innocence, their virginity, their security, and their faith. It is hard to think of a crime more heinous.

3. Priests who abuse minors usually have many victims.

> ## We saw victims who had been told by their abuser that their parents had sanctioned the priest's actions.

Another thing we learned about sexual abuse of minors is that the offenders typically have numerous victims. We heard from experts that the compulsion that drives some priests to molest or rape children is not curable, that treatment and supervision need to be intense and lifelong, and that the recidivism rate is extremely high. In the files of Philadelphia Archdiocese priests that we obtained by subpoena, we saw what must have been crystal-clear as well to Cardinals Krol and Bevilacqua and their aides: that many, many priests each have had many, many victims, often spanning decades.

The experts told us that, given the nature of the crime, victims who report their abuse represent merely the tip of the iceberg, and that abusive priests likely have preyed on many more victims who have not come forward. We heard reports, most of which the Archdiocese had also received, about 16 victims of Fr. Nicholas Cudemo, 14 victims of Fr. Raymond Leneweaver, 17 victims of Fr. James Brzyski, and 18 victims of Fr. Albert Kostelnick. We believe there were many more.

B. THE EVIDENCE PROVIDES MANY EXAMPLES THAT HELP ILLUSTRATE THE PATTERNS OF ABUSE.

There are many more Philadelphia-area priests who have molested and sodomized parishioners' children than are named here. We cannot in this Report describe the cases of every priest against whom allegations have been raised. But we have tried to include histories that reflect the depraved patterns, if not the full magnitude, of sexual abuse perpetrated by Philadelphia Archdiocese priests. Consider, for example, the cases of Frs. Brzyski, Cudemo, Chambers, Gana, Kostelnick, Leneweaver, Martins, and Sicoli.

FATHER JAMES BRZYSKI

It was Fr. Brzyski who told his victims that their parents knew and approved of his sexual abuse of their sons. The 6'5", 220-pound priest told this to a devout 12-year-old boy, "Sean," (the names of victims have been changed in this Report) whom he began anally raping in 1984. Sean, now a grown man, told the Jurors:

> I've harbored this feeling towards my mom for going on twenty years and to come to find out the other night that it's not—you know, it was—it wasn't true. She had no idea. She had absolutely no idea.
>
> So you know, I've been dealing with this. I've been hating her for twenty years for no reason whatsoever, and that's not right. That's my mom.

A top aide to Cardinal Bevilacqua described Father Nicholas Cudemo to the Grand Jury as "one of sickest people I ever knew."

Father Bryzski had started the abuse when Sean was 10 or 11 years old—fondling the boy's genitals and rubbing his own against the child in the corner of the sacristy where the altar boys dressed. Sean estimated that Fr. Brzyski molested him "a couple of hundred times." The abuse progressed from fondling to oral sex to anal rape.

Sean testified that he was scared, but he was devout. He believed that to say anything bad about a priest was a mortal sin, and that he would go to Hell if he told. So he said nothing, and continued to suffer the abuse even as its severity increased. His parents expressed pleasure that he was spending time with the priest. The abuse continued for seven or eight years.

Another of Fr. Brzyski's victims, "Billy," told the Grand Jury that his deepest wish was to return to who he had been before the priest first thrust his hands down the 11-year-old's pants. He wanted God back, and his parents, and the joy of celebrating Easter and Christmas. He wanted to believe in Heaven and morality. He described how Fr. Brzyski's abuse had "turned this good kid into this monster." He began to think of himself as two different people. He told the Jurors:

I had no God to turn to, no family, and it just went from having one person in me to having two people inside me.

This nice Billy...that used to live, and then this evil, this darkness Billy...that had to have no morals and no conscience in order to get by day by day and, you know, not to care about anything or have no feelings and to bury them feelings so that you could live every day and not be laying on the couch with a depression problem so bad that, you know, four days later you'd be in the same spot.

The Archdiocese files had the names of 11 boys who had been reported as victims of Fr. Brzyski. Three of his victims who testified before the Grand Jury provided names of still others they knew of. Sean told Jurors that he saw as many as a hundred photographs of boys, ages 13 to 16, many of them nude, which Fr. Brzyski kept in a box in his bedroom. One of the pictures was of Sean.

FATHER NICHOLAS CUDEMO

A top aide to Cardinal Bevilacqua described Father Nicholas Cudemo to the Grand Jury as "one of sickest people I ever knew." This priest raped an 11-year-old girl. He molested a 5th grader in the confessional. He invoked God to seduce and shame his victims. He maintained sexually abusive relationships simultaneously with several girls from the Catholic school where he was a teacher. His own family accused him of molesting his younger cousins.

Complaints of Fr. Cudemo's sexual abuse of adolescent girls began in 1966, with a letter to Cardinal Krol describing a three-year "affair" between the priest, then in his first assignment, and a junior at Lansdale Catholic High School. More allegations followed in 1968 and 1977, the latter alerting the Archdiocese to another long-term sexual relationship with a schoolgirl, and her possible pregnancy.

Father Cudemo began abusing another girl, "Ruth," in the late 1960s when she was 9 or 10 years old. When she was 11, he began to rape her. He would then hear her confession. He convinced the child that she could not survive without him, and that only through her confession was she worthy of God's love. When Ruth became pregnant at age 11 or 12, he took her for an abortion. He abused her until she was 17. She has suffered severely ever since.

Father Cudemo taught at three high schools—Bishop Neumann, Archbishop Kennedy, and Cardinal Dougherty—being transferred each time because of what were recorded in Archdiocese files as "particular friendships" with girls. He was then recycled through five parishes, and twice promoted by Cardinal Bevilacqua to serve as a parish pastor. The Grand Jury heard of at least 16 victims.

FATHER GERARD CHAMBERS

Father Gerard Chambers was accused of molesting numerous altar boys, and of anally and orally raping at least one, during 40 years as a priest in the Archdiocese. Beginning in 1994, four of his victims came forward to the Archdiocese to talk about their abuse. (The victims were from his 14th and 15th assignments—Saint Gregory, in West Philadelphia; and Seven Dolors, in Wyndmoor.) One victim, "Benjamin," told the Archdiocese that Fr. Chambers plied him with alcohol and cigarettes and then abused him, "hugging, kissing, masturbating" him and engaging in "mutual fondling of the genitals." This happened in the church sacristy, at Fr. Chambers' sister's house, and in the priest's car.

> **Often there were several boys involved in a weekend or on a trip, and Fr. Gana would have them take turns coming into his bed.**

Another victim, "Owen," has tried to commit suicide and has been institutionalized at a state mental hospital. Father Chambers anally and orally raped him when he was 12 years old. Owen was, and continues to be, especially devout. He suffers delusions because he cannot reconcile his faith in the Church with what happened to him. Two of his brothers, "George" and "Francis," were also victims of Fr. Chambers and are still haunted by their abuse more than 40 years later. They described to the Grand Jury how the abuse ruined their family—each boy withdrawing and suffering in silence, even though they knew, they said, on some level, that Fr. Chambers was abusing them all. They could not tell their parents, who taught them to be

in "awe" of priests. Rather than confide in anyone, George said they just "stuffed it down." But he began drinking at age 13, and still suffers from serious depression.

The victims named several other boys from Saint Gregory whom the priest had abused. One of the brothers testified that he believed Chambers "sexually abused every altar boy and quite frequently those who weren't altar boys."

FATHER STANLEY GANA

Father Stanley Gana also sexually abused countless boys in a succession of parishes. One victim, "John," who testified before the Grand Jury, had gone to Fr. Gana in 1977 because the then-14-year-old had been sexually abused by a family friend. Father Gana used his position as a counselor and the ruse of therapy to persuade the boy to have physical contact with him. This "therapy" slowly progressed to full-fledged sexual abuse, involving genital touching, masturbation, and oral and anal sodomy. It continued for more than five years. Father Gana abused John in the rectory, at a house at the New Jersey Shore, on trips, and at the priest's weekend house in the Poconos. Often there were several boys involved in a weekend or on a trip, and Fr. Gana would have them take turns coming into his bed. Sometimes he would have sex with John and another boy, "Timmy," at the same time.

Father Gana abused Timmy for nearly six years, beginning in 1980, when the boy was 13. The priest ingratiated himself with Timmy's parents. He was a frequent dinner guest and he often brought gifts to the family. He hired Timmy to work in the rectory, took him on trips with John and other boys to Niagara Falls and Disney World, and for weekends to the Poconos. Timmy's parents pressured their son to spend time with Fr. Gana and constantly told Timmy that he should be grateful for all the priest did for him. Timmy found it impossible to avoid or report his abuse. He knew that his parents' view of priests could not be reconciled with his reality—the obese priest pushing the boy's scrawny, undeveloped body across a rectory bed so that his face was pressed against the carpet, ignoring the boy's cries of pain, and forcibly penetrating him anally. Timmy was sure his parents would not believe him.

In 1992, training to become a priest himself and in his final year of seminary, Timmy told Cardinal Bevilacqua's Secretary for Clergy, William Lynn, and another aide about his years of abuse by Fr. Gana. But, after hearing from the seminary dean that he thought Timmy "might sue the diocese for pedophilia," Cardinal Bevilacqua ordered an investigation—of the seminarian. The probe failed to prove any wrongdoing on Timmy's part, but the Cardinal refused to allow the victim to complete his studies and forced him to seek ordination outside the diocese. Father Gana remained an active priest in the Archdiocese until 2002.

FATHER ALBERT KOSTELNICK

The Secret Archives file (where the Archdiocese, in accordance with Canon law, recorded complaints of sexual abuse by priests) for Father Kostelnick contained numerous reports that he sexually fondled young girls. The reported incidents spanned 32 years, beginning in 1968, when he fondled the genitals and breasts of three sisters, ages 6 to 13 years old, as he showed slides to their parents in the family's darkened living room. The three sisters also reported, in 2002, that Fr. Kostelnick had fondled their other sister as she lay in traction in a hospital following an automobile accident in 1971. They said the injured girl had to ring for the nurse to stop her molestation.

In 1987, Fr. Kostelnick was reported to the police for fondling an 8-year-old girl in an offensive manner. Cardinal Bevilacqua learned of additional complaints in 1988 and 1992, yet he allowed the priest to continue as pastor of Saint Mark parish in Bristol. The priest admitted in 2004 to the Archdiocese Review Board that his "longstanding habit" of "fondling the breasts of young girls" continued after these victims' complaints were ignored in 1992. In 1997, Cardinal Bevilacqua honored the serial molester at a luncheon at the Cardinal's house and set him loose as a senior priest in a new parish, Assumption B.V.M. in Feasterville. By the time Fr. Kostelnick was finally removed from ministry in 2004 (after Cardinal Bevilacqua's tenure had ended), the Archdiocese had heard reports about at least 18 victims.

FATHER RAYMOND LENEWEAVER

At Saint Monica parish in South Philadelphia, Fr. Leneweaver named a group of altar boys whom he abused the "Philadelphia Rovers" and had T-shirts made up for them. He took the 11- and 12-year-olds on outings and, when he was alone with them, he molested them. He anally raped at least one boy. He repeatedly pulled another out of class at the parish grade school, took him to the school auditorium, forced the boy to bend over a table, and rubbed against him until the priest ejaculated. Another time in his rectory bedroom, Fr. Leneweaver pulled the boy's pants down, smeared lubricant on his buttocks, and thrust his penis against the boy's backside. Each time the priest's crimes were reported to the Archdiocese, he admitted his offenses. By 1975, he had confessed to homosexual activity with at least seven named children with whom he was "seriously involved." He told Archdiocese officials of others he was involved with "in an incidental fashion."

Cardinal Krol transferred this chronic abuser four times after learning of his admitted abuses. Predictably, Fr. Leneweaver continued to abuse boys in his new parishes. When he finally requested a leave from ministry in 1980, Cardinal Krol wrote a notation on a memo to his Chancellor:

His problem is not occupational or geographical & will follow him wherever he goes. He should be convinced that his orientation is an acquired preference for a particular method of satisfying a normal human appetite. —An appetite which is totally incompatible with vow of chastity + commitment to celibacy.

While this note shows that the Cardinal understood the compulsive nature of pedophilia and knew the likelihood that Fr. Leneweaver would abuse boys wherever he was assigned, the parents of his victims could not imagine such abhorrent behavior from a priest. They could not have conceived of the truth—that Fr. Leneweaver had been transferred to Saint Monica after admitting to the abuse of another boy at a previous assignment. The father of one victim beat his son until he was unconscious when the boy tried to report Fr. Leneweaver's actions. The devout father, trusting priests and the Church more than his son, repeated as he beat the boy, "priests don't do that."

They could not have conceived of the truth—that Fr. Leneweaver had been transferred to Saint Monica after admitting to the abuse of another boy at a previous assignment.

FATHER NILO MARTINS

Father Martins was a Brazilian pediatrician and religious-order priest who came to the Archdiocese in 1978. In May 1984, he was assigned as an assistant pastor at Incarnation of Our Lord in North Philadelphia. On a Saturday afternoon in early February 1985, he invited a 12-year-old altar boy, "Daniel," up to his rectory bedroom to watch television, ordered the boy to undress, and anally raped him.

Daniel, now a Philadelphia police officer, testified that as he cried out in pain, the priest kept insisting: "Tell me that you like it." Daniel told the Grand Jury that he saw blood and was terrified. When the priest was done, he gave Daniel a puzzle as a present and told the boy to get dressed and leave.

Daniel, who had an unhappy home life and an abusive stepfather, went down to the church and cried. A young priest he considered a friend, Fr. Peter Welsh, saw him and asked what happened. After Daniel finished telling him, Fr. Martins entered and approached the two. Father Welsh then left the boy, took Fr. Martins' confession, and never returned to talk to the boy.

A few days later, Daniel confided in his lay math teacher at the parish grade school. The teacher was horrified and immediately informed the pastor, Fr. John Shelley. The teacher also encouraged Daniel to tell his parents. Frightened that he might be beaten if he told his mother and stepfather, Daniel asked Fr. Welsh to go with him to tell them. Father Welsh said he was busy. The pastor, who should have reported the boy's rape to police, or at least to his parents, also refused to accompany the boy to his house. Daniel finally got up the nerve to tell his mother. At her urging, he called the police.

The next day, when Daniel went to the church—as he did everyday to be with his friends—Fr. Shelley told him that he was not welcome anymore. The 12-year-old victim of a brutal anal rape by a priest was no longer allowed to be an altar boy. As word circulated, children at school called him a "faggot" and laughed as they said, "Ah, you got fucked in the ass." Even a teacher, Sister Maria Loyola, he said, started referring to him in class as "Daniella," prompting the class to laugh. When he asked her to stop calling him that, she gave him a demerit.

The 12-year-old victim of a brutal anal rape by a priest was no longer allowed to be an altar boy.

Daniel said he just wanted to disappear. Unable to change schools, he dropped out emotionally—withdrawing socially and failing academically. Father Martins pleaded guilty to involuntary deviate sexual intercourse and corruption of the morals of a minor. Deported back to Brazil, he did not serve his prison sentence.

FATHER DAVID SICOLI

Father Sicoli paid for tuition, computers, and trips to Africa and Disney World for parish boys he took a particular liking to. He invited several to live in his rectories with him, and he gave them high-paying jobs and leadership positions in the Church's youth group, the CYO. Some of them in interviews insisted that nothing sexual took place with the priest. But others, now grown, told the Grand Jury that Fr. Sicoli sexually abused them and treated them as if they were his girlfriends. From the start of his priesthood, and continuing through 2001, priests who lived with Fr. Sicoli warned the Archdiocese about his unhealthy relationships with boys.

Four victims from Immaculate Conception in Levittown, where Fr. Sicoli was assigned from 1978 to 1983, testified that he had sexually abused them when they were 12 to 16 years old. All of them said that Fr. Sicoli had plied them with alcohol and then abused them. Three told of being taken to a bar, the Red Garter, in North Wildwood, New Jersey. After Fr. Sicoli got the boys drunk, he asked them to drive him home—even though they were only 14 years old. On separate occasions, with all three, the priest feigned sickness in the car and asked them to rub his stomach. He then requested that they go "lower" and rub his crotch. The abuse these victims reported included mutual masturbation and oral sex. They said that Fr. Sicoli acted jealous and immature and threatened to fire them from their rectory jobs if they did not do what he wanted.

Despite reports in Fr. Sicoli's Secret Archives file of inappropriate relationships with these four victims and five other boys, Cardinal Bevilacqua appointed the priest to four pastorates between 1990 and 1999. At each one he seized on a favorite boy, or a succession of favorites, on whom he showered attention, money, and trips. Three of these boys lived with Fr. Sicoli in the rectories with the knowledge of Msgr. Lynn.

In October 2004, the Archdiocese finally removed Fr. Sicoli from ministry following an investigation by the Archdiocesan Review Board, which was created in 2002 to help assess allegations of abuse. The Review Board found "multiple substantiated allegations involving a total of 11 minors over an extensive period of time beginning in 1977 and proceeding to 2002."

OVERVIEW OF THE COVER-UP BY ARCHDIOCESE OFFICIALS

For a more complete picture of the actions taken by the Archdiocese to hide priest sexual abuse—from parents, potential victims, and the public at large—it is necessary to read the Case Studies in Section V of this Report. This Section, however, will provide an outline of the careful methods by which the Archdiocese accomplished its concealment of these crimes, and thereby facilitated the abuse of even more Archdiocese children.

A. ARCHDIOCESE LEADERS WERE AWARE THAT PRIESTS WERE SEXUALLY ABUSING HUNDREDS OF CHILDREN, AND THAT THEIR CONTINUED MINISTRY PRESENTED GREAT DANGER.

Grand Jurors heard evidence proving that Cardinals Bevilacqua and Krol, and their aides, were aware that priests in the diocese were perpetrating massive amounts of child molestations and sexual assaults. The Archdiocese's own files reveal a steady stream of reports and allegations from the 1960s through the 1980s, accelerating in the 1990s (with nearly 100 allegations in that decade), and exploding after 2001. In many cases, the same priests were reported again and again.

Notes in Archdiocese files prove that the Church leaders not only saw, but understood, that sexually offending priests typically have multiple victims, and are unlikely to stop abusing children unless the opportunity is removed. Cardinal Krol displayed his understanding of sexual compulsion when he wrote, in the case of Fr. Leneweaver, that the priest's problem would "follow him wherever he goes." Cardinal Bevilacqua noted in the file of Fr. Connor, an admitted child molester, that the priest could present a "serious risk" if allowed to continue in ministry (which he was). Notes in the file of Fr. Peter Dunne show that Cardinal Bevilacqua also was aware that therapists recommend lifelong supervision and restricted access to children for pedophiles. (Fr. Dunne, a diagnosed pedophile, did not receive such supervision and was permitted to continue in parish ministry.)

Secretary for Clergy William Lynn displayed his understanding of child molestation when he told Fr. Thomas Shea that "the evidence of the medical profession" makes it "very unusual for such instances [of sexual abuse] to be with only one youngster." Cardinal Bevilacqua and his staff also knew from experience that most victims do not report their abuse until many years later, if at all.

B. ARCHDIOCESE LEADERS EMPLOYED DELIBERATE STRATEGIES TO CONCEAL KNOWN ABUSE.

In the face of crimes they knew were being committed by their priests, Church leaders could have reported them to police. They could have removed the child molesters from ministry, and stopped the sexual abuse of minors by Archdiocesan clerics. Instead, they consistently chose to conceal the abuse rather than to end it. They chose to protect themselves from scandal and liability rather than protect children from the priests' crimes.

For most of Cardinal Krol's tenure, concealment mainly entailed persuading victims' parents not to report the priests' crimes to police, and transferring priests to other parishes if parents demanded it or if "general scandal" seemed imminent. When Cardinal Bevilacqua took over as Archbishop in February 1988, concern over legal liability had joined fears of scandal. Dioceses across the country were grappling with the implications of a 1984 case in which a Louisiana diocese paid $4.2 million to nine victims of a pedophile priest.

Cardinal Bevilacqua was trained as an attorney. (He holds degrees in Canon law from Pontifical Gregorian University in Rome, Italy, and in American law from St. Johns' University Law School in Queens, New York.) The Grand Jurors find that, in his handling of priests' sexual abuse, Cardinal Bevilacqua was motivated by an intent to keep the record clear of evidence that would implicate him or the Archdiocese. To this end, he continued many of the practices of his predecessor, Cardinal Krol, aimed at avoiding scandal, while also introducing policies that reflected a growing awareness that dioceses and bishops might be held legally responsible for their negligent and knowing actions that abetted known abusers.

To protect themselves from negative publicity or expensive lawsuits—while keeping abusive priests active—the Cardinals and their aides hid the priests' crimes from parishioners, police, and the general public. They employed a variety of tactics to accomplish this end.

1. Archdiocese leaders conducted non-investigations designed to avoid establishing priests' guilt.

At first, Grand Jurors wondered whether Archdiocese officials, including Cardinal Bevilacqua and his aides, were tragically incompetent at rooting out sexually abusive priests and removing them from ministry. Secretary for Clergy William Lynn suggested, for example, that accusations made against Fr. Stanley Gana in 1992—of anal rape, oral sodomy, and years of molestation of adolescent boys—"must have fallen through the cracks," since Fr. Gana remained a pastor three more years until another allegation surfaced. Soon the Jurors came to realize that sexual abuse cases in the Philadelphia Archdiocese did not fall "through the cracks" by accident or mistake.

> **The only "investigation" conducted after a victim reported being abused was to ask the priest if he did what was alleged.**

The Secretary for Clergy, whom Cardinal Bevilacqua assigned to investigate allegations of sexual abuse by priests, routinely failed to interview even named victims, not to mention rectory staff and colleagues in a position to observe the accused priests. The only "investigation" conducted after a victim reported being abused was to ask the priest if he did what was alleged. If the accused priest, whose very crime is characterized by deceit and secretiveness, denied the allegation, Archdiocese officials considered the allegation unproven. Monsignor Lynn professed to the Grand Jury that he could not determine the credibility of accusations—no matter how detailed the victims' descriptions, or how many corroborating witnesses there might be, or how many similar accusations had been made against a priest by victims who did not know each other, or how incriminating a priest's own explanation of the events.

The reason for Msgr. Lynn's apparent lack of judgment, curiosity, or common sense in refusing to acknowledge the truth of abuse allegations became evident when Cardinal Bevilacqua testified. The Cardinal said that, when assigning and promoting priests, he disregarded anonymous or third-party reports of sexual crimes against children that were contained in many priests' files. The Cardinal, like his Secretary for Clergy, claimed to be unable to determine whether the reports were true. He told the Grand Jury that he could not know without an investigation. And yet the staff, with his approval, never truly investigated these reports—no matter how serious, how believable, or how easily verified. This was the case even when victims were named and other priests had witnessed and reported incidents. The Cardinal conceded under questioning that allegations against a priest were generally not labeled "credible" unless the priest happened to confess.

The Grand Jury is convinced that the Archdiocese could have identified scores of child molesters in the priesthood simply by encouraging other clergy to report what they witnessed—for example, incidents in which they saw fellow priests routinely take young boys, alone, into their bedrooms. We heard from many victims that their abuse had been witnessed by other priests. Fellow priests observed Frs. Nicholas Cudemo, Craig Brugger, Richard McLoughlin, Albert Kostelnick, Francis Rogers, James Brzyski, and John Schmeer as they were abusing young victims. None of these witnesses helped the children or reported what they saw. Father Donald Walker confirmed what we came to believe—that the Archdiocese had an unwritten rule discouraging "ratting on fellow priests."

We were initially incredulous when Cardinal Bevilacqua insisted that Msgr. Lynn was very intelligent and competent. After all, the Secretary for Clergy's "investigations" did not bother with witnesses, nor did they seek the truth or falsity of allegations, unless the priest happened to confess. But after reviewing files that all contained the same "incompetent" investigation techniques, it became apparent to the Grand Jurors that Msgr. Lynn was handling the cases precisely as his boss wished.

2. The Cardinals transferred known abusers to other parishes where their reputations were not known and parents could not, therefore, protect their children.

a. The decision whether to transfer a known abuser was determined by the threat of scandal or lawsuit, not by the priest's guilt or the danger he posed.

Father Donald Walker was one of three priests in Cardinal Krol's Chancery Office charged with investigating and handling sexual abuse allegations against priests. He explained to the Grand Jury how, during his tenure, the Archdiocese's primary goal in dealing with these cases was to reduce the risk of "scandal" to the Church. The Grand Jurors saw this pattern for ourselves as we reviewed the files of priests accused of molesting minors. Whether an accused molester stayed in his position, was transferred to another parish, or was removed from ministry, the Archdiocese response bore no consistent relationship to the seriousness of his offense or the risk he posed to the children of his parish. Rather, the decision was based entirely on an assessment of the risk of scandal or, under Cardinal Bevilacqua, legal liability.

We saw this vividly illustrated in the case of Fr. John Mulholland. In 1970, Archdiocese managers had reason to believe that Fr. Mulholland was taking parish boys at Saint Anastasia in Newtown Square on vacations and engaging in sadomasochistic behaviors with them. An adviser to the church's youth group, the CYO, had warned the managers and given the names of many of the boys involved. Believing at first that Fr. Mulholland's reputation for "play[ing] around with boys" was widespread, Archdiocese officials decided he would have to be reassigned because of "scandal." Many of the parents of these boys, however, never imagined what was going on and opposed Fr. Mulholland's transfer. When the Archdiocese officials realized that there was no hue and cry, they decided to let Fr. Mulholland stay in the parish where they had been told he was committing his abuse. The reason for the change of heart was recorded in Church documents: "the amount of scandal given seemed to lie only with a very small minority."

While Archdiocese memos recording abuse allegations often omitted the names of victims or the nature of the priests' offenses, they almost never failed to note the degree of scandal or whether the victim had told anyone else. When scandal threatened, the Archdiocese would take action. During Cardinal Krol's administration, this almost always meant a transfer to another parish and the managers' memos unabashedly recorded the motive. In Fr. Joseph Gausch's file, for example, one of his many transfers was explained this way: "because of the scandal which already has taken place and because of the possible future scandal, we will transfer him in the near future."

Cardinal Bevilacqua's decisions, like his predecessor's, were similarly dictated by an assessment of risk to the Archdiocese. In the case of Fr. Cudemo, multiple victims came forward in 1991, reporting to the Archdiocese that the priest had abused them when they were minors. One he had raped when she was 11 years old, another he had had a sexual relationship with for 14 years, beginning when she was 15. The priest's Secret Archives file contained at least three allegations previously made against the priest. As more and more victims came forward, Cardinal Bevilacqua steadfastly refused to remove Fr. Cudemo as pastor of Saint Callistus parish. Only when some of the victims threatened to sue the Archdiocese and Cardinal Bevilacqua did he finally ask the priest to leave his parish. After the lawsuit was dismissed because the statute of limitations had run, the Cardinal permitted Fr. Cudemo to resume ministering.

b. Parishioners were not told, or were misled about, the reason for the abuser's transfer.

When Fr. Brennan was removed from an assignment in 1992 because of allegations of improper behavior with several parish boys, one parishioner remembers being told to pray for the Father because he was "being treated for Lyme Disease."

The Archdiocese's purpose in transferring its sexually abusive priests was clear—to remove them from parishes where parents knew of their behavior and to place them among unsuspecting families. The obvious premise of this pattern was the Church officials' understanding that parents would never knowingly allow their children to serve as altar boys, or work in rectories, or be taken to the New Jersey Shore by men they knew had molested other boys. The result of the Archdiocese's purposeful action was to multiply the number of children exposed to these priests while reducing the possibility that their parents could protect them.

Cardinal Bevilacqua had a strict policy, according to his aides, that forbid informing parishioners— either those whose children had recently been exposed to a sexual offender in his old parish or the parents of potential victims in a newly assigned parish—about any problems in a priest's background. The Cardinal, in fact, encouraged that

parishioners be misinformed. When Fr. Brennan was removed from an assignment in 1992 because of allegations of improper behavior with several parish boys, one parishioner remembers being told to pray for the Father because he was "being treated for Lyme Disease." Even the pastors of the new parishes, who might have supervised the abusers if aware of their history, were usually told nothing.

c. Sexual Offenders were transferred to distant parishes where their reputations would not be known.

If a priest was particularly notorious or a former victim was vigilant and vocal, the Archdiocese would transfer the priest to an especially distant parish, in hopes of escaping notice. Thus, after Fr. Leneweaver had abused boys in parishes in Philadelphia, Delaware, and Chester Counties, Chancellor Francis Statkus lamented that "the latest incident eliminates his usefulness in his ministry in the area of Chester County," and explained that he was to be transferred next to Bucks County "because it is one of the few remaining areas where his scandalous action may not be known." A notation in Fr. Leneweaver's file stated that his reassignment would not be announced, making it unlikely that anyone could forewarn the parents in his new parish.

Cardinal Bevilacqua used a similar strategy in 1992, when considering a reassignment for Fr. Michael McCarthy. The Cardinal just months earlier had received allegations that the priest had regularly taken students from Cardinal O'Hara High School to his beach house, plied them with liquor, slept nude in the same bed with them, and masturbated the boys and himself. The Cardinal had an aide tell the accused priest that, despite the allegations against him, he could be "appointed pastor at another parish after an interval of time has passed." That new parish, according to the Cardinal's instructions, "would be distant from St. Kevin Parish so that the profile can be as low as possible and not attract the attention of the complainant."

If a priest was arrested or convicted and his crimes publicized in the news, more extreme measures were needed to return the abuser to ministry among uninformed parishioners. Thus, when Archbishop Bevilacqua was deciding where to assign Fr. Edward DePaoli after his conviction for possessing child pornography, he wrote: "for the present time it might be more advisable for [Fr.

DePaoli] to return to the active ministry in another diocese." The Archbishop explained that this move would "put a sufficient period between the publicity and reinstatement in the active ministry of the Archdiocese of Philadelphia." He arranged for Fr. DePaoli to be assigned to a parish in New Jersey for three years.

d. The Archdiocese harbored abusers transferred from other dioceses.

Cardinal Bevilacqua also reciprocated with other dioceses, as part of what an aide referred to as the "tradition of bishops helping bishops." For five years, beginning in 1988, Cardinal Bevilacqua secretly harbored a New Jersey priest, Fr. John Connor, at Saint Matthew parish in Conshohocken so that the bishop in Camden could avoid scandal there. Cardinal Bevilacqua, despite an earlier acknowledgement that Fr. Connor could present a "serious risk," did not inform Saint Matthew's pastor of the danger. In fact, he told the pastor that Fr. Connor had come to the parish from another diocese because his mother was sick and he wanted to be near her. The pastor never knew, until he read it years later in a newspaper, that Fr. Connor had been arrested in his home diocese of Camden for sexually abusing a 14-year-old. As a result of his ignorance, the pastor did not worry, as he should have, when Fr. Connor showered attention and gifts on a boy in the parish grade school.

> The Archdiocese managers, however, never reported a single instance of sexual abuse—*even when admitted by the priests*—and did everything in their power to prevent others from reporting it.

3. Archdiocese leaders made concerted efforts to prevent reports of priest abuse to law enforcement.

The hundreds of allegations of sexual abuse by priests that the Archdiocese has received since 1967 have included serious crimes—among them, the genital fondling and anal, oral, and vaginal rape of children. Sometimes the abuse was ongoing at the time it was reported. The obvious response would have been to report such crimes to law enforcement, to allow police to investigate and to stop the perpetrators. The Archdiocese managers, however, never reported a single instance of

sexual abuse—*even when admitted by the priests*—and did everything in their power to prevent others from reporting it.

Cardinal Bevilacqua was asked repeatedly when he testified before the Grand Jury why he and his aides never reported these crimes to law enforcement. His answer was simply that Pennsylvania law did not require them to. That answer is unacceptable (as well as the result of a strained and narrow interpretation of a law specifically intended to require reporting sexual abuse of children). It reflects a willingness to allow such crimes to continue, as well as an utter indifference to the suffering of the victims. Such thinking is the reason, for example, that Fr. Leneweaver, an admitted abuser of 11- and 12-year-old boys, was able to receive a clean criminal record check and teach Latin at Radnor Middle School last year.

Not only did Church officials not report the crimes; they went even further, by persuading parents not to involve law enforcement—promising that the Archdiocese would take appropriate action itself. When the father of a 14-year-old boy reported to Cardinal Krol's Chancellor in 1982 that Fr. Trauger had molested his son and that he had told someone in the Morals Division of the Police Department (the father was himself a detective), the Chancellor succeeded in fending off prosecution. Chancellor Statkus informed the Cardinal: "Convinced of our sincere resolve to take the necessary action regarding Fr. T., [the victim's father] does not plan to press any charges, police or otherwise." (What Cardinal Krol did upon receiving this information was what he had done a year before, when Fr. Trauger had attempted to anally rape a 12-year-old boy from his previous parish: the Cardinal merely transferred the priest to another parish, where his crimes would not be known.)

Once in a while priests engaged so publicly in abusive acts that their crimes could not be concealed—such as when police in Rockville, Maryland stopped Fr. Thomas Durkin—a Philadelphia priest who was visiting the area—in the middle of the night. At the time of the police encounter, the priest was chasing a half-dressed 16-year-old boy through the streets. The teenager had run from their shared bedroom to escape Fr. Durkin's sexual advances. In that case, the Archdiocese had to rely on the local diocese to intervene to keep the police from taking action. Having successfully hidden its priest's crime and prevented the prosecution of it, the Archdiocese then permitted Fr. Durkin to continue in ministry despite his admission that he had abused other boys as well.

4. Church leaders carefully avoided actions that would incriminate themselves or the priests.

Some of the Archdiocese leaders' actions or inactions, which initially might have seemed merely callous or reckless, we soon came to realize were part of a deliberate and all-encompassing strategy to avoid revealing their knowledge of crimes. Church officials understood that knowing about the abuse, while taking steps that helped perpetuate it, made them responsible for endangering children.

Many victims, for example, told the Grand Jurors that they were treated badly by the Secretary for Clergy when they reported their abuse. After recounting their nightmarish experiences to the Archdiocese managers, the victims were surprised at the lack of outrage toward the priest or compassion toward the victim. They had wanted desperately to be believed and hoped for an apology. They expected that the Archdiocese, once informed, would make sure the offenders would never again hurt the children of their parishes. Instead, the Church official charged with assisting the victims often questioned their credibility and motives. When victims needing reassurance that the abuse had not been their fault asked Msgr. Lynn whether their abuser had other victims, the Secretary for Clergy refused to tell them—or lied and said they were the only one. Cardinal Bevilacqua's highest aide, Vicar for Administration Edward Cullen, instructed his assistant, James Molloy (who at times displayed glimpses of compassion for victims), never to tell victims that he believed them. Doing so would have made evident the Church officials' knowledge of other criminal acts and made later denials difficult.

Archdiocese leaders even left children in dangerous situations with known abusers rather than reveal their culpable knowledge by intervening to protect a child. Thus, when Archdiocese managers learned, on two separate occasions, that parish boys were on camping trips with Frs. Francis Trauger and John Mulholland—priests they had just been told were abusers—they did nothing to interrupt the camping trips. Nor did they do anything afterwards to keep the priests away from the boys or to warn their parents.

Cardinal Krol's Assistant Chancellor, Vincent Walsh, sat silently while parents from Saint Anastasia in Newtown Square voiced support for Fr. Mulholland, asking that the Archdiocese reconsider its decision to transfer the priest to another parish. These parents vouched for Fr. Mulholland's interest in their sons: one was grateful that the priest had taken his child on vacation without asking for money from the parents, another that the priest had helped his son gain entry to a sought-after school. At the time of the meeting, Fr. Walsh knew what the parents did not: that these teens had been reported as possible victims of Fr. Mulholland's sadomasochistic behavior. The Assistant Chancellor said nothing to warn the unsuspecting parents, and Cardinal Krol left Fr. Mulholland in their parish.

In another case, when a school psychologist learned from a third party that Fr. Brzyski had sexually abused a student, he informed the Archdiocese that it was important to the boy's mental health to talk to him about the abuse. Archdiocese officials, at that time, had already received numerous reports of Fr. Brzyski's assaults on altar boys, and the priest had admitted having sexual relations with this particular victim. Still, the Archdiocese managers refused to allow the psychologist to help the boy. Rather than acknowledge the abuse they were pretending not to know about, they chose to let the boy suffer.

When Msgr. Lynn learned that a priest and a teacher at Saint Matthew's parish were concerned in 1994 because Fr. Connor was still visiting a young boy in the parish after the priest was mysteriously transferred back to Camden, the Secretary for Clergy informed the Archdiocese's lawyer, but not the boy's mother. Similarly in 2002, Msgr. Lynn, knowing Fr. Sicoli's long history of inappropriate relations with adolescent boys, left two teenage brothers living with the child molester in his rectory rather taking action that might have alerted the boys' mother to the danger.

5. Archdiocese officials tried to keep their files devoid of incriminating evidence.

Even in their internal files, Archdiocese officials tried to limit evidence of priests' crimes and their own guilty knowledge of them. Under Canon law, the Archdiocese was required to maintain special files—in "Secret Archives," kept in a locked room accessible only to the Archbishop, the Secretary for Clergy, and their aides—that recorded complaints against priests such as those involving sexual abuse of minors. Church officials could not, therefore, simply conceal priests' crimes by never recording them. The managers did, however, record information in ways that often masked the nature of the reported abuse and the actions taken in response. Written records of allegations often left out the names of potential victims, while euphemisms obscured the actual nature of offenses. An attempted anal rape of a 12-year-old boy, for example, was recorded in Archdiocese files as "touches." The Grand Jury often could not tell from memos reporting "boundary violations" and "unnatural involvements" exactly what the Church officials had been told.

In addition, many of the communications discussing priest sexual abuse were oral. Under Cardinal Bevilacqua's policy, aides would inform him immediately when abuse allegations came into the Archdiocese, but not in writing. His initial response and instructions were not recorded.

6. Church leaders manipulated abusive priests' psychological evaluations to keep them in ministry.

a. Officials used therapy and evaluation to give false reassurances.

When confronted with allegations that they could not easily ignore, Church officials sometimes sent priests for psychological evaluations. A true determination of a priest's fitness to minister was not, however, their main purpose. Cardinal Krol's use of these evaluations for public-relations purposes was blatant. He often transferred child molesters to new parishes *before* evaluations finding them mentally fit—usually with no convincing evidence—were completed or received by the Archdiocese. We saw this in the cases of Frs. Trauger and Leneweaver.

Father Leneweaver was transferred to his last assignment even when the evaluation did not declare him fit. Cardinal Krol found the evaluation useful nonetheless, as his Chancellor explained in a memo, so that "the faithful of West Chester," the priest's old parish, would be reassured "that the case of Father Leneweaver is being carefully

studied and that he was not being reassigned routinely." On another occasion, when the mother of one of Fr. Leneweaver's victims complained that her son's molester had merely been recycled to a new parish, Chancellor Statkus wrote that he "assured her that truly Father Leneweaver was appointed in accord with medical advice, and that he [had] undergone therapy and medical attention."

b. Cardinal Bevilacqua instituted a test that falsely purported to exclude pedophiles.

By the time Cardinal Bevilacqua became Archbishop in Philadelphia, it was no longer possible to tell victims' parents that an abusive priest had been treated and was now fit for a parish assignment. The Cardinal was aware of the nature of pedophilia—that it cannot be cured, that sexual abusers of children often have hundreds of victims, that the abusers need lifelong treatment and supervision, and that they need to be kept away from children. In 1985, he had been given a copy of a report, the Doyle-Mouton-Peterson "Manual," and had discussed it with one of the authors, Fr. Thomas Doyle, who testified before the Grand Jury. The report contained several medical articles on sexual disorders, as well as legal and pastoral analyses. The authors were hoping to alert the U.S. bishops to the problems presented by pedophilia among priests and to help bishops know how to handle cases as they arose.

Cardinal Bevilacqua, however, used this knowledge about pedophilia not to protect children, but to shield the Archdiocese from liability. Central to his scheme was a policy designed to sound tough: Based on what was known about sexual abusers, he would not give an assignment to any priest who was diagnosed as a pedophile (someone with an enduring sexual attraction to prepubescent children) or an ephebophile (someone with an enduring sexual attraction to adolescents). But then he and his aides made a mockery of evaluation and therapy to avoid reaching these diagnoses. In the absence of a formal designation of pedophilia or ephobophilia, Archdiocese officials perverted logic to reach the converse of the Cardinal's "rule"—if a priest was not diagnosed a pedophile, he *would* be given an assignment. Never mind the Church leaders' full knowledge that the priest had abused children.

Church-affiliated centers would often fail to diagnose priests as pedophiles if they claimed to be acting under the influence of drugs or alcohol, or had sex with adults.

In fact, a failure to diagnose a priest as a pedophile is not the same thing as determining that he is *not* a pedophile. We repeatedly saw situations where treatment facilities found evidence to suggest pedophilia, but did not have sufficient information to make a conclusive diagnosis. This was especially problematic when the "treatment facility" did not use up-to-date tests and technology in making its diagnoses, and instead relied primarily on self-reports of the priests. The Archdiocese-owned Saint John Vianney Hospital was such a facility. In other words, to determine if a priest was a pedophile, the "treatment" facility often simply asked the priest. Not surprisingly, the priest often said no.

In addition, Church-affiliated centers would often fail to diagnose priests as pedophiles if they claimed to be acting under the influence of drugs or alcohol, or had sex with adults. According to one of Fr. Gana's victims, who had been forced to have oral and anal sex with the priest beginning when he was 13 years old, Secretary for Clergy Lynn asked him to understand that the Archdiocese would have taken steps to remove Fr. Gana from the priesthood had he been diagnosed as a pedophile. But Fr. Gana was not only having sex with children and teenage minors, Msgr. Lynn explained; he had also slept with women, abused alcohol, and stolen money from parish churches. That is why he remained, with Cardinal Bevilacqua's blessing, a priest in active ministry. "You see..." said Msgr. Lynn, "he's not a pure pedophile."

As a result of these policies, as the Cardinal himself acknowledged, "it was very rare that a priest would diagnose as such [a pedophile]." And yet, the Philadelphia-area priesthood harbored numerous serial child molesters. The Cardinal's litmus test was, on its face, grossly inadequate to protect children. It did, however, serve the Cardinal's purpose. He was able to say that he had a policy of not assigning pedophiles to the ministry.

c. Church officials interfered with evaluations.

Cardinal Bevilacqua's policy afforded easy opportunities for Archdiocese managers to manipulate treatment and diagnoses to keep abusive priests in the ministry. Secretary for Clergy Lynn often failed to provide incriminating information to therapists about priests he sent for evaluation. No Church-affiliated therapists spoke to victims or witnesses. The Cardinal allowed priests to shop for diagnoses, granting requests for second opinions when the priest was dissatisfied with the first.

The Grand Jurors find it significant that, according to the records we reviewed, the Archdiocese stopped using the Saint Luke Institute in Suitland, Maryland, a facility it had used often in the past that does use up-to-date evaluation tools. The relationship with Saint Luke ended in 1993 after it diagnosed Fr. McCarthy as an ephebophile. (The priest had admitted to therapists that he was sexually attracted to adolescent males.) Thereafter, Church officials began referring sexual offenders almost exclusively to the Archdiocese's own Saint John Vianney Hospital for evaluation—a facility under Cardinal Bevilacqua's purview and supervision and more attuned to his priorities.

The risk, however, was not that the priest might further harm the victims—it was that he might apologize to them.

d. The Cardinal attempted to evade personal liability for retaining abusers by claiming to rely on therapists' recommendations.

When asked by the Grand Jury why he placed obviously dangerous men in positions where they could abuse children, Cardinal Bevilacqua repeatedly testified that he relied on the advice of therapists. Those therapists, however, more often than not worked for him. That they understood their role as protecting the Archdiocese from legal liability was evident in many of the files we reviewed.

The therapists at Saint John Vianney, for example, warned in their "psychological evaluation" that returning Fr. John Gillespie to his parish, where he had abused two current parishioners, could present a risk. The risk, however, was not that the priest might further harm the victims—it was that he might apologize to them. Archdiocesan therapists warned: "If he pursues making amends with others, he could bring forth...legal jeopardy." In a similar vein, Msgr. Lynn asked the therapists "evaluating" Fr. Brennan at Saint John Vianney: "Should Father remain in his present assignment since there seems to be much gossip throughout the parish about his behavior?"

Even when therapists did recommend meaningful action, moreover, the Cardinal did not always follow their advice—especially when it conflicted with that of the Archdiocese's lawyers. We saw this in the case of Fr. Dunne (one of the few diagnosed pedophiles), who remained in ministry for seven and a half years after the Archdiocese learned he had abused several boys. Cardinal Bevilacqua first had Chancellor Samuel Shoemaker pressure a Saint John Vianney therapist to make an "accommodation" in the hospital's initial recommendations that Fr. Dunne be removed from parish ministry and that he be supervised 24 hours a day. The therapist "accommodated" by reversing himself on both recommendations.

The Cardinal also had the priest sent for a second opinion when the first therapist diagnosed him as a pedophile. When the threat of a lawsuit finally forced Cardinal Bevilacqua to remove Fr. Dunne from ministry, therapists once again advised the Cardinal that the priest should be carefully supervised. Instead, Cardinal Bevilacqua chose to follow the advice of the Archdiocese lawyer who counseled that "for civil law liability" reasons, the Archdiocese should not try to supervise the abuser, but should "take every step we can to distance self."

7. Church leaders invented "Limited Ministry," which they documented in Archdiocese files but did not enforce.

Another feature of the Bevilacqua administration's handling of priest sexual abuse was a practice known as "limited ministry." Like the "no pedophile" policy, limited ministry was designed to make it look as though the Archdiocese was trying to protect children. Once again, we find that the true purpose was to protect the Archdiocese—from criticism that it was simply transferring abusive priests from parish to parish as Cardinal Krol had done and, more importantly, from legal liability. We also find that the practical

effect of knowingly creating a false safeguard was to endanger more Philadelphia-area children.

Limited ministry was designed to allow priests who had sexually abused children, but were "not diagnosed as pedophiles," to continue in ministry. Most often such priests were officially assigned to nursing homes, hospitals, or convents. In practice, however, their official assignments were rarely full-time, and the priests had freedom to help out in parishes all over the Archdiocese. The supposed limitations on their ministry—in many cases not enforced—were never publicized, so unwitting pastors eager for help welcomed the priests and let them have unrestricted access to parish children.

In Fr. Gana's case, for example, the Archdiocese made a point of documenting in its files that he was only permitted to minister at his official assignment—as chaplain of a monastery. In practice, Msgr. Lynn granted him permission to fill in and celebrate Mass anywhere in the Archdiocese. The only restriction was that he should not minister in his old parishes in Northeast Philadelphia where he had abused boys—and where his former victims might see him. Even this slight limit on his ministry was not enforced. Father Gana was soon seen celebrating Mass in his old parish.

Cardinal Bevilacqua took other actions that were designed to give the appearance of imposing limits on priests and acting responsibly to protect parishioners, but which he knew would leave children in danger. Thus, when his Vicar for Catholic Education, Msgr. David Walls, was accused of and admitted to sexually abusing minors in 1988, Cardinal Bevilacqua asked him to resign his high-profile job. The Cardinal explained his decision this way:

Among the more immediate reasons was the fear that the parents of recent victims were not likely to take action of a legal nature as long as the Archdiocese has acted strongly. Since he would not be away on an inpatient basis and if he is restored to his previous position as Vicar, it would appear that the Archdiocese had not considered this a serious matter and had taken no reasonable action. This perception of inaction could very well trigger the parents to resort to some kind of further procedure through court action.

After making this show of concern in order to fend off legal action, Cardinal Bevilacqua allowed Msgr. Walls to remain unmonitored in a parish residence in Bryn Mawr—with no formal assignment, few obligations, and limitless unsupervised time in which to procure new victims. For 14 years after learning of the priest's admitted sexual offenses against minors, Cardinal Bevilacqua permitted him to live in the parish rectory, to celebrate Mass with altar boys, to hear confessions, and to counsel parishioners and others through Catholic Human Services.

8. Archdiocese officials used investigation and intimidation to fend off lawsuits and silence victims and witnesses.

The treatment of victims who reported abuse to the Archdiocese offered yet more evidence of the Cardinals' preoccupations and priorities. Secretary for Clergy Lynn, often taking direction from the Archdiocese's attorneys, treated victims as potential plaintiffs. Not only did they not receive apologies acknowledging their abuse, but many were bullied, intimidated, lied to, even investigated themselves.

The victim of Fr. Gana's, who was barred from Saint Charles Borromeo Seminary and forced to seek ordination outside the diocese after accusing his abuser, is one example of a victim subjected to investigation and intimidation. Proving that their "investigations" of accused priests were purposefully incompetent, Archdiocese leaders conducted an extremely thorough probe of Fr. Gana's victim. They aggressively scrutinized second- and third-hand reports (the kind Cardinal Bevilacqua found unworthy of further investigation when leveled against priests accused of serious sexual abuse of children) of homosexual contact (possibly hugging and kissing) between the victim and a fellow seminarian. Monsignors Lynn and Molloy spent several weeks interviewing students, teachers, and administrators at the seminary. Despite this investigation, they could not substantiate the rumors. They succeeded, however, in humiliating and silencing

the victim. Cardinal Bevilacqua, who had complete power over the seminarian's future in the priesthood, punished the victim by refusing to allow him to become a priest in the Archdiocese.

In another case, an investigator hired by the Archdiocese's law firm accused a victim of Fr. Furmanski's of being motivated by money. He suggested to the victim's wife that if her husband persisted with his allegation, the wife's employer would find out about a criminal conviction in the victim's past. The investigator told her it could affect her employment.

Monsignor Lynn's questioning of victims often seemed more like cross-examination than a compassionate, or even dispassionate, interview. With coaching from the Archdiocese's legal counsel (recorded in a memo of a conversation between Msgr. Lynn and the attorney), the Secretary for Clergy questioned and re-questioned one of Fr. Schmeer's victims in accordance with the lawyer's instructions to "get details—even unimportant." (The investigator hired by the Archdiocese's law firm also investigated this victim, collecting records of taxes, relatives, and two divorces.) Monsignor Lynn asked a victim of Fr. Gausch's whether it was possible he had "misinterpreted" the priest's actions of putting his hands on the then-12-year-old boy's penis. The Secretary for Clergy asked this, knowing that Fr. Gausch had a thick Secret Archives file of prior allegations of abuse dating back to 1948, which included letters he had written about boys whom he was sexually abusing or desired.

When Msgr. Lynn met with Fr. Gausch in 1994, he assured the priest that "the Archdiocese supported him and that he would investigate a little more the background of [the victim]." Probing victims and their families was a common practice. Records show Msgr. Lynn, as late as the summer of 2004, suggesting that some of Fr. Schmeer's victims be investigated.

The Secretary for Clergy also suggested possible defenses—even for admitted child molesters—that might embarrass or discourage a victim from pressing an allegation. Interviewing Fr. Thomas Shea, who had previously confessed to sexually abusing at least two boys, Msgr. Lynn suggested that perhaps the priest "was seduced into it" by his 5th- or 6th-grade altar boy victim.

Victims were not the only ones bullied by Archdiocese leaders intent on suppressing the truth. Witnesses were, too. A nun in Saint Gabriel, Sister Joan Scary, expressed concerns about the safety of children in her parish who were exposed to a priest convicted of possessing child pornography. After she tried to pressure the Archdiocese officials to act and began talking to parents, she was fired as director of religious education.

9. The Cardinals shielded themselves from direct contact with victims.

We are aware of no case in which Cardinal Krol met with an abuse victim or his or her family. Cardinal Bevilacqua also shielded himself from contact with victims. He was the head of the Philadelphia Archdiocese 14 years before he would meet with a victim, and even then it was a non-Archdiocesan victim (who could not, therefore, sue him), whom he met during a meeting of the United States Conference of Catholic Bishops in 2002.

> The Cardinal misled the public when he announced in April 2002 that no Philadelphia priest with accusations against him was still active in ministry—when in fact several still were.

One of Fr. Gana's victims asked to meet with Cardinal Bevilacqua in 1995. He requested the meeting because he found it inconceivable that the man who anally and orally sodomized him when he was 14 years old would still be a priest if the Cardinal had been informed. Monsignor Lynn's suggestion that such a meeting might be possible was flatly rejected by the Cardinal, who had another aide inform the Secretary for Clergy that it "would be setting a precedent, i.e. for the Cardinal to meet with such individuals. His Eminence [the Cardinal] cautioned about such a recommendation and noted that there must be other means of letting [the victim] know that his Eminence was informed, other than for his Eminence to meet with him personally."

10. Even in 2002, Cardinal Bevilacqua continued to mislead the public and give false assurances.

Cardinal Bevilacqua continued to try to hide all he knew about sexual abuse committed by his priests even in 2002, after the scandal in Boston drew attention to the problem nationally. He had his spokeswoman tell the Philadelphia media in February 2002 that there have been only 35 priests in the Archdiocese credibly accused of abuse over the last 50 years—when in fact the Archdiocese knew there were many more. (We were able to substantiate allegations against at least 63 abusers, and reviewed many more reports that on their face seemed credible, but could not be fully verified after so many years). The Cardinal misled the public when he announced in April 2002 that no Philadelphia priest with accusations against him was still active in ministry—when in fact several still were. He certainly was not credible when he claimed before this Grand Jury that protecting children was his highest priority—when in fact his only priority was to cover up sexual abuse against children.

11. Before the Grand Jury, Cardinal Bevilacqua continued to mislead about his knowledge of and participation in the cover-up.

In his testimony before the Grand Jury, Cardinal Bevilacqua was still attempting to evade responsibility for placing known sexual offenders in parishes where they had easy access to hundreds of children brought up to honor, trust, and obey priests. He often suggested that he might not have known all the facts and that he delegated the handling of these matters to his Secretary for Clergy. He repeatedly claimed to have no memory of incidents and priests that we will never forget.

He repeatedly was not forthright with the Grand Jury. For example, in the cases of Fr. Connor and Msgr. Walls, documents clearly established that Cardinal Bevilacqua knew that the priests had admitted abusing minors. They also established that he alone was responsible for subsequently placing or leaving the priests in parishes where they would present a severe danger to children. In both cases, when there was no plausible deniability, Cardinal Bevilacqua took the unsatisfying position that he did not know that the victims of the priests were minors. He declined to reconsider this claim even when confronted with a memo he had written about his concern that *the parents* of Msgr. Walls' victims might sue the Archdiocese—thus obviously indicating knowledge that the victims themselves were not adults.

C. THE ARCHDIOCESE'S STRATEGIES FOR HANDLING ABUSE CASES MULTIPLIED THE NUMBER OF VICTIMS AND INCREASED THE HARM DONE TO THEM.

In concealing the crimes of sexually abusive priests while keeping them in ministry, the Cardinal and his aides did not merely fail to protect children from terrible danger. They greatly increased the danger and the harm to Archdiocese children. When Cardinals Krol and Bevilacqua promoted and celebrated known abusers—rapists and molesters of children—and left them in positions as pastors, parish priests, and teachers, they in effect vouched for their holiness and trustworthiness and encouraged parents to entrust their children to them. When Church leaders hid allegations against priest child molesters and deliberately placed them in parishes where unsuspecting families were kept in the dark, they minimized parents' ability to protect their children. When they transferred the priests to new parishes to avoid scandal, they greatly increased the numbers of potential victims.

When they withheld from parents knowledge of their child's abuse, they sentenced that child to years of lonely suffering. By not reporting the crimes to law enforcement, they frustrated safeguards designed to protect children in society at large.

What makes these actions all the worse, the Grand Jurors believe, is that the abuses that Cardinal Bevilacqua and his aides allowed children to suffer—the molestations, the rapes, the lifelong shame and despair—did not result from failures or lapses, except of the moral variety. They were made possible by purposeful decisions, carefully implemented policies, and calculated indifference.

D. DIOCESES THROUGHOUT THE UNITED STATES EMPLOYED THE SAME STRATEGIES TO CONCEAL THEIR PRIESTS' CRIMES AND KEEP ABUSERS IN MINISTRY.

As further evidence that Church leaders' practices reflected deliberate policies, the Grand Jury learned that the methods used to keep known child molesters in parishes, schools, and other

assignments were not unique to the Archdiocese of Philadelphia. We reviewed newspaper articles from dioceses around the country describing procedures so identical to those employed in Philadelphia that the similarities could not be coincidental. The actions that endangered and harmed innumerable children in the Philadelphia Archdiocese were not solely the result of morally bankrupt local Church officials. They were part of a national phenomenon. Church leaders in many different dioceses somehow reached the same conclusion—that it was in their interest to leave priests in positions where they could continue to sexually assault the Church's young rather than take steps necessary to stop the abuses.

News articles from across the nation reproduced in Appendix F describe the same non-investigations of abuse reports coupled with claims that the allegations were not substantiated, the same refusal to report to police even admitted rapes and other molestations, the same misuse of Church-related treatment facilities to launder sexual offenders and place them back in parishes, the same practice of transferring abusive priests to new parishes where parents would be unaware of the danger, the same policy of not informing families about known child molesters in their parishes, the same false claims that the ministries of admitted abusers were "restricted," and the same lack of effort to enforce those supposed restrictions.

We read about Church leaders who transferred accused child molesters out of state, or even allowed them to leave the country, after victims reported their crimes to police and arrests were imminent. We read about retaliation by the Church hierarchy against employees who reported priests' sexual crimes. We learned that it was common for dioceses to ignore treatment facilities' warnings and recommendations, even as bishops used psychological evaluations to justify returning abusers to parishes. We learned of other bishops who falsely assured their dioceses that priests were not ministering—when in fact they were. A 2002 survey by *The Dallas Morning News* found that 111 American bishops, including all eight cardinals who led U.S. dioceses, had kept "priests on the job after admissions of wrongdoing, diagnoses of sexual disorders, legal settlements, even criminal convictions."

It surely was not a coincidence either that, in the first four months of 2002, when these common strategies were first exposed in Boston, more than 170 priests—implicated in sexual abuse and knowingly retained in active ministries—were finally removed from their assignments around the country. Among the news reports included in Appendix F:

—California, a bishop reprimanded a priest for writing a letter of apology to an 11-year-old girl he had molested. After a transfer to a rural parish and a promotion to pastor, the priest was accused of abusing three victims at his new assignment, including a 3-year-old girl. The diocese's lawyer sought to deflect responsibility from Church leaders, stating that a psychiatric evaluation of the priest, who admitted abusing 25 children, did not "render any diagnosis of pedophilia."

—In Connecticut, Church officials and other priests ignored obvious signs of sexual involvement with children—such as a priest's habit of having boys spend the weekend with him in his bed in the rectory. A bishop testified that "allegations are allegations," yet made no effort to substantiate them. Abuse reports were typically considered credible only if the priest confessed.

—In Massachusetts, the Boston Archdiocese accused a priest's young victims of being negligent for allowing their own abuse.

—A psychiatric hospital with a long history of treating sexually abusive priests from around the country accused the Church of deceiving therapists into providing reports that were then used to keep abusive priests in ministry. The hospital's chief of psychiatry charged that pertinent information relating to a priest's prior sexual misconduct was sometimes withheld and that therapists' warnings were disregarded.

—In New Hampshire, Church officials insisted that a priest continue ministering and working with children, even after he admitted sexual misconduct and asked for help. A teenage boy described a road trip with the priest and three other boys as a "rape fest." A grand jury found that decisions to reassign offending priests "were always made at the top," by the bishop.

—In a California diocese, Church officials shuffled abusers from parish to parish and diocese to diocese. They welcomed a convicted child abuser from out of state, knowing that he faced another allegation. When he was accused again, they sent him to a New Mexico rehabilitation center with a notation: "No one else will take you." The diocese dumped one of its own serial molesters in Tijuana.

The news articles sampled in Appendix F show that Church leaders have employed well-orchestrated strategies for decades and in all parts of the country to keep sexual offenders in ministry while minimizing the risk of scandal or legal liability. The laws of our states apparently have fostered a climate in which the Church has found it more advantageous to allow the perpetuation of priests' crimes than to end them. Only because some states have now permitted lawsuits to proceed in cases where crimes had been successfully concealed for years has the Church begun removing sexual abusers it had known about for years.

SELECTED CASE STUDIES

FATHER JOSEPH GAUSCH

Father Joseph Gausch began serving as a priest in the Philadelphia Archdiocese in December 1945 and, based on the Secret Archives file provided, he started to abuse young boys almost immediately thereafter. The abuse included fondling, masturbation, oral sex, and attempted anal rape. It occurred in sacristies, rectories, and on outings. On one occasion in 1974, after Fr. Gausch admitted to Archdiocese officials that allegations of child molestation were true, Chancellor Francis J. Statkus wrote in a memo that, "because of the scandal which already has taken place and because of the possible future scandal, we will transfer him in the near future."

There is every reason to believe that Fr. Gausch continued his reign of terror throughout his 54 years of service in the Archdiocese. Yet, because of the manner in which complaints of abuse were handled, neither the Grand Jury nor anyone else will be able to determine just how many victims this priest left in his wake.

FATHER PETER J. DUNNE

Father Peter J. Dunne, ordained in 1954, served the Philadelphia Archdiocese as a teacher, pastor, administrator of a school for delinquent boys, and assistant director of the Archdiocese scouting program for 40 years. He remained a parish priest for seven and a half years after Archdiocese officials learned, in 1986, that he had sexually abused an altar boy who had been in the priest's Boy Scout troop. During those seven and a half years, Father Dunne was diagnosed as an untreatable pedophile. He personally paid $40,000 to silence a victim. The Archdiocese was warned repeatedly that he had many victims, that he was most likely continuing to commit sexual offenses, that he should not be in a parish setting, and that he should not be around children or adolescents.

Yet, not until a former victim threatened a lawsuit did Cardinal Bevilacqua in 1994 finally remove Father Dunne from his assignment at Visitation B.V.M. in Norristown.

In an effort to escape legal liability, the Cardinal chose not to place Father Dunne in a supervised living situation as his therapists strongly urged. A committee of Cardinal Bevilacqua's advisers concluded that "overwhelming evidence of pedophilia is here!" But, rather than take action to protect present and future victims, the Cardinal responded to concerns that the Archdiocese might risk being held liable for the priest's crimes if it tried to supervise him. Cardinal Bevilacqua permitted Father Dunne to retire to his rural cabin where he was known to take boys for sleepovers.

FATHER MICHAEL J. MCCARTHY

Cardinal Bevilacqua named Fr. Michael J. McCarthy pastor of Epiphany of Our Lord Church in Norristown in September 1992—nine months after learning that the priest was accused of molesting several students from Cardinal O'Hara High School when he was a teacher there in the 1970s. The Cardinal had been informed that Fr. McCarthy had taken boys to his New Jersey beach house, plied

them with liquor, slept nude in the same bed with them, and masturbated the boys and himself.

Cardinal Bevilacqua responded by having his assistant, Msgr. James E. Molloy, assure the priest, ordained in 1965 and then parochial administrator at Saint Kevin parish in Springfield, that the Cardinal did not "doubt...Father McCarthy's ability to be pastor." The only concern expressed by the Cardinal before promoting Fr. McCarthy to a pastorate was that his parish should "be distant from St. Kevin Parish so that the profile can be as low as possible and not attract attention from the complainant." In the priest's Secret Archives file at the time of his assignment to Epiphany was another accusation, made in 1986, by the mother of a recent O'Hara student.

In May 1993, Cardinal Bevilacqua removed Fr. McCarthy from his pastorate at Epiphany, but not because of his abuse of children. The Cardinal said he removed the priest for keeping homosexual pornography in his closet—but he had launched an investigation of Fr. McCarthy only after a large financial contributor complained to the Archdiocese. The contributor, a travel agent, had protested that Fr. McCarthy was acting as an agent himself and had taken away business she usually received from Epiphany's travel club.

Child pornography—including 111 magazines, 14 8mm films, and 11 videotapes—was seized from under Fr. DePaoli's bed. At the time he was teaching morals and ethics at an Archdiocese high school.

The Saint Luke Institute, in Suitland, Maryland, diagnosed Fr. McCarthy as a homosexual ephebophile—someone sexually attracted to adolescents. Secretary for Clergy William Lynn questioned the diagnosis, but Saint Luke refused to alter its finding. Church records suggest that the Archdiocese, which had used Saint Luke extensively to evaluate and treat priests, thereafter curtailed its relationship with the Institute.

FATHER EDWARD M. DEPAOLI

Father Edward M. DePaoli, ordained in 1970, was convicted in 1986 of receiving child pornography through the mail. A 1985 search by U.S. Postal Inspectors of his rectory room at Holy Martyrs Church in Oreland turned up an estimated $15,000 worth of pornography. Child pornography—including 111 magazines, 14 8mm films, and 11 videotapes—was seized from under Fr. DePaoli's bed. At the time he was teaching morals and ethics at an Archdiocese high school.

Father DePaoli's criminal behavior, and the Archdiocese's concealment of it, followed familiar patterns, including transfers to parishes where parents were unaware of the priest's past, official intimidation of a concerned witness, and the filing of records claiming restrictions that were not enforced.

After his arrest in 1986, Fr. DePaoli went for treatment, which proved unsuccessful. He was diagnosed with a sexual compulsion and relapsed repeatedly—purchasing child pornography even while residing at a treatment center.

In February 1988, Archbishop Bevilacqua ignored the advice of the priest's doctor and the Archdiocese's Chancellor to keep Fr. DePaoli in Philadelphia for therapy. Instead, he arranged an assignment for the priest in Colonia, New Jersey, where his crime and sexual addiction would be unknown to his parishioners.

Father DePaoli eventually returned to Philadelphia in 1991 and continued to minister until December 2002, though without a formal assignment for part of the time. He was allowed to minister despite reports to the Archdiocese that his addiction to pornography continued, that he made sexual comments about an 8th-grade girl during a sermon, and even that he had molested a 12-year-old girl years earlier.

A nun in 1996 informed officials that she was worried about the safety of the children in her parish. She was fired for speaking out.

Father DePaoli's ministry, however, continued. The Archdiocese was well aware that he was performing marriages and baptisms, hearing confessions, concelebrating Mass, and preaching nearly every Sunday at Saint Gabriel of the Sorrowful Mother in Stowe, where he had resided in the rectory since 1995.

Yet, in December 2002, when news stories reported that the convicted collector of child pornography was still ministering, Cardinal Bevilacqua claimed the priest was being disobedient.

The Cardinal had his spokesperson, Catherine Rossi, tell reporters that Fr. DePaoli had been stripped of all his priestly duties immediately after the 1985 incident, but fail to mention that they had been fully reinstated before Fr. DePaoli returned to active and unrestricted ministry in 1988.

After telling a victim he believed her allegation that the priest had molested her, Cardinal Bevilacqua assured the public that he was "not a danger to anyone."

FATHER FRANCIS P. ROGERS

The Grand Jury will never be able to determine how many boys Father Francis P. Rogers raped and sexually abused in his more than 50 years as a priest. Nor, probably, will we or anyone else be able to calculate the number of boys the Archdiocese could have saved from sexual abuse had it investigated potential victims rather than protecting itself from scandal and shielding this sexually abusive priest. We have learned of at least three victims who we believe would not have been abused had the Archdiocese taken decisive action when it learned of Fr. Rogers' "familiarity" with boys. We find that the Archdiocese received a litany of verifiable reports beginning shortly after Fr. Rogers' 1946 ordination and continuing for decades about his serious misconduct with, and abuse of, boys.

One of his victims described waking up intoxicated in the priest's bed, opening his eyes to see Fr. Rogers, three other priests, and a seminarian surrounding him. Two of the priests ejaculated on him while Fr. Rogers masturbated himself. Then Fr. Rogers sucked on the victim's penis, pinched his nipples, kissed him, and rubbed his stubbly beard all over him. The former altar boy, whom Fr. Rogers began abusing when he was about 12 years old, remains haunted by memories of the abuse more than 35 years later.

Father Rogers' file demonstrates that the Archdiocese responded to reports of his crimes with a shameful half-century of transfers, excuses, and finger-wagging threats that did nothing to deter the priest from indulging his self-acknowledged "weakness" and that exposed every boy in his path to the very real and horrible possibility of sexual abuse.

FATHER FRANCIS X. TRAUGER

One night in a Poconos motel in the spring of 1981, Fr. Francis X. Trauger repeatedly tried to anally penetrate a 12-year-old altar boy and for hours manually manipulated his penis. After the 5th-grader's parents reported the abuse through their parish pastor, the Archdiocese recorded the event this way: "They shared the same bed and there were touches."

The pastor passed on other allegations against the priest, involving another boy. The Archdiocese report stated: "same bed: touches." A few days later, Fr. Trauger himself told an Archdiocese official that "two similar events" occurred that spring with still two other boys. Subsequent years saw Church officials record other reports of "touches" and "camping."

The Archdiocese's use of such delicate euphemisms had the effect of concealing the true nature of Fr. Trauger's crimes. Whether the result of intentional obfuscation or a refusal to interview victims directly, the Archdiocese's responses to abuse allegations effectively shielded the priest from legal or criminal action and facilitated decades of sexual predation.

Ordained in 1972, Fr. Trauger was transferred eight times during his long career, each time to a parish with a school attached, each time without a warning to parish parents about the priest's predilections. Six of the transfers occurred after 1981, when the Archdiocese began recording abuse allegations.

MONSIGNOR FRANCIS A. GILIBERTI

Monsignor Francis A. Giliberti, ordained in 1970, was said by his students at Cardinal O'Hara High School to run a "sort of boot camp to stop masturbation" at his beach house in New Jersey. His methods, he bragged to one student, included walking in on boys while they were masturbating.

The priest abused at least two students who went to him for help, fearing damnation because of their "masturbation problem." One victim described how Msgr. Giliberti insisted on "inspecting" the boy's penis to determine whether it was "traumatized," ordered him to make himself erect, and offered to perform oral sex. The priest told the

other student he could introduce him to gay men. These activities took place in the mid-1970s, and were reported to the Archdiocese in 2002.

Both victims who came forward were traumatized by Msgr. Giliberti's abuse. One doused his penis with lighter fluid and set it on fire, his self-loathing was so intolerable. The other lived through years of suicidal tendencies, alcoholism, and failed relationships. Both were incensed by what they saw as the hypocrisy of their Church.

Following these allegations, Cardinal Bevilacqua permitted Msgr. Giliberti to continue as pastor at Nativity B.V.M. in Media without restrictions on his access to children and without informing the parish of the allegations against him. On April 25, 2002, one week after the first victim brought his detailed accusations to the Archdiocese, Cardinal Bevilacqua was quoted at a press conference assuring the public that no priest "credibly accused of misconduct with a minor" has remained in ministry. In December 2003, the allegations against Monsignor Giliberti were determined to be credible and he was forced to retire.

FATHER JOHN H. MULHOLLAND

In August 1968, a mother brought to the pastor of Saint Joseph's Church in Hatboro two letters written by the parish's recently reassigned associate pastor, Fr. John H. Mulholland, to her son while he was at summer camp. Amid cut-out illustrations of chains, ropes, and people suffering various forms of bondage, the priest wrote to the boy:

Plan and prepare to break me on vacation. If you can get me to beg to be punished by you even more and beg to be your slave—I will offer a just homage payment—such as—you can be my financial bookkeeper for the school term, possessing the checkbook with signed blank checks—or an outright fee each month of maybe 10% of the balance. You really have no imagination—this is your chance—take over—become master in fact as well as word—make me know what it means to squirm, sweat and fear and to understand what slave means.

In the other letter, the priest discussed plans for proving submission by "kneeling next to toilet when master craps then wiping ass with paper

In the other letter, the priest discussed plans for proving submission by "kneeling next to toilet when master craps then wiping ass with paper then with tongue."

then with tongue. Also being forced to lick master's ass and kiss it frequently."

At the time the mother brought the letters to the rectory, her son was on a two-week trip with Fr. Mulholland. The letters mentioned several other parish boys and suggested that they also participated in sado-masochistic rituals with Fr. Mulholland. After the boy returned from the trip, the Archdiocese's Vicar General, Gerald V. McDevitt, recorded that he "confessed a relationship with Father."

Yet Msgr. McDevitt told Fr. Mulholland that the Archdiocese's response to learning that its priest victimized parish boys with his sick behavior would "depend on the attitude the mother of the boy took and how far she would want to follow up the matter." Archdiocese officials did nothing.

Two years later the Chancery received a report that a boy at Fr. Mulholland's next parish "was being strung up and Father Mulholland [was] piercing him or at least jabbing him with some instrument all over his body." Again, Archdiocese officials left the priest in place.

The Archdiocesan Review Board in 2004 found that "Reverend Mulholland's letter to a young boy in his parish," though "quite disturbing in its language regarding issues of power, descriptions of human excrement and use of restraint," did not "fall under the definition of sexual abuse as contained in the *Essential Norms*."

Ordained in 1965, Fr. Mulholland apparently has never undergone even the Archdiocese's concept of treatment. He remains at last report an active priest with unrestricted faculties in the Philadelphia Archdiocese.

MONSIGNOR JOHN E. GILLESPIE

Church officials in 2000 considered Msgr. John E. Gillespie a risk. He had admitted molesting several boys over his many years as a priest. But what appeared to worry Archdiocese leaders and therapists more than the danger Msgr. Gillespie posed

to parishioners was his stated desire to "make amends" to his victims. An apology might have helped the victims heal and the priest find peace. But it might also expose the Church to scandal or liability. Archdiocese officials were determined to prevent such an admission of guilt.

In 1994, two brothers—now middle-aged men—confronted Msgr. Gillespie and accused him of repeatedly fondling their genitals nearly 40 years earlier at Immaculate Conception parish in Levittown. Monsignor Gillespie, pastor at Our Lady of Calvary in 1994, informed Secretary for Clergy William J. Lynn. He also showed Msgr. Lynn letters he had written to his victims, apologizing, explaining, and trying to persuade them that events had not happened precisely as the victims remembered. The Secretary for Clergy instructed the priest not to write to the victims again.

The Archdiocese received more allegations against Msgr. Gillespie in 1997 and January 2000. In February 2000, after the priest admitted inappropriately touching several boys, Archdiocese-affiliated therapists concluded that Msgr. Gillespie "would be a risk to have in parish work," not only because of the sexual abuse and its impact on the victims, but also because of his "drivenness to make amends." Again, he was ordered not to apologize to his victims.

Monsignor Gillespie was still pastor at Our Lady of Calvary in February 2000 because Cardinal Bevilacqua had ordered no further investigation or action in response to the earlier allegations. The Cardinal asked for Msgr. Gillespie's resignation as pastor only after learning that the priest had admitted victimizing two current parishioners at Our Lady of Calvary and wanted to "make amends" to them. Archdiocesan therapists warned: "If he pursues making amends with others, he could bring forth difficulty for himself and legal jeopardy."

Upon Msgr. Gillespie's resignation as pastor, the Cardinal bestowed on the 73-year-old priest the title of Pastor Emeritus of Our Lady of Calvary. Monsignor Gillespie continued to minister, including hearing confessions of schoolchildren. It wasn't until Msgr. Lynn received a report, in November 2001, of yet another victim that the Secretary for Clergy wrote: "I told Monsignor Gillespie that because of these rumors, and in order to preserve his reputation and the reputation of the Church, I thought it might be best if he retire."

FATHER JOHN J. DELLI CARPINI

In 1998, Fr. John J. Delli Carpini began writing homilies and speeches for Cardinal Bevilacqua. He also became a writer in the Cardinal's Communications Office, working for its director, Catherine Rossi, and helping to represent Archdiocese views during a time that sexually abusive priests were becoming a national scandal. He did so even though, as Cardinal Bevilacqua well knew, Fr. Delli Carpini had just a few months before admitted to molesting a 13-year-old boy from his first assignment at Saint Luke the Evangelist in Glenside. Cardinal Bevilacqua tried to conceal his association with Fr. Delli Carpini and also made sure that the priest kept quiet his authorship of the Cardinal's homilies and pronouncements. This arrangement continued until March 2002.

Before writing for Cardinal Bevilacqua, Fr. Delli Carpini taught at Roman Catholic High School and was a dean at Saint Charles Borromeo Seminary for 12 years. The molestation he admitted began in 1977 when the boy was an 8th-grader in Saint Luke's parish; it continued for seven years. When the victim informed the Archdiocese of his abuse in 1998, he also reported that he had seen Fr. Delli Carpini in the act of molesting a 15-year-old, and had walked in on the priest as he appeared to be preparing to abuse an 8-year-old boy.

Cardinal Bevilacqua permitted Fr. Delli Carpini to continue in ministry anyway, and to live in a parish rectory. He did so after receiving a psychological evaluation reporting "a sexual disorder and a severe personality disorder." Attempting to justify these decisions to the Grand Jury, the Cardinal testified that he generally relied on the advice of therapists to decide whether a priest guilty of abuse should be given an assignment. The documents in Fr. Delli Carpini's file, however, show that it was Cardinal Bevilacqua who made the initial determination to keep him in ministry. The therapists, who worked for the Archdiocese, then tailored the priest's treatment to fit the Cardinal's decision.

FATHER THOMAS J. SMITH

Father Thomas J. Smith, who engaged in depraved and sadistic behavior with many boys in previous parishes, lived until December 2004 at the rectory of Saint Francis of Assisi, a parish with a grade school in Springfield. He was permitted to celebrate daily and Sunday Masses and hear confessions.

On March 12, 2004, the Archdiocesan Review Board unanimously found credible allegations that "Smith took at least three boys playing the role of Jesus in the parish Passion play into a private room, required them to disrobe completely," pinned loincloths around them, and then, during the play, encouraged "other boys in the play to whip the Jesus character to the point where some of the boys had cuts, bruises and welts." These actions, the Review Board found, "occurred in multiple parish assignments with a number of different boys over a number of years." The board also credited reports that Fr. Smith had told boys that the rules of a club where he took them required that the boys and priest be nude to enter the club's hot tub.

Also contained in the priest's Secret Archives file were reports that Fr. Smith regularly took boys camping and that he had fondled the genitals of at least one of those boys with whom he shared a tent. There were details from one of the victims who played Jesus in the Passion play, describing Fr. Smith, with pins in his mouth, kneeling in front of, and very close to, the boy's genitals. The victim said that Fr. Smith would sometimes prick him with the pins until he bled.

When Cardinal Bevilacqua learned of these accusations in May 2002, he chose to leave Fr. Smith in residence, and ministering, at Saint Francis of Assisi parish. Two and a half years later, after receiving additional reports that Fr. Smith had abused other boys, the Archdiocese removed the priest from active ministry.

FATHER FRANCIS J. GALLAGHER

Father Francis J. Gallagher was arrested in Sea Isle City, New Jersey, on December 28, 1989, for soliciting sex with two young men—ages 18 and 20 years old. He later admitted to sexually abusing two adolescent brothers.

With information about the priest's abuse of minors in Archdiocese files, Archbishop Bevilacqua appointed Fr. Gallagher, in May 1991, as parochial vicar at Immaculate Conception, a parish with a school in Jenkintown. In 2000, Fr. Gallagher was transferred to another parish with a school—Mary, Mother of the Redeemer in North Wales. In choosing this parish for Fr. Gallagher, Secretary for Clergy William Lynn noted that "because of past difficulties, he needs to be in Montgomery or Bucks County."

Cardinal Bevilacqua never limited Fr. Gallagher's ministry or restricted the priest's access to minors. Not only were parishioners not warned about Fr. Gallagher's past, but deliberate efforts were made to place him among unsuspecting families. As with other priests, the Archdiocese did not act in the absence of pressure from parents or fear of scandal. Church officials did not act even when the priest's abuse of minors was admitted and possibly ongoing. There is no indication in Archdiocese records that efforts were ever made to identify Fr. Gallagher's known victims, to ascertain if their abuse was continuing, or to notify their parents.

Father Gallagher, ordained in 1973, remained an active parish priest until March 2002 when publicity from the scandal in Boston prompted the Cardinal to remove several priests still ministering despite histories of abusing minors.

FATHER THOMAS F. SHEA

It was a victim's lawyer who, on October 26, 1994, brought the first recorded sexual abuse allegation against Fr. Thomas Shea to the attention of the Archdiocese. By November 2, 1994, the accused priest was at Saint John Vianney Hospital for evaluation, never to return to his Philadelphia parish, Saint Clement, or to active ministry. The Grand Jury would commend this prompt handling of a sexually abusive priest, except that it merely illustrates what Cardinal Bevilacqua did when a victim's lawyer was involved—and what he did not do in other cases.

Documents in the Secret Archives file of Fr. Shea, who was ordained in 1964, reveal why Archdiocese officials acted promptly in this case.

They clearly did so not to protect the children of the Church, but only because legal action was threatened. A contemporaneous case—that of Fr. Stanley Gana, who was sent for evaluation as a sexual offender at the same time as Fr. Shea—demonstrates how differently cases that did not immediately threaten the Archdiocese with public scandal or legal liability were handled. Cardinal Bevilacqua had received reports four years earlier that Fr. Gana had molested and anally sodomized an altar boy for years, beginning when the victim was 13 years old. Yet the Cardinal did not remove Fr. Gana from ministry until 2002, seven years after Fr. Shea's forced retirement.

FATHER JOHN A. CANNON

Father John A. Cannon, ordained in 1948, molested teenage boys at a Church summer camp from 1959 through 1964. Eight boys reported the sexual abuse in 1964. Father Cannon admitted to some, but not all, of the sexual abuse. The Archdiocese responded by ordering the priest to "desist" and by transferring him to a different parish, with no restrictions on his conduct. In 1992, one of the priest's victims contacted Archdiocese officials to report the continuing effect of Fr. Cannon's abuse. The victim was assured that in cases such as Fr. Cannon's, sexually abusive priests are removed from their present situation, evaluated and treated, and not allowed again to work with children.

That was not true in the case of Fr. Cannon. He failed to undergo treatment, yet Cardinal Bevilacqua allowed him to continue teaching at a girls' school in Holland, Pa., until he retired in February 2004. In March 2004, following an Archdiocesan Review Board inquiry that found the reports of Fr. Cannon's victims credible, the priest's faculties were restricted.

FATHER MICHAEL C. BOLESTA

The case of Fr. Michael C. Bolesta, who was ordained in 1989, might at first seem distinctive: the Archdiocese hierarchy appeared unusually responsive to the allegations against him. The Grand Jury finds, however, that its intent—as usual—was to shield a sexually abusive priest from criminal prosecution. And the effect—once again—was to facilitate the priest's continued predations.

When a group of parents in July 1991 accused Fr. Bolesta of improper sexual behavior with as many as 10 teenage boys, Cardinal Bevilacqua's delegates, Msgrs. James E. Molloy and William J. Lynn, were immediately dispatched to interview the complaining parishioners at Saint Philip-Saint James Church in Exton. In response to a separate request by the parents of grade school children in the parish, the Archdiocese sent a counselor to talk with the 7th- and 8th-graders, some of whom had been involved with Fr. Bolesta as altar boys.

The reason for this unusual show of concern? The parents had taken their complaints to the Chester County District Attorney, and county detectives had arrived unannounced at the church rectory. The detectives informed Pastor John Caulfield that the accusations against Fr. Bolesta were numerous, including "a lot of touching" and grabbing at least one boy's genitals. They asked pointedly what the Archdiocese was going to do about it. The pastor immediately notified the Secretary for Clergy, John J. Jagodzinski, and offered his opinion that the parents would drop the criminal charges if the Archdiocese acted.

In contrast with their normal practice, Church officials this time sought out the names of victims. But the victims whom Msgrs. Lynn and Molloy sought out were those whose parents had gone to the District Attorney. In conducting their interviews, they did not press reluctant victims for the details of their encounters, but did ask what the parents wanted the Archdiocese to do. Their purpose, clearly, was not to discover or prevent criminality. It was to stop a criminal investigation from going forward.

The parents told Msgr. Molloy they wanted to be sure that Fr. Bolesta would never again be assigned where he would have access to children. The Cardinal's delegate repeatedly assured that "the practice is when there is doubt, we err on the side of caution." Apparently reassured, the parents did not pursue their criminal charges. Meanwhile, Msgrs. Molloy and Lynn kept Fr. Bolesta apprised of the families' intentions and the Archdiocese's efforts to avert legal action, informing him at one point: "we are not completely out of the woods yet as far as a lawsuit is concerned."

The Cardinal's managers advised Fr. Brennan to "keep a low profile," but never restricted or supervised his access to the youth of his various parishes.

The true extent of Church officials' concern for Fr. Bolesta's victims—past and potential—became clear when assignments were made the next spring (in 1992). After his delegates had reassured victims' parents that "every caution will be exercised" in future assignments, Cardinal Bevilacqua appointed Fr. Bolesta parochial vicar at Saint Agatha-Saint James, a parish in West Philadelphia. Among his pastoral duties was to minister at Children's Hospital of Pennsylvania.

FATHER ROBERT L. BRENNAN

Father Robert L. Brennan, ordained in 1964, was made a pastor by Archbishop Bevilacqua in 1988. Since that time, the Archdiocese has learned of inappropriate or suspicious behavior by Fr. Brennan with more than 20 boys from four different parishes. He was psychologically evaluated or "treated" four times. Depending on the level of scandal threatened by various incidents, Cardinal Bevilacqua either transferred Fr. Brennan to another parish with unsuspecting families or ignored the reports and left the priest in the parish with his current victims. The Cardinal's managers advised Fr. Brennan to "keep a low profile," but never restricted or supervised his access to the youth of his various parishes.

When Cardinal Bevilacqua retired, Fr. Brennan was still a parochial vicar at Resurrection parish in Philadelphia, despite reports from parish staff that he had inappropriate contact with several students from Resurrection's grade school. In June 2004, Fr. Brennan was appointed Chaplain at Camilla Hall, a retirement home for nuns.

Douglas Rushkoff

GOD HAS LEFT THE BUILDING

THE SELF-IMPOSED DEATH OF INSTITUTIONAL JUDAISM

I'M A JEW. Or, at least I was last time I checked.

But the official (read: wealthiest) institutions of Judaism would say that I'm not, and, most likely, neither are you. No, it's not because my mom's not Jewish (the usual, racist, excuse), but because—like so many other intelligent, engaged people on the bagel-fueled island of Manhattan—I don't happen to belong to a synagogue. As a result, they'd label me "lapsed" or, in the optimistic language of the market researchers charged with saving Judaism, "a latent Jew."

Well, actually, these days they're calling me an atheist, Israel-hater, and anti-Semite. And not because I'm saying anything bad about God, Israel, or Judaism, but merely because I'm asking that we be allowed to discuss these ideas, together.

We all know that there's some sticking points to being Jewish in America today—particularly with what's going on in Israel. Luckily, Judaism has a wealth of built-in mechanisms for confronting the lure of fundamentalism, nationalism, and tribalism. But in my effort to show Jews some of what is so very progressive and relevant about their dwindling religion, I have instead provoked their most paranoid, regressive wrath.

What I'm learning, I'm sorry to say, is that today's Jewish institutions have more to fear from Judaism than they have to gain. That's why they're going out of their way to keep Judaism from actually happening.

I'VE WRITTEN ABOUT media and culture for the past ten years. Interactivity has always been my passion—especially the way the Internet turned a passive mediaspace into a freewheeling conversation. Instead of depending on the newscaster or sponsor for our stories, we were free to tell our own. I wrote eight well-received books about what was happening to our culture and how to navigate its new "do-it-yourself" terrains.

> **What I'm learning, I'm sorry to say, is that today's Jewish institutions have more to fear from Judaism than they have to gain.**

Then, just a few years ago, it occurred to me that Judaism had attempted to do the same thing to religion. The mythical Israelites of the Torah left their idols behind in order to forge a new way of life—one where they weren't depending on the gods to do everything for them. Judaism abstracted God so that people could become thinking, active adults. What made Judaism so radical—so sacrilegious in its day—is that it proclaimed that people can actually make the world a better place. God may have given us great hints on how to be holy people, but the rest is up to us.

See, the reason why Jews have such a hard time explaining Judaism, "the religion," is that we aren't about beliefs. All we really have is a process—an ongoing conversation. You get initiated, a bar mitzvah, by proving you can read the Torah and speak somewhat intelligently about it. No statements of faith required—just literacy and an opinion about what you've read earn you a place at the table. Then you get to argue with the old guys.

Judaism is not set in stone but to be reinterpreted by each generation.

That's right: Judaism boils down to a 3,000-year-old debate about what happened on Mount Sinai and what we're supposed to do about it. Judaism is not set in stone but to be reinterpreted by each generation. All you have to do is continually smash your false idols (iconoclasm), refuse to pretend you know who or what God is (abstract monotheism), and be nice to people (social justice). In a sense, Judaism isn't a religion at all, but a way human beings can get *over* religion and into caring about one another.

Sounds good, anyway.

But like so many so-called latent Jews in America today (we account for over 50 percent of the total), I had a hard time finding places where this sort of Judaism is still practiced. They exist, but more likely in an apartment living room or school basement than a sanctuary. The vast majority of messages coming out of mainstream Judaism concern post-Holocaust issues like the dangers of intermarriage, the threat of assimilation, and the need to protect Israel. Worst of all, as I'm learning, these subjects are not even up for discussion.

Jewish philanthropies spend millions of dollars and hours counting Jews and conducting marketing research on how to get young people to stop marrying goys and start supporting Israel. If they spent even half this effort actually *doing* Judaism, they might find that they attract a whole lot more people to their cause. In an era when spirituality is about breaking the illusion of self,

who wants to be part of a religion or a people that are turned so inward? Judaism's greatest concern, these days, is itself.

Most of my friends abandoned Judaism as soon as they were allowed to, for precisely these reasons. Having found some useful truths in there, however, I was loath to throw out the baby with the bathwater. I figured I owed it to myself, and to Judaism, to revive the conversation. "Can we talk?" I've been asking in my lectures, articles, and even a book. Apparently not.

Don't get me wrong: A great majority of the people I've been speaking to in synagogues and bookstores around the US about my ideas agree with what I have to say. Even the rabbis. "If that's Judaism," I've been told many times, "then count me in!" A half-dozen Torah discussion groups have formed among people who met at my bookstore appearances. But the people running Judaism's more established institutions—the philanthropies, federations, and periodicals that speak for the Jewish people in America today—are so threatened by the notion of an open conversation about Judaism that they can't help but go on the attack.

"Along comes Douglas Rushkoff," announced one of my intellectual role models, Anne Roiphe, after I wrote a *New York Times* op-ed about organized Judaism's self-defeating obsession with race and numbers. Treating Jews as an endangered species in dire need of a breeding program, I argued, was hardly a good strategy for attracting more young, successful, and universal-minded people into the fold, if that's even the object of the game.

She called me "silly" and cited the existence of Tay-Sachs disease as evidence of a Jewish "race" that requires protection. Why couldn't she have spoken to one geneticist before making such an unfounded remark, in print, no less? (Throw a few-thousand people into a ghetto for a few-dozen centuries, and they'll develop some diseases. In fact, most scientists have abandoned the concept of race, altogether.) She went on to cite the Jewish concern with "the degree of Jewishness of one's parents" as proof that Judaism is a race. Huh? It's the Jewish concern with the degree of Jewishness of one's parents that's the problem!

I've been amazed as I've watched otherwise rational, well-spoken people revert to childlike circularity when confronted by the inconsistencies in their own religious outlooks. I know: That's why they call it religion. But Judaism was supposed to be a smarter solution. A thinking person's answer to religiosity. A conversation. That's why, more than their inane remarks or beliefs, what disturbs me about the reaction of Judaism's gatekeepers is their refusal to make a place for me—and the majority of American Jewry—at the Jewish table. "Along comes Douglas Rushkoff"? To what? The official mahjong tournament, already in progress and closed to everyone else? Like, who dubbed you Pope of the Jews?

I do feel for these people, and I can understand the wish to believe that we are direct descendents of the mythical characters described in the Torah. But, forty-two years circumcised, I refuse to be treated as an outsider for seeing the great benefits of contending otherwise—as Judaism itself suggests we do.

They're not budging. In the first major review of my book, *Nothing Sacred: The Truth About Judaism*, in a Jewish publication, a critic for the *Jerusalem Report* called me a "yoga-practicing atheist Jew from New York's East Village," right in the lead paragraph![1] I was called an atheist because, like most thinking adults, I don't believe in an all-powerful creature with the white beard who rejoices in animal sacrifice. I get that. But the yoga-practicing and East Village parts? Is that supposed to be evidence of how far I've strayed—in neighborhood and exercise regime—from the Upper West Side where Jews belong?

It was certainly evidence enough for mainstream Judaism to take action. The United Jewish Appeal Federation of New York—headquarters of the biggest, most central Jewish organization in America—yanked an interview that one of their writers had conducted with me from their website, along with all mention in their calendar of a benefit I was scheduled to speak at in their auditorium for a Jewish social justice charity. All because, according to the editor, "a heightened sensitivity to some of

the topics we discussed emerged here at UJA-Federation once it was actually posted." (Gotta love the Internet: The entire interview was immediately reposted to a webzine called Jewsweek, along with an account of the whole fiasco. A week later, the excised text reappeared on the UJA site, albeit with a new title and a framing paragraph about how "Douglas Rushkoff likes to sound off." A UJA representative now says that the only problem with the original interview was the title.)

I do feel for these people, and I can understand the wish to believe that we are direct descendents of the mythical characters described in the Torah.

I'm not the only one facing such knee-jerk reactions from the institutions dominating public Jewish discourse. Rabbi David Wolpe, a respected and published rabbinic scholar now on the pulpit at Temple Sinai in Los Angeles, made headlines for daring to suggest to his congregation that the Exodus may not really have happened the way it's described in the Bible. Or at all. Although this question has been pondered out loud by rabbis ever since there were rabbis, today it is too dangerous a topic, and Wolpe is decried as a "silver-tongued devil." Why?

Because Jews are afraid, and the institutions that should be helping them conquer their ignorance are instead stoking it in order to further solidify their grasp on Judaism's future. The darker the picture they can paint of Judaism's plight—the further synagogue membership dwindles, the greater Israel's peril—the more money they raise. Every suicide attack on Israel and each negative report on intermarriage statistics lead to a surge in donations.

So it's in the fundraisers' interest to foster panic instead of discussion and to turn their agendas into inviolably sacred truths. Yet they are not entirely to blame. It is we who must challenge

darker the picture they can paint of Judaism's
ight—the further synagogue membership dwindles,
e greater Israel's peril—the more money they raise.

these holy assumptions if we're going to break free from top-down religion and start to think for ourselves, again, the way Judaism demands.

THE FIRST FORBIDDEN TOPIC is race. The Jews' crucial error has been to accept our enemies' contention that we are a race. We're not. The first character in the Torah to mention an "Israeli people" was Pharaoh, looking for an excuse to kill off people he's afraid won't support him in a war. The concept of "Jewish blood" was invented during the Spanish Inquisition, so that they would still have an excuse to slaughter former Jews who had completely converted to Catholicism. Best yet, it was Hitler, gently reworking a bit of Jung, who claimed that Jews' "genetic memory" would keep them from ever fully accepting the natural German order.

Two millennia of being treated as a despised race might convince any people that it's true. Ironically, Jews were being persecuted, at least in part, for their very refusal to accept such false boundaries. Local gods, ethnic purity, and national religions meant nothing to this amalgamation of formerly disparate tribes. Moses' wife was black, for God's sake. How much clearer can the story get about race not being the issue here?

By hanging onto racehood, Jews get to hang onto an immature understanding of chosenness. ("I *like* knowing that God loves us the best," a woman told me after a recent talk.) Along with being God's chosen people, however, come the racism and elitism that undermine our ethics but empower our central authorities. After all, if Judaism is not a race, then who exactly are we not supposed to intermarry with? No, they won't tell you that this whole matrilineal descent business isn't part of Judaism at all, but a remnant of the Roman census conducted in the second century. Assimilation has always been the Jews' best strategy. Our mandate in the Torah is not to protect ourselves from others but to "share our light" with them.

Part of the reason we don't know any of this is that we've relegated our Judaism to our authorities.

The Reform movement was a great idea when it arose in the 1800s in Germany. Judaism was built to be reformed. Problem is, some of the reforms were designed for little purpose other than to make Jewish worship look less weird to any Christians who might happen to drop by. So a spirited, participatory free-for-all was turned into church: Rabbis put on robes, stood on a stage in front of the room, and engaged in boring, monotone responsive readings with the congregation. All the problems of Christianity, without the salvation.

Worse, this set-up induced what Freud would call "regression and transference." The audience of spectators regressed to a childlike state and transferred parental authority onto their rabbis, who became more like priests administering the religion to their congregants.

The concept of "Jewish blood" was invented during the Spanish Inquisition, so that they would still have an excuse to slaughter former Jews who had completely converted to Catholicism.

No matter. Reform Jews figured that someone wearing a black hat, probably somewhere in Israel, was doing the "real thing." And so checkbook Judaism was born, through which Americans could practice their religion by proxy. Little did they know that their money was going to some of the most stridently Zionist sects around and forcing the Israeli government to cow even further to their bizarre demands.

WHICH BRINGS US to the real reason we can't talk about Judaism today: Israel. Note—I'm not suggesting that Israel shouldn't exist, but many readers will already think I've just said that. They cannot even see these words that say otherwise. Our problem is not with the Israelis but with our insistence—as Americans—in justifying a nation's existence with our religion. By forcing the Torah to serve as an accurate historical chronicle of the Jewish claim to disputed territories, Jews turn themselves into fundamentalists who have no choice but to interpret their texts literally. "Abraham got this piece from God in Genesis, and Jacob got this piece from the Pharaoh..." The transdimensional nature

> **Problem is, some of the reforms were designed for little purpose other than to make Jewish worship look less weird to any Christians who might happen to drop by.**

of Jewish myth—as profound as that of any Eastern religion—is reduced to a mere real-estate deed.

This literalism is a problem. Fundamentalists believe that Jews must be in control of the entirety of biblical Israel in order for the messiah to return to earth. This is why extremist Orthodox from Brooklyn race with gun in hand to settle the West Bank. It is also why the American Christian fundamentalists are responsible for funding a majority of Jewish immigration from Russia to Israel. They want to bring on the End of Days and get to Armageddon already.

But because many Jews refuse to look a gift horse in the mouth, everyone from Bush to Falwell becomes our allies. Fear, desperation, and a history of persecution make for strange bedfellows.

To free ourselves from this ultimately self-defeating conundrum, American Jews must come to understand our own unwitting complicity in this pact with, well, the devil. We must engage with the possibility that Israel, the nation, may not be the ultimate realization of Jewish ideals as much as a necessary compromise of these principles. Israelis get this; New Yorkers seem to have a little more trouble with it, because we insist on seeing Jerusalem as somehow more sacred than Manhattan.

There are certainly better arguments to be made for a Jewish homeland than the assertion that the "one and true God" gave it to us. (That's not what abstract monotheism was invented for, anyway. She's not just *our* God—she's everyone's.) After centuries being exiled or worse by nation-states with their own official religions, one obvious Jewish strategy was to create our own nation, with its own official religion. Although long characterized by an independence from territory and local gods, Judaism might not be completely wrecked by the temporary suspension of these values for the greater priority of survival.

Yes, Israel may be truly important to the Jewish people and, as a potential laboratory in ethical nation-building, to the whole world, but its current

and inappropriate centrality to the Jewish faith makes it a topic that cannot be approached or discussed openly. Like the synagogue and the Jewish bloodline, Israel has become an idol.

As a result, many American Jews feel that to question the religious or political authority of Israel—to suggest, as I have, that God might not have invented the nation-state—is akin to blaspheming Judaism or forgetting the Holocaust. So, as the Jewish authorities have made abundantly clear to me, we are to remain silent.

> **By forcing the Torah to serve as an accurate historical chronicle of the Jewish claim to disputed territories, Jews turn themselves into fundamentalists who have no choice but to interpret their texts literally.**

But I *can't* remain silent. It's against my religion. Indeed, it's time we apply a little Judaism to Judaism—before it's too late.

Life for Jews in America in the twenty-first century is as good as it has ever been, anywhere. This means it's up to us. Only by reviving the inquiry and activism that are truly central to Judaism can we serve as antagonists rather than passive supporters of everything from blind fundamentalism to the Bush regime's designs on the Middle East and the world. Just because the Jews will inevitably be blamed for provoking these crusades doesn't mean we have to make the accusation true.

No, resistance is our tradition, and it's a continuity worth fighting for. At this point, it's more important to me that I do Judaism than that I get to call myself Jewish. So call me what you like. I've got work to do.

---

1. A year later, she emailed me an apology for the review. She said she had been a recent convert to an extreme form of Judaism and had finally come up against the horrible racism at the core of this religion and its people. "You were right," she said. Of course, she again misunderstood the whole point. It's her extremism on both ends of the spectrum that got her into so much trouble.

Nasrin Alavi

REFORMATION HYMNS

ISLAM, IRAN, AND BLOGS

IRANIAN BLOGGER LBAHRAM ASKS:

What have the likes of me learned after 12 years of formal religious education? What is the outcome of being consistently bombarded with sacred information in this Islamic Republic of ours?

1. When you talk about your religion for over 20 years, its problems will be highlighted.

2. Religious education is the best way to create agnostics in the modern world. Just look around at the people you personally know who went to the infamously strict Islamic schools, like Haghani, Kamal, Moofid, etc.

3. Even those most addicted to religion will at some stage overdose.

4. The problem is not with Islam but with a few of our radical fellow Muslims.

The other day I saw a construction worker fast asleep next to a cement mixer; he appeared to have developed a deaf ear to all that noise. After so many years of being bombarded with religious facts you just stop hearing them.

Those who lived through the Islamic Revolution almost a quarter of a century ago are now a minority. More than 70 percent of Iran is under thirty, and for this population, literacy rates for young men and women stand well over 90 percent, even in rural areas. It is the voices of this educated youth that come through the phenomenon that is the Iranian blogosphere.

The Internet has opened a new virtual space for free speech in Iran, a country dubbed the "the biggest prison for journalists in the Middle East" by Reporters sans Frontières (a/k/a Reporters Without Borders). With an estimated 700,000 blogs, Farsi is now the fourth most popular language for keeping online journals. A blogger asks: "Has everyone noticed the spooky absence of graffiti in our public toilets since the arrival of weblogs?" But unlike graffiti, Iran's blogs are boundless and global.

> **"Religious education is the best way to create agnostics in the modern world."**

In the last ten years over 100 media publications, including forty-one dailies, have been closed down. Yet today, with tens of thousands of Iranian weblogs, there is an alternative media that for the moment defies control. Even though the subject matter of many blogs may seem tame by universal standards, most surpass the limitations imposed by state censorship. There is an endless variety of bloggers who are fans of everything from Harry Potter to Marilyn Manson.

Iran's flowering youth are described by leading Iranian philosopher Ramin Jahanbegloo (head of the Department for Contemporary Studies at Iran's Cultural Research Bureau) as the "fourth generation," who are moving away from political Islam towards an "Iranian secularism" based on Islamic traditions and Persian cultural history. Testament to Jahanbegloo's thinking are the countless Iranian voices in the blogosphere who time after time try to partition the regime's deeds from their own Islamic belief systems. The following quote is by a young journalist who was threatened by the extremists for his writing:

> In the name of God.
>
> I commence with the name of a supreme God, the God of Zoroaster, Moses, Jesus and Muhammad, the God of life itself. On the eve of the holy month of Ramadan when we are all the guests of God, the stench of fear, terror and revenge is in the air.
>
> This air is the air of the Middle Ages when the tyrant clergy in the name of holy dictates and the protection of their faith would burn the bodies of worthy men and women....
>
> What is this Islam of yours, that through its fight for righteousness has filled the world's atmosphere with the stench of decomposing corpses?
>
> I tell you that the Shia are purely the followers of one God and no one else.
>
> Your protestations are that you will safeguard the honor of the blood that was shed in the eight-year war with Iraq. No Iranian can forget those years which are a testament to the bravery of our youth.... They did not die for your contrived Islam but for the defense of their homeland and you are not the same breed as those blessed men....
>
> If my pen and my literary activities are so harrowing to you that you want to kill me and now threaten me with a bullet... If my pen is the menace, I will resort to writing in my own blood: long live freedom, equality, peace and democracy, long live Iran and Iranians!
>
> Your worship of the Supreme Leader is worthless, and as for your threats, I am not "a willow that will quiver at such breezes."

> "I have never feared death.... My fear is to die in a land where the gravedigger's wage is higher then the price of an individual's freedom"[1]

ISLAMIC REFORMATION OR BUST

In February 2005 a young cleric and blogger, Mojtaba Lotfi, was sentenced to three years and ten months for posting "lies" on his website. Based in the holy city of Qom, Lotfi and a group of young theologians at the seminaries had dared to grapple with such thorny notions as the need for Islamic reform, twenty-first-century Islamic jurisprudence, and human-rights abuses by state clerics, as well as how to deal with social problems such as the use of ecstasy and the spread of HIV. Yet it was an article entitled "Respect for Human Rights in Cases Involving the Clergy" that earned Lotfi a prison sentence. One thing Iran's state clerics are rather sensitive about is being accused of being unjust and un-Islamic by other clerics.

However, Lotfi is not a lone voice. Abdollah Nouri was imprisoned for publishing sacrilegious articles. Eshkevari was accused of apostasy. Mohsen Kadivar was incarcerated for calling for the autonomy of political life from religion. These outspoken critics of the regime are all prominent members of the Shia clergy, as are many political dissidents in Iran today, and they are not on the fringes of society. Religious people complain that the mosques were full before the Revolution but are now often empty. Dissident clerics argue that the Islamic Republic's failings have brought about a loss of Islamic values, because people associate the system with the religion. As the prominent Islamic scholar Hadi Eghbal says in his blog [ghabel.persianblog.com], twenty-five years of rule by the clerics in Iran "has not made Islam stronger, but it has brought about a decline in the position of the clergy and religion in society."

Ayatollah Taheri, the principal spiritual leader of Isfahan, Iran's second most populous city, has described the regime as "an enemy of Islam and humanity." In July 2002, resigning from his post after twenty-five years as the Friday prayers leader of Isfahan, he condemned the ruling clerics for corruption and incompetence, adding that the only reason for his public protest was to defend the faith, which had been marred in the eyes of ordinary people because of its association with a so-called Islamic government.

Grand Ayatollah Montazeri is one of the most senior-ranking religious figures in Shia Islam. Under total house arrest until very recently, he has in effect also joined the blogging bandwagon by posting regular commentaries, as well as his memoirs and damning indictments of the regime.

Despite the general (and erroneous) belief in a unified Shia clergy, the dozen or so Grand Ayatollahs in the world have their own groups of followers and take very different positions, even at times issuing religious edicts, or *fatwas*, that contradict one another. Yet only a tiny section of these Grand Ayatollahs is affiliated with the ruling clerics in Iran. And some, like Montazeri, have openly questioned the legitimacy of the Supreme Leader's absolute religious power.

Taking their cue from older theologians, clerics such as Kadivar and Eshkavari (and groups of young seminarians in Qom) are now questioning whether the mosques should be mixed up with a discredited and unpopular ideological regime. Many now openly speak of the need for an Islamic Reformation. Some argue that these clerics are at the heart of the battle over Iran's future and perhaps even eventually the future of Shia Iraq, advocating pluralism over an intolerant dogmatism. Ultimately these clerics possess the knack to hit Iran's theocracy where it hurts.

THE FREEDOM TO BE "BLASPHEMOUS"

While blogging gives some Iranians the freedom to defend their faith, for others it provides an outlet for their resentment and disapproval of a religious system that governs every aspect of their lives. Blogger Satgean writes:

> I don't know what this Allah of ours is, that we call the most beneficent and merciful ... that condemns you to burn in hell if you don't obey his commands....
>
> I am neither Allah nor beneficent and merciful, but when I see my fellow men under pressure,

displaying their limitations, I feel such a heavy weight of embarrassment on my shoulders that I cannot straighten my back to look them in the eyes ... and if I can, I try to help them....

> I don't try to make them totally lose the plot by terrifying them with hellfire....
>
> In truth, I don't understand the "beneficent and merciful" bit and what good it does to us Muslims.

Blogger Fozool:

> I shit on the whole of Hezbollah ... and your distorted Islam and its ideology that you use to diminish a human being through torture.
>
> All your bollocks analyses are obsolete.... This generation has finally, after 23 years, realized what sort of hole it's in....
>
> The student demonstrations are proof that 23 years of brainwashing from primary school to university cannot even save you today....
>
> People put an ayatollah and the clergy on the same level as pimps and thugs, and they would shove the whole lot of you up a donkey's arse if they could.

Blogger Deev:

> Good tidings.... Today "Ayatol-shit" Hakim, the head of Iraqi Shias, was assassinated. Thank you, God, as there is one less Mullah in the world....
>
> Yet, I wouldn't have been too unhappy if these senseless Iraqis could have experienced the misery of living under an Islamic Republic as we have for 25 years ... but I'm jealous in a way.... Why don't our Mullahs die off so easily?

Although tame by Western standards, the off-the-cuff remarks of bloggers concerning the "sacred" Supreme Leader are denounced as blasphemous in the Islamic Republic of Iran. Blasphemy carries the death penalty, as do a variety of offenses, from murder, rape, and armed robbery to drug trafficking, adultery, and apostasy.

It remains to be seen how long a small group of aging clerics can impose their desire for an Islamic state on a society in which the majority of people are under thirty and have no memory of the Revolution. A young blogger addressing the "Leader of the Revolution" writes:

Your Holiness,

Have you ever fallen in love? Have you ever gazed into the crimson of the wine, when you can still feel the spot where she kissed you on your eyelids? Have you ever danced? Have you ever had Maz Maz [Iranian chips] dipped in Mast Moseer [a dip]? Have you ever worn jeans? Do you know what Mum roll-on deodorant is? Have you ever cried at night? How many years did you go to school? Have you ever made *abghosht* [an Iranian stew]? Have you ever got a barbeque going? Tell me, what is Newton's Third Law?

How many times has the scent of springtime in Shiraz [a southern Iranian city] driven you wild? Have you ever kissed a dog? Have you ever listened to Persian classical music? Or what about rap? Do you ever whistle?

Have you ever kissed her neck? What about behind her ears?

Have you ever downloaded an MP3 from the Internet? Do you ever ask the guy at the kiosk selling cigarettes how he's doing? Ever walked through town at midnight? Have they ever raided your home and confiscated your books?

Have you ever been forced into exile? Has it ever happened that you just can't get the pattern of those tiles in your mother's kitchen out of your head (for three nights in a row), but you just can't remember the color? Have you ever called your mother up from far away and asked her to describe the color of those tiles—at the mention of which you both uncontrollably sob?

Have you ever longed for the windows of your apartment in Tehran?

CHILDREN OF THE REVOLUTION

It is no secret that most of the rulers in the Middle East are out of synch with their youth, and Iran is no exception. But while many Arab countries are ruled by authoritarian leaders who are nonetheless more liberal than many of their citizens, people in Iran have already experienced the fullness of a radical regime. Ayatollah Khomeini came to power promising independence and a classless Islamic society. Iran's average annual oil income has more than doubled since the Revolution, but most indicators of economic welfare show that it has steadily declined, and the Iranian economy has been described as akin to the crony capitalism that grew from the ruins of the

Soviet Union, controlled by a few state clerics who have amassed enormous wealth since 1979. While others in the region may dream of political Islamic utopias, Iranians understand the limitations of theocratic rule and have been there and done that.

Blogger khojaste writes:

Twenty-five years ago on a day like this, the first happy day of a New Year without a dictator, our parents said "yes" to something they had no understanding of: to an *Islamic Republic*.

A regime in which "Marxism would be taught at university by a Marxist lecturer" (a quote from Islamic Republic, a publication by Ayatollah Motahari [one of the founding theologians of the revolutionary state, President of the Constitutional Council of the Islamic Republic of Iran, and a member of the Revolutionary Council. He was assassinated soon after the Revolution]).

A regime in which "a Zoroastrian woman would have identical legal rights to a Muslim man" (a quote from a documentary shown nationwide on January 11, 2004, on State television. On the program, a Zoroastrian woman—a lawyer, incidentally—twenty-five years ago gave this statement as her reason and guarantee in voting for an Islamic Republic).

But today I can't stop wondering why my mother didn't ask: "What exactly is this Islamic Republic?" Why didn't she ask: "How do you guarantee what you are promising us today?"

A quarter of a century later, the regime's attempt to shield Iranians from the West's "cultural invasion" has backfired magnificently. The country's youth is now almost obsessed with the Western culture that they have been deprived of for so long. Young people who aspire to a more Western lifestyle have even turned events like St. Valentine's Day into a local festival. Iran's former Deputy-President Ali Abtahi, a mid-ranking Shia cleric, greeted the new cause for celebration for young lovers in Islamic Iran in his blog [webneveshteha.com] by writing that although there are many irritated by all this, "We cannot deny the reality. And anyway the Islam that I know encourages life and love."

Blogger Siprisk tells us:

The Revolution finally brought the clerics on the scene, stripping them bare so that they could perform their magic shows ... and this same revolution will kick the clerics out once and for all from the political scene....

Europe struggled for five centuries to banish religion and superstition from political and social life, making a lot of sacrifices along the way. Our country will be the first country in the Middle East to go on this journey in a relatively short time frame. We must make this hard and hazardous journey ourselves. There are no chains harder and stronger than the chains of religion and tradition....

The revolution is unstoppable until it reaches its final destination: the rebirth of a humanitarian culture and a democracy. Towards the end of the revolution, no cleric will be able to go to a village and tell the people: "They didn't allow us to have Islam." Believe me, defending religious rule will be impossible then. This rebirth has to happen in our country.

VIRTUALLY UNVEILED

After the 1979 Revolution, women were viewed as central to the project of changing the public morality, and wearing the veil became mandatory. Yet two and a half decades later, girls mock the strict guidelines by wearing their compulsory headscarves way back over their heads to reveal as much (illicit) hair as possible; meanwhile, the obligatory *manteau* gowns are getting shorter and tighter, to the point that they are no longer the black cloaks considered the ideal revolutionary *hejab*. Here blogger Atash (Fire) describes her encounter with the Morality Police:

I could feel the searing sun like a piece of burning coal on my veil.... My veil and my long robes make me smell like a corpse.... I walk on the street but can't see the end.... Far, far away, a group of trees are doing a choreographed dance....

And I, on the street, I'm walking.... Passersby, those in cars, can't see me, as if I'm here but I'm not.... Far, far away, I can see a mirror that has taken up the width of the street.... And the nearer I get to it the more distant I become.... I'm walking in a scorching heat that rips the breath out of you....

I catch a glimpse of myself, lighter, lighter, and lighter.... With each step in my mind's eye, I no longer feel the burden of my walk.

I'm wearing a white short-sleeved top, green shorts, and a scented straw hat.... I no longer smell like a corpse or like my grandmother's damp basement.

I walk freely and am spreading my fragrant sweet dreams among people who cannot see me.... They're running to get away from the harsh, searing sun.... What ecstasy....

There is a hand on my shoulder that abruptly swallows my world.... The toxic street voice with rage barks: "Pull your veil forward!" I hear it, but I don't want to hear it.

The street filth puts his hand in his back pocket to show that he's searching for something.... His mime does not frighten me. He pulls out a transmitter from his putrid shirt pocket and this time pointing at his black patrol van, with fury, hollers: "What do you say now?"

As I was stranded between two worlds...at high noon...I was hungry and thirsty...in an endless street where right at the end the trees were doing a choreographed dance.... My veil moved and came forward.... A few steps away my veil moved back again.

Prior to the Revolution, many traditional families refused to send their daughters to university. They believed it would violate their Islamic way of life. In those days, most educated working women didn't wear Islamic covering, but the majority of women did, especially in the provinces. Paradoxically, mandatory veiling may have helped some women to gain an education, especially in traditional families, as they didn't need to go through a drastic cultural makeover to leave the house or enter the workplace.

In 1936, when the Shah tried to make it law that all women should cease to wear their veils, he failed due to popular outrage. In 1975 women's illiteracy in rural areas was 90 percent and more than 45 percent in towns. Today, the nationwide literacy rate for girls between fifteen and twenty-four has risen to 97 percent.

In 2003 Shirin Ebadi—an Iran-based human rights activist—caused an uproar among Iran's ruling clerics when she attended the Nobel ceremony to accept the Peace Prize *unveiled*. She even received public death threats from extremist groups. Yet Ebadi has spoken out against the French ban on

Islamic headscarves in state schools. "If there is a law [against headscarves], only extremists will profit from it, as it would be an excuse to prevent their daughter's education," she said. "The better the girls are educated and the more they go to school, the more emancipated they will become."

TRUMPING THE CLERICS

A committed Muslim, convinced that change in Iran must come peacefully and from within, Ebadi has battled for an interpretation of her faith that is compatible with democracy. For her efforts, Ebadi writes that she has been imprisoned and threatened with death by those who denounce her "as an apostate for daring to suggest that Islam can look forward and denounced outside the country by secular critics of the Islamic Republic, whose attitudes are no less dogmatic." Yet she is far from friendless in Iran. After receiving the Nobel Peace Prize in 2003, Ebadi was greeted at Tehran airport by a joyous crowd numbering "hundreds of thousands."

Ebadi writes in her memoir, *Iran Awakening* (2006):

> As I was defending the [divorce] bill to the commission, an imperious, traditionalist cleric sitting next to me gathered his robes and turned to address me: "Why have you written that male consent is not required for divorce?"
>
> "Because it's not," I said. "And I'll prove it to you." I pulled out the *Shahr-e Lomeh*, the Shia Textbook of Jurisprudence. "This is the book you study in the seminary, and on which you are tested in becoming a mullah," I stated. "It says nowhere in here that male consent is required. So why are you insisting it is?"

For trumping this cleric with his own seminary's books, Ebadi was ejected from the session at the Iranian parliament. In another court battle, the judge sternly warned her, "Do not criticize Islamic law," to which she responded: "I am only asking if justice has been served."

More recently in Tehran (May 31, 2006), a group of women's rights protestors presented the authorities with a tight dilemma. As is the norm in such protests, at the outset all placards were to be removed. But this time the women were ready. They had ingeniously used white headscarves printed with bold red slogans to cover their hair—the authorities could not remove them.

Some people believe the regime is immune to change, but many others, especially women, are experts at finding ways around the constraints of the patriarchal system. These women activists are less interested in whether or not to wear the veil and more concerned with gaining access to education, wider employment opportunities, equality at work, and better healthcare for their families.

Since the Revolution, many other women have fought for democracy within the confines of an ideological state. They have dared to continue crossing the line, and in doing so they are steadily shifting Iran's cultural and political landscape.

HEROIC WOMEN VS. EVIL MUSLIM MEN

The Revolution's impact on women has been entirely paradoxical, as it has both opened up new possibilities for them and at the same time instituted the most repressive controls on their lives. Although they're discriminated against, Iranian women continue to play a considerable role in everyday life. A third of all doctors, 60 percent of civil servants, and 80 percent of all teachers in Iran are women. However, this cannot be explained through the tirelessly used Western media paradigm of brave, heroic women subjugated by a post-9/11 caricature of a brutal Muslim male.

Reading the intimate, online commentaries of Iranians, we are sometimes granted a rare glimpse of life beyond the crude stereotypes:

> To my wife on our sixteenth wedding anniversary.
> We have struggled and yet we have survived.... We have been humiliated, but we have not lost our dignity....
> Do you remember when we were first married? We rented this room in south Teheran and had to share a toilet with the landlord.... There was no bathroom and we had to use a public bath....
> Do you remember that time when we took all the money we had and went to a posh restaurant uptown? We had a wonderful meal and gave the rest of the money as a tip to the waiter.... We had no money left for a taxi ... so we walked all the way home across the whole town.... We had a lot of energy then....

Do you remember the time our son was born? Through all that bombing and war ... in that climate of death we built a new life.... And the evening our daughter was born.... With two kids and work, you still went to university and you were top of your class....

Do you remember getting war rations for dried milk? To prove that you had no milk, you had to show your breasts to the "sister" at the *Komiteh* every week ... but we would not have that.... "We'll work overtime and buy dried milk on the open market.... But we're not showing your breasts to anyone!"

I said all this stuff so you know that I haven't forgotten... our mutual troubles, growth and love can never be destroyed. We are just starting ... with more energy than ever before....

We will go forward to change a world that was unjust for our children and make it a fairer place for our grandchildren.

BEHIND THE HEADLINES

Yet at a time when headlines scream of a global crisis and a new era where Cold War rivalry is replaced by the clash of civilizations, such earthly voices are drowned out and rendered irrelevant. The Islamic world and especially Iran are under a media spotlight. More recently the protests across the Islamic world against the Danish cartoons of the Prophet Muhammad have been used to stress this looming clash of civilizations. On February 6, 2006, a small (albeit violent) demonstration outside the Danish embassy in Tehran was a top news story in much of the world. Among the protesters was blogger Saleh Meftah, a member of the Iranian Basij (revolutionary militia). The following day he wrote in his blog about the thrill and the fun-filled atmosphere of the attack, posting smug photos of himself taken inside the embassy compound.

When the story of Saleh's escapades was written up on Roozonline, a popular Iranian Internet news daily, the "counter" for his blog, which had been showing an average of thirty-one readers per day, suddenly shot up to 2,872 visitors. Roozonline recounted how Saleh had described the preparations the night before the attack and how "he and his friends used two cars and seven motorcycles to scout the Danish embassy to coordinate their efforts with the embassy guards," while naming members of the student Basij who were "knowledgeable in planning, preparations and even help inside the embassy attacks."

On the streets of Tehran, only the brave or the foolhardy would dare to confront a member of the Basij. But in this cyber-sanctuary, within a period of only two days, hundreds of angry comments were left on Saleh's page. The following is just a tiny sample:

• I cannot hide my hatred of you and your actions. It's your bestial breed that gives Westerners cause to insult our dear Prophet and faith.

• You've written here that, as you read the comments, "I am proud that the enemies of the Revolution are attacking me." Listen, you godless fool.... What enemies!! They are ordinary people who are telling you how they feel ... your fellow countrymen!!!!

• Unlike Iran, in the West what is published in a newspaper is not dictated by the regime. I agree with you that the cartoons are offensive but the best strategy is to ignore the ignorant. But as you're still young, I feel that it may not be too late to talk to you before it's too late ... before you start seeing a divine light like our dear President. When you attack an embassy, you are attacking a whole nation. Do you honestly feel that what you did was justified and something to be proud of?

• You, Basij, just don't learn. No matter how many of you fill up our universities like flies through [government] quotas, you still don't seem to get wise to that fact you are being played. You talk of bringing the true face of the Revolution to the Westernized northern [affluent] suburbs of Tehran by setting fire to that embassy. My brother! While there, you should have opened your eyes. For your mentors and this nation's tormentors mostly live behind those neighboring grand high walls. But I also want to say that I commend you for not deleting the messages here and for upholding the democratic principle of free speech. This is all we want: to be allowed to speak out and not to be beaten to death for it. And this is a great chance for you to realize what people honestly think of you. Thank you.

Ordinary Iranian Muslims may well be dismayed by images of their Prophet dressed as a terrorist, his turban a bomb with a lit fuse, but the twelve million citizens of their capital, Tehran, were far from lit up with rage. Most don't support violent attacks on European diplomatic missions and have stayed away from the demonstrations. In any case, Iranians have no real freedom to gather in public; only a week earlier, hundreds of Tehran bus workers were imprisoned in an effort to crush their strike. In these circumstances, an attack by a 400-strong mob whose members act with impunity, injure police officers, and burn a car at the embassy compound cannot be seen as a spontaneous protest by the people, but is rather a foreign-policy directive from an extremist establishment trying to isolate Iran internationally for its own ends.

But again, as is the norm, the Western news coverage had us believe that this mob of 400 in a city populated by twelve million people represented the mood of the Iranian street.

REALITY VS. PERCEPTION

There is a vast gap between reality and the Western perception of Iran. Following the election of the hardline President Ahmadinejad in June 2005, this chasm widened further.

When Mohammad Khatami was in office (1997–2005), Western political commentators often highlighted the toothless nature of Iran's presidency. But Mahmoud Ahmadinejad's election in June 2005 saw him quickly elevated to the position of the West's "worst nightmare," and as such, he has become a central factor in the new Iranian political equation. Ahmadinejad's provocative speeches against Israel, calling for it to be "wiped off the map," have sent jitters across the world.

Ahmadinejad has tried to represent himself as a champion of the Arab street, and it may perhaps be no accident that his Holocaust-denial speech was made at a summit in Saudi Arabia attended by most Muslim nations. Since his election, Arab newspapers have been awash with their support for Ahmadinejad and what they see as the West's double standards in hounding Iran while allowing Israel to possess a potent nuclear arsenal. Arab columnists out of harm's way and writing from the sidelines can enthuse and cheer Ahmadinejad, but many in Iran are aware of the dangers facing their country as a result of their new leader's stance. Former President Khatami has criticized Ahmadinejad, saying, "Those words have created hundreds of political and economic problems for us in the world."

Iran has an abysmal human rights record. It may be hard to believe, but Iran also has the largest Jewish community in the Middle East outside of Israel. Under the present constitution, religious minorities, including Iranian Jews, must have an elected representative in Parliament. The *Jerusalem Post* has reported that "most of the Jews still resident in Iran are quite happy to be there and despite the anti-Israel hatred that often translates itself into anti-Jewish feeling, generally speaking, they are not persecuted" (May 5, 2004). The next year, the *Jerusalem Post* reported on Iranian Jewish immigrants to Israel who were moving back "'home' to Teheran" (November 4, 2005).

The Iranian Jewish exile Roya Hakakian has published a beautifully written memoir (*Journey From the Land of No*) about her life in Tehran before and after the Revolution. She has said that while growing up in Tehran, she never experienced anti-Semitism: "The people who persecuted Jews in Iran were the same people who persecuted anyone who didn't fall in line with the Government.... Our neighbors never turned on us and we always maintained close ties."

Naturally, there has been widespread condemnation of the President's Holocaust-denial claims on the Internet. A writer on the group blog Sheepish lamented:

The myth of the holocaust, the myth of the extermination of Jews, the myth of Hiroshima, the myth of the Serbian massacres, the myth of those gassed in Halabjeh. The shameful myth of humanity.

While another writes:

Perhaps Ahmadinejad has never seen aging Jewish men and women, who sixty years after WWII, still recount with trembling voices and tearful eyes how they were separated from their parents and sent to Auschwitz ... and he has not seen on their wrinkled arms their hacked-out prisoner numbers.... Where are those "ever-ready" defenders of Islam ... those who see Islam threatened and endangered to the point of extinction by even the slightest loosening of moral standards and who keep calling on others to revolt in defense of the integrity of their faith? Don't they have a problem with their Islam's accord with Nazism?

While Ahmadinejad was calling for a conference to assess the scale and consequences of the Holocaust, Hossein Derakhshan, the "godfather" of the Iranian blogosphere, traveled to Israel in a symbolic gesture of peace. He wrote:

> As a citizen journalist, I'm going to show my 20,000 daily Iranian readers what Israel really looks like and how people there live. The Islamic Republic has long portrayed Israel as an evil state, with a consensual political agenda of killing every single man and woman who prays to Allah, including Iranians.
>
> As a peace activist, I'm going to show the Israelis that the vast majority of Iranians do not identify with Ahmadinejad's rhetoric, despite what it looks like from the outside.
>
> I'm going to tell them how any kind of violent action against Iran would only harm the young people who are gradually reforming the system and how the radicals would benefit from such a situation.
>
> During my visit, I'm going to blog in both English and Persian, take a lot of pictures and record numerous video and audio reports and make a few podcasts.

Iran's President, described by George W. Bush as an "odd man," has caused further astonishment and much media debate around the world with his references to Mahdaviat (belief in the coming of the Mahdi, a messianic figure). In a video recording, Ahmadinejad even talks of being surrounded by a divine light as he addressed the United Nations General Assembly in September 2005. This has caused much ridicule in the blogosphere, with bloggers referring to their President as "luminous Mahmoud" or "the incandescent."

Iran's leading (and recently exiled) satirist, Ebrahim Nabavi, has joked that conversations in Iran's communal taxis would go something like this: "In the Rafsanjani era, they're all thieves. In the Khatami era, they're all useless, and now with Ahmadinejad, they're all mad."

But Ahmadinejad's apocalyptic visions have proved even more controversial in religious circles. According to Shia Islamic belief, the Mahdi will appear alongside Moses, Jesus, and Muhammad on Judgment Day. Yet Shia scriptures also abound with condemnations of any prediction by mere mortals of the Mahdi's arrival. The former parliamentary speaker and cleric Mehdi Karroubi, in an interview with the reformist *Sharg Daily* newspaper (January 7, 2006), fiercely attacked the new government's profane references to the Mahdi; he even cast doubt on the revolutionary credentials of the President's spiritual leader and mentor, Ayatollah Mesbah-Yazdi: "In the first ten years of the Revolution, Mesbah was not known.... Wherever he was, I don't know. If anyone knows, they should tell us."

Bootleg tapes showing Ahmadinejad's mystical belief in his own mission are available in Iran and can be viewed on the Web, yet the risks of adverse public opinion and an outcry from the seminaries led government spokesman Gholamhossein Elham to dismiss the tapes as forgeries made to discredit the President. Even the fervent Ahmadinejad and his backers realize that Iran is not a Saddamite society where a political leader can enforce his delusions upon the population.

"BUT THEY ELECTED AN ISLAMIC RADICAL"

A deluge of flustered media reports seemingly asks us to believe that the Iranian people have confirmed their radical Islamic sensibilities by electing Ahmadinejad. Iranians are routinely portrayed on news broadcasts as crowds chanting, "Death to America and Israel!" in archival footage shot during Friday prayers. Yet according to surveys by Iran's own Ministry of Culture and Guidance, fewer than 1.4 percent of the population actually bothers to attend Friday prayers.

Iran is also perhaps one of the few countries in the Middle East where people don't attribute their hardships to their undemocratic United States–backed rulers. A major national poll in 2002, commissioned by the then-reformist Parliament, revealed that 64.5 percent favored resumption of talks between Iran and the United States. As a result, three separate Iranian institutes, including the National Institute for Research Studies and Opinion Polls (Nirsop), were closed down, and the researchers involved soon found themselves in prison. Three years later, Abdolah Naseri, the former director of the state news agency, Irna, was put on trial for revealing that the regime's *raison d'etre*, enmity to the US, is not shared by the majority of Iranians.

Those who took part in that survey seemingly believe in Iran's integration into a global economy that can offer jobs and prosperity. Equally, Mahmoud Ahmadinejad's electoral draw was based on promises of a better economic future. He had tapped into the vein of popular anger against corruption and cronyism, appealing to the minds and hearts of jobless youth and underpaid workers by promising food and housing subsidies for the poor.

Only months after his election, the populist powers of the man who famously donned a street sweeper's uniform in camaraderie with the workers were already in danger of eroding as union workers were arrested, basic groceries and metro subway prices went up, and the much-publicized government loans for newlyweds were as good as abandoned.

Ahmadinejad comes from and is endorsed by the hardline core of the regime that has ultimately controlled power in Iran since the Revolution. His ability or inability to keep his campaign promises will be a critical challenge for Iran's revolutionary elite. One young blogger writes:

> I pray for Ahmadinejad's protection and well-being everyday. If allowed to run his course uninterrupted, by the time of the next election [2009] we will see a beleaguered and discredited President, the definitive collapse of all this revolutionary mumbo jumbo, and the ultimate demise of extremism. It is only then that you will see this society flower.

A NATION OF ISLAMIC MARTYRS

Ahmadinejad continually talks of the glory days of the Iran-Iraq war (1980–88) and of a "new Islamic Revolution," at a time when even most of his contemporaries appear to have moved on. Iranians have lived through a recent violent revolution and a war with Iraq, bleak years that they logically don't want to encounter again.

The roads, streets, and narrow alleyways of Iran have been renamed after the hundreds and thousands of dead that the locals of these neigh-borhoods still vividly and fondly remember as young boys. As one blogger puts it:

> The Americans fight and go to war to prove to the world that they are cheerful, beautiful, and sophisticated humanitarians. The Palestinians fight, as this is all they can do to defend their homes. We fought so that men who represent God ... will have more chance of racketeering. We fought against another Muslim country to defend this Islam.

Blogger Shargi perhaps sums up the views of many when she says:

"God invented war so that Americans can learn geography."

> I hate war. I hate the liberating soldiers that trample your soil, home, young, and old under their boots. Believe me, I love freedom. But I believe that you have to make yourself free. No one else can free you.

In a jibe against an American threat, one blogger writes: "God invented war so that Americans can learn geography."

In the aftermath of the Iran-Iraq war, a baby boom was encouraged. According to Ayatollah Khomeini, a country whose youth were ready for martyrdom "could never be destroyed." Although the population has indeed more than doubled since the 1979 Revolution, to almost 70 million, this master plan has not come to pass.

Blogger baba.eparizi writes:

> When the most ruthless are the victors and not the wise ... the story is truly of a bloody vicious struggle.... The ruthless killings at the dawn of the Revolution ... the assassinations ... eight years of devastation and war ... the bombing of towns ... the dastardly killings of prisoners en masse in the 1980s.... These are all the bloody roots of our story. Yet today these blood feuds are fading from the minds of a new generation ... a generation that was created to fight for God ... a generation that was created for martyrdom is suddenly aware of its predicament and the world around ... and no longer believes in the endless wars of his forefathers.... A new generation is pressing forward to destroy the old formula.

ONLY IN IRAN

Ahmadinejad's attempt to bury the "unknown martyrs" of the Iran-Iraq war in public places illuminates the other realities of contemporary Iran. To keep "alive the memories and sacrifices of those who lost their lives fighting for Iran," the new government has also tried to bury these unknown soldiers around Iran's university campuses. But this has met with such a strong student backlash around the country that in May 2006 officials announced that no more burials were planned.

At Sharif University (March 13, 2006), hundreds of students attempted to create a human chain around the graves to prevent the soldiers from being interred. A photograph of a protester, posted to a student's blog, shows her with a banner that reads: "They want me dead, so they can say I was one of them and that I existed because of them."

These youth are perhaps the greatest challenge to the Islamic radicals, as they are part of a new generation of Iranians fonder of the truth than of martyrdom. A student blogger writes:

> I was able to read my blog last night and my heart started shaking.... I had no idea so many of you were following my reports from campus....
>
> But today I want to write about hope.... I want us to believe that we can all make a difference....
>
> An old lady turned up yesterday among the demonstrators.... It brings a smile to my face when I remember her...because she stopped so many students from being beaten to a pulp.... She just kept going up to the Basij and pleading with them, "My son, for God's sake, stop beating those kids!"... You have no idea how much this meant to us....
>
> Let us finally break this chain of hate ... even against those who hit and arrest you.... All the children of Iran ... believe even in our smallest efforts.... I have to tell you that my generation, we don't want to be anyone's heroes or martyrs for freedom. We want to live, and the Basij are a part of my generation, too.

Since his election, President Ahmadinejad has been under a frenzied Western media spotlight, his every move and directive making headlines. He was even reported to have banned Western music. But the gap between the president's desires and what actually takes place is vast.

Among Tehran's maddening traffic, the trance-techno soundtracks of homegrown pop sensation Benyamin relentlessly boom out of rickety taxis and flashy cars, but you won't hear him on state radio or television. Benyamin is detested by much of the older generation, Iranian literati and conservative clerics alike. He sings about love, boredom, but also about his faith with tributes to Shia imams. His popular demographically driven "reformation" hymns, which couldn't have been aired before the Islamic Revolution, reveal so much about Iran's journey in the past generation. If any attempt were made to broadcast them in Shia regions of Iraq today, they might well trigger riots similar in scale to those unleashed over the Danish cartoons of the prophet Muhammad.

What is happening in Iran is more significant and more sustainable in the long-run than the mere overthrow of dictators; that, as we are witnessing in Iraq, is the easy part. A generational change threatens the survival of radicals. Yet while the gap between the rulers and the ruled widens, fanatics have raised the volume of their hardline rhetoric, desperately trying to reassert Iran's radical credentials.

The West must realize that it is the Iranian people and the bourgeoning youth of Iran who will determine the future of their country. An actual military attack against Iran (in addition to the obvious disastrous repercussions) will only set back society by another quarter of a century, unifying Iran's youth with the most hardline elements of the regime.

Today the Western media, through a prism of fear and stereotype, have further empowered the likes of Ahmadinejad in a confrontation in which Islam is seen to be pitched against the West. Yet the West must realize that radical Iran survives in isolation and conflict. As Ahmadinejad appears to be doing his best to provoke the West, a clash of civilizations is not yet inevitable—but pick up his gauntlet and it's a pretty good start.

Baby Boomers in the West have had enormous impact, driving change and transformation across the Western world; Iran's new up-and-coming youth may well prove as significant and influential, not only for their society but for the entire region. It seems possible that Iran, which a quarter of a century ago introduced a bemused world to radical Islam, may yet surprise the world all over again.

3

BIBLE TALES

Ruth Hurmence Green

THE GOD FROM GALILEE

Editor's Note: The late Ruth Hurmence Green was sixty-four years old when her first book, The Born Again Skeptic's Guide to the Bible, *was published in 1979. Put out by the Freedom From Religion Foundation, it has become their bestselling title, going through three editions and staying in print nonstop for almost thirty years now. This Norman Rockwell grandmother—raised Christian, but skeptical since childhood—simply read the Bible cover to cover and relayed what she found. She came "to the shocked realization that it is opposed in every way to what one had perceived it to be, having heard it excerpted and 'interpreted' from childhood." Before reading the entire Bible, she had taken Christianity with a grain of salt. Afterward, she was a full-fledged atheist.*

For this anthology, I had considered writing an essay about the Jesus one finds in the Gospels, but I quickly realized that I would merely be retreading what Ruth had already covered:

- *Jesus repeatedly said that his Second Coming and the End Times would happen almost immediately, that many who were listening to him speak would live to see these events.*
- *Jesus refused to heal a Gentile little girl, only relenting when her mother begged him.*
- *At three different times, Jesus was asked what a person must do to be saved, enter heaven, etc. Each time, he gave a completely different answer.*
- *Jesus, "the Prince of Peace," declared: "I came not to send peace but a sword."*
- *Jesus never condemned slavery, even though he constantly talked about it.*
- *Peter and Paul both denied the Virgin Birth by stating that Joseph was Jesus' biological father.*
- *And—as the commercials say—much, much more, complete with chapter-and-verse references to everything.*

Others said, This is the Christ. But some said, Shall Christ come out of Galilee?
—John 7:41

JESUS BASES HIS MINISTRY upon the assumption that the end of the world is imminent and that he will return shortly and establish the kingdom he preaches. In the Gospel of Matthew alone, Jesus refers to this concept at least six times. "From that time Jesus began to preach, and to say, Repent: for the kingdom of heaven is at hand" (Matthew 4:17). These words of warning are an exact repetition of those of John the Baptist, whom many mistake for the Messiah (Matthew 3:2).

Again Jesus asserts: "There shall be some standing here, which shall not taste of death, till they see the Son of man coming in his kingdom" (Matthew 16:28).

Sending his Disciples out onto the circuit, Jesus reminds them: "For verily I say unto you, Ye shall not have gone over the cities of Israel, till the Son of man be come" (Matthew 10:23). Again Jesus asserts: "There shall be some standing here, which shall not taste of death, till they see the Son of man coming in his kingdom" (Matthew 16:28). He makes it clear, after describing his early triumphant return: "This generation shall not pass till all these things be fulfilled" (Matthew 24:34).

In Galilee Jesus repeats: "The time is fulfilled, and the kingdom of God is at hand" (Mark 1:15). "The hour is come, and now is, when the dead shall hear the Voice of the Son of God" (John 5:25). Finally: "If I will that he tarry till I come, what is that to thee?" (John 21:22). Here Jesus speaks of the Disciple John to Peter. Paul and the other evangelist Apostles take up Jesus' clarion prediction, still echoed today.

As a natural accompaniment to the wording of impending doom, verbal pictures of the End are majestically painted by Jesus on several occasions. His second coming will bring about the redemption of the Jews from the Gentiles, and the establishment of the Jewish kingdom of God. In the words of Jesus:

> And when ye shall see Jerusalem compassed with armies, then know that the desolation thereof is nigh. Then let them which are in Judea flee to the mountains...and let not them that are in the countries enter thereinto. For these be the days of vengeance, that all things which are written may be fulfilled. But woe unto them that are with child and to them that give suck [the usual biblical disregard for women] in those days; for there shall be great distress in the land, and wrath upon this people. And they shall fall by the edge of the sword and shall be led away captive into all nations: and Jerusalem shall be trodden down by the Gentiles, until the time of the Gentiles be fulfilled. (Luke 21:20–24)

Jesus' narrow world surfaces. He limits the area of his Second Coming to Jerusalem and a tiny Judea, as he gives details.

The recital of this Armageddon is somewhat different in Matthew and also elaborates upon the accompanying condition of the heavens. After the terrible tribulation (for which some religious sects store up provisions), the sun and *moon* will be darkened, and the stars shall *fall*. Then all shall see (with no light?) the Son of man coming in the clouds. His angels shall come with trumpet sounds (and flashlights?) and gather up the elect from the four winds (Matthew 24).

These descriptions by Jesus point up the fact that he was abysmally ignorant of science and the universe and was no more cognizant of knowledge to be discovered later than the average superstitious Jew of his day. He makes no mention of atomic power; the armies will use swords and have no air cover; stars can fall, and the sun loses its heat and light, and life will still remain on the earth and clouds in the heavens, upon which he can float down into the four winds. As the Son of God, or God if you will, he has none of the information which people have been able to acquire through their own efforts during the centuries since then (in spite of the opposition of the Church). Why didn't Jesus know everything there is to know?

He doesn't even seem to know the season or day of his return to earth, for he says the elect should pray it is not in winter or on the Sabbath.

He doesn't even seem to know the season or day of his return to earth, for he says the elect should pray it is not in winter or on the Sabbath. Yet they do not take these predictions of Jesus concerning the last days seriously, or they would all move near mountain ranges, and Christian women would hesitate to bear children as they prepare for the imminent end of all things. Jesus was not omniscient, obviously.

Jesus' description of the day when he will return to establish his mythical kingdom is almost a word-for-word repetition of these passages attributed to the prophet Zechariah:

> Behold, the day of the Lord cometh, and thy spoil shall be divided in the midst of thee. For I will gather all nations against Jerusalem to battle; and the city shall be taken, and the houses rifled, and the women ravished; and half of the city shall go forth into captivity, and the residue of the people shall not be cut off from the city. Then shall the Lord go forth, and fight against those nations... And ye shall flee to the valley of the mountains... yea, ye shall flee...and the Lord my God shall come, and all the saints with thee. And it shall come to pass in that day, that the light shall not be clear... And the Lord shall be king over all the earth. (Zechariah 14).

Joel also foretells the Day of the Lord when the Gentiles shall come under the domination of Jehovah: "For the day of the Lord is near in the valley of decision. The sun and the moon shall be darkened, and the stars shall withdraw their shining. The Lord shall roar out of Zion, and utter his voice from Jerusalem; and the heavens and the earth shall shake... Judah shall dwell forever, and Jerusalem from generation to generation" (Joel 3:15,16,20). (Judah fell 2,600 years ago.)

Almost all the prophets predict such a Day of the Lord when the new kingdom of Zion will be accomplished, whose subjects shall include all other nations under the God of the Jews. Familiar with these traditional expectations, Jesus with his customary respect for the Old Testament, coupled with his goal of clothing himself with the prophecies, feels compelled to make his statement: "that all things that are written may be fulfilled" (Luke 21:22).

He is bound always to address himself to the establishment of a *kingdom*, since a kingdom with a descendant of David as ruler is what the prophets all promise and what the Jews all expect will be the ultimate future stronghold of a triumphant Jewish nation (Zion). Jesus could not have laid claim to the Messiahship without portraying himself as the king-to-be when Israel would be redeemed from the domination of her conquerors. His reference to the days of vengeance are directly from the prophets: "For the day of vengeance is in my heart, and the year of my redeemed is come" (Isaiah 63:4).

Either Jesus patterned his Second Coming after the prophetical Day of the Lord, or the prophets had been given inside information about it several hundred years before even the *birth* of the self-proclaimed Redeemer.

Statements of Jesus about what the Church chooses to call Judgment Day make one wonder if definite plans for it have been formulated. Conflicting verses of scripture leave the questions of when, where, and by whom judgment will take place unanswered. Jesus says in Luke 13:28: "There shall be weeping and gnashing of teeth [sure thing] when ye shall see Abraham, and Isaac, and Jacob, and all the prophets, in the kingdom of God, and you yourselves thrust out." To the unsaved whom he is addressing, it would appear that the Jews mentioned have already been judged or that they were admitted to heaven without benefit of judgment. (Incidentally, the spiritual bodies Jesus says the elect will have are apparently identifiable, if further conclusions are drawn from these words of Jesus, words which Paul later ignores when he maintains that none who lived before Christ is eligible for eternal life.)

Referring again to a Jewish patriarch, Jesus says that he will not accuse people to the Father but that Moses will: "Do not think I will accuse you to the Father: there is one that accuseth you, even Moses, in whom ye trust" (John 5:45). In Moses Jews are given for a judge a murderer, a military leader who ordered the slaughter of innocents and the wresting of lands from their rightful inhabitants, and a man not deemed fit enough by God to set foot in the Promised Land.

Although Jesus has claimed in the above statement that he himself will not accuse, he later says: "But whosoever shall deny me before men, him will I also deny before my Father which is in heaven" (Matthew 10:33). Jesus repeats the claim that he will do the judging: "When the Son of man shall come in his glory, and all the holy angels with him, then shall he sit upon the throne of his glory: And before him shall be gathered all nations [quite a crowd]: and he shall separate them one from another, as a shepherd divideth his sheep from the goats" (Matthew 25:31,32). Again: "For the Son of man shall come in the glory of his Father with his angels; and then he shall reward every man according to his works" (Matthew 16:27). Yet again: "The Father...hath given him [the Son] authority to execute judgment." (John 5:27).

Retreating from his role as judge, however, Jesus on another occasion gives the job to the angels: "The Son of man shall send forth his angels, and they shall gather out of his kingdom all things that offend, and them which do iniquity; And shall cast them into a furnace of fire: then shall be wailing and gnashing of teeth" (Matthew 13:41,42). (Will parents be snatched from children and children from parents?)

Finally, to add to the confusion, Jesus delegates the Disciples: "Ye shall also sit upon twelve thrones, judging the twelve tribes of Israel" (Matthew 19:28). Apparently judgment of Gentiles is of little concern, and that will certainly cut down on a very crowded calendar. (Population of this world is already over 6.5 billion.)

Jesus has much to say about judgment and eternal punishment in order to establish fear as a motivation for belief in his role as Savior of a sinful humankind, thus coupling fear of physical punishment with a sense of guilt, two powerful persuaders in any cause. It is somewhat of a contradiction to believe that judgment of human behavior will even be necessary, since one message of the Gospels is that belief in Jesus as the Redeemer is all that is required for salvation: "For God so loved the world, that he gave his only begotten Son, that whosoever believeth in him should not perish, but have everlasting life" (John 3:16). Judgment as portrayed in the New Testament is immediate once it starts, without trial or consideration of contributing conditions, a system with no bill of rights and no degree of guilt or punishment, although there do seem to be lesser and greater rewards. Here on earth, judges often find it difficult to pronounce sentence fairly, and long jury trials are frequently necessary to determine guilt, but divine judgment is cut and dried, and the accused before the throne of *grace* can expect no mercy or pity from their heavenly father, no consideration of heredity or environmental influence.

JESUS TRIES TO convince John the Baptist that he (Jesus) is the Messiah by buttering up John and speaking highly of him to the people, although in some passages of the Gospels John seems to

In some scriptures, John is not all that convinced that Jesus *is* the Messiah, as he sends from prison to ask Jesus if he is.

accept without question that Jesus is such, especially when God as a pigeon lands on Jesus' head (Matthew 3:16 and John 1:32-34). John could be expected to recognize the Messiah with ease since John supposedly has been given the privilege of announcing the long-awaited arrival of the Redeemer. But Jesus passes out compliments: "Verily, I say unto you, Among them that are born of women [includes nearly everyone] there hath not risen a greater than John the Baptist" (Matthew 11:11). He says John is a prophet risen from the dead (Jews expected prophets to reappear in this way), but John denies that he himself is either a prophet or the Messiah, as many think.

It is possible that Jesus sees John as a rival; at least he does not seem very upset when John is beheaded. In some scriptures, John is not all that convinced that Jesus *is* the Messiah, as he sends from prison to ask Jesus if he is. Jesus then instructs these inquirers to tell John of all the great works that have been done: "Then Jesus answering said unto them, Go your way, and tell John what things ye have seen and heard: how that the blind see, the lame walk, the lepers are cleansed, the deaf hear, the dead are raised..." (Luke 7:22 and Matthew 11).

Jesus doesn't seem to know whether he will get more followers by preaching heaven or by preaching hell. He is not very specific in his descriptions of either one. Heaven is a very desirable place with unimagined delights and is supposed to contain many mansions which Jesus himself is going to prepare. (This finishing project ought to insure some construction workers getting through the pearly gates early.) When Jesus is questioned about human relationships that will prevail in Paradise, he gets by with an explanation that the bodies will be angelic: "They are as the angels of God in heaven" (Matthew 22:30). Because angels are able to function as human beings and are sometimes mistaken for them, the saints may expect to appear much as they did on earth, with the possible addition of a halo and a bunch of feathers at each shoulder, but whether in the buff or robed in white perma-press is not clear.

Christians pretend little interest in details about their everlasting fate, but each probably has "a little list" of questions too frivolous, in his or her estimation, to admit. Jesus says they will recognize each other, but will they have any kind of relationship with one another? (There will be no marrying or giving in marriage.) If there is no relationship, what is the appeal of heaven, and if there is, will the saved miss their skeptical relatives in hell? (There shall be no sorrow.) Will the resurrected be the age they were at death—newborn, a senile ninety-five? Will they have bodily functions? (They will live in mansions and eat at tables.)

Will they have shape and form? (Otherwise how to recognize each other?) Will faces have wrinkles and lines; will bodies be chubby, skinny, short, tall, male, female, of different races? (All Bible angels are male.) Will lost limbs be replaced, infirmities erased, ugly features beautified, emaciated bodies restored? Jesus says that occupants of heaven can converse with occupants of hell (Luke 16:19–25), but Paul would seem to make that impossible by saying that Jesus descended into the "lower parts of the earth" (hell) before he ascended "far above all heavens" (Ephesians 4:9,10). Will children go to hell, as the early Church fathers taught (graphically describing their agony)? If not, what is the cutoff age?

With so little knowledge of the heavenly abode, Christians still make sacrifices (no longer literally) in order to reach it. Of the tortures of hell, Jesus is more informed, and he regularly foretells of the weeping and wailing and teeth-gnashing awaiting all who deny him as the Savior even John the Baptist was not sure Jesus was.

Making it plain that he considers Satan a rival, Jesus admits his existence, is carried through the air and tempted by him for forty days, and refers to him often: "Simon, behold, Satan hath desired to have you" (Luke 22:31). He cures a woman whom he says: "Satan hath bound, lo, these eighteen years" (Luke 13:16). Jesus also declares that hell was prepared for the devil and his angels, of which there are vast hosts (Matthew 25:41). Jesus makes it clear that they are powerful antagonists of God. Satan actually is treated by Jesus and the Apostles as an evil and dangerous "he's every-where" mischief-maker who vies with God for the hearts of men, most of the time successfully. Hell is described as having gates and as being both a lake and a furnace.

JESUS SPENDS MUCH of his brief ministry casting out devils or unclean spirits. He is not very knowledgeable about medicine, attributing many ailments, from epilepsy to insanity, to the possession of the body by spiritual demons. He has power over them and tries to give some of his followers the same power, although the Disciples are not always successful at exercising it. At times the touch of Jesus' hands will heal, also; then again at other times a little spit works, or the hem of his garment. (Such transference of power is a concept originating in pagan magic.)

Many unlikely stories abound in the Gospels of Jesus' experiences with healing by the banishment of devils that inhabit people of that day. One of the most elaborate accounts is found in Luke. Shortly after the episode in which he calms the waves, Jesus enters a city and meets a man "which had devils a long time," a man who lived in no house and ran around naked (a not-uncommon biblical practice). Jesus commands the unclean spirit to come out of the sufferer, but the spirit cries out (oh, yes, they can speak): "What have I to do with thee, Jesus, thou Son of God most high?" (The man's name is Legion, because so many devils possess him.)

The devils beseech Jesus to cast them into a herd of swine, and after he does so, the swine "ran violently down a steep place into the lake and were choked" (Luke 8). (Quite a loss to the owner of the pigs, whether a Gergesene or a Gadarene!)

Continuing in this vein, the Disciples try to heal a child possessed of a devil and fail. Jesus impatiently asks that the child be brought to him. "And as he was yet a coming, the devil threw him [the child] down and tare him. And Jesus rebuked the unclean spirit, and healed the child" (Luke 9:38–42). Again: "And devils also came out of many, crying out, and saying [devilishly], Thou art Christ the Son of God. And he rebuking them suffered them not to speak: for they knew that he was Christ" (Luke 4:41). But: "Unclean spirits, when they saw him, fell down before him, and cried, saying, Thou art the Son of God" (Mark 3:11).

Obviously these unclean spirits (the devil's angels who used to live in heaven?) are a good source of miracle-working for Jesus, and it is handy that they frequently announce his identity.

Obviously these unclean spirits (the devil's angels who used to live in heaven?) are a good source of miracle-working for Jesus, and it is handy that they frequently announce his identity. E.g., some of them make their home in a man in a synagogue (of all places), saying:

Let us alone; what have we to do with thee, thou Jesus of Nazareth? Art thou come to destroy us? I know thee who thou art, the Holy One of God. And Jesus rebuked him, saying, Hold thy peace and come out of him. And when the unclean spirit had torn him, and cried with a loud voice, he came out of him... And immediately his fame spread abroad. (Mark 1:23–28)

Jesus seems to have no difficulty "casting out" these little devils, but one wonders where they go when no unfortunate animals are nearby. Into other persons, apparently, for Jesus tells the Disciples to "raise the dead, cast out devils" (Matthew 10:8). How easy can it be?

SOME CONTEMPORARIES THOUGHT Jesus to be just another prophet: "And the multitude said, This is Jesus the prophet of Nazareth of Galilee" (Matthew 21:11). And: "Many of the people therefore when they heard this saying, said, Of a truth this is the Prophet. Others said, This is the Christ. But some said, Shall Christ come out of Galilee? ... So there was a division among the people because of him" (John 7:40–43). "Search and look," said the Pharisees, "for out of Galilee ariseth no prophet." These words spoken to Nicodemus are indicative of the problems faced by Jesus in proving that he fulfilled the prophecies foretelling of a Messiah. Jesus could hardly breathe in and out once without remarking that some occurrence or occasion fulfilled an Old Testament prophecy. Throughout the Gospels he makes a conscious effort to establish that he is the awaited Redeemer (whom the Jews expected to save them from the Gentiles).

In Matthew alone Jesus alludes to these prophecies thirty-one times. He also admits that he follows certain patterns of behavior *purposely* to fulfill a familiar-to-all prophecy of a Messiah-to-come, forecast by the fortune-teller prophets of the Old Testament: "I am not come to destroy, but to fulfill" (Matthew 5:17).

Jesus is thought at times to be a prophet risen from the dead: "And they said, Some say that thou art John the Baptist: some say Elias (Elijah); and others Jeremias (Jeremiah), or one of the prophets" (Matthew 16:14). Jesus also thinks of himself as a prophet or at least takes seriously this belief of some of his fellow Jews, for he says at one time: "Nevertheless I must walk today, and tomorrow, and the day following: for it cannot be that a prophet perish out of Jerusalem" (Luke 13:33). Can he be both prophet and God?

Throughout the Gospels he makes a conscious effort to establish that he is the awaited Redeemer (whom the Jews expected to save them from the Gentiles).

THE DISCIPLES, WHO are frequently skeptical although they hear even *devils* identify Jesus as the Son of God, confront Jesus with a prophecy from Malachi that says Elias must return before the Messiah comes, but Jesus answers that: "Elias is come already, and they knew him not" (Matthew 17:12). Here Jesus is claiming that John the Baptist was Elias. In fact, he so states while John is still alive: "This is Elias which was for to come" (Matthew 11:14). But John tells the priests: "I am not the Christ. And they asked him, What then? Art thou Elias? And he saith, I am *not*. Art thou that prophet? And he answered, *No*" (John 1:20,21, emphasis added). Jesus describes himself many times as the Son of man, a title applied to prophets, of whom Elijah was traditionally supposed to be the one who would recognize and identify the Messiah.

Throughout the Gospels Jesus stresses that he is both the Son of God and God himself: "He that believeth on the Son hath everlasting life" (John 3:36). And: "All things are delivered to me of my Father" (Luke 10:22). But: "I and my Father are one" (John 10:30). And: "...even as we are one" (John 17:22).

Jesus and God and the Holy Ghost make up the Trinity, that dogma of the Church which became necessary to retain the monotheism of Christianity. It was one of the mystic concepts invented to clothe the Christian religion with that "mystery" of which the New Testament is enamored. Such enigmas are meant to put comprehension of Christian theology out of reach of the masses, who are summarily commanded to "avoid foolish questions" and fall back on puerile trust, leaving to the clergy the intellectualism and privilege which are required for understanding.

Without the Trinity, Christianity might be seen as having three gods, and Satan, seemingly more powerful than all of them, might have to be allowed to be the fourth. Indeed, some scriptures challenge the Trinity quite effectively: "My Father is greater than I" (John 14:28). And: "I love the Father" (John 14:31). These statements are attributed to Jesus.

JESUS IS OFTEN CONFRONTED by the question of how his teaching relates to the Mosaic law and to secular law. Throughout the Gospels he struggles with answers. Finally, in a superficial manner, he tries to solve the whole problem with one brief remark: "Render unto Caesar the things which are Caesar's" (Mark 12:17).

Such a stand leaves a great deal open to further question as to separation of Church and State, and the argument about whether the Church should take political attitudes remains a bitter one today.

At times Jesus preaches that God must have the highest allegiance, in connection with which

idea he says that up until the time of John the Baptist the law prevailed, but since then the "kingdom of God" is taught. In line, however, with his predilection for contradicting himself, he on another occasion assures the Pharisees (strict adherents to the God-given Mosaic law): "Think not that I am come to destroy the law or the prophets" (Matthew 5:17). He expands this theme: "Till heaven and earth pass, one jot or one tittle shall in no wise pass from the law..." (Matthew 5:18). To add to the confusion, he then proceeds to defend the Disciples when they break the Mosaic law, and at times he amends it to excuse his own actions.

The conflict which arises between the "morality" of obeying civil law and the "morality" of following religious beliefs when the two are in opposition is recognized by Jesus, but he does little to resolve it: "In vain do they worship me, teaching for doctrines the commandments of men" (Matthew 15:9).

Jesus does not sanction any challenge of the State by its citizens, although it is clear from his words that a very oppressive class system existed among the Jews of his day.

JESUS DOES NOT SANCTION any challenge of the State by its citizens, although it is clear from his words that a very oppressive class system existed among the Jews of his day. New Testament scriptures teem with talk of kings, rulers, lords, and masters, and their servants, many of whom are slaves. The teaching of Jesus is concerned with instructions of how all members of that society should conduct themselves in their present situation. No one in servitude is encouraged to rebel against it, and the division of the culture into the rich and the poor, also obvious from Jesus' words, is not considered by him to be a situation that should be changed, except by reliance upon charity and welfare.

The unique appeal of Christianity to early converts was the promise that the next world would be a place where the class ranking would be reversed. In the meantime, the underprivileged, subservient, and poverty-stricken were to content themselves with their social position and not threaten the hierarchy. Jesus repeatedly reprimanded

EVERYTHING YOU KNOW ABOUT GOD IS WRONG

the scribes and Pharisees for their ill-treatment of the laity, but reform was to be voluntary and undertaken as a way of avoiding hell.

Jesus addresses himself to the Hebrew class system which imprisoned his contemporaries: "The servant is not greater than his lord... If ye know these things, happy are ye if ye do them" (John 13:16,17). Bible attitudes would not be popular with labor organizations today. John the Baptist advises: "Be content with your wages" (Luke 3:14). Servants have no civil rights in the parables Jesus tells. Speaking of the need to be on watch for the last days, he paraphrases: a servant who, failing to anticipate his master's return, and

> shall begin to beat the men servants and maidens, and to eat and drink and be drunken; the lord of that servant will come in a day when he looketh not for him,... and will cut him in sunder...and that servant, which knew his lord's will, and prepared not himself, neither did according to his will, shall be beaten with many stripes. But he that knew not, and did commit things worthy of stripes, shall be beaten with few stripes. (Luke 12:45–48)

Such scriptures give a vivid impression of Jesus' attitude toward the working class. Their bodies belonged to their masters, who were free to mete out corporal punishment to suit their own sadistic tendencies. The Gospels contain much talk of high and low rank. Jesus tells a parable in which the following instruction is offered: "When thou art bidden of any man to a wedding, sit not down in the highest room; lest a more honorable man than thou be bidden of him... For whosoever exalteth himself shall be abased; and he that humbleth himself shall be exalted" (Luke 14:8–11). Jesus was prone to take advantage of every opportunity to "put down" people of importance when he was describing Paradise. At other times they are often heroes of his narratives.

Several parts of Jesus' Sermon on the Mount give much consolation to servants, and also the poor. The effect, if not the purpose, of many of the teachings, is to keep the underdogs in their miserable estate and reasonably resigned to it. The poor especially have little chance of acquiring any assets, and Jesus declares their situation hopeless—there will always be poor people. There certainly always will be if Jesus' recommendations for dealing with poverty are followed.

His primary palliative is for the rich to give everything they have to the poor. In spite of the fact that Jesus holds out heaven as the reward for compliance, no one seems to take him seriously, probably not seeing what will be gained by creating a surrogate group of indigents. Having abandoned the poor to their fate, Jesus defends Lazarus' sister when she pours on his head a whole box of "ointment of spikenard very precious." When there is a murmuring that the ointment might have been sold and the proceeds given to the poor, Jesus chides: "Let her alone; why trouble ye her? she hath wrought a good work on me. For ye have the poor with you always..." (Mark 14:3–7).

Another time he has kind words for a poor widow who puts two mites in the temple treasury, choosing to ignore the observation of some spectators that it may be unfortunate that the temple to which she has just contributed "all the living that she had" was "adorned with goodly stones and gifts" (Luke 21:1–5).

Jesus sees the poor as objects of charity. They can serve as a stepping stone to Paradise for all those who take pity on them: "But when thou makest a feast, call the poor, the maimed, the lame, the blind: And thou shalt be blessed, for they cannot recompense thee: for thou shalt be recompensed at the resurrection of the just" (Luke 14:13,14). Paul later echoes this sentiment when he says it is better to give than to receive. That may be, but it is also much less humiliating. Neither Paul nor Jesus considers the psychological plight of those who must always be the *objects* of that commendable charity. Their degradation does not detract from the rewards their benefactors will enjoy in the next life.

To be fair, Jesus does seem to indicate that just the fact of being poor will assure one of a place in heaven. He tells a story of a rich man "which was clothed in purple and fine linen" and a beggar at his gate who waits for crumbs from the rich man's table. When the scene changes, the beggar is in Paradise, and the rich man is in that place where all persons cursed with wealth will eventually be (Luke 16:19–31). Heaven and hell are not reward and punishment! They are equalizers!

THAT HIS TEACHING WAS intended strictly for the Jews is the obvious conclusion reached from the emphasis Jesus placed on the audience he sought. To the Samaritan woman (Samaritans were descendants of Jews who had intermarried with people of Mesopotamia and Asia Minor), Jesus flatly asserts: "For salvation is of the Jews" (John 4:22). He has little time for the Gentiles, although he occasionally associates with some of them.

An episode related in the scriptures is cruel proof of the fact that the Jews were his chosen audience: Jesus refuses to listen to a Gentile woman (or to answer her) when she begs him to heal her daughter. Pressed, he finally explains: "I am not sent but unto the lost sheep of the house of Israel. It is not meet to take the children's [Jews'] bread and to cast it to dogs [Gentiles]." After she further humiliates herself, he finally agrees to heal the child. Not satisfied with being rude and practicing heartless discrimination, he then exploits the occasion by delivering a speech on the power of faith (and persistence?) (Matthew 15:22–28). Christians worship a God who refused to heal a *sick child*, until he was pressured!

Jesus also gives definite instructions to his workers when he sends them out to spread the word: "Go not into the way of the Gentiles...but rather to the lost sheep of the House of Israel" (Matthew 10:5,6).

In John 12:15 it is said that Jesus fulfills the Old Testament prophecy (always does): "Fear not, daughter of *Zion:* behold, *thy* King cometh, sitting on the ass's colt" (emphasis added). And Jesus also gives definite instructions to his workers when he sends them out to spread the word: "Go not into the way of the Gentiles...but rather to the lost sheep of the House of Israel" (Matthew 10:5,6). At the Last Supper Jesus limits the realm to come: "And I appoint unto you a kingdom...that ye may eat and drink at my table in my kingdom and sit on thrones judging the twelve tribes of Israel" (Luke 22:29,30). Just prior to this, he has described the

behavior of Gentile kings and told the disciples: "Ye shall not be so" (emphasis added).

Belatedly, the authors of the Gospels have Jesus, just before the ascension, instruct the Disciples to enlarge the audience: "And he said unto them...that repentance and remission of sins should be preached in his name among all nations." But this change of policy must be suspect, for Jesus throughout almost his entire ministry says that he has come as the Messiah of the Jews.

JESUS LIKES TO TELL stories to prove a point, and these stories the Bible calls parables. He may have gotten the idea from Ezekiel, whose contemporaries remarked upon this habit of his that manifested itself during Ezekiel's few waking hours. The Disciples are curious about why Jesus uses this method of communication, and his answer is that *they* may know the *mysteries* of heaven but that others are not given that knowledge—all this in spite of the likelihood that the Disciples were not for the most part known for their perceptive qualities. And, of course, they are all men—no woman could be expected to be able to comprehend anything as complex as the mysteries of heaven. And with the Disciples and Jesus no longer around, *no one* on earth can, apparently, understand them. (How could Paul?)

From these words of Jesus to the Disciples, one gathers not only that God is so complicated that he is unfathomable but that favoritism is shown in the revelation of the intricacies of everything pertaining to the divine: "Therefore speak I to them in parables: because they seeing see not; and hearing they hear not, neither do they understand" (Matthew 13:13). Why bother to preach at all, if it is futile? Not to mention the put-down of his contemporaries by a "man" who is himself apparently not well-educated and whose intelligence is rated poorly by his neighbors and fellow citizens: "And the Jews [of his hometown] marvelled, saying, How knoweth this man letters, having never learned?" (John 7:15 and Mark 4:33).

Jesus as much as says that people can't understand anything but storytelling. Even so, several of the parables are foggy and meaningless, so much so that even the privileged Disciples have to ask for explanations: "His disciples came unto him saying, Declare unto us the parable of the tares of the field" (Matthew 13:36). Jesus also admits that he speaks in parables to fulfill a prophecy (Matthew 13:35). There must be *some* reason to speak in such a manner that the truth is obscured.

Several of the parables are foggy and meaningless, so much so that even the privileged Disciples have to ask for explanations.

The contents of the parables are frequently characterized by violence and injustice. Jesus does not disapprove of social conditions inherent in the contents as long as they make a point. E.g., Jesus tells a parable about a king who *sells* a man who owes him money and at the same time *sells* the debtor's wife and children. Although he uses the parable to make some comment on forgiveness, Jesus expresses no moral indignation whatever toward the selling into slavery of human beings (Matthew 18). Another time he tells a story of an employer who becomes angry at the protests of workmen who receive the same pay for working all day as those who work one hour. The employer is supposed to represent the kingdom of heaven where "the last shall be first and the first last" (Matthew 20:16). No unfairness is attributed to the employer by Jesus, even though the employer arbitrarily states that he will pay as he pleases. Jesus seems to feel that such an attitude is just.

If rewards in the next world are as inequitably distributed, it would seem repentance at the last minute would be the wise course to follow. This same unfairness is inherent in the parable of the prodigal son (Luke 15). Certainly any father would be happy to see a philandering son return to the fold at long last, but his prejudice, while understandable, is hardly admirable, and the loyal son would have just cause for indignation.

One of the most violent and unfair of the parables, and one of the most far-fetched, is the story of the marriage feast which servants do not wish to attend and for which reluctance they are massacred. This grisly tale continues, as "guests" are forced in from the street to view the wedding rites. One such kidnapped soul, who understandably is not attired in a wedding suit, is bound and cast into darkness for being improperly clad (Matthew 22:1–14). The moral of this tale of atrocities is again that many are called but few are chosen!

That Jesus should use such reprehensible deeds to illustrate his principles tells the reader something of his personality. Episodes of bestial behavior and occasions for revenge have a fascination for him. Such an impression is compounded not only by his choice of material but to an even greater degree by a realization that he feels no repugnance for it. The performers in some of his parables are liars, assassins, wealthy oppressors, ingrates, con artists, slave-beaters and slave-merchants, autocrats, and torturers. Victims of the wickedness present in all this do not win Jesus' sympathy. They are pawns in the literary conceit he has chosen to employ, and he occasionally endorses the villain of the piece. The parable that tells of the householder and the husbandmen in Matthew 21 is especially gory.

The performers in some of his parables are liars, assassins, wealthy oppressors, ingrates, con artists, slave-beaters and slave-merchants, autocrats, and torturers. Victims of the wickedness present in all this do not win Jesus' sympathy.

Even the parable of the Good Samaritan is about highway muggers. Here again there seems to be acceptance of the crime, and Jesus ignores the racist bigotry of the Jews of his day, who made it unlawful to associate with Gentiles and despised Samaritans. The point he seems to belabor here is that the object of the racism is to be commended for not harboring resentment.

After completing one of these gruesome sermonettes, Jesus usually departs abruptly, leaving his audience to contemplate as much on the horrid details as on the murky moral.

At the conclusion of one parable, the final words of a nobleman (!) are: "Unto everyone which hath shall be given; and from him that hath not, even that he hath shall be taken away from him. But those mine enemies, which would not that I should reign over them, bring hither, and slay them before me." Jesus invents this parable to illustrate his own philosophy, and he deliberately puts these words into the mouth of a despot who is punishing his servant (slave) for an honest error in judgment, an error which represented a financial loss to his master. This king's retaliatory treatment of the erring servant, and his concluding edict proclaiming death by the sword for any disobedient subject, has been described by Jesus to serve as an illustration of recommended behavior. (This nobleman had become the ruler of his "enemies" by going into a far country to "receive for himself a kingdom.") (Luke 19:11–27).

In several of the parables one looks in vain for any compassion and understanding, for any trace of ordinary human kindness. The humans aren't very kind, and the storyteller doesn't come off very well, either. These parables are brutalizing. They cannot be told to children (which is why Sunday schools must dwell on Old Testament fairy tales and Jesus the Magician). In no way can they ennoble. Even hardened adults will shudder at their ferocity, and sensitive readers will look elsewhere for inspiration.

The few women who appear in the stories Jesus tells are usually victims of slave-masters and kings, but at least one parable mirrors the position held by women in Palestine. *Ten virgins* await their one bridegroom, but five of them fail to bring extra oil for their lamps and have gone to buy more when the tardy bridegroom arrives. These "foolish" virgins implore the bridegroom, sequestered with the other five: "Lord, Lord, open to us." He, self-righteous to a fault, makes a very formal reply, under the circumstances: "Verily I say unto you, I know you not." Jesus is the steely fellow, for whose arrival at the end of the world all must be prepared (Matthew 25:1–13). This allegory is played out by Christian congregations in which at a certain age young girls become "brides of the Church."

When Jesus is not proclaiming his divinity to anyone who will listen, he enigmatically sometimes conceals it and asks others to do so: "Then charged he his disciples that they should tell no man that he was Jesus the Christ" (Matthew

16:20). After his transfiguration, he cautions: "Tell the vision to no man, until the Son of man be risen again from the dead" (Matthew 17:9). Again, upon another occasion: "And he straitly charged them that they should not make him known" (Mark 3:12). At times, after performing miracles, he asks for secrecy: "And he charged them straitly that no man should know it." These were his orders after he had raised the daughter of the synagogue ruler from the dead (Mark 5:43).

Following the healing of a deaf mute: "He charged them that they should tell no man: but the more he charged them, so much the more a great deal they published it" (Mark 7:36). Perhaps in that admonishment lies the chief purpose behind the pretended desire for secrecy. There are two other possible reasons for Jesus' request that healings not be aired about. One is fear for his life, and another is to keep doubt at a minimum.

Whatever the reason, the secrecy itself is contrary to his command: "Let your light so shine before men that they may see your good works, and glorify your Father which is in heaven" (Matthew 5:16). And the following claim of his would seem to belie hiding his light under a bushel: "The works that I do in my Father's name, they bear witness of me" (John 10:25).

DESPITE BELIEF TO the contrary prevalent today, Jesus was not a booster for family life. In the scriptures he treats his mother and siblings with something less than affection and respect. He does not marry or father children. After laying down rules about adultery and divorce, he proceeds to predict some rather astonishing effects that belief in him will have upon the family as an institution: "For I am come to set a man at variance against his father, and the daughter against her mother, and the daughter in law against her mother in law. And a man's foes shall be they of his own household" (Matthew 10:35,36). From the time he is twelve years old and doesn't bother to tell his mother that he is remaining in the temple, he seems to have no close ties to his family and discourages his converts from having any with theirs.

He demands that they drop everything immediately to become his followers: "And he said unto another, Follow me. But he said, Lord, suffer me first to go and bury my father. Jesus said unto him, Let the dead bury their dead... And another also said, Lord, I will follow thee; but first let me go bid them farewell, which are at home at my house. And Jesus said unto him, No man, having put his hand to the plough, and looking back, is fit for the kingdom of God" (Luke 9:59–62). Two of his disciples actually leave their father mending the fishing nets (Matthew 4:21,22).

It is a real puzzle where Christians today get their exalted view of the Christian family. And few Bible readers will understand the worshipful position accorded to Mary, for Jesus was rude to his mother at the marriage feast: "Woman, what have I to do with thee?" (John 2:1–4). And he was even more uncivil when she and his brothers waited at the edge of a crowd to speak to him, posing a question to his Disciples: "Who is my mother? And who are my brethren?" and indicating that the Disciples were now his family (Matthew 12:46–49). Then he added that all who do the will of God, "the same is my brother, and sister, and mother."

THE ATTITUDE OF JESUS toward women in general is ambiguous in the extreme. At times he seems to regard them as they exist under the Mosaic law. Again, he upholds them. Sexism on his part cannot be condoned, since he supposedly came to earth as the moral example for all time to come, and bias that prevailed in the treatment of women during the period of time he spent as a human being should not have influenced him to conform to it. Although such treatment might have been the custom of that day, Jesus' behavior standards should surely have been timeless.

He has a touching scene with *children*, in which they get just about as high an approval rating as it is possible to award, since everyone else is cautioned to be as naïve as they are, but woman receives little praise and that only when she is performing some act of servitude, such as pouring oil on Jesus' head or washing his feet and drying them with her hair, or even giving her last mite to the poor (Mark 14:3–9; John 12:3). Or not ceasing to *kiss* Jesus' feet (Luke 7:45).

It's what Jesus *doesn't* say that is more a key to his attitude toward women than what he says or does. For instance, he doesn't say that Eve was wrongly blamed; he doesn't say that the Mosaic law is cruelly demeaning of women; he doesn't say that women need not submit to their husbands in everything; he doesn't say that wives may ever divorce their husbands or marry again if their husbands divorce them for "fornication"; he doesn't say that there are no witches, and in any case they should not be burnt to death; he doesn't say that a hapless girl thought not to be a virgin when she is wed should not be stoned or burnt to death (and her despoiler allowed to go free); he doesn't say that ten virgins should not belong to one bridegroom.

The Gospel of John tells a story of a woman caught "in the very act" of adultery, who is brought before Jesus in the temple. The self-righteous scribes and Pharisees, whom Jesus habitually labels adulterous, prepare to stone her according to the Mosaic law. Jesus looks up from scratching in the dirt with his finger and admonishes: "He that is without sin among you, let him first cast a stone at her" (John 8:7). These scribes and Pharisees, as well as most other Hebrew men, did not think of themselves as sinners, so it was a risky proposition that really changed nothing about the status of women in Jewish society of the time.

It would have been a wonderfully opportune occasion for Jesus, since he was surrounded by people listening to him teach, to have spoken out against the inexcusable cruelty of a law that would kill a woman in an excruciating way for a minor "sin" that was indulged in by even the temple priests. By not doing so, he failed to protect any other women in a similar situation, who might even be falsely accused. He had succeeded only in saying: Judge not.

Jesus was not moved to inquire about the other partner in the act, who had been permitted to go free, and he asked for no details, such as whether the woman had been a victim of force or held at knifepoint. It is all too obvious that Jesus spoke the truth when he said he came to uphold the law of Moses.

He makes snide remarks about harlots, and, according to John 4:29, he knows every woman's marital status and sexual secrets, but he is big-hearted about female sexual peccadilloes and frequently blames them on possession of women's bodies by devils, which he expels. In Jesus' eye, as

In Jesus' eye, as with his contemporaries, the _man_ is seldom at fault in any sexual situation, and the woman has to promise never to be naughty again.

with his contemporaries, the _man_ is seldom at fault in any sexual situation, and the woman has to promise never to be naughty again.

It must be concluded that Jesus was the usual male chauvinist of his day. Although he traveled about with women, none was a disciple, and none will sit at his table in heaven. Finally, it is clear that he shared the sexist conviction of Jewish men of Bible days that sexual relations with women were unholy, for he gives extra commendation to eunuchs, especially those who castrate themselves "for the kingdom of heaven's sake" (Matthew 19:12).

AT TIMES JESUS gives cryptic answers, and at times he is very wrong. When certain church elders among the Jews ask by what authority he preaches, a natural enough question, he replies by in turn asking them a question which puts them on the spot in such a way that they refuse to answer it. His verbal shrug follows: "Neither tell I you by what authority I do these things" (Matthew 21:27). Most of the time he is repeatedly naming God as his authority, without even being asked.

In another instance, when asked for a sign, although he habitually describes many happenings as signs and can hardly make a move without declaring it a sign, he says to the Pharisees and scribes: "An evil and adulterous generation seeketh after a sign; and there shall be no sign given to it, but the sign of the prophet Jonas" (Matthew 12:39). By this answer Jesus says he meant that he would be in the earth three days just as Jonah was in the whale's belly three days. Actually, Jesus was to be in the grave a little over one day and two nights.

Cryptic replies to earnest questions, when it would seem clarity would better serve a sincere advocate, are difficult to justify. They are in the same key as some of Jesus' behavior and instructions, often mysterious, and the Gospels are packed with discrepancies and errors concerning him. Perhaps the most obvious error that can be attributed to Jesus' teaching and ministry, however, has to lie in his prediction that he would return to earth within a very short time and before his generation should pass away.

THE MANNER IN WHICH Jesus chooses his Disciples is incomprehensible and surely open to criticism when one considers that care and discrimination would ordinarily be shown at such a time. Apparently he picks them up, total strangers or at the most mere acquaintances, as he is strolling about the countryside. Several are fishermen, one is a publican, and that is about all one is given to know about them. The Gospels do not even agree upon their names. One is left to wonder what Jesus knew about their backgrounds and to conclude that he wasn't interested in finding out very much about them. That one of them proves less than loyal is not surprising.

Jesus himself loses patience with the Disciples several times for their lack of faith, failure to understand, and inability to perform miracles. He is driven to cursing them and calling them names. Not exactly a model of patience himself, he vents his wrath upon them: "O faithless and perverse generation, how long shall I suffer you?" (Matthew 17:17). Acts 4:13 says they were "unlearned and ignorant men."

One Gospel gives a list of their names but not of their occupations, although most seem to be of humble origin, admittedly uneducated and simple, thus readily fitting into the ideal mold for Christians as outlined by Jesus and later by the Apostles. They seem to be completely irresponsible, for they traipse along with a total stranger (?) at a moment's notice, dropping everything, quitting their employment, gathering no belongings, not worried about a livelihood, and not permitted by Jesus to say good-bye to their families or make provisions for them. The two brothers who abandon their father in the fishing boat don't give him a backward look.

Although they are unable to understand Jesus at times, he doesn't hesitate to tell them that they are privileged to have knowledge of spiritual enigmas that cannot be mastered by others. And their possibly rather limited mental capacities will not preclude their enthronement in heaven as the judges of the Jews. When Jesus sends them and seventy other followers out as missionaries to those fellow Jews, he instructs them to sponge off friends and sympathizers for food and lodging, as he does. It is possible to be even nervier, and Jesus is, criticizing his hostess Martha for working in the kitchen (probably preparing a spur-of-the-moment repast for her unexpected guest) instead of listening to an egotistical Jesus utter words about mansions in heaven, in the kitchens of which she has a hunch she is really going to be stuck.

Since not only the Disciples but most, if not all, of the leaders of the new sect are probably, to put it generously, not exactly pillars of wisdom, it is to be expected that Jesus will gear his preaching to all who are willing to become childlike and to accept him on faith that requires the abandonment of reason and of truth: "Verily I say unto you, Except...ye become as little children, ye shall not enter into the kingdom of heaven" (Matthew 18:3). Jesus makes a further case for ignorance: "I thank thee, O Father...that thou hast hid these things from the wise and prudent, and has revealed them unto babes" (Luke 10:21). Education and knowledge gained from maturity lead to eternal damnation, because they threaten blind faith, and achievement in this world assures one a place far down on the class scale in heaven, as the first shall be last and the last shall be first.

The faith of the Disciples in Jesus as the Messiah is so precarious, even after months of close association with him, that their belief does not solidify until they are partaking of the Last Supper: "Now are we sure that thou knowest all things, and needest not that any man should ask thee: by this we believe that thou earnest forth from God. Jesus answered them, Do ye now believe?" (John 16:30,31). The final days of destiny give the Disciples an opportunity to show themselves to be men of integrity, but they desert Jesus to a man, after one of them betrays him.

Peter comes off the worst, and his three-times denial of Jesus is reminiscent of two former occasions when Jesus lost his temper with Simon Peter: "Get thee behind me, Satan: thou art an offence unto me" (Matthew 16:23). But Jesus says he will build his church upon Peter, even though Peter is not the most beloved of Jesus, and Jesus knows in advance that Peter will deny him three times.

Women follow Jesus and the Disciples from city to city (fan-club groupies?), and Jesus, if he had been a good judge of character, should have made some of them Disciples, as they courageously remain loyal and believing, coming to the scene of the crucifixion and meeting Jesus the morning of the resurrection. They received few accolades, but the sniveling, cowardly Disciples sit on heavenly thrones.

> He has no patience whatsoever with anyone who doesn't listen to him and unhesitatingly pronounce him the Messiah, although some pretenders at the time claim the same title.

"FOR I AM MEEK and lowly in heart" (Matthew 11:29). Jesus may have thought of himself that way, but these are not adjectives which come to mind when reading the account of his ministry in the Gospels. He continually makes it abundantly clear that he has been sent by God, is God, and will return in clouds of glory to claim a kingdom. That's meek?

He has no patience whatsoever with anyone who doesn't listen to him and unhesitatingly pronounce him the Messiah, although some pretenders at the time claim the same title. Others have continued to do so. He even warns of false Messiahs, so it is not to be wondered at that the Jews wanted a little proof, especially the priesthood, which he was trying to unseat or reform.

He calls unbelievers fools, wicked, perverse, adulterous, and "whited sepulchres" ("which indeed appear beautiful outward, but are within full of dead men's bones, and of all uncleanness" (Matthew 23:27)), and with relish assigns them to eternal torment. If his contemporaries believed with the ease he expected of them, the Jews probably would have accepted a Messiah long before Jesus appeared on the scene. To anticipate instant belief and welcome on their part was naïve and showed little understanding of human nature by Jesus. His quick temper, impatience, and resort to violence on occasion, along with his contemplation on the fate of the unbelievers, sometimes make it impossible for the love to show through, although the Gospel of John tries to smooth it all over and give the world a Savior full of loving compassion.

Christianity was established by the sword, and Jesus brought it: "I came not to send peace but a sword" (Matthew 10:34). The Jews had a history of violence, and Jesus was well-versed in that history. He doesn't hesitate to pick up a whip and drive the merchants and moneychangers from the temple area. These capitalists were assigned a permanent place in the temple courtyard, where they sold pigeons and animals for the sacrifices demanded under the Mosaic law, as a convenience to worshippers. Far better if Jesus had condemned the whole idea of the useless slaughter of innocent creatures to appease a vindictive Jehovah.

He calls all who pray on street corners hypocrites, but ministers pray in public today, even at football games, and no doubt some of them are sincere; surely not all are "serpents" and "vipers." They might be incensed at being so described.

Another show of temper and violence occurs on a walking trip when Jesus, suddenly hungry, finds a fig tree bearing no fruit (Mark 11:13 says it is out of season). Furious, Jesus curses it: "Let no fruit grow on thee henceforward forever." The innocent tree proceeds to wither away on the spot (Matthew 21:19).

Not satisfied to downgrade individuals who don't believe, Jesus damns whole *cities* which fail to put out the welcome mat: "Woe unto thee, Chorazin! Woe unto thee, Bethsaida!... And thou, Capernaum...shalt be brought down to hell" (Matthew 11:20–23). All of this hardly sounds like the "Prince of Peace."

Any humility which might surface is properly smothered in such pronouncements as: "In this place is one greater than the temple" (Matthew 12:6). And: "Behold, a greater than Jonas is here" (Matthew 12:41). And: "Behold, a greater than Solomon is here" (Matthew 12:42). These are all words spoken by Jesus to describe himself.

Aforementioned parables of horrendous bloodiness and pointless brutality fall from the lips of this self-proclaimed deity and would match any presentation on television today; yet Christian groups trying to sanitize current entertainment keep the Bible accessible to all ages.

JESUS IS ADDICTED TO MAKING rash promises which involve conditions and occurrences contrary to what most people regard as natural laws. Such seeming order is sufficient evidence for many persons to envision some sort of supernatural being. Some consider it to be, for them, the *supreme* evidence. Jesus seems to fail to understand that reliance upon so-called miracles might tend to foster doubt and questioning about whether a hoax could have been perpetrated. "Unnatural" happenings depend for their verification on witnesses, whose reliability, of necessity, is open to doubt. Witnesses may be victims of their imaginations, gullibility, or intentions, or even of poor eyesight and faulty hearing, and they may not be accurate reporters.

Categorically, at any rate, he assures: "Whatsoever ye shall ask the Father in my name, he will give it you" (John 16:23).

Perhaps Jesus does realize that miracles arouse suspicion in rational minds, and thus his insistence upon faith and childlike confidence. Categorically, at any rate, he assures: "Whatsoever ye shall ask the Father in my name, he will give it you" (John 16:23). He proceeds to elaborate upon this by saying that faith as large as a mustard seed will move mountains. But bulldozers and dynamite are still being manufactured, and few have seen a large mound of earth and rock moved without them. The idea that any favor sincerely requested of God will be granted is rather frightening, and one can only hope that all requests are of a benevolent nature. The validity of the promise would surely be put to the test should two mustard-seed faith-possessors want an identical mountain moved in opposite directions at the same time.

A God whose mind is so easily influenced is a God without plan or wisdom or ability to see into the future, a God who, contrary to some scripture, *is* after all changeable. Such a deity precludes any conception of order in the universe, although human experience has been that some kind of order and natural law exist.

Besides giving his Disciples, and seventy other appointed missionaries, the ability to raise from the dead and drive out those elusive evil spirits, Jesus gets carried away and expands: "Behold, I give unto you power to tread on serpents and scorpions...and nothing shall by any means hurt you" (Luke 10:19). Just before he is taken up into heaven, he goes even further: "In my name shall they [the saved] cast out devils; they shall speak with new tongues; They shall take up serpents; and if they drink any deadly thing, it shall not hurt them; and they shall lay hands on the sick, and they shall recover" (Mark 16:17,18).

Unrealistic claims such as these, added to the suggestion that becoming a eunuch is considered worthy in the kingdom of heaven (Matthew 19:12) and that offending eyes should be plucked out, sinful hands and feet chopped off, and families forsaken (Matthew 19:29), have led to lonely lives spent in monasteries and convents, self-mutilation, faith healers, and weird cults among those who take these words literally, and to apologetic shrugs among those who pick and choose what they consider to be practical and admirable in the teachings of Jesus. Thousands of suicides and willing martyrs, taking the promises and instructions of Jesus seriously, sought to assure themselves of a heavenly abode. Many even included their children in this plan for salvation.

CHRISTIANS LIKE TO speak of being "born again" in the "spirit," and many say it is a universal requirement for that "pie in the sky." True, Jesus does make that assertion, but, as he often does, he then contradicts himself and says: "I came not to call the righteous, but sinners to repentance" (John 3:3, Mark 2:17). Many times his actions are opposed to his teaching, some blatantly so, such as shortly after telling listeners not to call anyone a fool (Matthew 5:22), he himself says to his pet targets, the scribes and Pharisees: "Ye fools and blind" (Matthew 23:17).

At least once he is intentionally devious (John 7:2–14). His brothers plan to attend the Feast of the Tabernacles in Jerusalem and urge Jesus to accompany them and perform some of his miracles. Unbelievers in him themselves ("For neither did his brethren believe in him."), they suggest that he "shew thyself to the world." But Jesus, saying his time has not yet come, tells his brothers to go without him, leading them to believe that he does not plan to attend. After they leave, however: "Then went he also up unto the feast, not openly, but as it were in secret." He preaches there in the temple, but he is not captured for the same reason that his time has not yet come. It is little wonder there is so much disagreement about the character of Jesus that arguments persist, even among theologians.

> **Many times his actions are opposed to his teaching, some blatantly so, such as shortly after telling listeners not to call anyone a fool (Matthew 5:22), he himself says to his pet targets, the scribes and Pharisees: "Ye fools and blind" (Matthew 23:17).**

His teaching of the need to be born again denies the ability of God to create perfection at the first attempt; all born of God are imperfect and need to be improved. Since heaven was the scene of civil war, and considering that the first generations of humankind had to be destroyed as faulty, God begins to come across as a consummate blunderer. Actually, Paul implies that rebirth is meaningless, when he says the New Jerusalem is populated by the "firstborn," who have always been of the elect (Hebrews 12:22,23). Predestination scripture negates any need for rebirth.

THE SPAN OF HUMAN LIFETIME has increased greatly since Bible days. Some persons are living even into their nineties, and they are spending those years in a material world and environment. Adjustment to that world so that reasonable contentment, if not enjoyment, is possible would seem to be of necessary concern to material bodies requiring material things. Yet Jesus teaches that life here on earth is of secondary (actually *little*) importance and that all time and energy should be expended in preparation for an ill-defined eternal existence in heaven.

The small amount of information about the reward he holds out for abandoning earthly pursuits seems to suffice for Christians. He tells them that they will be subjects of a kingdom where some will be greater than others (just like earthly monarchies) and that all will be able to see him. Other than that, Jesus lets the chief attraction of heaven be that it is not hell.

The instinct of self-preservation is so strong in humanity that any promise that abolishes death "has a wondrous attraction" for them, as the old hymn observes. The idea that existence of any sort should continue *forever*, though, would seem to be mind-boggling, if not terrifying, and can Christians be happy in this world living in fear that loved ones are damned? Or will the ecstasy of heaven be all the more intense as the saved contemplate their better fate in contrast to that of their more unfortunate fellows? The Revelation says they will shout Alleluia (Revelation 19:3).

One must keep in mind when reading the admonitions of Jesus that he labored under the illusion that life in this world was nearly over for everyone. Just as soon as he finished preparing those mansions, he intended to come back and gather up the saints, or let the angels do it. So perhaps the following statements of his are understandable, after all: "He that hateth his life in this world shall keep it unto life eternal" (John 12:25). "And every one that hath forsaken houses, or brethren, or sisters, or father, or mother, or wife, or children, or lands, for my name's sake, shall receive an hundredfold and shall inherit everlasting life" (Matthew 19:29). "Whosoever he be of you that forsaketh not all that he hath, he cannot be my disciple" (Luke 14:33). (Why such contempt for the world that God created?)

Jesus discourages any ambition other than this attainment of future reward: "For what is a man advantaged, if he gain the whole world, and lose himself…?" (Luke 9:25). Any position of importance achieved in this world will be a liability in the next, for "the first shall be last." Jesus outlines the goal of every Christian: "Seek ye first the kingdom of God" (Matthew 6:33).

LUKE TRACES JESUS' genealogy through seventy-five generations back to Adam (although anthropologists have found evidence that human beings were around a bit previous to that time). Jesus claims, however, that he existed before the world began. It is incomprehensible that Jesus as God should even have a genealogy, but it was necessary, to establish him as the Messiah, that his ancestry should extend to David, at least. Jesus as both divine and the heir (by succession) to the throne of a reunited Jewish nation is a throwback to pagan human-god mysticism, but the Jews have refused to accept him as either God or king. (The Hebrew Messiah is nowhere *clearly* defined as to concept in the Bible.)

AT TIMES JESUS must have exuded charm and authority, for he is said to attract *multitudes* and worshipful followers of both sexes. Far from having the gentle personality traditionally attributed to him, however, he is often overbearing and condescending in the scriptures, with traits not usually associated with the sublime deity of love and compassion. Although he does exhibit these latter traits at times, an impartial student of his sometime behavior might apply other adjectives to the Jesus of the Bible: impatient, heartless, imperious, vengeful, vain, rude, misinformed, quick-tempered, inconsistent, given to violence upon occasion, smug, and scornful. From the Gospels, the reader can fashion a Jesus to his or her liking.

A parasite upon society during his ministry, he is at the same time a welcome guest. He is appealing, and he repels. He soothes, and he stirs up. He makes sense, and he rants. He weeps at the death of a friend, and he consigns untold numbers of his "children" to *eternal* torment. He curses his Disciples, and they lean on him lovingly. He gives good advice, and he recommends impractical behavior. He loves, and he has "enemies." He brings the Word, and he comes with a sword. He bears a promise of joy, and he bestows a terrible burden—fear and guilt.

SEVERAL HUNDRED YEARS, which saw much controversy (even persecution) over the identity and doctrines of Jesus, produced the final New Testament, although even then not one acceptable to all. And the final agreement upon the Creeds had brought the warring factions into a semblance of a whole, which has not prevented almost continuous formation of sects whose adherents translate the faith as they see it into various rules for sipping, nibbling, kneeling, sprinkling, dunking, babbling, fasting, tithing, ring-kissing, bell-ringing, healing, snake-handling, self-chastising, aisle-rolling, confessing, and supplicating, the lot linked up with other complex guidelines for dress and diet, ad infinitum.

METAPHORICAL AND ANALOGICAL descriptions of himself are characteristic of Jesus' preaching. In the Gospel of John, alone, he uses over twenty complimentary cognomens:

THE SON OF MAN	1:51
THE SON OF GOD	3:18
LIVING WATER	4:14
SPIRIT	4:24
THE MESSIAH	4:26
CHRIST	4:26
A PROPHET	4:44
THE BREAD OF LIFE	6:35
LIGHT OF THE WORLD	9:5
THE DOOR	10:9
GOOD SHEPHERD	10:11
GOD	10:30
THE RESURRECTION AND THE LIFE	11:25
THE WAY, THE TRUTH, AND THE LIFE	14:6
PRINCE OF THIS WORLD	12:31
MASTER	13:13
LORD	13:13
SPIRIT OF TRUTH	14:17
HOLY GHOST	14:26
THE COMFORTER	14:26
THE TRUE VINE	15:1
THE HUSBANDMAN	15:1

MANY OF THE BEHAVIOR rules laid down by Jesus are guilty of an impractical morality that would make of human beings spineless, passionless, unresponsive robots. Some of the more traditional rules for good conduct, if not all, are borrowed from the Mosaic law and from the Book of Proverbs, which may have been appropriated from the Gentiles, and from philosophers such as Confucius, Plato, and Aristotle, who lived a few hundred years before Christ.

Jesus softened some of the harsher demands of the Mosaic law, stiffened the one about divorce, and got into trouble when he undermined the authority of the Jewish tribal priesthood. The

Sermon on the Mount (or on the Plain, where Luke 6:17 locates it) contains most of Jesus' moral precepts and is so long it is thought to be a summary of several dissertations. To follow these precepts literally one would have to be a person practicing no discrimination or evaluation based upon reason or experience.

Here are some ways Jesus tells people to act throughout the Gospels:

1. Accumulate no wealth or possessions. There is no need for them. Besides you would run the risk of getting rich. If you do, be sure to give it all away.

2. Make no plans. Give no thought to the morrow. Do not buy groceries or cook. Don't buy patterns or sew. Just stand there like a lily. God will feed and clothe you.

3. Be gloomy and mournful.

4. Be self-righteous and put-upon, holier than thou. Parade your perfection in such a way as to invite persecution.

5. Be smug and know that you are the salt of the earth and the light of the world. Let everybody know this.

6. Do behave so you can be high up in the class system in heaven.

7. Think of yourself as a gross sinner. Nearly every thought you have and almost everything you do must be regarded as a sin that will require repentance and forgiveness.

8. Take no pleasure in this world. Constantly point toward the kingdom of God, the coming of which is imminent.

9. Be sure to *believe* that someone else bought your way into heaven by being tortured to death, a death in which you had a hand. Be comfortable in that concept of salvation.

10. Agree with everyone else.

11. Don't admit to having sexual urges. If a sight of a member of the opposite sex arouses you, pluck out your eye.

12. Be a eunuch, if you want to win special approval of God.

13. Don't have *deep* love for your family. Abandon them, if you want to receive an "hundred-fold" and attain everlasting life in heaven for sure.

14. Be retiring, do not lead, take a back seat, do not assert yourself. Be a jellyfish. Do not be proud of your accomplishments.

15. Love everybody. Have no special feeling for those who might otherwise endear themselves to you.

16. If a criminal robs you of $50, give him another $50.

17. Don't use your reason or your mind. Remain as a child, with no moral sense, ability to discriminate or make rational decisions, or experience to guide you.

18. Be gullible and credulous. Do not question or philosophize.

19. Don't resist any attacker. Let him abuse you again.

20. If you lose a lawsuit, pay double what you are assessed.

21. If someone kidnaps you and takes you five miles, offer to go ten.

22. Love all those who mistreat you. This will encourage them to continue, since they have now discovered how to win your admiration and affection.

23. Don't declare your charitable giving for income tax credit.

24. Avoid the "dogs" and "swine" of this world. Save your uplifting thoughts for worthy persons.

25. Don't worry or rebel at misfortune (which will be your special lot). Be content and passive, confident you have a heavenly father who loves you so much that if you don't grovel, he'll throw you into a furnace (lake?) of fire forever.

26. Behave as you please most of your life and say you're sorry at the end. That way you'll get your reward before more exemplary persons at the seat of judgment.

27. Do not achieve prominence in this world, for the first shall be last in the next.

28. For special approbation, refrain from eating, pour oil on your head, and wash your face. Then take a gift to the church.

JESUS SPOKE MANY harsh words. Several examples follow:

1. "Ye serpents, ye generation of vipers, how can ye escape the damnation of hell?" (To the scribes and Pharisees) (Matthew 23:33).

2. "Woman, what have I to do with thee?" (To his mother) (John 2:4).

3. "O faithless and perverse generation, how long shall I suffer you?" (To the Disciples) (Matthew 17:17).

4. "Who is my mother, and who are my brethren?" (To the Disciples when his family waits to speak to him) (Matthew 12:48).

5. "Let the dead bury their dead." (To a Disciple who wants to bury his father) (Matthew 8:22).

6. "Woe unto thee, Chorazin! Woe unto thee, Bethsaida!... And thou, Capernaum...shalt be brought down to hell." (To unfriendly cities) (Matthew 11:21–23).

7. "An evil and adulterous generation." (Of the scribes and Pharisees) (Matthew 12:39).

8. "And he that hath no sword, let him sell his garment, and buy one." (To the Disciples at the Last Supper) (Luke 22:36).

9. "And whosoever shall not receive you...when ye depart out of that house or city, shake off the dust of your feet." (To the Disciples) (Matthew 10:14).

10. "And the brother shall deliver up the brother to death, and the father the child: and the children shall rise up against their parents, and cause them to be put to death." (Speaking of the dissension to be caused by Christianity) (Matthew 10:21).

11. "But whosoever shall deny me before men, him will I also deny before my Father... Think not that I am come to send peace on earth: I came not to send peace but a sword. For I am come to set a man at variance against his father, and the daughter against her mother, and the daughter in law against her mother in law. And a man's foes shall be they of his own *household*" (Matthew 10:33–36).

12. "O generation of vipers, how can ye, being evil, speak good things?" (To the Pharisees) (Matthew 12:34).

13. "The Son of man shall send forth his angels, and they shall gather...all them which do iniquity; and shall cast them into a furnace of fire: there shall be wailing and gnashing of teeth" (Matthew 13:41,42).

14. "I am not sent but unto the lost sheep of the house of Israel... It is not meet to take the children's [Jews'] bread, and cast it to dogs [Gentiles]." (To a Canaanite woman who asks him to heal her child) (Matthew 15:26).

15. "Wherefore if thy hand or foot offend thee, cut them off, and cast them from thee: it is better for thee to enter into life halt or maimed, rather than having two hands or two feet to be cast into everlasting fire. And if thine eye offend thee, pluck it out" (Matthew 18:8,9).

16. "Let no fruit grow on thee henceforward forever." (To a fig tree that bore no fruit out of season) (Matthew 21:19).

17. "Woe unto you that laugh now! for ye shall mourn and weep." And: "Woe unto you, when all men shall speak well of you!" (To a multitude) (Luke 6:25,26).

18. "Ye fools and blind." (To the scribes and Pharisees) (Matthew 23:17).

19. "And woe unto them that are with child, and to them that give suck in those days." (Speaking of the last days) (Matthew 24:19).

20. "For, behold, the days are coming in the which they shall say, Blessed are the barren, and the wombs that never bare, and the paps which never gave suck." (To his female friends, warning them of the last days) (Luke 23:29).

21. "Then shall he [the Son of man] say also unto them on the left hand, Depart from me, ye cursed, into everlasting fire, prepared for the devil and his angels" (Matthew 25:41).

22. "Get thee behind me, Satan: thou art an offence unto me." (To Peter) (Matthew 16:23).

23. "If a man abide not in me, he is cast forth as a branch...and men cast them into the fire, and they are burned" (John 15:6). These words became the justification (command!) for burning heretics alive.

ACCORDING TO THE BIBLE, Jesus and the devil are in constant competition for the "souls" of humankind. So the legends behind Christian theology imply and so Jesus himself teaches. He repeatedly warns against Satan and temptation, and he dies to bring about Satan's death. If this goal had been achieved, all who lived after Jesus' death would have been saved, but a literal or figurative devil is still very much alive and active in Christian dogma.

The Bible implies that Satan has a large host of angels or spirits at his command, dedicated to the task of abetting human beings in disobeying or disbelieving God. The Bible reader must ask himself or herself which is the more powerful today—Jesus or Satan (if all persons who are not Christians are considered to be in the hands of the devil). Although the largest single religion, Christianity, in its three main divisions of Eastern Orthodoxy, Roman Catholicism, and Protestantism (as well as Quakers, Mormons, Jehovah's Witnesses, and other small sects), claims only about one-third of the world's population today. That leaves approximately 4.4 billion people alive at the present time, including all members of other religions, destined for hell. And the fastest-growing religion today is Islam.

The devil of the Bible was able to change himself into a snake, bring sin into the world and turn every human creature away from God, and make it necessary for a Supreme Deity to be tortured and killed. He could perform miracles—fly through the air, transport God to the tip of a steeple, find a mountain that overlooked the entire earth, possess that world and offer it to God in return for his allegiance, and get into people's bodies and speak aloud. He made the earth tremble and shook kingdoms, made the world a wilderness and destroyed cities. He challenged God and escaped from the "pit."

The lesson of the New Testament is that Satan made everyone evil, and God had to come up with a scheme to redeem man from Satan's clutches. But so far Satan is still far ahead, and if Jesus should return today, he would be able to claim for his kingdom only one person for every two belonging to Satan, even assuming that every Christian will be saved.

As of today, Satan is twice as powerful as God in the struggle for the souls of his own creatures.

The existence of hell, as long as it has even one occupant, attests to the victory of Satan over God. And as of today, Satan is twice as powerful as God in the struggle for the souls of his own creatures. Chains may await Satan, but he will share them with most of humankind, according to the Christian Bible.

The victories that *are* won by God through Jesus must be gained entirely by the sole efforts of those who believe in the sacrifice described in the New Testament, since God either cannot or does not choose to banish Satan and sin from the earth by himself.

A DIRECT COROLLARY can be drawn between Jesus as Savior and the tradition of Judaism and the Mosaic law whereby the sins of the congregation of Israelites could be expiated by transferring them to an animal, which was then put to death on the altar (Leviticus 4:13–21).

Jesus may also be seen as the embodiment of the primitive practice of transferring the sins of a group to an animal or human scapegoat which then was banished or even put to death as a means of expelling all past wrongdoing committed by members of a society, a custom which often took place once a year at the beginning or end of a season. That animal or human being was sometimes endowed with divinity, and thus a man-god might die as a scapegoat and become a "redeemer." The Jewish Day of Atonement on the tenth day of the seventh month of every year was ordered by God to be set aside for a ceremony wherein the priest (originally Aaron) should "lay both his hands upon the live goat, and confess over him all the iniquities of the children of Israel, and all their transgressions in all their sins, putting them upon the head of the goat, and shall send him away by the hand of a fit man into the wilderness" (Leviticus 16:21).

Mythology documents many pagan customs involving the killing and "resurrection" of incarnate gods for purposes other than the expiatory ones of some human sacrifices, and the sacramental eating of the body of Christ in the Eucharist and Communion rites is reminiscent of a heathen tradition of dining on the effigy of a tribal god and thus becoming partly divine. Just so Christians today either figuratively or in fact believe that they enter into a mystical union with the body of Christ by eating his flesh and drinking his blood (so instructed by Jesus himself) (Luke 22:19,20).

PAGAN RELIGIONS IN different parts of the world embraced many suffering saviors and many virgin births. And the "death" and "resurrection" of vegetation were symbolized in practices which found their counterparts in Christian legends. Nature, the heavens, the waters, the earth, and the seasons controlled by the sun combined in the minds of superstitious savages and in the rituals of even advanced cultures to nurture beliefs in magic and in religions characterized by mysticism.

An even cursory examination of mythology throughout the world will reveal an astonishing similarity between the traditions and dogma surrounding Christ and the Church and the ancient superstitions of paganism. Peoples throughout the ages came to invest the elements and nearly every common plant and animal, as well as many hypotheses, with spirits, which gradually took on ever more human characteristics, sometimes metamorphosing into actual human beings and often eventually into gods and goddesses. The bull, ram, calf, and lamb were all deities at times. In such a way Jesus may have been perceived as the lamb of God.

The old songs which tell of being "washed in the blood of the Lamb" are possible plagiarisms from these heathen ceremonies which deified animals and used their blood to purify people, buildings, and altars. The Old Testament Jews sprinkled the blood of sacrificial animals upon the altar and vail of the tabernacle in the belief that such blood would cleanse and sanctify.

Jesus was depicted in early Christian art as a fish, and Christianity still uses the fish in its symbolism, seemingly unaware of the pagan origin of such display. The nature-worship common to pagan cultures in some instances imparted divine power to water as necessary to life. It was natural to transfer this power to creatures associated with streams, lakes, and seas, and fish became sacred. Much of the New Testament relates to water, fish, fishermen, boats, and storms at sea. Jesus describes himself as Living Water and promises to make the disciples "fishers of men."

Tree-worship also evolved from nature-worship, and gods were envisioned as the trees themselves or as fastened to them, just as imaginary spirits were believed to inhabit other natural objects. The idea of a god hanging on a tree was the inevitable heritage of descending superstitious generations who were bound to inject it into their own worship systems. Jesus used the tree analogy (vine) to depict himself and spoke of believers and unbelievers as branches in different conditions: "That ye bear much fruit, so shall ye be my disciples" (John 15:5–8). This analogy was also used by Paul: "For if thou wert cut out of the olive tree which is wild by nature, and wert graffed [sic] contrary to nature into a good olive tree: how much more shall these, which be the natural branches, be graffed [sic] into their own olive tree?" (Romans 11:24). There are numerous references to "hanging on a tree" in the scriptures of both Testaments, and even the crucifixion is referred to as Jesus being "hanged on a tree" (Acts 5:30, Acts 10:39). The cross of Christianity, in any case, is a familiar pagan symbol that has existed in some form in almost every society, including the most primitive.

The theory has been debated that Christ was manufactured as a sun god, a theory which has a direct tie-in with pagan worship built around the seasonal cycles of nature and vegetation. And Christ's resurrection is linked to the season of rebirth. Upon such a possibility and upon the related Zodiac and its twelve signs, familiar to the "wise men" of Babylonia, Egypt, and Assyria, it has been widely claimed here rests the foundation for yet another explanation of Jesus being symbolized as the Light of the World with twelve disciple satellites, and for other facets of both Judaism and Christianity.

It is obvious from examination of mythology and paganism that Jesus Christ may be a myth or that he has been so clothed in the vestments of magic and fable that his resemblance to the myth saviors and heathen gods-incarnate cannot be ignored. Certainly the above theories do not prove that Jesus did not live as a real person in the Holy Land 2,000 years ago, but it is impossible not to be influenced by the paucity and fragility of the evidence that Jesus existed as a Palestinian Hebrew.

Historical data on Jesus is admittedly meager and open to dispute, unless one accepts the contradictory and undocumented Gospels as proof. Scarcely a line about Jesus' physical appearance or everyday life beyond incidents which relate specifically to his ministry or role as Savior can be found in any part of the New Testament, let alone the Gospels. There is no "homey" discourse about him as a growing child or maturing adult and hardly anything at all about his family or family life, and the reader must inevitably wonder—was there really a person Jesus? Or was there just a Christ cult that had been building at a time when cultism and mysticism were flourishing in the Middle East?

The part which mythology plays in Christian theology and the unsubstantial proof of a Jesus who sojourned on earth must in the long run be evaluated by interested parties to their personal satisfaction.

CONSIDERATION OF THE BIBLICAL Jesus logically leads to an assessment of the God of Christians as he emerges in the New Testament personification. The conclusion reached could conceivably be that by bringing their god down to earth for an extended time as a human being, by making their deity flesh and blood, they have diminished "him" with the brush of myth and superstition. Just who "they" are probably cannot be specifically determined but must include every assenting Christian to a certain extent.

Christendom has not only a human god (like pagan deities) but a supernatural god whom it is possible to describe and delineate in terms of human attributes, a god who can never differ from a human being, or superhuman being at best. By bringing him down from the upper regions assigned to the good guys, by divesting him of his infinity and majesty and godliness, and by assigning to him human characteristics, Christians tarnished the divinity of their deity. The traits attributed to him as a human being remained the divine traits of their God, who could not escape humanness or be superior to it, for he had already exhibited himself in the flesh. And those who choose to depict Jesus as the epitome of compassion and sweetness of character ignore the claim of Jesus himself that he was the incarnate Old Testament Lord, with all of Yahweh's meanness, partiality, jealousy, and vengefulness—the deity who chose to show special consideration to one people, who slaughtered thousands, drowned and tortured babies, violated women, expressed admiration for merciless despots and ruthless conquerors, rewarded villainous deeds, abetted duplicity, and forced his behavior rules upon a helpless nation.

Christians are obligated to obey that Mosaic law also, for it was bequeathed by their God and categorically endorsed by Jesus, who said he came to fulfill it and that not one tittle of it should fail. He made his position very clear: "For had ye believed Moses, ye would have believed me: for he wrote of me. But if ye believe not his writings, how shall ye believe my words?" (John 5:46,47).

By upholding the Mosaic law, Jesus sanctioned slavery; sacrifices; the burning of witches; the stoning of young women, disrespectful and stubborn children, heretics, and Sabbath-breakers; circumcision; polygamy and concubinage; and innumerable other discriminatory and heartless acts. But the Old Testament Lord was not yet monstrous enough for Christianity—no, he must debase himself further by fashioning a place of eternal pain for all those who choose to deflate his precarious ego. Hanging on a cross as a man, he had to bring further proof of his depravity to a people already his slaves. That the majority of this people refused to believe he would so disgrace himself should have been no surprise to an omniscient deity.

The God of the Christians and the *mother* of their God belong to a Semitic race which comprises much less than one percent of the world's population, and twelve thrones in the Christian heaven are occupied by twelve more members of that race. The Christian deity and the Christian heaven are very provincial in the sense that they pertain to any one particular race or nation, but the Christian God was not only a human Jew but chose to show partiality to the people of that race.

The Christian God was *dead* for part of three days. "He" wears clothes, eats at a heavenly table (kosher), and lives in a mansion with many angel-servants. A favored few of his saints will be greater than others. This God is superstitious and ignorant of science—he was an exorcist—who thought the sun could stand still and the moon had light of its own. He was a tempter and tricker, even a deceiver.

He makes threats. He is partial to one sex and actually refused adamantly for a time to heal a Gentile. He belittles family life and relationships. He encourages people to mouth nonsense, handle snakes, drink poison, and mutilate their bodies. He curses cities, even a tree, and persons who don't agree with him. He destroyed 2,000 pigs without paying for them. More importantly, the Christian God seems incapable of banishing evil from the world, or doesn't choose to, teaching that bloodshed redeems.

It is possible that any attempt by a people to define its gods automatically detracts from their godliness.

BEFORE HE DEPARTED this vale of tears, as God's habitat for humanity this side of the grave has been described, the Savior of the entire world might have been expected to leave very lucid instructions as to how salvation might be achieved. And from his lips on various occasions do fall words that supposedly pinpoint "the way." Such words should leave not the smallest doubt, for they deal with *everlasting* happiness or inevitable *everlasting* torment. Let these words be examined!

When a lawyer questions Jesus about the requirements for eternal life (in heaven, one assumes), Jesus asks the lawyer what "the law" says, no doubt referring to the Mosaic law. The lawyer answers: "Thou shalt love the Lord thy God with all thy heart, and with all thy soul, and with all thy strength, and with all thy mind; and thy neighbor as thyself." Jesus replies: "Thou hast answered right: this do, and thou shalt live" (Luke 10:25–28).

No mention of belief in himself as the Son of God or the Redeemer of the world from sin! In other words, one does not have to be a Christian to be saved. Love for God and fellow beings suffices.

Consider, then, Jesus' words at another time: "He that believeth on the Son hath everlasting life; and he that believeth *not* the Son shall not see life; but the wrath of God abideth on him" (John 3:36). To Nicodemus, Jesus also expounded: "He that believeth on him is not condemned; but he that believeth not is condemned already, because he hath not believed in the name of the only begotten Son of God" (John 3:17,18).

No mention of love of God and neighbor! Unquestioning belief is all that is necessary for salvation. There are no other stipulations.

Jesus' above statements are categorical, but in at least one sense the two requirements are at odds, for Deism and Christianity are not one and the same in every case, not by far. For, although Christianity may imply love of God and one's neighbor, such love does not necessarily imply Christianity. Thus, Jesus himself is presented in the scriptures as denying the need of anyone for a Savior.

But that is not yet the end of the puzzle. Jesus continues to put up conflicting guideposts: "The hour is coming, in the which all that are in the graves shall hear his voice, and shall come forth; they that have done good, unto the resurrection of life, and they that have done evil, unto the resurrection of damnation" (John 5:28,29). No mention of belief in Jesus Christ *or* of love of God and neighbor! Now only good deeds assure one of "life." No need here, or in above rules, to be reborn!

Perhaps Jesus intended to leave the impression that love of God and humanity, *plus* belief in himself as the Savior and Son of God, *plus* good deeds, are *all* necessary for assignment to heaven. But he comes a long way from claiming that. Each requirement stands alone in the course of his ministry. And those other admonitions about being born

again and being converted simply make the conditions mandatory for salvation the more perplexing. If there are cut-and-dried rules for playing the game of life (and there should be when the stakes are so high that defeat leads to damnation), the referee fails to transmit them to the players.

CHRISTIANITY CHOOSES TO include the virgin birth of Jesus in its dogma, but biblically it is a circumstance narrated in only two of the Gospels and completely ignored in the rest of the New Testament. Not only ignored, but denied! And denied so explicitly that it is obvious that paganism, whose gods were frequently born of virgins, was parent to the idea. Matthew and Luke are responsible for the claim that Jesus' mother was a virgin, impregnated by the Holy Ghost, but then both of these Gospel-writers are brazen enough to give the Bible reader long (and completely different) genealogies of Jesus from Joseph to David and beyond.

Matthew wanted to make Jesus more authentic by tying in a virgin birth with a prophecy from Isaiah, but that same virgin birth was not compatible with the Jewish tradition (and with other prophecies) that the Messiah would be of the house of David. Matthew has a special gift for concocting stories to fit prophecies; perhaps that talent makes it possible for him to go to a great deal of trouble to establish Jesus' descendancy from David, without an apology, just before he gives his account of the virgin birth, concluding the genealogy thus: "So all the generations from Abraham to David are fourteen generations; and from David until the carrying away into Babylon are fourteen generations; and from the carrying away into Babylon unto Christ are fourteen generations" (Matthew 1:17). This genealogy serves no purpose, if Jesus was not the son of Joseph.

Luke recognizes his own dilemma, at least, and adds a parenthetical aside to his introduction of Jesus' genealogy (which lists fifteen more generations to David than were named by Matthew): "And

Jesus himself began to be about thirty years of age, being, as was supposed, the son of Joseph" (Luke 3:23). Mark describes a scene that takes place when Jesus visits his own country. His former neighbors exclaim: "Is not this the carpenter, the son of Mary, the brother of James, and Joses, and of Juda, and Simon? and are not his sisters here with us?" (Mark 6:3). No one recalls on this occasion or even hints at anything unusual about Jesus' parentage. How did Matthew and Luke know about a virgin birth? Was it revealed only to them?

John realized the peril involved in the claim of a virgin birth (or he was also not aware of such a claim), for he not only makes no mention of it but promotes the counterclaim—that Jesus was descended from David. *He* reports Jesus' countrymen saying: "Is not this Jesus, the son of Joseph, whose father and mother we know?" (John 6:42). John also gives an account of another incident: "Philip findeth Nathanael; and saith unto him, We have found him, of whom Moses in the law, and the prophets did write, Jesus of Nazareth, the son of Joseph" (John 1:45). John even suggests that Jesus was not born in Bethlehem, when he repeats the arguments of a group of doubters: "Hath not the scripture said, That Christ cometh of the seed of David and out of the town of Bethlehem, where David was?" (John 7:40–43). The story used by the Gospel of Luke to have Jesus born in Bethlehem was that Joseph had to pay his taxes in the city of David, because Joseph was "of the house and lineage of David" (Luke 2:4). Apparently the populace believed that Jesus was born at home in Nazareth. Deliberate mishandling of facts surrounding Jesus' birth reeks of invention, even fraud.

The conflict about Jesus' origin was so embarrassing that Peter and Paul both denied the virgin birth indirectly, and in fact no biblical mention is made of it beyond what appears in Matthew and Luke. Here are Peter's words: "Men and brethren, let me freely speak unto you of the patriarch David... knowing that God had sworn with an oath to him, that of the fruit of his loins, according to the flesh, he would raise up Christ to sit on his throne" (Acts 2:29,30). Paul has no doubts of Jesus' lineage: "Of this man's [David's] seed hath God according to his promise raised unto Israel a Savior, Jesus" (Acts 13:23). And: "Concerning his son Jesus Christ our Lord, which was made of the seed of David, according to the flesh" (Romans 1:3). Paul was not one to glorify womanhood by painting Mary as a virgin.

In all fairness to Peter and Paul, it is possible that the virgin birth became a figment of the imagination after their time, if the Gospels were written later than Acts or the Epistles. A real or imaginary hero becomes more fabulous with the passage of the years. But that still does not explain the fact that Luke, author of a genealogy of Jesus in the book that bears his name, is also supposed to have been the author of the book of Acts, in which the virgin birth is not spoken of, and in which both Peter and Paul flatly assert that Joseph was Jesus' natural parent.

Jesus would seem to settle the whole issue when he speaks to St. John in the Revelation: "I Jesus have sent mine angel to testify unto you these things in the churches. I am the root and the offspring of David..." (Revelation 22:16). It's a wise child that knows its own father, perhaps, but Jesus was a very wise child (Luke 2:40).

JESUS AS THE HUMAN sacrifice offered up by his father was the duplication of an ancient pagan practice of offering the firstborn son to be put to death as an act of homage and appeasement to tribal gods. This tradition and custom was supposed to be the target of the Lord's wrath in the Old Testament that was directed against the worshipers of Baal and Moloch. Elimination of the "groves" and altars where children were made to "pass through the fire," and eradication of this abominable ritual, along with the gods who demanded it, were given as the justification for and purpose of the Jewish conquest of Palestine. Worship of the monotheistic, "nice" Hebrew Lord was to be substituted for heathen ways.

Nevertheless, scripture says that the ancient Hebrews themselves frequently ascribed to the frowned-upon method of worship, and the Old Testament God required it for himself on occasion, as for instance when Abraham was told to sacrifice Isaac, and Jephthah was made to burn his only child to death (Judges 11:30–39). The prophet Micah reveals how this concept of child-by-the-father human sacrifice persisted in Jewish tradition at the time parts of the Old Testament were written:

> Wherewith shall I come before the Lord, and bow myself before the high God? shall I come before him with burnt offerings, with calves of a year old? Will the Lord be pleased with thousands of rams, or with ten thousands of rivers of oil? shall I give my firstborn for my transgression, the fruit of my body for the sin of my soul? (Micah 6:6,7)

Thus, the God of the Bible, who is portrayed in the Old Testament as the relentless enemy of human sacrifice among the heathen, turns himself, in the shape of his own son, into the New Testament equivalent.

Although dedication of the firstborn to the Lord as a human sacrifice to atone for sin was gradually replaced by dedication of the firstborn male offspring to serve in the temple or in some related religious capacity, the idea of actually putting the victim to death lived on to its final conclusion—the Son offered up by the Father in an act of atonement for sin. Thus, the God of the Bible, who is portrayed in the Old Testament as the relentless enemy of human sacrifice among the heathen, turns himself, in the shape of his own son, into the New Testament equivalent.

Behavior that is hideous and reprehensible in part of the Bible becomes in a later part an act of divine love and beauty. But the Christian Redeemer is the same human sacrifice of those pagans who practiced infanticide as a necessary part of their religion, and there is no escape from that fact. The derivation of Christian doctrine from paganism is too obvious to admit of argument. The human sacrifice of Jesus is just one evidence of it.

JESUS HAS TAKEN on a benignity and a gentle sweetness in societies which seek the lost cohesiveness of other days. He is the sympathetic companion who proffers the love and support which could formerly be extracted from the mutual empathy felt by people in a less harried, more personal era. But, how did Jesus himself want to be visualized? Here are his instructions: "But I will forewarn you whom ye shall fear: Fear him, which after he hath killed hath power to cast into hell; yea, I say unto you, Fear him,..." (Luke 12:5).

Jesus must inevitably emerge from the scriptures as the angry rejected prophet of doom who looks forward to having his revenge. That he had an abrasive side to his personality is obvious not only from the fact that he could not get along with his own family and was often at odds with the Disciples but also from the evidence that he was not even liked or respected by his Nazareth neighbors. One would have thought that such a wondrous child who had arrived with an angelic fanfare, who had been announced as the Savior of the whole world, and whose destiny had been sensed by distant Zoroastrian priests, would have been carefully watched in awe during his childhood and youth, but among his own family and townspeople he enjoyed no deference. The attitude of the latter is so humiliating to him that he is unable to perform any miracles among them. He explains that a prophet is without honor in his own land and in his own house (Matthew 13:54–58).

Such treatment may have accounted for his bitterness and readiness to assign his detractors forevermore to hell. It is ironic that this self-proclaimed Messiah of the Jews should find himself today still rejected by his own people and proprietor of a heaven where few of his fellow Jews will spend eternity with him. He will have the obligation of committing *them* to the flames, while he welcomes to his kingdom a preponderance of Gentiles, who received little of his attention on earth.

But surely the omniscient Lord of the Old Testament Jews (the Chosen People) could foresee this outcome of his new promise!

Gary Greenberg

WHO WROTE THE GOSPELS?

(HINT: IT WASN'T MATTHEW, MARK, LUKE, OR JOHN)

ASKING "WHO WROTE THE GOSPELS?" may seem like a strange question. Pick up any New Testament and it will tell you at the beginning of each Gospel who the author was. There we find, in order of appearance, the attribution of these Gospels to Matthew, Mark, Luke, and John, all of whom were elevated to sainthood. Church tradition also tells us that Matthew and John were two of the Twelve Apostles, Mark was a secretary to the Apostle Peter when he preached in Rome, and Luke was a companion of the Apostle Paul. (Paul was not one of the Twelve Apostles, nor was he a companion of Jesus during his lifetime.)

All in all, this Church tradition boasts quite a stellar cast of writers with a good claim to a reasonable amount of historical credibility, authors who were either eyewitnesses or intimate with eyewitnesses to the mission of Jesus and its aftermath. Unfortunately, all of this information is almost certainly wrong.

Each of the four Gospels was written anonymously. No author's name appears on any of the earliest partial or full copies of these texts (through at least the fifth century), and none of the authors give any personal information about themselves. The Gospel of Matthew, for example, refers to the Apostle Matthew in the third person, giving no evidence that the author and the Apostle were the same person.[1]

The Gospel of John, at 21:24, a passage that many scholars consider to be an addition to the Gospel added later by a different author,[2] claims as a source for the Gospel someone known as the "Beloved Disciple" but does not say who this person was. Elsewhere in the text we find several references to the acts of the Beloved Disciple, but nowhere does the author of the Gospel of John give any hint that he and the Beloved Disciple were one and the same person.[3] While the Gospel of John clearly distinguishes between Peter and the Beloved Disciple, and obviously rejects any connection between Judas Iscariot and the Beloved Disciple, it doesn't give us any direct evidence as to which of the Apostles or other disciples of Jesus we can identify with this revered individual.

Each of the four Gospels was written anonymously.

If any of the Twelve Apostles or one of their close associates had written a report about the activities of Jesus, one would expect such a work to have become an instant classic in Christian circles, widely copied, distributed, and cited, and the author frequently mentioned by name by other Christian writers (even if that disciple's name didn't appear in the text). Yet, on the basis of writings from the first four

Several falsified documents have even made their way into the New Testament.

centuries of Christianity, it appears that until the last years of the second century, Christian scholars had no idea who wrote the New Testament Gospels. It is only at this later stage that some Christian scholars began to associate these four Gospels with the traditional identifications of the authors. But those who made these identifications either utilized unreliable sources or simply asserted that the identification was correct without any evidence to support the allegation. Prior to that time, Christian writers appear to have thought of these four Gospels generically as the "memoirs" of the Apostles,[4] without any specific attribution, and identified them by characteristics of the text, such as "the Gospels with the genealogies"[5] (i.e., Matthew and Luke).

We should also note that these weren't the only four Gospels circulating in Christian circles. In the first couple of centuries of Christianity we have indications of over thirty different Gospels circulating, many falsely attributed to either Apostles or to other persons mentioned in the Gospels.[6] Among the most important of these other Gospels, primarily due to their priority, were the Gospel of Peter and the Gospel of Thomas. The Gospel of Thomas may have been highly popular in Gnostic Christian circles and may have been widely distributed in Christian communities. The Gospel of Peter had been widely circulated in Syria and apparently read as scripture in some churches. Toward the end of the second century, it came to be seen as possibly containing heretical claims about Jesus and fell out of favor in proto-orthodox circles. Most scholars would date the authorship of these two texts to the early years of the second century or perhaps the last years of the first century,[7] with a few scholars arguing that one or the other was written prior to the four canonical Gospels.[8]

The forgery of Gospels and letters and other writings in the name of Apostles and other figures from the time of Jesus appears to have been something of a cottage industry in Christian circles during the first few centuries. Several falsified documents have even made their way into the New Testament. Most New Testament scholars who study these issues believe that approximately half of the letters

attributed to Paul were not written by him, nor was the second letter of Peter written by that Apostle, nor did Jude write Jude, nor did James write James.[9] The letters of Paul that scholars acknowledge as authentic include 1 Thessalonians, Galatians, Philemon, Philippians, 1 and 2 Corinthians, and Romans.[10] These seven Pauline letters appear to be the earliest Christian writings that we know of, generally dating to the early 50s.[11]

MATTHEW AND MARK

The identification in Christian tradition of Matthew and Mark as the authors of the respective Gospels attributed to them seems to derive from an unreliable claim from an early second-century Christian writer named Papias. Our evidence about his attribution comes from the fourth-century Church historian Eusebius.[12] While Eusebius cites Papias' testimony favorably with respect to the Gospel origins, he appears to have little regard for Papias' intelligence, calling him a man "of very limited understanding."[13]

According to Eusebius, who claims to have had copies of Papias' books, Papias set out to collect the traditions about the teachings of the Apostles.[14] He himself had never met any of the Apostles and he relied on oral traditions from the elders of his day for information,[15] suggesting that these various elders were unaware of any writings attributed to the Apostles who knew Jesus. He mentions the existence of Christian writings but does not consider them as reliable as what the elders had to say.[16] This strongly suggests that these other known Christian writings weren't attributed to the apostolic circle that knew Jesus.

Papias, says Eusebius, wrote of a tradition given to him by one of the elders concerning two texts, one written by someone named Mark, whom he alleges to have been a secretary to the Apostle Peter, and the other written by the Apostle Matthew. Eusebius quotes him, regarding Mark, as follows:

Mark having become the interpreter of Peter, wrote down accurately, though not in order, whatsoever he remembered of the things said or done by Christ. For he neither heard the Lord nor followed him, but afterward, as I said, he followed Peter, who adapted his teaching to the needs of his hearers, but with no intention of giving a connected account of the Lord's discourses, so that Mark committed no error while he thus wrote some things as he remembered them. For he was careful of one thing, not to omit any of the things which he had heard, and not to state any of them falsely.[17]

Eusebius then says that Papias added the following remark about Matthew:

So then Matthew wrote the oracles in the Hebrew language, and every one interpreted them as he was able.[18]

These two quotes comprise all of Papias' known commentary on the alleged origins of the Gospels of Mark and Matthew.

In the late second century, the Christian writer Irenaeus repeats the claims made by Papias, that Matthew wrote his Gospel in the dialect used by the Hebrews and that Mark, the disciple and interpreter of Peter, wrote the other Gospel.[19] But he doesn't tell us where he got this information. His reference to Matthew being written in the Hebrew dialect and to Mark being the "interpreter" of Peter, that odd word also used by Papias, indicates that Irenaeus used Papias as his source.

Shortly thereafter, in the early third century, Origen, one of the most learned and respected of ancient Christian writers, says that Matthew wrote his Gospel in Aramaic and it was published for believers of Jewish origin.[20] (Aramaic was the language used by Hebrews in the time of Jesus.) He also refers to Mark, Luke, and John as the authors of a Gospel. He adds the claim that this Mark was the one mentioned in Peter's second epistle as being his son.[21] But, like Irenaeus, he doesn't say where he got this information. He does, however,

indicate that in his own time it was the traditional view and that he accepted it.[22]

This is the state of the evidence in the fourth century for associating the Gospel of Matthew with the Apostle Matthew and the Gospel of Mark with an associate of the Apostle Peter. The evidence suggests that an undocumented tradition tracing to Papias and his contemporaries in a particular community became Christian dogma, and with each subsequent mention of the claim by a Christian writer, its authenticity became reinforced. The problem is that the validity of the claims by Papias, Irenaeus, and Origen are historically questionable.

An important problem with Papias' description of Mark's Gospel is that he describes it as "not in order," referring apparently to the sequence of events in Jesus' life, when in fact Mark's Gospel is clearly presented in an orderly fashion. It seems unlikely that someone who had read the actual Gospel of Mark would think of it as unorderly. Closely related to the question of what text Papias was referring to is the fact (noted previously) that there was probably in circulation at that time a Gospel of Peter. Papias provides no evidence of any specific content that can be attributed to this alleged Gospel of Mark. It is possible, therefore, that Papias' source had in mind the Gospel of Peter, which may have been a popular text at the time of Papias' inquiry, rather than the one we now refer to as the Gospel of Mark.

The attribution of a Gospel to Matthew presents another difficult problem: the claim that Matthew wrote his text in Hebrew or Aramaic. It is overwhelmingly accepted among New Testament scholars that the author of the Gospel of Matthew wrote in Greek and that the text bears no indicia of having been translated into Greek from Aramaic.[23] So, whatever text Papias is talking about, it is not the Gospel of Matthew as we now know it. While it might be argued that Papias actually is referring to an Aramaic translation of the Greek version of the Gospel of Matthew, and evidence indicates that Aramaic translations existed at some point in time (but almost certainly not before the second century), that seems unlikely since it should've been known that the text was originally written in Greek and translated into Aramaic, rather than the other way around. As with his references to a work by Mark, here, too, there is no citation to any of the content of the written work so that it may be compared to what we now know as the Gospel of Matthew.

In sum, then, at the beginning of the second century we have an unidentified source giving Papias an oral tradition alleging that there were Gospels written by Matthew and Mark. But Papias never saw these written works, the description of their contents is clearly erroneous, and Eusebius considers Papias to be something of a dunce.

Despite these historical difficulties, Papias seems to be responsible for the trend, developing in the late second century and continuing into the early third century, to identify the authors of these two Gospels as Matthew and Mark, and to further identify Matthew as one of the Twelve Apostles and Mark as the secretary to Peter.

LUKE

The author of Luke specifically says that at the time he began his effort many others had already set down orderly accounts of what had been "handed on to us by those who from the beginning were eyewitnesses and servants of the word."[24] But he makes no particular claim that any of the Apostles had written a Gospel. In fact, his language suggests that the written sources he has came from persons other than the original witnesses and that these sources relied on oral traditions that may have been handed down by people who may have been eyewitnesses. He asserts that he decided to investigate matters and prepare an orderly account for someone named Theophilus, so that he may know the truth.[25] Who this Theophilus was, we don't know. His name may have been a metaphor for the Christian movement or the Christian reader of his text.[26] Luke doesn't name his sources nor tell us when he is citing a source. Tradition holds that Luke was a companion to Paul, but the author of Luke makes no such claim and never says that he got any particular information from Paul.

Despite the lack of any noted association with Paul, the New Testament Acts of the Apostles, universally accepted as written by the author of the Gospel of Luke, presents a clue that the author may have traveled with and known Paul. This evidence may have been responsible for the early Christian tradition that Luke was Paul's companion. At several points in Acts the author uses the term "we" when talking about some activities of Paul.[27] This use of "we" has led to the idea that Luke was with Paul at the time these events occurred and was writing a first-hand account of what took place. On the other hand, the "we" passages may simply reflect the author's use of one of the many written sources he refers to and from which he took the "we" passages.

In opposition to the idea that Luke was a close companion of Paul, most New Testament scholars recognize that much of Acts' account of Paul's activities conflicts with Paul's own version of the same or similar activities as reflected in Paul's letters.[28] The author of Acts seems to have had no knowledge of Paul's letters or any intimate knowledge of Paul's works from personal observation.[29] He appears even to have misunderstood Paul's theology.[30]

If the author of Luke-Acts knew Paul, it appears that the acquaintance was casual at best. The author of Luke, therefore, would seem to be somewhat removed from the Apostolic circles that emerged after the death of Jesus. If he was a companion of Paul, the many errors he makes with respect to Paul's career and teaching suggest that he should be read cautiously at best with regard to his accounts of Jesus. If he wasn't a close companion of Paul, that should make us even more wary.

JOHN

As noted above, the Gospel of John has a passage that suggests that the Beloved Disciple was the source of the Gospel text, but the Gospel doesn't identify who the Beloved Disciple was. His identity is one of those interesting issues that Johannine scholars like to kick about.

The first evidence we have connecting the authorship of John with the Apostle John appears in the late second century, from the aforementioned Christian writer Irenaeus. In the passage in which he seems to rely on Papias for the claim that Matthew and Mark wrote the respective Gospels attributed to them (see above), he also makes the claim that the Beloved Disciple was named John, but he doesn't say how he knows this.[31] Nor does he quite say that this disciple was the Apostle John, although it would be hard to imagine that Irenaeus did not believe this to be the case. Nevertheless, by the fourth century this identification had become widely accepted among Christians.[32]

In considering the possibility that the Apostle John may have been the Beloved Disciple, we should note that the Gospel of John never refers to the Apostle John by name. To the argument that the author didn't need to mention the Apostle's name since he referred to him as the Beloved Disciple, I would make the following observation. In the other Gospels, John is also known as the son of Zebedee, and on one occasion the Gospel of John makes a casual, offhand remark about the presence of the "sons of Zebedee" and some other disciples without any hint that one of the sons of Zebedee was the Beloved Disciple.[33]

That the author of the Gospel of John used an earlier written text by a different author for at least some of his work can be inferred from John 7:22, which reads: "Moses gave you circumcision (it is, of course, not from Moses, but from the patriarchs), and you circumcise a man on the Sabbath." In this passage, John attributes a quote to Jesus in which Jesus mistakenly places the origin of circumcision with Moses rather than Abraham, and the author of John includes a correction noting that circumcision originated with the patriarchs (but doesn't specifically mention Abraham).

Why would the author of this passage include a quote from Jesus that contains an error together with a correction unless either 1) the author believed Jesus had made the error or 2) the author relied on a written source that he had copied from and that source already contained the error? Since the author of John clearly believes that Jesus is incapable of making a mistake and since it is highly unlikely that Jesus, raised in an orthodox Jewish family in an orthodox Jewish environment, would make such an error, the most probable explanation is that the author relied on a written source in which the error was already present.

It is also evident that the author of John is reasonably familiar with Jewish law and tradition and, therefore, would have known that Abraham was responsible for the practice of circumcision. So, why would he attribute the invention to the patriarchs in general (including Isaac and Jacob) rather than just Abraham? Here the most likely explanation would seem to be that the correction also was already in his written source, which suggests that the author of the source text had made the correction to a still earlier text. This implies that the passage in John is twice-removed from the original author. It was this secondary written source that the author of John received, and since it was technically correct in that Abraham was one of the patriarchs, he left the passage unchanged.

Implicit in this mistake is that the author of the original passage may not have been a knowledgeable Jew and, therefore, was very unlikely to have been one of the twelve disciples, all of whom should have been quite familiar with the origin of circumcision. Also implicit is that the secondary author, who cited the patriarchs as the source, was more knowledgeable about Jewish tradition than the first author but still not as knowledgeable as an ordinary Jew living in Galilee or Judea would have been. Again, that eliminates the likelihood that one of the twelve disciples wrote this passage. It further suggests that the authors of the earlier written sources were nowhere around Jesus during his lifetime and probably lived outside of the Jewish communities in Judea and Galilee.

If we can draw that conclusion about this passage, how sure can we be that much else in John's Gospel came from a Jewish disciple from Galilee close to Jesus? After all, how likely is it that the author of John would add a separate text, containing errors and not authored by the Beloved Disciple, to an existing Gospel supposedly written by the Beloved Disciple, and act as if they were from one and the same pen? The most likely conclusion is that the author of John relied on a number of written sources, at least some of which had no connection to Jesus' inner circle.

WHEN WERE THE GOSPELS WRITTEN?

If we can't be sure who wrote the Gospels, it would be helpful to know when they were written. Were the authors personally familiar with the events, or did they have to rely on earlier sources for their information? If the latter, then how good were these sources? Were they written close in time to the events in question, before several competing traditions and theologies developed, or on a later occasion, after a wide range of conflicting views emerged? Once the link to the traditional identity of the authors is broken, these questions become more difficult to resolve.

The best evidence would be written copies of some portion of each of the Gospels that could be dated or citations to the Gospels by some author whose writing can be dated. Extant evidence of this sort, however, leaves a very wide range of possible dates for authorship.

Prior to the third century, the only written evidence for the existence of any of the Gospels is a few papyri fragments from the Gospel of John. The earliest of them, no larger than an index card, has been dated on the basis of writing style to about 135–150 C.E.[34] This suggests the latest possible date for that writing of that Gospel. We don't begin to see evidence for the existence of the other Gospels until about the third century. Our earliest complete Gospels date to the fourth century.[35] While we don't have evidence associating the Gospels with particular authors until about the end of the second century, references in the

Patristic literature suggest that the texts themselves were in circulation earlier than that point. How much earlier is the problem to be resolved.

In establishing a latest possible date, one criterion used by scholars is the absence of any reference to the great Jewish revolt of Bar Kokhba at about 132 C.E. and the devastating impact on the Jews when the Romans eventually put down the rebellion and barred the Jews from Jerusalem, their holy city. This suggests to many scholars that the Gospels were almost certainly written before this revolt.

Prior to the third century, the only written evidence for the existence of any of the Gospels is a few papyri fragments from the Gospel of John.

As to the earliest likely date, scholars have attempted to date the Gospels on the basis of themes and events mentioned in the text and on the apparent chronological relationship of the Gospels to each other. (See "The Synoptic Problem" on the next page.) For Matthew, Mark, and Luke, one of the chief criteria for dating the Gospels involves the issue of whether the Gospels contain references to the Roman destruction of the Jewish Temple in 70 C.E.

Mark 13:2 records a prophecy by Jesus, to wit, "Do you see these great buildings? Not one stone will be left here upon another; all will be thrown down." A variation of this prophecy also appears in Matthew 24:2 and Luke 21:6. In addition, Matthew 22:7 has Jesus say, "The king was enraged. He sent his troops, destroyed those murderers, and burned their city." In Luke 19:43 Jesus says, "Indeed, the days will come upon you, when your enemies will set up ramparts around you and surround you, and hem you in on every side."

Those who believe these passages were written after the fact of the Roman capture of Israel and the destruction of the Jewish Temple, date the Gospels to sometime after 70 C.E.

As to Matthew and Luke, the overwhelming majority of scholars accept that Matthew 22:7 and Luke 19:43 refer to the destruction of the Temple and tend to date Matthew and Luke from around 75 to 85. As to Mark, most scholars believe it was written either during or shortly after the outbreak of hostilities in 66 C.E. But some scholars dispute these interpretations and argue that if the Gospels were written after the destruction of the Temple, the authors would've made more explicit reference to the destruction. This latter group argues for a pre-70 C.E. date for all of the Gospels.

Raymond Brown, one of the most respected Christian scholars, however, has observed that while there are occasional attempts to move the Gospel dates earlier, none of the proposals has gained much of a scholarly following.[36] He also notes that there is a growing tendency to date Mark after 70.[37]

A number of scholars also believe that the emphasis in the Gospels on the conflict between the Pharisees and the followers of Jesus suggests that the events reflect the period after the destruction of the Temple, when the Pharisees became the most influential Jewish religious authority and probably became the chief Jewish opponents of Christianity in the post-Temple period, as opposed to the pre-war period when several Jewish religious schools of thought flourished. (The leading philosophical opponents of the Pharisees, the Sadducees and Essenes, were wiped out during the Jewish revolt. The Sadducees, had they survived, almost certainly would have opposed Christianity. Yet they are virtually invisible in the Gospels. Mark and Luke mention them just once, both describing the same minor incident. John doesn't mention them at all. Matthew has only a little additional material to add. We don't know enough about the Essenes to know how they would've reacted, but they were an ultra-orthodox Jewish group.)

Dating the Gospel of John is more difficult because we don't have any clear chronological landmarks cited, such as the Temple destruction. The tendency is to argue that the enhanced nature of its theology and Christology and themes, such as the expulsion of Christians from Jewish synagogues and the absence of any Jewish groups other than the Pharisees and priests, suggest a post-70's environment. Another question that scholars raise is whether or not the author of John knew the other Gospels. If he did, then John would have to be dated after at least one of the other Gospels. The broad scholarly consensus is that John dates to about 90–110 C.E.

WHERE WERE THE GOSPELS WRITTEN?

Tradition places the authorship of Mark in Rome. Though possible, this view probably reflects the unreliable report of Papias concerning Mark as a secretary to Peter in Rome. A number of scholars have suggested Syria or the northern Transjordan.[38] A few scholars have suggested Galilee, but Raymond Brown, in his survey of the evidence, finds the argument unconvincing.[39]

As to Matthew, most scholars would probably place its origin in Antioch, in Syria, a city that had a very large Jewish population.[40] Luke's special interest in Paul's activities (as reflected in Acts) suggests that Luke probably addressed Pauline churches in Greece or Syria, where Paul conducted his missions.[41] As to John, the majority of scholars would probably place it in the Greek city of Ephesus, with some suggesting a Syrian locale.[42]

The broad scholarly consensus is that none of the Gospel authors wrote from Judea or Galilee or addressed themselves directly to persons from those areas.

THE SYNOPTIC PROBLEM

Scholars refer to the Gospels of Matthew, Mark, and Luke as the "Synoptic Gospels." This is because if you place the three Gospels side by side, you'll see that a large number of stories appear in all three Gospels. It is often the case in these triplicate accounts that at least two, if not all three, of the Gospels share some of the same key words and phrases. It is also the case that in many instances at least two, if not all three, place the collection of stories in the same chronological sequence. Even where sequences vary in one Gospel or another, we find frequent key word or phrase agreements within the stories.

To get an idea of the relationship between these three texts, consider these statistics. Mark has 661 verses, Matthew 1,068, and Luke 1,149.[43] Of all the verses in Mark, 80 percent have close parallels in Matthew and 65 percent in Luke.[44] This means that approximately one-half of Matthew overlaps Mark, and over one-third of Luke overlaps Mark. Scholars refer to those verses appearing in all three Gospels as "the Triple Tradition."

The large amount of agreement between the three Gospels as to story, word usage, and sequence very strongly suggests that there must have been some written source for the Triple Tradition. This would indicate that either all three Gospels had access to a similar written source that preceded the Gospels or that one of the Gospels had some sort of source relationship to the other two. In the latter case that would mean either two of the Gospel authors, independently of each other, used the third Gospel as a source, or one of the Gospel authors used one of the other Gospels as a source and the third author used at least one of the other two as a source.

Trying to figure out the relationship of the three Synoptic Gospels to each other is known as the Synoptic Problem. In attempting to resolve this issue, we have a number of clues.

While similar usage of wording appears in most of the parallel stories in the Triple Tradition, there are several situations in which one of the Gospels differs from the other two in that there is either a change in some of the wording or some additions to or omissions from the wording. The changes usually clarify an ambiguity, enhance a Christological understanding, or correct an error in one of the other Gospels. As a general proposition, where such changes exist you often find that either Mark and Matthew agree against Luke, or Mark and Luke agree against Matthew, but rarely do Matthew and Luke agree against Mark. This would suggest that of the three Gospels, Mark may represent the earliest written form of the Triple Tradition, with the other two making changes to the earlier written text.

Since, very often, the changes in either Matthew or Luke reflect a clarification of some ambiguity in Mark's text, show an enhanced Christology over Mark's text, or correct an error, we have another clue that Mark must represent an earlier written form of the Triple Tradition. After all, as a general principle, one shouldn't expect Mark to frequently take a higher form of Christological teaching and transform it into a lower form of Christology, continuously take clear phrasings and make them ambiguous, or take a reported fact and change it to something erroneous.

In a similar vein, there are occasional significant changes in the order of the stories in the Triple Tradition. On some occasions, again, Mark and Matthew agree against Luke, and on others Mark and Luke agree against Matthew, but rarely, if ever, do Matthew and Luke agree against Mark. This, too, suggests that Mark represents the earliest written form of the Triple Tradition as to the order of the stories.

Another argument in favor of Markan priority is that Mark has a less elegant form of Greek than Matthew or Luke, and if he had been copying from the others it is unlikely that he would've rendered their Greek in a more primitive fashion. Scholars also wonder why Mark would omit so much material from Matthew and Luke in his own account if he had used either one of them for a source.

The study of the Synoptic problem constitutes a major branch of Gospel studies. The literature is enormous and the arguments many and complex. Nevertheless, the vast majority of New Testament scholars support the following conclusion: Mark was written first, and Matthew and Luke, independently of each other, used Mark as a written source.

Q AND THE DOUBLE TRADITION

In addition to the Triple Tradition of the Synoptic Gospels, we have what is known as the "Double Tradition." This refers to a substantial amount of material that appears in both Matthew and Luke but doesn't appear in Mark. Again, we have a good deal of agreement as to language and some lesser degree of agreement on the order of the stories. However, there is enough material in the Double Tradition to suggest that Matthew and Luke, assuming that they wrote independently of each other, must have had access to a common written source that either was not available to

Mark or wasn't used by him. Approximately 20 percent of Matthew and Luke falls into this category.[45]

It is the overwhelming consensus among scholars that the Double Tradition stems from a common written source but that the text has been lost to us. Scholars refer to this common source as Q, a nickname believed to have been derived from the German word *Quelle*, meaning "source." (A few scholars believe that Luke used Matthew as a source and therefore reject Q as necessary to resolve the Double Tradition problem.)[46]

Q, therefore, is a hypothetical written text that circulated prior to the writing of Matthew and Luke. Scholars attempt to reconstruct it from the material in the Double Tradition. Q studies form another major branch of Gospel source analysis, and despite the lack of a source text, the scholars examine such issues as the original written language, the order of the stories, where the text was written, whether it was written as a single text or developed in stages, and which text belongs to which stage of development. The general consensus, subject to some debate, is that Q was written in Greek, went through at least three stages of development, and that Luke probably represents the original sequence of stories in most instances.

Scholars refer to the idea that Matthew and Luke used Mark and Q as source material for their Gospels as the Two-Source Theory.

As with Mark, we have no good information about what sources the Q author relied upon. Both Q and Mark appear after the development of many oral traditions, many of which may have been unreliable. How much of the unreliable material found its way into Mark and Q is one of the difficult problems that historians face. However, because Mark and Q are independent of each other and both precede Matthew and Luke, if we can find evidence for a particular tradition in both earlier sources we can at least date that tradition to one that probably arose before any of the Synoptic Gospels were written. Whether we can trust the earlier tradition presents a different question.

THE M AND L SOURCES

After removing the Double and Triple Traditions from both Matthew and Luke, each has some material not appearing in the other. Approximately one-third of Matthew and about forty percent of Luke fall into this category. The bulk of this extra material can be accounted for by the lengthy accounts of the birth of Jesus that appear in both Matthew and Luke but not in Mark or Q.

Whether either of these two authors had a written source for this extra material or relied upon oral traditions or imagination is a matter of speculation. The material appearing in Matthew that doesn't appear in Mark or Luke is generally referred to as M, and the material appearing in Luke but not in Mark or Matthew is referred to as L.

Scholars refer to the idea that the Matthew and Luke derive from Mark, Q, M, and L as the Four-Source Theory.

If we eliminate the nativity stories from both Matthew and Luke, neither of which appears in Mark or Q, then we find that almost everything else in Matthew and Luke is copied from either Mark or Q. If Matthew was an apostolic eyewitness and Luke was so well-informed by Paul, how come each relies almost exclusively on the written versions of Mark and Q for their accounts of the life of Jesus?

Another problem raised by the texts of Matthew and Luke is that both authors routinely and frequently edit Mark, changing his facts or claims. Obviously they didn't consider Mark to be an inspired source who accurately recorded what Peter told him. Yet they relied on Mark for a substantial amount of what they say about Jesus' lifetime. This clearly suggests that neither the author of Matthew nor the author of Luke had close apostolic ties to the mission of Jesus.

CONCLUSION

The evidence that the authors of the four canonical Gospels were Matthew, Mark, Luke, and John, two of whom were allegedly Apostles of Jesus, one of whom was a secretary to Peter, and one of whom was a close companion of Paul, rests on extremely shaky historical ground. With the exception of Papias' account, we have no evidence prior to the end of the second century that any of these four Gospels were written by any of the four traditional authors. Papias' evidence is almost worthless. It is based on an oral tradition that written texts by Matthew and Mark existed. Papias never saw the texts and gives us no quotes from either text for comparison with the existing Gospels. Further, what he does tell us about the content is at odds with what we know about both texts. Finally, Papias' credibility as a reliable scholar is called into question by the one source who cites his account, the fourth-century Christian historian Eusebius, who considered Papias rather dim-witted.

As to the identities of the authors of Luke and John, there are no credible historical accounts that tell us how these two names came to be associated with the authorship of the two Gospels attributed to them. The Gospel of John, in a passage of questionable authorship, cites an unidentified individual, the Beloved Disciple, as the author. Who this individual was is unclear, but internal textual evidence suggests he was not the Apostle John.

A text-critical analysis of Matthew, Mark, and Luke, the "Synoptic Gospels," shows that Matthew and Luke relied heavily on both Mark and another document nicknamed Q for almost all of their own Gospels (with the exception of the nativity scenes and a few other brief passages). Such reliance clearly suggests that they were not writing as eyewitnesses but relying on generally circulating texts. That the authors of Matthew and Luke freely alter what Mark wrote suggests that they didn't hold him to be a close apostolic source who wrote with inspired authority.

Who wrote the Gospels remains an open question, but the evidence available shows that none of the authors were witnesses to what happened or had any direct connection to the apostolic circle of Jesus.

1. Matt 9:9, 10:3.

2. For some discussion of this issue, see Brown, R.E. *An Introduction to the Gospel of John.* Francis J. Maloney (ed.). New York: ARBL/Doubleday, 2003: 192–6.

3. John 13:23, 19:26, 20:2.

4. Justin Martyr, *Dialogue*, CVI; ECF 1.1.6.3.0.106.

5. Eusebius, *Historia Ecclesiastica*, 6:14, citing the writings of Clement, who wrote around the end of the second century or early third century.

6. These include the Gospel of Peter, the Gospel of Thomas, the Gospel of Mary, the Infancy Gospel of James, the Infancy Gospel of Thomas, the Gospel of Bartholomew, the Gospel of Matthias, and the Gospel of Judas.

7. See, for example, Ehrman, B.D. *Lost Scriptures: Books That Did Not Make It Into the New Testament.* Oxford: Oxford University Press, 2003: 20, 32.

8. Crossan, J.D. *Who Killed Jesus?: Exposing the Roots of Anti-Semitism in the Gospel Story of the Death of Jesus.* San Francisco: HarperSanFrancisco, 1996: 24, 26.

9. See, for example, Brown, R.E. *An Introduction to the New Testament.* New York: ARBL/Doubleday, 1996: 5–7, 726, 749, 762.

10. See, for example, Brown (1996): 5; Ehrman, B.D. *The New Testament: A Historical Introduction to the Early Christian Writings.* New York: Oxford University Press, 2000: 262.

11. See, for example, Brown (1996): 5.

12. Eusebius, 3.39.14–16.

13. Eusebius, 3.39.13.

14. Eusebius, 3.39.3.

15. Eusebius, 3.39.2.

16. Eusebius, 3.39.4.

17. Eusebius, 3.39.15.

18. Eusebius, 3.39.16.

19. Irenaeus, *Adversus Haereses*, 3.2.1; ECF 1.1.7.1.3.2.

20. Eusebius, 6:25.4–5.

21. Eusebius, 6:25.4–5.

22. Eusebius, 6:25.4–5.

23. Brown (1996): 210.

24. Luke 1:2.

25. Luke 1:3–4.

26. Theophilus means "God-lover."

27. See Acts 16:10–17, 20:5–15, 21:8–18, 27:1–29, 28:1–16.

28. Brown (1996): 268.

29. Brown (1996): 324.

30. Ehrman (2000): 138.

31. Irenaeus, 3.2.1; ECF 1.1.7.1.3.2.

32. *Anchor Bible Dictionary*, sv. "John, Gospel of."

33. John 21:2.

34. Brown (2003): 209.

35. These are the Codex Sinaiticus and Codex Vaticanus.

36. Brown, R.E. *The Death of the Messiah: From Gethsemane to the Grave—A Commentary on the Passion Narratives in the Four Gospels* (2 vols.). New York: Doubleday, 1994: 4 n 1.

37. Brown (1994): 4 n 1.

38. Brown (1996): 162.

39. Brown (1996): 162.

40. Brown (1996): 172.

41. Brown (1996): 226.

42. Brown (1996): 334.

43. Brown (1996): 111.

44. Brown (1996): 111.

45. Brown (1996): 265.

46. Goodacre, M. *The Case Against Q.* Harrisburg, PA: Trinity Press International, 2002: 10–1.

Bobbie Kirkhart

BRIDGING THE LEAP OF FAITH

"For God is not the author of confusion..."
— (1 Corinthians 14:33, KJV)

I GREW UP IN A teetotaling Methodist church in the dry state of Oklahoma. This presented a problem, as the Bible is virtually soaked with wine. The miracle at Cana (John 2:1–10), where Jesus turned the water into wine, was a particular enigma. "Why would a nice young god like Jesus turn pure, sweet water into the devil's drink?" Some opined that, while he turned the water into wine, he didn't drink it. For most, this was not a good enough explanation, as he still enabled others to drunkenly ruin a perfectly good wedding reception, when everybody knows that orange juice concentrate with lemonade, canned pineapple juice, and ginger ale is just perfect for the occasion. You can even add some strawberry sherbet to float in the punch bowl for added sweetness and color. Palestine, after all, already had plenty of wine but was severely lacking in strawberry sherbet.

I don't know whether it was my mother, the preacher, or one of the women in the Mary-Martha Circle who figured it out, but the problem was solved when it was decided that Jesus didn't really turn water into wine; he just purified the water. Pure water was scarce in Palestine, the thought went, and people who had never tasted it would surely think it was the finest wine.

As explanations go, it wasn't much of one, but it did solve the problem of cognitive dissonance, that discomfort we feel when we know that what we know just ain't so. Psychologists tell us that we deal with that distress by "discovering" new facts. This idea is not just a facility of Christians—indeed, it is the generator of many of our great scientific discoveries and almost all of our UFO sightings—but belief in ancient holy texts is certainly one good reason for the phenomenon, and the biggest lies we hear are frequently the lies we ask someone to tell us.

"Why would a nice young god like Jesus turn pure, sweet water into the devil's drink?"

By and large, the wisdom of the itinerant preacher, the sewing circle, and the back-porch philosopher has given way to the blogger, the listserv moderator, and the chat-room junkie, so to find out how the world is coping with the Bible's uncomfortable anecdotes, my own experience is greatly enhanced by the Internet. Things look absolutely right and real on a webpage, but the approach to truth doesn't seem to have changed much from when I was a child in the 1950s in the whipping strop of the Bible Belt. When it comes to

> **It is the fundamentalists, clinging to their belief that the Bible is literally true, who need a J.P. Holding to tell them that, yes, the Bible is literally true and a great moral guide, but you just have to understand that it doesn't always mean what it says.**

logic and truth, the consensus is that two wrongs can make a right.

The Bible presents a lot of problems for those who love their families. Indeed, Jesus is supposed to have said, "If any man come to me, and hate not his father, and mother, and wife, and children, and brethren, and sisters, yea, and his own life also, he cannot be my disciple" (Luke 14:26, KJV). The wise ones of cyberspace are unanimously sure that when Jesus said "hate," he really meant, "not love as much as you love me." Unfortunately, the translators always put "hate"—or the older ones, "hateth"—as the verb. I looked at a dozen translations and didn't find an exception. In the original Greek of the New Testament, the word is *miseo*. According to *Thayer's Greek-English Lexicon of the New Testament*—one of the standard works in this area—*miseo* means "to hate, pursue with hatred, detest." Still, even for an atheist like me, it's good to think he didn't *really* mean hate.

Potentially more troublesome is the story of Jephthah (Judges 11:28–40, RSV), who was at war when he was visited by "the Spirit of the Lord." He promised the Lord: "If thou wilt give the Ammonites into my hand, then whoever comes forth from the doors of my house to meet me, when I return victorious from the Ammonites, shall be the Lord's, and I will offer him up for a burnt offering." Well, indeed, he smote the enemy "with a very great slaughter. Thus the children of Ammon were subdued before the children of Israel," and Jephthah went home. Darn it, who should come first to greet him but his only child, a daughter, "with timbrels and with dances." Somehow, he hadn't counted on this. Having expected something more disposable, like a dog or a slave, he said, "Alas, my daughter! you have brought me very low, and you have become the cause of great trouble to me; for I have opened my mouth to the Lord, and I cannot take back my vow." The daughter understood. A promise is a

promise, after all, but she asked for a couple of months to go into the mountains and mourn her virginity. Here is the most surprising part of the story: "And at the end of two months, she returned to her father," and less surprising, if you know the Old Testament, "who did with her according to his vow which he had made." Interestingly, the narrator thinks it's important to note that she was still a virgin.

J.P. Holding explains that, even though the ordinary reader might think that this is a story of a man who got God to help him kill a bunch of people (that part, Holding seems to find absolutely true and perfectly acceptable) and in return executed his only daughter as a burnt offering, it really didn't happen that way at all.[1] First, and this is obsessively important to Holding, there is no evidence that the Holy Spirit actually inspired the vow. Second, Jep didn't know a person would be the first to greet him. After all, human sacrifice is a bad thing, and if he had known, he would never have made the promise. Holding sort of skates around the question of whether God, who knows everything, knew a human would greet Jep. He says that if Jep had foreseen this, then God would have been guilty "by endorsement."

All this makes little difference, because, even though Holding concedes that "(m)any commentators think" Jep sacrificed his daughter, he didn't really do it. His proof? The girl lamented her virginity. After all, nobody facing death would care about a little thing like that. Okay, well, maybe Antigone and a few dozen other literary characters, but no nice Jewish girl in Holding's Bible.

Jep's story isn't really a problem for most modern Christians. It's likely that a higher percentage of atheists than Christians know the story of Jephthah, and the average Christian would dismiss it as the primitive fable it is. It is the fundamentalists, clinging to their belief that the Bible is literally true, who need a J.P. Holding to tell them that, yes, the Bible is literally true and a great moral guide, but you just have to understand that it doesn't always mean what it says. Still, the average Christian is committed to the idea that the Bible is a holy book that teaches right from wrong. While they can dismiss the more preposterous tales, they do run into a conflict with the Bible's parenting advice, which leans heavily toward physical punishment.

"I think that sometimes it comes down to what we mean when we say different words," says Pastor Crystal Lutton.[2] She's a smart woman who believes in modern parenting techniques, and she knows a lot of meanings for the different words in the Bible. She invests a lot of words, herself, in explaining what Solomon meant when he said, "Withhold not correction from the child: for if thou beatest him with the rod, he shall not die. Thou shalt beat him with the rod, and shalt deliver his soul from hell" (Proverbs 23:13–14, KJV). The Hebrew word being translated as "rod" (shebet) might mean a walking stick, shepherd's crook, or scepter, she explains, but she thinks it is the latter. She has alternate definitions for almost everything except "beatest," which she concedes does refer to "striking," but she notes that it is followed by "he shall not die." Since a person who is beaten can die, she is sure that Solomon is using the term metaphorically.

Short of true open-minded investigation and real testing of conflicting ideas, Pastor Lutton may exemplify the best use of this human facility to develop information that reconciles the dissonance. Modern research is clear that corporal punishment has only short-term results, at best, and does long-term damage, at worst, so I personally applaud anything that enables Christians to become good parents.

Of course, God himself was rather punitive with children. Take this story of the prophet Elisha: "He went up from there to Bethel; and while he was going up on the way, some small boys came out of the city and jeered at him, saying, 'Go up, you baldhead! Go up, you baldhead!' And he turned around, and when he saw them, he cursed them in the name of the Lord. And two she-bears came out of the woods and tore forty-two of the boys" (2 Kings 2:23–24, RSV). I'm indebted to Eliezer Segal, who recalls the teachings of the Midrash[3]

that, in fact, the fault lies with the leaders of the town who did not give their distinguished guest a proper escort out of town.[4] I guess a proper escort would have overcome the bears, even when they were sent by God. Some interpretations go further, insisting that Elisha's taunters were not children but were adults "with unsavory backgrounds who were guilty of an assortment of heinous sins." Segal doesn't buy it himself, but his account proves that such rationalizations of scripture are not new and are not exclusively Christian.

In these days when religious belief has become a political issue, the tale of Sodom and Gomorrah gets bandied about a lot. You know the story. Lot took in two travelers, angels perhaps.

> But before they lay down, the men of the city, even the men of Sodom, compassed the house round, both old and young, all the people from every quarter: And they called unto Lot, and said unto him, Where are the men which came in to thee this night? bring them out unto us, that we may know them. And Lot went out at the door unto them, and shut the door after him, And said, I pray you, brethren, do not so wickedly. Behold now, I have two daughters which have not known man; let me, I pray you, bring them out unto you, and do ye to them as is good in your eyes: only unto these men do nothing; for therefore came they under the shadow of my roof. (Genesis 19:4–8, KJV)

Then God struck the men of Sodom blind, told Lot and his family to leave, rained fire on Sodom and neighboring Gomorrah, turned Lot's wife into a pillar of salt, and later his daughters got him drunk and raped him, but that really gets into another story.

The idea that the mob wanted to "know" the strangers sexually is so ingrained in modern citings that one cyber-sage comes up with a whole different interpretation of the story, one that goes well beyond the necessary or reasonable.

"Grumpy" writes on a discussion board: "(T)he story is not about homosexuals, it is a story of the conflict between Ba'al and the Jews."[5] I hadn't heard this interpretation involving the Canaanite deity Ba'al before, so I asked my good friend, Bible scholar Bob Price.[6] He wrote, "Actually, I have never heard of the interpretation you mention.

However, even if it were true, it would seem to be yet another case of genocide-mongering. But there is a theory I find quite reasonable re: Sodom and Gomorrah that gives no aid and comfort to anti-gay forces and is probably superior historically anyway." He makes the point, as do others, that failure to protect the guest in ancient desert tribes was a crime similar to horse theft in the old American West. His argument that "know" was probably not meant sexually is persuasive, "since 'to know' means 'to have sex with' 10 times out of 900 plus in the Hebrew OT [Old Testament]. It does once even in the immediate context of the story, when Lot describes his virgin daughters as those 'who have not known man.' But it also uses it in the other way in the previous chapter, part of the same story, when God says of Abe, 'him alone of all the earth have I known,' i.e., chosen. Does this mean God was having homosexual trysts with the Patriarch Abraham? The mere word settles, even suggests, nothing by itself." Bob adds this note, "And of course the word 'sodomy' is not ancient but merely derives from the anti-gay reading (I should say MISreading) of the passage."

"Grumpy" didn't need his new interpretation, after all.

The daughters' rape of Lot is wrong, of course, but Rick and Eileen Beltz of Biblestudy.org ask us to consider the circumstances.[7] "Lot's daughters must have thought it was the end of civilization and that they were some of the only people then living. They were obviously greatly concerned about the future of their family (and possibly the human race). This concern led them to do what they did." More interesting is their assertion that Lot was not an alcoholic because "Lot is considered a good man, righteous in God's eyes." Knowledge that the two are incompatible must come as a shock to more than a few people, including George W. Bush, Ted Kennedy, and Mel Gibson.

Lot's wife becoming a pillar of salt prompts another kind of cognitive dissonance. There is simply no known mechanism which turns a human being into a pillar of salt. "Jesus, Dinosaurs and More" bills itself as "a webpage of Scientific evidence supporting the Biblical account of Creation." In it we learn that the land had many salt deposits, one of which must have engulfed Lot's wife in the explosion.[8] It seems that when God declares war on a town, he, too, may cause collateral damage.

As tempting as the above webpage is, and as entertaining as some of its "proofs" are, most are just that: assertions that claim to prove what the reader already believes, that scientific observation is wrong and the Bible is right. The above attempt to reconcile fiction with fact is an exception.

For most well-educated Christians, the big miracles, such as the Creation or Noah's Ark, are easy to accept as myth. There is just too much knowledge of evolution to square the Bible with reality. It's all those little miracles that conflict with our modern understanding of the world. If God performed miracles then, why not now? Some eagerly seek modern-day miracles and are easily taken in by confidence men of all kinds, especially faith healers. Most, however, note that "modern-day miracles" give way to logical explanations, and they seek to protect the value of the Bible by finding explanations for its miracles.

The crossing of the Red Sea (Exodus 14:21–29) is, of course, a puzzlement. Back in 1992, climatologists Doron Nof and Nathan Paldor offered analyses supposedly demonstrating how a wind could have parted the Red Sea, as described in the Bible.[9] They may have been the first with the actual statistics, wind charts, and oceanographic models, but I remember such explanations from scientists when I was a child, well before 1992. Similarly, many people have suggested that the event might have taken place on the "Sea of Reeds," a shallow arm of the Red Sea, although there is no certainty about which shallow arm might have been so called. Both of these explanations ignore the complete lack of evidence that the Jews were ever in Egypt, as the Moses story claims.[10]

The press probably pleases the populace with its uncritical reporting of stories that support religion. They rationalize that they later print corrections if the story isn't true, so no harm is done. So it is with the accounts of men swallowed whole by big fish or whales, as Jonah allegedly was, that come up every few decades. Perhaps the most famous one concerns a ship called *Star of the East*, which lost, then found in the belly of a whale, a crew member named James Bartley. Never mind that the *Star* wasn't a whaling ship, that there was no James Bartley on the register, that the captain's wife said it was a sea tale, or that subsequent versions changed the details. The story was first reported and debunked in the latter part of the nineteenth century, but it is still circulated.[11]

The New Testament is the source of more serious cognitive dissonance, however. Jesus was God, or he wasn't. Gods can do supernatural things, or they are not gods. (Okay, there is a small but growing group that says their god has no supernatural powers. I'll let them explain how that is a god, because it certainly beats me.) We live in the real world, or we don't. This brings up problems from virgin births to divine resurrections.

The Christian Virgin Birth is just too hard. The Hindu deity Krishna was born of a virgin. Julius Caesar's mother was a virgin. The Gnostics didn't believe Mary was a virgin. So it is explained away as a cover story for an unplanned pregnancy or it is taken on faith without examination.

Recently, our old friend Doron Nof, of Red Sea fame, came up with an account of how Jesus might have walked on water (Matthew 14:25–32). On *Seed* magazine's website he explains, accurately as far as I know (but then, what do I know?), that during the time of Jesus' life, weather was much cooler and there was a cold spring, so an ice flow on the Sea of Galilee was entirely possible, although not likely at any given time.[12] Quite honestly, Nof explains:

My view is that the Bible is a historical book and was written and re-written many times, probably. I think that (this particular miracle) is perhaps based on something natural that happened, but not frequently enough for people to get used to it. Again, this is my view. It doesn't mean it's the correct view, but that's the view I took before I started that research. It doesn't mean other people need to view it that way.

Jesus' raising of Lazarus (John 11:43–44) is a problem for several reasons. The point is made that Lazarus had been dead four days. This makes Jesus' resurrection after three days seem the lesser miracle and raises all sorts of possibilities. Of course, in those times, it was hard to tell if someone was really dead. I've been told that Lazarus was likely entombed prematurely, and Jesus merely cured his illness after he had lain in the tomb for four days.

The resurrection of Jesus is the biggest problem, because it is crucial to the whole Christian idea that we can overcome death, that Jesus was (is) God, and all the things that this implies to the true believer. The people I've heard rationalize the resurrection are not Christians in that sense. They are much more likely people who want to believe that Jesus lived and was a great teacher. They think the Prince of Peace is a wonderful moral guide, but they tend to ignore the aforementioned "hate thy family" Jesus, the one who has "not come to bring peace, but a sword" (Matthew 10:34, RSV).

These folk just can't buy the resurrection. After all, in this very well-documented period of history, wouldn't an executed criminal/cult leader who came back to life have made the papers? Still, if the whole story is untrue, they have lost the last remnants of the faith of their fathers. This may explain why as many as 40 percent of non-Christians told the 2000 Harris poll that they believe in the resurrection of Jesus.[13] I'm guessing that they mean they believe the stories were told by people who believed it. Still, most polls show a significant number of Christians who do not believe that Jesus recovered from his execution. The Religious Tolerance website gives a list of alternate ideas:[14]

- The Swoon Theory: Jesus was only unconscious and was whisked away by followers before the Romans could learn that their execution had failed;
- The Stolen Body Theory: his corpse was stolen by followers;[15]
- The Vision Theory: it was all an hallucination shared by many people;
- The Catholic Modernist Theory: "the entrance into life immortal of one risen from the dead is not subject to observation; it is a supernatural, hyper-historical fact, not capable of historical proof";
- The Reserpine Theory: Jesus used this or another drug to lower his body temperature and give the appearance of death.

They also include the Myth Theory, which says that the New Testament writers made up the whole thing (duh!), and Bishop John Shelby Spong's Midrash interpretation that, yes, they made it up but it has symbolic truth.

This is a pretty good list, but they left out my favorite theory. Some years ago, I heard a lecturer at a Secular Humanists of Los Angeles[16] gathering forward the obvious explanation, overlooked all these centuries—Jesus was a twin!

Oh, well, I guess there's no end to it. The human mind acquires new falsehoods more easily than it discards old ones. When I was a child, my favorite story was the miracle of the loaves and the fishes (Matthew 14:14–21). The Sunday school taught it as "The Little Boy Who Gave His Lunch to Jesus," but none of the biblical accounts includes a child. The hook for me wasn't the fact that a kid was involved; it was trying to visualize the five loaves and two fish passed among the multitude, being taken and eaten without being consumed. They simply passed them out and yet kept them in the baskets (one wag suggests they cloned the fish). I spent hours trying to visualize this miracle, until one day I heard my mother, a true believer if ever there was one, saying that perhaps the sharing of food encouraged everyone in the crowd to share what they had been hoarding.

This kind of radical thinking in my religious home brought about another kind of cognitive dissonance, one that was finally solved in early adulthood by hard-headed rationalism. Although I have to salute anyone who tries to bring their fictions closer to fact, I'll take rationalism over rationalizationism any day.

1. <www.tektonics.org/gk/jepthah.html>

2. <aolff.org/sparetherod.html>

3. Jewish commentaries on the Hebrew Scriptures compiled between 400 and 1200 C.E.

4. <www.ucalgary.ca/~elsegal/Shokel/010531_BearsBottles.html>

5. <forum.physorg.com/index.php?showtopic=5071&st=15>

6. Dr. Robert M. Price, professor of theology and scriptural studies at the Johnnie Colemon Theological Seminary, is the author of numerous books of biblical scholarship, including *The Widow Traditions in Luke-Acts*, *Deconstructing Jesus*, *The Incredible Shrinking Son of Man*, and *The Da Vinci Fraud*.

7. <www.biblestudy.org/question/was-lot-alcoholic.html>

8. <www.angelfire.com/mi/dinosaurs/lotswife.html>

9. Nof, Doron, and Nathan Paldor. "Are There Oceanographic Explanations for the Israelites' Crossing of the Red Sea?" *Bulletin of the American Meteorological Society* 73 (1992): 305–14. They expanded on this in: Nof, Doron, and Nathan Paldor. "Statistics of Wind Over the Red Sea With Application to the Exodus Question." *Journal of Applied Meterorology* 33 (1994): 1017–25.

10. In their articles, Nof and Paldor concede that they're not out to prove that the crossing did or didn't happen, just whether it could've happened. Believers tend to ignore this, citing their research as evidence that it did happen.

11. Adams, Cecil. "Have Any Real-life Jonahs Been Swallowed by Whales and Lived?" "Straight Dope" column, 14 Sept 2001.

12. <www.seedmagazine.com/news/2006/05/jesus_on_ice_placeholder_for_p.php>

13. <www.harrisinteractive.com/harris_poll/index.asp?PID=112>

14. <www.religioustolerance.org/resurrec7.htm>

15. The motivation for this is not given on the website, but I have heard two: Some think they wanted to create the illusion of a resurrection, while others believe they were sparing the body from desecration by infidels.

16. Forerunner of the Center for Inquiry West.

Neil Gaiman and **Steve Gibson**

JOURNEY TO BETHLEHEM

Editor's Note: In 1987—the year before his classic comic series The Sandman *would start, and well over a decade before he would pen the most honored fantasy novel of all time,* American Gods*—Neil Gaiman wrote almost half of the comics in the graphic anthology* Outrageous Tales From the Old Testament *from London's Knockabout Publications. A roster of artists illustrated Gaiman's faithful renditions of the atrocity stories to be found in the Good Book: Jephthah sacrificing his daughter to God, massacres and mass rapes committed by the Israelite Tribe of Benjamin on orders from God, ad nauseam.*

Steve Gibson—who would soon illustrate for the children's comic Oink!*—teamed up with Gaiman to put into images one of the most disgusting, soul-killing stories of the Bible (which is saying a lot): Judges chapter 19, in which a man from the Tribe of Levi, his concubine, and his servant are traveling from Bethlehem to a remote part of Ephraim. They stop for the night in Gibeah because it belongs to another Israelite Tribe, the Benjamites. An old man, who isn't a Benjamite, is the only one who'll give them lodging, but wouldn't you know it—in an echo of the Sodom fable—a group of men gathers outside the old man's house, demanding sexual access to the Levite. The old man begs them not to violate his male visitor, instead offering the crowd his own daughter, whom he assures them is a virgin, and the Levite's concubine (verse 24). Eventually, the concubine is thrown to the wolves, and she is "abused" until sun-up. Managing to drag herself to the old man's door, she dies from the vicious, all-night gang rape she has just endured. The Levite then hacks her into twelve pieces, sending the body parts to different areas throughout Israel.*

Regarding this particular comic, Gaiman has said: "I very nearly sent a publisher in Sweden to prison, for printing a bible story I had retold (the story, from the Book of Judges, contains a very nasty rape and murder, which we depicted as a very nasty rape and murder) which fell foul of a Swedish law forbidding the depiction of violence against women." From what has filtered out regarding the case, the prosecution appears to have presented the images from the top half of page 136 in isolation; the defense pointed out that these are simply literal illustrations of a biblical story (indeed, the words accompanying those images are an exact quote from verse 25 of the King James Version). The publisher avoided prison.

EVERYTHING YOU KNOW ABOUT GOD IS WRONG

4

I WAS THERE!
(TRUE ENCOUNTERS WITH RELIGION)

Tasha Fox

WITH THE SWORD

ATTENDING A MUSLIM STUDENTS' CONFERENCE

WHAT DO STUDENTS DO on Valentine's Day at one of America's biggest, boldest, bawdiest, most in-your-face universities? The University of California at Berkeley, after all, has been home to a popular academic course on male sexuality which included a strip-club field trip and an assignment in which classmates assessed snapshots of each other's genitals, trying to guess whose was whose. Since 1997, the *Daily Californian* has run a weekly sex column whose riffs on rimming, morning-after manners, and top-quality lube are the independent campus-paper's main attraction. Naked protesters pose in Sproul Plaza, supporting causes. Generations of Cal students have tarried in a local housing co-op's clothing-optional pool. It's that kind of campus: smart. Sex-positive. Smirking. And it wants the world to see.

Which is why so many aspects of the sixth annual Muslim Students Association West Conference on campus on Valentine's weekend 2004 were so startling. The strictly gender-segregated seating, for one. The no-leg-or-arm-flesh-showing, for another. Berkeley is usually warm in mid-February, a freak false summer that sears for a few days every year before the temperature plummets again and the March rains begin. Valentine's weekend was French-kiss warm. Students not attending the conference slouched past the columned, pale façade of monumental Wheeler Hall in strappy tank tops and shorts and sandals, sipping iced Starbucks. Holding hands,

they stepped around the clusters of headscarfed young women lunching together under trees, the young men in *kaffiyehs* and flowing cotton shirts conferring along the wide, white steps. Except for those moments when a group of guys or girls knelt four or five abreast toward Mecca, passersby might not even have noticed that a conference was afoot.

Except for those moments when a group of guys or girls knelt four or five abreast toward Mecca, passersby might not even have noticed that a conference was afoot.

The event certainly hadn't been massively advertised. I almost didn't hear about it myself. I stopped being a student here years ago. One day in town I was musing to a friend, wondering what might be new these days on campus, when a student walking ahead of us turned around. This serious young man in a polo shirt said that every year hundreds of Muslim students from throughout the West Coast convene at one campus for one weekend, that this year they were convening at Berkeley, and that if I was curious I should come and see.

FOUNDED IN 1963 and now boasting chapters at over 150 North American colleges and universities, the Muslim Students Association (MSA) is one of Islam's most prominent youth groups worldwide. According to the MSA-National website, its goals include helping students "to implement Islamic programs and projects...and educate, mobilize, and empower students to struggle against injustice and oppression." The site also notes that "MSA-National is a non-profit, 501(c)(3), tax-exempt organization that finances itself mainly by fundraising activities. We do not receive funding from overseas governments." Yet critics, such as *The Two Faces of Islam* author Stephen Schwartz, charge that MSA is linked to Saudi Arabia and, as such, is a channel for the radical, puritanical, Saudi-based Wahhabi brand of Islam that fuels jihad today.

Such fierce claims seem at odds with the mild and welcoming mien of MSA chapters' websites. "Our major events, such as Islam Awareness Week, Eid Dinner, Fast-a-thon and more," reads the University of Michigan MSA homepage, "provide students with both exciting and illuminating experiences...and promote the cultural, ethnic and ideological diversity that characterizes the religion." The University of Wisconsin MSA advocates "activism for the betterment of humankind as a whole" as, "with the help of Allah, we will educate students of all backgrounds about our beautiful religion of Islam." "Whether it is general announcements, prayer times, or our MSA events that you are looking for," the Purdue MSA offers warmly, "*insha-allah* you will find it here. Please feel free to contact us via email and to make any comments that will *insha-allah* help us to make our website and our organization better." Companionship beckons, such as at "Sisters' Chai Time!!" offered by the Texas A&M MSA: "Need a break and more time to relax? Well, here's your chance! Join us for the upcoming Sisters' Chai Time.... The sisters will get together and drink different types of tea, eat delightful snacks, and be entertained with cute tea party games!... Hope to see you girls there! Note: This is a sisters only event." At Bryn Mawr: "The MSA has made great head way [sic] in making the Muslim presence on campus recognized. We have fought for and attained a Muslim Student lounge.... This lounge is open to all members of the MSA as well as Muslim faculty and staff."

Many MSA chapters vow a commitment to outreach, "to promote understanding between Muslims and people of other faiths on campus," as the MIT MSA puts it. The University of Tennessee MSA asserts: "Islam has long been a misunderstood religion in the west. We aim to set the record straight and clear up the many misconceptions."

Blazingly clear is the fact that this is a deeply religious organization. The Kaaba at Mecca is emblazoned across the homepages of MSA chapters at Colorado State, Kansas State, Duke, the University of Chicago, and many more. Koranic verses, the Star and Crescent—whoever thinks Christians are the only ones talking about abstinence and the afterlife on campuses these days is still living in the Reagan era. "MSA exists for the sake of Allah and Allah only," affirms the Arizona State University MSA. At Rensselaer Polytechnic Institute, "the MSA unveiled its new campaign to enhance and solidify the MSA's commitment to its central mission (Allah willing)...to realize Islam through words, actions and intentions to Muslims and non-Muslims on the Rensselaer campus and in the society at large for the love of God... (all thanks are due to Allah)." The University of New Hampshire MSA offers a printable flier titled "The Spread of a World Creed."

THEY HAD COME TO Berkeley that sunny weekend from Washington and Oregon, from LA and San Diego and Las Vegas and in between, nearly a thousand, most of them on buses. The $30 admission fee included a weekend's worth of workshops, lectures in Wheeler's vast auditorium, prayer sessions, a name tag, and meals. I thought: *Deal.* Flashing back to myself at eighteen, I remembered lost afternoons spent staring out the windows in Wheeler's classrooms at blackbirds, not at the works of Dickens on my desk, nor at Joyce, his rosary-popery jibes virtual hieroglyphs to a California Jew.

It was announced that no photographic or recording equipment was permitted at this event. I felt a chill.

But now Wheeler was transformed. The massive doors at either end of its lobby opened onto the huge auditorium where I remembered going to see *King of Hearts* and *Hearts and Minds* and *Desert Hearts* and, one spring night, clamoring for an in-the-flesh, standing-room-only chance not to understand Michel Foucault. For the conference, the big door on the left bore a hand-lettered sign reading, "BROTHERS ENTRANCE," the one on the right a sign reading, "SISTERS ENTRANCE." As a series of lectures was about to start, young men poured through the left-hand door, young women through the right, a swirl of scarves. And just like that, the vast space filled up, an invisible but invincible vertical line bisecting it: On the left, row upon row of close-cropped heads, neat beards, the occasional skullcap; on the right, no hair in sight.

A palpable camaraderie infused the air like a scent: all those smiles, those eager, intelligent eyes, sleek shoes in the latest styles. Brotherhood, sisterhood: I envied them.

The speakers were assembling onstage. An emcee announced that one of the orators in this program, Imam Jamil, would speak to us later via phone hookup because he couldn't be there in person—he was in jail.

Imam Jamil. It didn't ring a bell.

"He's under lockdown," the emcee said. "But he was a slave of Allah before he was incarcerated and when he is released he will continue."

A chorus swelled from the men's side: "Allah *akbar*."

"There are some," the emcee said of Imam Jamil, "who are scared to even mention his name." But "if we don't work for his cause, it is us who are incarcerated. We don't submit to the wills of other people—we are working for the sake of Allah. If we aren't scared of anybody, Allah's will will be implemented in this land. Are we going to work for Allah, or are we going to work for other people?"

"Allah *akbar*."

It was announced that no photographic or recording equipment was permitted at this event. I felt a chill. This was Wheeler Hall, friendly old harbor of *Hearts and Minds* and Emily Dickinson classes, in the middle of a campus where everyone is always talking about freedom, about rights. In Sproul Plaza, in 1964, the Free Speech Movement was actually *born*. No recordings? No pictures? At a public event, at my alma mater?

MSA security guards flanked the stage. And along each outermost aisle, MSA members—a woman on our side, a man on the men's—strode up and down, clasping the only cameras in evidence and scanning the rows, stopping now and then to snap pictures, unsmiling, stern, as if to study them later. The female photographer bent at the waist to snap me. Once. Twice. My arms in long sleeves, which was a lucky accident, my brown hand holding a pen. *Snap*.

As we awaited the phone hookup that would connect us with the mysterious Imam Jamil, another figure assumed the stage: Charismatic, wearing rings, it was Amir Abdel Malik Ali, affiliated with a mosque in nearby Oakland. Later I would read articles calling him "notorious," a "firebrand"—articles reporting that he was a favorite speaker at campus events nationwide. But on Valentine's Day he was just a name to me, a name on a program.

He got his first burst of applause after decrying "the white man, who is the enemy." He polished it by addressing any unseen Zionists, conservatives, or other opponents in the audience: "Your days are numbered in the apartheid state of Israel and in America."

Oh, Israel. I *knew* that would come up.

"Allah *akbar*," chorused the conferencegoers.

"The Zionist Jews done really messed up," Ali mused. "I'm talking about the Zionist Jews, not all Jews, not the Jews who are down with us—because not all Jews are Zionists. I have to say that, otherwise I'll get called an anti-Semite."

Folks laughed.

The war in Iraq had been underway for a year at that point, and Ali said he'd read in the paper recently "that if things go wrong in Iraq, there'll be a backlash against Jews in America." He rocked pertly behind the mic.

"Let the backlash begin."

At other schools, Ali has reportedly used similar rhetoric, sometimes specifying that Jews per se aren't the problem, just Israel-supporters, but nevertheless sometimes railing against "Jewish money" and "the Jew." It's easy to see why listeners call him incendiary; he keeps invoking the Holocaust. At the University of California at Irvine in May 2006, he presented a program called "Israel: The Fourth Reich." It's easy to see, too, why people call him an agitator. At California State University, Long Beach, in early 2006, he reportedly told a crowd, "We'll strap bombs if we have to." That Valentine's Day in Berkeley, he told the students, those hundreds of chemistry majors and engineering majors and political science and literature and sociology majors: "You should also learn how to fight with the sword."

He described the scenario that would crop up again and again throughout the weekend: the vision of a future world dominated by Islam. Not just the Iberian Peninsula regained but the whole globe.

"The enemies of Islam," Ali intoned, "know that when we come back to power, we're gonna check 'em. They're gonna be checked."

THE PHONE HOOKUP was good to go but scratchy, so through the static, a voice strained to be heard over loudspeakers. Before being cut off by an operator, Imam Jamil inveighed his listeners to "stay conscious and ask Allah to raise the Muslims and give us victory over the disbeliever."

Victory? Waaait. Because the disbeliever was...me. My eyes swept the hall: its familiar cathedral grandeur, artfully sloping floor, lofty ceiling, paneled walls. High-tech lighting that bathed us all like liquid pearls. I remembered myself here at eighteen: bangles and faded jeans. And now swords, power, victory.

Snap.

A representative from the "Imam Jamil Task Force" announced that "Imam Jamil...has the potential of uniting North America."

But who the ... ?

Googling later, I would learn that he had been H. Rap Brown, the Black Panther Party's Justice Minister, legendary in the 1960s, and both loved and feared for his catchphrase, "Violence is as American as cherry pie." Arrested after a New York shootout, Brown discovered Islam in Attica Correctional Facility, where he spent much of the 1970s. In 2002, by then known as Imam Jamil Abdullah al-Amin, he was convicted of killing a Georgia sheriff's deputy. He was given a life sentence.

The buffet dinner, a selection of curries with rice and soft bread, included in my ticket price and served outdoors on a lawn, where girls ate with girls, and boys with boys, was delicious.

THE NEXT MORNING, bright and early after a fruit-punch-and-pastry breakfast, we filed toward the auditorium. Workshops were in progress elsewhere on campus—political, religious, social. I had tried some the night before, but what with all the Koranic references and Middle Eastern history, I was way out of my depth. These addresses in the aud were the main events anyway, and nearly everyone was there. Friends greeted friends in the lobby. In the restroom, where I ducked to tuck my short hair under a bandanna, two young women flanked me as I was heading for the door.

"Are you having a good time?" one of them asked.

"Do you find the speakers interesting?" ventured the other, in a native-Cali drawl much like my own. They wore *hijabs*, flared jeans, and thigh-length tailored blouses, and they leaned close, breathing into my face, as if we were pals. I looked like such an outsider. Curiosity flashed like scribbled lightning in their eyes. That's how college students are, body language all languorous and confident and cool, eyes ricocheting everywhere.

"Uh-huh," I said. "Thanks."

> In the restroom, where I ducked to tuck my short hair under a bandanna, two young women flanked me as I was heading for the door.

ABDEL MALIK ALI was back. Again he was going on about a caliphate. Students must focus on the formula, he said, "for how we come to power. From an Islamic movement we graduate to an Islamic revolution, then to an Islamic state."

"Allah *akbar*."

"We must," said Ali, "be in power.... When it's all over, the only one standing is gonna be us."

"Allah *akbar*."

"We ain't gonna lose. We must implement Islam as a totality." In his envisioned future, "Allah controls every place—the home, the classroom, the science lab, the halls of Congress."

Other speakers throughout the morning—student leaders, local Muslim teachers, a professor—

echoed his urgings. During the lunch break, I wandered across the plaza toward a drinking fountain in the glade where, as a sophomore, I used to sit licking chocolate cones from nearby Yogurt Park—sometimes with my roommate and sometimes with my boyfriend, watching buskers and Frisbee games and the latest pro-choice rally ("Get your hands! Off my body!") and Jonathan Richman, when he used to breeze through. As I neared the fountain, a man caught my eye. Sparse hair silver at the temples, sleek briefcase and cardigan: not a student, I deduced. After a day and a half of strict gender-segregation, I jumped when he said hi. It already felt wrong.

He'd tagged me as a nonstudent, too, and lobbed a guess.

"Reporter?"

"No."

"Not an academic then, I hope." He gave that reedy, faux-self-effacing sort of laugh that academics use and handed me his card. Professor at a private college back East.

"I'm working on a book," he said, "about religion in schools. How do you like it?" He gestured broadly at Wheeler with its clusters of young people on the stairs. He was smiling, as if none of this had anything to do with us.

I shrugged. "It scares me."

"Scares—?" His jaw and shoulders jerked, that electric, excited shimmy seen among boys at boxing matches.

He was working on a book.

THE TITLE OF THE conference's crowning event borrowed a buzzword from Marxism: *struggle*. And the series of speakers whose lectures comprised "Muslim Students in the Struggle" indeed talked of striving, with one basic objective: world domination. One young man sketched out his vision of the day "when we are called upon to rock the West like it's never been rocked before."

A female student from San Diego urged her female listeners "to re-establish the Islamic state.

If you think about the sister's greatest role, it's to be a mother...training the children who will lead that revival. It's a promised revival; it's going to happen. We know that. It's a fact. The mission will be fulfilled."

Another speaker jeered that Anti-Defamation League infiltrators were somewhere among us in the auditorium, keeping tabs. If that was true, they were wearing disguises.

Abdel Malik Ali strode back to the mic. The first order of business, he declared, was "to step up," to "work on building Islamic infrastructures in the USA now."

"Allah *akbar*."

Infrastructures. *But*, I thought, *this is a secular country, right?* Spring break isn't called Easter vacation anymore, and that extra check you get in December isn't a Christmas bonus. From student lounges and Sisters' Chai Time to infrastructures: wow. This didn't feel like my old school anymore. This didn't feel like a school at all. I didn't like the look in Ali's eye. I didn't like the photographer in the aisle. I didn't like the rules. I didn't like the idea of having to wear long sleeves on hot days until the end of time.

"There will be some poop-butts," Ali mused with broad gestures and a wry smile, "who will not want to live under *sharia* law and will leave."

Ah. Well. Leave. In that future of his. Overpacked into rowboats, the poop-butts, like Cubans.

But first, the neoconservatives would have to be dealt with.

"Neocons," Ali intoned, "are all Zionist Jews."

"Allah *akbar*."

"They really blew it, y'all."

He surveyed the crowd. It was big. It was young. It was brilliant. Today's Muslim students, he proclaimed to the boys on the left and the girls on the right, will be the parents of tomorrow's Muslim children. Babies, sweet, growing up under the sun.

"And they should," he cried, "be militants."

Jeff Sharlet and **Peter Manseau**

BROWARD COUNTY, FLORIDA

"Who knows the power of your anger?"
— Psalm 90:11

"ARE YOU A PREACHER?" Dawnia DaCosta might have asked that night, the lilt of Jamaica in her voice as much of an enticement as the curves of her hips and her breasts. And Lucious Boyd, a preacher of sorts, would have smiled.

"My daughter was a virgin!" Dawnia's mother told us three years later. It wasn't an assertion; it was an accusation. How could the Lord take an innocent? How could the Lord take one who'd not yet been blessed by love? God's will. She spat the words out and ground them into the floor.

We sat silent, staring at them. We'd come to the southern tip of Florida looking for Santería, the Cuban religion of African gods doubling as Catholic saints, of chicken bones and love candles and goat blood on the streets outside the INS building every morning, prayers to the Virgin Mary and her Yoruba alter-ego, Ochun, to let a brother or a sister, or a daughter, come to the promised land. Instead we'd found Dawnia's mother. She didn't need candles; she didn't need chicken bones—all she wanted was blood.

"A virgin!" Dawnia's mother said. "Lord, how she felt!" She spoke of the last time she'd seen her daughter alive, before Dawnia left for church one Friday night three years ago.

"Are you a preacher?" Dawnia might have asked. In Lucious Boyd's reply, she would have noted the erudition of his tone, his long American vowels. "Yes, I am a preacher," he might have answered; and from what the witnesses tell us about the dark-skinned girl who climbed into a church van with the light-skinned black man, how she wavered before getting in as if on the edge of faith, we know she was excited, and afraid.

She spoke of the last time she'd seen her daughter alive, before Dawnia left for church one Friday night three years ago.

Faith is dangerous. Friday night, 2 A.M.: Dawnia just now coming home from church, Faith Tabernacle Pentecostal United, a church of Caribbean exiles making good in America. She's a big girl, handsome, known for her bright laughter and her powerful lungs. She loves Jesus; she loves her church. Friday night, nowhere else she'd rather be. She's twenty-one, going to be a nurse, so God-fearing she won't even wear slacks, but she loves to party, loves to pray, loves to sing. She's an alto. She sings solos.

Friday night, her throat is itching. She wants to let it loose; she wants to pray; she wants to sing;

she has the solo. "There is power, power, wonder-working power, power in the blood of the Lamb!" It's a song; it's a prayer; it's a vibration in her bones.

The clock creeps into the morning. The choir decamps to a Denny's, where they drink coffee and laugh about life back on the islands; then they shift to the parking lot, short bursts of song escaping their lips between goodbyes like hiccups of gospel. Dawnia gets behind the wheel, alone with her solo. She cruises through the warm, dark Florida morning, her windows down while she sings. There is power in the blood. Her voice shakes the car so hard she doesn't notice it sputtering. Then it rolls to a stop. She's run out of gas.

Faith is dangerous. Dawnia walks down the highway in the dark; cars whiz by; nobody stops; just as well. She keeps company with the Lord. She sings to keep herself safe. "There is power in the blood, power, power, wonder-working power!" She comes to a ramp, exits the highway on foot, walks out of the dark, into the white light of a gas station. She sees a turquoise van. A church van, "Generation of Hope" written on its side. In it is a man with broad shoulders and dark eyes; they spot her wandering, and he rolls up beside her. His eyebrows are raised; his lips are set in a careless smile.

"Are you a preacher?" Dawnia might ask. The man would laugh. No, not really, but he does give sermons at the funeral home he runs with his family. He's a businessman, but solace is his trade. Isn't that about the same thing? Dawnia gets in the van.

Faith is dangerous. Three A.M. Dawnia's gone. Her mama's awake. She wants her daughter. Dawnia, her eldest, Dawnia, her strongest.

"She is physically strong," her mother told us, sitting in her beauty parlor between a pawnshop and a gun store, making a fist out of her daughter's strength. "She is always with me," she said. Three years later, she still saw Dawnia nodding to Lucious Boyd's pious words; felt her daughter's shoulders tensing as he drove past her car without slowing down; heard her praying—Oh my God, help me!—as his hands pushed her down to the floor of the church van—Jesus, help me!—as his face came from above like the maw of an animal—God—as he tore into her like the Beast himself—Please!

"I pray for him to suffer," Dawnia's mother said. "May the Lord make that so."

Dawnia's church prayed with her: "Let him suffer," they prayed, a chorus of hate so deep it didn't so much stain their faith as transform it. Even before they knew his name, the day they found Dawnia's body, naked, raped, stabbed, run over, and oddly, tenderly, wrapped in a shroud of bedsheets, they prayed for him. The day the police caught him, they prayed for him; every day of his trial they sat in the back of the courtroom and prayed for him; the day the jury said *guilty* they prayed for him, and now, the Sunday after the verdict, a new holiday they called "Victory Day," they prayed for him. Let him suffer, thank you, Jesus; give him the chair, thank you, Jesus; make him bleed, thank you, Jesus. They were a prayer in a red dress, a red suit, red suspenders. "It's the color of Jesus' blood," said the reverend of Faith Tabernacle, as if that explained why he and his church had chosen it as the special color of their celebration. "Today we're celebrating Jesus," a congregant said. "Today we're wearing red for justice."

Red is the color of their prayer. Red is the color of blood. And there is power in the blood, that's what they sang. A choir forty-five strong at the front of the church; the band bursting out of its corner; the women in the pews sizzling in their seats until like popcorn they hopped into the air. Thank you, Jesus! That's an S like a Z, Jee-zus! That's a red, bloody Jesus; say it again! A boy in a black suit over a red shirt put his hands in the air and let his fingers flutter like butterflies until the spirit filled them and they turned into talons. There is power in the blood! The soloist wore a red skirt suit and a red hat shaped like that of a pilgrim. "There is power!" she sang. "Power! Power! Power!"

From somewhere in the choir loft, tambourines rose up and rippled across the singers like a school of silver fish. The drummer banged his way past the Plexiglas shield designed to contain him; the piano player, a teenage boy, splashed across the keys as if skipping stones on water. Two rows ahead, a tall man with the heavy jaw and thin frame of an undertaker rocked back and forth, his arms glued to his sides, his hands like paddles.

Then the bass simmered. The choir quieted. The reverend preached. "She has been justified!" He was the biggest man in the church, his legs alone taller than the full height of a boy, his head as wide and thick as the dark mouth of a cannon, his words shaped like an Englishman's. "My God," he said. "We can rejoice!"

Later, we'd sit with him in his office, lost in deep leather chairs, straining to see him behind the bronze eagle that swooped from a pedestal over his neatly piled sermons. His god, he said, was a loving one, and God's love was like a lion, like a fighter plane. The reverend loved fighter planes; he loved his new country's F-16s. "Do you understand," he asked us, one hand in a fist pressed against the black marble of his desk, the other stroking its sheen, "what this nation, under God, can do to God's enemies?" If we hadn't before, we did then, under the anger of the reverend's glare.

In the pulpit, the reverend roared his adopted American creed: "You can run, but you can't—"

"HIDE!" his congregation shouted.

"Let us sing!" the reverend commanded.

The soloist shook her head hard, and her red pilgrim hat punched the air. In her hand there was suddenly a red handkerchief like a splash of blood. "We won!" she sang. Red scarves burst into the air around the church like so many gunshots. "We won! We won! We won!"

In the front row, a half a dozen white men, detectives and a prosecutor, special guests for Victory Day, nodded their heads; they knew this song. The lead singer pumped her hands: "We won the war! We won the war! We won the war!"

"Yes," said the reverend. "Yes!" The choir subsided, folded up into twitching quiet like wings behind his shoulders. "Did we not know it would be so?" The guitar player twanged, warned, played a blues. "The wise man Solomon says in Ecclesiastes, 'But it shall not be well with the wicked, neither shall he prolong his days!'"

"Yes!" The congregation shouted with joy.

"St. Paul tells us in Romans, chapter twelve"—

"Tell us!" screamed a woman in the back pew. "St. Paul tells us in Romans chapter twelve, verse nineteen, 'It is written, Vengeance is mine, I will repay, sayeth the Lord!'"

"St. Paul tells us in Romans chapter twelve, verse nineteen, 'It is written, Vengeance is mine, I will repay, sayeth the Lord!'"

The congregation roared. "Jesus!"

"And does it not say, in Galatians chapter six, verse seven"—Oh yes, the congregation said, women crying and men dancing. "'God is not mocked! For whatsoever a man soweth! For whatsoever a man soweth, that he shall also reap!'" A flurry of keyboard and a burst of rumbling bass followed the words. The reverend waited. He looked at the pews, his congregation of exiles and immigrants, Jamaicans and Antiguans, their skin so dark, their souls so white. The reverend did not know what it meant to be "black" until he came to this country. He wished not to know. He was not black; he was a man. Just like, he'd told us—especially like—the white men who filled the first pew. The detectives. The prosecutor. These powerful men, who had listened to the power of the Lord, heard the power of Faith Tabernacle. The reverend stared at the white men. "I am well-pleased," he said, "with what God has done. With what God is about to do."

"Isaiah!" A man in the back shouted the prophet's name.

The reverend ignored him. "I will say now that we have the blessing of dignitaries among us." The white men shifted in their seats. "These men," said the reverend, "who have done"—he paused—"so much. I have not seen one flaw in these men. If it exists, I am not looking. I have not seen one such flaw—such as racism." The prosecutor nodded.

The man in the back again shouted the prophet's name, like a bullet fired at the altar. What did he mean? Nobody cared. Why did people say the sheriffs shot black people as if they were dogs? Nobody knew. Why didn't they put Lucious Boyd away when they thought he'd killed a black whore? That didn't matter. What mattered was power. The power of prayer, the power in the blood, the power of Faith Tabernacle to make white men do their will.

The guitar thrummed, and the red handkerchiefs waved. At the reverend's invitation, the prosecutor stepped up to the pulpit. He was nearly as big as the reverend, with dark hair going silver, boyish cheeks, narrow-set eyes that beamed concern. And teeth. Bright white teeth.

"I'm seeing a whole lotta red out there!" he shouted. The guitar leapt up behind him. "Can you hear me?" he called. YES! Can you hear me? YES!

He reminded them he'd been there before, campaigning. Two years ago, didn't even know what church he was in, when the reverend had pointed a finger at him and demanded, "What are you going to do?"

"Only then did I realize that I was in Dawnia DaCosta's church. And when I knew that I came up—you remember?—I came up to the pulpit, and I said, 'I will do everything in my power to make sure justice is done!'"

"Thank you, Jesus!"

"Yes! And in return, I asked for one thing—what was that?"

"Oh Lord! Justice!"

The prosecutor, who would not comment on his plans to run for higher office, who was a lector in his Catholic church, the racial mix of which he told us he had never noticed, who loved hockey and his two children and his wife, none of whom he had brought that morning to Faith Tabernacle, who said there were no bad parts of his town, the prosecutor had asked for one thing.

Votes? No, no.

"Your thoughts and your prayers!"

"Power in the Blood" resumed, the red-hatted woman belting, "We got it! We got it! We got it!" A woman in the second row of the choir let her long hair fly as she slammed her torso backwards and forwards like a wet rag snapping. The detectives danced, hips and shoulders this way, then that. Despite ourselves, we did too, even though it made us feel like accomplices, two more lightning rods for the power Faith Tabernacle meant to draw down from the sky and up from the grave. We got it whether we wanted it or not, though what it was we couldn't say. They'd already had deliverance; that's how they'd come to America. And they were certain each and every one of them was saved. What did they want? Not chicken bones, not candles, and not a creamy white Christ bleating, "Forgive!" They

wanted blood. To get it they needed power. "We got it! We got it!" They needed the D.A. who stacked their young men up in jails like piles of sugarcane. "We got it!" They had it, and now the D.A. felt it, the power they had. We could see it in the way his bones seemed to shake free of their joints and the way his bright white teeth sparked electric, as Faith Tabernacle anointed him—old women running to him, young men seizing him, the choir singing for him, the pastor smiling at him. He gave his smile back to the pastor. It was as though, both would later claim, there was no more black and white between them. Just red. A wave of it that could take Lucious Boyd to the chair, the prosecutor to the judge's bench, and the reverend to a brand-new marble pulpit.

LUCIOUS BOYD DIDN'T say a word at his sentencing hearing a few days later. "Nice to see you, Mr. Boyd," the judge said; Lucious Boyd simply nodded. We sat in the visitor's gallery, ten feet away. He had sleepy eyes and a broad jaw, a face that spread out like an alluvial plain, handsome but tired; his skin was as gray as it was brown. Every day of the trial he'd worn a new suit, but now he wore a prison-issue coverall, beige. It rounded his shoulders and made his chest look hollow, but still he smiled, even for the prosecutor, just as he had smiled at the reverend when the reverend had sat in the gallery, praying for justice and power and blood. Why not? They'd won the war, to them went the spoils. Lucious was a preacher himself. He knew the cost of a covenant. He knew a deal had been struck on the foundation of his body. Over his bones the reverend and the prosecutor would not just shake hands but bind themselves together in order to build a bright red temple.

Sentenced to death, Lucious Boyd would never hear its choir. Nor would Dawnia's mother. "I don't need that church no more," she told us when we went to her beauty parlor and sat in an empty room behind the styling chairs, lit by cold blue fluorescent bulbs. She had hated Victory Day. As far as she was concerned, "Power in the Blood" belonged to Dawnia. And she had hated the things people had said to her there. "People say God use Dawnia as a sacrifice. People say God use her to kill Lucious." She paused, for a moment too angry to speak. "But people use God in a wrong way."

From *Killing the Buddha: A Heretic's Bible* (Free Press, 2004).

MY WEEKEND WITH OSHO

OSHO IS ONE OF THE MOST WEIRD—and worrying—extreme religious groups around. They now market themselves as a meditation and alternative-therapy group, but in reality they are a cult who follow the teachings of a discredited guru, Bhagwan Shree Rajneesh, and follow some bizarre and dangerous practices. After a long period in the wilderness, they are once again on the rise, attracting new followers to their bases around the world—including Osho Leela, an old Manor House in Dorset in the South of England, which I visited in late 2005.

FASCIST BOOT CAMP: OREGON, USA

Back in 1985, Margaret Hill, a former mayor of Antelope, Oregon, had the measure of Bhagwan Rajneesh. "He is a crook," she said. There were few people around then who would have disagreed with her.

Hill was being interviewed by a *New York Times* reporter who'd gone to investigate the chaos that the Indian guru and his followers had wreaked during their four-year tenure just outside her hometown.

In brief, the facts were these:

The Indian guru Bhagwan Shree Rajneesh had arrived in America in 1981 (along with twelve tons of luggage), claiming that he needed to enter the country for "medical reasons." He was accompanied by around 7,000 disciples, who settled in a 60,000-acre, $6-million ranch on semi-desert scrubland just outside of Antelope. Almost immediately, things took a turn for the weird.

To the surprise of everyone around him, Rajneesh stopped talking (or, as he put it, he determined on a course of "speaking through silence"). The day-to-day running of the huge community then fell to his follower, Ma Anand Sheela.

Sheela took to wearing robes and calling herself "queen." Fences, complete with guard towers, went up around the compound, and disciples armed with Uzis patrolled the Bhagwan's residence.

Many of the commune's members were forced to work twelve hours a day for no pay. While they succeeded in clearing and planting 3,000 acres of land, building a 350-million-gallon reservoir, a ten-megawatt power substation, and a functioning dairy farm, only Sheela and her coterie seemed to live in any comfort. The others had to endure unbearable hardships.

The most bizarre incidents occurred outside the ranch in the town of Antelope itself. There were so many people living on the ranch that they were able to force the results of the 1984 local elections and take over Antelope's local council. They decided to rename this hitherto upright Oregon backwater Rajneeshpuram. When attempts were also made to rig local county elections by shipping thousands of homeless people onto the ranch, resistance to the Sannyasins (as Osho's followers were known)[1] grew stronger. Sheela responded by having her followers dump salmonella into the salad bars of several local restaurants. Antelope, therefore, gained the dubious distinction of being the site of the first successful bioterrorism attack in US history.

Eventually, Rajneesh emerged from his silence and attempted to distance himself from his disciples. He said that Sheela had been running the place like a "fascist concentration camp" and went on the talk show *Good Morning America* to suggest that those with him were "fellow travellers" rather than followers. He also called on the FBI to conduct an independent investigation into the ranch. The FBI quickly found an extensive eavesdropping system that was wired throughout the commune residences, public buildings, and offices. They also uncovered a secret laboratory where experiments had been run on the manufacture of HIV, as well as salmonella. Oddest of all, they found that Rajneesh's bedroom was rigged so that he could receive nitrous oxide—laughing gas—while he lay in bed.[2]

Sheela confessed to having a rather "bad habit" of poisoning people and was sent to jail. Bhagwan Shree Rajneesh himself was charged with criminal conspiracy, thirty-four counts of making false statements to federal officials, and two counts of immigration fraud. He paid a $400,000 fine and was given a ten-year sentence—suspended on the understanding that he would leave the United States. When he left, he declared that he "hoped never to come back."

Many of his followers, meanwhile, were simply abandoned on the ranch. Most of these people had given over their life savings. They had been promised that their money would be returned when they left or when the ranch started generating an income. Of course, the money was never returned. Somewhere along the line, however, Bhagwan Rajneesh had managed to amass no fewer than ninety-three Rolls Royces.

"Now he has left two groups of followers in the lurch when the going got tough," the plain-speaking Margaret Hill told the man from the *New York Times*. (Rajneesh had moved to Oregon primarily to escape a large tax bill he faced at his original commune in India.) His cult had been disgraced, discredited, and, finally, displaced. It seemed that the end had come. Few organizations would have been able to recover from the kinds of scandals they'd been engulfed in, no matter how fanatical their devotees. Few would even have had the gall to stick around.

Somewhere along the line, however, Bhagwan Rajneesh had managed to amass no fewer than ninety-three Rolls Royces.

PARADISE: PUNE, INDIA

All of the antics in Oregon were a far cry from the cult's humble beginnings just over a decade before in India. In 1971, Mohan Chandra Rajneesh (a former philosophy teacher at the University of Jabalapur, who had quit his job to dedicate himself to his full-time calling as a spiritual leader) assumed the modest title of Bhagwan Shree Rajneesh, meaning "The Blessed One Who Has Recognized Himself as God." He had a simple commandment: "Enjoy!" Unlike more ascetic gurus who have emerged from India in the 1960s and 1970s, Rajneesh demanded little from his followers in the way of renunciation—and lots in the way of carnal pleasure.

The ashram he established in Pune (in west central India) in 1974 quickly became a New Age mecca.

It attracted thousands of young Western disciples sold on the charismatic teacher's mercurial wit and unusual brand of Eastern mysticism. Marked by their happy expressions and orange clothes (dyed at the Bhagwan's instigation to reflect the color of the sun), they quickly spread

They wore blindfolds—or nothing at all—and explored their deepest selves by screaming, fighting, and, inevitably, having sex.

their guru's teachings and popularized his unique forms of taboo-breaking therapies. In these sessions, known as Dynamic Meditations, pupils were encouraged to destroy their religious and social conditionings to find out who they really were. They wore blindfolds—or nothing at all—and explored their deepest selves by screaming, fighting, and, inevitably, having sex. Broken limbs were common, as were broken relationships. The latter came thanks to the teachers' propensity for encouraging students to watch their partners having sex with another person—so they could confront the emotions that this betrayal provoked.

In spite of, or maybe even because of, these extreme practices, the "Rajneeshees" continued to expand in number. Soon they spread across Europe and the US, often in stately homes like the one they named Medina Rajneesh in Suffolk, where 400 of the Bhagwan's followers established themselves in the early 1980s—seemingly in utopian contentment.

At his peak, Rajneesh laid claim to 250,000 followers. His Orange People were the cults' cult. They fulfilled every cliché—sex, drugs, tribal music, and crazy clothes. Their leader was the very image of the guru, with twinkling eyes, a long, flowing beard, and a priapic fondness for his flock. And just like most cult leaders, he left a trail of broken families, ruined minds, and wrecked lives.

Even before the Antelope episode, there had been plenty of signs that all was not well in paradise. One of Bhagwan Shree Rajneesh's more chilling suggestions was that prominent female followers should get sterilized so that they could better practice his teachings. Ugly rumors of child abuse and the destruction of family life slowly began to surface. The growing anti-cult movement of the late 1970s and early 1980s also warned that the group's communal living practices and intensive "meditations" were akin to brainwashing.

The disaster in Oregon was just the tipping point. For a long time, the communes around the world had been gaining momentum for a rapid descent.

As soon as Rajneeshpuram imploded and Rajneesh fled to India, many more of his communities around the world dissolved. Most of them were embroiled in scandals of their own. Bhagwan's English followers, for instance, had developed a marked fondness for the drug ecstasy, which the Indian guru had recommended as a spiritual elixir. It's widely believed that they were the first to bring it into the UK, and members began producing it on an industrial scale.

Meanwhile, the original commune in India limped on, but Rajneesh was a shadow of his former self. In 1985, he declared that his religion was dead—and that it had, in fact, been invented by his followers. He said that he was glad not to have to pretend to be enlightened anymore. Then, in December 1988, he told his followers that his body had become host to none other than Guatama Buddha. However, when the Buddha disapproved of his use of the Jacuzzi, Rajneesh banished him from his body and said that he was now Zorba the Buddha instead. In 1989, he changed his name for the last time to Osho. He died the next year, bedridden and addicted to laughing gas. He left a simple post-mortem instruction to his disciples: "Stick me under the bed and forget about me."

OSHO RETURNS—EVERYWHERE

For a long time, it seemed that the man last known as Osho had indeed been forgotten—or was at least regarded as little more than a bad memory. In 2004, for instance, when Tim Guest published *My Life in Orange*, his autobiographical account of his childhood in the UK commune Medina Rajneesh, it read like an obituary for the group.[3] As the blurb on the jacket put it, they represented "a lost moment of madness in the cultural history of the West." The press presented them as nothing more threatening than a fascinating museum piece, and in nearly all of the coverage this excellent book produced, the cult was written about firmly in the past tense.

Osho was a busted flush. Nothing to worry about anymore.

The trouble is that, in direct contradiction of his last known command, Osho's followers who remained did not forget about him. They just laid low for a few years, licking their wounds, waiting for the fallout from all the scandals to blow over.

Without anyone really noticing, they've once again grown into a huge multinational organization.

These followers—who now call their faith "Osho," as well—forgot about all the bad stuff. Like nearly all durable religions and other belief systems, Osho has developed a distant and shaky relationship with history. Those facts that don't suit their cause seem to have been conveniently forgotten (or at least banished), while a new narrative has taken their place.

Osho/Rajneesh, we are now told, with the cult's Christian-like habit of talking about their dead master in the present tense, "is not a guru." He is just the man who gives people the space to take "responsibility" for their own lives—and thus "find total freedom."

So that's clear.

The Oregon days, meanwhile, when they are mentioned, are explained rather differently than the way newspapers, witnesses, locals in Oregon, the FBI, and even Osho/Rajneesh himself saw things. The article most frequently cited on Osho websites ("The Story of Osho—Master, Mystic, Madman" by Amit Jayaram) describes how the guru and his Sannyasins "transformed the face of a timeless desert" into a green and beautiful land. Then they came under attack from "a bigoted government" that used every "foul means" at its disposal to destroy the nice old guru and his cult. Meanwhile, the residents of the nearby "ghost town" of Antelope joined this conspiracy and harassed the innocent Sannyasins.

So *that's* why the ranch collapsed and they all had to leave. The US "government," it's claimed, even tried to poison Osho/Rajneesh with the drug thalium. (He himself came up with this theory and was convinced of it right up until his dying day, even though he exhibited none of the usual symptoms of thalium poisoning. For instance, he still managed to hang on to his hair and lustrous grey beard, even though thalium induces rapid and catastrophic hair loss.)

Osho/Rajneesh's followers have been busy at more than rewriting history. They've also been steadily regrouping over the last decade, attracting new members and spreading out again all over the world. Without anyone really noticing, they've once again grown into a huge multinational organization.

In short, Osho is back.

ALONGSIDE THE HUGE center in Pune (which never closed down, even in the cult's darkest days), there are now known Osho-based communities in Iran, Thailand, Holland, Italy, Argentina, Taiwan, Patagonia, Germany, Brazil, South Africa, Denmark, France, Mexico, Canada, and all over the UK and the US (where there are large retreats in Colorado, New York, and, naturally, California).

If you were to read the websites that promote these communes without knowing anything about the group's past, you could easily mistake them for perfectly legitimate New Age therapy centers. Of course, it's understandable that they don't market themselves as a crazy cult with a terrorist history, but that doesn't mean such comprehensive—and fundamentally deceptive—rebranding isn't troubling.

The Pune commune in India, for instance, looks on its website like little more than a resort—and they encourage visits from anyone and everyone: "This lush contemporary 40-acre campus is a tropical oasis where nature and the 21st Century blend seamlessly, both within and without," the website gushes. "With its white marble pathways, elegant black buildings, abundant foliage and Olympic-sized swimming pool, it is the perfect setting to take time out for yourself."

Sounds lovely. And if that doesn't convince you, they even provide a plug from *Elle* magazine:

Every year thousands of people visit this luxurious resort…. A very comfortable paradise where you can stay a long time, with low-budget hotels nearby and very good food in the commune, with meditations free. The atmosphere is really like a fairy tale. A paradise where all your emotional, bodily and spiritual needs are met. I can advise everybody to visit for a few days and walk around that beautiful garden where everybody is friendly.

It's only when you delve deeper into the site that you find the odd stuff about the need to wear red robes during the day—because the color maroon, when worn by many people meditating together, "adds to the collective mental energy," and because loose robes are comfortable in the tropical climate. Oh—and you have to take an AIDS test before you can enter the campus. That's right, an AIDS test.[4]

Even with these strange restrictions and the bizarre nature of the meditations that "guests" are invited to partake in, many people who visit the "resort" have no idea what they're getting into. I recently horrified a personal acquaintance who had visited the center in all innocence on a trip around India by telling her about the history of the friendly looking old man whose picture hung on every wall. Up until that point, she'd still been convinced that Osho Pune was nothing more than an eccentric resort—even if the AIDS test had made her feel awkward and she had found it strange how many of the people there had changed their names.

IT'S NOT JUST spiritually inclined tourists who have been taken in. In Holland one of Osho's most prominent followers, a man who calls himself Veeresh, runs something called a Humaniversity, which terms itself "an international centre for therapy, training and personal growth." Here they run a series of courses designed to help create "people people," easily able to work with others and who will, the literature says, "develop and refine many positive and beautiful qualities to become heartful, dynamic, resourceful, juicy, creative and humorous."

As well as fostering these useful, if eccentrically labelled skills, the Humaniversity runs a large addiction center. All very commendable—although it may set alarm bells ringing among those who know about other cults' involvement with addiction treatment and the way they recruit from the ranks of the homeless and hopeless.

This addiction treatment has also gained Veeresh a degree of legitimacy that other Osho followers have so far failed to attain. In May 2006, for instance, Veeresh was visited by John E. Sheehan, vice president of Phoenix House Programs, one of the biggest and most respected drug and alcohol relief organizations in the world.

An even bigger coup came when Veeresh appeared on BBC Radio in March 2006. Presented as a "spiritual therapist," Veeresh described the Osho Humaniversity he leads as a training, meditation, and therapy center and claimed not to follow a religion.

The talk was most notable for Veeresh's unintentional hilarity. When asked about hugging, he replied: "Yeah, yes, that's what we teach. We're a hugging school. I love hugging. When I met you, I thought that you looked like this image of the Johnny Walker bottle, whisky bottle. Yeah, yeah, you're a warm guy. I like you, man. I like your voice; I heard it for the first time yesterday."

He went on to suggest that all members of the UN should hug before and after meetings ("that would be so beautiful man, wow!") and explained at length how he once threatened to break his son's legs.

Odd as Veeresh may have appeared to Johnnie Walker's traditionally rather staid audience, the fact remains that it's a show listened to by millions in the UK. It marks a new high in the UK for Osho's disciples' continuing quest to present themselves as modern, dynamic therapists rather than an old-fashioned cult.

A JUICY WEEKEND: DORSET, UK

The continuing success of Osho's rehabilitation can be measured by the fact that on the very day I'm writing these words, there's a recommendation to visit the Osho Leela commune in the glossy magazine section of the London *Guardian*, one of Britain's bestselling quality broadsheets. It's the third recommendation in as many years from the paper, and just one of the many that get printed around the world every year by journalists who know little about the group's true nature. "Consider getting your festival fix at the Great British Yoga Festival in Dorset," counsels the writer, next to a photo of the Osho Leela building. Judging by the article, it all sounds like good, healthy fun with talks, workshops, "nice cups of herbal tea," and lights out by 9:30 P.M. The worst thing that's likely to happen to you is that your hair might end up being braided. Anyone clicking on the yoga festival website, meanwhile, will learn that Osho, rather than being a crook, is a "great mystic and teacher."[5]

Of course, as Margaret Hill from Antelope could tell you, the reality of Osho is very different. And, from my own personal experience, I know that there's a bit more to worry about at their communes than hair-braiding.

I spent a weekend at Osho Leela in the autumn of 2005. I was there specifically because I'd developed an interest in the group while writing a book about cults, cranks, and religious eccentrics, *The Joy of Sects*,[6] but I signed up in the guise of a normal punter. I wanted to keep my identity as a journalist with an interest in cults quiet, both so that they would allow me to visit in the first place and because of a vague sense of paranoia about my own safety.

> **The majority of the fifty or so people who had gone to the party didn't think the Osho group was odd at all—for the very good reason that they didn't know anything about its true nature.**

Using the group's website, I put my (false) name down for a "A Yes! Party" [*sic*], just like anyone else can. Described as "mini-festivals," the Yes! weekends offer meditations, workshops, and, according to the promotional literature, "much laughter, play and dancing—not forgetting the great food and cuddles." They are regular events open to the general public and which strangers to the group are actively encouraged to attend. This last element was good news for me, as it meant I could get an inside glimpse into life in Osho Leela without having to declare my interest. More to the point, since so many of the participants were going to be first-timers, it provided a great opportunity to witness first-hand the process by which a normal person can become involved with Osho.

I also hoped to be able to find out why anyone would want to have anything to do with Osho when so much about it and its history seemed downright crazy to me. The answer to this question turned out to be simple. The majority of the fifty or so people who had gone to the party didn't think the Osho group was odd at all—for the very good reason that they didn't know anything about its true nature.

There were several categories of attendee. First, the actual members of the household, who were generally in charge of things. Working closely with them, but performing more menial tasks in the kitchens, gardens, and around the house, were the "volunteers."[7] Then there were the regular visitors who had taken on Sannyasin names and paid large amounts of money to keep coming back to various events. There were also a few people who had been on two or three visits to Osho Leela, and finally there was a large contingent of first-timers like me.

Even the regular Sannyasins seemed to know little about the organization that they were devoting their lives to. There was a limit to how far I could press them about the unmentionable episodes in Antelope, since I was keen not to let on that I was a journalist, but the overwhelming impression I took was that they regarded Osho Leela simply as a place for therapy where they could make friends and kick-start a new life (they often seemed to have ended up in Osho's embrace after personal tragedies: nervous breakdowns, divorces, bankruptcies). Many (particularly a few goaty fifty-something male divorcees) also seemed to regard it as something of an advanced singles' club, frequently dropping lascivious hints throughout the weekend and, as I was eventually to discover, engaging in some decidedly "blue" practices.

Out of the less-regular attendees, a few had been attracted out of an interest in Osho the guru, and a few more were regulars on the UK spiritual circuit and seemed to have a vague idea what Osho was about. Most, however, had not even heard of Osho the person, let alone what he had done. Indeed, videos were shown throughout the weekend with the specific purpose of introducing newbies to the old guru. (Curiously, the one I watched made no mention of guns, nitrous oxide, or Rolls Royces).

The question of why—and how—people with absolutely no knowledge of Osho could end up there is harder to answer. Some seemed to have turned up pretty much on a whim. One girl I spoke to, Jo, said that she had signed up for the party after a brief Internet search. She'd been looking for a therapy weekend, having been treated to one in a hotel once before, where she'd been pampered, massaged, and spent most of her time in the steam room. She'd enjoyed this experience so much, she said, that she wanted something similar again and since Osho Leela had seemed to be the cheapest "therapy center" with easy rail access in the South of England, she'd decided to give it a try.

Naïve as Jo appeared, she did at least have a more savvy friend at home. "He's dead worried about me," she said. "He told me, if it's a cult or anything, you leave, girl."

In spite of this advice, Jo was staying. Osho Leela wasn't quite what she'd been expecting, but she was having a very "interesting" time and wasn't planning on leaving until the weekend was finished.

But if Osho Leela isn't a cult, I don't know what is.

THE MOST STEREOTYPICALLY "cultish" of the weekend's activities were the trademark Osho meditations. Sometimes they were reminiscent of the kind of reality TV exercises employed to humiliate the contestants; at other times they were pretty worrying.

For instance, on my first morning in Osho Leela (after a sleepless night spent in a dorm above a room where techno music blared until 4:30 A.M.), I got up early (7:00) to take part in the infamous Dynamic Meditation, a practice carried through from the good old/bad old days of Osho/Rajneesh.

This meditation was split into fifteen-minute stages.

The first was called "Chaotic Breathing." As intense, arrhythmic drumming sounds boomed out of the stereo (accompanied by other indefinable sounds in the high registers), we were told to breath in and out, hard and fast and in no regular pattern. Several of the participants quickly became wet with sweat, while snot dripped down their fronts.

The disorienting music and hyperventilation induced a panicky, intense atmosphere in the room, one that was only heightened when the second stage was introduced by a loud crash on the stereo and the room erupted around me.

When this next stage had been explained for the benefit of the newcomers, we'd been told that the idea was to expunge all bad thoughts and negative energies from the brain. To do this mind-cleansing, we were expected to shout, scream, and swear at the top of our voices and use our bodies to "let out" our anger. So it was that the people around me began beating cushions (left in the room specifically for the purpose) against the floor, or they used them as protection as they pounded their fists against the walls. A couple of Sannyasins stripped down to their shorts, writhing and stomping, the polished wooden floor around them becoming ever slicker with sweat. One man started spinning round and round on a cushion. A woman lay on her back, her legs furiously pedalling in the air. The noise and pressure were immense. A few other first-timers were looking as self-conscious and uncomfortable as I felt, but most were throwing themselves into it, the hysteria in the room pushing everyone to respond with ever-greater energy.

After all that stress it came as something of a relief that the next stage was just plain, old-fashioned daft—if a little tiring. To the accompaniment of pulsating music, we had to bounce up and down on our heels for another fifteen minutes, our hands in the air, going "Oooh! Oooh! Oooh! Oooh!" until a voice (Osho himself, recorded before his death) shouted: "Stop!"

Next came fifteen minutes of complete silence. The calm was broken only by the labored breathing of participants recovering from their exertions—and one particularly percussive fart around the ten-minute mark. I didn't laugh. The atmosphere forbade it. I noticed when we entered the final stage—fifteen minutes of dancing to fast, soaring Indian music—that several people had tears running down their cheeks.

Afterwards, I was exhausted—and the people around me, who had been participating in all earnest rather than with journalistic skepticism, looked drained. I was surprised by how full-on the experience had been, especially since I thought that the Sannyasins must have softened things considerably for the benefit of the inexperienced attendees at the Yes! Party. The stories of broken limbs and group sex from the 1970s and 1980s were beginning to seem far less outlandish....

ALONGSIDE THE MEDITATIONS, several other characteristics of the weekend were likely to affect participants' minds and emotions. One of the first things we were told upon arrival was that English people never hug properly. A proper Osho hug, we were informed, was far better. The correct procedure was to make "a foot sandwich" so that your legs are interspaced with your partner's, then twist so that your chest is pressed against theirs and hold still. During this time, the experienced Sannyasins would let out deep sighs and pornstar-style "ahhh" noises. After a good thirty seconds of squeezing, the embrace was released so that you could move to the next person. The whole thing generally went on for about quarter of an hour—long enough to ensure that you hugged every person in the room at least once.

There was a hugging session in the evening when we arrived, another directly after the Dynamic Meditation, another after lunch.... I tried to avoid them as much as possible but still ended up taking part in five. I learned the aroma of more complete strangers' armpits in one weekend than I had in the whole of the rest of my life. And if this enforced intimacy felt like an assault on my boundaries, that was exactly intended. One of the first things that Dhyano, the founder of the commune and leader of that weekend's activities, explained was that to refuse a hug was to "come on all English": with all that cold reserve and all those dreadful hang-ups about personal space. It was thinking with the head instead of the heart. Keeping a safe distance was weak. "None of us die safe at Osho," he declared proudly.

Most anti-cult activists say that the breaking down of boundaries and the intense physical- and emotional-bonding exercises—like the Osho hugging—are a common characteristic of most dangerous cults. It's one of the primary ways they create a tie to the group—a tie of guilt and fear (as much as affection) for anyone who might be thinking of leaving.

"Babies die without love," Dhyano told us. "In orphanages children can't survive." No evidence was provided to support these bizarre claims, nor his most alarming pronouncement: "If you're alone, you will wither and die."

THE COROLLARY TO THIS intense bonding within most cults is the creation of an extreme "us and them" mentality between the group and the outside world. The frequent references made over the course of the weekend to the deficiency of English nature and the superiority of the sannyasin way was indicative that such conditioning was on the agenda at Osho Leela. Even more emphatic was the workshop I attended following the Dynamic Meditation. The subject was "nonviolent communication."

Nonviolent communication, we were told, is "a way to learn how to listen empathically and communicate our authentic feelings and needs." In reality, it's a method that stigmatizes everyday language—and, therefore, everyone who speaks it (that is, everyone who hasn't taken the course—i.e., almost everyone outside Osho).

The workshop teacher, a man called Michael, arranged on the floor a series of cards with words and phrases printed on them, such as "Demand," "Threat," "You are," "I am," "Punish," "Sorry." These, we were told, are examples of "jackal" language. Words that bad people use. Attaching two puppets—a giraffe and a "naughty jackal"—to his hands to help make his points, Michael explained that he wanted us to talk with our hearts rather than our heads (the need not to think being another theme that was cropping up again and again over the weekend). He warned us to be "self-full" rather than "selfless" or "selfish" and to beware the kind of language—heavy in demands and hard logic—that "jackals" would use to trick us. We weren't supposed to say "sorry," because that is "a demand for absolution." We weren't supposed to use the verb "to be" too often, as that "labelled" people.

> was really touched by the way you brought me
> at dinner. It satisfied my inner need for beauty."

These language strictures resulted in some strange combinations. For instance, Michael suggested that instead of saying, "That was a good dinner" ("a meaningless and labelling construction"), we should say to the cook: "I was really touched by the way you brought me that dinner. It satisfied my inner need for beauty."

Of course, it was ridiculous and laughable. But no one else was smiling. By the end of the workshop, Michael had even managed to reduce one girl to floods of tears as she was made to relive an argument she'd recently had with a friend and asked to think of the "nonviolent" way of resolving it. There was no doubting that she was taking all this very seriously even though Michael had made her wear a pair of giraffe ears and talk what was, essentially, nonsense.

BRAINWASHING IS A controversial subject. Ever since American GIs captured during the Korean War returned home, talking about how great communism is, there's been hot debate about what constitutes brainwashing—and whether, indeed, it actually works. Anti-cult groups are convinced that some sinister organizations have been using mind control techniques for years, but medical opinion is divided. The term is too emotive—with its redolence of Cold War propaganda and paranoia—and it's too hard to test "brainwashing" situations in a controlled way for any theories to be completely scientific. Another problem is that some people seem far more open to mind control than others, leading many who've researched purported brainwashing cults to conclude that people have to *want* to be indoctrinated, or at least be open to suggestion, before mental coercion can occur... in which case it's not really coercion at all.

However, while the jury is still out on brainwashing, as any good-cop/bad-cop torture team can tell you, there are definitely a few things you can do to alter people's mental state and to make them more open to suggestion and manipulation. Deprive them of sleep. Exhaust them mentally and physically. Subject them to extremes of pain and pleasure. Be nice to them, then scream at them like a maniac....

The attendees at the Yes! Party all encountered varying degrees of this treatment. The meditations were all physically tiring, as well as mentally exhausting; the highs and lows of the screaming sessions followed by intense group-hugging must have played fury with participants' dopamine levels. The jumping, dancing, and cushion-pummelling ensured that most participants were reduced to sweating, quivering messes.

> The jumping, dancing, and cushion-pummelling
> ensured that most participants were reduced to
> sweating, quivering messes.

Meanwhile, even by Saturday afternoon, with a full (largely sleepless) twenty-four hours still to go, the wakefulness enforced by the all-night music and dancing was already taking its toll on the bleary-eyed, puffy-skinned people who wondered zombie-like around the compound. The strange atmosphere of the weekend was only increased by the sight of men and women passing out in chairs, dozing off while eating dinner, and, in the case of the "art class" I took part in after the nonviolent communication workshop, lying flat on their backs and snoring while other people scribbled on the floor around them.

In Osho's defense, I should note that this constant, loud music and impossibility of getting a good night's sleep was the only unavoidable facet of the weekend. Nobody *had* to take part in any of the other activities, and they were free to leave at anytime. Indeed, I sneaked away to visit a local pub on Saturday afternoon instead of taking part in a group "Love Meditation" (a high point in my weekend).

All the same, even if there were no rules about attendance and there was certainly no physical coercion, there was a lot of peer pressure to take part in everything, ensuring that Osho ticked yet another box on most cult-watchers' checklists.

I noticed several people around my dorm being

We had to go around the room, encountering as many different people as possible, shouting and screaming that we hated them—alongside any other obscenities that sprang to mind.

questioned intensely throughout the weekend. They were forced into making excuses about why they hadn't been to various meditations and left looking embarrassed and even ashamed. I personally had been cornered several times by the end of the second day and told that I needed to participate more and try harder.

"The more you put in, the more you get out," one man I'd never met before yelled at me, naked and dripping with sweat in the communal dorm, angry that I'd missed the afternoon's activities when I'd slipped out to the pub.

"You've just got to do it.... No point in half-measures. Come on!" someone else urged me less than five minutes later. And so it went on.

Meanwhile, although some people who had come back from the "Love Meditation" that I'd skipped looked like all their Christmases had just come at once, others looked ashen-faced and sullen, especially those who were visiting Osho Leela for the first time. "It was a bit much," said a man called John (who only the night before had been bright-eyed and telling me how much he'd been looking forward to having a new experience that weekend). He didn't think he was going to come to Leela again. He wasn't even going to try the main event of the weekend—the following morning's Aum Meditation.

THE AUM MEDITATION took place on Sunday morning. I already had a reasonable idea of what to expect thanks to a session the night before in which Amira, one of the full-time residents, explained the meaning and techniques behind the various unusual rites we were expected to perform. All the same, nothing could have completely prepared me for the real thing.

As performed at the Yes! Party, the Aum was three hours long, split into twelve stages of fifteen minutes.

The first stage was called the "Return To Hell." We'd been told in the pep talk that as in the shouting stage of the Dynamic Meditation, the aim of the exercise was to get rid of all our "negative emotions" by "continuously exhausting" ourselves. The difference was that this time we had to go around the room, encountering as many different people as possible, shouting and screaming that we hated them—alongside any other obscenities that sprang to mind.

The reason for all this, we were told, was that "cancer arises from unexpressed anger," so we needed to get rid of it. The frenzied shouting, combined with another weird soundtrack on the stereo, created one of the most unhinged scenes I have witnessed in my career.

And that was just the beginning. The second stage was far quieter but more unsettling in its way. It was called "Heaven." Now we were expected to go around the room, telling each person individually that we loved him or her, with just as much passion as we had been screaming at them in the previous stage. "I love you," I had to say to complete strangers, looking them straight in the eye. It felt like a betrayal of all the people outside Osho whom I really did love.

One man fell at my feet in a convulsive fit.

The third stage, "Second Wind," involved fifteen minutes of running on the spot, arms in the air. It was physically tiring but a relief after all that forced intense interaction and emotional display. The same went for the fourth stage, "Kundalini Rising": fifteen minutes of continually shaking the entire body, which certainly looked (and felt) strange but was relatively innocuous compared to what followed. Labelled "The Cuckoo's Nest," this was the strangest of all the sections of the meditation. It involved fifteen minutes of acting "as mad as you can be." We were told to scream, shout, cry, jump, have tantrums, act like a mental patient if we could....

The reason for this?

"You'll never go mad if you freak out."

The practice was just as dubious as the science. Most people in the room were whipped into a state of extreme hysteria. Some even started going into spasms. One man fell at my feet in a convulsive fit.

He was foaming at the mouth, so the Sannyasins in black T-shirts (who were there to ensure that nothing went wrong during the Aum) took him to one side of the room and propped him up on cushions.... And when he came around, they sent him back into the maelstrom.

We descended from that sharp emotional peak with fifteen minutes of dancing, then fifteen minutes of crying (which we'd been told the night before "helps the brain chemistry turn from depression to feeling good"), and then fifteen minutes of laughing. The laughing stage was creepy. It felt like being in a room with fifty people doing impressions of the Joker from *Batman*. Or forty-five, I should say, because a handful of people had been unable to stop the uncontrollable weeping they'd entered during the crying stage.

The ninth stage was called the "Dance of the Lovers" and rather alarmingly entailed dancing in a "sensual and sexual way" with other people around the room. We'd been asked to "allow" ourselves "to take a risk." I had no desire to do anything of the sort, but it turned out, I didn't have much choice.

Already shattered from all that had gone before, I moved to the side of the room, intending to keep out of things. Most other participants joined in near-orgies, dry-rutting as a deep, Barry White-esque voice boomed over the sound system about how "nice and sexy" everyone was feeling and how much we all loved Osho...to the accompaniment of moaning sounds and crazy trance music. Several girls were crying. They didn't seem to like it, either. My attention was diverted from their plight, however, when two (much older) female Sannyasins came towards me. I told them I wanted to be left alone, and according to the explanation we'd been given the night before, that should have been that. Instead, they grabbed me, sandwiched me, and started frotting me.

I'm aware that this "Sam-sandwich" sounds pretty funny. And I'm sure that the look on my face was absolutely priceless while it was going on. As the cliché goes, I can laugh about it now, but at the time it was terrible. At the time, it seemed less like a good dinner-party anecdote and more like molestation.

The only way out seemed to be to overpower the two overenthusiastic ladies, a prospect I was beginning to seriously contemplate when I was rescued by the sudden malfunction of the stereo system. As the CD began to skip, I was able to push myself clear without using too much force, spending the rest of that particular stage by the water cooler, feeling very odd indeed.

The three remaining stages were all extreme and unpleasant in their way, too, but by then my attempt at objective observation had collapsed, my one aim being to keep my mind clear and just endure the meditation until I was free to leave. I went though it all on autopilot: fifteen minutes of chanting *ohm* in a circle, fifteen minutes of complete silence, and then that Osho favourite, fifteen minutes of intense hugging.

It was three hours I never want to repeat. Judging by the faces of others around the room, it had had a similarly intense effect on them. But our experience palls in comparison to what the full-time Sannyasins put themselves through and what it really means to be a dedicated follower of Osho today.

Amira had hinted darkly during his pep talk the night before the Aum Meditation that "The Dance of the Lovers" could get much more serious. Even more unsettling was his proud declaration that the Aum should really go on for days. He himself had been on a five-day Aum marathon. For three of those days, he'd gone without sleep ("a *big* thing for heightening emotions," he explained). He'd only finally stopped when, he said, "one guy became completely catatonic."

BY THE END of the Aum, I was eager to leave, already convinced that despite their efforts to forget the past, the Osho group was already repeating it (to paraphrase George Santayana). I also felt that I'd been made to throw off quite enough of my "typically English" reserve.

The excitement wasn't quite over, however. During Amira's evening talk about the Aum, I'd taken the opportunity to snap a few photos of the

"You better not publish those photos, man," he said.

Sannyasins who were helping him to demonstrate the weird rites. That turned out to be a mistake. Soon afterwards I'd been approached twice in quick succession—first by Amira himself, then by Dhyano, the commune's founder. They'd both demanded to know (in as aggressive a way as possible for people who insisted on communicating "nonviolently") why I was taking pictures and what I intended to do with them. The following morning, as I sat panting in the main hall with all the other people who'd taken part in the Aum, Dhyano made me raise my hand, informing everyone that a "snapper" was present and making sure they all got a good look at me.

It was time to leave.

I made my exit soon after the meeting was over, and my already tired and paranoid brain had decided that sticking around was going to, at the very least, cost me my camera and what little dignity I had left.

My last contact with an Osho follower came as I packed my bag and hurried out of the dormitory.

"You better not publish those photos, man," he said. "There are governments that want to shut us down. They don't like people supporting themselves or being happy."

I should have asked in return what possible harm would come through publication of the photos if Osho had nothing to hide. It might have been pertinent, too, to inquire why, if Osho Leela was a mainstream therapy center as it purported to be, they'd object to someone explaining what went on there. I could also have pointed out that no one had seemed at all "happy" to me and that the only people supporting themselves were the group leaders, while most other people appeared to be parting with an awful lot of money.

Of course, by the time I'd thought of all that, it was too late. I was already in my car, eager to put a good few-hundred miles between Osho Leela and myself. When the heat was on, I'd simply made a weak joke about how my photos probably wouldn't be good enough to print anyway (true

enough, as it turned out) and wished him luck for the future (he was another man drawn in by Osho following a recent bankruptcy). My feeling of culpability and personal dishonesty added to the already uneasy mix of fatigue, paranoia, and disorientation that the weekend had instilled. My conscience was clear on one point, however; the story of Osho Leela was one that should be told. I'm convinced that it's still a cult and potentially dangerous for anyone that goes there.

---

1. "Sannyasin" is the name given to Osho devotees after they have given up their old name and taken a new one approved by the cult. Hence, all the Amiras, Sheelas, Dhyanos, Pragits, and Jamusheens etc. that will appear in this narrative.

2. Osho was a laughing-gas addict for most of the rest of his life. Trivia fans will be interested to learn that it's been estimated he took more than any other person before or since, largely through spigots attached to the walls wherever he lived.

3. I had a brief correspondence with Tim Guest while writing this article. While extremely helpful and courteous, he felt unable to contribute any comment on Osho now, saying: "I'm quite keen to leave the world of sannyasins behind, as in my experience those still connected to the movement tend to get very aggravated with people who have a different take on Osho than them."

4. AIDS became a major bugbear of Osho's during the later years of his life—hardly surprising given all the free love that he encouraged. He described the virus as a spiritual malaise as well as a disease and became increasingly anxious that it get nowhere near him.

5. Just type "Osho meditation" into Google to see how many there are. I later asked the journalist who wrote this article if he'd heard of Osho's history. He hadn't. He also said he now thought Osho were "possibly unsavoury" and that he was "concerned" and "disappointed" that the yoga festival provided a link to the Osho website on its own site.

6. My chapter on Bhagwan Shree Rajneesh forms the bulk of the first two parts of this article.

7. The volunteer I managed to speak to was a recent immigrant to the UK and spoke little English, but did manage to tell me that sometimes he was "allowed an hour off" from work, when he could go for a walk. His story in itself was probably worth an article, if only I'd had been able to speak to him properly.

Earl Kemp

JUNGLE DRUMS OF THE EVIL I

FATE AND MOTHER NATURE, my constant companions and true gods, took me on long, leisurely trips to far-off exotic places where I could indulge my lifelong research into comparative religions. I couldn't believe the things I encountered...poor, starving people giving their last penny to the Church, walking on their knees—bloody and shredded—for blocks just to be privileged enough to give that last penny to the obscenely rich Church. The Vatican, itself a depository of the world's riches, robbed, pilfered, and stolen from everywhere and housed there for the benefit of the very few.

Islamics in North Africa, treating me with respect and recognizing my earnest search for knowledge, showing me how they responded to Allah by facing Mecca at fixed times of the day and in ritualistic adoration.

In Japan I had a number of close friends who tried to explain Buddhism to me, and took me with them to their shrines and on visits to pay respect to those incredible fat-bellied statues.

In Mexico I spent quite a bit of time with *brujos* and *brujas*—white witch doctors—and skirted around the fringes of Santería, almost devil-worshiping, only it was far too bloody and ridiculous for me to seriously contemplate. I did, though, thoroughly appreciate their belief that consuming large amounts of cannabis could make one invisible. I really tried, but remained very noticeably in sight.

Also in Mexico, living amid the Wichole Indians of Jalisco, I learned the truer meanings of meditation augmented by ingesting the sacred peyote.

In Jamaica I was taught the ecstatic delights of ganja-laced Rastafarianism while listening to the wailing tunes of Bob Marley.

For a surprisingly long time I was a member of the Maccabees, studying Hebrew, making proper responses to the rote readings, and celebrating their special holidays.

I did, though, thoroughly appreciate their belief that consuming large amounts of cannabis could make one invisible.

And, at the bottom of the pit of homogenized knowledge, I determined that most of them were quite similar except for the names of God and the things one was expected to do for him.

The more I learned, the surer I was that I was God. Fortunately for me, I was a much more benevolent deity than the one a large number of brainwashed humanity thought existed but doesn't.

Yet there was still one religion that I felt compelled to explore, just in case I belonged there and didn't yet know it. The elusive, mystical Macumba!

Spirits and gods became saints, Mary, and Jesus. Out of this, Macumba was born.

BRAZIL HAD BEEN a cherished dream for me for many years...going there...being one with the people...perhaps living there for the rest of my life. Many times I not only dreamed of doing just that but also researched the possibilities and checked on land prices and cost-of-living expenses. I even had at least two positive plans to proceed as fast as I could toward those goals.

Rio de Janeiro was, in my thoughts, the ultimate place in which to live out the rest of my god-like days.

I went there at the first opportunity, loaded with loot, with real intent never to return to the USA. I found it ideal for all of my purposes. The people were beautiful, warm, sensual, and responsive, especially the women, who seemed to undulate with a samba rhythm that pulsed through their entire bodies. Copacabana, Ipanema, Sugarloaf...my kind of town.

While I knew a smattering of Spanish, I couldn't understand a word of Portuguese. Fortunately, for my first tour of Rio, I was traveling with Toni Austin, a beautiful young schoolteacher from New York City and a devout Catholic. She taught Spanish but knew enough Portuguese to converse almost fluently everywhere we went. And, more to the point, being a devout Catholic, she was also very interested in examining Macumba to see how it differed from her personal indoctrinations. In the end, the differences almost blew her away.

BACK IN THE SIXTEENTH century, when the Holy See was running roughshod over most of the New World with torture chambers and a "we will kill you if you don't accept our God" mentality, the African slaves who were brought to Brazil in the 1500s decided on a quick fix that has lasted until now and served them well. Their masters forbade them to practice any religion or spirit-worship they might have brought with them in the transition to South America, and ordered them to accept the doctrines of the Catholic Church as their own.

Of course they didn't...they only appeared to do so by mixing their true beliefs with Catholicism. Spirits and gods became saints, Mary, and Jesus. Out of this, Macumba was born. Even after the slaves were freed in 1888, this syncretic religion lived on.

The owners allowed the slaves to continue their rituals of drum-beating that literally were the origins of the samba, the musical rhythm of the saints, the undulating sounds that most Brazilians unconsciously march to.

The black spirit-worshipers brought two denominations with them to Brazil. One of them was named Candomble and the other Umbanda—an updated version of Niteroi—and the two of them merged and became Macumba, the word literally meaning "Sanctuary."

The factions were almost like two sides of the same coin. Umbanda was the side that represented all things good, and Quimbanda was the evil side, toward which all its powers were devoted.

These African-based spirit-worshipers represent the very basic elements of the myths on which these two divisions are based. For the people who believe in those solid dualistic foundations, the entire universe is divided into just those two elements, good versus evil, and they relate to each other through intangible and mysterious ways to defend and attack each other. Both Candomble and Umbanda possess enough power to counteract the other.

Ironically, a large amount of the energy expended in paying attention to Macumba and observing its admonitions is centered on love, sex, and individual happiness. A little hex here and a little hex there could lead to the little sex that was constantly missing.

The rituals and objectives of Macumba are focused a great deal less on things divine and celestial and a great deal more on the commonplace annoyances that plague day-to-day life for the average citizen of Rio de Janeiro, a densely populated, major metropolis wherein the constant inequality separating the haves and the have-nots breeds a lot of resentment and envy. All kinds of harmful vibrations rest heavily upon the citizens, causing all manner of stress and collateral physical and mental damage to the true believers. And make no mistake about that...they are indeed true believers, and they take the "evil eye" quite seriously, confident in the fact that it can gaze upon them at any time, anywhere, and without warning, crippling them extensively, preventing them from achieving their more sought-after goals.

he next taxi driver in line merely crossed himself atholic-style and turned his back to us.

I FOUND THE CONCIERGE at the Sheraton Rio to be particularly condescending, but then most of them are. He referred me to a couple of fantastic nightclubs, for instance, where the floorshows began promptly at midnight and weren't over until 4 A.M. Where the dancers and musicians and partygoers intermingled to pulse-pounding rhythms of loud jungle music reinforced by double-strength alcoholic drinks. By the time the performance is over, it doesn't matter that you don't understand any Portuguese—the body language, the sensuality, the overt sexuality have all been enough to have you standing on your feet, pounding the tabletop along with the heartbeat of the crowd.

It was only when Toni and I asked the concierge to refer us to a Macumba church on Sunday morning that he balked. Guidebooks said there were more than 65,000 Macumba churches in Rio alone, with uncountable millions of "Catholics" congregating there. Nevertheless, the concierge pretended that he didn't know what it was, that there was no such thing, that I was somehow very mistaken, and, above all, he admonished me to "not go there at all...."

Outside the four-star hotel, I approached the first taxi in line at the designated spot near the curb and asked the driver to take Toni and me to the closest Macumba church. He stared at me in astonishment and shook his head in a definite *no*.

The next taxi driver in line merely crossed himself Catholic-style and turned his back to us.

The third driver walked away without responding in any fashion.

Frustrated, Toni and I walked away from the hotel down a side street, finally stepping to the curb and flagging a passing taxi. This time we got in before the driver could drive away. In her halting Portuguese, Toni told him to take us to a Macumba church.

The driver was aghast. At first he flatly refused, but as Toni kept insisting and I kept flashing more and more money at him, he reluctantly agreed, turning the next corner and heading across town to we knew not where. After a short drive, he pulled the cab to the curb and opened the door for us.

"This is as far as I can go," he said. "Past this point only danger lies for me, and it's much worse for you." He crossed himself, as if doing so would protect him from those unknown evils lurking there in wait, already shining their all-seeing evil eye upon him and questioning his motives in bringing us heretics this close.

"It's the big building you see there just at the corner, a block away," he said, turning his back on the structure before the evil eye could recognize him and mark him forever. "On the second floor."

I overpaid him, and we walked to the church through the early morning pedestrians, our hangovers still throbbing in our heads from the previous night's—this morning's—reveling with the samba and the befeathered, braless chorus line we had eagerly joined in our own abandonment.

There was a regulation storefront of some sort on the ground floor, and we found a flight of stairs leading up to the sanctuary itself. Just as we entered the church, moving into some form of anteroom, we were met by what could, under other circumstances, be a barroom bouncer. He was firm and unmovable and insisted that we had no right being there at all.

Toni, in Portuguese, persisted and insisted upon our right to enter the sanctuary and to observe the services. Finally, and obviously under duress, he said that we could go inside but first it would be necessary for Toni to put on a dress because the denim jeans she was wearing—or any form of masculine attire—were not permitted on a female. From a huge closet full of clothes he selected a tent-like, flower-print mumu and told Toni to put it on over her blouse and jeans. It dragged the floor and completely covered her very unmasculine pants.

We were also told to remove our shoes and carry them with us into the sanctuary. As we entered the doorway, a second bouncer separated us. It seems that men and women aren't allowed to sit together inside the sanctuary but were separated by a wide aisle right through the center, sort of like groom's side/bride's side at stateside weddings.

SITTING THERE ALONE, with all the other church-goers visibly shrinking away and glaring accusingly toward us, without the comfort and security of each other, I felt weakened and vulnerable. Later, Toni confessed that she did, as well.

It was, however, the pure Catholic trappings that did the most harm to Toni while not bothering me at all. For all practical purposes, the inside of the sanctuary looked like the inside of every small-town Catholic church I had ever visited. The same high-arched ceiling, large stained-glass windows, and familiar statuary.

Only they were all black. My very first black Jesus on the cross, a black Mary mother of same, blacks in stained glass, with the old, familiar saints all as equally black. The shock to Toni was visible from across the aisle—I could see her grimacing in pain, the fear of her own religious indoctrination grabbing at her with forceful, almost tangible threats.

Candles burning in votive glasses gave off a faint, sweet aroma that conflicted with the adrenaline-rush, anticipation perspiration coming profusely from the devotees. Somewhere in the distance beyond the drummers and musicians, floral incense was burning.

The service began with the Gira, a form of sacred dance with music and the ever-present beat of African drums. It is within this performance that the dancers connect with and raise the souls of the dead to take possession of them and guide them through the consultations of the day.

There was a "Mother," the Babalao, the spiritual guide of the church, the high priestess incarnate. The Mother and a number of mediums performed this dance. Some were men, but men never get to be Babalaos. Macumba was created as a matriarchal religion. All of the dancers were barefoot and dressed in white cotton dresses or pants, with white bandanas covering their heads like slaves from the early 1500s.

The dance itself was circular, with all of them moving around the area, undulating and dipping in unison. It is through this dance that they receive spiritual guides to lead them through the rest of the ceremonies. As the spirits of the dead overtook the dancers, they switched into a rapid, shaky rhythm, indicating that they were possessed.

As the spirits of the dead overtook the dancers, they switched into a rapid, shaky rhythm, indicating that they were possessed.

The Mother and the mediums separated and moved to stools placed around the floor in specific areas. Sitting upon those low, little stools, from inside their white cotton attire they produced cigars or pipes and plastic lighters—and proceeded to light up, inhale, and relax.

I was seated quite near the front of the church, on the aisle in the second bench. The smoke from Mother's rancid old pipe was clearly troublesome, mingling as it was with the tinge of dirty feet and rotten shoes I kept trying to ignore. I couldn't figure out what type of herb was in that pipe, and I thought I was pretty up on things like that in those halcyon days.

Following the dance, the devotees from the audience who had paid a fee were then allowed to approach at random the Mother or one of the mediums (guides, counselors) for help with their individual problems. By twos, they isolated themselves and delved into the devotee's concern. This was Macumba's counterpart to the part of Catholicism that really jolted Toni: the confessional. The Macumba devotees crouched on their haunches before the medium on the stool. They whispered confidentially for a bit. The medium made a few hand passes close to the devotee, touching them rarely and reluctantly, telling them their pleas have been answered.

It could be the usual—"Make her fall in love with me," or, "My upstairs neighbor has put a hex on me so I can't sleep. Take it away and put it on him," or, "Make me rich and handsome." All the normal things that plague most of us, just a little askew and apart from reality.

The guides purified the devotees, promised to make their wishes come true, and received tokens of the devotee's appreciation slipped into their hands during the hand passes of the purification process.

When there are real problems, major sicknesses to be eradicated, tangible demons to be exorcised, stronger measures are necessary. While Toni and I watched the services unfolding in that Macumba sanctuary, a number of live chickens were sacrificed...and one nanny goat.

Only the Babalao can make these sacrifices. They took place very quickly; you could've missed any of them completely by turning your head aside for just a moment. They were clean kills, almost antiseptic. The Mother was so adept from long years of practice that hardly any blood was shed, no drops or crimson spatter on her pristine, white cotton clothing. And, though I was watching quite intently, I never saw the instrument used for the killings.

There was one brief view of fresh red blood from the goat's slaughter, but minions from offstage dashed in and removed all traces and dashed out again in just a few seconds. They removed the dead animals with as much dispatch. I often wonder what happened to the meat of the animals sacrificed in that one Macumba church alone. Hopefully, it was used to feed the needy like the meat after bullfights.

Then, with a slowly fading jungle drumbeat, the entire service concluded, the devotees' urgent needs attended to, and worshipers began leaving the bench seats and the sanctuary. Toni and I paused in the anteroom long enough to return her borrowed mumu to Omar the cloakroom attendant before putting on our shoes and heading down those stairs as quickly as we could.

I looked back, just once, as we were nearing the street corner. At just that moment, like in a special-effects scene from a movie, the Sunday morning sun struck the lone evil eye in glorious stained glass high atop the church. The bouncing ray of that sunbathed, all-seeing evil eye struck me dead center before I could turn the corner and escape its devious clutches forever.

Within only minutes and a block away from the church, we flagged a taxi to take us back to the Sheraton Rio.

There was one brief view of fresh red blood from the goat's slaughter, but minions from offstage dashed in and removed all traces and dashed out again in just a few seconds.

IN OUR ROOM, cuddling an ice-filled champagne bucket holding a pitcher of grand-larceny room-service martinis, Toni and I settled back to relax and passed one of the four big indica doobies that the bellhop just happened to have on him in case we were interested.

The luxurious taste of the Stolichnaya mingled with the heavenly skunkweed flavor of the indica as it swirled around us, enveloping us in glorious ecstasy as we writhed there on the Sheraton Rio's queen-sized bed.

The ever-increasing, pulsing beat of jungle drums seemed to be coming from all around us as I did my best godlike thing while we eagerly waited for the Rapture to come with a divine orgasmic rush of lust.

Photos and Text by **Kristan Lawson**

SACRED SPOTS

CORPSES, THORNS, BMW COFFINS, A HYMEN-RESTORING SPRING,

AND OTHER RELIGIOUS RELICS AND PLACES

Photographer's note: Cameras are forbidden at many of these sites, so some of these pictures were taken surreptitiously. Specifically, forbidden photos were snapped of the thorns from the Crown of Thorns, the ghostly handprint, the mural in the church of Santo Stefano Rotondo, the grotto of the Last Judgment, the sacrificial BMW, and the mummified Capuchin monk (the ban on photographing the Capuchin monks may no longer be in place).

Preserved body of Santa Zita, in the Church of San Frediano (Lucca, Italy). Zita was a poor thirteenth-century servant girl whose saintliness was based not on any tragic martyrdom or flamboyant miracles but rather on her humility and simplicity. When her body was exhumed 300 years after her death, it was found to be "incorrupt," or undecayed. It was put on display in her favorite church, and it's been there ever since in a glass coffin. Over the years, her corpse has begun to crumble a bit, but she remains one of the better-preserved saints in Europe.

Ghostly handprint on a German religious book, in the Museum of the Souls of the Dead, in the church of Santa Cuore in Suffragio (Rome, Italy). In traditional Catholic theology, good people who nonetheless die with minor sins on their souls end up in Purgatory, sort of a temporary hell where the sins are expiated before the deceased can finally enter heaven. The expiation process can be helped along and accelerated by the prayers of those still alive. But not everybody remembers to pray for relatives still stuck in Purgatory, which—though temporary—is still as terrible as hell for the time you're there. So, some souls, eager to escape to heaven as soon as possible, will reach out from Purgatory to remind the living to keep those prayers coming. The standard reminder technique is to lay a spirit hand on whatever book a relative happens to be reading at the time. Because Purgatory is, literally, as hot as hell, the spirit hand will burn an impression into the pages. Rome's Museum of the Souls of the Dead houses the world's only collection of such objects, which include not only books but nightgowns and hats, all bearing the telltale burned handprints of spirits suffering in Purgatory.

Preserved body of Santa Zita, in the Church of San Frediano (Lucca, Italy).

Ghostly handprint on a German religious book, in the Museum of the Souls of the Dead, in the church of Santa Cuore in Suffragio (Rome, Italy).

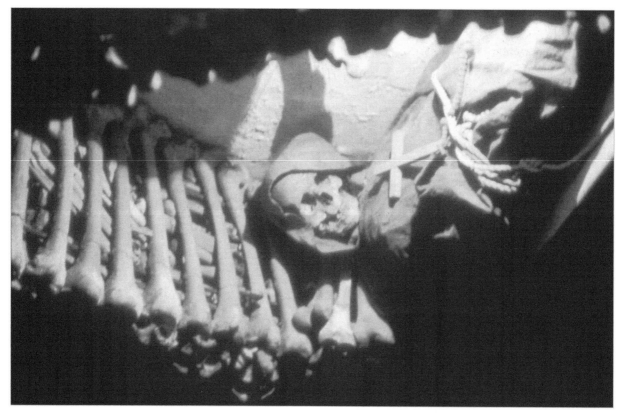

Mummified Capuchin monk, in the crypt of the Chiesa Immacolata Concezione (Rome, Italy).

Two thorns from the Crown of Thorns, in the church of Santa Croce in Gerusalemme (Rome, Italy).

Gruesome religious mural, in the church of Santo Stefano Rotondo (Rome, Italy).

EVERYTHING YOU KNOW ABOUT GOD IS WRONG

Mummified Capuchin monk, in the crypt of the Chiesa Immacolata Concezione (Rome, Italy). The basement of this antique church has served for centuries as an ossuary for the bones of deceased Capuchin monks. While most of their skeletons have been disassembled and rearranged in geometric patterns around the crypt, a few lucky brothers have been left intact, where they lounge for eternity in bone-lined niches along the wall.

Two thorns from the Crown of Thorns, in the church of Santa Croce in Gerusalemme (Rome, Italy). This little-known church contains the greatest collection of alleged relics from the crucifixion of Jesus anywhere on earth. Among the many relics on display are bits of the True Cross, a nail that affixed Jesus to the Cross, the original "INRI" sign, the finger of St. "Doubting" Thomas, who touched the wounds of the resurrected Christ, and much more—including the two thorns pictured here, taken from the Crown of Thorns that the Roman legionnaires were said to have placed on Jesus' head. The origins of most of these relics are obscure, and their authenticity is unknown.

Grotto of the Last Judgment (Brantome, France).

Gruesome religious mural, in the church of Santo Stefano Rotondo (Rome, Italy). The round church of Santo Stefano Rotondo is among the oldest in Italy, dating to the fifth century C.E. A thousand years after it was built, the artists Niccolo Pomarancio and Antonio Tempesta covered its interior walls with the most violent religious imagery ever seen in a church. This particular scene apparently depicts the "Slaughter of the Innocents," when Herod ordered his soldiers to kill all the babies in Bethlehem because one of them might grow up to become the King of the Jews. In 1845, Charles Dickens visited the church and wrote what remains the most famous description of its murals: "But S. Stefano Rotondo, a damp, mildewed vault of an old church in the outskirts of Rome, will always struggle uppermost in my mind, by reason of the hideous paintings with which its walls are covered. These represent the martyrdoms of saints and early Christians; and such a panorama of horror and butchery no man could imagine in his sleep, though he were to eat a whole pig raw, for supper. Grey-bearded men being boiled, fried, grilled, crimped, singed, eaten by wild beasts, worried by dogs, buried alive, torn asunder by horses, chopped up small with hatchets: women having their breasts torn with iron pinchers, their tongues cut out, their ears screwed off, their jaws broken, their bodies stretched upon the rack, or skinned upon the stake, or crackled up and melted in the fire: these are among the mildest subjects."

Grotto of the Last Judgment (Brantome, France). Brantome's series of underground chambers and cliffside grottos was carved by an order of medieval monks sometime around the twelfth century. Into the soft chalk walls are carved a series of bizarre religious bas-reliefs whose purpose and significance are still unknown. Chief among them is this massive throned figure above two horn-playing angels and a crowned head. It is thought to be among the earliest known representations of the Judeo-Christian God himself. (Traditionally, Jews are forbidden to create depictions of God, a prohibition followed by early Christians, as well.) By the Renaissance, artists like Michelangelo felt free to depict God, but in the Middle Ages it still wasn't permitted, which is why the Grotto of the Last Judgment is so remarkable.

The Spring of Kanathos, Aghia Moni convent (Nafplion, Greece).

Girls praying at the Lover's Rock shrine (Hong Kong Island, Hong Kong).

EVERYTHING YOU KNOW ABOUT GOD IS WRONG

Sacrificial BMW, Yuen Yuen Institute (Tsuen Wan, Hong Kong).

The Spring of Kanathos, Aghia Moni convent (Nafplion, Greece). The Greek goddess Hera, according to legend, restored her virginity every year by bathing in the magical Spring of Kanathos. Long after Greece was Christianized, even up to the twentieth century, young brides-to-be who were already sexually active would bathe in the spring before getting married, in the belief that it would restore their virginity not just metaphorically but physically—enough to convince their husbands of their wedding-night purity. Incredibly, the spring still exists and is now (fittingly) on the grounds of a Greek Orthodox convent, where the nuns use the water for drinking. The spring emerges from a small shrine on the side of a hill next to the convent, then trickles into the pool depicted here. Despite its legendary association, the site is completely ignored by tourists. It is not known whether the nuns allow bathing in the pool.

Girls praying at the Lover's Rock shrine (Hong Kong Island, Hong Kong). Lover's Rock—known as Yan Yuen Sek in Cantonese—is a natural thirty-foot-high outcrop overlooking the Wan Chai District on Hong Kong Island. Because of its naturally phallic appearance, since time immemorial it has been used as a "love shrine," where women and girls go to pray for success in attracting men. Even in the hustle and bustle of twenty-first-century Hong Kong, Lover's Rock remains popular among locals—such as this trio of teenage girls making offerings in hope of getting boyfriends.

Sacrificial BMW, Yuen Yuen Institute (Tsuen Wan, Hong Kong). The Yuen Yuen Institute in Hong Kong's New Territories is a combination Taoist, Buddhist, and Confucian temple complex that specializes in elaborate funerals. Locals believe that any representative object burned at a funeral will arrive in the afterlife to the benefit of the deceased. Hence, an endless parade of papier-mâché luxury goods go up in flames at the Institute's death rituals. In this scene, workers pour a bag of "hell money" (faux cash sent to the dead) into a mini BMW sedan. After it's been burned, the person whose funeral this is can drive around forever in the hereafter, spending like a king.

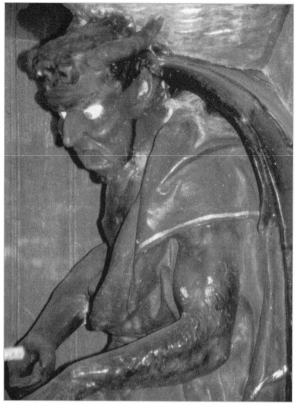

Statue of the Devil in the village church (Rennes-le-Château, France).   Sheela-na-gig, on the Church of St. Mary and St. David (Kilpeck, England).

Statue of the Devil in the village church (Rennes-le-Château, France). According to the book *Holy Blood, Holy Grail*, Rennes-le-Château is the starting point for the panoramic Christian conspiracy tales of Jesus and Mary Magdalene, the Holy Grail, and the rest of it, later popularized by *The Da Vinci Code*. When the local priest Bérenger Saunière uncovered a mysterious "treasure" (said to be the secret of the Holy Grail) at the end of the nineteenth century, he set about remodeling the village church with a mystifying variety of blasphemous artwork, including biblical scenes with intentional errors, and depictions of the Devil himself, such as this statue by the church's front door. What's it all mean? Deciphering the mystery has become a major industry unto itself.

Sheela-na-gig, on the Church of St. Mary and St. David (Kilpeck, England). Appearing on churches in Celtic areas (mostly England, Ireland, and France) starting around the twelfth century, these sexually explicit figures—always showing a woman holding open her vagina—have an unknown purpose. Some scholars believe they are a pre-Christian magical figure meant to scare off evil spirits and be a good-luck charm for the church; others say Sheelas are sly clues left by the artisans of the day that they still maintained their pagan beliefs. Perhaps most prosaically, they may simply be warnings to women not to engage in licentious behavior. (There are other, similar "cautionary" carvings on churches of the era showing drunkards and fools.) The Sheela-na-gig of Kilpeck is by far the most famous one in the world; her clean lines and cartoonish simplicity make her the iconic prototype for all Sheelas. She decorates one of the church's corbels, which are stone roof supports running along the tops of the exterior walls; she is joined by dozens of other comical and intriguing carvings on either side of her.

EVERYTHING YOU KNOW ABOUT GOD IS WRONG

Robert W. Pelton

TAKING UP SERPENTS

A PHOTO GALLERY OF SNAKE-HANDLERS

Editor's Note: When you're taking a gander at the stranger aspects of religion, you simply can't ignore the snake-handling Christians. Followers of a certain subset of Pentecostalism, mainly in the American South, place a whole lot of emphasis on Mark 16:18, words supposedly spoken by Jesus about those who would be his followers: "They shall take up serpents; and if they drink any deadly thing, it shall not hurt them; they shall lay hands on the sick, and they shall recover." They also put Luke 10:19 into action: "Behold, I give unto you the power to tread on serpents and scorpions, and over the power of the enemy: and nothing by any means shall hurt you." Lastly, there's Hebrews 11:34, which reports that faith "Quenched the violence of fire."

So, by Jove, during services they hold, fondle, walk on, wear, and otherwise antagonize deadly snakes, usually rattlers, copperheads, and cottonmouths. They sip strychnine and caustic chemicals, such as drain cleaners, and they hold flames to their bare flesh.

Determining how many people have died from these practices is essentially impossible, given the extremely Irural locations of most churches, their independence from each other, their often unofficial nature, plain old secrecy, and the probable willingness of some local doctors to list another cause of death. In Serpent-Handling Believers *(University of Tennessee Press, 1993), Thomas Burton tallies 71 deaths by snake bite and "some half-dozen" fatal poisonings in the history of the movement, though the true totals are undoubtedly higher. As for how many people are in the movement, statistics are again so unreliable as to be next to worthless. Burton writes that "a reasonable estimate might be several hundred actual handlers," while total membership has been guesstimated as high as 2,000.*

During the first half of the 1970s, Robert W. Pelton, who was writing books on unusual religious practices, and Karen W. Carden gained rare access to snake-handling services in West Virginia, Georgia, Tennessee, Michigan, Ohio, and elsewhere. They snapped lots of photos, which ended up in Snake Handlers *(1974) and* The Persecuted Prophets *(1976) (the images you see here).*

As I've written before, to the surprise of some, I actually have a certain respect for the cobra-coddlers. After all, other fundie Christians claim that they take the Bible absolutely literally, but only these people have the stones to walk it like they talk it.

Brother Jimmy Ray Williams.

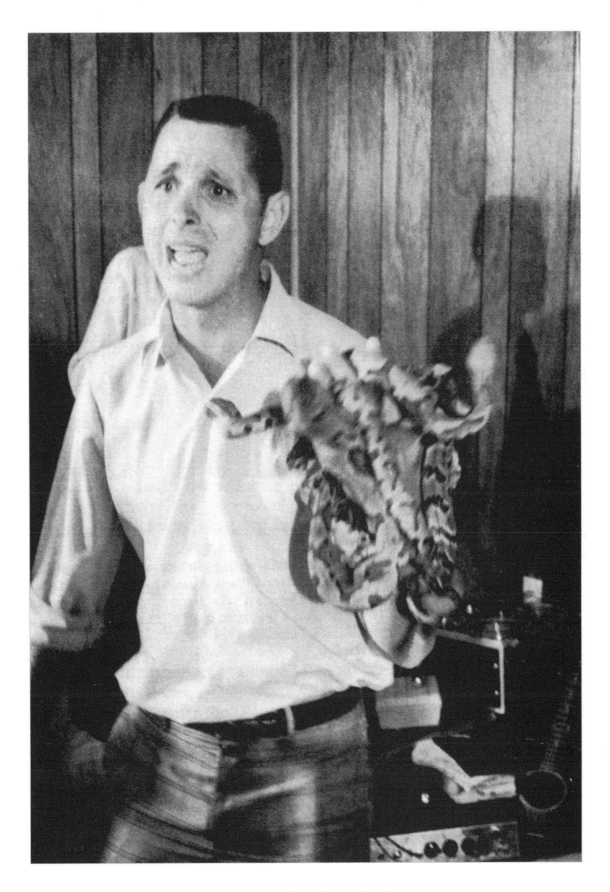

Brother Gene Sherbert of the Holiness Church of God In Jesus Name, Kingston, Georgia.

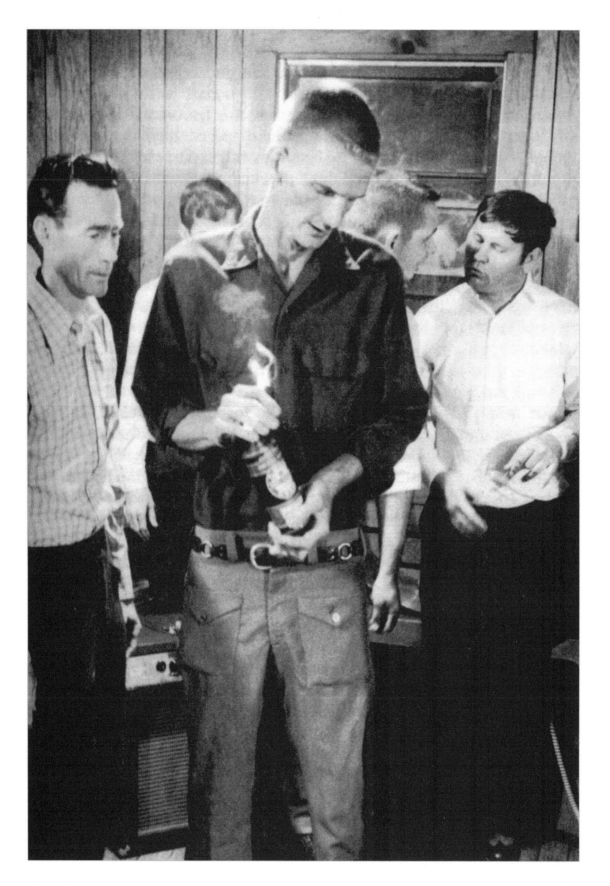

Brother Billy Lemming, devout Christian serpent handler from Kingston, Georgia, holds a torch to his hand. "We go by the eleventh chapter of Hebrews where it says by faith the violence of fire is quenched," Billy reveals.

EVERYTHING YOU KNOW ABOUT GOD IS WRONG

Sister Lucille Dishner of Athens, West Virginia. Next to her is her daughter, wife of Brother John Holbrook.

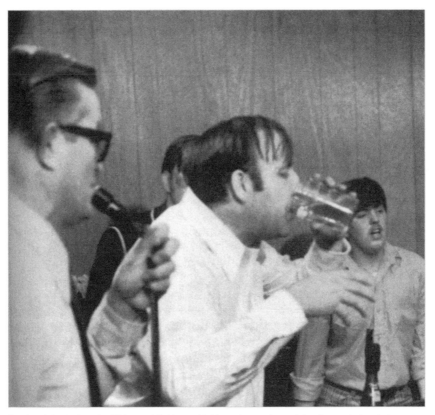

Brother John Holbrook of Warren, Michigan, drinking a heavy dose of deadly strychnine during services. "In a revival, it's drunk just about every night," explains John.

5

GOD-FREE LIVING

Dianna Narciso

THE HONESTY OF ATHEISM

SOME TIME AGO, after American Atheists president Ellen Johnson made an appearance on a national news program, an acquaintance of mine opened a conversation by saying, "I saw your leader on television last night." I was duly confused. Few, if any, atheists look to any particular person or organization as representative of their "beliefs."

But, then, atheists aren't so very different from any other group of people. While I've heard, and made, attempts to label us as fiercely independent, in reality we're pretty much like everybody else. As in the religious community, there are atheists who congregate with the like-minded and those who don't feel the need. Like the religious with their labels, atheists disagree on exactly what atheism is and who is and isn't an atheist. One thing that sets atheists apart, I suppose, is that, while the religious may claim other people of their faith are not *truly* a part of the flock, it is often atheists themselves who claim not to be atheists. I've yet to hear a Christian say he isn't one—in fact, they all seem to be clamoring for defining rights to the word. On the other hand, many atheists run from their label as if it's diseased.

A lot of atheists just don't like the word. They use various other labels to get around it: humanist, freethinker, agnostic, nonreligious, secularist, materialist, and rationalist, to name a few. When put on the spot during the early stages of my atheism, I once told a woman, "We're not church people" in a polite attempt to turn down an invitation. Sometimes polite is an excuse for gutless.

Often we use one of our other labels as a "polite" way of saying we're atheist. For some reason, using the word that best describes our position with regard to the existence of gods is considered in-your-face—rude. Some atheists use these other terms because they don't want to alarm the general public. While I can sympathize, it's clear that the general public wouldn't be so outraged by the word if we'd use it more freely.

Often we use one of our other labels as a "polite" way of saying we're atheist.

While it's frustrating to have atheism misunderstood and mischaracterized by the religious, to hear it maligned by fellow atheists is disheartening. Much of the trouble in which atheists find themselves can be laid at their own feet, it would seem. Too many insist that atheism requires an absolute certainty or belief that gods do not exist. They prefer the word *agnostic*, mistakenly thinking it describes a skeptic, a doubter, or a person who just doesn't know.

Atheist has a long history as the term used for anyone refusing to fall in line and worship whatever gods are in vogue at the time.

The reality is that atheism is the only intellectually honest position a person can take—it is the only logical stance.

ATHEIST HAS A LONG history as the term used for anyone refusing to fall in line and worship whatever gods are in vogue at the time. The polytheists called monotheists atheists for not worshiping local gods; their behavior was considered, at best, rude. The Romans, for instance, called the Christians atheists. With the growth of monotheism, atheism and paganism were seen as one and the same and reviled as evil.

Historically, the word was not intended to describe a person who "believed in no gods." No, the word *atheist* was generally used to describe a person who "does not believe in" one or more particular gods. Atheists of today, by virtue of living in a world in which the vast majority of god characters are no longer proposed as real, don't believe in *any* gods. There are only a few left, after all, to not believe in.

In today's America, there is a line not to be crossed in religion. Believe what you will about God or gods and you will be, at the very least, tolerated, but abandon belief in deity altogether, and you've committed an unforgivable act of reason. You have dared to suggest that the natural world is all there is. This will not do.

The agnostics are better tolerated because they seem to be saying they aren't sure. It is preferred that you be certain there is a god. To be unsure is admitting that you're at least open to the possibility, but to be certain there is no god is to be unreachable. Adamancy in belief is good; adamancy in unbelief is evil.

This is a strange hypocrisy of belief. With it, you can claim you have knowledge when you don't, and call it reality. But you can then say someone who lacks your belief is making a claim of knowledge, and call such certainty delusion.

One reason that atheism is so misunderstood by religionists is because it must be. They can't fight its logic and honesty when properly defined, so they make it mean what they feel comfortable attacking. The meaning of atheism is confused by atheists as a result of living in a society in which the term has been so maligned.

All our troubles with the word boil down to the difference between belief and knowledge. Atheism is nothing more, nor less, than a lack of belief in deity. Theism is "belief in deity." Regardless of whatever else a person believes or doesn't, if he does not *believe* in gods, he is atheist.

An atheist could believe in astrology or alien abduction or elves. He wouldn't be a rationalist atheist, but he'd be atheist just the same. A person could admit he has no idea whether or not there is a god, but as long as he doesn't believe there is one, he's an atheist.

Believe what you will about God or gods and you will be, at the very least, tolerated, but abandon belief in deity altogether, and you've committed an unforgivable act of reason.

ATHEISM IS NOT A RELIGION. Atheists like to say, "If atheism is a religion, then baldness is a hair color," or, "If atheism is a religion, then not collecting stamps is a hobby." This doesn't mean that atheists can't have religions, but their religions would be godless—and they would be individual choices, not something all atheists share.

Some atheists distinguish between strong and weak atheism: Strong atheists claim no gods exist; weak atheists just don't believe in any. There is no real difference between these types of people. Either way, neither believes in gods.

Some say that strong atheists "believe" there is no god. I would hope they mean to use the word "believe" as a synonym for "think," though it's not the same thing. To believe there is no god is just as delusional as believing there is one—when we properly define the word *believe*. Note the subtle difference between believing there is no god, and not believing there is a god.

The strong atheist is not one who "believes" there is no god. Instead, unlike the believer, the strong atheist bases his claim on evidence. In that respect, the basic difference between the strong and weak atheist is the weak atheist's hesitation to either state the obvious, or examine it. That is where the honesty of atheism lies. There is no evidence for the existence of gods and some good evidence that they don't exist. The honest position is to admit that. All atheism asks of a person is the honesty to admit that no one knows whether or not there is a god—no one—and from that, to refrain from the delusion of belief.

Many claim the position of not knowing is merely agnosticism—but they're wrong. Let's take a moment here to realize that people use labels the way they want to use them. The other reason atheism is so misunderstood is that language is a fluid thing. We're constantly hashing out just what it means to wear a certain label, and unfortunately that process results in the invention of more labels—a few interestingly perfect, others completely useless, and some creating more havoc in an already confusing topic.

Agnosticism, for instance, in the public mind is doubt, being on the fence, not sure if there is a god or not. In the true sense of the word, as T.H. Huxley coined it, agnosticism is a claim of lack of knowledge about the existence of gods. The Gnostics of history claimed direct knowledge of God; Huxley, believing atheists claimed knowledge that there was no god, decided to call himself agnostic: He claimed to have no knowledge of the existence of any god.[1]

But Huxley was an atheist, whether he understood the word or not, because he didn't believe there was a god. When he said that atheists and believers had "solved the problem of existence"— atheists claiming knowledge that God did not exist, theists that it did[2]—he was wrong.

It is only by demanding that atheism requires

certainty, or *knowledge*, that gods do not exist, that a person would find need for a word that describes a lack of knowledge of gods' existence. At their origins, atheism admits a lack of belief, while agnosticism admits a lack of knowledge. We are all without knowledge of gods—the agnostics are just the ones who admit it.

Defining gnosticism as "declaring knowledge of the existence of god or gods," there are agnostic theists who admit they have no knowledge of God's existence but still believe it exists. There are agnostic atheists who admit they have no such knowledge and logically refrain from belief. Naturally, there are gnostic theists who claim knowledge of God's existence and believe one exists. One would think there would be no gnostic atheists—those who claim they have knowledge of the existence of one or more gods but refrain from belief in them—but no doubt, they're out there rationalizing their disconnect daily.

In a 2003 Harris Poll, four percent of those calling themselves atheist/agnostic claimed to be absolutely certain there is a god.[3] I have conversed with a few former "Christians in rebellion." They claimed they knew all along that God existed, but they were either angry with him or just didn't want to live by his rules, so refused to worship him. They called this "atheism" once they returned to the flock. (This attitude would explain why so many people claim atheists know God exists and are only angry at him or want to lead licentious lives, as people often project their own failings onto others.)

Whether or not that unexpected four percent in the Harris poll was due to rebellious believers, functionally neurotic atheists, people using a strange definition of agnosticism, or people accidentally giving the wrong answer, we'll never know.

Of the four choices in the gnostic/agnostic, theist/atheist range, gnostic theism is the most perplexing proposition. Belief is an active acceptance of something without evidence, or despite it. If you have enough evidence for a position, you don't need belief. I don't have to believe that being hit by a car can kill you; I've got lots of evidence of that—enough to know it's true. I don't have to believe my spouse loves me—he shows me by his actions that he does. I don't need faith in the sun's shining to expect it to do so—it has done so every day of my life. I have confidence in these areas, not belief. Confidence in something is only warranted when there is evidence to support it. Evidence is based on observation and repeatability. Belief is faith—acceptance without evidence.

If the gnostic truly had the knowledge he claims to have, he could share it with others; it would be factual, testable, and reliable because that's what knowledge *is*. If he had the knowledge he claims, he would not need the belief. We don't believe knowledge—we *know* it. And we know it because it is repeatable and based on observable evidence. Yes, much knowledge is probabilistic. There is no absolute certainty in matters other than logic or definition, for example; there are degrees toward certainty. Knowledge is what you have when you come very close to certainty.

Unfortunately, believers have managed to equate knowledge and belief—their belief is considered knowledge. But let the atheist claim that gods do not exist due to lack of evidence, and he is pounced upon with demands for proof there is no god. "You can't know everything," they say, "but you must think you know everything to say there are no gods." This is twisted logic.

Often atheists do make the claim that there is no god. We base this position on observation and evidence. There is just as much evidence for fairies as there is for gods, and yet we aren't expected to *believe in* fairies. No one tells us that we must open our hearts to the reality of fairies before we'll see that fairies are very real. And more importantly, we aren't expected to prove they don't exist if we say we don't believe in them.

We have no knowledge of fairies—no evidence of their existence. We have stories about fairies, but that's all. When you don't have knowledge about something, you either remain without an answer or position regarding it, or you just *believe* what you've been taught or told or dreamt up. Only when you have knowledge, can you honestly take a position or claim to have an answer.

That is why belief in gods is disingenuous, and atheism is honest. There is no evidence for the existence of gods, despite the claims of believers. To *believe* is to dissuade oneself from seeking the truth.

BELIEF IN GOD has become so ingrained in our society that it is the accepted norm. People in the United States, for the most part, don't like atheism, to put it mildly. We could debate the various reasons why: It casts light on their own doubts; they believe it threatens the moral fabric of our nation; they think it's Satanic; whatever—they don't like it, and people tend to revile and slander what they don't like. For many, atheism is a steadfast refusal to accept the reality of the Christian God's existence. And that is, apparently, unforgivable and worthy of contempt.

> **There is just as much evidence for fairies as there is for gods, and yet we aren't expected to *believe in* fairies.**

According to the 2004 American Mosaic Project, a survey of US households conducted by the University of Minnesota Department of Sociology, atheists are this country's least-trusted minority. Americans rank atheists far below Muslims, gays and lesbians, and recent immigrants when identifying those who share their vision for America and those they'd like their children to marry.[4] These results should not surprise atheists.

Religious claimants are rarely asked to show any evidence for their belief, or even to describe what they mean when they use the word *God*. But when forced to confront skeptics, theists are adamant that there is ample evidence that a god exists. And in their endeavor to elaborate, we come to realize that the word *evidence* can be just as maligned as *atheist*.

The "evidence" given for the existence of God comes in our culture from Christian apologists, but it can easily be transferred to other religious notions of God or gods:

- Everything has a cause, so there is a God, who doesn't have a cause.
- Life exists, so God exists.
- Miracles happen, so God made them happen.
- The Bible is so fabulous God must have written it.

- Biblical prophecy can only be explained by the existence of God.
- Answered prayer proves God exists.
- Subjective experience proves God exists.
- The effects of belief prove the belief is true.
- The spread of Christianity proves God is the one, true God, and Jesus was his son.

These arguments are taken very seriously by very serious people. Volumes are written on them. Syllogisms are presented and debated. It's all good fun for some, but these arguments can be dismissed very easily. They all require a leap of faith from what is unknown to an answer that has no evidentiary support.

For example, if everything has a cause, God must have one also. If God doesn't have to have a cause, some things are obviously exempt. To say that only God is exempt is cheating. To say that only things that "begin" to exist have a cause and that God never "began" is cheating. Saying everything has to have a cause proves nothing except that you're assuming what you think will further your argument. If it has been shown that the universe had a beginning, it tells us absolutely nothing about whether or not there is a God. In other words, even if everything did require a cause, we still wouldn't know what that cause is.

Michael Shermer, in his book *Why People Believe Weird Things: Pseudoscience, Superstition, and Other Confusions of Our Time*, outlines twenty-five fallacies that lead to errors in thought and allow people to accept invalid ideas as truth. Among these fallacies are the belief that bold and forceful statements and the use of scientific language make a claim true, problems with placement of the burden of proof, reasoning after the fact, rationalization of failures, and an inability to distinguish truth from false analogies, coincidence, and appeals to ignorance.

Belief in the veracity of the aforementioned "evidence" for gods is nothing more than Shermer's fallacies at work. We have no evidence for the existence of gods. What people have is lack of knowledge and lots of faith. People react credulously to their incredulousness—the unknown is a vacuum that for millions of people must be filled with *something* to banish the gnawing discomfort of not knowing.

Millions either refuse to accept the factual evidence of evolutionary theory, for example, or are unable to understand it. They can't imagine that life arose for no reason and without the guidance of some greater being—so they *believe* there was one. People have a lot of emotion invested in life, and they can't tolerate the thought of it simply, permanently ending—so they *believe* there is more after death. There are so many questions people can't answer, so they *believe* the answers given to them by religions.

BELIEF IS DELUSION. Belief is based on your feelings and ignorance, not on any factual evidence. If you had factual evidence for what you believe, you would not have to believe it—you would *know* it, and we could all share in that knowledge. We would all come to the same conclusion, the same god, the same story.

We now can see the error of the theist promoting his god:

> Theist: Believe in him.
> Atheist: He obviously doesn't exist.
> Theist: You atheists think you know everything.
> Atheist: I don't have to know everything to assume your god doesn't exist. All I have to do is listen to you tell me to believe in him. If I have to believe in him, it's glaringly apparent he does not exist.
> Theist: Stop bashing me for my faith!
> Atheist: Yeah, yeah, whatever.

There is no evidence that a god exists. If there were, we would all know that a god exists. Sure, there would still be deniers, just like those who refuse to accept the evidence of evolutionary theories. And that's what many believers would like to make of atheists: deniers. The difference is that we have a great deal of evidence for evolution; it can be found in the museums of natural history, in magnificent and scholarly tomes and journals, and most important, in the fossil record. There is no such evidence offered for their *belief*, only assertions.

We must always remain open to new evidence that would enhance our knowledge. But until such evidence arrives, the intellectually honest position is to refrain from believing in propositions for which it is lacking. To lack belief in what you can't know is to embrace the reality that can be known—to revel in the vastness of the unknown, to wonder, to muse, to imagine...and then return to what we know, to live as best we can in the face of it.

But this is unacceptable for the believer, who insists we all share his delusion. If you refuse, he'll claim you have your own. You will occasionally run into the senseless individual who will, with a straight face, tell you that there is no difference between lacking a belief and having one. Do not talk to such people. They can see your lips move, but there's someone else in their heads doing your talking for you, so just forget it.

Atheists don't *know* that gods don't exist; we're just fairly certain of it based on a severe lack of evidence for them. Believers try hard to paint the atheist into a position of absolute certainty so they can better attack him. Believers figure that atheism is a belief just like theirs, only opposite. "After all," they claim, "everyone believes something." Delusion needs company to survive. In company, it can hide and spread in the shadows of ignorance. We must bring it out into the light.

Atheists don't *know* that gods don't exist; we're just fairly certain of it based on a severe lack of evidence for them.

THERE'S A TRIGGER, somewhere in the human brain, I'm sure, that people just miss. Their thinking dances around it, avoiding logic by every means possible. One day though, for some of us, something hits it. Someone says something like, "I don't know how we got here and neither do you," and the trigger fires, and they suddenly, though too often

only briefly, understand lack of knowledge, lack of certainty, lack of belief. They get that it's all just different stories: the Jewish story, the Christian story, the Muslim story, the Hindu story, the Wiccan story; and they get that the atheist just doesn't believe the stories are true.

Unfortunately, it rarely sticks because if they're all just stories, then the atheist is right. If we don't really know, then the atheist is the only one looking at the situation honestly. If no one knows, belief is just delusion, a salve for the mind, a bedtime story to soothe us into sleep.

And if no one knows, maybe the material world really is all there is. Maybe we really do cease to exist when we take our final breaths. Fear creeps in and sets the blocks of belief back in their places and the dishonesty begins anew. We can not honestly admit we don't know because we can't accept that we're a part of this earth and we will die.

"What a sad state of affairs," the believers lament. Perhaps. But sad doesn't mean false anymore than comforting means true.

And so, we come to the truth at hand. As there is no evidence for gods (admitted by the theists who tell us we must believe in it before it will seem real to us, and as having to believe in anything is verification that it has no evidence for it and is therefore delusional), the only intellectually honest position one can take is that of atheism.

I myself do not believe in belief.

1. Hastings, James (ed.). *Encyclopaedia of Religion and Ethics*. 1908. Pertinent quotes can be found at [www.infidels.org].

2. Ibid.

3. The Harris Poll #59, 15 Oct 2003. Can be found at [www.harrisinteractive.com].

4. American Mosaic Project main page [www.soc.umn.edu/amp/]. An article on the results published by American Atheists can be found at [www.atheists.org].

Greta Christina

COMFORTING THOUGHTS ABOUT DEATH THAT HAVE NOTHING TO DO WITH GOD

SO HERE'S THE PROBLEM. If you don't believe in God or an afterlife; or if you believe that the existence of God or an afterlife are fundamentally unanswerable questions; or if you do believe in God or an afterlife but you accept that your belief is just that, a belief, something you believe rather than something you know—if any of that is true for you, then death can be an appalling thing to think about. Not just frightening, not just painful. It can be paralyzing. The fact that your lifespan is an infinitesimally tiny fragment in the life of the universe, and that there is, at the very least, a strong possibility that when you die, you disappear completely and forever, and that in 500 years nobody will remember you, and in five billion years the earth will be boiled into the sun: This can be a profound and defining truth about your existence that you reflexively repulse, that you flinch away from and refuse to accept or even think about, consistently pushing to the back of your mind whenever it sneaks up, for fear that if you allow it to sit in your mind even for a minute, it will swallow everything else. It can make everything you do, and everything anyone else does, seem meaningless, trivial to the point of absurdity. It can make you feel erased, wipe out joy, make your life seem like ashes in your hands. Those of us who are skeptics and doubters are sometimes dismissive of people who fervently hold beliefs they have no evidence for simply because they find them comforting—but when you're in the grip of this sort of existential despair, it can be hard to feel like you have anything but that handful of ashes to offer them in exchange.

But here's the thing. I think it's possible to be an agnostic, or an atheist, or to have religious or spiritual beliefs that you don't have certainty about, and still feel okay about death. I think there are ways to look at death, ways to experience the death of other people and to contemplate our own, that allow us to feel the value of life without denying the finality of death. I can't make myself believe in things I don't actually believe—heaven, or reincarnation, or a greater divine plan for our lives—simply because believing those things would make death easier to accept. And I don't think I have to, or that anyone has to. I think there are ways to think about death that are comforting, that give peace and solace, that allow our lives to have meaning and even give us more of that meaning—and that have nothing whatsoever to do with any kind of God, or any kind of afterlife.

Here's the first thing. The first thing is time, and the fact that we live in it. Our existence and experience are dependent on the passing of time, and on change. No, not dependent—*dependent* is too weak a word. Time and change are integral to who we are, the foundation of our consciousness, and its warp and weft as well. I can't imagine what it would mean to be conscious without passing through time and being aware of it. There may be some form of existence outside of time, some plane of being in which change and the passage of time is an illusion, but it certainly isn't ours.

And inherent in change is loss. The passing of time has loss and death woven into it: Each new moment kills the moment before it, and its own death is implied in the moment that comes after. There is no way to exist in the world of change without accepting loss, if only the loss of a moment in time: the way the sky looks right now, the motion of the air, the number of birds in the tree outside your window, the temperature, the placement of your body, the position of the people in the street. It's inherent in the nature of having moments: You never get to have this exact one again.

And that's a good thing, too. Because all the things that give life joy and meaning—music, conversation, eating, dancing, playing with children, reading, thinking, making love, all of it—are based on time passing, and on change, and on the loss of an infinitude of moments passing through us and then behind us. Without loss and death, we don't get to have existence. We don't get to have Shakespeare, or sex, or five-spice chicken, without allowing their existence and our experience of them to come into being and then pass on. We don't get to listen to Louis Armstrong without letting the E flat disappear and turn into a G. We don't get to watch *Groundhog Day* without letting each frame of it pass in front of us for a twenty-fourth of a second and then move on. We don't get to walk in the forest without passing by each tree and letting it fall behind us; we don't even get to stand still in the forest and gaze at one tree for hours without seeing the wind blow off a leaf, a bird break off a twig for its nest, the clouds moving behind it, each manifestation of the tree dying and a new one taking its place.

And we wouldn't want to have it if we could. The alternative would be time frozen, a single frame of the film, with nothing to precede it and nothing to come after. I don't think any of us would want that. And if we don't want that, if instead we want the world of change, the world of music and talking and sex and whatnot, then it is worth our while to accept, and even love, the loss and the death that make it possible.

Here's the second thing. Imagine, for a moment, stepping away from time, the way you'd step back from a physical place, to get a better perspective on it. Imagine being outside of time, looking at all of it as a whole—history, the present, the future—the way the astronauts stepped back from the earth and saw it whole.

Keep that image in your mind. Like a timeline in a history class, but going infinitely forward and infinitely back. And now think of a life, a segment of that timeline, one that starts in, say, 1961, and ends in, say, 2037. Does that life go away when 2037 turns into 2038? Do the years 1961 through 2037 disappear from time simply because we move on from them and into a new time, any more than Chicago disappears when we leave it behind and go to California?

It does not. The time that you live in will always exist, even after you've passed out of it, just like Paris exists before you visit it, and continues to exist after you leave. And the fact that people in the twenty-third century will probably never know you were alive... that doesn't make your life disappear, any more than Paris disappears if your cousin Ethel never sees it. Your segment on that timeline will always have been there. The fact of your death doesn't make the time that you were alive disappear.

And it doesn't make it meaningless. Yes, stepping back and contemplating all of time and space can be daunting, can make you feel tiny and trivial. And that perception isn't entirely inaccurate. It's true; the small slice of time that we have is no more important than the infinitude of time that came before we were born, or the infinitude that will follow after we die.

But it's no less important, either.

I don't know what happens when we die. I don't know if we come back in a different body, or if we get to hover over time and space and view it in all its glory and splendor, or if our souls dissolve into the world-soul the way our bodies dissolve into the ground, or if, as seems very likely, we simply disappear. I have no idea. And I don't know that it matters. What matters is that we get to be alive. We get to be conscious. We get to be connected with each other, and with the world, and we get to be aware of that connection and to spend a few years mucking about in its possibilities. We get to have a slice of time and space that's ours. As it happened, we got the slice that has Beatles records and Thai restaurants and AIDS and the Internet. People who came before us got the slice that had horse-drawn carriages and whist and dysentery, or the one that had stone huts and Viking invasions and pigs in the yard. And the people who come after us will get the slice that has, I don't know, flying cars and soybean pies and identity chips in their brains. But our slice is no less important because it comes when it does, and it's no less important because we'll leave it someday. The fact that time will continue after we die does not negate the time that we were alive. We are alive now, and nothing can erase that.

Paul Krassner

CONFESSIONS OF AN ATHEIST

Editor's Note: Paul Krassner has been skewering and defying authority for a half-century now, and he's known primarily as a satirist and trickster. His legendary magazine (later a newsletter), The Realist, *infamously mixed fact and parody so artfully that readers often couldn't tell which was which. But Krassner's crucial place in the history of secularism is often overlooked. From its beginning during the Eisenhower administration in 1958— thus predating the Counterculture—*The Realist *courageously served up hardcore atheism, usually in the form of acid satire on religion but sometimes via frontal attacks (including articles by Madalyn Murray O'Hair).*

THE PARADOX OF my own peculiar spiritual path is that I'm an unbeliever who engages in constant dialogue with the deity I don't believe in. For example, as a stand-up satirist, before I walk on stage to perform, I always look in the mirror and pray out loud to the deity I don't believe in: "Please, God, help me do a good show." And then I always hear the voice of God come booming back at me: "*Shut up, you superstitious fool!*"

I had developed that habit of communicating with my imaginary friend when I was a kid who actually *believed* in an all-knowing, all-powerful Being. It was *his* idea to have extra skin on people's elbows so they could bend. I wondered whether he had intended for boys to button their shirts one way and for girls to button their blouses another way.

My faith disappeared when I was thirteen. I was working early mornings in the candy store on the ground floor of our apartment building. My job was to insert different sections of the newspaper into

the main section. On Sundays rows and rows of piles of papers were stacked high, and it would take me hours. On the day after the United States dropped an atomic bomb on Hiroshima, I would read that headline over and over and over and over again. That afternoon, I told God I couldn't believe in him any more because he had allowed such devastation to happen.

"*Allowed? Why do you think I gave humans free will?*"

> **When I got beaten up by the class bully because I was Jewish, I told him, "I'm *not* Jewish. I don't believe in God."**

"Okay, well, I'm exercising my free will to believe that you don't exist."

"*All right, it's your loss!*"

So at least we would remain on speaking terms. Our previous relationship had instilled in me a touchstone of objectivity that could still serve to help keep me honest. I realized, though, that whenever I prayed, I was only talking to myself. And when I got beaten up by the class bully because I was Jewish, I told him, "I'm *not* Jewish. I don't believe in God."

"That doesn't make any difference," he replied. "You're stilll Jewish."

THE ONLY THING I can remember from my entire college education is a definition of philosophy as "the rationalization of life." For my term paper, I decided to write a dialogue between Plato and an atheist. On a whim, I looked up "atheism" in the Manhattan phone book, and there it was: "Atheism, American Association for the Advancement of." I went to their office for background material.

The AAAA sponsored the Ism Forum, where anybody could speak about any "ism" of their choice. I invited a few acquaintances to meet me there. The event was held in a dingy hotel ballroom. There was a small platform with a podium at one end of the room and heavy wooden folding chairs lined around the walls. My favorite speaker declared the Eleventh Commandment: "Thou shalt not take thyself too goddamned seriously." Taking that as my unspoken theme, I got up and parodied the previous speakers. The folks there were mostly middle-aged and elderly. They seemed to relish the notion of fresh young blood in their movement.

However, my companions weren't interested in staying. Had I left with them that evening in 1953, the rest of my life could have taken a totally different path. Instead, I went along with a group to a nearby cafeteria, where I learned about the New York Rationalist Society. A whole new world of disbelief was opening up to me. On Saturday night I went to their meeting. The emcee was a former circus performer who entertained his fellow rationalists by putting four golfballs into his mouth. He also recommended an anti-censorship paper, *The Independent*.

The next week, I went to their office to subscribe and get back issues. I ended up with a part-time job, stuffing envelopes for a dollar an hour. My apprenticeship had begun. The editor, Lyle Stuart, was the most dynamic individual I'd ever met. His integrity was such that if he possessed information that he had a vested interest in keeping quiet—say, corruption involving a corporation in which he owned stock—it would become his top priority to publish it. Lyle became my media mentor, my unrelenting guru, and my closest friend. He was responsible for the launch of my own magazine, *The Realist*. The masthead announced, "Freethought Criticism and Satire."

"Thank you, God," I said.

"*God never says 'You're welcome,'*" he replied.

I NOW LIVE IN A SMALL TOWN in California. The official slogan was recently changed from "People, Pride and Progress" to "Clearly Above the Rest," and so heaven would be the theme of the Chamber of Commerce installation dinner at the Miracle Springs Hotel. The waiters and waitresses would be dressed as angels. The stage in the hotel ballroom would be overlain with a cottony white cloud, enhanced by a fog machine. There would be a blonde angel playing the harp. And I was invited to perform.

At 7 P.M., the salad would be served. At precisely 7:15, a clatter of pots and pans would be heard, then I would be thrown out of the kitchen, directly into that heavenly scene in the banquet hall. Oh, yes, and I would be dressed as the devil, who had been kicked out of heaven. The devil isn't merely a metaphor. The latest poll indicates that 68 percent of Americans believe Satan exists.

I rented a devil's costume—red pants, shirt, bowtie, jacket, cape, tail, and horns, with a golden three-prong pitchfork—which I donned in the staff bathroom. I looked in the mirror, pulled my hair into a point on my forehead and said—to the image of Satan— "Please, God, help me do a good show." I may have been the personification of evil, but for an instant it felt like God and the devil were in perfect harmony. And then I heard the voice of God boom out: "*You must be kidding!*"

6

DOING GOD'S WORK

Sam Jordison

"IRISH GULAGS FOR WOMEN"

THE CATHOLIC CHURCH'S MAGDALENE ASYLUMS

A CHANCE DISCOVERY SET in motion the chain of events that led to the unravelling of the mystery of Ireland's Magdalene Asylums.

In 1993 a mass grave was uncovered on the grounds of a Catholic nunnery in the north of Dublin. The grave was found on land that the Good Shepherd nuns from High Park Convent had sold to a developer, to build the kind of brash new development that has characterized Ireland's economic miracle during the past fifteen years. At first it was thought that 133 bodies had been buried—we now know that there were 155. They were all female.

Extraordinarily, even though most of these women had died as recently as the 1960s and 1970s, the nuns were unable to name forty-five of them or to provide death certificates for eighty. Since the nineteenth century, it's been illegal in Ireland to not register any death that occurs on your premises, but even so, the Irish government did nothing. Nor was any investigation made. Instead, the Department of the Environment quickly granted the nuns an exhumation certificate so that the bodies could be removed and the building work could continue. Even when the exhumation was carried out and a further twenty-two bodies were found, no action was taken. It was a flagrant avoidance of legal requirements, but no more than typical in a country where until very recently the Roman Catholic Church had been at least as powerful as the state.

While the Church may have escaped the law, history at least was catching up with it. When it became known that the bodies had been discovered, Dublin families streamed to the convent, hoping to identify long-lost daughters, sisters, and mothers. Their personal tragedy soon became a public scandal as the press wondered aloud what had happened to all those women—and why. The answers to their questions were shocking. A country already reeling from the revelation that up to a quarter of its population had been physically and sexually abused by members of the Catholic priesthood now had to contend with yet another dark secret.

> When it became known that the bodies had been discovered, Dublin families streamed to the convent, hoping to identify long-lost daughters, sisters, and mothers.

THE BACK-STORY AND PURPOSE of the Magdalene Asylums, also called Magdalene Laundries, were fairly easily discovered.[1] Taking their name from the biblical figure Mary Magdalene (who was supposed to have been a prostitute turned penitent in Christian mythology), they were first established as a refuge for "fallen women," intended to take prostitutes from the streets and "reform" them using the twin persuasions of hard work and religious instruction.

Victims of rape and incest were sent to the laundries, as were any women who had children out of wedlock.

Originally, these holy washhouses hadn't been just an Irish phenomenon. Indeed, the first was built in 1641 in France by the Catholic order of the Sisters of Our Lady of Charity of the Good Shepherd of Angers (known more simply as "the Good Shepherds"). That was more than 100 years before the first Irish institution, the Dublin Magdalen Asylum, opened in 1767 (some ten years after a similar institution had opened in London). Other institutions were built all over Europe and the United States.

Nor were the laundries exclusively Roman Catholic. Protestant orders ran almost as many of them in the early years of the nineteenth century. However, crucial theological differences affected the running of the asylums as time wore on.

Because of the Catholic belief in grace and the need to be in a state free from sin before death, the two orders of nuns who controlled the institutions in Ireland—the Good Shepherds and the Sisters of Mercy—began to steer a new course. It became less and less of a priority to reform the "penitents" (as the women were branded) or to send them back into the world. After all, the best way to keep them away from temptation and the presence of sin was to keep them under the careful supervision of the nuns in the laundries.[2]

Further inducement to keep the women prisoners for life came as the laundries grew increasingly profitable. The fact that they were functioning washhouses was no accident. The women were told that they were literally washing away the stain of their "sins"—as well as, usefully enough, earning money to provide for their own upkeep and for the enrichment of the convents that presided over them. The longer that women stayed in the institutions—any youthful independent spirit broken by a life of drudgery—generally the more useful they became as workers.

This money-making potential of the laundries, when combined with the peculiarly anti-sex zeal of their Catholic managers, also encouraged mission creep. At first the nuns had only housed prostitutes, but they began to expand their remit, taking charge of many other kinds of women and girls whom they labelled as "fallen." In this task they could count on the easy compliance of the local population, whose fiercely traditional brand of local Catholicism was quick to see sin and eager to condemn it. Sex outside of marriage was in the same category as murder: a "mortal sin."

Victims of rape and incest were sent to the laundries, as were any women who had children out of wedlock (and there were plenty of those since the Church had banned sex education, as well as contraception). Even virgins were taken in: "pretty" girls denied their freedom on the basis that they had the *potential* to be "temptresses" or, most absurdly of all, because of a "love of dress."[3]

In all, an estimated 30,000 women were imprisoned in Ireland's Magdalene Asylums ("estimated" because no proper records were kept).[4]

ATTEMPTS HAVE BEEN MADE to justify the Magdalene Asylums on the grounds that they were symptomatic of their times. The desire to reform prostitutes in the nineteenth century was a common one, and the nuns did at least provide the women a place to live and a shelter from the frequent horrors of the streets.

However, even in the late 1800s, the hypocrisy inherent in the system was easy to see. No one ever suggested, for instance, that the love of dress displayed by female members of the British Royal Family (who then had sovereignty over Ireland) was sinful. Fortunately, as time went on, most of the world realized that the laundries were out of step—and most were closed down.

The sad exception was in Ireland. There, in the 1920s, under de Valera's newly independent, Catholic-dominated government, the Magdalene Asylums actually began to expand. They continued to take in women up until the 1970s, and the last one shut down in 1996. While the rest of the developed world was celebrating the Summer of Love, women in Ireland were having their freedom taken away for looking too pretty.

The very existence of Magdalene Asylums within living memory is unsettling enough. Even many people in Ireland were shocked to hear that they existed. Certainly, the majority of people I've spoken to who weren't involved with the laundries tell me that they didn't know anything about them until the scandal broke in the 1990s.

While the rest of the developed world was celebrating the Summer of Love, women in Ireland were having their freedom taken away for looking too pretty.

Other writers, however, have argued persuasively that more people were aware of the asylums' existence than like to admit it now. Social history professor Frances Finnegan, the author of the first major history of the Irish Magdalene Asylums, *Do Penance or Perish*, states explicitly that "the idea that society is blameless—that the Magdalene Asylums were so shrouded in secrecy that the public was unaware of what was taking place—is a myth."[5] She notes that the phrase, "Be good or I'll send you to the laundries," was a common threat to badly behaved children. Furthermore, while many of the families who did send their daughters away claimed that the girls had "emigrated," the truth couldn't have been hard to work out.

Whether or not people knew about the laundries before the scandal broke, beyond doubt is that the revelation of what went on inside the buildings horrified Irish society—not to mention the world. They were in short, and in the words of so many survivors, "hell on earth."

Discovering this inside story was a slow process. By the time the story hit the news in 1993, with the discovery of the mass grave at High Park, most of the women who had been through the laundries were old and frail. Few were able to properly express themselves anyway; one of the most upsetting consequences of life inside the Magdalene Asylums was that they had received very little education. Most important, they were afraid—afraid of the stigma attached to publicly declaring themselves to have been "fallen women," afraid of the continuing power of the Church in their communities (or, indeed, afraid of the nuns, since they still housed many of the women). Also, thanks to years of religious indoctrination, they were afraid of the consequences in the next life of criticizing the Church.

"The shame of being a Magdalene still runs so deep in Ireland nobody would [talk]," explains Steve Humphries, the maker of the documentary *Sex in a Cold Climate* and the man who perhaps did the most to eventually uncover the story. His film, first shown on British television in 1998, was instrumental in finally changing the atmosphere sufficiently so that some women felt able to tell their stories.

Humphries was so successful because he managed to track down four women who had escaped the laundries and since fled to the UK. Their testimony is devastating.

One of these women, Martha Cooney, was put away by the local priest and her family after she'd complained to a cousin that she'd been raped. "They got rid of me very quickly," she says. She'd broken a cardinal rule, as she discovered to her cost: "The biggest sin in Ireland was to talk." She was made to work so hard in the laundries that she got varicose veins in her hands at just fifteen years of age. When she did anything that the nuns perceived as wrong, she was made to bow down before them and beg for forgiveness. She spent four years inside an asylum until a family member rescued her in 1945. She has never felt able to marry. "I never wanted anybody to have power over me, or chain me ever again," she explains.

"They were very vicious, some of them nuns," she says.

Phyllis Valentine, an orphan, was judged a danger because of her good looks and was transferred from her orphanage to an asylum. It was years before she found out that her attractiveness was the reason for her detainment. She recalls punishments and girls being "punched," "slapped," and beaten with a leather belt. "They were very vicious, some of them nuns," she says. "They were really cruel to us. And we never did anything wrong."

In 1964, after eight years of incarceration at the Sisters of Mercy asylum in Galway, and after months of determined rebellion, self-starvation, and trouble-making, the nuns found her so much of a handful that she was released. She married at twenty-five, but her sex life was ruined from an overhanging conviction that the act was "wrong," a psychic scar from the laundry. "I felt ashamed every time he touched me," she says. "The nuns had taught us that it was wrong to let a man touch you. They never prepared us for the outside world."

Christiana Mulcahey went to the same Galway asylum ten years before Phyllis Valentine. Her perceived crime was to have given birth outside of wedlock. She agreed to talk to Humphries only because a recent diagnosis of terminal cancer had freed her from any consequences. Like many other Magdalenes, she had been forcibly separated from her baby while still breastfeeding. She went, in her words, "absolutely berserk" when she discovered one day that her child had been adopted. She was informed that the baby had been placed for adoption with a "good Catholic family" (many hundreds of babies were sent to Catholic families in the United States, who were almost entirely ignorant of their original circumstances).

Phyllis Valentine explains that there was nothing unusual about Mulcahey's story; it happened often, and it was always heartbreaking. The mothers, she says, were "desperate to find out where their children were—absolutely desperate." But they rarely did. "It was really very sad, but all the girl could do was to cry. There was nothing else to do but cry."

Adding to the hurt, Mulcahey had been hoping that she could still have a life with the baby's father. "I lost out on him," she says. "I would have married him. I loved him." After three years in the asylum—during which a priest sexually abused her—she became one of the few people who successfully escaped, slipping out a side gate when a cowherd was bringing cows into the asylum. She fled to Northern Ireland and became a nurse. She never saw her lover again, although she was finally reunited with her son shortly before her death in 1997, having kept his existence a secret from her new family for more than fifty years.

The fourth woman to talk to Humphries, Brigid Young, managed to avoid entering a laundry directly, but she didn't escape its influence. She grew up in an orphanage attached to the Magdalene Asylum in Limerick. One day "just for talking to a Magdalene" (she had spoken to a "penitent" at the

The Mother Superior of the convent beat her with a purpose-made black rubber baton and forcibly cut off her hair.

laundry door and agreed to help her see her baby, who was in the orphanage with her), she was given "a severe beating." The Mother Superior of the convent beat her with a purpose-made black rubber baton and forcibly cut off her hair. Afterwards, the head nun forced Brigid to look into a mirror, in spite of the blood flowing into her eyes. "I'll never forget what looked back at me," she says. "Totally devastating. My face all swelled up. Under my chin, all cut up where she had stuck the scissors...." The Mother Superior was triumphant. "And you're not so pretty now!" she exclaimed. Later, when a priest masturbated on her dress, Young was so afraid of being sent to the Magdalene Asylum that she told no one. In 1956 she left the nuns' charge. Her later marriage collapsed as a result of the abuse she had suffered.

"It haunts you," she says.

ALONGSIDE THESE STORIES of personal tragedy, *Sex in a Cold Climate* also helped to build up an image of everyday life inside the Magdalene Asylums—an image that gradually became clearer as more people started talking to the press in the documentary's wake.

As well as denying them their freedom, the nuns stripped away the women's and girls' right to their very individuality. When they arrived, their clothes were taken away and replaced with drab, heavy Victorian smocks (even in the latter half of the twentieth century) made from coarse material. They were also given new names (generally taken from Catholic saints, although some, bizarrely, were given masculine titles). This renaming of the girls had the incidental effect of making it harder for their families to track them down—especially because they were frequently moved without anyone being informed. Since a request from a family member was just about the only recognized way of getting out of the asylums, these obscuring measures often resulted in the girls being imprisoned for life—with no trial, no judgment, and often no understanding of what they were supposed to have done wrong.

Under Irish law, the nuns had no legal right to imprison their charges. Women and girls were supposed to enter the asylums voluntarily, but most were sent to them by priests, their families, or directly from Industrial Schools (where they were supposed to have been under the protection of the Church and so kept away from the kind of "sins" they were being punished for in the laundries). Even a report commissioned by the Irish government, the 1970 Kennedy report, questioned the validity of the "voluntary" placements and noted that the girls were kept unaware of their true rights.

Escape, meanwhile, was extremely difficult. The "penitents" were kept inside towering walls (more than twenty feet high in many of the institutions), topped with glass and barbed wire. If they did manage to get outside, the girls were often forcibly returned to the asylums by the local police. And even if they did get back to their homes, they were generally rejected and then returned by outraged family members. The only real escape came in leaving Ireland completely.

If they did manage to get outside, the girls were often forcibly returned to the asylums by the local police.

"I would rather have been down the women's jail," Mary Norris (one of the survivors who came forward after the scandal broke) told the *Irish Independent*. "At least I would have got a sentence and would know when I was leaving."

Meals were eaten wordlessly to the sound of biblical readings, the "penitents" stationed away from the sisters, whose food was invariably better.

Until the 1970s, the women, regardless of age, were referred to as "children." They had to call the nuns "mother." A priest writing in 1931 neatly summed up the contempt inherent in this patronizing relationship:

> It may be only a white-veiled novice with no vows as yet; and it may be an old white-haired penitent giving back to God but the dregs of a life spent in sin. It matters not. In the Home of the Good Shepherd the one is ever the "Mother" while the other is always the "Child."[6]

This quote further highlights one of the greatest tragedies of the whole system: the way the women were indoctrinated with the idea that they were "sinners" and "penitents." They were taught that they were outcasts and that any sexual abuse they might have suffered was their own fault. The hardship of their lives was said to be no more than they deserved. They were also told that if they tried to leave the asylums, they were literally taking the road to hell. Indeed, if they wanted to avoid the fiery Catholic underworld, the best course of action was to debase themselves completely, obey the nuns in everything, and constantly pray for their own souls. They also had to—quite literally in some cases—work themselves to the bone.

It was a real slog, with hours of scrubbing (often of bloody sheets—and worse—from the hospitals that made up a large part of the laundries' clientele), hours of hanging, and hours of ironing. The days were strictly time-tabled, with several hours of prayer on top of around ten hours of physical work in the washing rooms, six days a week.[7]

"You'd have to handwash—scrub," Josephine McCarthy—who was in a Magdalene Asylum in the 1960s—explained to the makers of a CBS documentary in 1999. "You'd have no knuckles left. Ironing—you would be burnt. It was just hard work."

For most of each day, the women were forbidden to speak or to communicate with each other. Nuns were stationed around the work areas to watch for any transgressions. Punishments were frequent and, by all accounts, brutal.

"Those places were the Irish gulags for women," says Mary Norris. "When you went inside their doors, you left behind your dignity, identity, and humanity. We were locked up, had no outside contacts, and got no wages although we worked ten hours a day, six days a week, fifty-two weeks a year. What else is that but slavery? And to think that they were doing all this in the name of a loving God! I used to tell God I hated him."

Phyllis Valentine too recalls how she had asked to be paid after her first week in the laundry. "They just laughed at me," she says.

This failure to pay the women for their labors is thrown into stark relief by the huge profits that the asylums made. The accounts of the Sunday's Well Good Shepherd asylum in Cork show that the laundry was making a profit of hundreds of thousands of dollars in today's money annually during the 1950s and 1960s.[8] The books also show that nearly all of this money was spent on the nuns and their increasingly fancy internal chapel, rather than on their imprisoned workforce. The laundries stopped making such vast profits only from the 1970s onwards, thanks to the advent of cheaply available automatic washing machines and driers. Indeed, many commentators, not to mention survivors, have attributed the Magdalene Asylums' eventual decline to the arrival of the washing machine.

Thus it was money that closed down the laundries, rather than any ideological objections to their existence or any realization of their injustice on the part of the nuns.

> **"Those places were the Irish gulags for women. When you went inside their doors, you left behind your dignity, identity, and humanity."**

IN SPITE OF THE HORROR of revelations about life inside the Catholic Church's Magdalene Asylums, next to nothing has been said or done by the Vatican. At first, there wasn't even an apology. Journalists hunting for comment were met with silence. Only Ireland's outspoken liberal prelate Bishop Willie Walsh of Killaloe publicly recognized the wrong that had been done, telling ABC News that "the Magdalene Laundries were in some instances a form of slavery... a source of pain and shame." My own attempts to get a statement from the Vatican or the Conference of Religious in Ireland (the umbrella organization for all monastic orders in the country) came to nothing.

The Vatican was moved to speak, however, in 2003 when the director Peter Mullan released *The Magdalene Sisters*. This film, inspired by the documentary *Sex in a Cold Climate*, and made in consultation with a number of survivors, as well as a former nun (who had left the Church in dismay at what she saw in the laundries), provided a harrowing depiction of the life its young subjects had to endure. It won the best film award at the Venice Film Festival and was watched by a third of the Irish adult population. The Catholic Church was unable to ignore it, so they denounced it. The Vatican newspaper *L'Osservatore Romano* declared it an "angry and rancorous provocation" that misrepresented religious leaders. The Catholic League in America labeled the film "anti-Catholic propaganda" and barracked Miramax for distributing it. Elsewhere, the old canard was reeled out that the film was biased because it didn't do anything to promote the good work that the Catholic clergy do around the world.

One scene in particular, where a group of nuns mock their charges' naked bodies, was heavily criticized as exploitation. In fact, the filmmakers and many survivors were adamant that if anything, the film understated the reality. In *The Magdalene Sisters*, the nude parade is presented as a one-off, but according to many survivors, that kind of thing happened to them weekly. "They enjoyed us stripped naked," Brigid Young says.

The survivors themselves lamented the extent to which the reality of their lives had to be watered down to make it bearable for cinema audiences. "Plenty of people will think the events in the film have been exaggerated to make it more dramatic," Mary Norris explained to the *Irish Independent*. "But I tell you, the reality of those places was a thousand times worse. There's a scene in which a girl is crying in the dormitory, and another goes over to her bed to comfort her. That could never have happened. You weren't allowed any private conversation. Again, in the film the girls get glimpses of the outside world and even ordinary people who don't live in the laundries. In reality, we were totally incarcerated. You could see nothing except sky."

Meanwhile, Mary-Jo McDonagh, who spent five years in a Magdalene Asylum in Galway (after being molested by a neighbor), told the London *Guardian*: "It was worse in the Magdalens, much worse than what you see. I don't like to say it, but the film is soft on the nuns."

Director Peter Mullan openly admits that he left out some of the most harrowing material for the sake of the audience, and tells the story of how one sixty-five-year-old woman said to him: "It's not nearly bad enough. You didn't show it as it really was. We were only babies. It was a lot worse. It was horrendous."

IN THE AFTERMATH of the film *The Magdalene Sisters*, the survivors did at least get something of an apology, not from the Vatican or the perpetrators themselves, but better than nothing. It came from the Sisters of Mercy of the Americas—the US branch of the organization that ran the Irish asylums that weren't run by the Good Shepherds. "It's not proper to hide from anything," said a spokeswoman for the organization. "We're all human, we've all made mistakes. We do reach out and apologize to anyone who may have been abused at the hands of our sisters, or any sisters."

For a while it even seemed as if the remaining survivors were going to get some compensation for their years of slave labor. In 2002, following the numerous Catholic sexual abuse scandals that emerged in Ireland in the 1990s,[9] an independent Redress Board was set up with the stated intention to "make fair and reasonable awards to persons who, as children, were abused while resident in industrial schools, reformatories and other institutions subject to state regulation or inspection."

Surprisingly, very few of the Magdalene survivors were considered to be within the ambit of this board (the main exceptions being those who were transferred directly from the Industrial Schools).

"They were completely ignored," explains Mari Steed, a spokeswoman for the Justice for Magdalenes group, whose own biological mother spent a number of years in the Sunday's Well asylum in Cork. "Basically, in 2002, it came down to a decision from a chief justice [the Honorable Mr. Justice Sean Ryan] who determined that the Magdalene women were, in fact women"—i.e., they were too old—"and were 'voluntarily' sent to these institutions. As such, he felt that they were not entitled to the redress given to other victims of institutional abuse."

Steed and the survivors were unimpressed by this decision. "If these women 'voluntarily' submitted to a life doing industrial laundry," she asks, "why when some tried to leave or escape were they dragged back by the *gardai* [i.e., Ireland's National Police Service]?"

"Many were not legal adults when they entered," she adds, noting that none of the various scenarios for which women were sent to the laundries (being the victims of rape, having babies out of wedlock, being too pretty, or getting deemed "flirtatious") "seem very voluntary, either."

In addition to this injustice, the women have lately had to contend with further setbacks. Perhaps the most damaging is the controversy following the publication of the book *Kathy's Story* by Kathy O'Beirne. A misery memoir in the mold of James Frey's *A Million Little Pieces*, full of painful stories and horrific accounts of abuse within the Magdalene system, the book was an international bestseller.

Unfortunately, claims have been made that *Kathy's Story* resembles Frey's work in more than just its explicit storytelling. The Good Shepherd nuns, who ran the High Park asylum in Dublin in which O'Beirne says she spent several years, have claimed that many of the stories O'Beirne tells are untrue and that she didn't spend any time in any of their institutions.

Although they had kept an undignified silence when the first attempts had been made to uncover the story of the Magdalene Asylums, and declined all press interviews when their laundries first hit the headlines, the Sisters seized this opportunity to put the boot in.

"We are very careful about confidentiality as people's reputations are sacred to us whether they are dead or alive. Our girls came to us because they needed help," High Park's senior archivist told the Irish *Sunday Independent*. "Kathy should produce evidence of where she was and when. Where is the child's birth certificate? Why has it taken 30 years to find? I am very sorry, the girl is clearly very traumatised."

The *Sunday Independent* was happy to report the story almost entirely from the nuns' viewpoint, portraying them as victims "appalled" by the allegations being made against them, not even mentioning the verifiable suffering about which they have been silent for so many years (revealed by numerous news outlets, documentarians, and twenty years of primary-source research by professor Frances Finnegan.)

When I spoke to Kathy O'Beirne, she did at least make the point that her book has kept the issue of the Magdalene Asylums firmly in the public eye, and like James Frey she pointed out how helpful it has been to many of her readers who have themselves suffered abuse. She is also able to defend herself on the grounds that plenty of other people with complicated upbringings in Industrial Schools and Magdalene Laundries are unable to produce their correct birth certificates and documentation. O'Beirne also claims that many of her records were destroyed in a fire. Sadly, however, there are several aspects of the book that other more neutral observers have declared "do not pass the smell test."

"It's all the truth," protests O'Beirne. "We know it's the truth. They [the Church] know it's the truth." At the time of writing, she faces an uphill struggle to prove her case. It seems likely that the case will go to court. There is, however, no doubting that O'Beirne carries a lasting trauma from whatever it was that happened to her in her youth, and an enduring hatred for the abusive members of the Catholic clergy. "They're just sick. They're the disciples of the devil," she kept repeating when I spoke to her. "They should be ashamed."

AS IT IS, THE NUNS have shown no sign of repentance, although, unsurprisingly, the asylums they ran still cast a long shadow over many lives. The survivors will, of course, never forget. Indeed, many of them are so institutionalized by their time in the laundries that they are unable to fend for themselves and still live in the care of the same orders of nuns who used to hold them enslaved. There are also the hundreds (or possibly even thousands) of children who were forcibly separated from their mothers. Most of them will never find their mothers—or even find out who they were.

There have at least been some happier stories. There are the women like Christina Mulcahey, who managed to escape the system and went on to lead a fulfilling life and raise a family of her own—not to mention telling her story to a wide and sympathetic public and eventually tracking down her long-lost son.

Others, too, have been reunited with their lost babies. Mari Steed from Justice for Magdalenes, for instance, eventually found her mother after a ten-year search.

"I am one of the very lucky ones who met with absolute joy in my reunion," she says. "My mother had been eagerly awaiting my 'return' one of these days and was not at all put out by my finding her."

She insists that there is hope for those still looking and encourages them to persevere, albeit with the following warning: "Guard yourself against unrealistic expectations, because sometimes you're not always met with a warm welcome. The shame and stigma of unwed pregnancy in Ireland was so heavy back then that many women have never outed themselves to subsequent husbands or children."

So it is that most of the women who passed through the Magdalene Asylums never have told

"The shame is not mine; the church should be ashamed."

their stories, and never will. As Mary Norris told the *Irish Independent*:

> Many survivors refuse to talk about what they went through, but I've never been ashamed to have been in one of those places. The shame is not mine; the church should be ashamed. They say now they're sorry—what they mean is, sorry they were found out.

There has been no apology. No state enquiry. Most of the 155 women found in the mass grave at the High Park Laundry still have no death certificate. More graves, still uncovered, are said to be scattered around Ireland.

---

1. Not least because, before the scandal broke, several of the institutions handed over their records to social history professor Frances Finnegan, who made it her mission to bring this shadowy history into the light, talking to journalists, helping to inform the TV programs that would eventually explain the laundries to the world, and eventually publishing the definitive history, *Do Penance or Perish: A Study of Magdalen Asylums in Ireland* (Congrave Press, 2001).

2. This was all explained in the handbook of the Good Shepherds: "The greater number of our children we know desire to return to the world. The thought that they will be once more exposed to the danger of going astray...is a sorrow for a Religious. We should then, make every effort to induce them to remain in the asylum opened to them by Divine Providence, where they are assured the grace of a happy death..." (*Practical Rules for the Use of the Religious of the Good Shepherd for the Direction of the Classes* by Mother St. Euphrasia Pelletier, 1898: 182–3. Cited in Finnegan: *Do Penance*.)

3. As shown in the records investigated by Frances Finnegan. *Do Penance*: 195.

4. Ibid.

5. Ibid: 46.

6. Ibid: 42.

7. Sundays were given over to yet more religious contemplation.

8. Raferty, Mary, and Eoin O'Sullivan. *Suffer the Little Children: The Inside Story of Ireland's Industrial Schools*. New Island Books, 2000: 290.

9. Including the exposure of the systematic mistreatment of thousands of children in the country's Catholic-run Industrial Schools and hundreds of cases of priestly pedophilia, as well as the stories from the Magdalene Laundries.

John Gorenfeld

"END OF THE WORLD PROPHET FOUND IN ERROR, NOT INSANE"

A FAILED PROPHET'S SURVIVAL HANDBOOK

THOUGHT ABOUT BECOMING an an end-of-the-world prophet? It's not the make-or-break enterprise you might think, as much as your gut feeling may be that mobs of angry parishioners await the fortune-teller who talks them into making room on the calendar for the final trumpets, the Rapture, World War III, the return of Jesus, global computer meltdowns, or post-game shows on life hosted by great messiahs stepping out of the pages of history—only for the poor dupes to find themselves paying bills the next week.

Time and again, it hasn't worked that way. The beauty of blown prophecies is that failure is the beginning of success. That is, *if* you adopt the techniques of history's most successful faulty prophets. Through time-tested rebranding methods, they've reinvented failure as proof that they were righter than anyone could have imagined.

The very glue holding your congregation together can be a mistaken prediction and what you've invested in it. Thousands of apostles of Shaini Goodwin of Tacoma, Washington, known to admirers as the "Dove of Oneness" and to the *Tacoma News Tribune* as a "cybercult queen," hold out for a Judgment Day that will justify all of her bad guesses.

Every year is supposed to be the year it happens: the revelation of NESARA (the National Economic Security and Reformation Act), a secret bill purportedly signed by President Bill Clinton. We are just a hair's breadth away. When the gag order is lifted, NESARA will free the world from debt, stop the Iraq War, and—according to one Utah group of adherents, filmed in the documentary *Waiting for NESARA*—unmask Republicans as space aliens masquerading as fiscal conservatives.

The beauty of blown prophecies is that failure is the beginning of success.

For other bad prophets, it turns out it's the thought that counts. Maybe the seer was on the right track but just jumped the gun, the sense is, and interest heightens in the original questions he raised. Just consider theologian William Miller. His followers believed his prediction—based on calculations he derived from the Book of Daniel—that Jesus would return between March 21, 1843, and March 21, 1844. This misfire was soon followed by the Great Disappointment of 1844, when a crowd of 100,000 people, many of them sober, respectable reformers and abolitionists, assembled to see the end-times that Samuel S. Snow, a Millerite (that is, a follower of Miller), had marked down for the 22nd of October. Supposedly using a more precise version of Miller's formula, Snow had worked out the exact day, and after some initial hesitancy Miller enthusiastically endorsed this specific prediction. As the clock ticked and everyone waited awkwardly for Christ, someone pointed out that the Holy Land had a seven-hour time difference. The sting of failure was worse for all the mockery they took from the townspeople: "What, not gone up yet?"

No, they were still here. For now. And yet Miller's bad guesses, far from leaving a foul taste in everyone's mouth, made them newly anxious about the great return they'd prepared themselves for. It even inspired the creation of new denominations, including the Seventh Day Adventists and the Jehovah's Witnesses, a church that has since slated Jesus' return for 1874, 1914, 1918, 1941, 1954, *and* 1975. And Miller awakened the fascination with the Rapture that today drives sales of Tim LaHaye's *Left Behind* books, which sell in the tens of millions, several years after the year 2000 failed to deliver on the millennial holocaust of non-Christians wished for by many Americans.

How can your sect rebound from failed prophecy in better shape than ever? According to one school of science, the answer starts with understanding the principle of *cognitive dissonance.*

You mostly find that term thrown around these days in Internet political debates, in which bloggers profess amazement that their foes can simultaneously hold conflicting beliefs. They reach for a formal name for what it is that permits (for example) Judith Miller, the *New York Times* reporter who predicted that WMD would be found in Iraq, to exclaim in an interview with Salon, after no weapons had been found: "I was proved fucking right. That's what happened. People who disagreed with me were saying, 'There she goes again.' But I was proved fucking right."

"Cognitive dissonance" is a term coined by researchers from the University of Chicago who, under the leadership of one Dr. Leon Festinger, infiltrated a prophecy group in the 1950s: a fellowship of believers sure that a tidal wave was about to kill millions. In their humane but unsparingly detailed 1956 account, *When Prophecy Fails*, they described their efforts to find out just how far personal investment in strong convictions will go when what the material world calls "evidence" becomes the enemy.

CHRISTMAS EVE, 1954, and Dr. Charles Laughead stood waiting for the disaster outside a home on South Cuyler Avenue in the western suburbs of Chicago, hemmed in by a media circus. A week ago, this neighborhood was supposed to have become the basin of a new sea, along with most of the central United States. It didn't, but the tidal wave must be crashing over the Great Lakes soon. The stakes were too high for him to change his mind now.

"I've given up just about everything," he'd said in recent days. "I've taken an awful beating in the last few months, just an awful beating."

He'd been laughed at and fired from his job at the medical school. The administration didn't like that he was upsetting medical students with his warnings that North America was about to be cleaved into western and eastern islands and flooded with a new ocean that would make Cook County a reef before graduation. With an upbeat, can-do spirit, he preached at the group's meetings that "the boys upstairs," rescuers beyond our solar system, would spirit away humans who were ready to hear the call.

Other believers wept when silence came instead of cataclysm. But Laughead wasn't about to quit now. He rallied the group, discarding despair in favor of twentieth-century PR. He phoned reporters. A press release, sent to newspapers across the country, read: "Due to the confusion which has arisen from the prophecy we have decided to unite forces to complete the prophecy…"

The story went national. The *Chicago Daily Tribune* wrote, in an article headlined "SECT EXPECTS TO DEPART THIS EARTH TONIGHT":

> Mrs. Dorothy Martin, 707 S. Cuyler Av., Oak Park, said yesterday she, Dr. Charles Laughead, 44, and other associates have received word from "the space brothers" that they will be "lifted up" from the face of the earth tonight.
>
> Mrs. Martin said the group will gather in front of her home at 6 P.M. "We have been instructed to sing carols while we wait to be lifted up," she said.

Dorothy Martin alerted them first to the space-landers coming to retrieve them from the flood. Soon, settling down across the earth, including in the suburbs of Chicago, the "peapod ships" would evacuate eight to ten souls each. The space arks would leave behind a new sea filling the bowl between the Alleghenies, the Catskills, and the

Rocky Mountains. There would be a "washing of the top to the sea, for the purpose of purifying it of the earthling, and the creating of the new order.... [A]ll things must first be likened unto the house-cleaning...."

No metal was allowed on board. No bra clasps; therefore, no bras. Men cut the zippers from pants. As the expected exit date neared, and everyone stood ready, Dr. Laughead discovered that one of the undercover psychologists was still bezippered, and performed last-minute surgery—hands trembling, according to the report.

A prophet faces a thousand humiliations. This week proved no exception. Jokesters kept making phone calls, claiming to be spacemen with names like Captain Video, calls that Laughead refused to rule out, though his daughter insisted otherwise: that the aliens wouldn't be making contact under the call sign of TV's then-famous space ranger. But everyone was so coiled up for first contact, and ready to hear from the aliens in coded signals, that the signs lay everywhere. After a boy phoned and invited the seekers to a party, Mrs. Martin decided this was it. "Put your coats on," she said and led a delegation across town, only to return, disappointed. Then there was the cheap shot the *Tribune* took, saying the Laughead kids must not think Armageddon was coming, seeing as how they'd set up ornaments in the living room for Christmas morning.

What was Dr. Laughead going to do about presents? The phone rang and another awkward exchange took place, transcribed verbatim in the Festinger report:

NEWSMAN: Dr. Laughead, I wanted to talk to you with reference to this business about—you know—your calling the paper to say you were going to be picked up at six o'clock this evening. Ahh, I just wanted to find out exactly what happened.... Didn't you say they sent a message that you should be packed and waiting at 6 P.M. Christmas Eve?
DR. LAUGHEAD: No.
NEWSMAN: No? I'm sorry, sir. Weren't the spacemen supposed to pick you up at 6 P.M.?

DR. LAUGHEAD: Well, there was a spaceman in the crowd with a helmet on and a white gown and whatnot.
NEWSMAN: There was a spaceman in the crowd?
DR. LAUGHEAD: Well, it was a little hard to tell [...]
NEWSMAN: [...] Did you talk to him?
DR. LAUGHEAD: No, I didn't talk to him.
NEWSMAN: Didn't you say you were going to be picked up by the spacemen?
DR. LAUGHEAD: No.
NEWSMAN: Well, what were you waiting out in the street for, singing carols?
DR. LAUGHEAD: Well, we went out to sing Christmas carols.
NEWSMAN: Oh, you just went out to sing Christmas carols?
DR. LAUGHEAD: Well, and if anything happened, well, that's all right, you know. We live from one minute to another.
NEWSMAN: [...] Uh, well how do you account for the fact that they didn't pick you up?
DR. LAUGHEAD: As I told one of the other news boys, I don't think a spaceman would feel very welcome there in that crowd...

The tidal wave and the peapod ships never came. Soon the doctor's aggrieved sister tried to have him committed to an asylum. But at his hearing, a psychologist testified that the doctor "showed no obvious illusions or hallucinations and his conduct and manner seemed entirely normal."

"END OF THE WORLD PROPHET FOUND IN ERROR, NOT INSANE," reported the *Tribune*. Police, however, briefly considered charging the duo with contributing to the delinquency of minors—Chicago Police Chief Kearin explaining, it said in the paper, that "children of the neighborhood had talked to Mrs. Martin about space travel with the result that some of the youngsters had trouble sleeping afterwards."

YEARS LATER, Dr. Laughead would roam the Americas, still seeking the space brotherhood, whom he believed to be linked to an ancient South American civilization. Meanwhile, Leon Festinger and his team had begun to assemble a theoretical framework for understanding why the seekers hadn't disbanded in shame after the failure of their prophecy but instead proselytized even more fervently about their saviors from deep space.

Reaching back to early failed prophecies in the Christian world, as well as the story of William Miller, they came to the conclusion that given the right set of conditions—including great personal investment in preparing for the end—what kicks in is Festinger's syndrome (a/k/a, cognitive dissonance). Failed prophecy might make a church redouble its efforts at proselytizing, instead of questioning its premises:

> **"The individual will frequently emerge, not only unshaken but even more convinced of the truth of his beliefs than ever before."**

Suppose an individual believes something with his whole heart; suppose further that he has a commitment to this belief, but he has taken irrevocable actions because of it; finally suppose that he is presented with evidence, unequivocal and undeniable evidence, that his belief is wrong: What will happen? The individual will frequently emerge, not only unshaken but even more convinced of the truth of his beliefs than ever before. Indeed, he may even show a new fervor about convincing and converting other people to his view.

Since then, *When Prophecy Fails* (which changed the names of its subjects) has been the love-it-or-hate-it starting point for all other studies of bad prophecy. Other scholars have repeated the original experiment, often succeeding to some measure, though sometimes proposing new conditions to account for when this reaction is likely to happen, or not happen.

In the last few decades, a more forgiving school of researchers has grumbled at Festinger's unsparingly literal approach. Outsiders don't get to decide if a prophecy fails or not, its adherents say.

One major figure in this gentler approach to prophecy is Dr. G. Gordon Melton of Santa Barbara. His passion for proving the sanity and rationality of new religions has even taken him to Japan on the dime of the Aum Supreme Truth church, there to maintain that the group couldn't possibly have gassed Tokyo subway commuters in 1995 (as they did) to hasten the apocalypse. Adopted by Festinger's critics, Melton's influential view, developed in the mid-1980s, is that failed prophecies don't fall flat so much as they become "spiritualized." They are transformed from literal predictions into deeper visions of the hidden cosmos.

Whatever the quibbles, however, Festinger's general idea—that faith is often invigorated by disconfirmation—still stands strong, even if the predicted result—more proselytism—hasn't always been the pressure valve for the new burst of faith. Whether it happens, though, seems to depends on a number of factors, including the degree of ridicule to which the group has been subjected and whether the religion offers more than just apocalyptic predictions as something to fall back on, such as tradition or community.

THE LUBAVITCHERS OF BROOKLYN, the subjects of another study, were able to go on as usual after a major prediction by some of its adherents failed to materialize, and one scholar wanted to know why. In 1991, just after Saddam Hussein was driven from Kuwait, the Hasidic Jewish group put up fliers proclaiming that the Messiah walked in Crown Heights in the person of the white-bearded sage Rabbi Menachem Schneerson:

DRAW YOUR OWN CONCLUSION
These are amazing times. The Iron Curtain has crumbled. Iraq is humbled. The people of Israel emerge from under a rainstorm of murderous missiles. An entire beleaguered population is airlifted to safety overnight. A tidal wave of Russian Jews reaches Israel. Nations around the world turn to democracy. Plus countless other amazing developments that are taking place in front of our eyes. Any of these phenomena by itself is enough to boggle the mind. Connect them all together and a pattern emerges that cannot be ignored. The Lubavitcher Rebbe emphasizes that these remarkable events are merely a prelude to the final redemption. The era of Moshiach is upon us. Learn about it. Be part of it. All you have to do is to open your eyes. Inevitably, you will draw your own conclusion.

Even after Schneerson fell into a fatal coma in 1994, believers guessed that he'd descended into the world of death only to begin his unification of all souls and his work on earth. He would soon gather together his powers, spring to life, and save the world of the living. When it didn't happen, an official proclamation explained that he lay suspended in a "state of concealment," like when Moses was on the mountaintop and couldn't be seen.

After his death, some held out for resurrection; some privately acknowledged to Simon Dein, a psychiatrist who studies the cultural aspects of religion, that they'd made a mistake; but *Lubavitch Magazine* said that it was their naysayers who were discredited. They pointed to an acceleration of Lubavitch activity all over the world, as new temples went up in Schneerson's honor. And some maintain he is the Messiah, even if he hasn't ended war and suffering. Among many there was an agreement that, whatever you thought of these events, there was no doubting that a miracle had happened. Dein's conclusion: These were "sane people who try to reason their way through facts and doctrine." Their prediction had become spiritualized.

THE "CHURCH OF THE TRUE WORD" tried everything.

At one point it comprised 135 splinter Baha'i survivalists in Montana, led into fallout shelters to await mass nuclear death and the return of Jesus. Over a span of several years, True Word leaders Leland Jensen and Neal Chase predicted so many dates for World War III and other misadventures that studies of the group have names like "When the Bombs Drop" and "When the Bombs Still Haven't Dropped."

By the 1990s, blown predictions had become a lifestyle. Indeed, Leland Jensen, the group's soothsayer, had covered every possible base in explaining why everyone was still alive. Researchers keeping tabs on Jensen's excuses tallied up a list so all-encompassing that it covers just about every justification ever applied to an inaccurate prophecy.

1) It really did happen, just not in the material world.

If God's world is the spirit and ours is just matter and flesh, how can you expect to use our reason as the measuring stick?

In keeping with this popular axiom, Jensen predicted that Halley's Comet would start ripping apart earth's cities on April 29, 1986, raining down deadly chunks for a year. When it harmlessly passed by instead, Jensen explained that it "did take place. A spiritual stone hit the earth."

The Jehovah's Witnesses similarly defended the 1844 date of Snow and Miller's failed Second Coming prophecy by arguing that this date was when Christ arrived—in the second apartment of a sanctuary in heaven. And a 1914 prediction date was explained later as the time that Jesus' kingdom began—but in the *spirit* world.

2) It really did happen, only in a much more ordinary way than you expected.

The "bowl of wrath" that was supposed to be flung into the air by the seventh angel turned out, according to Jensen and Chase, to be all the news coverage touched off by their explosive predictions.

3) Just testing.

Famously, God was just messing with Abraham when he asked him to knife his own son. Why not take a page from him? When World War III wasn't declared on time, Church of the True Word leaders said their warning was "God's fire drill."

A variation is to shame followers by telling them they blew God's test. On the morning of June 18, 1975, a Japanese prophet/healer named Katsuichi Motoki appeared on a radio station, explaining that if an apocalyptic earthquake didn't hit Japan that morning, he'd "take the blame and dissolve the sect."

It turned out to be a nice day. "We are saved," cried out the apostles as they made for Motoki's "Shrine of the Fundamental Truth." But when they got there, they found Motoki bleeding to death, having tried to commit ritual suicide, samurai style, after his failed prophecy. Had he offered his life to the spirits for saving Japan? They admired his sacrifice.

The next month, out of the hospital, he gathered them together and chewed them out.

"All of you are failures," he said. "Why? You thought that if God's prophecy did not materialize, you would be so scorned and slandered...."

They'd thought only of themselves—that was what mattered. Their self-consciousness had shamed

God. And Motoki had taken the heat for their lapse of belief. "God had transferred the cataclysm to my own body," he explained, describing a vision in which he morphed into the islands of Japan.

It worked and he kept his group. Of the twenty-one who lived at his dorm, he retained seventeen.

4) The numbers were off.

Sometimes it's easiest just to say you forgot to carry the one. On May 6, 1980, the *Chillicothe Constitution-Tribune* of Missouri reported, under the headline "DOOMSDAY IS RESCHEDULED FOR WEDNESDAY MORNING," that "the prediction of a holocaust for April 29 at 5:55 P.M. was in error because sect members were not interpreting Biblical time references correctly." Jensen's messenger didn't fear ridicule. "They laughed at Noah," he said. Jensen reiterated that on the following Wednesday the world would be rocked by either nuclear detonation or an assassination.

In London in 1524, there was some commotion over fortune-tellers who predicted that a flood would wipe out the city; 20,000 people were said to have left, including the wealthy. Later, instead of drowning the soothsayers, there was widespread agreement that they'd calculated incorrectly and that the true date was 1624, according to Charles Mackay, author of the great 1841 book *Extraordinary Popular Delusions and the Madness of Crowds*.

Mackay devotes a chapter to English prophecies of doom, including the story of the chicken whose egg came out marked "CHRIST IS COMING." That led to a stir until it was discovered that the words had been written in human-made ink, then stuffed back into the bird.

5) Who said anything about being prophets?

Hey, they just took a stab at the stuff. Chase and Jensen didn't have a direct line to God. "We can't be false prophets because we don't claim to be prophets," said Chase and Jensen after one nuclear war turned up missing. "We simply interpret what is already there in the Bible."

6) Erring on the safe side.

The nuke prophets said it was their moral responsibility to warn humanity, regardless of whether the end came. Faced with the choice of embarrassment or letting everyone die horribly without warning, wouldn't you choose the embarrassment?

NOW THAT YOU'VE SEEN how the world's most successful failed prophets turn poorly phrased predictions into success, let's see if you can identify time-tested disconfirmation dynamics in this case study.

Once upon a time, a con man, Clyde Hood, went to prison for tricking his victims into signing up for bogus "prosperity plans." But just as dupes of Nigerian email scams imagine that nonexistent millions must still be in a suitcase somewhere in Abuja, some of Hood's victims refused to believe that the money was a fantasy.

Hood had even pled guilty to swindling and making it all up. But victims clung to the idea that the wealth was winging its way to them.

Enter Shaini Goodwin, a woman in the Pacific Northwest whose online "Dove Reports" describe the machinations of secret plots, supposedly revealed to her by top sources, kept from us by secret gag orders, that will soon release the fund to the world.

By day the excuses grew evermore complex.

Any day now, the checks would come.

Any day now, the forces of darkness would stop holding back the checks.

Any day now, Christ himself would return in a spaceship, bringing news that in 2000 President Clinton had signed a secret law, with the heavenly acronym NESARA, abolishing the Internal Revenue Service. The National Economic Stabilization And Recovery Act would forgive all debt and topple the Bush Administration.

From lack of evidence came a volcano of faith. The conspiracy theory has now spread across the Net to thousands of websites.

Waiting For NESARA, a little documentary by Salt Lake City filmmakers Zeb and Elisa Haradon, films a Utah group who weren't the original scam victims but were converts to the beliefs that grew out of the con: the Open Mind Forum, a group that meets at a Kentucky Fried Chicken to giddily await the announcement of NESARA.

"Some people have asked, 'Why does Jesus need a spaceship?'" a grandmotherly lady tells us. Well: "It might be more comfortable..."

But I'm getting ahead of myself. You need to go on Google for yourself and see, because words can't do justice to the scope of this thing. Type in "NESARA," which turns up an amazing 118,000 hits as of this writing. You need to see a picture of one of the rallies these people throw in Washington, DC, and in foreign countries, plastering NESARA signs on trucks that they rent to circle Capitol Hill, demanding the government reveal "the true NESARA law."

Sometimes someone drives by and gives them a thumbs-up, which they interpret as a wink from a politician in the know.

Typical of many NESARA websites—headlined "The Public Announcement of NESARA in the United States is Imminent!"—is the one maintained by a soul going under the name "Patrick Bellringer" to elude identification. He claims to have been told in a vision from God that the hidden law was passed "in a secret joint session of Congress with the walls of the House Chambers lined with Navy Seals and Delta Force."

Members tune in to updates from the Dove, who says that the "White Knights," supernatural avatars, will step in any day now to reveal the law and bring about a New World Order. In one message left on Dove's dial-a-prophecy answering machine, a supposed alien being is heard to explain that 9/11 was a plot to stop the prophecy of NESARA, saying in an extraterrestrial voice: "HUMANS HAVE TO GET OVER THEIR ANGER. WE WERE THERE INSTANTLY TO BEAM THEM UP OUT OF THAT BUILDING."

The group in the documentary, which has little to fall back on, eventually breaks up. The discussion leader is ridiculed on a local talk-radio station, where a caller sneers at him: "Who are these White Knights—the Knights of Columbus?"

"That's pretty cute," he says, trying to brush it off.

Even worse, it's pointed out to him that if the aliens make us all rich, it'll just lead to inflation. And then, of course, NESARA fails to be revealed.

"We have to go with the flow," Jim tells the group in explanation. "Plans change."

That was years ago. But the Dove continues to claim victory is at hand. In mid-2006, she posted that the evidence just kept coming: "About 90 percent of Navy SEALs are aware of the true NESARA law," she wrote, suggesting that it's "possible to confirm that the new 'rainbow' currency has already been printed."

Goodwin called me about this article, beginning the conversation by asking if my phone was tapped. Assured we were on a secure line, Goodwin told me that the US Congress was "attempting to move this forward, but there's so much control from the US Supreme Court." Former Fed chief Alan Greenspan and former Treasury Secretary Paul O'Neill had confirmed NESARA's existence, she claimed. "If they were publicly to discuss NESARA they would be arrested," she said; the situation is "as serious as a heart attack."

AND IT GOES ON and on. In April 2000, Trinity Broadcasting Network evangelist Benny Hinn "prophecized" that God Almighty was "fulfilling His plan" for Syria's Hafez Al-Assad to sign a peace treaty with Israel: "They have to, because God says they will." It was a reason for viewers to send him checks. When Assad died two months later without having signed a treaty, Hinn backpedaled and said, in a flourish worthy of Spinal Tap: "It was God's plan for it *not* to happen, really."

The end has been nigh as far back in time as anyone can remember. The slip-ups are at least as old as the Assyrian clay tablet from 2800 B.C.E. that said, citing the disgusting morality of the times: "Our earth is degenerate in these latter days. There are signs that the world is speedily coming to an end." While archaeologists have no signs of whether this ancient version of Benny Hinn did well for himself, preachers in our time have unmistakably made a fortune regardless of—or is it because of?—bogus prophecies.

Our own Hinn reaped $89 million in donations in 2003, despite having predicted that a devastating earthquake would hit the East coast in the 1990s, that American gays would be wiped out by fire in 1995, and that the Rapture was less than two years away in the fall of 1990.

And that Jesus would be arriving in the next two years.

That was in 1997.

Thérèse Taylor

FAITH AND CURSES

God is jealous, and the Lord revengeth; the Lord revengeth, and is furious; the Lord will take vengeance on his adversaries, and he reserveth wrath for his enemies.
   —Nahum 1:2 (KJV)

THE BIBLE CITES the word of God as, "Behold I set before you, the blessing and the curse" (Deuteronomy 11:26). We all hope to see blessings, and religious teachers tell us of them. What of the curses?

Curses are not remote in pagan antiquity nor lost as a means of expressing religious feeling. The infliction of harm, whether by God or his agents, is definitely part of the history of religions that we would consider mainstream.

In 1986, during an Israeli election campaign, voters in the holy city of Jerusalem were treated to an advertisement which showed "a group of rabbis, including Rabbi Josef clad in gold brocaded robe and a black felt Ottoman-style hat murmuring religious curses against their opponents. The committee regulating election coverage allowed this, but cut out a section where the rabbis threatened that the wrath of God would fall on those who did not vote for Shas."[1]

Some people will do anything to win an election.

Shas, a political party in Israel, is notorious for mixing religion, superstition, and appeals to fanaticism. Their constituency is the Oriental Jews—a community marked by tribal loyalties and familiarity with the folk religion of the Middle East—a religion of jinns, spirits, insights from holy men, and visits from the souls of the dead.

The infliction of harm, whether by God or his agents, is definitely part of the history of religions that we would consider mainstream.

Religious curses might be expected from Shas. But they are not alone in this. Shas is merely openly articulating a belief found in most major religions, but which tends to be downplayed by contemporary clerics.

Shrines of the Virgin Mary, writings by Protestant divines, holy legends of the Sufis, and other religious literature contain evidence for the belief that it is not just wrong to defy God's representatives on earth. It is also dangerous.

CHRISTIANITY

Early Christianity made free use of curses, and a whole form of canonical literature was built up around them. In 1916, H. Martin wrote a detailed article about theological curses for the *American*

Journal of Philology. This writer explained: "The Christian world has never fully obeyed the injunction 'swear not at all.' On the contrary, we find the Christian from the beginning proficient in cursing as well as in blessing and his stock of imprecations and epithets proves to be quite as rich and varying as that of his pagan forbears...."[2]

The subject of Christian maledictions has been understudied. It is an aspect of the faith seen as unimportant, or as an anomaly, but the 2006 study *Early Christian Historiography: Narratives of Retribution* looks at the early centuries of Christian history and "the conflict between retributive logic and what began to emerge as the central features of the Christian faith: forgiveness and redemption."[3]

This oscillation between damning the wicked, or offering them unconditional love, is especially marked in Christianity. It persists to this day. The established churches now claim their faith as solely based on love. However, irregular and populist movements, such as fundamentalist groups, have revived practices such as exorcism and cursing. These can give warrant to the most violent actions in the name of religion.

THE VIRGIN MARY

The mother of Jesus is honored throughout Christianity and especially revered in Catholicism and Eastern Orthodoxy. She is universally seen as a figure of ideal motherhood, of love and mercy.

The notion of ideal motherhood has altered over the centuries, and few Christians are aware that until the late eighteenth and early nineteenth centuries, Mary was often honored in shrines and legends which celebrated her ability to inflict harm.

In Brittany, the Celtic area of France, traditional Marian shrines abound. Altars sacred to the Virgin Mary and her mother, Saint Anne, sustain the faithful by numerous miracles and messages of hope and devotion. Amongst these, a shrine with the title of Our Lady of Hatred might seem startling. However, it is an historical fact that this shrine existed, and until the late nineteenth century it was frequented by pilgrims who believed that if one said "Ave Maria" three times at the shrine, one could bring about the ruin of one's enemies.[4]

This is an aspect of Celtic Christianity, but such tales can be found elsewhere, most especially in the Mediterranean. The scholar Michael P. Carroll has written a book, *Madonnas That Maim*, partly about Italian beliefs regarding people being cursed if they offend the Virgin Mary. Some examples:

The Madonna del Popolo, Bologna: A soldier urinates against a wall on which had been painted an image of this Madonna. He is struck blind and suffers strong pain "in the parts that offended the Madonna." He repents and is healed.

... The Madonna della Vendeta, Naples: During a siege of Naples, Pietro Aragonese hurls a cannonball against a sanctuary of the Virgin. The ball bounces back and kills him.

... The Madonna di Baracano, Bologna: Two soldiers play at dice, and the loser strikes an image of the Virgin with a stone. The impious soldier is struck by lightning, and the surviving soldier is hanged, along with the corpse of his companion.[5]

St. Alphonsus de Liguori's classic book of Marian devotion, *The Glories of Mary*, informs us: "In the year 1611, in the celebrated sanctuary of Mary in Montevergine, it happened that on the vigil of Pentecost the people who thronged there profaned that feast with balls, excesses, and immodest conduct." Their house of entertainment suddenly burst into flames, and more than 1,500 people were killed. "Five persons who remained alive affirmed upon oath, that they had seen the mother of God herself, with two lighted torches set fire to the inn."[6]

St. Alphonsus was a theologian who maintained a special emphasis on Mary's merciful intercession. He also, in his general religious writings, stressed that Christianity was a religion of forgiveness and love. The above anecdote might appear to be out of place in his thinking, but he would not have included it if he didn't think it was valid and meaningful. His great respect for the Virgin Mary included the supposition that she could bring about the deaths of those who violated her shrine.

During the nineteenth century, the legends of Virgin Mary shrines were refined by the authorities of the Catholic Church, and malign miracles and curses were taken out of the story.

Notre Dame de Médous, who has a shrine in the Hautes Pyrénées, appeared to a visionary in 1648. The shrine was founded after a series of visions experienced by a local widow, Liloye. Our Lady of Médous requested devotions, and in order to demonstrate her power, caused the town to be struck with plague. This ensured that her orders were obeyed. In the nineteenth century, the shrine legend was revised, and clerics wrote explanations of how Our Lady had appeared during an epidemic of the plague and had miraculously halted the epidemic.[7]

The educated Catholic priests who reformed the legends of Mary shrines during the nineteenth century were part of a culture that sentimentalized maternity and the domestic sphere. They were part of the same generation that read the novels of Charles Dickens and stopped taking children to public executions. Of course they did not appreciate stories of Mary as a vengeful and arbitrary queen—the type of authority figure who ruled homes, feudal estates, and whole kingdoms in pre-Enlightenment Europe.

The faithful, especially those who lived in rural poverty, had attitudes that were slower to change. For instance, in 1814, Notre Dame de Redon-Espic appeared in the French province of Périgord, to a peasant girl. The vision predicted the death of the visionaries' parents, and then of a landlord who had threatened her with a stick. Soon after, they died in an epidemic, and this helped to establish the truth of the vision among the local population.[8] Traditional Catholics of rural France accepted this story without question. They saw nothing untoward in it.

The Virgin Mary is the highest of the saints, and offending *any* of the saints might be risky. One of Mary's followers, who shared the disconcerting powers granted to her in Mediterranean culture, was St. Rita of Cascia (1381–1457), born Rita Mancini in a small village in Umbria.

Rita was devoutly religious and had always wanted to become a nun. This ambition was thwarted by her parents, and she was forced into an arranged marriage at the age of twelve to a man known only as "Ferdinand." Rita was married for eighteen years, during which she patiently endured her husband's violent temper and improvident ways. She bore two sons, who, as regretfully noted by her clerical biographers, greatly resembled their father.

It seems that Ferdinand was a trial to many people, not just his wife. He was waylaid outside of Rocca Porena and stabbed to death. Rita immediately and generously forgave his murderers. She then realized that her sons were plotting a violent revenge, in the tradition of vendetta.

St. Rita decided to pray for her sons. She prayed that if God would not alter them, he would remove them from the perils of this world, and "she saw her two sons fall one after another victims to her prayers that pierced the heavens."[9] Both soon died of illness.

As a current pamphlet explains, the death of the sons was providential: "Her prayers were again answered and, within a year, both sons died, leaving Rita completely on her own. With her earthly responsibilities behind her, she could now live for God alone."[10]

Having achieved independence, St. Rita went on to excel. She was a complete success in religious life and became a respected public figure. Her shrine, where her body is entombed, is one of the most visited holy sites in Italy. Apparently without irony, the devotional literature assures us: "Because Rita was a wife and a mother, many women relate to and find comfort in her life story."[11]

A Catholic preacher has commented that St. Rita did, in effect, curse her sons, but that "a judge lawfully curses a man with a just penalty; the Church curses with anathema; prophets cursed evil doers in Old Testament to inspire repentance."[12]

This preacher easily relates the miracle wrought by St. Rita's prayers to orthodox Christian standards. Not everyone would be so content, and it seems significant that the contemporary British writer David Sox, in his scholarly guide to holy places, *Relics and Shrines*, repeats the story of St. Rita's life but merely notes, without further explanation, that her husband and sons died.[13] He instead concentrates on the examples of kindness and inspirational teaching found in her life story. This account is more in keeping with current expectations about the lives of saints.

In the contemporary world, the maleficent powers of the Virgin and the saints appear to have faded and are no longer an active part of Catholic belief. Yet when researching the history of the visions at the Marian shrine at Lourdes in the 1990s, I noticed that people still repeated stories about the sudden deaths of those who had disrespected the Grotto. The Grotto of Lourdes itself is said to be haunted by many spirits, and few people from the town will go there at night. An oral tradition of these supernatural beliefs is therefore maintained but gains no official recognition by clerical authorities.

Protestant thinkers, who dismiss veneration of the Blessed Virgin and the saints, do not have the same fund of holy stories to draw on and tend to take their curses directly from Scripture. They have had no difficulty in finding examples, from God cursing Cain (Genesis 4:11–12) to Jesus cursing the fig tree (Matthew 21:19). In 1649, Milton wrote a fierce pamphlet, *The Tenure of Kings and Magistrates*, which called upon Englishmen to execute King Charles. If they did not do so, they themselves were cursed, and Milton cites Jeremiah from the Bible: "Cursed be he that doeth the work of the Lord deceitfully, and cursed be he that keepeth back his sword from blood."[14]

IN THE HOLY LAND

The former Prime Minister of Israel, Ariel Sharon, has the distinction of being formally cursed, in an elaborate religious ceremony, by his fellow Jews. During 2004–2005, his policy of withdrawing the settlements from Gaza was opposed by extremist elements among the settlers. Many cursed him informally, but a select few arranged a Kabbalistic religious ceremony during which they called upon God to send the angels of death after Sharon.

The curse inflicted on Sharon was known as the *pulsa denura* ("lashes of fire") in the Aramaic language used for these rites. It was a vivid and exotic ceremony. A group of men went into a graveyard at midnight, where, by candlelight and under the cypress trees, they recited prayers and evoked the curse. This took place in July 2005.

Israeli politics tends toward extremes, but even in Israel, a death curse on the Prime Minister caused outraged public comment. Some wanted the cursers to be charged under an anti-terrorist law which forbids "incitement," but the Attorney General considered the case and found that no existing law applied to it.

As Israelis debated the issues in the media, several points emerged. Scholars pointed out that the *pulsa denura*, although claimed to be very ancient, is probably a recent invention; there are no records of it earlier than 1905. It is derived from the traditional rite of excommunication, whereby an evil-doer is cast out of the community. A columnist in the *Forward* pointed out in 2004 that a similar ceremony had been inflicted on Saddam Hussein during the Gulf War of 1991, "but Saddam is still alive, if not particularly well, 13 years after being fire-whipped."[15] Scholars were reassuring and defined all this as merely an attempt to work off negative feelings.

Others scoffed openly and asked what the Kabbalists would do next—were they going to create a *golem* to run for public office? But, as more letters appeared in the media, one Israeli after another said that they were afraid of the *pulsa denura*, and that they knew of cases which proved its power.

Then, on January 4, 2006, Sharon collapsed with a major stroke. He went into a prolonged coma, and his doctors hold out no hope that he will ever recover.

People who deal in death curses are not restrained by notions of good taste. Baruch Ben-Yosef, one of the participants at the July *pulsa denura*, told the *Jerusalem Post* that he and the groups spent all night celebrating after hearing that Sharon was ill.[16]

The Kabbalists who cursed Ariel Sharon are participants in a minority stream of Judaism, which promotes the belief that supernatural—even magical—feats can be performed by those who master sacred texts. Most Jewish authorities are critical of this, viewing such claims as superstition or even outright humbug. They also claim that the *din rodef*, a religious license for a Jew to kill another Jew, is hedged with conditions, so that it is largely a theoretical warning and should almost never be justified in real life.

Throughout Jewish history, many scholars have pondered the curses found in Scripture, where the prophets, and the words of God, pronounce awful sentences on various sections of humanity. Judaism acknowledges that divine punishments are a part of providence and sees the workings of justice in this.

In a philosophical reading, the Jewish scholars have pointed out that some statements typically rated as curses may really be blessings. They point out a statement from the Zohar: "Within the place of greatest despair is found the concealed deliverance."

A Jewish preacher pointed out that this is "interesting and perplexing," but he invited people to consider:

> When one truly despairs of life, if one treats that despair not as a curse but as a blessing, he is "delivered;" relieved from the never-ending sense-less pursuit of material bliss and pleasure-seeking, and free to serve Hashem [the Lord] with a heart uninhibited by the daily grind that slowly eats away at our days and years.... Of course we can't completely ignore life's daily needs and details. But if we lived each day with this attitude, how much of it would really matter? Would we care if the caterer botched up the centrepiece at our son's bar-mitzvah?... If we lived today as if it were our last, how would our davening [reciting of prayers] be different? Our Torah? Our attitude towards life?[17]

This teaching shows a paradox, whereby curses and blessings can lead to the same place—a deliverance from care to live without being ruled by expectations and desires.

SACRED THREATS IN THE ISLAMIC WORLD

Islamic religious literature offers many examples of curses and maledictions called down by holy men, and sometimes women, on God's behalf.

Like Christianity, Islam is divided on the basis of significantly different theological interpretations. The minority Shia branch of Islam is reckoned to have a cultural affinity with Roman Catholicism, as both believe in the veneration of saints and attendance at their tombs and shrines. Like Catholics, Shias worship only God, but some aspects of their devotions to holy figures have popular traditions which incorporate many strands of legends and folklore. Like Hassidic Jews and Roman Catholics, Shias believe in intercession—that is, holy people who have died can intercede for us before the throne of God and be a conduit for blessings. One therefore finds, within Shia Islam, more individualized stories of blessings, whimsies, and favors associated with various mortals who channel divine powers on earth.

The twelve imams of the Shia tradition are revered by their followers as the "holy household." They were the descendants of the Prophet, believed by their followers to be the true rulers of the Islamic world, selected by God. Deprived of their rights by the machinations of tyrants, who deposed and persecuted them, they left messages for their followers, and the last of them—the twelfth imam—was finally taken into "occulation," where he awaits the messianic age when he will return to rule the earth.

The twelve imams are said to have faced persecution with fortitude, and each one is said to have been martyred. They enjoined their followers to practice patience and to await divine deliverance. imam Ali, the first of the imams, is said to have recommended of true believers that "they treat their friends and their enemies the same."

These elevated virtues would seem to place the imams well above acts of malice or revenge. Yet, as with some of the Catholic saints, popular tradition has an inclination to add, to their miraculous abilities, tales of their ability to inflict harm.

The eleventh imam, Ali Naqi, is described thus in a learned source:

> Imam Ali Naqi's conduct and moral excellence were the same as those displayed by each and every member of this sacred house. Whether in imprisonment, confinement or freedom, in every case these sacred souls were engaged in worship and in helping the poor and the needy. Totally refraining from desire, greed and worldly ambitions,

they lived dignified in misfortune, dealt fairly even with their foes.[18]

The above text stresses traditional virtues, and books about Imam Al-Hadi give a picture of a mild-mannered philosopher who spent much of his life under house arrest, or worse. He advised his followers to show resignation in all circumstances, as "Allah made the worldly life a place of trial, and the afterlife a place of reward."[19] He pondered the virtue of true restraint, rather than merely being subject to outside forces: "Patience is to possess yourself and control your anger when you are in a position to express it."[20] To judge by these sources, Al-Hadi's severities were limited to his letters, where he maintained that the death sentence was appropriate for capital crimes.[21]

In contrast to these austere teachings, more colorful anecdotes circulate. In these dramatic and folkloric stories, people are told of the imam not as a remote and exemplary person, but as a wonderworker who can transform reality. A Shia devotional text states:

> Abul Qassem ibn Abul Qassem Al-Baghdadi narrates our next incident from the life of the Imam quoting Zaraarah, the Orderly of Mutawakkil who said, "There came a magician and juggler to the court of Caliph Mutawakkil al-Abbasi who was supposed to be an expert in making things disappear and in such other tricks and buffoonery."

The magician uses his tricks to mock the imam, making bread disappear when he reaches for it.

> Seeing this, Imam Ali an-Naqi (A.H.S.) cast a wrathful glance on the pillow on which there was a picture of a lion...and addressed the lion, "What are you looking at, eat up this magician"! As if the lion was waiting for a command from the Imam (A.H.S.) that it immediately pounced upon the magician and within a matter of seconds, it ate and gobbled him up and then went back to its original shape of a picture!![22]

This story allows the audience to participate in Imam Al-Hadi's virtues through the pleasing spectacle of the mocking magician being punished. Instead of an austere message of "totally refraining from desire, greed and worldly ambitions," as in the canonical account, here we have the imam dealing with his foes by magical curses.

The lion had a strong presence in pre-Islamic Middle Eastern pagan religions, and this may be why it is the being which springs to life from an image. Ancient statues of lions are dotted over Persia and even to this day are associated with supernatural tales.

Invocation of the Names of Allah is a traditional way to attract blessings, but an exclusive concentration on one particular attribute—Ya-Qahhar (Oh Destroyer)—is supposed to have given the Sufi teacher Osman Baba the power to kill those around him. "If he threw a piece of cotton at someone and it hit him, he would die."[23] The people complained to a senior religious leader, who told them to take a piece of cotton and throw it back at Osman. They did so and he, in his turn, was the one to die.

Such stories are found in many Islamic accounts of the lives of sufis, prophets, and inspirational figures. Tales of people who drop dead after disrespecting a copy of the Koran are also common. Many people in the Islamic world are convinced that the artist responsible for the most infamous Danish cartoon, mocking the Prophet Muhammad as a terrorist, later caught fire and died in his bed.

CURSES

What are the common features of these curses, which range from Christian antiquity to contemporary Jerusalem?

They all depend upon a notion that people are vulnerable to unseen powers. The hatred, rejections, and rivalries which others feel toward us can, through spiritual means, be linked to supernatural forces. The ordinary then becomes the extraordinary, and banal circumstances—such as an old man having a stroke—are no longer random events.

Curses, ultimately, offer some hope of justice.

Curses, ultimately, offer some hope of justice. If wrongdoers can be struck down by God, then they suffer for the misdeeds that have made others hate them. The patterns of life are given meaning, and all misfortunes which follow sin are defined as a punishment. The spectacle of suffering is easy to accept if the victim is also a culprit.

When we purge all mention of curses, malediction, and harm from religion, we are left with lofty ideals that don't quite correspond with life. But when curses are taken literally, one has an overwhelming impression of superstition and malice, dressed up as faith.

Modern clerics, when they leave curses behind, also abandon some of the powerful forces of awe that make humanity aware of a reality beyond its own existence. Also, the notion of supernatural danger, ignored by mainstream religion, then becomes marginalized into New Age, fundamentalist, and other alternative sects. They preserve an aspect of religious experience bleached out of the respectable, ordinary, and safe ways of the mainstream. Curses remain one of the ways by which we explain our experiences and communicate with each other and the deity. They will never disappear.

1. Colvin, Marie. "Ultra-orthodox Hold the Key to Israel's Future; Israeli Election." *Sunday Times* (London), 6 Nov 1988.

2. Martin, H. "The Judas Iscariot Curse." *American Journal of Philology* 37.4 (1916): 434.

3. Trompf, G.W. *Early Christian Historiography: Narratives of Retribution.* Equinox Publishing, 2006.

4. Devlin, Judith. *The Superstitious Mind: French Peasants and the Supernatural in the Nineteenth Century.* Yale University Press, 1987: 18.

5. Carroll, Michael P. *Madonnas That Maim: Popular Catholicism in Italy Since the Fifteenth Century.* Johns Hopkins University Press, 1992: 73.

6. Liguri, Alphonsus. *The Glories of Mary*: 659. Cited by the email list _Catholic_no_EACW ("A list for Catholics who are fed up with the new liberalist views being forced on us."), 26 May 2006. <groups.yahoo.com/group/1_Catholic_no_EACW>.

7. Théas, A. *Notre Dame de Medoux; aujourd'hui Notre-Dame d'Aste.* Tarbes, 1896.

8. Gibson, R. *A Social History of French Catholicism, 1789–1914.* Allen & Unwin, 1990: 146.

9. Condon, Fr. Joannes L., O.S.A. *Life of St. Rita of Cascia.* Washbourne, 1917: 75.

10. Heater, James, and Colleen Heater. *The Pilgrim's Italy: A Travel Guide to the Saints.* Inner Travel Books, 2002. Excerpts posted at the publisher's website <innertravelbooks.com>.

11. Ibid.

12. Hathaway, Fr., FSSP. "Homily 26 September 2004: Seventeenth Sunday After Pentecost—On Cursing (Part 1)." Website of Mater Dei Latin Mass Community, Roman Catholic Diocese of Dallas <web2.airmail.net/carlsch/MaterDei>, 4 Oct 2004.

13. Sox, David. *Relics and Shrines.* Allen and Unwin, 1985: 133.

14. "Introduction. *The Tenure of Kings and Magistrates.*" Milton Reading Room, Dartmouth University website <dartmouth.edu/~milton/>.

15. Philologos. "Cracking the Whip." *Forward*, 24 Sept 2004.

16. Katz, Yaakov. "Extremists Boast They Cursed Sharon." *Jerusalem Post*, 6 Jan 2006.

17. Hoffmann, Rabbi Eliyahu. "Inspiration—On the Spur of the Moment." Torah.org, no date.

18. Shabbar, S.M.R. "The Tenth Imam Ali Ibn Muhammad (Al-Naqi, Al-Hadi) (AS)." Al-Islam.org, no date.

19. Shareef al-Qurashi, Baquir. *The Life of Imam Ali Bin Muhannad Al-Hadi.* Translated by Abdullah al-Shahin. Ansariyan Publications, 2005: 141.

20. Ibid.: 139.

21. Ibid.: 89.

22. From a Shia pamphlet, which states: "This has been taken from the book *Mukhtar al-Kharaij wal Jaraih*, p. 210."

23. Feidlander, Shems. *Ninety-nine Names of Allah.* HarperCollins, 1993: 11.

7

THE MOST POPULAR SIN

Lawrence E. Gichner

VOLUPTUOUS ECSTASY ON THE TEMPLE

EROTIC ASPECTS OF HINDU SCULPTURE

Editor's Note: Information on Lawrence Gichner (1907–1992) is scarce. He was known as the "Ambassador of Antiquities" and was involved with the Smithsonian, likely as a consultant. In the late 1940s and 1950s, he self-published three limited-edition books on the erotic aspects of Chinese, Japanese, and Hindu culture, complete with photos of the art and artifacts being frankly discussed. What's the big deal, you may ask? As hard as it may be to comprehend now, a mere 50 to 60 years ago, publishing pictures of Hindu statues or Chinese vases of an erotic nature was almost suicidally risky in the US. Sure enough, the prudes in power noticed Gichner's short, pioneering works—his home was raided and his material was confiscated.

Erotic Aspects of Hindu Sculpture (1949), the start of the trilogy, seems to be the first American book devoted exclusively to the subject, and it was certainly the first to contain photographs of these centuries-old statues. Virtually no one in the US had ever seen images of the artwork adorning the temples of the oldest existing religion, the world's third-largest. Gichner broke the blackout, and he paid a price.

Even now, the statues are more than explicit enough to raise an eyebrow. Sure, we can look at hardcore porn in about three seconds on the Web, but these are religious, devotional statues created ages ago. What was their purpose? Gichner examines the various theories, ending with the idea that they were designed to show men and women how they can literally achieve physical enjoyment and symbolically achieve spiritual enlightenment. As religion professor Jeffrey S. Lidke has more recently written: "Ultimately, for Hindus, sexuality is not one thing and spirituality another. They are, rather, two aspects of the very same fire, a fire that both gives rise to life and makes possible its transcendence." [1]

IN A LAND OF FEW old books, little written history, and no recorded annals, the rock-cut temples of India present a record of the people's erotic customs and the philosophy which explained their acts. For the Hindus regarded Love as God and recorded their acts of love upon the outer walls of their temples. They made public what other cultures concealed and preserved for examination in imperishable stone the records of many tribes

> **For the Hindus regarded Love as God and recorded their acts of love upon the outer walls of their temples.**

and races, their manners, customs, and religious practices. Here, perhaps, is the largest single store of material for the psychologist or anthropologist who seeks the evidence of the erotic habits of former times.

The great subcontinent of India, for a period of a thousand years, from the reign of Asoka in 250 B.C.E., enjoyed a remarkable expression of religious fervor expressed in the construction of countless temples. These varied greatly in size and form—from humble structures to exalted piles of sculptured stone, from simple rock-hewn caves to complicated structures of vast dimensions. Some remain in a state of preservation, others are but heaps of tumbled stones. Working closely with the architects who designed these temples were the sculptors who covered the surfaces of their walls with exuberant carvings. For hundreds of years the song of the sculptor's chisel rang through the land, until throughout its length and breadth there were made complicated records in stone of the lives and loves of the myriad gods. Though the subjects were divine, inspiration and models sprang from the lives of the people who made that record. Man can portray only what he knows. Sculpture requires the portrayal of physical form, though metaphysics may explain these as symbols of abstract truth. Thus we find among the record of the battles and triumphs of the Hindu gods, also that of their love life; of the manner in which they translated into acts the powerful sex drive and the many ways in which its physical aspects could be manifested.

> **In their drive to destroy the unbelievers, the Muslims slaughtered with merciless ferocity the Hindu population, and many parts of the country became entirely deserted, the Hindu temples left to the destroying hand of time and nature.**

In 1194 the Muslims fell upon India, which, disunited and chaotic, could offer little resistance. The Muslim conquerors, forbidden by their religion to create images of any living being, viewed with horror the Hindu temples and the carvings upon their walls. What temples could not be converted into mosques were razed with fanatical zeal. In their drive to destroy the unbelievers, the Muslims slaughtered with merciless ferocity the Hindu population, and many parts of the country became entirely deserted, the Hindu temples left to the destroying hand of time and nature.

Will Durant, in the *Story of Civilization*, describes the manner in which the conquest was carried out. In his account of an expedition by the Turkish chieftain Mahmud, who each winter descended from the mountains to the plains of India, where he

> filled his treasure chest with spoils and amused his men with full freedom to pillage and kill. At Mathura (on the Jumma) he took from the temple its statues of gold encrusted with precious stones, and emptied its coffers of a vast quantity of gold, silks and jewelry; he expressed his admiration for the architecture of the great shrine, judged its duplication would cost one hundred million dinars and the labor of two hundred years, and then ordered it to be soaked with naptha and burned to the ground.

Protected from invasion by the natural defenses of the Vindhya hills and the dense jungles of Central India, the temples in the south were not destroyed. It is there that the greater part of the sculptures, which form the basis of this study, are to be found.

Five hundred years after the Muslims, the British came to India. They, especially the missionaries, were profoundly shocked by the public display of what many regard as "obscene" carvings. The advisability of destroying these sculptures was even debated in Parliament, but it was British colonial policy not to interfere with established religious practices of the peoples in the colonies. The British

218

went beyond noninterference and when they withdrew from India in 1947, left behind an invaluable survey of India's archaeological and architectural treasures. This systematic record has helped preserve the treasures themselves, if not from disintegration due to natural climatic conditions, at least from apathy and neglect due to ignorance.

The Muslims and the climate are not alone to be blamed for the destructions. The people of India aided in the process. They used the temples, as did the Romans of the Middle Ages with the great buildings of Imperial Rome, as quarries from which they took stones for their own purposes. Temple columns, stones, and carvings served to build roads and the walls and steps of their dwellings. The Mahrattas purloined the stones to build their own temples, and the Portuguese assisted the hand of time with their own fanaticism by barbarously mutilating many temple carvings.

Each community in India had (and has) its temple, not only as a place of worship but also as a center of social contact. Here the latest news was exchanged and discussed, and they could and did see and examine the numerous sculptures which were their books, source of knowledge, and model for their own behavior. These sculptures not only urged the Hindu on to a life of sacrifice, they portrayed a way of life which would bring pleasure to others and to himself. The lesson which these sculptures taught the Hindu was toward the enjoyment of the senses, rather than the denial of them.

Hindu thought has always insisted upon the importance of sex and its physical manifestations. Thus, the temple decorations contain many carvings which demonstrate the various positions of the marital embrace. They convey that the physical and mental aspects of life must be in perfect harmony for complete fulfillment. Pleasure and fulfillment are not the only aspects of this teaching, for to the Hindu procreation is the most important single act leading toward the individual's happiness and his significance in the scheme of his society.

In the Hindu marriage ceremony, the couple vows before the priest and the sacred fire to provide food, clothing, and bodily pleasure for one another. Only after marriage does a man become a full-fledged citizen. Then, as a man, it is his duty to beget and raise a child. A husband's happiness increases in accordance with the number of children he has, and a devout Hindu must have at least one son, who after his father's death must crack the deceased's skull, that the spirit may be liberated. To the women, too, early marriage and childbearing are of vital importance. The Hindu woman, when denied the blessings of fruition, rushes from temple to temple seeking relief from her barrenness, and she will accept any nostrum in the frantic hope of attaining fertility.

Furthermore, every Hindu man looks to sexual intimacy with his wife for pleasure and relaxation from the dull, relentless struggle for existence which makes up the lives of so many Hindus. Poverty permits him no other pleasure than this, which at the moment at least, costs him so little and is so readily available.

As a result of this relentless racial and individual urge to procreation symbolized in a multiplicity of shrines which house the objects of his veneration, the Hindu worshiper lays his offerings before images of the lingam and the yoni, the male and female reproductive organs. To the Occidental this form of worship seems to be the simple aboriginal superstition of an agricultural and pastoral people who pay tribute in such manner to the forces of generation.

Yet, Hindu worship is individual, not congregational. The student seeking a single interpretation of the images and rituals soon discovers that none exists. Each commentator is influenced by his education and background. Those who justify the use of such images do so for widely differing reasons, and those who condemn them find a variety of reasons for wishing them destroyed. Some Occidentals are stirred by these images to noble ecstasies, others in turn fall prey to anxiety. The practicing Christian in particular finds it difficult to accept calmly these sculptures, because Christian theology contains the concepts of "immaculate conception," "virgin birth," and carnal knowledge is the "original sin."

In studying these sculptures one must continually bear in mind that the Hindu who raised these structures and covered them with sculptures did so for the greater glory of his gods. He would never have covered them with what he regarded as obscenities. Those of other religions must approach them with sympathy and tolerance in an effort to discover the meaning which the builder intended.

Vatsayana, a religious student in Benares during the early centuries of the Christian era, wrote the *Kama Sutra* (Aphorisms on Love), a guide to virtue, wealth, and pleasure. Love, he teaches, lies in the enjoyment of the five senses of seeing, hearing, feeling, tasting, and smelling assisted by the mind together with the soul. The object of the enjoyment of woman is twofold: pleasure and progeny. Woman, to derive satisfaction from coition, must be prepared. At the time of sexual enjoyment any embraces or gestures that are conducive to the increase of love or passion should be practiced.

Some students believe that the temple figures were intended to portray graphically the various methods of sexual congress described in the *Kama Sutra*, but there are embraces described which do not appear in sculpture, while others are represented which are not mentioned in the *Kama Sutra*.

TO THE QUESTION, "What is the meaning behind these sculptures?" the answers are various. They can be classified, for clarity, under four brief headings progressing from the idea of defilement to significant philosophy:

1. Judgments based upon foreign standards.
2. The "good life" similar in principle to Epicureanism.
3. "Practical" usage.
4. A way to obtain spiritual knowledge.

Some of the earliest writings to which we have access were produced by Christians and Christian missionaries. To understand correctly their horrified reactions and cries of "revolting representations," "moral depravity," "shameful indelicacies," "disgusting obscenity," "flagrant indecency," and "loathsome nastiness," it is necessary briefly and objectively to review their backgrounds and basis for condemnation.

JUDGMENTS BASED ON WESTERN STANDARDS

Christianity over the centuries has varied in its ideals and standards of life. Hundreds of existing sects today attest to the truth of this statement. It is true, however, that though not all, many have held to the belief that sex is the evil in physical man. He was unconscious of sin until he indulged in this "evil." A mighty conflict arose between the flesh and the spirit.

Sidney C. Tapp in the *Sexology of the Bible* says, "An ocean of carnality within us is continually lashing against the shores of our spiritual natures, the soul; and these mighty waves of Carnality and Sensuality drown the voices of the Divine within us. The deliverance of the Soul from the error of the senses—the lust of the flesh—is salvation."

With such an attitude toward sex, we can readily understand the reactions of Captain Edward Moor, when in 1794, he wrote in his narrative these observations:

We are totally unable, and equally unwilling to convey a full idea of these monstrous delineations; it must therefore suffice to say, that there is a great variety of not only human nudities in the most indecent, uncleanly situations, but men and beasts, and beasts and women, exposed in the most shameful combinations that a brutal imagination could suggest, in all the filthy attitudes of unnatural depravity.

James Mill, in his *History of British India* (1826), believed the sculptures encouraged the loosest morality. He wrote:

A religion which subjects to the eyes of its notaries the grossest images of sensual pleasure, and renders even the emblems of generation objects of worship; which ascribes to the supreme God an immense train of obscene acts: which has them engraved on the sacred cars, portrayed in the temples, and presented to the people as objects of adoration, which pays worship to the Yoni. and the Lingam, cannot be regarded as favorable to chastity.

Other writers from Christian Europe and America felt these stone carvings were studies in flagrant indecency which only tended to inflame the passions of youth, which, in a hot climate, needed restraints rather than stimulants.

Robert Edward Treston Forrest (1834–1914) in the seventieth year of this life advised B.C. Mahtab, Maharaj-Adhiraj of Burdwan, to

clear his estate of these foul images. They are a scandal and a reproach. Representations of the human organs of generation, of the act of coition, would not be allowed to be publicly exhibited in any civilized country. They would be dealt with by the police as contrary to public decency. Let him think of the effect of these things, being under the observation of all from childhood, being worshipped by the women. Their presence in the land keeps morality and decency at a very low level.

In the fall of 1836 Ferdinand De Wilton Ward sailed from Boston as missionary to the native of southern India. Fourteen years later he published *India and the Hindoos* in which he gave his views of their manners and customs. Much that he saw did not please him, and in his zeal for reform and demolition Ward denounced the gods of India. He said they were

false to their word, thievish, licentious, ambitious, murderous, all indeed that is repellant, malignant, and vile, (their own writers being judges,) is it surprising that there is perjury, and injustice, and wickedness the land over? Ah no! The people are bad, many of them very bad; but they do not and cannot equal their own gods in wickedness. Their deities must be changed ere their moral condition can be materially and generally improved. The Bible must supplant the narratives of their false divinities; their temples, covered now with sculptures and paintings which crimson the face of modesty even to glance at, must be demolished; the vile lingam must be leveled to the ground; the festivals, in which are re-enacted shameless events in the lives of Krishna, and others like him, must be abolished; the scenes

now passing before the eyes of that nation, sanctioned by divine example, must cease. Then will India rise from her deep moral depression.

"Hinduism seems the greatest abomination of the earth," wrote Frederick Courtland Penfield, onetime US Ambassador to Austria-Hungary, after a season's sojourn in the subcontinent. Apparently disappointed that he was unable to unravel the mysteries of the East in a fortnight of travel, he says in *East of Suez*:

Each faith offers admirable precepts and teachings, and prolonged study of them produces a feeling of respect for all true believers. But a season of travel in India, entered upon with the desire to dispassionately study the Hindu religion in the land of its overweening strength, produces only bewilderment and mental nausea. The more determined one many be to lay bare the gems of this faith and its administration by the Brahmins, the keener will be his disappointment, for not a redeeming feature will he find, and he may quit India smarting with regret over wasted time. To such an investigator Hinduism must forever he remembered as paganism steeped in idolatry. More, its gruesome sacrifices will provoke only disgust, perhaps equalled by that called forth by the unspeakably coarse temple carvings and ornamentation of the cars of Juggernaut.

I have been acquainted with Indian gentlemen proud to be known as Hindus, and have been amazed to hear them avow devotion to the hideous idolatry that absorbs a great part of the time of two hundred million people in India alone. If the strong arm of England were not raised over the great empire of the East the suttee right and child sacrifice would unquestionably prevail today. To a westerner, Hinduism seems the greatest abomination of the earth.

THE "GOOD LIFE" WITHIN THE CONCEPT OF EPICUREANISM

Since before the dawn of recorded history philosophers have discussed their conceptions of the "good life." Each religion claims to possess the answer.

Of the Indian sculpture under discussion, no more lovely examples exist according to K. de B. Codrington than the little couples of figures that adorn the Badami pillar-capitals. In the year 570

C.E., Mangalesa, in dedicating this temple to Vishnu, described it as "a shrine beyond the dreams of men and gods." Today it is less picturesquely referred to as Cave No. III.

Codrington, writing in *Indian Art and Archaeology*, makes this comment: "'Protestants at heart, too often we shut the doors of our religion against delight. In India loves decorate the temple and the fact is worthy of deep consideration."

The family unit has been considered by many as the basis of the good life. Children, the fruit of family union, are a positive part of the picture. To be assured children, members of many cults performed fertility rites, as do many primitive people today, and this has become an integral part of their customs.

In a *Journey Over Land to India*, Donald Campbell, who commanded a regiment of cavalry in the service of his Highness the Nabob of the Carnatic, described "pure and spotless women" kissing an enormous phallus under "the belief that it promotes fecundity."

Already by the first century, the Indians had an extensive literature on the art of love. These books described in amazing detail the size and proportions of the genitalia; classified them in groups and prescribed the types of male and female parts that blended best together for connubial happiness. In addition, various postures for sexual congress were detailed and instructions given as to which was to be assumed according to the time of the month and the fullness of the moon.

Written in all seriousness, these books were in the best scientific tradition of their time. Each generation is indebted to its predecessors for having handed on to them the accumulated knowledge of the past. If these things seem amusing to us, we should remember that, were we living in the first century, we would have accepted these books with all the earnestness of those who turned to them for enlightenment and knowledge.

Several present-day commentators believe with Hugh George Rawlinson that "the reliefs on the walls of the temples at Konarak and Bhuvaneswara are frankly erotic, and are based on the "Kamasastra [i.e, *Kama Sutra*], the Indian Ars Amatoria." Some feel they constitute a complete set of illustrations for these Sanskrit erotic treatises.

Dr. Ernest Theodore Block, in writing on the Black Pagoda at Konarak in *The Archaeological Survey of India*, makes this pithy observation:

The walls of the mandapa (of the temple) as is well known, are covered with a multitude of human figures of varying sizes, illustrating all the various bandhas taught in the Kamasastras. It looks almost as if King Narasimha I (1238–1264 C.E.), who built the temple, had taken a special fancy to the class of Sanskrit literature and for this reason ordered the masons to supply a complete set of illustrations for those books in honor of the god for whom he erected such a magnificent temple. It should, however, be born in mind that the word "obscene" and the notion it conveyed were unknown to the ancient Indians. In all the productions of the Kalidasa and of many another famous Sanskrit poet are numerous scenes and descriptions, the true meaning of which would be too difficult to explain to an audience of ladies but there is not the slightest reason to suppose that anyone in antiquity took exception, either to these or to the realistic carvings of the Black Pagoda. Nothing indeed could be more unjust than to decry the people, who made them, as indulging in immorality, gross as the figures may seem to modern ideas.

Many different explanations are given for the meaning of these temple decorations, and it is amusing to note that taken singularly, often each by itself sounds logical and applicable. A Christian Bishop Missionary reports a Brahmin's explanation for these representations as "intended to teach the vulgar that from the enjoyment of animal pleasures, the lowest condition of man's nature, they must gradually ascent to intellectual and spiritual attainments."

Others indicate that these figures illustrate the worldly and sinful thoughts one must leave behind on entering the temple, and to strengthen their argument, they say these carvings are only found on the outside of the structures and never on the inside, where simplicity of detail prevails.

Still others quite naïvely explain that these groups were there because they were particularly amusing to the people and attracted them to the temple.

PRACTICAL USAGE

Many people, at a loss to understand why these figures have a place on sacred buildings, after long search and inquiry, have found as the answer that these figures are meant to resist the evil effects of the jealous gaze of observers, to ward off evil spirits that may desire to possess the building, and to protect the structure against lightning, cyclone, or other dire visitations of nature.

Among the serious writers who advance this theory is Wilber Theodore Elmore who, in his study, *Dravidian Gods in Modern Hinduism*, states:

> The Dravidian idea of the evil eye is that there are innumerable evil spirits waiting at all times to do harm. These spirits appear to be very much dependent on human suggestion and initiative. If special attention is directed to any object or person, and especially if something complimentary is said about it, some listening spirit will take notice, and thinking the object is desirable for itself, or out of jealousy and evil-mindedness, will bring about some evil.
>
> One can scarcely be more tactless in India than to praise a man's crops or cattle or child. The proper thing to do is not to appear to pay too much attention to that which interests one, or if it is necessary to mention it, to point to some defect. This is one of the reasons for wearing ornaments, and it is always in order to praise or notice the ornaments on a child, as this will keep attention away from the child itself. The gracious friend always addresses one with the words of commiseration because he is looking so poorly. The European is often disappointed because his Indian friends see nothing but faults in his new horse or house, when he expects them to praise it.
>
> With the idea of making the spirits think an article is worthless, some flaw is left in everything. No house is ever completed. The weaver leaves a flaw in his cloth. The brickmaker daubs his kiln with unsightly spots of lime. The placing of obscene figures and carvings on idol cars and temples is often explained in the same way.

Writing two years later in 1915, Ernest Binfield Havell, in his study *The Ancient and Medieval Architecture of India*, has this to relate:

> The decorative sculpture on the temples at Khajuraho and elsewhere is sometimes grossly obscene, a fact which might mislead Europeans into forming a wrong judgment of the ethics of Hindu religion. It is no doubt true that some Hindu sects, especially in the decadent period, indulged in the most depraved ritualistic practices, but Indo-Aryan religion should not be convicted of immorality on that account. There must naturally be a different outlook in sexual matters among a social and religious duty than there is in Europe, where a considerable proportion of both sexes remain celibate. A Vishnu temple was a symbol of the active or dynamic principle of nature, and most of the external sculpture was popular art interpreting vulgar notions of the philosophic concept, but not necessarily implying any moral depravity. The indecency was generally introduced on account of the popular belief that it was a protection against the evil eye. There was never any obscenity in the sculpture of the sacred images worshipped within the sanctum and elsewhere.

A WAY TO OBTAIN SPIRITUAL KNOWLEDGE

Portrayal in the events of the lives of the gods.
To demonstrate ceremonial ritual.
Let us keep in mind the fact that India is a large

country with millions of people and thousands of temples. Again and again we find that India displays in the sun what others hide in the dark.

A sojourner in India for twenty-five years as missionary of the American Board, Reverend Dr. David Oliver Allen (1800–1863), in his *India, Ancient and Modern*, believed the figures to represent the play functions of the gods who were unrestricted by moral laws. Dr. Allen writes of his first-hand observations:

I saw in one celebrated temple a great number of stone statues, in one part of it a long series of them, representing the amours of Krishna, which were of the most obscene character, which if exhibited or offered for sale, as statues, or pictures, or engravings, or in any form, or described in any language in this country, would subject the exhibiter or seller to severe but merited punishment from the laws. And yet such representations make a part of the Hindu religion, as publicly exhibited and celebrated. To reasoning and arguments about the worship of such gods the Hindus reply, (They were not men but gods, and so were not subject to moral laws as we are. They could do as they pleased. Actions which would be sinful in us were not sinful in them, for being subject to no law they could do what they pleased without doing any wrong or committing any sin.)

Dr. Allen believed these amours to be those of Krishna. Another authoritative writer, John Nicok Farquhar, M.A. (1861–1929), who was literary secretary to the National Council of the Young Men's Christian Association, in his *Crown of Hinduism* accredits the actions instead to Vishnu and Siva in these words:

The great temple-gateways of South India known as *gourams* and the temple-towers of Central India (it is to the devastation wrought by the Mohammedans that we owe the fact that obscene sculptures are scarcely to be seen in North India) are in many cases covered with sculpture of indescribable obscenity; while here and there, as in the metropolitan Vishnuite shrine, Srirangam, at Trichinopdy, the internal walls and ceilings are, in Hopkins' phrase, "frescoes with bestiality"—frescoes representing the pleasures of Vishnu's heaven.

The extraordinary thing is that the obscene sculptures, the foul frescoes, the dancing-girls, and the offensive symbols are found, not in private buildings, but in the temples, the high palaces made holy by the living presence of the gods. The inevitable conclusion is that neither Vishnu nor Siva has ever been regarded as having such a character as would be shocked by such things. Even the greatest philosophers failed to feel any incongruity between these temples and the ethical Brahman of their theology.

In 1917, during a lecture by Lady Katharine Stuart on "Tomorrow in India," Sir Arundel Tagg, K.C.S.I., arose to sagely suggest that one should look *through* the figures for their meaning. His remarks as reported in the *Asiatic Review* were:

With regard to the question of the study of the Hindu religion, there were difficulties in their way. In South India and elsewhere one often saw outside of temples and within them and on the cars various representations which excited repulsion and deterred the spectator from further investigation. But apart from this there were Hindu symbols of the deepest significance and interest, if, we would and could look, not only *at* the symbols, but *through* them to their meaning.

Looking through the represented act of sexual congress, there are those who see the symbolic union of the individual and the world soul.

And looking through the represented act of sexual congress, there are those who see the symbolic union of the individual and the world soul. Among those holding this idea is Ernest Binifield Havell, a former principal of the Government School of Art and Keeper of the Art Gallery in Calcutta. He wrote in his book, *Ideals of Indian Art*, as follows:

It would be wrong to infer that the obscenities which occasionally disfigure Hindu temples are necessarily indicative of moral depravity. In the matter of sexual relationship Indian civilization, in every stratum of society, holds up a standard of morality as high as Europe has ever done.

> **"Not merely are female forms felt to be equally appropriate with male to adumbrate the majesty of the Over-Soul, but the interplay of all psychic and physical sexual forces is felt in itself to be religious."**

The ideas connected with sex symbolism in Hindu art and ritual are generally misinterpreted by those who take them out of the environment of Indian social life. In the Upanishads sexual relationship is described as one of the means of apprending the divine nature, and throughout Oriental literature it is constantly used metaphorically to express the true relationship between the human soul and God.

Holding to this same idea of the spiritual oneness of the individual in relation to the Universe was the profound scholar Ananda K. Goomaraswamy (1877–1947), who in addition felt that the deeper symbolism lay in the great lesson, that voluptuous ecstasy also has its due place in life. A master in language as well as a recognized authority on art, Coomaraswamy's beliefs are very well expressed in these paragraphs from his *Arts and Crafts of India and Ceylon*:

In nearly all Indian art there runs a vein of deep sex-mysticism. Not merely are female forms felt to be equally appropriate with male to adumbrate the majesty of the Over-Soul, but the interplay of all psychic and physical sexual forces is felt in itself to be religious. Already we find in one of the earliest Upanishads,

"For just as one who dallies with a beloved wife has no consciousness of outer and inner, so the spirit also, dallying with the Self-whose-essence-is-knowledge, has no consciousness of outer and inner."

Here is no thought that passion is degrading—as some Christian and Buddhist monks and many modern feminists have regarded it, but a frank recognition of the close analogy between amorous and religious ecstasy. How rich and varied must have been the emotional experience of a society to which life could appear so perfectly transparent, and where at the same time the most austere asceticism was a beloved ideal for all those who sought to pass over life's Wandering! It is thus that the imager, speaking always for the race, rather than of personal idiosyncrasies, set side by side on

his cathedral walls the yogi and the apsara, the saint and the ideal courtesan; accepting life as he saw it, he interpreted all its phenomena with perfect catholicity of vision. Perhaps for Western readers the best introduction to such Indian modes of thought is to be found in the writings of William Blake, who in one and the same poem could write

"Never, never I return
Still for victory I burn."
"Let us agree to give up love
And root up the infernal grove."

He, in his day, could have said with the Bengali poet of our own, that "what I have seen is unsurpassable," regarding with equal enthusiasm the Path of Pursuit and the Path of Return—Affirmation and Denial.

The Indian sex-symbolism assures two main forms, the recognition of which will assist the student of art: first, the desire and union of individuals, sacramental in its likeness to the union of the individual soul with God,—this is the love of the herd-girls for Krishna; and second, the creation of the world, manifestation, lila, as the fruit of the union of male and females cosmic principles—purusha and shakti.

The beautiful erotic art of Konarak clearly signifies the quickening power of the Sun, perhaps not without an element of sympathetic magic. Popular explanations of such figures are scarcely less absurd than the strictures of those who condemn them from the standpoint of modern conventional propriety. They appear in Indian temple sculpture, now rarely, now frequently, simply because voluptuous ecstasy has also its due place in life; and those who interpreted life were artists. To them such figures appeared appropriate equally for the happiness they represented and for their deeper symbolism. It is noteworthy, in this connection, that such figures, and indeed all the sculptured embroidery of Indian temples, is confined to the exterior walls of the shrine, which is absolutely plain within: such is the veil of Nature, empirical life, enshrining One, not contracted or identified into variety. Those to whom all such symbols drawn from life itself appeared natural and right, would have shrunk in disgust from the more opaque erotic art of modern European salons.

1. Lidke, Jeffrey S. "A Union of Fire and Water: Sexuality and Spirituality in Hinduism." In *Sexuality and the World's Religions*, ed. by David W. Machacek and Melissa M. Wilcox. Santa Barbara, CA: ABC-CLIO, 2003: 110.

WANTING THE TOPMOST PEACH

THE EROTIC POETRY OF THE SIXTH DALAI LAMA

THE SIXTH DALAI LAMA (1683–1706, maybe 1746)

Rigdzin Tsangyang Gyatso. *Gyatso*, the lineage. *Rig-dzin* means "treasure." *Tsangyang* came from a pre-cognitive dream that a monk had about him. It means, "having a voice like God's." The sweetness of these songs in Tibetan has always been associated with his voice-melody. They are treasured throughout the Himalayan region, and up until the 1950s, when street-singing was outlawed by the Chinese communists, they were heard in the markets of Lhasa. The reality they embody, of being drawn simultaneously by the clarity of meditation and by the delights of desire, and the ground they find that mixes those, is felt as the great gift of his art. The songs are modeled on anonymous folksongs sung in a lilting manner. They treat love problems in simple images and plain, intense speech. His street name, Dangwang Bangpo, means "one who has a good sensual appetite."

The early part of Tsangyang Gyatso's life was lived in secret confinement with his tutors, evidently to preserve the politically expedient illusion that the Fifth Dalai Lama was still alive and on retreat. In 1697 at the age of fourteen, his public life began. He was enthroned with great ceremony as the Sixth Dalai Lama. But he turned out to be a unique sort of holy man. He seems to have formally "given back" the monastic vows he took. He lived in the Potala (the monastery palace) but dressed as a layman. He wore rings and blue silk, instead of the red and yellow of the monks. He kept his hair long, and on most days was to be found out in the archery field with his friends. He had a free-roving spirit, and he loved to take short journeys "according to his will." He is best remembered now, of course, for his nights, which he spent with many different partners, aristocratic women from Lhasa and peasant girls from Shol, the village at the foot of the Potala. His love-life and the poems he wrote from within it are a cultural treasure. It was an honor to have the Sixth Dalai Lama visit one's daughter for a night. Houses were painted yellow as a sign that the privilege had occurred, and it is said that a good percentage of the houses were yellow, as opposed to the traditional white.

It was an honor to have the Sixth Dalai Lama visit one's daughter for a night.

There are many different tones in his love songs—urgency, caution, tenderness, wry humor, confusion, pleading—the variety found in all love poetry. We get a sense of a growing, energetic human being, amused by his predicament, being so young and carrying such light. There's an interesting contemporary account of a traveler (Lelung) who came to a house late where the Sixth Dalai Lama and his retinue were. All the attendants were drunk and behaving stupidly, but Tsangyang was "completely clear, writing songs, and singing them without flaw, not in the least affected by the alcohol." And the man who caused the early downfall of the Sixth reminisced remorsefully, "He had wonderful charm, and he was tremendously bold. He knew he was not destined to live beyond the age of twenty-five." The word "bold" is used here in the sense of someone who acts with courageous resolve on the difficult path toward enlightenment. Tsangyang Gyatso was an honest, and open, rebel, who would no doubt laugh at any attempt to characterize his behavior. He was not chaste. He was not profligate. He had a fine sensitivity and a taste for the company of any and all elements of the human community.

I hear Shakespeare, Sappho, Byron, Keats, Wyatt, Elvis, and Van Morrison in these poems, Chaucer, Ovid, Emily Dickinson, and the troubadours. He is not simple! And he's still very controversial: a tantric master, a libertine, or some as yet unnameable mixture? In 1706, he was publicly declared by one governing element *not* to be the incarnation of the Great Fifth, deposed, and led off toward China. Monks loyal to him, though, freed him and took him to the summer palace. After a short siege he surrendered himself to avoid more fighting, and the journey toward China resumed. According to Chinese records, on November 14, 1706, he died and was cremated near Lake Kokonor. But the story doesn't end there.

Fifty years later in Mongolia, a book appeared which claimed to be his secret biography, saying that he didn't die in 1706 but magically escaped, assumed a disguise, lived in a hermit's cave, and then began a new life as a wandering pilgrim, traveling to Nepal, India, throughout Tibet and China, and living finally as an abbot of a Mongolian monastery. The secret biography is evidently very plausible and accepted as genuine by the current Tibetan community in exile. After his disappearance in 1706, the Chinese tried to replace him with their own candidate for "the true Sixth," but the stand-in was never accepted by the Tibetan people. The lineage continued out of Lithang, as Tsangyang Gyatso had predicted it would in a poem sent secretly back from the exile journey to an unidentified woman.

The brother of the current Dalai Lama tells the story of how an old man came to Tsangyang's tent opening there as he was camped by Lake Kokonor in 1706. "Who are you?" asked the young Dalai Lama.

The old man replied, "Sengge," which means "lion." The name of the nearby lake meant "joy."

"The lion's happiness. A sign that I should leave my people here, so they can be happy." And saying this, he left, never reclaiming his place as the Sixth Incarnation, though several times he is said to have appeared in Tibet in various disguises. At the following year's New Year festival in Lhasa, for example, the ruling regent saw a beggar and bowed as he would only bow to the Dalai Lama. People noticed and cried out, but the beggar disappeared. The same thing happened with the state oracle at Nechung. He suddenly turned and paid homage to a particular man in the crowd, who immediately vanished. The legend continues, how he traveled as a mendicant to the shrines of India and also worked as a shepherd for a wealthy Mongolian lady. One day she complained that a wolf was killing the sheep. Armed with just a small knife, he went into the hills and brought the animal back alive. "Here is the wolf. Punish him however you wish."

Tsangyang's legend-laced wandering is what he leaves us, along with the short poems, which are themselves close to the texture of his moving. Perhaps the truth he embodies is that, more than scriptures and religious disciplines, life-lived is the great teacher. We have the shape of a foundation, but his temple remains a mystery.

Michael Tatz suspects that Tsangyang's actual diary of the early years exists, or a copy, and that the diary is the ultimate source of the songs. If that precious document does exist, it could clarify some of the problems in the poems. Perhaps it will appear. The cloak of mystery still very much surrounds the Sixth. The Thirteenth Dalai Lama in conversation with Charles Bell said, "Tsangyang Gyatso used to have his body in several places at once, in Lhasa, in Kongpo, and elsewhere. He has one tomb in Alashan in Mongolia and another in Drcpang in Tibet. Showing several bodies at the same time is disallowed now because it causes confusion in the work."

Whatever the truth, the multiple energies that compose the Sixth Dalai Lama are powerfully elusive. They confuse normal concepts of identity, and they make his poetry very alive to the touch.

Sources

• Aris, Michael. *Hidden Treasures and Secret Lives: A Study of Pemalingpa (1450–1521) and the Sixth Dalai Lama (1683–1706).* Delhi: Motil Banarsidass, 1988: 107–226.
• Norbu, Thubten Jigme, and Colin Turnbull. "A Riddle of Love." In *Tibet.* New York: Simon & Schuster, 1968: 279–94.
• *Songs of the Sixth Dalai Lama.* K. Dhondup, translator. Dharmsala: Library of Tibetan Works, 1981.
• Tatz, Michael. "Songs of the Sixth Dalai Lama." *Tibet Journal* 6.4 (1981): 13–31.
• *Wings of the White Crane: Poems of Tshangs dbyangs rgya mtsho (1683–1706).* G.W. Houston, translator. Delhi: Motilal Banarsidass, 1982.

Even the stars can be measured,
their arrangements and influences.

Her body can be lovingly touched,
but not her deep longings.

Those cannot be understood
by science.

Lassoes can catch the wild horses
that flee over the hills.

But nothing, not even incantations,
can hold a wild beloved

who has stopped loving
her lover.

If the one I love gives up everything
to study the teachings,
I'll take the holy path too.

I'll live in a secluded retreat
and forget how young I am.

I listen intently
to what my teacher says,
but beneath that concentration

my loving slips
out of the room
to be with you.

Your stallion trots on the slippery ice,
over deep-frozen and nearly-frozen water.

When you move toward the beauty of
        a new lover,
be careful that your secret legs
don't scatter and fall!

Lover waiting in my bed
to give me your soft, sweet body,
do you mean well?

What will you take off me,
besides my clothes?

What appears in Spring
fades in the Fall.

The blue-green bees
don't mourn that destiny.

My lover and I will not always be together,
but we don't cry about it.
Wanting this landlord's daughter
is wanting the topmost
peach.

Back when I was lucky,
I could hoist a prayerflag,

and some well-bred young woman
would invite me home.

She shone her whole smiling face
at the crowd in the tavern.

Then, from the delicate corners
of her eyes, she spoke
love-secrets to me.

One who loved me
has been given in marriage to another.

My body grows thin and sick
with what now cannot be.

I often see my lost lover in dreams.
I will ask a shaman to search in there
and bring her back to me.

Is this girl human,
or did she come from a stem
on the branch of a peach tree?

Her love opens and withers and falls
just as quickly as those flowers.

On the third day, the moon appears
like my lover in white silk.

By the fifteenth day, our meeting
has grown brighter and more direct.

Excerpted from Stallion on a Frozen Lake: Love Songs of the Sixth Dalai
Lama. *Coleman Barks, translator (Athens, GA: Maypop Books, 1992).*

Animals of all kinds can be tamed
with bits of meat and bread.

But this tavern tigress, when you think
she's satisfied, she rises
to snarl again.

My lover and I, we meet in complete
privacy, in the southern valley forest.

Then I hear some parrot in the market
jabbering our secrets.

While I live in the monastery palace,
I am Rigdzin Tsangyang Gyatso,
honored in the lineage.

When I roam the streets of Lhasa,
and down the valley to Shol,

I am the wildman, Dangzang Wangpo,
who has many lovers.

Pure snow-water from the holy mountain.
Dew off the rare Naga Vajra grass.

These essences make a nectar
which is fermented by one
who has incarnated as a maiden.

Her cup's contents can protect you
from rebirth in a lower form,

if it is tasted in the state
of awareness it deserves.

I have never slept
without a lover.

Nor have I ever let
one drop of sperm come.

EVERYTHING YOU KNOW ABOUT GOD IS WRONG

Jack Murnighan

"FONDLING THE FELLOWS IN FOLLY"

IN WHICH GOD WONDERS, WHY BE GAY
WHEN STRAIGHT SEX IS SO GREAT?

AH, THE HISTORY of Christianity: multiple millennia of mischief, molestation, malfeasance, and quite a few other "m"-words, morality only occasionally among them. Yes, I'm painting the picture darkly, but it's hard to get over St. Augustine having Pelagius declared a heretic in the early fifth century for saying that a good life could earn you a place in heaven or, worse, the English Church's sixteenth-century persecution of Dame Julian of Norwich—an anchoress—for suggesting that God is Love and that his love applies to all. Hers is one of the most beautiful notions to emerge in any theology, but it was rejected out of hand, and, according to some accounts, Julian was burned at the stake. Thinking back over the last five centuries and seeing what the world is now, we can only imagine, had Julian's notions taken root, how different it all could have been.

Day to day, however, the biggest complaint against Christianity, both by many of its practitioners and those dating them, is its relationship to sexuality. Not many religions, especially in the West, are body-positive, and the various disciples of Jesus clearly have no love for what Milton called our "perfidious bark." But, tucked away among Christianity's chastisements, repressions, flagellations, and guilt, there is a curious little gem—deep within a heavy-handed homiletic poem (i.e., a sermon with meter)—that, while condemning one type of sexuality, actually makes a pretty strong case for the kind many of us know and love.

The set-up itself is interesting: God is kicking back on the celestial La-Z-Boy, shotgunning a nectar with his only son, our Savior, asking him about life on earth. The Heavenly Father confesses that he doesn't really get this homosexual sex thing that seems to be becoming rather popular (especially in those two famous cities of the plain), and he asks Jesus to explain why people are doing it thusly. Jesus says he has no idea, and God then comes back with the following little monologue in which—careful reader take note— he pretty much says, I can't believe they do it that homo way since I made the hetero way so gosh-darn fun.

So what is clearly intended to be a condemnation of same-sex practices ends up being an incidental endorsement of the much more conventional joys of the flesh.

So what is clearly intended to be a condemnation of same-sex practices ends up being an incidental endorsement of the much more conventional joys of the flesh. My guess is that's not what

"Each male making mate of men like himself"

the anonymous fourteenth-century English author (who might also have written the better-known *Sir Gawain and the Green Knight*) was trying to achieve. But who would think that the lips of the Lord would give us a promo of the one thing which, historically, has had the least need to advertise.

Here are the choice lines, reworked into modern English but retaining most of the alliteration of the original.

From *Cleanness*
translated by Jack Murnighan and Andrew Cole

> The great sound of Sodom sinks in My ears
> And the guilt of Gomorrah goads Me to wrath
> I shall research that rumor and see for Myself
> If they have done as is heard on high.
> They have learned a lifestyle that liketh Me ill,
> And found in their flesh of faults the foulest,
> Each male making mate of men like himself
> Fondling the fellows in folly as if they were female.
> Yet I designed them a deed and devised them to do it
> And deemed it in My dominion the dearest of dances
> And set love therein, making such sex the sweetest.
> The play of paramours I portrayed Myself,
> And made one manner much merrier than all others:
> When two who are true tie to one another
> Between a male and his mate such mirth may be made
> That paradise proper would prove hardly preferable.
> They must take to each other in the manner most true
> Stealing to a secluded spot, sight unseen,
> And the flame of their love will fire up so free
> That all the sorrows of this life will not it slake.

Kristan Lawson

THE PRIVATE PARTS ON THE POPE'S ALTAR

THE VATICAN, IT IS WHISPERED, harbors secrets. Forbidden archives overflowing with banned books and suppressed manuscripts—not to mention the world's biggest collection of antique porn—languish in locked storerooms hidden deep in the recesses of the Holy See's *sanctum sanctorum*. Or so the legends say. But these areas of the Vatican are completely off-limits to visitors, so the odds of someone like you or me ever seeing them are practically nil.

Which is a tad disappointing.

Yet the Vatican's strangest secret is not hidden at all. In fact, quite the opposite: It's smack-dab in the center of one of the most heavily visited spots in the world. Crowds of gawking tourists and pilgrims brush by it all day, sometimes briefly looking right at it but never really *seeing* it. Of the four million people every year who unwittingly visit the site, perhaps only a handful understand what they're looking at.

Someone—it might have been Agatha Christie—once said that the best place to hide something is in plain sight. Never has that aphorism been more successfully put to the test than in the case of the indecent carvings on Christendom's most sacred altar, which have been there for the last 400 years.

Consider this.

In the observable universe, only one planet is known to harbor life: earth. And on earth, only one species has ever attained consciousness:

the human race. And the highest form of human consciousness, according to most cultures, is spirituality. And the form of spirituality with the most adherents, and by far the greatest historical importance and influence, is Christianity. And the center of Christianity is Rome. And the focal point of Christianity in Rome is the Vatican. And in the Vatican, the seat of Christendom is the Basilica of St. Peter. And the Basilica of St. Peter is so named because it was built atop the tomb of St. Peter, chief among the Apostles, Jesus' chosen favorite, the acknowledged founder of the Christian church. And recent archaeological discoveries revealed that St. Peter is indeed buried in the exact center of the Basilica. And built directly on top of St. Peter's grave is the High Altar, also called the Papal Altar: a structure considered so holy that only the Pope himself is allowed to touch it.

Yet the Vatican's strangest secret is not hidden at all.

By this reckoning, the Papal Altar is the most sacred spot in the entire universe. Sure, other religions have their holiest of holies—Judaism's

Western Wall, Islam's Kaaba, and so on—and even Christianity has other contenders, including the Church of the Holy Sepulchre in Jerusalem and the Church of the Nativity in Bethlehem. But for palpable religious power, architectural magnificence, and historical import, nothing can top the High Altar of St. Peter's.

But wait—there's more. On the structures enclosing this High Altar are carvings created by the artist whom many consider the greatest sculptor of all time: Gian Lorenzo Bernini, he of the orgasmic *Ecstasy of St. Theresa*, among countless other masterworks.

So there you have it: the most sacred altar in the precise center of the most important church of the most significant religion in the world. Just what, exactly, did the greatest sculptor of all time carve there? Care to venture a guess?

Would you believe...female genitalia? In explicit detail? And not just once, but *eight times*?

WHEN YOU ENTER St. Peter's for the first time, you are overwhelmed by its sheer scale. The arched ceilings are impossibly high, the gold-and-marble walls impossibly regal, the artwork impossibly beautiful. Every niche boasts yet another larger-than-life saint, flawlessly rendered by this or that Renaissance genius. Towering Latin inscriptions loom overhead, radiating sanctity and majesty even to those who can't understand a word. Travelers and supplicants are swallowed up by the Basilica's vastness.

And in the center of it all, where the nave and transept meet, is something unexpected: a heavy, dark bronze canopy held up by four slender, spiraling columns which, as you approach, you slowly realize are almost ridiculously tall, reaching as high as a five-story building. This peculiar structure is the Baldacchino, the sacred canopy that covers the High Altar. A holy gazebo. St. Peter's Baldacchino is not the only one in the world; many cathedrals and large churches have their own *baldacchini*. Originally they were made of cloth, supported by wooden poles: simple coverings meant to demarcate hallowed ground. Over time the *baldacchino*—called a "baldachin" in English—evolved from a flimsy, temporary canopy into a permanent structural edifice.

In 1624, as part of a series of renovations at the

The Vatican's High Altar with the Baldacchino.
Credit: eva bd of Wikipedia

Vatican, Pope Urban VIII commissioned his favorite artist, the young Bernini, to design and build a *baldacchino* over the new High Altar, which itself had been installed only a few years beforehand by a previous Pope. (Interestingly, the new High Altar completely encased the previous High Altar, which in turn encased the preceding one, and so on, presumably all the way back to 326 C.E., when the first shrine was constructed on top of St. Peter's grave.) Here the Pope alone conducts the most sacrosanct of Catholic rituals, on Easter and a select few other holy days—which is why it is sometimes referred to as the Papal Altar, since no one but the Pontiff is permitted to use it.

Bernini outdid himself, creating the Baldacchino to end all *baldacchini* (earning itself a capital "B" to distinguish it as *the* one and only *baldacchino* that mattered). Using bronze ripped from the still-standing Pantheon (the ancient Roman temple to all gods), Bernini succeeded in turning nearly 14,000 pounds of metal into an airy and frilly simulacrum of a cloth canopy. The striated columns twirl skyward, festooned with an absurd profusion of baroque details—leaves and sunbursts and cupids and doves and faux-tassels amidst a plethora of inscrutable Papal emblems. It's all so overwhelming that most modern visitors just stand and stare upward, trying to absorb the magnificence until their neck muscles give out.

But the Baldacchino itself, finished in 1633, is actually of little importance to this story. As far as we're concerned, it serves only one function: to distract visitors from something even more interesting below. In fact, it's because of the Baldacchino that so few notice the carvings that are the focus of this chapter. Turn your attention now to something seemingly more pedestrian: the marble bases on which the Baldacchino's four columns rest and which stand at the four corners of the High Altar's platform.

Compared to the splendor around them, the four column-bases are somewhat unremarkable at first glance. The two outward-facing sides of all four bases (hence, eight sides in total) feature figurative carvings which, upon close inspection, are all nearly identical but subtly different from each other. Take a look at the photograph on the following page (which I snapped myself) and ponder each of the elements of the series' first carving.

Pope Urban VIII was born Maffeo Barberini, a member of Florence's powerful Barberini clan. When he was named Pope, he combined the Barberini insignia and the Papal emblems to create his own special coat of arms. The altar carvings all show a stylized version of Urban VIII's unique coat of arms but with strange and subtle alterations. The top portion comprises the Papal emblems: a crown, specifically called the Papal Tiara, above the two crossed keys to the Kingdom of Heaven which, according to the Bible, Jesus symbolically gave to Peter while telling him: "And I also say to you that you are Peter, and on this rock I will build My church, and the gates of Hades shall not prevail against it. And I will give you the keys of the Kingdom of Heaven" (Matthew 16:18–19, NKJV). Below that is a shield on which rest three bees—the Barberini insignia.

So much for what Urban VIII's coat of arms was *supposed* to look like. As you can see, Bernini added two conspicuous elements: a woman's face above the bees, and what looks like convoluted bodily organs below. In each of the eight panels, the face and the organs change slightly. They're meant to illustrate, of all things, the process of giving birth.

Competing theories, as we shall see, debate the meaning of the carvings, but all of them concede that the figure's lower portion is supposed to represent a woman's "naughty parts." In fact, the bees are also supposed to represent elements of her body. The face at the top is her face (obviously); the shield is her torso; the two top bees are her breasts; the lower bee is her navel; and the volutes at the bottom are her genitals.

And look closely at those genitals. While Bernini presumably was not allowed to be sexually explicit in his depiction, he did get away with a stylized representation of a woman's reproductive organs in detail that is remarkably anatomically correct. What's especially noteworthy is that the vagina is depicted in what looks like a cut-away view; the top wall is not shown, revealing the interior vaginal canal. To the sides of the vagina are folds representing the labia minora and labia majora. And at the top is a protuberant nub that could represent the clitoral hood.

Through the course of the eight panels, a series of changes takes place in each of the elements as the pregnancy progresses. In the first panel, the woman's face is young and smiling. With each successive scene, her mouth opens, and she begins to either grimace or scream in pain. Her "belly" (the shield with the bees) swells and broadens. And her vagina opens up and spreads. In the final panel, a baby's face replaces hers, and the belly and genitals return to normal.

BERNINI'S SCULPTURAL SERIES, therefore, unquestionably shows a woman's pregnancy, labor, and childbirth. But why? And why, of all places, on the High Altar of Christendom?

The first carving of the series. Credit: Kristan Lawson.

EVERYTHING YOU KNOW ABOUT GOD IS WRONG

The answer to that question is not easy to find. Biographies of Bernini make only passing reference to the altar carvings; some don't mention them at all. It's almost impossible to find photos of them in any book about Bernini or St. Peter's Basilica, no matter how comprehensive. One of the difficulties is that we don't know for sure whose hands actually carved the designs. Bernini was the man in charge, and he certainly was a master sculptor. But he was helped by a small army of assistants, including his rival, Francesco Borromini, and Bernini's brother-in-law, Agostino Radi, both of whom conceivably could have actually wielded the chisel to render Bernini's design, as a few scholars have speculated. Even so, the general consensus is that Bernini either did the actual carving himself or made the design and assigned its rendering to an underling.

Most catalogs of the artwork on display in the Vatican similarly gloss over these particular carvings, a few mentioning them briefly as being merely the Papal coat of arms. Guidebooks point visitors to the Baldacchino above but almost universally ignore the altar carvings. One is tempted to speculate that this silence is intentional, a suppression of the embarrassing evidence. But here and there, in obscure sources (mostly in Italian), the carvings are mentioned, and answers are given. The problem is, they don't all agree on the details—though one thing on which they almost all *do* agree is that the carvings indeed depict a woman's genitalia.

In my survey of rare, old sources, I eventually uncovered no fewer than four different explanations as to the origins of Bernini's design. The first theory is the most commonly cited, though it's not completely clear which of the four is most likely to be true.

Theory 1: The carvings depict the troubled pregnancy of the Pope's niece.

Pope Urban VIII had a niece who was experiencing a difficult pregnancy. Everyone expected it to end badly, for her to die in childbirth. In desperation, Urban VIII made a public vow to God that he would bequeath improvements to the High Altar if God would intervene and allow mother and child to survive the birth. Miraculous or not, the birth went smoothly, and Urban VIII followed through on his promise. He hired Bernini to create a new *baldacchino*. But it was Bernini, aware of the circumstances of his commission, who came up on his own with the idea of depicting the successful pregnancy on the column's bases and revealed them as a surprise to the delighted Pope.

While this charming story seems on the surface the most likely to be the real explanation behind the carvings, a few troubling details cast doubt. First off, the mysterious niece is never named—which is odd, since the Barberini family was very well-known, and if Maffeo Barberini had a brother, who had a daughter, we almost certainly would know their names. Secondly, one needs to keep in mind exactly where this is: the High Altar in the Vatican. Would a Pope really allow such a personal, trivial, and (some would say) obscene artwork to be permanently displayed at such a high-profile sacred location? If there's no greater significance to the story beyond that of some relative of a Pope having a baby, it seems quite odd that it would be immortalized on the most important altar in the Catholic world. Why not depict the Virgin Mary's pregnancy, if a pregnancy is to be depicted at all? Why not depict the martyrdom of St. Peter? Or Jesus? Or any other significant religious scene? What's so important about little Miss Barberini that she trumped the Savior of mankind?

Theory 2: The carvings depict the scandalous pregnancy of Pope Joan, history's only female Pope.

The legend of Pope Joan—which has been popularized recently in TV specials and books—tells of a young woman from England who disguised herself as a man, traveled to Germany (or in some versions, Greece) in the ninth century, became a famous ecclesiastical scholar, and was eventually elected Pope in 853 C.E. Serving under the name John VIII, she reigned for only two years, as in 855 she gave birth in public after going into labor while riding a horse. Her true gender thereby revealed, she was stoned to death by outraged Romans.

The existence of Pope Joan is still debated, though most scholars insist that her story is nothing more than a legend; detailed, reliable chronologies of the succession of ninth-century Popes leave no room for the two-year reign of a "secret" Pontiff, male or female. Even so, the Catholic Church itself seemed for centuries to accept the story as possibly true, and it wasn't until the fifteenth century that it officially repudiated the fable. By 1624, when these carvings were made, the Church's unequivocal position was that no such person as Pope Joan ever existed. Why then portray her in the most obvious place imaginable?

(Interestingly, Pope Joan lives on in our culture as the High Priestess in the tarot deck. In the first tarots, the High Priest and High Priestess cards were called the *Pape* and *Papesse*—the Pope and Popess. The very concept of a "Popess" was based on the legend of Pope Joan.)

The Pope Joan theory might be the most colorful explanation, but it is also the least likely. Nowhere else in any Catholic iconography is Pope Joan depicted. The Church even had previously removed and destroyed the only other statue elsewhere in Rome that was rumored (probably falsely) to portray her. Why would it then put her right in the middle of St. Peter's, even as some kind of not-so-"secret" clue about the existence of this historical embarrassment?

Theory 3: The carving is an allegorical representation of the Church giving birth to Truth.

This theory is put forth by Catholic writers fishing around for a respectable, nonsexual interpretation of Bernini's creation. It doesn't actually show a real woman's body, they say, but rather just a symbol of how the Catholic Church is the mother of Truth. Alternately, a few writers claim that the scene shows how humanity (represented by the young woman) suffers while awaiting salvation (the birth).

Nice try, but I'm not buying it. The face of the woman and her distorted expressions are too personalized, too specific to be merely an allegorical figure, which are almost always idealized, symmetrical, and glamorous. (The Statue of Liberty is perhaps the most famous statue of an allegorical figure.) Why would Bernini portray the Catholic Church or humanity in general as a grimacing girl?

Theory 4: The carvings celebrate the "Sacred Feminine" that secretly lies at the heart of Christian theology.

This is the theory that everyone wants to be true. And by "everyone," I mean feminists, neo-pagans, postmodern intellectuals, conspiracy theorists, *The Da Vinci Code* fans, and anybody who likes "weird stuff." The unambiguous maleness of the deity in Judeo-Christian beliefs has often bothered critics of monotheism, who argue that before the religion of Abraham arose, humans saw God or the gods as having both male and female aspects. This ur-Goddess, as championed by followers of anthropologists such as Marija Gimbutas, was a pancultural counterpart to and companion of the male figure we now know as "God." As this theory holds, the three main monotheistic religions—Judaism, Christianity, and, later, Islam—came along and quashed this divine feminine, creating a patriarchal culture and all the subsequent misery of the modern world. But hidden within the masculine theology is a buried thread of the Sacred Feminine, for those who care to look.

Here we could spin off into *Holy Blood, Holy Grail* territory and speculate about Sophia, the feminine counterpart to Christ in Gnostic beliefs, and all the cryptic clues to the real meaning of Christianity, but no—hang on a minute. Let's go back to Bernini's sculpture. It's just a girl. And Bernini almost undoubtedly devised the design himself—Urban VIII was no artist. What would the conversation have been between the two?

"Gian Lorenzo, I want you to build a big bronze canopy over the new Papal Altar."

"Sure thing, Maffeo—whatever you say."

"Oh, and while you're at it—on the bases of the canopy's columns, could you carve eight depictions of the Divine Goddess that lies at the heart of Christianity, a forbidden secret that we've been trying to suppress for 1,600 years? I want to make sure everyone knows about this."

"Can I show her genitals in explicit detail?"

"Of course! What good is Sacred Femininity without some nice genitals?"

But ponder this: In Islam, the only site that is comparable to the High Altar is the Kaaba, a tall, brickwork cube housing what is believed to be a meteorite. It is considered the holiest site in the world. The *hajj*—the pilgrimage to Mecca—revolves around the Kaaba, which every able-bodied Muslim must see at least once in his or her lifetime. When Muslims around the world "turn toward Mecca" to pray five times a day, they are specifically turning toward the Kaaba. The meteorite—called the Black Stone, or al-Hajar-ul-Aswad—is visible through a small window on the outer southeastern corner of the Kaaba. And here's the kicker: The window and its silver frame are in a distinctly vaginal shape—a circular hole in the center, with tapering, curved lines above and below, accentuated by being exposed in a gap in the Kaaba's cloth covering, which also looks quite crotch-like. How oddly coincidental is it that the two holiest sites of the two largest patriarchal, monotheistic religions both have symbolic female genitalia on them?

Also intriguing is the theory that the organic convolutions in the High Altar carvings *start out* representing female genitalia, but as the pregnancy nears its conclusion, they morph into the face of a "Green Man" (a pagan life-spirit occasionally found on churches starting in the medieval era, most commonly in the Celtic parts of Europe). With a little imagination, it is easy to visualize a foliate face in the penultimate of the eight carvings. The Divine Feminine, in this theory, is shown giving birth to Life itself.

SO THERE YOU HAVE IT. Four theories, none of them satisfactory.[1] But the sculptures are undeniably there, in plain view, begging for some kind of expla-nation. Of the four possibilities given in the literature, the first very well might be the most likely: that the carvings simply portray a real young woman, a relative of the Pope, going through her pregnancy. Adding to this likelihood is Urban VIII's notorious nepotism: He gave lucrative Church positions and assignments to his family members and was not above turning the Papacy into a private Barberini fiefdom. It's entirely within what we know of Maffeo Barberini's character to have been so crass as to immortalize a minor family incident in the most conspicuous place imaginable. Or at least, he wouldn't have complained if young Bernini tried to curry papal favor by flattering the Barberinis unbidden.

Whatever the origin and rationale for the explicit carvings around the High Altar, the one indisputable fact is simply that they *exist*, which by itself is bizarre in the extreme.

The next time you visit the Vatican, remember: Look for the genitals.

A later carving in the series. Credit: Kristan Lawson.

1. Mention should be made here of the only scholarly article ever written in English about the carvings: "The Stemme on Bernini's Baldacchino in St. Peter's: A Forgotten Compliment" by Philipp Fehl (*Burlington Magazine*, CXVIII, 1976, pages 484–91). (The word *stemme* means "coat of arms" in Italian.) Fehl goes into as much detail as is known about the official history of the carvings but dismisses the possibility that the convolutions at the bottom represent genitalia. In fact, the entire article is devoted to disparaging that concept, brushing it aside as a "cicerone's tale" (i.e., a story told by travel guides meant to titillate the visitor). Instead, Fehl claims, the lower portion is "the distorted face of a flayed satyr." While it is true that the carving in the second-to-last of the eight panels does indeed acquire a jaw and look rather like a face, as mentioned above, it more resembles a "Green Man." And the other seven lack the jaw or facial structure that one would expect in the skinless head of a satyr, or any head. But in his attempt to sanitize the meaning of the carvings, Fehl introduced something even more bizarre than a woman's private parts: Why would an image as grotesque as a "satyr's flayed face" be on Christianity's High Altar? Is a horror show an improvement over a peep show?

8

SOUNDS AND WORDS

Dan Barker

IT AIN'T NECESSARILY SO

MUSIC'S DEBT TO NONBELIEVERS

"RELIGION HAS INSPIRED such great music," we often hear. "Secular music doesn't compare."

During a debate on religion and society, I was asked: "Doesn't faith have the capacity to inspire people to great acts? No atheists come to mind who have been important in the formation of classical or Romantic art or music."

John Philip Sousa, known as the March King, agreed. He felt that "atheistic composers could not be inspired to great things." His own compositions, which include "The Stars and Stripes Forever," came from a "higher power," he insisted. "The Unseen Helper sends me a musical idea, and that Somebody helps the public to lay hold of my meaning."[1]

Religious writers indeed have produced some beautiful music. Although I don't believe in the object of adoration of Schubert's "Ave Maria," I do find the melody quite haunting and appealing—musically, emotionally. I admire the art, if not the words. Vivaldi was a priest, and he composed some gorgeous sacred melodies.

But religion has also inspired a lot of junk. I find the droning, pentatonic "Amazing Grace," a song adored by millions, to be banal and manipulative, and the lyrics insulting. (Knowing that the composer, the "wretch" John Newton, was a Christian slave-trader does not help.) If religion gets the credit, it should also get the blame. Like the face that only a mother could love, some truly horrible hymns,

insipid worship songs, awkward anthems, macho militaristic marches, and tiresome, simplistic chord progressions have been spawned by religion. With much of it, beauty is in the eye of the believer.

Not all "religious" music is what it seems. Some of it was inspired not so much by faith as by hunger. Often, the only way a composer could make a living was to write for the powers who were commissioning the music: the king and the church. Some sacred music was originally popular secular music recycled for religion. Some religious music was actually created by nonreligious composers, and some was written by composers who later became unbelievers. Of course, a lot of secular music was composed by believers.

Nonbelievers, in fact, have immensely beautified (not beatified) the musical landscape.

Granting the place of sacred music in history, is religion the only real inspiration? Is music written by nonbelievers less beautiful? What did Sousa think about the operas of Verdi or the symphonies of Brahms? How did he feel about Vaughan Williams' *The Lark Ascending* or Gershwin's *Rhapsody in Blue*? What would he have thought of "Over the Rainbow" or "White Christmas"? Are these not "great things"?

> **When his friend Ignaz Moscheles returned a manuscript to Beethoven with the words "The end with the help of God" written at the bottom, Beethoven wrote in reply: "Oh, man, help thyself!"**

Nonbelievers, in fact, have immensely beautified (not beatified) the musical landscape. "Inspiration" turns out to be a purely natural phenomenon. A brief survey of the lives and views of some beloved composers and songwriters will dispel the myth that only religion can inspire truly great music.

CLASSICAL COMPOSERS

WOLFGANG AMADEUS MOZART (1756-1791)

The young Mozart was indeed a believer, but he grew up to discard his faith. Son of a Catholic musician, the child prodigy conducted his first original Mass at age twelve in Vienna, was later made a Knight of the Golden Spur by the Pope, and was concertmaster to the Archbishop of Salzburg for many years. However, accused of neglecting his religion, he resigned the appointment in 1781. Mozart rejected many of his earlier religious views and then joined the Freemasons, who required only a minimal belief in a deistic god, and who were condemned by the Catholic Church.

During his short life, Mozart created a treasure trove of innovative, beautiful music: operas, masses, oratorios, cantatas, ballet music, vocal ensembles, marches, dance music, chamber music, more than seventy piano sonatas and works, and more than fifty symphonies.

Although probably not an atheist, the mature Mozart had little use for religion. Referring to the orthodoxy of his youth, he said: "That is all over, and will never come back."[2] He refused to ask for a priest when dying. His wife sent for one anyway, who refused to attend. He was buried in a pauper's grave, and nobody knows the exact location of his remains.

If Mozart's music was "inspired," why have so few others been equally "inspired"? Credit should go where credit is due: Mozart was a musical genius.

LUDWIG VAN BEETHOVEN (1770–1827)

Beethoven was born into a Roman Catholic family. After working as an assistant organist, he studied in Vienna under Haydn. Beethoven was an admirer of Goethe, who rejected Christianity in favor of a pantheistic viewpoint. When his friend Ignaz Moscheles returned a manuscript to Beethoven with the words "The end with the help of God" written at the bottom, Beethoven wrote in reply: "Oh, man, help thyself!"[3] "Ode to Joy," in his Ninth Symphony, sets to music the humanistic words of Friedrich Schiller, artistically invoking pagan gods, not the god of the bible. The English translation, by the way, makes the lyrics more "Christian" than Schiller or Beethoven intended.

Biographer and friend Anton Schindler wrote that Beethoven was "inclined to Deism." Although, at the insistence of religious friends, he received Catholic ministrations near his death, Beethoven reportedly said in Latin, after the priest left: "Applaud, friends; the comedy is over."[4]

The composer Sir George Macfarren—principal of the Royal Academy of Music—described Beethoven as "a free thinker."[5] According to prolific atheist writer and researcher Joseph McCabe, the *Catholic Encyclopedia* chose to omit Beethoven.

"There is no record of his ever attending church service or observing the orthodoxy of his religion," writes biographer George Marek.

"He never went to confession…. Generally he viewed priests with mistrust."[6]

"Beethoven was not a churchgoer and was suspicious of any sort of orthodoxy, religious or secular," writes Bill Cooke. "He composed very little religious music, in the narrower sense of the term. His most ostensibly religious piece was the *Missa Solemnis* which was…a hymn to Deism, and evokes the ideal not of humanity managing to qualify for entrance into a distant heaven above, but, in the words of Paul Griffiths, of a 'sovereign humanity in ultimate concord here on earth.'"

HECTOR BERLIOZ (1803-1869)

Identified with the French Romantic movement, the mature Berlioz was a nonbeliever who was impressed with religious form but motivated by human passion. He acknowledged that his earliest experiences with music were connected with religious ritual, Christian as well as pagan. He was "innately romantic," experiencing emotions deeply during his entire life. This showed itself when, as a child, he wept at passages of Virgil, and later in a series of love affairs. As a young man, he briefly fell under the spell of the Catholic religion, "though his beliefs will not survive into adult life," writes biographer David Cairns.

Berlioz was the son of a physician. As a young composer, "when not copying parts (which he did 'till his thumbs ached') he read the materialist philosophers and physiologists whose works were in his father's library—Locke, Cabanis, Gall—and found confirmation for his own disbelief in a personal God..."[7] Among his friends were skeptics Alexandre Dumas, Victor Hugo, and Honoré de Balzac.

When he was twenty-three, his unrequited love for the Irish Shakespearean actress Henrietta Smithson was the inspiration for his *Symphonie Fantastique*. His love letters to her were so overly passionate that she initially refused his advances. However, the symphony which these emotions are said to have inspired, and the autobiographic, "romantic" nature of this music, was considered sensational by listeners. Smithson finally agreed to marry Berlioz after she had attended a performance of the *Symphonie Fantastique* and realized that the work was his depiction of his passionate letters to her. This work was clearly not motivated by a love for God—unless God is a redhead.

Berlioz, like nonbelievers Verdi and Brahms, also wrote a funeral mass. Cairns writes of the Requiem composed by Berlioz:

> Though it is not the work of an orthodox believer, it has Wordsworth's "visionary gleam." Berlioz spoke of himself as an atheist, at most as an agnostic. The passionate faith of his boyhood did not survive long into his adult years. (If he had a god it was Shakespeare: "It is thou that art our father, our father in heaven, if there is a heaven," he will cry out,

in one of the most harrowing moments of his existence.) But the very loss left a permanent mark.

As further evidence of his disdain for religion, he wrote in a June 1824 letter to Jean-François LeSueur: "Then, when I wished to set about this mass [of which I have spoken], I remained so cold, so icy in reading the *Credo* and the *Kyrie* that, more than convinced that I would not be able to do anything tolerable in this frame of mind, I gave it up."[8] (The *Credo* is the Nicene Creed, and the *Kyrie* is a well-known prayer; both are often set to music for Catholic Mass.) In a letter from Paris, July 22, 1862, to Princess Sayn-Wittgenstein, Berlioz wrote: "Like you, I have one of the theological virtues, Charity; but unlike you, I have not the other two [Hope and Faith]...."[9]

Other works of Berlioz currently in the standard orchestral repertoire include *La damnation de Faust*, the symphony *Roméo et Juliette*, the song cycle *Les nuits d'été*, and his symphonic viola concerto, *Harold en Italie*.

Berlioz was inspired by life, beauty, love, and passion, not by religious belief.

ROBERT SCHUMANN (1810-1856)

German composer Robert Schumann's father was a bookseller who encouraged his young son to read the humanistic works of Schiller, Goethe, and many freethinkers, such as Byron. Schumann gave up Christian beliefs as a student. He was educated at Leipzig and Heidelberg Universities for a law career. Unable to resist the pull of music, he first trained to be a pianist, then threw himself into composition. He founded the journal *Neue Zeitschrift für Musik* in 1834, which he edited for around nine years, an influential contribution to the promotion of progressive thought on music. His famous "Scenes from Childhood" was composed in 1838.

He married his beloved Clara Wieck, a talented concert pianist and composer, in 1840. (See note about Clara Schumann in Brahms section.) During that year he composed approximately 150 songs, many based on romantic tales. In 1841, he turned to orchestral music, in 1842 to chamber music, and in 1843 to choral music, including a secular oratorio and Goethe's *Faust*. His *lieder* set to

Robert Schumann, 1839 lithograph by Joseph Kriehuber.
Credit: Wikimedia Commons.

music words by such freethinking writers as Goethe, Heine, and Kerner.

Schumann had a devastating nervous breakdown, attended by hallucinations and suicidal impulses, in 1854. Although tended by Clara and his young protégé and friend, Johannes Brahms, he did not recover, and died in a sanitarium two years later. Writing about a goodbye walk Clara and Brahms took with Schumann before checking him into a hospital toward the end of his life, Brahms biographer Jan Swafford notes: "Naturally they stopped at the Beethoven statue that Schumann had been visiting nearly every day; the monument was his church and his altar."

GIUSEPPE VERDI (1813–1901)

The great Italian composer Giuseppe Verdi was a hearty skeptic, an altar boy who grew up to say: "Stay away from priests." Biographer Mary Jane Phillips-Matz documents Verdi's "anticlericalism and refusal to believe in God or any higher power." Instead of following the Church, "he put his faith in land, gold, and his compositions."

The great Italian composer Giuseppe Verdi was a hearty skeptic, an altar boy who grew up to say: "Stay away from priests."

Verdi's wife, Giuseppina Strepponi, was quite aware of his irreligious views. "For some virtuous people," she wrote of him, "a belief in God is necessary. Others, equally perfect, while observing every precept of the highest moral code, are happier believing in nothing." She also wrote:

> He is a jewel among honest men; he understands and feels himself every delicate and elevated sentiment. And yet this brigand permits himself to be, I won't say an atheist, but certainly very little of a believer, and that with an obstinacy and calm that make me want to beat him. I exhaust myself in speaking to him about the marvels of the heavens, the earth, the sea, etc. It's a waste of breath! He laughs in my face and freezes me in the midst of my oratorical periods and my divine enthusiasm by saying "you're all crazy," and unfortunately he says it with good faith.

(Of course, if atheism is the lack of belief in a god, then Verdi was indeed an atheist. He was certainly at least agnostic.)

Verdi wrote about the human condition, not religion. When the young composer did write for Church performances, he was sometimes accused of "substituting 'profane words' for the 'Holy words' of the text." His operas were often censored by the Church and the government, especially early in his career, but as his reputation solidified, Verdi refused to bow to religious and political pressure. He wrote what he wanted.

His first opera, *Oberto*, was produced at La Scala in 1839. Many operas would follow, including *Rigoletto*, *Il trovatore*, *La traviata*, and *Les vêpres siciliennes*, which was criticized by clergy. The composer of *Don Carlos*, *Aida*, *Otello*, and *Falstaff* was acclaimed internationally and regarded by contemporaries as the greatest Italian composer of his century.

As an anti-Papist and a rationalist whose beliefs were well-known, Verdi avoided writing ecclesiastical music. He was elected to Parliament (1861–1865) and sympathized with the nineteenth-century campaigns for freedom. At the end of his successful career, Verdi shared his wealth, endowing the city of Milan with two million lira in 1898 to establish a home for aging musicians. Twenty-eight thousand mourners showed up for his nonreligious funeral, which, according to his request, was conducted without "any part of the customary formulae."[10]

JOHANNES BRAHMS (1833–1897)

How many parents, soothing their children to sleep with "Brahms's Lullaby," know they are singing a melody written by a nonbeliever?

Brahms, the great German composer who was often called the "third B" (after Bach and Beethoven), had no faith in a god or religion. He was most often influenced by philosophy and literature, and inspired by nature. "A great deal of his music," writes biographer Jan Swafford, "in its inspiration and spirit, rose from mountains and forests and open sky." The melody for the finale of Symphony No. 1 in C Minor actually traces the shape of the Alps, as Brahms viewed them during a hike. "Music was Brahms's religion," Swafford observes.

> **"Such a man, such a fine soul," Antonín Dvořák said of Brahms, "and he believes in nothing! He believes in nothing!"**

"Such a man, such a fine soul," fellow composer Antonín Dvořák said of Brahms, "and he believes in nothing! He believes in nothing!"[11]

Brahms occasionally used biblical texts but only for artistic reasons. After the death of his mother, he wrote *Ein deutsches Requiem* using text from the German bible, but he selected only those words that relate to this life and to those who grieve. It starts, "Blessed are they that mourn, for they shall be comforted," and avoids talk of eternal salvation. Noticing this secular spin, conductor Karl Reinthaler wrote to Brahms:

> Forgive me, but I wondered if it might not be possible to extend the work in some way that would bring it closer to a Good Friday service... [W]hat is lacking, at least for a Christian consciousness, is the pivotal point: the salvation in the death of our Lord....

"Brahms was not about to put up with that sort of thing," Swafford writes. "He was a humanist and an agnostic, and his Requiem was going to express that.... Even if the words come from the Bible, this was his response to death as a secular, skeptical, modern man."

Brahms replied to Reinthaler: "As far as the text is concerned...I would dispense with places like John 3:16.... I have chosen one thing or another because I am a musician, because I needed it...but I had better stop before I say too much." He had already said too much! To reject John 3:16 ("For God so loved the world, that he gave his only begotten Son...") is to reject Christianity.

"[H]e downplays the theology of some verses he does use, saying, 'I can't delete or dispute anything' from Scripture," Swafford writes. "With that he obliquely confesses that even the hints of resurrection lingering in his texts are not his own sentiments. At the end of his Requiem, the dead are not reborn but released."

However, in order to "placate the pious," Swafford writes, the young Brahms (who in later life would never have tolerated such intrusions) permitted a compromise during the first performance of the Requiem on Good Friday, 1868. A female soloist sang, "I know that my Redeemer liveth," from Handel's *Messiah*. "Hearing that effect," Swafford continues, "may have helped Brahms conclude that the piece could use a nice solo for a female voice. But when he added that solo after the premiere, it still pointedly made no allusion to the eponymous founder of the Christian religion."

In other works, Brahms referred to pagan deities. "Let the race of man, Fear the gods! They hold the power, In eternal hands" (from *Gesang der Parzen*). However, Swafford notes: "The gods he spoke of were his personal ones, his real religion: Bach, Mozart, Beethoven, Schubert, and the others."

To a friend, Brahms, who never married, said, "Apart from Frau Schumann I'm not attached to anybody with my whole soul!... Is that not a lonely life! Yet we can't believe in immortality on the other side. The only true immortality lies in one's children." (Clara Schumann, the virtuoso pianist and composer, though she may have been a nominal believer, also had little use for the church. "Performing was her religion," Swafford observes. "If there is such a thing as a secular saint, surely she was one.")

When Karl Lueger was elected mayor of Vienna in 1895, turning Austria formally anti-Semitic from then until Hitler, Brahms remarked to his friends: "Didn't I tell you years ago that it was going to happen?... Now it's here, and with it the priests' economic system. If there was an 'Anticlerical Party'—that would make sense! But antisemitism is madness!"

"Brahms's Lullaby" (*Wiegenlied*), one of the best-known melodies in the world, was inspired by romantic, not religious, feelings. It was written in honor of the birth of a child to Brahms' friends Bertha and Artur Faber in 1868. Years earlier, Brahms had briefly fallen in love with Bertha, and during the playful courtship she often sang him a lilting Viennese melody. The romance ended, but the friendship endured, and the melody Brahms composed was a counterpoint to the earlier love song that she would remember singing to the composer. When he presented the gift, Brahms included this note to her husband: "Frau Bertha will realize that I wrote the 'Wiegenlied' for her little one. She will find it quite in order...that while she is singing Hans to sleep, a love song is being sung to her." Bertha was the first person to sing "Brahms's Lullaby," both love melodies dancing flirtatiously in her head.

When Brahms died, there was no deathbed conversion, no regret for having lived a godless life. He did achieve a kind of immortality, not in children or in heaven, but in the gorgeous music he left behind.

GEORGES BIZET (1838–1875)

Georges Bizet, the French musical prodigy, entered the Paris Conservatoire at age nine. Over the next decade he won virtually every prize available, including the Prix de Rome, yet refused a career as a concert pianist in order to compose operas. He wrote about thirty, none particularly successful, until he composed *Carmen* in 1875, based on Prosper Mérimée's novella about a Spanish Gypsy girl. *Carmen* was controversial not only because of its humble subject matter and passionate sweep, but for the fact that the libretto was written in French rather than the customary Italian and (scandalously) could be understood by the audience. Criticism and a lukewarm reception closed the play after a brief run, although the composers of that day praised it.

Bizet was a rationalist. Biographer Winton Dean writes that as a young man, struggling with his religious and philosophical views, Bizet was asked by his Academy to write a Mass. Preferring to write a comedy, he replied:

I don't want to write a mass before being in a state to do it well, that is a Christian. I have therefore taken a singular course to reconcile my ideas with the exigencies of Academy rules. They ask me for something religious: very well, I shall do something religious, but of the pagan religion.... I have always read the ancient pagans with infinite pleasure, while in Christian writers I find only system, egoism, intolerance, and a complete lack of artistic taste.

Nine years later, he wrote:

Religion is a means of exploitation employed by the strong against the weak; religion is a cloak of ambition, injustice and vice.... Truth breaks free, science is popularized, and religion totters; soon it will fall, in the course of centuries—that is, tomorrow.... In good time we shall only have to deal with reason.[12]

Three months after the opening of *Carmen*, while the failed opera was still playing to empty houses, the dejected writer, who suffered from ill health, died of a heart attack at the age of thirty-six, never knowing that *Carmen* would become one of the best-known, best-loved, and most-produced operas in history.

Instead of religion, which divides, Bizet gave us something better: music that is adored throughout the world.

SIR EDWARD ELGAR (1857–1934)

Although born and raised in England as a believing Roman Catholic, composer Edward Elgar eventually discarded his faith toward the end of his life. Most of his works were religious in nature, such as the oratorios *The Dream of Gerontius*, *The Apostles*, and *The Kingdom*, although he would come to regret having written them. Composer Frederick Delius reports that Elgar told him "it was a great pity that [Elgar] had wasted so much time and energy in writing those long-winded oratorios." Delius himself, who greatly admired Nietzsche, remarked to a friend that Elgar "might have been a great composer if he had thrown all that religious paraphernalia overboard. *Gerontius* is a nauseating work, and, of course, tremendously influenced by Parsifal."[13]

After the unsuccessful premiere of *The Dream of Gerontius*, Elgar, a waning believer, wrote to a friend: "I always said that God was against art & I still believe it."[14]

The Apostles and *The Kingdom* were intended to be the first two parts of a trilogy, but Elgar never finished it. "By the time he commenced work on *The Kingdom*," writes professor Byron Adams, who considers a loss of faith to be a bad thing,

> Elgar's enthusiasm for completing the trilogy had begun to fade, as had his faith. Paradoxically, the excursion into biblical exegesis that Elgar did during the creation of *The Apostles* and *The Kingdom* could have played a part in the unraveling of the composer's already frayed beliefs. Elgar possessed an intuitive intelligence but he was unversed in systematic theology: his training as a Catholic had been liturgical and doctrinal. For such a quick but undisciplined intellect, the contradictory speculations advanced by the various authors that Elgar consulted, including such sceptics as Ernest Renan, may have caused only distress.

In other words, reading the bible turned Elgar into an unbeliever. French philosopher and theologian Ernest Renan's *Life of Jesus* (1863), which Elgar read, is a critical analysis of the New Testament, attempting to explain the miracles in natural terms.

Elgar viewed composition as a natural exercise, claiming that he was trying to set the environment to music. Robert Buckley, his first biographer,

reports that "when he was nine or ten years old Edward Elgar was discovered sitting on a bank by the river with pencil and a piece of paper whereon were ruled five parallel lines. He was trying, he said, to write down what the reeds were singing."[15] All through his life, he used to sit outside and dream, and listen. Beneath a quotation from the "Woodland Interlude" from his cantata *Caractacus*, he wrote: "This is what I hear all day—the trees are singing my music—or have I sung theirs? It is too beautiful here."[16]

Elgar's full-blown nonbelief in his later years was revealed when he learned he was dying. Adams writes:

> Arthur Thomson, the Birmingham doctor who delivered the fatal diagnosis of cancer to the composer, reported that Elgar "told me that he had no faith whatever in an afterlife: 'I believe there is nothing but complete oblivion.'" Approaching his final dissolution, Elgar expressed in a lucid moment the perfectly rational desire to be cremated and have his ashes scattered at the confluence of the Severn and Teme rivers, a request in direct conflict with the doctrines of the Roman Catholic Church of which he was still a member. Only when Elgar lapsed into unconsciousness due to heavy doses of morphine did his daughter summon a priest to administer the Viaticum.... Betrayed by friends and family, manipulated by ruthless commercial interests and without consolation, Elgar died on 23 February 1934, and was buried next to his wife in the cemetery of St Wulstan's Roman Catholic Church in Little Malvern.

RICHARD STRAUSS (1864–1949)

German composer Richard Strauss began piano lessons at age four and composition by seven. He studied music and philosophy for two terms at Munich University and launched into a life-long career as conductor. His teenage composition was influenced by the work of Robert Schumann, and his piano quartet of 1884 was completed following a consultation with Johannes Brahms. As an adult, Strauss was influenced by Franz Liszt and Richard Wagner. He excelled in the tone poem, such as *Also sprach Zarathustra* (most famously used in the film *2001: A Space Odyssey*), ostensibly setting to music Nietzsche's and his own nonreligious views, earning harsh criticism from the Church. His opera *Salome*, based on the play by Oscar Wilde, was a sensation not just because of the "blasphemous" subject matter but also because it was a musical stretch. Another Strauss opera is the much-performed *Electra*. His compositions include *Till Eulenspiegels lustige Streiche*, as well as many *lieder*.

Strauss wrote his first songs as a wedding present for his wife, Pauline von Ahna, whom he married in 1894. He composed the Olympic Hymn for the 1936 games in Berlin. He was briefly appointed head of State Music (without his consultation) by the Third Reich. He was barred from working with his librettist, Stefan Zweig, who was Jewish, and it is believed he maintained silence about the Nazis in part because his grandchildren were part-Jewish. He received warnings about his private letters, which were screened by authorities. Strauss spent much of the war in Vienna, moving to Switzerland at the war's conclusion. He conducted for the final time when he turned eighty-five.

"[Strauss] did not believe in God, and he saw no spiritual dimension in his art," music critic Alex Ross wrote in the *New Yorker*.

"His funeral was in Munich on 12 September [1949]," notes biographer Michael Kennedy. "There was no Christian symbolism of any kind."

RALPH VAUGHAN WILLIAMS (1872–1958)

"There is no reason why an atheist could not write a good Mass," Ralph (pronounced "Rafe") Vaughan Williams said.[17] Indeed, the prolific British composer, who helped compile *The English Hymnal* and who wrote religious music that is performed in liturgies and worship services around the world, was himself not a believer. "Although a declared agnostic," his wife Ursula wrote of him, "he was able, all through his life, to set to music words in the accepted terms of Christian revelation as if they meant to him what they must have meant to George Herbert or to Bunyan." She reports:

He had been confirmed at Charterhouse, taking it as a matter of course in his school career, and he continued to go to church fairly regularly "so as not to upset the family." This attitude did not affect his love of the Authorized version of the Bible. The beauty of the idiom of the Jacobean English was established in his mind long before he went away to school and, like the music of Bach, remained as one of his essential companions through life. He was far too deeply absorbed by music to feel any need of religious observance. He was an atheist during his later years at Charterhouse and at Cambridge, though he later drifted into a cheerful agnosticism: he was never a professing Christian.

Ralph's grandmother was a sister of Charles Darwin. As a child, he spent considerable time in his famous granduncle's home in Down. Hearing about *The Origin of Species*, he asked his mother what it was about. She answered: "The Bible says that God made the world in six days, Great Uncle Charles thinks it took longer: but we need not worry about it, for it is equally wonderful either way."

At Cambridge, Ralph spent more time with music than religious duties. Ursula writes:

In those days attendance at Chapel was compulsory, and one morning when Ralph's absence had been noted he was sent for by authority:

"I did not see you in Chapel this morning, Mr. Vaughan Williams."

"No, Sir."

"Perhaps, however, you were in the organ loft?"

"Yes, Sir, I was."

"Well, you can pray as well in the organ loft as in any other part of the Chapel."

"Yes, Sir—but I didn't."

Just as the tune of the English folk song "Greensleeves" has been used as a dance, a hymn, and a political ballad, music itself is neither religious nor nonreligious. While compiling *The English*

Hymnal in his early thirties, finding lyrics in want of a melody, "some tunes he wrote himself but these he did not sign and they appeared anonymously in the first edition. He searched for the best versions of the older tunes, and he adapted folk songs, continuing the ancient practice of the Church of taking secular music and using it for her own purposes."

Ralph Vaughan Williams' real world was artistic, not supernatural. Two of his best friends were the dancer Isadora Duncan and the composer Maurice Ravel, both nonbelievers. He didn't think art had to point to anything beyond itself. His widow insists:

> He was passionately anxious to discourage the critics from inventing "meanings." He would have liked to print Mendelssohn's saying that "the meaning of music is too precise for words" on every concert programme at which his works were played. He could not stop the questions and, rightly or wrongly, he never allowed the idea that lay behind the last movement of this [Sixth] symphony to be known to the critics who speculated on its historical and philosophical origin. Yet, as silence followed the final whisper of the last notes, it seemed as if the whole audience must guess the riddle:
>> And, like the baseless fabric of this vision,
>> The cloud capp'd towers, the gorgeous palaces,
>> The solemn temples, the great globe itself,
>> Yea, all which it inherit, shall dissolve
>> And, like this insubstantial pageant faded,
>> Leave not a wrack behind. We are such stuff
>> As dreams are made on, and our little life
>> Is rounded with a sleep...

Ralph's last day, at the age of eighty-six, was spent at the piano with a composer friend, discussing music. "It was all very ordinary, usual," his wife reports, "and like many other nights had been and we did not guess that before dawn death, not sleep, would claim him." Vaughan Williams, whose secular life was simply "rounded with a sleep," added hundreds of songs and other compositions, including the popular *The Lark Ascending* and nine symphonies, to the world's treasure of music.

MAURICE RAVEL (1875-1937)

Ravel was a French pianist, orchestrator, and a major composer of the twentieth century. He is probably best known to the general public for the seductive *Boléro*.

"Although born of Catholic parents and baptized as an infant," writes pianist and music professor Arbie Orenstein, "Ravel was not a practicing Catholic and did not accept the last rites of the Church. He apparently was an agnostic, relying upon his inner conscience and moral sensitivity." Since he gave generously to charity and hated all forms of racism, his parish priest once told him, "Monsieur Ravel, you are the most Christian of my parishioners," even though Ravel called himself an atheist.[18]

In a 1920 letter to his friend Ida Godebska, Ravel wrote: "I spoke with Pierette Haour, an atheist like myself, about what you had written concerning the benefits of religion," although another friend (composer Alexis Roland-Manuel) seemed surprised at Ravel's self-description and claimed that he was "certainly not an atheist, but rather a confirmed agnostic." In either case, he was a freethinker who did not believe in a god.

Ravel's works contain a notable absence of religious references and forms. He was most commonly inspired by nature, fairy tales, folk songs, and classical and Oriental legends. He planned an opera about Joan of Arc (which was never completed) but was not interested in its religious significance: "I am thinking about Joan of Arc. The famous novel of Delteil inspired me, and the plan of the music is almost completed.... [N]ature and humanity, closely dependent, offer innumerable possibilities of musical interpretation."

When Ravel died, his body was interred at the cemetery of Levallois-Perret without religious ceremony.

SERGEI PROKOFIEV (1891–1953)

The prolific Russian composer Sergei Prokofiev produced eight complete operas (including *War and Peace*), eight ballets (including *Romeo and Juliet* and *Cinderella*), seven symphonies, eight film scores, nine concertos, twenty-three suites, twelve vocal-symphonic compositions, fifteen overtures and poems (including *Peter and the Wolf*), fifteen pieces for instrumental ensembles, fifteen pieces for voice and piano, eleven piano sonatas, twenty-four other piano works, and a sonata for solo violin. Not one was religious.

Prokofiev gave up on the idea of religion at an early age. Biographer Harlow Robinson writes:

Neither of Prokofiev's parents was particularly religious. This was more surprising in his mother's case, since she came from a very devout peasant family, and her sisters were faithful churchgoers. His father came from the less religiously inclined merchant class, and his education at the university—oriented toward science and technology—did nothing to strengthen his faith in Russian Orthodoxy. Maria Grigorevna's natural skepticism and cynicism, strengthened by the harsh reality of Russian provincial life and her own family's struggles, led her eventually to openly question and even mock church dogma, rather than to embrace it. Prokofiev inherited these skeptical sentiments from her. One should remember, too, that atheistic attitudes were almost universal among the progressive intelligentsia in Russia in the years leading up to the Revolution.

"Generally speaking," Prokofiev said, "I was reserved in dealing with questions of the heart, and that trait showed up here, too; I waged the battle for religion internally, without sharing it or discussing it with anyone." After attending religious services with one of his aunts in a crowded, stuffy church smelling of incense, he fainted and had to be taken outside. "My fainting spell frightened me and cooled my desire for the church," he reported. "At home we didn't talk about religion. So, gradually the question faded away by itself and disappeared from the agenda. When I was nineteen, my father died; my response to his death was atheistic. The same was true when...I lost a close friend.... I took this 'farewell' very bitterly, the farewell of a human consciousness that had departed finally and forever."[19]

Robinson writes of the chess-playing composer:

The love of rationality, mathematical organization and logic characteristic of Prokofiev's personality and working methods stems in part, at least, from his rejection of emotional, irrational and religious explanations for the way the world works. Fuzzy promises of happiness in the world hereafter were alien to his uncompromisingly rational, disciplined, here-and-now attitude.... Unlike so many Russian composers before him, Prokofiev never wrote a single explicitly religious setting—no requiems, vespers, choruses or pieces of the Russian Orthodox liturgy. The opera *The Fiery Angel* revolves around religious-spiritual issues, but it is fictional and uncomplimentary in its treatment of institutionalized religion.

Robinson notes: "The history and ritual of religion, if not its emotional appeal, had always fascinated Prokofiev; he found the elaborate Vatican ceremony of a papal reception intriguing. No doubt it supplied him with appropriate atmosphere for *The Fiery Angel*."

Like so many other composers, Prokofiev died thinking about his music, making arrangements for the copying of a revision of the Fifth Piano Sonata and his last ballet, *The Stone Flower*. Knowing his life was ending, he also put his papers in order. His final recorded words were a touching apology to his wife for his sickness having caused her such trouble. He died the same day Stalin died, March 5, 1953. His passing, eclipsed by Stalin's, was noted at a small civil funeral accompanied by the music of his F Minor Sonata for Violin and Piano.

> **"His friend and protégé, Leonard Bernstein, would tease him by saying that he was not a 'real Jew.'"**

AARON COPLAND (1900–1990)

Aaron Copland—the great American composer of numerous ballets (including *Appalachian Spring*, which won the Pulitzer Prize for Music), operas, symphonies and orchestral works (including *El salón México*), concertos, film scores (including *Of Mice and Men*), chamber music, and piano and choral works—was not religious. Professor Howard Pollack writes:

[A]lthough retaining strong memories of the music he heard in the synagogue and at Jewish weddings, Copland evidenced little direct connection with Judaism or Jewish culture. He was neither religious nor observant. He rarely attended a synagogue service. In fact, in a 1974 letter, he reminded a young friend that he had "resigned from the Jewish church."... His friend and protégé, Leonard Bernstein, would tease him by saying that he was not a "real Jew." To all appearances, and by all accounts, he was what many might call a secular humanist.

Copland was born into a well-off family of Jewish immigrants in New York City. "The expectation," professor Leon Botstein writes of the family, "was that Copland's generation would live in America as American citizens of Jewish descent and perhaps faith. Judaism as a religion became increasingly adhered to in an often nominal and merely symbolic manner."

"He had spent time before his bar mitzvah in a synagogue, but only periodically," Botstein continues. "He emerged as an adult without an ongoing connection to religion."

Copland did write a few "Jewish" compositions, but this "clearly paled both in size and importance to his involvement with American themes and subjects," Pollack reports. Furthermore,

> only four date from his maturity, and three of these...were commissioned as such.... But in any case, as it turned out, *Vitebsk* proved his only mature work on a Jewish theme undertaken on his own initiative, and that piece reflected on the social conditions of East European ghetto life as opposed to the legacy of ancient Israel or the Jewish-American experience.[20]

However, many critics (including Pollack), knowing Copland was from a Jewish family, try to spot "prophetic statements" or "the Mosaic voice" or "Hebraic ideas" in some of his compositions, although we have no real evidence that this was Copland's intent. "All agreed that there was nothing explicitly Jewish in the obvious sense... Yet there was something Jewish in the musical style nonetheless," Botstein suggests of Copland's music. Would these same critics, knowing that Copland was also a homosexual, say that there is something "gay" in his musical style? The fact that an artist is born into a religious family does not mean that the art is therefore "religious."

The Protestant sentiments of the text of melodies such as "Simple Gifts" from *Appalachian Spring* reflect, of course, the beliefs of American Shaker settlers, not Copland's own world view.

Copland himself, rather than claiming "inspiration," wrote:

> To explain the creative musician's basic objective in elementary terms, I would say that a composer writes music to express and communicate and put down in permanent form certain thoughts, emotions and states of being. These thoughts and emotions are gradually formed by the contact of the composer's personality with the world in which he lives. He expresses these thoughts...in the musical language of his own time.[21]

Aaron Copland lived and died as a nonbeliever. His will specified that his funeral service, if any, be "non-religious."

DMITRY SHOSTAKOVICH (1906–1975)

"Have atheists ever built any hospitals?" believers sometimes ask. Of course they have—all over the world. The most obvious example is the Soviet Union, an officially atheistic state in which hundreds of hospitals were constructed. In spite of the faults of Soviet Communism, especially the totalitarianism of Stalin, the Soviet people were like anyone else, and they accomplished many humanitarian acts and produced marvelous art.

Just as composers under theocratic or religious cultures were sometimes compelled to write for the church, others have been obliged to write for the state. One example is Dmitry Shostakovich, perhaps the greatest composer from the Soviet era.

Born in St. Petersburg with a heritage of proud Siberian roots, Dmitry's family initially welcomed Lenin and the Revolution as a chance for real freedom, equality, and peace on earth. Although he became privately disillusioned with the excesses of Stalin, Shostakovich had little choice but to go through the motions, eventually joining the Communist Party and fulfilling many official functions as a representative of the government, due to his celebrity status as a great composer. He didn't care about politics, except where he could use his connections to truly help people. What he really cared about was music.

"Music is what motivated him. This alone remained constant throughout a turbulent, often tortured life," writes biographer Laurel E. Fay.

"For me there is no joy in life other than music," Shostakovich wrote to a friend. "All life for me is music."

The prolific and tireless Shostakovich wrote nine operas and ballets, thirty-seven film scores, fifteen symphonies, hundreds of works for choral, solo, piano, concerti, incidental music, chamber and instrumental music. He is one of the most admired composers of the twentieth century.

When Stalin decreed that all art should adhere to a strict aesthetic of programmatic "Soviet realism," subservient to the republic, some of Shostakovich's works were considered "ideologically suspect," condemned as too decadent or "Western" in their bold experimentation. Although his music was acclaimed internationally, Shostakovich was twice officially denounced by the government and forced to make a public apology in which he humbly promised to return to a more melodic style that spoke to "the people." Seeking folk tunes that he thought would please Stalin, at one point Shostakovich turned to Jewish music. "The appearance of these works, at a time when appalling revelations about the Holocaust were filtering out and when home-grown anti-Semitism was assuming more menacing dimensions is hardly coincidental," writes Fay. "Shostakovich's aversion to anti-Semitism in any form was deeply rooted." He also related to the flattened scale degrees in much of that music.

However, just before he was ready to perform his new composition, Shostakovich realized his mistake. "By late January 1949," writes Fay, "Stalin's campaign against 'rootless cosmopolitans' escalated rapidly into a virulent campaign against Jewish culture and Zionism in the press. Shostakovich's near-disastrous timing, the tragic irony of his attempt to redeem his recent promises by favoring the folklore of the 'wrong' ethnic group, must have become appallingly clear to him. To contemplate public performance of *From Jewish Folk Poetry* then became absurd. Shostakovich prudently shelved the work."

Shostakovich was forced to announce a "program" for most of his works, although he would often privately deny that the music really "meant" what it officially meant.

Many of Shostakovich's themes were drawn from literature, such as Shakespeare, Burns, Pushkin, and the controversial Yevtushenko, who railed against Russian anti-Semitism. "Every morning," he wrote to a student, "instead of morning prayers, I reread—well, recite from memory—two poems by Yevtushenko, 'Boots' and 'A Career.' 'Boots' is conscience. 'A Career' is morality. One should not be deprived of conscience. To lose conscience is to lose everything. And conscience needs to be instilled from earliest childhood."

Shostakovich began creating a piece based on the Psalms of David, but never finished it. For the state, he sometimes composed symphonies praising the war. He was never motivated by religious feelings. He did not believe in God.

His Fourteenth Symphony was dedicated to Benjamin Britten, whom Shostakovich admired greatly for his music, if not his choice of lyrics. The dedication "was not simply a token of professional respect," writes Fay.

In a real sense, it was his creative response to [Britten's] *War Requiem*, a work he considered "nearly" great. For the nonbeliever Shostakovich, where the genius of Britten's requiem flagged was in its offer of consolation in the hereafter, eternal rest, the promise of "In paradisum deducant te Angeli" (May the angels lead thee into Paradise) contained in the final measures of Britten's score. Once, after listening intently to the recording of the *War Requiem*, Shostakovich had been heard to remark: "You can't achieve anything without God." When asked if he believed in God, his reply was swift and firm: "No, and I am very sorry about it." As unprecedented and unexpected as was this unvarnished musical treatment of death, it is not surprising that some people found (and continue to find) the stark realism of Shostakovich's Fourteenth Symphony and its denial of spiritual redemption profoundly disturbing.

Shostakovich valued *this* world, not an imagined supernatural realm. Even his Eighth Symphony (a "war symphony") was a celebration of life: "I can sum up the philosophical conception of my new work in three words: life is beautiful," he said during a 1943 interview. "Everything that is dark and gloomy will rot away, vanish, and the beautiful will triumph."

In spite of incredibly strict artistic constraints by the state, and disdaining any sense of religious transcendence, Dmitry Shostakovich, by virtue of his natural human drive for beauty, managed to create a body of work that truly rises above and endures.

POPULAR AMERICAN SONGWRITERS

LYDIA MARIA CHILD (1802–1880)

"Over the river and through the wood to grandfather's house we go" is the beginning of a song that many of us happily sing during the winter holiday season. The words were written by Lydia Maria Child, considered one of the "first women of letters" in the United States, who became a famous abolitionist, freethinking author, novelist, and journalist.

The daughter of a Calvinist, she joined the creedless Unitarians in 1820 but was unchurched most of her life. She ran a school, started the first journal for children, wrote several novels, then supported herself (and her husband) by writing popular how-to books such as *The Frugal Housewife*, *The Mother's Book*, and *The Little Girl's Own Book*. Her history, *The First Settlers of New England*, blamed Calvinist-based racism for the treatment of Native Americans.

An Appeal in Favor of That Class of Americans Called Africans recruited many to the anti-slavery movement but made Child a pariah in Boston society. Her two-volume *The History of the Condition of Women, in Various Ages and Nations* was published in 1835.

"It is impossible to exaggerate the evil work theology has done in the world," Child wrote in *The Progress of Religious Ideas*, a three-volume work that repudiated revelation and creeds.

> What a vast amount of labour and learning has been expended, as uselessly as emptying shallow puddles into sieves! How much intellect has been employed mousing after texts, to sustain preconceived doctrines!... What a blooming paradise would the whole earth be, if the same amount of intellect, labour, and zeal, had been expended on science, agriculture, and the arts!

In 1844, the second volume of her *Flowers for Children* introduced her most-remembered work, "The New-England Boy's Song About Thanksgiving Day." Although the title itself may be obscure, pretty much everyone knows at least the first verse:

> Over the river, and through the wood,
> To grandfather's house we go;
> The horse knows the way,
> To carry the sleigh
> Through the white and drifted snow.

At some unknown point, Child's words were set to the tune of a French folk song. Besides being passed to children by parents, teachers, and other kids as an oral tradition for over 160 years, the song is also heard by tens of millions of people each year on the animated special *A Charlie Brown Thanksgiving* (with "grandmother's" being substituted for "grandfather's").

Child later defined true religion as simply working for the welfare of the human race. At her death, her funeral was presided over by Wendell Phillips. John Greenleaf Whittier recited a memorial poem in her honor, and freethought journal *Truth Seeker* memorialized her.

STEPHEN FOSTER (1826-1864)

Stephen Foster wrote the first great American popular songs and was the first American songwriter to support himself from music sales, propelling the industry in its infancy. From the 1848 "Oh! Susanna," his first hit, through "Camptown Races," "Old Folks at Home" ("Way down upon the Swanee River"), "My Old Kentucky Home," "Jeanie With the Light Brown Hair," and many others, Foster produced a body of songs that has been remembered and sung longer than the works of any other American songwriters.

Irving Berlin honored Foster by quoting part of "Swanee River" in his first hit, "Alexander's Ragtime Band" (he had a picture of Foster on his office wall). George Gershwin paid him a similar tribute with his first hit song, "Swanee." They knew that if you wanted to tap into the culture of America, you had to start with Stephen Foster.

Little is known of Stephen Foster's inner religious views, but he lived and worked as if he were not a believer. He was a nonconformist, never joined a church, and rarely attended services. None of his music can be said to have been inspired by religious faith. The songs that he chose to write of his own volition were purely secular.

Toward the end of his life, when he was poor and hungry (he had sold his songs too early, before the age of royalty contracts), he was forced to find work wherever he could. He accepted an assignment writing Sunday school songs. "As his life hit rock bottom," biographer Ken Emerson writes, "Foster, who never expressed much interest in religion, who had resisted the urgings of his sisters Ann Eliza and Henrietta to join the church, wrote nearly thirty songs for Sunday Schools. He hadn't found God, but he had found a publisher." Those songs, which went into the *Sabbath School Bell No. 2*, were part of an endeavor to indoctrinate children with "catchy" music, sometimes setting religious words to secular melodies. "Sorrows Shall Come No More" is a rewrite of Foster's secular "Hard Times Come Again No More." "We Love the Happy School" was set to Foster's tune "Some Folks." (The fact that the lyrics were changed shows that the original songs were unsuitable for religious purposes.)

Perhaps the original lyrics to "Some Folks" (1855) give us a glimpse into Stephen Foster's liberal attitude of live-and-let-live, as well as his celebration of "life before death." Some of the words appear to be a rebuke to Puritanism:

Some folks like to sigh,
Some folks do; Some folks do.
Some folks long to die,
But that's not me nor you.
Some folks fret and scold,
Some folks do; Some folks do;
They'll soon be dead and cold,
But that's not me nor you.
  Long live the merry, merry heart
That laughs by night and day,
Like the Queen of Mirth,
No matter what some folks say.

The lyrics for his 1846 utopian song, "There's a Good Time Coming," don't point to an afterlife or a theocracy. They yearn rather for a time of tolerance, when religious divisiveness shall be eliminated:

Shameful rivalries of creed
Shall not make the martyr bleed,
In the good time coming.
Religion shall be shorn of pride,
And flourish all the stronger;
And Charity shall trim her lamp;
Wait a little longer.

Stephen Foster may not have been an atheist—it is hard to know—but he certainly lived like a nonbeliever and wrote as a humanist, inspired by a hope for *this* world.

SCOTT JOPLIN (1868–1917)

Although the history is thin, and the personal views of the King of Ragtime are hard to determine, we can be quite certain that Scott Joplin was not religious.

Joplin's early musical career took place in centers of entertainment, not in church. He played piano in a brothel, as well as in a club (the famous Maple Leaf) that was shut down due to pressure from local churches, whose pastors were ashamed of the "iniquitous practices" (dancing) taking place in that type of establishment. This charge would hound Joplin his entire life—and virtually every popular American songwriter to follow.

Ragtime was America's first uniquely national style of music, from which later styles would flow. (Irving Berlin's first hit song was "Alexander's Ragtime Band," although it is not in ragtime style.) Scott Joplin, born in Texas and raised in Missouri, didn't invent ragtime, but it was his incredible compositions that propelled the style to national prominence, especially after his 1899 "Maple Leaf Rag" became a huge hit, followed by dozens more, including "The Entertainer," which is still popular today. Joplin always considered his compositions to be "classical" music, not popular songs. Indeed, we all enjoy the music alone, without words.

Joplin never wrote religious music. He was married in a home, not a church, and his funeral wasn't conducted in a church.

A glimpse into Joplin's personal views might be found in the words of his opera *Treemonisha*, which was never completely performed during his lifetime. "The subject," writes biographer Edward A. Berlin, "is really the African-American community which, as seen by Joplin fewer than fifty years after emancipation, was still living in ignorance, superstition, and misery. The way out of this condition, he tells his intended audience, is with the education that can be provided by white society." He does not propose religion as the solution. "Ignorance is criminal," he tells his audience. Even the religious characters refer to the "Creator," not the "Lord God" or the "Jesus" of spirituals and hymns.

The main character in the opera is Treemonisha, a woman who promotes education. If she is not a modern feminist, she is certainly an example of the fact that a woman can be a leader of men, more persuasive than the useless pastor in town. Hoping to improve her community, she preaches against superstition and trickery. To the conjurer Zodzetrick, she says: "You have lived without working for many years, All by your tricks of conjury. You have caused superstition and many sad tears. You should stop, you are doing great injury."

Joplin named the pastor Parson Alltalk.

Joplin named the pastor Parson Alltalk. "Joplin does not succeed in making the Parson as comical as the name might suggest," Berlin writes, "but the Parson lives up to his name: all he does is talk, exhort the people to be good. He is totally ineffectual, unable to see his congregation's real needs and, being uneducated (as his dialect tells us), unable to provide leadership." This certainly reveals a freethought attitude on Joplin's part, championing knowledge over belief. The opera contains no gospel music, no hymns or religious melodies that would have been expected of such a community.

Why should Joplin have rejected the church, Berlin wonders. "Because the churches rejected what was important to him—ragtime, dance, and the theater." Whatever Joplin's private views may have been, it is clear that his music was not inspired by religion. "There is no harm in musical sounds," he said, reflecting the view of many composers that music simply speaks for itself. "It matters not whether it is fast ragtime or a slow melody like 'The Rosary,'" he continued, implying that there is no such thing as religious music or nonreligious music. Music is just music. And what great music it is![22]

JEROME KERN (1885–1945)

Jerome Kern is most responsible for making the Broadway musical different from anything that had ever come before, breaking entirely from European traditions, creating a style of singable melody that has come to be known as "American," the fount from which twentieth-century songwriters drank. The 1927 musical Show Boat (lyrics by Oscar Hammerstein) was groundbreaking in its integration of music and story. Songs such as "Ol' Man River" (Kern's favorite), "Can't Help Lovin' Dat Man," "The Way You Look Tonight" (1936 Academy Award, lyrics by Dorothy Fields), "Smoke Gets in Your Eyes," "All the Things You Are," "The Last Time I Saw Paris" (1941 Academy Award, lyrics by Oscar Hammerstein), "A Fine Romance," "Long Ago (and Far Away)," and dozens more Kern melodies have defined what it means to be a "standard."

This "inspired" songwriter—the "father of American music," as many have referred to him—did not believe in God.

Jerome Kern's parents were German-Jewish immigrants who had no use for religion. "Their marriage at Temple Emanu-El was the last religious function in either of their lives," writes biographer Michael Freedland. They gave their son no religious training, and "the Jewish faith, of which he never consciously felt himself a member," was simply social custom. "I don't let a single day pass without writing something," he once said, explaining why he worked on the Sabbath and on holidays.[23]

"His religion was his music and his lifestyle—his enjoyment of elegance and his voracious appetite for having a good time," Freedland writes. His daughter Betty said that her father was "charitable to a fault; a soft touch to everyone."

Kern's motto was, "Life is to be enjoyed." This outlook probably saved his life. When he was thirty, and recently married to a woman from England, he and his bride had planned to sail to Liverpool on May 1, 1915, on the SS Lusitania. They had heard the warnings that the ship might be attacked by German subs, but few people took much notice. While his wife made preparations for the trip, Jerome stayed up late the night before, partying with a crowd of theater friends, playing music, not getting home until early morning. He ended up oversleeping and missing the departure. (His polite young wife didn't want to disturb his sleep.) Six days later the *Lusitania* was torpedoed, with tremendous loss of life. "Had it not been for Jerome Kern's notorious love of late nights, he would doubtless have gone down with them—and would scarcely be remembered," Freedland comments. There is no indication that Kern thanked a deity or found religion after this stroke of good luck.

Instead, he partied more and worked harder. He wrote about 700 songs and more than 100 complete scores for shows and films during his life.

In 1929, he sold his entire collection of rare books—which he collected as a hobby—in a famous five-day auction, covered breathlessly by the press. He netted more than $1.7 million (at least $19 million in current US dollars), nine months before the stock market crashed. He was still a lucky nonbeliever.

In 1945, Kern was in New York City to begin consulting on the musical *Annie Get Your Gun* (concept by lyricist Dorothy Fields, eventually written by Irving Berlin), and after meeting with Richard Rodgers and Oscar Hammerstein for story ideas, he was walking down the street. When he reached Park Avenue at 57th Street, just outside the building of the American Bible Society, he collapsed on the sidewalk and never regained consciousness. Jerome Kern, the nonreligious founding father of modern Broadway songs, inspired by human drama, lived and died while working on the music he loved.

IRVING BERLIN (1888–1989)

How many patriotic Americans know that "God Bless America" was written by a man who did not believe in God? Or that it was intended as an *antiwar* anthem?

Irving Berlin is by any measure the greatest composer of popular American music, with hundreds of enduring hits, such as "White Christmas," "Anything You Can Do," "There's No Business Like Show Business," "Alexander's Ragtime Band," "I Love a Piano," "Always," "Blue Skies," "Let's Have Another Cup of Coffee," "Cheek to Cheek," "Marie," "Play a Simple Melody," "A Pretty Girl Is Like a Melody," and "Easter Parade."

Born in 1888 into a Russian-Jewish family who

Dan Barker stands in front of the Music Box Theater, built in 1920 by Irving Berlin and producer Sam H. Harris.

came to New York City in 1893 to escape religious persecution, he quickly shed his religious roots and fell in love with America. "Patriotism was Irving Berlin's true religion," notes biographer Laurence Bergreen.

"Though he is not a religious person," his daughter Mary Ellin Barrett writes in her family memoir, "doesn't even keep up appearances of being an observant Jew, he does not forget who his people are." Irving and his nominally Catholic wife, Ellin, were married in an unannounced secular ceremony at the Municipal Building, not a church or synagogue. They had three daughters. Mary Ellin recalls:

Both our parents would pass down to their children the moral and ethical values common to all great religions; give us a sense of what was right and what was wrong; raise us not to be good Jews or good Catholics or good whatever else you might care to cite, but to be good (or try to be) human beings.... When we grew up, she [my mother] said, we would be free to choose—if we knew what was best for us, the religion of our husband.... It wouldn't quite work out, when we "grew up," as my mother hoped. All three of us would share our father's agnosticism and sidestep our husbands' faiths.

The man who wrote "White Christmas" actually hated Christmas. "Many years later," Mary Ellin writes, "when Christmas was celebrated irregularly in my parents' house, if at all, my mother said, almost casually, 'Oh, you know, I hated Christmas, we both hated Christmas. We only did it for you children.'" (This also had something to do with the fact that they had lost a baby boy on December 25.)

Why did an agnostic humanist who loathed Christmas write the song "White Christmas"? Because he needed a number for the 1942 movie *Holiday Inn*, which called for a song for each major holiday celebrated in the US. "White Christmas" is not religious; it is not about the birth of a savior-god. It's about winter, the real reason for the season.

"God Bless America" was originally written in 1918 for *Yip, Yip, Yaphank*, a WWI show about the US Army. As he was finishing the musical, Berlin added a patriotic melody that he imagined the soldier characters would sing. Bergreen writes:

> But even as he dictated it to [his pianist Harry] Ruby, Berlin became insecure about its originality. "There were so many patriotic songs coming out everywhere at the time," Ruby recalled. As he wrote down the melody, Ruby said to Berlin, "Geez, another one?" Deciding that Ruby was right, that the song was too solemn to ring true for the acerbic doughboys, Berlin cut it from the score and placed it in his trunk. "Just a little sticky" was the way he described the song. "I couldn't visualize soldiers marching to it. So I laid it aside and tried other things."

The song was forgotten for two decades. During those years, Berlin's attitude toward war evolved.

In 1938, while the United States was resisting joining the new European conflict, Kate Smith was looking for a "song of peace" for her Armistice Day broadcast. Irving Berlin tried writing a couple of songs, but they were "too much like making a speech to music," he said.[24] It then occurred to him to dig up that discarded composition from 1918.

"I had to make one or two changes in the lyrics," Berlin said in an interview,

and they in turn led me to a slight change and, I think, an improvement in the melody.... One line in particular; the original line ran: "Stand beside her and guide her to the right with a light from above." In 1918 the phrase "to the right" had no political significance, as it has now. So for obvious reasons I changed the phrase to "Through the night with a light from above," and I think that's better.[25]

Just as "White Christmas" is not about Christ, "God Bless America" is not about God. It is about love for America. "'God Bless America' revealed that patriotism was Irving Berlin's true religion," Bergreen writes. "It evoked the same emotional response in him that conventional religious belief summoned in others; it was his rock." His choice of "God bless" was his picking up an American idiom, not expressing a personal belief.

Irving Berlin sometimes poked fun at faith. In 1922, confronting censors, he wrote "Pack Up Your Sins and Go to the Devil in Hades" for his *Music Box Revue*. During the show, a comedienne in a red devil suit dispatched jazz musicians to hell, singing, "They've got a couple of old reformers in Heaven, making them go to bed at eleven. Pack up your sins and go to the devil, and you'll never have to go to bed at all." The song is the perfect antidote to "God Bless America."[26]

Irving Berlin died quietly at home at the age of 101. He did not believe in an afterlife, but maybe he did jokingly wish for a hell, because "all the nice people are there," his lyrics report.

COLE PORTER (1891–1964)

Cole Porter, composer of hundreds of American show tunes and standards (he wrote both words and music), was a nonbeliever and openly gay. He was born into a nominally Protestant family. His father was "a good man but not burdened by religion," writes biographer William McBrien. His mother went to church as a matter of social habit.

Porter "was never a believer, and his several comments about his mother's attachments to Peru [Indiana] churches were dismissive."[27]

"Cole developed no deeply felt religious beliefs," McBrien continues. "On most occasions throughout his life, he spoke of 'pleasing the gods' or lamented, 'The gods are punishing me,' but he seldom referred to God, except to deny belief in Him. Even at seventy, he told his social secretary, Mrs. Everett W. Smith, that he found no comfort in trying to believe in a Supreme Being."

According to friend and biographer George Eells, a childhood friend remembered Porter visiting church one Easter Sunday as a teenager. "Cole talked all through the service. He was one of the most irreverent persons I've ever encountered—but so charming," she said. "While he talked, he cracked his ankle bones in a kind of castanetlike accompaniment. I'm certain he did it to draw attention to his new brown silk socks and snappy new footwear. He was quite the Beau Brummel—even then."

Eells writes that "most of Cole's other friends were led to believe that he was an agnostic who might have wished for the support and comfort of some religious conviction but who was unable to summon up belief."

After Porter became a well-known Broadway composer and internationally famous songwriter, he fell from a horse, which rolled over him and crushed his legs. Instead of submitting to amputation, Cole decided to endure more than twenty painful operations in order to be able to walk again. Observing how he dealt with pain, trauma, and drug-related depression, his secretary (a believer) remarked: "[T]he little boss had not the strength that comes in a time of need, of a bolstering religion of even a Buddhist, a Seventh Day Adventist, a Jehovah's Witness—anything to take the place of just nothing. Without faith one is like a stained glass window in the dark. How to reach his particular darkness is an enigma."[28]

She didn't realize that he was coping just fine without religion—he had expert medical care, plus his own inner determination, the strength of his many friendships, and the support of a caring wife. He and his wife, Linda, had a life-long, loving (though sexless) marriage, in which his homosexuality and lifestyle were acknowledged and encouraged.

How many conservative believers who love Porter melodies know that "You'd Be So Nice To Come Home To" was written for a dancer and choreographer named Nelson Barclift, with whom Cole had had a long, romantic relationship? Other Porter songs arose from relationships with men, such as Russian dancer Boris Kochno and architect Eddy Tauch.

Porter's 1953 musical *Can-Can* was a deliberate rebuttal to Puritanism.

Porter's attitude toward life is often reflected in his lyrics. "'Live and Let Live' is another hurrah for tolerance," writes McBrien, "and it may have been one way Cole salved his wounds after the critics' objection to the sexy scenes in *Out of This World*."

Porter spent much of his life battling censors. "Anything Goes" was criticized by churchgoers. Cole fought back but sometimes had to compromise. "Because of the censorship exercised by the Hayes office in the thirties," writes McBrien about the song "Easy To Love," "the original lyric 'So sweet to awaken with, / So nice to sit down to eggs and bacon with' had to be changed to 'So worth the yearning for / So swell to keep ev'ry home fire burning for.'" McBrien reports another change:

> In the most famous number from the musical *Jubilee*, "Begin the Beguine," Porter, possibly feeling the oppression of censorship, decided to change the penultimate line, "And we suddenly know the sweetness of sin," to: "And we suddenly know what heaven we're in."

Porter's 1953 musical *Can-Can* was a deliberate rebuttal to Puritanism. The thrust of the next year's *Silk Stockings* "is similar to *Can-Can*'s, and the theme the recurrent one of scorn for puritanism," McBrien observes. "*The Catholic News* deplored the scanty costumes of Gwen Verdon and thought that the replica of Sacré-Coeur in some sets 'must to the discerning offer apt and eloquent comment on the rest of the proceedings.'"

Let the religious right howl: The public loved Porter's art. And still does.

Though happy to "live and let live," Cole Porter occasionally took jabs at religion. In a letter to Barclift, Porter pointed out that "yesterday was the feast of St. Joseph" and remarked that he hasn't much use for such a day, as Joseph "resents being called the husband of the Virgin Mary & you know what she produced."[29]

Porter produced many enduring standards: "I Get a Kick Out of You," "You'd Be So Nice To Come Home To," "I Love Paris," "C'est Magnifique," "You Do Something to Me," "I've Got You Under My Skin," "In the Still of the Night," "My Heart Belongs to Daddy," "All of You," "What Is This Thing Called Love?," "De-Lovely," "Just One of Those Things," "Love For Sale," "Night and Day," "Don't Fence Me In," "True Love," "Every Time We Say Goodbye," and dozens more. Believers, nonbelievers, straights, gays, all of us have been enriched by the songs that this nonconformist gave us.

Eells reports that when Porter was admitted to the hospital for the last time, accompanied by his friend Robert Raison, a nurse who was filling out the admittance form asked Porter about religious affiliations:

"Put down none," Cole replied.

"Protestant?"

"Put down—none."

Raison spoke up to say that Cole had been a Baptist; why not put down Protestant?

Cole refused. Later, even when his condition had changed for the worse, he stood by his convictions.

Cole Porter's final words were: "Bobbie, I don't know how I did it."[30]

IRA GERSHWIN (1896–1983)
GEORGE GERSHWIN (1898–1937)

Neither of the Gershwin brothers was religious, yet who would deny that *Rhapsody in Blue*, *An American in Paris*, or *Porgy and Bess* have vastly enriched the world's art and beauty? (George wrote the music and Ira wrote the lyrics for most of their famous songs.)

"For a family of Eastern European Jewish immigrants," writes biographer Deena Rosenberg, "the Gershwins led a relatively secularized existence. At home they spoke only English, not Russian or Yiddish. Of the three sons, only Ira (who was born Isidore) had a bar mitzvah, and as he recalled it later, the ceremony did not mean much to him.... The Gershwins' Judaism was neither religious nor politicized. It was cultural and casual—and as such, it was a Judaism from which George and Ira never felt estranged."

Biographer Rodney Greenberg records:

The two brothers roamed all over New York City in their youth, absorbing the culture of Chinatown, Harlem and the West Side just as much as Italian, Irish and Jewish sources. They were not imbued with Jewish ritual and practice in their boyhood, when it would have had most effect. Rose [their mother] made sure the living-room curtains were drawn closed on the eve of sabbaths or festivals, so that her Jewish neighbours would be unaware she had not lit the ceremonial candles. Ira did seem to retain a fondness for one religious ceremony: the annual Passover *seder* meal...but we know from the harmonica virtuoso Larry Adler that, on the evening he was invited to Ira's house to celebrate the festival, Ira wore a silly top-hat like a vaudeville comedian, and had rewritten the ancient text for maximum comic effect.

George and Ira Gershwin wrote hundreds of songs, producing a huge number of standards, in what is now considered the Great American Songbook: "The Man I Love," "Somebody Loves Me," "'S Wonderful," "Fascinating Rhythm," "Oh, Lady Be Good!," "Someone to Watch Over Me," "Strike Up the Band," "How Long Has This Been Going on?," "I've Got a Crush on You," "Embraceable You," "I Got Rhythm," "But Not For Me," "They All Laughed," "Let's Call the Whole Thing Off," "They Can't Take That Away From Me," "A Foggy Day," "Nice Work If You Can Get It," "Love Walked In," "Our Love Is Here to Stay," and so many more. They wrote the songs and music for the ground-breaking opera *Porgy and Bess* (which was considered a flop at the time of George's death):

"Summertime," "I Got Plenty o' Nuttin'," "I Loves You, Porgy," and "It Ain't Necessarily So."

The lyrics to "It Ain't Necessarily So" (the title was suggested by George) are decidedly irreverent, taking the gospel "with a grain of salt." The song has become something of an anthem among non-believers: "The things that yo' li'ble to read in the Bible, it ain't necessarily so." An unpublished verse was held for encores:

> 'Way back in 5000 B.C.
> Ole Adam an' Eve had to flee.
> Sure, dey did dat deed in
> De Garden of Eden—
> But why chasterize you an' me?

Only a freethinker could write such irreverent words.

Regarding inspiration, George had this to say: "When we most want it, it does not come. Therefore the composer does not sit around and wait for an inspiration to walk up and introduce itself. What he substitutes for it is nothing more than talent plus his knowledge."[31]

George Gershwin had major plans for musicals and serious concert works when his life was tragically cut short at the age of thirty-nine by an undiagnosed brain tumor. (If it had been diagnosed, he still couldn't have been saved, even with today's medicine.) Before he lapsed into a coma, he was thinking and talking about his future work, ambitious projects. After George died, Ira continued to work and write songs for forty-six more years, concentrating on preserving the Gershwin estate, a "'s wonderful" legacy that celebrates humanity in the real world.

YIP HARBURG (1896–1981)

According to the American Film Institute's list of top 100 movie songs, "Over the Rainbow" is number one. It is the one song that "everybody knows." The music was written by Harold Arlen, and the words are by Yip Harburg, who also wrote the lyrics to "It's Only a Paper Moon," "Brother, Can You Spare a Dime?," "April in Paris," songs for many musicals and movies, as well as the lyrics and much of the screenwriting for The Wizard of Oz. He and Arlen won a 1939 Oscar for "Over the Rainbow."

Lyricists are songwriters, too, Arlen always insisted. A song without words is not a song. "Over the Rainbow" is a beautiful melody, but without those lyrics in that context, it would have been just another pretty tune, long-ago forgotten.

Songwriter E.Y. ("Yip") Harburg was born in New York's Lower East Side to immigrant Russian-Jewish parents. In school, he sat alphabetically in the desk next to his childhood friend and future lyricist Ira Gershwin, another nonbeliever who was to change the face of American popular music. Although he was raised Jewish, music very quickly replaced religion for Harburg. He explains part of the reason:

> My parents were Orthodox Jews, though not as strict as the Hassidim. To some extent, they were tongue-in-cheek Orthodox. My father did go to *shul* regularly and I usually went with him. Whatever religious feeling I had evaporated when I was about 15 in the face of a devastating personal crisis. I had an elder brother, Max, twelve years my senior—my hero—my inspiration.... Max became a famous scientist.... And then, at age 28, he died of cancer. My mother, broken by the shock, died [some years] after. The tragedy left me an agnostic. I threw over my religion. I began seeing the world in a whole new light.... The House of God never had much appeal for me.... Anyhow, I found a substitute temple—the theater.[32]

After the crash of 1929, Harburg turned to songwriting. While everyone advised "happy songs" to counteract Depression-era blues, Yip Harburg and Jay Gorney wrote a realistic, socially conscious number for the 1932 Broadway revue New Americana that acknowledged the long bread lines outside the theaters. "Brother, Can You Spare a Dime?" became a huge hit, echoing the despair of the working class. Some historians credit that song with helping Franklin D. Roosevelt's sweeping agenda.

Yip always viewed his songs as more than entertainment. He was often "caught at the art of sneaking social messages into his lyrics."[33] The lyrics "Barnum and Bailey world...phony as it can be" were actually chiding corporate and political powers. "I am a rebel by birth," Yip said. "I contest anything that is unjust, that causes suffering in humanity. My feelings about that are so strong, I don't think I could live with myself if I weren't honest [about that]."[34]

Edward Jablonski writes that Harold Arlen's relationship with Harburg "was kinetic and curious. They did not agree on political matters, and Arlen sometimes admonished Harburg over the 'propaganda' in some of his lyrics. Yet he never refused to set them to music."[35]

When Arthur Freed at MGM was looking for music for *The Wizard of Oz*, he jumped at the chance to work with Harburg. Although Freed was a "flag waver of the first order" and could not comprehend Yip's social imperative, he admired and respected his genius and whimsy with words.[36]

Freed handed control of the script and songs to Harburg. It was Yip who made the movie a brilliant success, rewriting whole scenes, replacing entire stretches of dialogue with song. Much of the movie—including the scene where the Wizard hands out medals—was written by Yip, though he is credited only as "lyricist." The film was a moderate success in its time, but after yearly broadcasts on television since the 1950s (where most of us first saw Judy Garland sing it), "Over the Rainbow" has become a global treasure. The US postage stamp commemorating Yip Harburg (released in April 2005) has the familiar words: "Somewhere over the rainbow, skies are blue..."

Cabin in the Sky (1943) was the first all-black Broadway musical to be adapted for the silver screen. With a score by Arlen and Harburg, it featured Lena Horne, Ethel Waters, and Eddie "Rochester" Anderson, as well as Louis Armstrong and Duke Ellington. Like many artists, Harburg was not immune from censorship woes. The song "Ain' It the Truth," recorded by Lena Horne, was removed from the movie with no explanation, but probably due to its freethought denial of the afterlife. It begins with:

> Life is short, short, brother!
>   Ain' it de truth?
>   An' dere is no other
>   Ain' it de truth?
>   You gotta rock that rainbow while you still got your youth
>   Oh! Ain' it de solid truth?

In 1944 Arlen and Harburg wrote the songs for *Bloomer Girl*, a feminist and early civil-rights Broadway musical, based on the pre–Civil War political activities of Amelia Bloomer. "There were so many new issues coming up with Roosevelt in those years," Yip said, "and we were trying to deal with the inherent fear of change—to show that whenever

a new idea or a new change in society arises, there'll always be a majority that will fight you, that will call you a dirty radical or a red."[37] This was the first musical over which Yip had full control, and he used his power to produce a smash hit with a social message that ran for 654 performances.

The wildly successful *Finian's Rainbow* was produced in 1947—conceived by Harburg and cowritten with Fred Saidy, with music by Burton Lane—as a socialist attack on capitalism and racial inequality. The show had a smash run of 725 performances on Broadway, introducing hits such as "How Are Things in Glocca Morra?," "Old Devil Moon," and "Look to the Rainbow." It was the first musical with a fully integrated chorus. Musical librettist Peter Stone wrote: "*Finian's Rainbow* was...extraordinarily political, [but] the audience had no idea of that.... If you ever want to reach people with a political tract, go study *Finian's Rainbow*."[38]

Yip was not a Communist, but he had many friends on the left. Although he had written patriotic songs, including "The Son of a Gun Who Picks on Uncle Sam," this did not shield him from the House Committee on Un-American Activities. When Harburg's name hit the Hollywood blacklist in 1950, he was shocked. "I had just been one of those vociferous guys who was fighting injustice and joining all the movements at the time," Yip said. "I am outraged by the suggestion that somehow I am connected with, believe in, or am sympathetic with Communist or totalitarian philosophy."[39] He was effectively barred from Hollywood for a decade.

Yip continued to work on Broadway, with shows like *Flahooley*, *Jamaica* (where Lena Horne finally got to sing "Ain' It the Truth?"), and the anti-war *The Happiest Girl in the World*. After the blacklist was over, he and Arlen wrote the music for the 1962 animated movie *Gay Purr-ee*, starring Judy Garland, Robert Goulet, Red Buttons, and Hermione Gingold.

Yip also wrote light satiric verses poking holes in all things sacred, with titles like "Atheist," "Do Unto Others?," and "How Odd of God." After being out of print a long time, these poems were republished by my organization in *Rhymes for the Irreverent* (FFRF, Inc., 2006).

Yip's children, Ernie and Marge, grew up to share their father's freethinking views. Ernie, a retired research scientist, told me a story about his dad's world view. Yip and his cousin Herman Meltzer were riding in a bouncing plane in bad weather when the pilot announced that they were having trouble, asking the passengers to prepare for a possible crash landing. Fearing the worst, Herman asked Yip, "Do you believe in God?"

Yip thought for a moment, then said, "I'll tell you when we land."

Nearing his eighty-fifth birthday, Harburg died in 1981 due to a massive heart convulsion while driving to a story conference for a film version of *Treasure Island*. In one of his poems (recently rediscovered), he had observed:

> They who live on love and laughter
> Don't mess around with the hereafter.

Yip Harburg did not believe in an afterlife "over the rainbow." He was inspired by beauty, hope, and humanity. He knew that there is a place in the human heart where "dreams really do come true" and hoped that our future would be free of fanaticism and violence.

JAY GORNEY (1896–1990)

The composer of "Brother, Can You Spare a Dime?" was—like the song's lyricist, Yip Harburg—a nonbeliever who ended up being blacklisted for his liberal views. Jay Gorney is the man who discovered Shirley Temple, for whom he wrote her first movie song, "Baby, Take a Bow" (in *Stand Up and Cheer*). He wrote such standards as "You're My Thrill" and "What Wouldn't I Do for That Man?," plus hundreds of popular songs for theater, film, and television.

"We were not a religious family," his widow Sondra Gorney told me in a telephone interview. They weren't married in a church or synagogue. His memorial was held at the Public Theater/New York Shakespeare Festival, not in a religious setting.

The son of Polish-Jewish immigrants who came to the United States to escape religious persecution when he was a child, Gorney became more involved with liberal human causes than with any religious heritage.

Because of his social views, Gorney was subpoenaed to testify before the House Un-American Activities Committee on May 6, 1953. To prove his loyalty to America, Jay told the committee that besides helping his father to learn about the

Constitution in preparation for citizenship, he had written a song in 1940 called "The Bill of Rights" that was being sung by American schoolchildren. He sang that song to the committee. It includes these words:

> Congress shall make no law respecting an establishment of religion,
> Or prohibiting the free exercise thereof,
> Or abridging the freedom of speech
> Or of the press
> Or of the right of the people peaceably to assemble
> And to petition the Government for a redress of grievances—
> That's the Bill of Rights. That's the Bill of Rights.
> Don't lose it!

Sondra describes the reaction in *Brother, Can You Spare a Dime?*, her biography of her husband:

> A surprised committee chairman's gavel banged loudly. Congressman Tavenner, a member of the committee, tried to stop Jay's singing and said, "It's rather unusual for a person to sing a song."
>
> "Well," said Jay, "you have allowed other singers in this committee from time to time. They have sung long songs—trained pigeons, I call them."

Rather than answer direct questions, Gorney took the Fifth Amendment. "It kept him out of prison but lost him his thriving career for the rest of his life," Sondra laments.

"Jay's entire life was dedicated to helping his fellow man and woman, as an artist and as a concerned human being," Sondra tells us. Music, for Gorney, was more than entertainment—it was a way to make *this* world a better place.

RICHARD RODGERS (1902–1979)

Richard Rodgers, one of the great composers of musical theater, was an atheist. He was born on Long Island, New York, to a prosperous Jewish family (with an atheist grandmother). While attending

Richard Rodgers, Irving Berlin and Oscar Hammerstein II, seated in back is Helen Tamiris; they are watching hopefuls who are being auditioned on stage of the St. James Theatre. (Caption from the *World Telegram*, 1948.) Credit: *World Telegram* photo by Al Aumuller via Wikipedia and the Library of Congress.

Columbia University, he met his first major writing partner, lyricist Lorenz Hart, then studied serious music at the Institute of Musical Art, known today as Juilliard. After the success of *The Garrick Gaieties*, Rodgers and Hart became a huge Broadway songwriting force. During the 1920s and 1930s they produced the musicals *Babes in Arms*, *Pal Joey*, and *The Boys From Syracuse*. After Hart's early death, Rodgers teamed up with Oscar Hammerstein II, who was also nonreligious, to create *Oklahoma!* and ten more musicals, including *Flower Drum Song*, *Carousel*, *South Pacific*, *The King and I*, and *The Sound of Music*, plus the movie *State Fair*. The Rodgers and Hammerstein musicals earned a total of thirty-four Tony Awards, fifteen Academy Awards, two Pulitzer Prizes, two Grammy Awards, and two Emmy Awards. After Hammerstein's death, Rodgers collaborated with Stephen Sondheim, Sheldon Harnick, and Martin Charnin. He wrote a total of thirty-nine Broadway musicals and 900 songs in his life and vastly improved the musical theater by seamlessly weaving music, words, and dance.

Many of the standards in the Great American Songbook flowed from musicals by Richard Rodgers: "Blue Moon," "Bewitched, Bothered and Bewildered," "Do-Re-Mi," "Getting to Know You," "My Favorite Things," "My Funny Valentine," "Some Enchanted Evening," "Have You Met Miss Jones?," "If I Loved You," "Isn't It Romantic?," "It Might as Well Be Spring," "Manhattan," "My Heart Stood Still," "Spring Is Here," "This Can't Be Love," "This

Richard Rodgers, one of the great composers of musical theater, was an atheist.

Nearly Was Mine," "With a Song in My Heart," and "You Took Advantage of Me."

Biographer Meryle Secrest reports that Richard Rodgers was married in his in-laws' home, not in a synagogue. His wife, Dorothy, said: "We are not religious. We are social Jews." Secrest continues: "Those around him knew that…Rodgers was an atheist. At the age of twelve [his daughter] Mary Rodgers Guettel asked her father whether he believed in God and he answered that he believed in people. 'If somebody is really sick, I don't pray to God, I look for the best doctor in town.'"

On the subject of "inspiration," Rodgers said:

That's a bad word for what happens to me when I write. What I do is not as fancy as some people may think. It is simply using the medium to express emotion…. This isn't a question of sitting on the top of a hill and waiting for inspiration to strike. It's work. People have said, "You're a genius." I say, "No, it's my job."[40]

When Richard Rodgers died, the marquees of Broadway went dark for one minute in his memory.

STEPHEN SONDHEIM (1930–)

Composer and lyricist Stephen Sondheim was born in New York City to nonreligious Jewish parents. "The school chosen for him," writes biographer Meryle Secrest,

had been founded by Felix Adler, a nineteenth-century social reformer who had begun life as a rabbinical student but who had decided that religion was inadequate to deal with the problems of the modern world. Being born into an observant household seemed to have left no mark on Etta Janet [his mother], or rather, seemed to have convinced her that she wanted nothing more to do with it…. [T]he Ethical Culture School was the ideal solution for parents uneasily poised between a strict adherence to old dogmas and atheism: although it was considered a radical school, it might have looked to both

Sondheims as the only alternative. As for religious instruction, Stephen Joshua Sondheim received none at all. He never had a bar mitzvah ceremony, he knew nothing about the observances of the Jewish calendar, and he did not enter a synagogue until he was nineteen years old.[41]

After his parents divorced, he moved at about age ten with his (unstable) mother to Pennsylvania, where their neighbor happened to be lyricist Oscar Hammerstein II. Serving as a surrogate father, Hammerstein took Stephen under his wing and inspired him to write music, critiquing his childish work and giving him invaluable pointers. Sondheim majored in music at Williams College and studied with composer Milton Babbitt. While only in his twenties, he wrote the lyrics for *West Side Story* and *Gypsy*. His first score as composer/lyricist was for *A Funny Thing Happened on the Way to the Forum*, a successful musical farce with some irreverent lyrics. That was followed by many other musicals, including *Anyone Can Whistle*, *A Little Night Music*, *Sweeney Todd*, *Sunday in the Park With George* (which was honored with a Pulitzer Prize for Drama, a rare accomplishment for a musical), *Assassins*, and *The Frogs*. His songs range from singable show-tune hits, such as "Send in the Clowns," to densely lyrical, operatic pieces relying on integrated music.

In "Comedy Tonight" from *A Funny Thing Happened on the Way to the Forum*, Sondheim urges:

Nothing with gods, nothing with fate;
Weighty affairs will just have to wait!
Nothing that's formal,
Nothing that's normal,
No recitations to recite;
Open up the curtain:
Comedy Tonight!

Sondheim seems to assert that religion is, well, boring. Real art, life, and entertainment are found in those things that make us laugh and love.

MANY OTHER POPULAR American songwriters appear(ed) to be completely nonreligious, though I haven't yet been able to find direct quotes:

Lyricist **Oscar Hammerstein II** (*Show Boat*, *Oklahoma*, *South Pacific*, *The King and I*, *The Sound of Music*) was the magnanimous son of a non-practicing Jewish father and a liberal, feminist, Presbyterian mother. Perhaps because of the mixed traditions, he kept his personal views to himself. He didn't attend religious services, didn't write religious music, became a surrogate father and mentor to atheist Stephen Sondheim, and enjoyed a lifelong collaboration with atheist composer Richard Rodgers. "Inspiration," he said, "comes to you when you are active, not when you passively wait for it."[42]

The same is true of **Lorenz Hart**, Richard Rodgers' first regular lyricist, a troubled genius who was probably an unbeliever, and who lived as if religion meant nothing to him. He wrote lyrics to hundreds of songs (such as "My Funny Valentine," "Blue Moon," and "Bewitched, Bothered and Bewildered") and many musicals (including *Babes in Arms* and *Pal Joey*), as well as music for dozens of films. Partly as a result of alcoholism, he died early, his last recorded words being, "What have I lived for?"

Composer **Edward Eliscu** ("Without a Song," "More Than You Know") was socially Jewish, possibly a believer but seemingly religiously indifferent. He spent his life working for social causes, which earned him a spot on the Hollywood/Broadway blacklist.

"Nothing with gods, nothing with fate; / Weighty affairs will just have to wait!"

Many songwriters who did have religious beliefs nevertheless lived godless lives in practice (that isn't an insult):

Composer **Harold Arlen** (*The Wizard of Oz*, *A Star Is Born* (1954), "Ac-Cent-Tchu-Ate the Positive," "It's Only a Paper Moon," "Stormy Weather," "I Love a Parade," and hundreds of other popular songs) was the son of a cantor, and although Harold occasionally expressed religious thoughts, he married outside the faith (deeply disappointing his father) and lived his daily life as a practical nonbeliever. He claimed that the melody for "Over the Rainbow" was a "gift from above," so he certainly had some kind of faith, though he didn't write religious music, finding his inspiration in the theater and the movies.

Lyricist **Dorothy Fields** ("The Way You Look Tonight," "On the Sunny Side of the Street," "I Can't Give You Anything But Love") was probably a believing Jew, and she sometimes claimed that her ideas came from on high. (She said that about the idea for *Annie Get Your Gun*, which would seem a strange subject for a god to inspire.) She didn't write religious music.

Hoagy Carmichael was nominally Protestant, though he rarely went to church. He seemed to be the most conservative in the industry—he once got in a fistfight with Humphrey Bogart over political differences. ("He was not a tough man at all offscreen, in my opinion," Hoagy said of Bogie.) He may have had otherworldly beliefs, but his music was this-worldly. He wrote the popular standard "Stardust," as well as "Georgia on My Mind," "Skylark," "The Nearness of You," "I Get Along Without You Very Well (Except Sometimes)," and dozens of singable standards.

The same is true of the prolific lyricist **Johnny Mercer**, who appeared to maintain the nominal Protestant faith of his Savannah childhood but lived as if there is no God. His songs "One For the Road" and "I Remember You" were inspired by a failed love affair with Judy Garland. He also wrote "Moon River," "Days of Wine and Roses," and "Laura."

Lyricist **Alan Jay Lerner** and composer **Frederick Loewe** (*Brigadoon*, *My Fair Lady*, *Gigi*, *Camelot*) both seemed to be completely nonreligious, though Lerner believed in ESP and Loewe once refused to buy a house because he thought it was haunted.

Probably the most religious of American popular songwriters was **Harry Warren** (*42nd Street*, "We're in the Money," "Chattanooga Choo Choo," "Lullaby of Broadway"), a rare Roman Catholic in the industry, whose faith, however, did not prevent him from getting a forbidden divorce.

Another Catholic was composer **Henry Mancini**, who seemed to have little use for religion, although he did sometimes donate to the Church. He was so unfamiliar with the ceremonies that he had to be coached when to sit and stand during his wedding. He never wrote religious music, and his many standards—including "The Pink Panther Theme," "Days of Wine and Roses," "Baby Elephant Walk," "Love Theme from Romeo and Juliet," "Peter Gunn Theme," "Moon River," and "Charade"—all draw inspiration from the movies and television, not the supernatural world.

MUSIC IS JUST MUSIC

Some composers and critics insist that there is no such thing as religious music. "We find that music, by itself," writes conductor David Randolph, "without benefit of a text, cannot reveal whether its intentions are sacred or secular, and the emotions evoked by the music—exultation, excitement, Joy [*sic*], sadness, and so forth—cannot be identified as either sacred or secular in origin. The overtures to many of Handel's operas are identical in style, form, and orchestration with the overture to his oratorio *Messiah*, and audiences are not impelled to think religious thoughts when listening to one of these works. The devotional frame of mind with which many listeners hear the overture to *Messiah* stems from their knowledge of the fact that it is part of a work whose text is on a sacred subject."

Randolph continues:

> Actually there is nothing, except possibly esthetic sensitivity, that could prevent a chorus of atheists from singing the "*Credo*" of Bach's *Mass in B Minor* and putting a "*non*" before each "*credo*"—meaning "I do *not* believe." There would be those who would object to this adaptation, but their objection would not alter the fact that Bach's music, though unchanged, would now lend itself with equal strength to conveying the steadfastness of the concept of disbelief.

Much "religious" music was originally written for secular purposes and later adapted to a religious text. "An outstanding example," writes Randolph, who has conducted *Messiah* 172 times,

> is the chorus "For unto us a Child is born," in Handel's *Messiah*. This music, despite the sacred atmosphere now associated with it, was originally a love duet composed to the Italian words: "*No, di voi non vo fidarmi, cieco Amor, crudel beltà.*" ("No, I no longer wish to trust you, blind love, cruel beauty.") The music occurring later in the chorus, for the words, "And the government shall be upon His shoulder," was originally a setting of words accusing a lover of faithlessness!

A footnote to the above paragraph reads: "Incidentally, here is the explanation of the awkward accent on the word 'For.' It was well suited to the original Italian word 'No,' but became inappropriate when Handel substituted the English text."

Randolph's book, *This Is Music: A Guide to the Pleasures of Listening*, is an insightful and useful introduction to music appreciation, stripping away many of the lofty "meanings" that so many professional critics pretend to notice, that we mere listeners are supposedly unable to grasp. "No series of notes," he writes, "can be demonstrated to contain, in itself, a religious thought or sentiment, just as none can be proven to be, per se, irreligious. All music is organized sound. All music is made up of the same ingredients. The difference lies in the ways in which they are organized."

Think of the melody to "Onward, Christian Soldiers," written by Arthur S. Sullivan of Gilbert and Sullivan fame. If I didn't know the words to this hymn, written in a style similar to Sullivan's comic tunes of pomposity and buffoonery, I could imagine it fitting quite well into *The Pirates of Penzance* ("Major-General's Song") or *The Mikado* ("Behold the Lord High Executioner"). Taken seriously—and Sullivan indeed wrote serious music, including hymns—"Onward, Christian Soldiers" betrays a chilling, intolerant, dangerously militaristic face of religion; but perhaps if we nonbelievers can pretend he was writing tongue in cheek, as he did with Gilbert, we can hear the song as the very model of a major mythic comedy.

PERSONALLY, I CAN IDENTIFY with composer Edward Elgar. When I was a Christian minister, before becoming an atheist, I used to write religious music. In the 1970s I composed a children's Christmas musical for Manna Music called *Mary Had a Little Lamb*. (Get it? Mary was the mother of Jesus, and Jesus was the "Lamb of God.") I followed this with an Easter musical called *His Fleece Was White as Snow* (the Passover sacrifice was an unblemished animal, typifying the death of "sinless" Jesus), both of which became bestsellers for that publisher for a few years. (I'm still getting royalties from those works.) I was planning to make it a trilogy, concluding with *Everywhere That Mary Went* (tracing the life of Jesus through the stories that mention his mother), but by that time, fortunately,

"The overtures to many of Handel's operas are identical in style, form, and orchestration with the overture to his oratorio *Messiah*, and audiences are not impelled to think religious thoughts when listening to one of these works."

my views had changed, and the world was spared those great insights.

I can also identify with Stephen Foster, who found it necessary to compose Sunday school songs. While I was a believer, I had sincerely written and produced a number of musicals for Gospel Light Publications' Vacation Bible School curricula. I was right in the middle of their 1984 project when I sent a letter of deconversion to all my friends, family, and colleagues. I included a little note to the project manager saying that I would understand if they wanted to find another composer to finish the project, now that I was an atheist. He told me that they had no choice but to continue the arrangement, since they were on a tight schedule and budget, and asked me to finish the songs. I reluctantly assented, feeling it would have been unprofessional to back out of a business agreement, and asked if I could use a pseudonym, to save us both the embarrassment. So, if you ever see a Christian VBS musical written by "Edwin Daniels," you will know that it was composed by an atheist. (Writing those songs, I confess, was a strange experience. I felt like a total hypocrite.) To the credit of Gospel Light, the manager did tell me that they thought I was merely going through a stage, a spiritual crisis, and that he was certain I would come back to Christ. I don't think we can accuse them of deliberately employing a nonbeliever. Regardless, I can testify that the creation of such music, which the religious publisher accepted and was performed by believers in churches and Christian schools, was purely artistic craftsmanship, not "inspired" by faith.

The reverse also happened to me. One of the songs I had presented to Manna Music in the early 1980s, "Happy as Can Be," was rejected by them. They thought it was too sugary and unrealistic, and they were right. It was pretty silly. However, after abandoning faith, I later took that same tune and wrote "Friendly Neighborhood Atheist," a song that I still perform. This "atheistic melody" composed by a believer ought to be enough proof that music is just music.

I HAVE LIMITED this survey to classical composers and mainly Tin Pan Alley American songwriters. The views of songwriters of folk, country, rock, jazz, Latin, hip-hop, and other more recent styles will have to wait for another article. In any event, I have certainly overlooked many examples and would appreciate hearing from readers who know of other nonbelieving composers of any era <dbarker@ffrf.org>.

John Philip Sousa thought nonbelievers can't write great music, but we know that ain't even remotely so.

---

1. Bierley. (Although Sousa did believe in God, he was not conventionally religious. "Inasmuch as Sousa did not attend church regularly in adulthood, especially while on the road, it would appear that he was not a religious man. He was, however, very much in tune with the Divine. Close friends often observed—quite accurately—that music was his religion. He sincerely believed that...a sermon could be preached with music as well as with words." "Specifically, he was Episcopalian, but his beliefs were broad. He believed in evolution.... [H]e put little stock in the literal interpretation of the Bible.... [H]e did not believe in the virgin birth." Bierley.)

2. Ulibichev.

3. Moscheles.

4. Nohl.

5. McCabe.

6. Haught.

7. Cairns.

8. Holoman.

9. Turner.

10. All quotations from Phillips-Matz.

11. All quotations from Swafford.

12. All quotations from Dean.

13. Adams.

14. Ibid.

15. Kent.

16. Ibid.

17. All quotations from Vaughan Williams.

18. All quotations in Orenstein.

19. Robinson.

20. Botstein.

21. Copland.

22. All quotations from Berlin.

23. All quotations from Freedland.

24. Bergreen.

25. Ibid.

26. It can be heard on the *Beware of Dogma* CD produced by the Freedom From Religion Foundation.

27. McBrien.

28. Eells.

29. McBrien.

30. Eells.

31. Jablonski, *Gershwin*.

32. Meyerson and Harburg.

33. Taylor.

34. Meyerson and Harburg.

35. Jablonski, *Harold Arlen*.

36. Harmetz.

37. Meyerson and Harburg.

38. Ibid.

39. Ibid.

40. Secrest, *Somewhere for Me*.

41. Secrest, *Stephen Sondheim*.

42. Fordin.

Bibliography

• Adams, Byron. "Elgar's Later Oratorios: Roman Catholicism, Decadence and the Wagnerian Dialectic of Shame and Grace." In Grimley & Rushton (below).

• Barrett, Mary Ellin. *Irving Berlin: A Daughter's Memoir*. Limelight Editions, 1994.

• Bergreen, Laurence. *As Thousands Cheer: The Life of Irving Berlin*. Da Capo Press, 1990.

• Berlin, Edward A. *King of Ragtime: Scott Joplin and His Era*. Oxford University Press, 1994.

• Bierley, Paul E. *John Philip Sousa: American Phenomenon*. Meredith Corporation, 1973.

• Botstein, Leon. "Copland Reconfigured." In Oja & Tick (below).

• Cairns, David. *Berlioz*. 2 vols. University of California Press, 2000.

• Child, Lydia Maria. *The Progress of Religious Ideas Through Successive Ages, Vols. I–II*. James Miller, 1855.

• Cooke, Bill. *Dictionary of Atheism, Skepticism, and Humanism*. Prometheus Books, 2006.

• Copland, Aaron. "A Modernist Defends Modern Music." *New York Times*, 25 Dec 1949.

• Dean, Winton. *Bizet*. Collier Books, 1962.

• Eells, George. T*he Life That Late He Led: A Biography of Cole Porter*. G.P. Putnam's Sons, 1967.

• Eliscu, Edward. *With or Without a Song: A Memoir*, ed. David Eliscu. Scarecrow Press, 2001.

• Emerson, Ken. *Doo-Dah!: Stephen Foster and the Rise of American Popular Culture*. Da Capo Press, 1998.

• Fay, Laurel E. *Shostakovich: A Life*. Oxford University Press, 2000.

• Forbes, Elliot, ed. *Thayer's Life of Beethoven*. 2 vols. Princeton University Press, 1967.

• Fordin, Hugh. *Getting to Know Him: A Biography of Oscar Hammerstein II*. Random House, 1977.

• Freedland, Michael. *Jerome Kern: A Biography*. Stein and Day, 1981.

• Furia, Philip. *Ira Gershwin: The Art of the Lyricist*. Oxford University Press, 1996.

• Furia, Philip. *The Poets of Tin Pan Alley: A History of America's Great Lyricists*. Oxford University Press, 1992.

• Furia, Philip. *Skylark: The Life and Times of Johnny Mercer*. St. Martin's Press, 2003.

• Gardner, Martin. "Lydia Maria (Francis) Child." In *Famous Poems From Bygone Days*. Dover Publications, 1995.

• Gaylor, Annie Laurie (ed.). *Women Without Superstition: "No Gods—No Masters"*. FFRF, Inc., 1997.

• Gershwin, Ira. *Lyrics on Several Occasions*. Limelight Editions, 1997.

• Gorney, Sondra K. *Brother, Can You Spare A Dime?: The Life of Composer Jay Gorney*. Scarecrow Press, 2005.

• Greenberg, Rodney. *George Gershwin*. Phaidon Press Limited, 1998.

• Grimley, Daniel, and Julian Rushton, eds. *The Cambridge Companion to Elgar*. Cambridge University Press, 2004.

• Harburg, Yip. *Rhymes for the Irreverent*. FFRF, Inc., in collaboration with the Yip Harburg Foundation, 2006.

• Harmetz, Aljean. *The Making of "The Wizard of Oz": Movie Magic and Studio Power in the Prime of MGM—and the Miracle of Production #1060*. Hyperion, 1998.

• Haught, James. *2,000 Years of Disbelief: Famous People with the Courage to Doubt*. Prometheus Books, 1996.

• Holoman, D. Kern. *Berlioz*. Harvard University Press, 1989.

• Jablonski, Edward. *Alan Jay Lerner: A Biography*. Henry Holt and Company, 1996.

• Jablonski, Edward. *Gershwin: A Biography*. Doubleday, 1987.

• Jablonski, Edward. *Harold Arlen: Rhythm, Rainbows, and Blues*. Northeastern University Press, 1996.

• Jablonski, Edward. *Irving Berlin: American Troubadour*. Henry Holt and Company, 1999.

• Kennedy, Michael. *Richard Strauss: Man, Musician, Enigma*. Cambridge University Press, 1999.

• Kent, Christopher. "Magic by Mosaic: Some Aspects of Elgar's Compositional Methods." In Grimley & Rushton (above).

• Latham, Alison, ed. *The Oxford Companion to Music*. Oxford University Press, 2003.

• Lerner, Alan Jay. *The Street Where I Live*. W.W. Norton and Company, 1978.

• Mancini, Henry, with Gene Lees. *Did They Mention the Music?: The Autobiography of Henry Mancini*. Cooper Square Press, 2001.

• Marek, George R. *Beethoven: Biography of a Genius*. Funk and Wagnalls, 1969.

• McBrien, William. *Cole Porter*. Vintage Books, 1998.

• McCabe, Joseph. *A Biographical Dictionary of Modern Rationalists*. Thoemmes Continuum, 1998.

• Meyerson, Harold, and Ernie Harburg. *Who Put the Rainbow in "The Wizard of Oz"?: Yip Harburg, Lyricist*. University of Michigan Press, 1995.

• Moscheles, Ignaz. "Ignaz Moscheles (1810–1814)." In *Beethoven: Impressions by His Contemporaries*, ed. by O.G. Sonneck. Dover Publications, 1967.

• Nohl, Ludwig. *Life of Beethoven*. Best Books, 2001.

• Nolan, Frederick. *Lorenz Hart: A Poet on Broadway*. Oxford University Press, 1994.

• Oja, Carol J., and Judith Tick, eds. *Aaron Copland and His World*. Princeton University Press, 2005.

• Orenstein, Arbie, ed. *Ravel: Man and Musician*. Dover, 1991.

• Phillips-Matz, Mary Jane. *Verdi: A Biography*. Oxford University Press, 1993.

• Pollack, Howard. "Copland and the Prophetic Voice." In Oja & Tick (above).

• Randolph, David. *This Is Music: A Guide to the Pleasures of Listening*. Creative Arts Books, 1994. (Originally published by McGraw Hill, 1964.) Available from the Masterwork and Art Foundation, 23 Pleasant Valley Road, Whippany NJ 07981.

• Robinson, Harlow. *Sergei Prokofiev: A Biography*. Northeastern University Press, 1987.

• Rodgers, Richard. *Musical Stages: An Autobiography*. Richard Rodgers Centennial Edition. Da Capo Press, 2002.

• Rosenberg, Deena. *Fascinating Rhythm: The Collaboration of George and Ira Gershwin*. Dutton, 1991.

• Ross, Alex. "The Last Emperor: Richard Strauss." *New Yorker*, 20 Dec 1999.

• Secrest, Meryle. *Somewhere for Me: A Biography of Richard Rodgers*. Applause, 2001.

• Secrest, Meryle. *Stephen Sondheim: A Life*. Delta, 1998.

• Smith, Warren Allen. *Who's Who in Hell*. Barricade Books, 2000.

• Sudhalter, Richard M. *Stardust Melody: The Life and Music of Hoagy Carmichael*. Oxford University Press, 2002.

• Swafford, Jan. *Johannes Brahms: A Biography*. Vintage Books, 1999.

• Taylor, Theodore. *Jule: The Story of Composer Jule Styne*. Random House, 1979.

• Turner, W. J. *Berlioz: The Man and His Work*. Vienna House, 1974.

• Ulibichev, A. *Mozart's Leben*, 1847.

• Vaughan Williams, Ursula. *R.V. W.: A Biography of Ralph Vaughan Williams*. Oxford University Press, 1988.

• Winer, Deborah Grace. *On the Sunny Side of the Street: The Life and Lyrics of Dorothy Fields*. Schirmer Books, 1997.

For proofing and invaluable suggestions to this article, I am indebted to Mary Ellin Barrett, Michelle DuVall, Fred Edwords of the American Humanist Association, Annie Laurie Gaylor, Ernie Harburg, Frank Huitt, Russ Kick, John Lombardo, Nick Markovich, David Randolph, Phyllis Rose, and John Widdicombe.

David V. Barrett

HOLY BLOOD, HOLY CODE

LIKE MANY OTHER PEOPLE, as I first read Dan Brown's *The Da Vinci Code*, I was mentally ticking off all the ideas taken from *The Holy Blood and the Holy Grail* (published in the US as *Holy Blood, Holy Grail*) by Michael Baigent, Richard Leigh, and Henry Lincoln, from *The Templar Revelation* by Lynn Picknett and Clive Prince, and from other sources—but mainly from *Holy Blood, Holy Grail* (hereafter: HBHG).

In February and March 2006 Baigent and Leigh went to the magnificent Victorian Gothic buildings of the Royal Courts of Justice on the Strand in London to sue Random House, publishers of *The Da Vinci Code* (under the Doubleday and Bantam/Corgi imprints), for infringing upon their copyright. I was at the court case (disappointingly held in a modern courtroom), which had some fascinating revelations we shall come to later. Unless otherwise stated, all quotations from Dan Brown below are from my own court notes.

The Da Vinci Code is one of the most remarkable publishing phenomena ever. It's sold tens of millions of copies in hardback ("over 40 million" is the most commonly bandied figure); it's led to a host of responding books, DVDs, and several TV documentaries, nearly all of them critical; it's had bishops and cardinals speaking out against it; its author has been in court accused of plagiarizing other novels and speculative history books; it's spawned

possibly the dullest film of the decade—and yet its fans are still raving about it.

Why has *The Da Vinci Code* caught the popular imagination to this degree? What is its religious significance? Why are the churches so antagonistic towards it? Just how factual is it?

How was the novel researched and written? What happened when Dan Brown faced Baigent and Leigh in court? What else is strange about *The Da Vinci Code* phenomenon?

This article explores these questions and more.

THE DA VINCI CODE'S HISTORICAL ACCURACY

The books criticizing *The Da Vinci Code* (hereafter: DVC) all spend a great deal of time pointing out the factual errors in the novel. There's a huge number of them.

During the court case, when Dan Brown was being questioned about the many lectures by the characters Robert Langdon and Sir Leigh Teabing in his novel, he said: "The novelist is not a historian, but I try very hard to get it right." This prompted gasps of suppressed laughter and some incredulous head-shaking by a number of people in the courtroom who had taken the trouble to check the facts that Brown clearly hadn't.

Here is just a small selection of some of Brown's historical screw-ups.

• Art scholars always call the famous artist "Leonardo," which was his name, and *never* "Da Vinci," which means "from Vinci," the Tuscan town in which he was born. Brown's wife, supposedly an art historian, really should have pointed this out to him.

In chapter eight Brown writes:

• Leonardo was "a flamboyant homosexual." Wrong. While in his twenties, he and four other artists were anonymously accused of sodomy with an artist's model, but they were all acquitted. There is no other evidence that he was gay—and being flamboyantly homosexual in strongly religious fifteenth- and sixteenth-century Europe would *not* have been a bright idea.

• "Da Vinci's enormous output of breathtaking Christian art." In reality, he produced fewer than twenty paintings, and many of those were unfinished.

• "Accepting hundreds of lucrative Vatican commissions." In fact, we know of *one*, and he didn't even complete that.

In chapter fifty-five Brown writes:

• "More than *eighty* gospels were considered for the New Testament." Actually, there were only a handful of other gospels, and few if any of them were ever considered for the New Testament.

• "The Bible, as we know it today, was collated by...Constantine" in 325 C.E. In fact, the first list of the New Testament canon as we now have it was written by Bishop Athanasius in 367 C.E. and the canon was not fixed until a synod in Hippo, North Africa, in 393 C.E.

• Until the Council of Nicaea, convened by Constantine in 325 C.E., "Jesus was viewed by His followers as a mortal prophet." Wrong. Most Christians viewed him as divine well over a century before that.

• "Constantine commissioned and financed a new Bible," editing out certain material. Completely incorrect.

• Leigh Teabing tells Sophie that two quotations from Leonardo's notebooks are about the Bible. In reality, one quote—"Many have made a trade of delusions and false miracles, deceiving the stupid multitude."—is from his attack on necromancy or black magic, while the other—"Blinding ignorance does mislead us. O! Wretched mortals, open your eyes!"—is actually criticizing people who don't study mathematics!

In chapter sixty Brown writes:

• "There exists a *family tree* of Jesus Christ" from Mary Magdalene and her daughter Sarah. There is no such thing, outside the creative imaginings of certain speculative historians.

• "The Sangreal documents include tens of thousands of pages of information. Eyewitness accounts of the Sangreal treasure describe it being carried in four enormous trunks." This is complete invention.

• "[T]he legendary *'Q' Document*—a manuscript that even the Vatican admits they believe exists... [is] possibly written in [Jesus'] own hand... a chronicle of his ministry." In fact, Q is a hypothetical document, believed by scholars to have been one of the sources of Matthew's and Luke's Gospels; it contained teachings of Jesus, but no scholar suggests it was written by him.

• "The Merovingians founded Paris." Actually, the Merovingians, who were a branch of a Germanic Frankish tribe, date to the late fifth century C.E.; Paris was founded by a tribe called the Parisii between 250 and 200 B.C.E., at least 600 years earlier. And there is absolutely no genuine historical link between Jesus and the Merovingians.

Elsewhere:

• In chapter twenty-three Brown writes that the Priory of Sion is "one of the oldest surviving secret societies on earth." In fact, it was founded in 1956 by a handful of Frenchmen, including Pierre Plantard.

• In chapter twenty-eight Brown repeats the myth that five million women were burned at the stake during the Inquisition. Current scholarly thinking puts the total number at around 40,000, of whom 20-25 percent were men, and many of them were executed in other ways.

• In chapter thirty-seven Brown says the true goal of the Knights Templar was "to retrieve a collection of secret documents" from under the Temple of Solomon in Jerusalem: "the one thing on which all academics agree is this: The Knights discovered *something* down there in the ruins." There is no evidence whatsoever that they even looked for anything, let alone found anything, and no academics claim they did.

> **"Blythe will be researching something which she will dump on me at some point for another book."**

• In chapter fifty-eight Brown calls "the Nag Hammadi and Dead Sea Scrolls...the earliest Christian records," which is wrong on three counts: The Nag Hammadi texts aren't scrolls and are considerably later than the New Testament texts, while the Dead Sea Scrolls aren't Christian at all (they're from the Essenes, a Jewish sect).

• In chapter seventy-four Brown says that the Tetragrammaton YHWH, the sacred name of God, was "derived from Jehovah," then gives a derivation for Jehovah. This is complete twaddle. The Jews never spoke the name of God, saying *Adonai* (Lord) instead. The "name" Jehovah is probably a sixteenth-century English invention, when a not-very-good scholar added the vowels from *Adonai* to the consonants YHWH, producing a hybrid and totally spurious name for God: Jehovah.

All of these from the novelist who says, "I try very hard to get it right." And most of these errors could have been checked and corrected in five minutes. It's just sloppy research.

HOW *THE DA VINCI CODE* WAS RESEARCHED

Since the novel first appeared, all the critics, including myself, have lambasted Dan Brown for his appalling quality of research. But we were wrong. The great revelation of the DVC vs. HBHG case at the Royal Courts of Justice was that Dan Brown didn't research *The Da Vinci Code* at all—his wife, Blythe, did. We learned quite a lot about how they worked.

Dan and Blythe Brown work in separate offices in their house. While he's busy writing one novel, she's busy researching the next. And often he doesn't even know what she's looking into; he told the court: "Blythe will be researching something which she will dump on me at some point for another book." That's real teamwork...

...but it might explain something about the trial. Over and over again, when asked questions, Brown would reply that he didn't know when something had occurred—everything from buying a book for research to completing stages of his novel. He couldn't remember; it was quite a while ago.

In fact, at that point, it had been three or four years ago. When Baigent and Leigh were on the stand, they were questioned about events of over twenty years ago, and the Random House barrister grew quite tetchy if they didn't have every answer at their fingertips, even criticizing Baigent for the slowness of his replies. In contrast, Baigent and Leigh's barrister showed patience and courtesy to Brown, despite his persistent forgetfulness. Several times, for instance, Brown complained that he wasn't sure what a particular document said because there was such a large number of them. True—exactly the same number that everyone else in the case—Baigent, Leigh, both legal teams, the judge—had to wade through.

He rarely answered "yes" or "no" in reply to a simple yes/no question, instead giving noncommittal responses. When asked, for example, "The markings in HBHG: Do you accept they are heavy on the pages we're looking at?" he non-replied, "There are certainly markings on that page, yes."

Throughout, it was his general level of ignorance, in the sense of not knowing, that was astounding. At one point the barrister pointed out that he had copied his wife's misspelling of Botticelli, to which Brown replied, "I don't remember precisely how to spell Botticelli." Then only a few minutes later he told the court, "My wife and I both studied art. Botticelli is a pretty famous painter." In which case, one wonders, how did they both manage to spell his name wrong?

He also showed quite astonishing confusion at times. I would never have believed the following exchange if I hadn't been sitting just a few feet from him. Baigent and Leigh's barrister was making the point that when other authors use someone else's work, they say so; for example, when Lynn Picknett and Clive Prince quoted words and ideas from HBHG in their book, *The Templar Revelation*, they always correctly attributed them to Baigent, Leigh, and Lincoln. Brown responded, "If you look in HBHG you'll see points referring back to *The Templar Revelation*." As HBHG was published fifteen years before *The Templar Revelation*, that seems just a little unlikely! The barrister, no doubt as surprised as everyone else, challenged Brown on this—and Brown replied, "Not in that particular case, okay, but I'm sure there are many others."

The reason for all this evasion and forgetfulness and not-knowing and confusion became clear when Brown explained in more detail how his books get written. Blythe Brown does all the research for her husband, copy-typing masses of material from books and the Internet, which he then incorporates into his novels. Sometimes she takes information from several places and writes her own summary, which she gives him. But unless it happens to be mentioned in the text itself, she rarely sources the material she gives him or says which book or books or websites she copied it from.

The first rule of research, to identify your sources: ignored.

With no sources and no context for Brown to assess the accuracy, validity, or significance of all this material, it's small wonder that (a) his novel is so full of errors and (b) he was so vague about it all in court.

Why was Blythe Brown never on the witness stand? According to Brown, he wanted to protect her from the glare of publicity, and in any case he would be able to speak on her behalf. Perhaps, but it was she who did the research. I find it incomprehensible that she wasn't a major witness in the case.

On the matter of just when in the research process Blythe Brown started taking material from HBHG, the judge said, damningly: "At the end of the day her failure to give evidence without any reasonable excuse is determinative on this issue."

THE JUDGMENT

Although Dan Brown himself wasn't on trial, the case at the Royal Courts of Justice hinged on whether (or how much) he had plagiarized HBHG. For those who say that you can't copyright history, Baigent and Leigh's skeleton argument at the beginning of the case made this point about HBHG: "It is a book of historical conjecture setting out the authors' hypotheses. It is not, however, an historical account of facts and it does not purport to be such."

Without going into too much detail, it wasn't a straightforward question of Brown copying chunks of text, which is easy to prove or disprove; instead, Baigent and Leigh claimed that Brown had substantially copied the *architecture* of their book. By this they meant the specific combination or pattern of different ideas that they had creatively brought together in their own book more than twenty years earlier. Their lawyers argued that there were fifteen central theme points in the two books where there was too much similarity to be acceptable.

My own opinion is that one of the most crucial points was the HBHG theory that the purpose of the Priory of Sion, supposedly a secret organization set up in the Middle Ages, was to protect the sacred bloodline of Jesus and Mary Magdalene. This idea was created by Baigent, Leigh, and Lincoln, and it lies at the very heart of the plot of DVC. But the judge, Justice Peter Smith, dismissed its importance. In his judgment he said of the idea "that the Priory of Sion were the protectors of the bloodline and equally the Holy Grail": "I am not sure that [this] is much of a point because it is merely a consequence of linking the bloodline with the Merovingian line which would then have the consequential effect of the Priory of Sion protecting both."

"I conclude that, in the main, the majority of the Central Themes were drawn from HBHG."

The judge missing the crucial significance of this point is especially strange, because throughout the court case he seemed more on top of the complex arguments than anyone else, including Baigent, Leigh, Brown, and their respective barristers—who are, incidentally, the top men in their field of intellectual-property rights. Several times I watched him cut through a morass of argument to state clearly the point at its center. Several times I heard him correct the witnesses and the barristers when they made a mistake. He knew what he was doing.

In his seventy-one-page judgment he states clearly that Dan Brown copied from HBHG when he was writing DVC and that "HBHG was the essential tool for the Langdon/Teabing Lectures" in the novel. He rules that ten of the fifteen central theme points were drawn from HBHG, saying: "I conclude that, in the main, the majority of the Central Themes were drawn from HBHG."

He states that "when the character of Teabing was created the US copy of HBHG possessed by Mr Brown and Blythe Brown was used as the primary vehicle for those lectures almost exclusively," and that "I regard the suggestion that Mr Brown and Blythe Brown created the Langdon/Teabing lectures from the other sources as completely unsustainable. It flies in the face of logic.... The conclusion is irresistible. Blythe Brown provided the material for the lectures with HBHG in her hands." And the judge says bluntly: "Language copying occurred and Mr Brown admitted it."

You'd think that would be clear enough. But after all this the judge ruled against Baigent and Leigh, and in favor of Brown. I've discussed this with a lot of people. I don't know anyone who followed the case and read the judgment who understands it. In the judge's words, "It flies in the face of logic." And indeed, a couple of months later the Court of Appeal granted permission for Baigent and Leigh to appeal this judgment. Although they lost the appeal in March 2007, they are said to be considering their legal options in other countries, including the US.

AND YET MORE QUESTIONS...

With Dan Brown's credibility as a serious writer shot to hell, and with the much-hyped film simply an embarrassment, why is *The Da Vinci Code* still so prominent? When the Emperor's underwear is in such grubby tatters, why are so many people still taken in by his dress-sense?

Just possibly, because DVC is one of the most successful marketing operations in the history of publishing.

In his judgment, the judge says that nearly two years before publication, an in-house exchange of emails at Doubleday about the synopsis of the planned novel "showed that internally the publishers clearly linked the Synopsis to many of the books that had in effect sprung from HBHG." The publishers understood the pedigree of DVC, even if its author didn't.

It emerged in the court case that when Dan Brown had written only 190 pages of manuscript, he sent these to his editor at Doubleday. These were edited down to 128 pages; they were printed out and put together in a package which was shown to Doubleday's sales staff, the people responsible for persuading stores to take the book. This is sometimes done for important nonfiction books, but how often is it done for a quarter-written novel, especially by an almost unknown author? Very, very rarely. The reps were given a product to push.

So was the publicity department. About the time that DVC was published, I was at a launch party for a nonfiction book by a friend of mine, put out by the same publishing group. I was talking to the publicity person, who should have been hyping my friend's book. Instead she was gushing about this new novel, a sensation, a *religious sensation*, which I really must read, I *must* review, she'd send me a copy immediately. That doesn't usually happen, either. For one thing, with publishers and imprints as large as Bantam/Corgi, who published DVC in the UK, different publicists handle fiction and nonfiction books. For another, it was discourteous to the author of the book actually being launched.

Dan Brown himself refers to this astounding publicity effort in his witness statement taken before the High Court proceedings began: "It is impossible to ignore the fact that *The Da Vinci Code* launch was one of the best orchestrated in history.

EVERYTHING YOU KNOW ABOUT GOD IS WRONG

"It is impossible to ignore the fact that *The Da Vinci Code* launch was one of the best orchestrated in history."

It is still talked about in the industry. Articles have been written specifically on *The Da Vinci Code* launch." And he notes: "There were more Advance Reader Copies given away for free of *The Da Vinci Code* than the whole print run for *Angels & Demons* [one of Brown's previous novels]."

It's almost as if DVC was deliberately created as a publishing sensation by its publishers, and that its explosive impact actually had little to do with the author himself.

Then he gets accused of plagiarism, not once but twice.

One could very nearly feel sorry for Dan Brown, this third-rate thriller writer suddenly flung into the limelight. He'd written three previous novels, none of them selling particularly well. Then he changed publishers and suddenly had all the might of a huge publishing company hyping a novel with a plot almost identical to one of his previous novels, before he'd even finished writing it. There were the phenomenal sales, which he wouldn't object to, but also the virulent opposition from the churches, from evangelical ministers and professors of religion and even a cardinal or two, plus all the articles and books tearing his own to shreds—an absolutely unheard-of reaction to any novel.

Then he gets accused of plagiarism, not once but twice. First, Lewis Perdue accuses him of swiping bits of his novels *The Da Vinci Legacy* and *Daughter of God*. (Perdue didn't sue Brown; strangely, Random House sued Perdue to obtain a declaratory judgment that no copyright infringement had occurred.) And then along come Baigent and Leigh, claiming that Brown had lifted the "architecture" of *Holy Blood, Holy Grail*.

In his initial witness statement in the case, Brown said of Baigent and Leigh and their claim against him: "I have been shocked at their reaction: Furthermore I do not really understand it."

That came over very clearly during his three days in the witness box. In conversation with me, many of the journalists in the packed courtroom commented on how completely out of his depth Brown appeared. He seemed bewildered by the entire proceedings. In fact, the brevity and tone of most of his replies gave the impression to those of us sitting on the press benches of an odd mixture of boredom, detachment, and irritation. It was as if he was affronted by the very situation of having to sit in this witness box in this courtroom in wintry England having to answer such impertinent questions from this barrister, who was clearly trying to tie him in knots. Why was he even there?

That answer seemed obvious to some of us. The bigger question was: Why had a poorly written hack thriller taken the world by storm? What was it in *The Da Vinci Code* that struck such a chord with its readers? And why were the churches so vehemently against it?

THE RELIGIOUS QUESTIONS

At the height of the DVC furor in Britain (which was mild compared to some countries), I interviewed the press secretary of an English Catholic archbishop about his reaction to the book. He was urging Catholics to stand up and fight for the truth of their beliefs against this "blasphemous," "scurrilous," and "grossly offensive" book. Well, that's his right. A few months later the Christian Council of Korea asked Sony to cancel their planned release of the DVC film in that country, accusing the filmmakers of disparaging the divinity of Jesus Christ. Film censors in Singapore barred people under sixteen from watching the film because they were afraid some children might see it as a factual movie. And a Catholic group in India called on Christians to starve themselves to death in protest of the film's release there. They hoped for thousands to attend a demonstration where they would burn effigies of Dan Brown. As I said, the British reaction was mild.

By now we all know that the idea in the novel that most upset Christians, especially Catholics, was that Jesus was married to Mary Magdalene (or, presumably even worse, *not* married to her!) and had a child by her. Though many Christians find that idea distasteful, if not shocking or even blasphemous, if Jesus was fully man as well as fully God, then why shouldn't he have had a normal human relationship? He performed other natural bodily functions, such as eating and sleeping, so why not sex? Theologically there's no real argument against it, though Bible scholars say there is absolutely no evidence that he was married and that as a messianic prophet, he probably wasn't.

The mass reaction to DVC, both positive and negative, surpasses anything previously seen in modern publishing. There have been other cases of religious reaction against a book, a play, or a film: Salman Rushdie's *The Satanic Verses*, the stage play *Jerry Springer: The Opera*, the Martin Scorsese film *The Last Temptation of Christ*, based on Nikos Kazantzakis' novel. And there was the Muslim furor against the Danish publication of some cartoons of Muhammad. But in each case these were orchestrated campaigns, a few voices inciting many, protesting about blasphemy.

Although the United States is currently still a church-going country, it's a generation behind Britain and the rest of the Western world, which have almost become post-Christian societies.

Blasphemy's a strange thing. If there is a One Creator God, then I'd have thought he'd be big enough to be able to cope with a bit of disrespectful barracking; he must be used to it by now. And surely, if he loves humanity, he'd be rather more upset by things like murder, rape, ethnic cleansing, and the destruction of our planet. Blasphemy has nothing to do with upsetting God; it's about upsetting other people, hurting their feelings by mocking something that's important to them. But people's feelings get hurt every day, for a thousand and one reasons. We learn to cope with it without punching the perpetrator in the face; that's part of growing up. But not, it seems, for religious believers.

The Catholic Church, rather foolishly, tried to get the film's makers to include a "health warning" about it being fiction, or to remove or water down its "heretical" aspects. Foolishly, because this just made the Church look as if it were running scared. The Christian churches have controlled what people believe for centuries, but in the twenty-first century it's no longer possible to stop people having enquiring minds. Of course there are questions about the beginnings of Christianity; there always have been, and Dan Brown was right in one thing—that the Church has never been prepared to discuss them openly. Now it is having to, and that can surely only be a good thing.

So we have two linked questions.

Why has there been such a huge interest in DVC? In the last few decades we've moved into a more questioning, pluralistic world. Except for fundamentalists, we're less inclined than we once were to believe what we're told, to passively accept dogmatic authority, teachings set in stone by other people; we're better educated and better informed than past generations, and we want the opportunity to make up our own minds about everything—including religion. The spirit of the 1960s is still alive; we want to kick back against authority. With the growth in pagan and other alternative beliefs of recent years, the thought of overturning the patriarchal rigidity of conventional religion has a strong appeal.

Why have there been so many Christian attacks on DVC? First, because deeply believing Christians, Catholics or evangelicals, are genuinely affronted by what they see as a blasphemous attack on the Truth. But second, I suspect that, consciously or not, they are aware of the very real threat to traditional mainstream Christianity today from both pluralism and paganism (and other new religions). Although the United States is currently still a church-going country, it's a generation behind Britain and the rest of the Western world, which have almost become post-Christian societies. In most of the developed world, Christianity is becoming just one of many minority faiths, with all religions being seen as equally valid, rather than one being true and all the others false. So when Christian churches see such massive popular interest in a book that, however clumsily, challenges conventional Christianity, they panic. Hence, the overreaction of most of the Christian criticisms of DVC.

Over twenty books have been written in the English language alone, criticizing DVC and its author. The majority are from Christian writers and publishers; Dan Brown has managed to unite both Catholics and evangelical Protestants against him. One of the better-written ones, *The Da Vinci Hoax* by Carl E. Olson and Sandra Miesel, castigates the novel as "custom-made fiction for our time: pretentious, posturing, self-serving, arrogant, self-congratulatory, condescending, glib, illogical, superficial, and deviant." (I don't think they liked it much…)

What a lot of these books miss in their affronted reaction is that it's actually very healthy to challenge "received wisdom." In fact, there are some ideas in DVC which are well worth examining. Whatever the faults of his novel, Dan Brown has achieved something quite remarkable in finally bringing to the attention of the ordinary Christian-in-the-pew things which every trainee priest in theological college, and every university student in a biblical criticism or early Christianity course, has been taught for decades: that the origins and early development of Christianity, including the eventual compilation of the New Testament, were nothing at all how we have been led to believe by priests and preachers in church. The creation of what became mainstream Christianity was a messy, untidy, argumentative, and very hit-or-miss affair. Very different early versions of Christianity slammed each other as heretical. Early theologians slugged it out at councils, sometimes almost literally. The exact balance of humanity and divinity in Jesus was argued exhaustively for centuries; so was the precise makeup of God, resulting in the compromise doctrine of the Trinity, a concept that would have been both incomprehensible and offensive to Jesus and his Jewish disciples. The New Testament was cobbled together with books written in other people's names (about half the epistles are forgeries), with texts rewritten and verses inserted to "prove" certain doctrines, and with disagreement about its exact content, let alone its meaning, for several centuries after Jesus' life and death.

All of this is vital, but most of the Christian critics of DVC ignore it or even dismiss it. In their eagerness to highlight Dan Brown's poor scholarship, some of them make equally fallacious statements. In *Cracking Da Vinci's Code* evangelical Protestant writers James L. Garlow and Peter Jones write:

"Orthodoxy follows a straight line from the teaching of Jesus in the thirties to the writings of Paul and the other apostles in the latter half of the first century, to the final decrees of the ecumenical synods in the fifth century," which is blatantly untrue. Catholic writer Steven Kellmeyer claims in *Fact and Fiction in The Da Vinci Code* that "the four Gospels…were all known to have been written by the people to whom they are attributed" and that Matthew was the first gospel to be written, both of which any first-year undergraduate knows are utter tosh. Both of these books, and many of the other Christian attacks on DVC, are led more by faith than fact.

The novel claims as fact much that is mere speculation, and it plays fast and loose with known history.

But there are also some critical assessments from biblical scholars, such as Bart D. Ehrman's excellent *Truth and Fiction in The Da Vinci Code*, which offer a readily comprehensible introduction to biblical criticism, and in the process provide a much more devastating critique of DVC than any of the Christian books. Similarly, historical novelist Sharan Newman takes Brown to task very comprehensively for his poor research in *The Real History Behind The Da Vinci Code*.

What was it that annoyed the critics so much, both the Christians and the academics? Mainly, it seems, Brown's assertion of historical factuality at the front of the book, tied in with the huge number of basic historical errors he made throughout it, a small number of which I listed above. The novel claims as fact much that is mere speculation, and it plays fast and loose with known history, as we've seen.

The *ideas* in the novel are well worth exploring, but the arguments Brown uses to put forward those ideas are so error-ridden that in places they're laughable. Ultimately, I think it's a great shame that DVC wasn't written by a better novelist, who would have researched it properly and made it a worthwhile novel—a well-thought-out challenge to traditional Christianity, instead of the mix-and-match smorgasbord of mistakes and misconceptions that is *The Da Vinci Code*.

Michael Standaert

"INCOMPLETE JEWS" AND

"INTERNATIONAL MONETARISTS"

VEILED ANTI-SEMITISM IN THE *LEFT BEHIND* SERIES

ONE OF THE DEEPEST antipathies that ardent Christians have had toward Jews through the ages derives from Jewish denial of Jesus Christ as the Messiah, a denial that has long fueled much of the anti-Semitism among Christian cultures. Most enlightened Christians, especially the non-proselytizing kind, don't obsess over this anymore. It's simply a non-issue. Furthermore, in an active sense, mainline Christian denominations have gone out of their way in the past half-century to rid their cultures of slurs referring to Jews as "deniers" or at its most virulent, as "Christ-killers." For most, it was the realization that fuel like this embedded in the minds of pre-secular Christian Europeans helped ignite everything from pogroms in Russia to the Holocaust under Nazi rule.

There were other aspects of anti-Semitism, the more secular class- and race-based notions (as opposed to the simply religious), that also aided in turning people from everyday bigots and haters into exceptional purveyors of genocide. For many Jews in Europe at the time were hardly religious at all. Being a "denier" wasn't really much of an issue, apart from the total denial of religious life in any way. Being bourgeoisie was an issue, as was, paradoxically, being a Marxist champion of the proletariat. Hitler, with his Germanic version of nationalism, attacked both Jewish bourgeoisie

(shopkeepers, bankers, businessmen) and socialist intellectual upstarts alike. Stalin's anti-Semitism feasted more on the flavors of ousting the bourgeoisie and later their minor remnants in the dekulakization campaigns, playing off popular anti-Semitic notions left over from Czarist days.

What united both ideologies, Nazism and Stalinism, in their anti-Semitism was, first, that Jews played central roles in their dramas. Second, these ideologies based the Jewish threat to their nations on wild conspiracy theories, namely the *Protocols of the Learned Elders of Zion*. Under these lenses, Jews were seen as the number-one scapegoats, as purveyors of secrecy and conspiracy, as intellectual troublemakers, as anti-nation internationalists, as unpatriotic, as outsiders, and as the ultimate "others." Today these same conspiracy theories are widely propagated throughout the Middle East by both Islamic fundamentalists and secular totalitarian regimes to use as propaganda against the state of Israel.

Considering what we know about how past uses of anti-Semitism in popular culture have later supported popular feeling against Jewish peoples, it is somewhat amazing how little has been said about these narratives within American culture. They are no more apparent today than in the hugely popular and successful series of Christian apocalyptic thrillers, the *Left Behind* novels.

Simply chalking off the books as a didactic screed against modern "secular" society, as many have done, likely misses the most dangerous aspect of the *Left Behind* books: the revival of anti-Semitism as a strong undercurrent in American society.

Over the past decade, the *Left Behind* novels, have sold around 70 million copies and have become the most successful Christian publishing phenomenon ever in the United States, outside the Bible. Written by Jerry B. Jenkins and Tim LaHaye, a prominent evangelical minister and political activist, the series culminated with the final, fifteenth book, *The Rapture*, appropriately enough, on June 6, 2006 (6/6/06). Three movies have been based on the books, with the third film, *Left Behind: World at War*, released straight to DVD, skipping theaters altogether. It didn't skip churches, however. Over 3,000 churches signed up for a special viewing the weekend before the official release.

For these books, LaHaye provides Jenkins with a detailed outline of prophecy based on the beliefs of dispensational premillennialism, a previously minor Protestant belief system that proposes a "Rapture" of "true believers" to heaven prior to a seven-year period of tribulation culminating in the return of Jesus Christ and the Battle of Armageddon between the true believers and Satan. These beliefs came into being only 150 years ago when Scottish preacher John Darby formulated the ideas, which were later disseminated in popular Bibles such as the *Scofield Reference Bible*. They found a home in Protestant fundamentalism in the US and were propagated throughout academic systems, mainly through the Dallas Theological Seminary. Besides LaHaye, fundamentalists Pat Robertson and the late Jerry Falwell are among the most well-known believers in these doctrines.

As a belief system, the "Rapture" itself is somewhat benign. All Christian denominations to some extent believe in the end of time when all believers will go to heaven, be it individually or en masse. The importance of how LaHaye has used it, however, is that "the Rapture" has become a powerful tool for activism due to the fact that the "end of time" is seen as close at hand. The idea that the return of Christ is imminent, not simply for the individual but for a large mass of believers, is a powerful ideological force when used by activists such as LaHaye for political ends.

Simply chalking off the books as a didactic screed against modern "secular" society, as many have done, likely misses the most dangerous aspect of the *Left Behind* books: the revival of anti-Semitism as a strong undercurrent in American society. LaHaye, in these books, has combined both the old anti-Semitic idea of Jews as "deniers" with Jews as being the leaders in anti-Christian "secular" society, nicely wrapped together with hints of conspiracy theories of Jewish world domination, *Elders of Zion* style.

In the prophecy-watching of dispensational premillennialism, Israel, Israelis, and Jews in general play central roles in the "End Times" drama. Their roles in this narrative mean that they must either be converted to the premillennialist version of Christianity or be led astray by the Antichrist. There is no nonfatal choice to remain Jewish. The only other option, for those who remain Jewish in this narrative, is to be destroyed by either the Antichrist, or in the end, by the militant avenger, the victorious Jesus Christ himself. A great part of this comes from the Christian fundamentalist belief in Jews as the "deniers" of Jesus as the Messiah, a concept, as mentioned above, that has long fueled anti-Semitism among Christians. In the *Left Behind* books, these "deniers" are seen as "incomplete Jews," a notion that is central to the novels, making Jews the pivotal players in this fantastical prophetic drama, much to their dismay. For these are "incomplete Jews" waiting to be turned into "believing Jews," meaning converts to this fundamentalist sect of Christianity.

A paradoxical aspect of dispensational premillennialism in real life is an overt support for the "State of Israel" by these believers, often called philo-Semitism, as opposed to anti-Semitism. This support lies in their belief that the current nation of Israel must expand and take possession of the land that was the biblical "Land of Israel," which accounts for their massive support of Jewish expansion of settlements, the return of Jews to Israel, and far-right messianic Jewish groups that have similar goals due to their own readings of prophecy. This support is also often called Christian Zionism. Far from being a love or respect for Judaism in its own regard, the end game for premillennialists is the idea that 144,000 Jews in the biblical, expanded State of Israel will convert to Christianity, becoming "believing Jews" and not the "incomplete Jews" they were before. The rest, sadly, will be eliminated.

Despite his explicit and repeated disavowal of anti-Semitism, LaHaye has made odd comments about Jews, saying to Slate.com journalist Jeffrey Goldberg, "Some of the greatest evil in the history of the world was concocted in the Jewish mind."

If we look at the conspiracy narrative side of the cube, the "secular humanist" denial of Jesus as the Messiah is the equal in this antipathy, and for those like LaHaye, nonreligious Jews have been the leaders in this secular humanist revolution. Leftward-leaning academia, media, and Hollywood, for LaHaye, have been led by these nonreligious Jews "infected with atheism."

Despite his explicit and repeated disavowal of anti-Semitism, LaHaye has made odd comments about Jews, saying to Slate.com journalist Jeffrey Goldberg, "Some of the greatest evil in the history of the world was concocted in the Jewish mind," and: "Sigmund Freud, Marx, these were Jewish minds infected with atheism." Goldberg, unsure of what LaHaye was getting at, asked him to explain "more about the Jewish mind." LaHaye responded: "The Jewish brain also has the capacity for great good. God gave the Jews great intelligence. He didn't give them great size or physical power—you don't see too many Jews in the NFL—but he gave them great minds."[1]

Through the mix of premillennialist theology and right-wing conspiracy, veiled references to Judaism and secular humanism actually end up fusing the two to create the "evil" portrayed by the Antichrist. If we go a bit further, in the *Left Behind* novels LaHaye plays with the ideas that the media, international banking, and entertainment industries are being run by Jews. For those versed in right-wing conspiratorial worldviews, the connections are readily available to be made. For those not so versed, it likely passes over their heads, at least on the conscious level.

What has happened during the past half-century with the theology of dispensational premillennialism is not only religious but also cultural and political. What has been introduced to this theology are some of the same well-worn conspiracy theories used by those interested in getting rid of Jews. LaHaye has been one of the leaders in uniting this mix of prophecy and conspiracy.

In one example of this melding, after the Rapture occurs in the first *Left Behind* book, the authors allude to a meeting called by a Jewish nationalist conference in Manhattan that is behind a "new world order government." This group, we are told, is looking to rebuild the Jewish Temple in Jerusalem and is reaching out to interfaith groups in order to gain support for the plan. In essence, this Jewish nationalist group, if you follow the narrative of the entire series, is partly responsible for the rise and eventual world domination of the Antichrist character.

On the next page, the authors easily turn to talk of "international monetarists" and their influence on the United Nations. For anyone familiar with conspiracy theories about Jews, this phrasing simply drops "Jewish" out of the frame of reference when talking about "international monetarists" (elsewhere in the book, "international bankers" is also used). Yet, due to the proximity of the pages before and after, which promote the theme of Jewish aid in some shadowy conspiracy to bring the Antichrist to power, the connection can rightly be made.

We see these terms in some of the most influential anti-Semitic literature, including Henry Ford's infamous *The International Jew: The World's Foremost Problem*. It contains the chapters "How

Jewish International Finance Functions" and "Jewish Power and America's Money Famine." In the latter chapter we find this passage:

> The internationalism of the Jew is confessed everywhere by him. Listen to a German banker: imagine the slow, oily voice in which he said:
>
> "We are international bankers. Germany lost the war?—what of it?—that is an affair of the army. We are international bankers."
>
> And that was the attitude of every international Jewish banker during the war. The nations were in strife? What of it? It was like a Dempsey-Carpentier bout in New Jersey, or a baseball game in Chicago—an affair of the fighters—"we are international bankers."
>
> A nation is being hamstrung by artificial exchange rates; another by the sucking of money out of its channels of trade; what of it to the international banker?—he has his own game to play. Hard times bring more plums tumbling off the tree into the baskets of the international bankers than does any other kind of times. Wars and panics are the Jewish international bankers' harvests.[2]

Another chapter, "The High and Low of Jewish Money Power," contains these passages:

> Rothschild power, as it was once known, has been so broadened by the entry of other banking families into governmental finance, that it must now be known not by the name of one family of Jews, but by the name of the race. Thus it is spoken of as International Jewish Finance, and its principal figures are described as International Jewish Financiers....
>
> To the International Jewish Financier the ups and downs of war and peace between nations are but the changes of the world's financial market; and, as frequently the movement of stocks is manipulated for purposes of market strategy, so sometimes international relations are effected for mere financial gain.

> It is known that the recent Great War was postponed several times at the behest of international financiers. If it broke out too soon, it would not involve the states which the international financiers wished to involve.[3]

And this: "The figures representing Jewish population in Great Britain and the United States indicate that the colossal power wielded by international Jewish financiers is neither consequent nor dependent upon their number."[4]

Hitler, an admirer of Henry Ford (the respect was mutual), also employed the phrase. In a pivotal speech to the Reichstag on January 30, 1939, he declared: "Today I will once more be a prophet: if the international Jewish financiers in and outside Europe should succeed in plunging the nations once more into a world war, then the result will not be the Bolshevizing of the earth, and thus the victory of Jewry, but the annihilation of the Jewish race in Europe!"[5]

At one point in the books, the character Buck Williams, an international journalist who later becomes a premillennialist believer and part of the Tribulation Force, happens to comment that "the Israelis hate Jesus."

The phrase "International Jewish Finance" also shows up in "Fascism and Jewry," a diatribe by the traitorous William Joyce ("Lord Haw-Haw"). The similar "international Jewish financiers" was used by leading Australian Fascist Eric Butler, and "International Jewish bankers" was the term of choice for US Congressman Louis McFadden, who made anti-Semitic speeches on the floor of the US House of Representatives. Type any of these phrases into Google, and you'll find that they're *still* being used on anti-Semitic websites.

At one point in the books, the character Buck Williams, an international journalist who later becomes a premillennialist believer and part of

"I'm being overrun by Jews."

the Tribulation Force, happens to comment that "the Israelis hate Jesus." This just kind of pops out of his mouth, uttered, in the context of the book, like something nearly as cliché as a phrase like, "the Lord works in mysterious ways." It's also a very odd thing for an Ivy League graduate and an international journalist of Williams' stature to say. When that type of remark comes out of a cardboard character like Williams, a later hero in the novel, and then on the next page the authors dive into remarks about secret meetings and "international bankers," it tends to take on the larger context of reinforcing these anti-Semitic generalizations.[6] Following this passage are repeated notions of "one world" conspiracy theories and shadowy references to "the power behind the power," that when built upon some of the veiled *Elders of Zion*–type references, charges these messages with a distinct anti-Semitic quality.

THERE ARE A NUMBER of problems with the way Israelis, and Jews in general, are depicted in this bestselling series, particularly the characters of Israeli scientist and secular Jew Chaim Rosenzweig and the soon-to-be reformed Rabbi Tsion Ben-Judah, who converts to premillennialist Christianity. For example, Rosenzweig creates a formula which makes Israel's deserts bloom, but he doesn't allow any other nation in the world access to his discovery. The authors, whether intentionally or unintentionally, leave his reasoning for this ambiguous. Is greed behind his secrecy? Is it his nationalistic and racial pride?

The reader also is treated quite often to the caricature of "Jew-speak" with the debating styles of a cartoonish Rosenzweig and later Ben-Judah, complete with boisterous exclamation-punctuated sentences and a halting style of ending sentences with a question mark (recalling the stereotype that Jews answer everything with a question).[7]

Drawing further on old-time conspiracy, the authors bring in the names of Joe Kennedy and the Rockefellers as reminiscent of the "power behind the power" embodied by the international banker character Jonathan Stonagal, who has the backing of "an international brotherhood of financial wizards," though it is unclear whether he is Jewish or not. Kennedy and Rockefeller are names which have long been intertwined with conspiracy theories about Catholic and Jewish power cabals.

"It still smells major to me," Buck said. "Rozenzweig was high on this guy, and he's an astute observer. Now Carpathia's coming to speak at the U.N. What next?"

"You forget he was coming to the U.N. before he became president of Romania."

"That's another puzzle. He was a nobody."

"He's a new name in disarmament. He gets his season in the sun, his fifteen minutes of fame. Trust me, you're not going to hear of him again.

"Stonagal had to be behind the U.N. gig, too," Buck said. "You know Diamond John is a personal friend of our ambassador."

"Stonagal is a personal friend of every elected official from the president to the mayors of most medium-sized cities, Buck. So what? He knows how to play the game. He reminds me of old Joe Kennedy or one of the Rockefellers, all right? What's your point?"

"Just that Carpathia is speaking at the U.N. on Stonagal's influence."[8]

A page after mentioning these names, between references to Orthodox Jews wanting to rebuild the Temple in Jerusalem and "international monetarists" setting up a one-world currency, Buck complains to his boss that he's "being overrun by Jews."

"You are short on sleep, aren't you, Buck? This is why I'm still your boss. Don't you get it? Yes, I want coordination and I want a well-written piece. But think about it. This gives you automatic entrée to all these dignitaries. We're talking Jewish Nationalist leaders interested in one world government—"

"Unlikely and hardly compelling."

"Orthodox Jews from all over the world looking at rebuilding the temple, or some such—"

"I'm being overrun by Jews."

The choice is clear: Remain an incomplete Jew and perish, or become a believing Jew and live with your new-found Messiah.

"—international monetarists setting the stage for one world currency—"[9]

Returning to the premillennialist fascination with the conversion of Jews, the figure of Rabbi Tsion Ben-Judah appears in the second book, *Tribulation Force*, to proclaim to the Jews over worldwide television that after three years of study he has found that the Messiah predicted by the Scriptures is indeed Jesus, that the Rapture has occurred, and that the legitimate study of Bible prophecy could only lead to Jesus. In the meantime, Orthodox Jews left and right throw off thousands of years of study to become converts to Christianity. We later hear from Rosenzweig, saying that the "religious zealots" in Israel "hate a person who believes that Jesus is Messiah." Toward the end of the series, Rosenzweig wonders how he had ever been so blind to the faith that now buttresses him, claiming "I was too intellectual," an absurd construction that equates intellectualism with a lack of faith.

Later in the novels, the Antichrist Nicolae Carpathia orders pogroms and death to any Jew in the world. These pogroms by the Antichrist essentially create a diversion about where the anti-Semitism lies.[10] It is never fully explained in the series of books how or why Carpathia has become an anti-Semite; it is simply understood that this is the case, all of a sudden, toward the end of the books. There is also an illuminating segment here where Carpathia's forces are rounding up Jews and Chinese Muslims in Zhengzhou, China. The choice for these unfortunates is either to convert to Carpathia's one-world religion or face the guillotine. A group of Christian believers, who had come to convert the remaining Jews before they were massacred, tells them reassuringly: "Resist the temptation to choose the guillotine without choosing Christ the Messiah."[11]

In the grand drama of the novels, the option to *choose Jewish* no longer remains. Either the Antichrist kills you or else the Christians, with their returning Messiah, will. The choice is clear: Remain an incomplete Jew and perish, or become a believing Jew and live with your new-found Messiah.

---

1. Goldberg, Jeffrey. "I, Antichrist?" Slate.com, 5 Nov 1999.

2. Ford, Henry. *The International Jew: The World's Foremost Problem*. vol. 3, ch. 61. Dearborn, Michigan: Dearborn Publishing Co., 1921.

3. Ford: *International Jew*. vol. 2, ch. 24.

4. Ford: *International Jew*. vol. 1, ch. 3.

5. "Hitler, Adolf." *Encyclopædia Britannica*. 2006. Encyclopædia Britannica Online. 21 Nov 2006.

6. *Left Behind*: 80.

7. Ibid.: 68.

8. Ibid.: 139.

9. Ibid.: 140.

10. *The Remnant*: 81.

11. Ibid.: 289, 294.

9

HOLY HISTORY

Bill Brent

MARTIN LUTHER GOES BOWLING

"ALLEGED BOWLING FAN Martin Luther supposedly wrote a ninepins rule book."[1]

It all goes together, doesn't it—bowling and beer, bowling and betting, bowling and...religion?

We can't shake for long the irresistible urge to bash objects with a ball, whether we're pitching at weighted milk bottles at the fair, playing pool/billiards, or bowling in any of its myriad variations. How many contemporary videogames are based on the notion of smashing something to smithereens with another object? The instinct to engage in bowling-style games is so primitive and hardwired that it cannot be stopped for long by any ruling authority, whether the church or the law—and both have tried mightily over the centuries. It is such a core aspect of humanness that even babies love to throw whatever we place in their tiny hands. So it makes perfect sense that men of the cloth would have taken advantage of this primal impulse.

Bowling at pins, which originated in Germany during the third century C.E., emerged not as a sport but rather as a religious ceremony.[2] William Pehle, a member of the German Bowling Society and Berlin Bowling Club in the late nineteenth century, wrote in his book, *Bowling*:

The ancient chronicles of Paderborn[3] reveal that the first bowling was done in the cloisters of cathedrals. It was the custom of the canons to have parishioners, in turn, place their pins at the end of the cloister. This represented the "Heide," meaning heathen. The parishioner then was given a ball and asked to throw it at the "Heide." If a hit was scored it indicated the thrower was leading a clean, pure life and was capable of slaying the heathen; if he missed, it meant that a more faithful attendance at services would help his aim.

Bowling at pins, which originated in Germany during the third century C.E., emerged not as a sport but rather as a religious ceremony.

There are many versions of this story, but one thing bowling historians agree on is that some version of a bowling game, using pins or clubs called *kegels*, was played in German churches for about 200 years prior to the fifth century C.E. As with most symbols, these early "bowling pins" were based on a practical need. A *kegel* was a club that served as a weapon or a walking stick, and as such, provided a means of bonking any devilish heathens a man might encounter on his way to church. In fact, the English word *kegler* is still used as a synonym for *bowler*. It is from the German *kegeln*, to bowl, which in turn derives from the Old High German *kegil*, a stake or peg.

Martin Luther, most famous as a religious reformer, is credited with reforming bowling, as well.

According to the most common version of the story, German life was pretty brutal in those times, so a man traveled with a club to protect himself and his family. These clubs became the first "bowling pins," perhaps by way of some enterprising preacher who seized upon their potent and eternal presence at his house of worship as an effective visual aid for teaching a spiritual concept.

In the ancient lesson of the *heide*, we can find mythos pertinent to our terrorist-tempered times. "Bowling down the heathen" is a *cri de Coeur*—a strike, if you will—against all that is vulgar, dangerous, and threatening to the safety of the village, and in particular the sanctity of the family, of whom the club-wielding father is the traditional protector.

MARTIN LUTHER, MOST FAMOUS as a religious reformer, is credited with reforming bowling, as well. As would befit any game or sport that satisfies a primeval urge, northern Europeans enjoyed many variations of the bowling game over the centuries. According to the *Encyclopedia Britannica*,[4] the pin count ranged anywhere from three to seventeen! Many bowling historians credit Luther with standardizing the rules of the game, which included fixing the number of pins at nine—not ten—in the version of bowling that is still played in many German bowling centers today. Rather than the triangular ten-pin formation we are used to seeing, the nine-pin formation was a diamond shape. The central pin in this formation became known as the "kingpin," and in some versions of the game, it was larger than the surrounding protective pins, and thus harder to topple.

According to one of his biographers, Luther was fond enough of the game that he had an outdoor bowling lane in the yard of his home, where his children sometimes played, and which he visited now and then, sometimes throwing the first ball.[5]

Bowling became an important part of German culture, and children were often taught that thunderstorms were due to St. Peter and the angels bowling.[6] Thus, the metaphor of St. Peter as the guardian of the pearly gates is akin to the older German church's use of the solemn *heide* game in order to gain access to heaven.

Perhaps this is where Washington Irving drew his inspiration in the early 1800s for his famous short story "Rip Van Winkle." The fiction derives from German folktales that Irving learned through his reading and travels. Resolved to transplant Europe's rich folk traditions to American soil, Irving sets his tale in the New World. While hiking in the Catskills, Rip and his dog meet a strange little man. Rip helps him carry a keg of beer to "a company of odd-looking personages playing at ninepins," just before he more than helps them drink their beer and consequently falls asleep for twenty years. (We'll return to the bowling/beer connection later.) Strangely, the bowling men maintain "the gravest faces, the most mysterious silence, and were, withal, the most melancholy party of pleasure [Rip] had ever witnessed." Consciously or not, Irving's description of the solemn bowlers hearkens to the German cloisters' *heide* tradition of yore. He also describes "the noise of the balls, which, whenever they were rolled, echoed along the mountains like rumbling peals of thunder," which parallels the German children's myth of angels bowling at the gates of heaven.

Likewise, there is a striking contrast between Rip's notorious sloth[7] coupled with his intemperate drinking at the bowling games (for which he is punished by losing twenty years of his life!) and the *heide* notion of diligence, that oh-so-Germanic notion that even life's simplest pleasures can be co-opted for the agenda of work and spiritual attainment. The Paderborn parishioners would nod approvingly upon hearing Irving's parable.

WE DON'T NEED HOLY sanction to locate bowling's spiritual overtones. Bowling is a participatory sport, widely acknowledged as America's most popular. While it is competitive, it also fosters team camaraderie and community spirit—*esprit de corps*. The pace of the game allows players time to relax, enjoy refreshments (beer and otherwise), and converse with one another. For the past hundred years, America has also been more amenable to including women in bowling than in sports such as football, basketball, or baseball. As the suffrage movement grew in the early twentieth century, so did the presence of women in American bowling.

In fact, bowling has influenced American social life ever since its arrival with the first Dutch settlers on Manhattan in the 1620s,[8] who played the game outdoors with nine pins and a ball. Eventually regular nine-pin games took place in an area on the southern tip of Manhattan still known as Bowling Green.[9]

For every co-optation by men of the cloth, bowling has probably been appropriated tenfold by barkeeps and racketeers.

Yet bowling has often been linked with licentiousness, in sharp contrast to its ancient setting in the German cloisters. For every co-optation by men of the cloth, bowling has probably been appropriated tenfold by barkeeps and racketeers. Bowling's long and checkered history as a venue for drunkenness, gambling, and even distraction from the national defense has resulted in the recurring enactment of laws against it.

In 1366, Edward III banned bowling games because they distracted his soldiers from their longbow archery practice.[10] However, London beheld its first roofed-over lanes around 1455, which marked the advent of modern bowling, in its all-weather, around-the-clock glory.[11] Yet it took only half a century for bowling's new indoor incarnation to cause a furor at the national level. Henry VIII issued a 1511 edict proclaiming, "the game of bowles is an evil because all the alleys are in operation in conjunction with saloons, or dissolute places, and bowling has ceased to be a sport, and rather a form of vicious gambling."[12] By contemporary mores, there is deliciously hypocritical irony in Henry VIII's imposition of a tariff on the game, effectively making it a rich man's activity, one which he himself enjoyed within the walls of his palace.

There is also a famous anecdote about Sir Francis Drake. Allegedly, on July 19, 1588, he was playing at bowls on Plymouth Hoe when a small, armed vessel sped into the harbor. The ship's commander had just seen the Spanish Armada off Cornwall. Drake told his scouts, in so many words, that there was still time for him to score more strikes before striking down the Spaniards. He did both.[13]

"In the cities of Hildersheim and Halberstam," one source states, "the clergy competed at the game with the town's divinity students—the first bowling league, of sorts."

Meanwhile, in Germany, bowling underwent a transformation from ritual to social recreation that was probably aided by the church. "In the cities of Hildersheim and Halberstam," one source states, "the clergy competed at the game with the town's divinity students—the first bowling league, of sorts."[14] Bowling was widely enjoyed as a festive part of village dances, country festivals, and even baptisms—about as far from Britain's disreputable "saloons" as one could get.

WHILE DRAKE and the Germany clergy may have felt confident that they were bowling on the right side of Providence, others have not been so sure. Not surprisingly, the Puritans forbade bowling, though some were tempted nonetheless. One confessed in 1658:

> To those concerned, I hereby say, I should not make confessions which are likely to be read from this page at some future time by public eyes but my conscience is troubling me, so I seek this way to ease it. The weather is tantalizing warm, but I was tempted to do so what I have refrained from doing before. This game of bowls has bewitched me, I fear. For I played it today and for funds. Yet, I was fortunate, for the bet was £10. Woe unto me! My fellow Puritans will be shocked if they hear of this, but the more reason for my confession. I like the game, my own ability to win, and the fine folks I met on the greens. May this confession do my soul good.[15]

EVERYTHING YOU KNOW ABOUT GOD IS WRONG

"This game of bowls has bewitched me, I fear."

In America, gambling associated with bowling led to an 1841 ban on the game of nine-pins that the Dutch had brought to Bowling Green over 200 years prior. Connecticut led the way, followed by New York, Massachusetts, and other eastern states. However, these new laws did not prohibit ten-pins! So the less popular ten-pin game began to replace nine-pins in the 1840s, and thus, the traditional diamond formation used in nine-pins gave way to the game with the triangular ten-pin target that is still enjoyed throughout America and most of the world today.[16]

The influence on bowling's popularity in America due to German immigrants—those descendants of the men who bowled for souls in the cloisters of ancient Paderborn—can hardly be overstated. As in London nearly four centuries prior, the arrival of indoor lanes to 1840s America made time and weather inconsequential factors. Even as attempts were made to outlaw nine-pins, Manhattan's new Knickerbocker Alleys enjoyed commercial success. Indoor bowling spread westward from New York City to Syracuse, Buffalo, Cincinnati, Chicago, Milwaukee, and St. Louis—all cities with large German immigrant populations, and all of which became bowling strongholds.[17]

In the twentieth century, America saw a huge rise in bowling's popularity, particularly spurred by the introduction of automatic pinsetters in 1952,[18] which increased the speed of the game and led to its peak during the 1961–62 season.[19] It is still America's favorite participatory sport in terms of annual attendance.[20]

Along with bowling's makeover as a wholesome form of recreation, a rich tradition of church-sponsored bowling leagues grew in America. A news story from October 2000[21] illustrates this point vividly, using that odd combination of schmaltz and reverence that frequently defines the bowling spirit. Note the Lutheran reference—and likewise to St. Peter:

> The miniature pins and palm-sized balls used for duckpin bowling may be unrecognizable to most of the country, but passion for the sport sometimes approaches religious fervor in the city of its birth.

Just ask members of Stephen and James' Evangelical Lutheran Church.

The congregation gathered on the maple wood lanes of Southway Bowling Center over the weekend to pay homage to the 61-year-old landmark, which will close for good on Saturday.

"We know in our heart and in our memories that God's grace was present with us each time we bowled," said Mel Tansill, a member of the church. "For this, we gather together today in his name to give thanks...."

Church leagues have competed for decades at Southway, just up the street from the church in the Federal Hill neighborhood....

On the altar next to the Bible and underneath a life-size painting of Jesus and St. Peter was a duckpin shrine, complete with pins, Tansill's bowling ball and bag from when he was 12, and a pair of size 7 bowling shoes. Next to that: A crinkled church-league roster from Nov. 26, 1948.

"We know in our heart and in our memories that God's grace was present with us each time we bowled."

On rare occasions, American churches contain bowling centers in their basements! St. Francis Bowling Center of St. Francis-St. James United School in St. Paul is one such place, boasting six lanes. It may be one of the last two church bowling centers left in the Twin Cities. According to the Reverend Stephen Adrian, pastor of St. Matthew's Church, "It was very much a part of the German parishes."[22]

No doubt.

Bowling has waxed and waned in popularity, manifesting in numerous variations over the centuries, yet clearly it is here to stay, along with dancing and war, two activities that more obviously share bowling's spiritual impulse, and have likewise transcended all moralists' efforts to suppress them. Of course, there is no way to establish a causal connection between Martin Luther's embrace of bowling as a wholesome family sport—whether or not he actually "wrote the book" on it—and his reinvention of Christianity. And yet, apparently his third-century predecessors in Paderborn recognized one guiding principle in the winning of souls:

If you can't beat 'em, join 'em.[23]

1. Luby, Mort Jr. "Pharaoh or Foul?" *Bowlers Journal International*, June 2004.

2. Weiskopf, Herman. *The Perfect Game*. Englewood Cliffs, NJ: Prentice-Hall Books, 1978: 22, 25. See also: Fraley, Oscar. *The Complete Handbook of Bowling*. Englewood Cliffs, NJ: Prentice-Hall Books, 1958: 96–101.

3. A Westphalian city in northwestern Germany.

4. "Bowling." Retrieved June 18, 2006, from *Encyclopædia Britannica* Premium Service.

5. Ibid.

6. Ball, Ann. *Encyclopedia of Catholic Devotions and Practices*. Huntington, IN: Our Sunday Visitor Publishing, 2003: 593.

7. Irving calls Rip Van Winkle "one of those happy mortals, of foolish, well-oiled dispositions, who take the world easy, eat white bread or brown, whichever can be got with least thought or trouble, and would rather starve on a penny than work for a pound."

8. For the introduction of nine-pin bowling to America, *How to Talk Bowling* by Dawson Taylor (New York: Galahad Books, 1987: 11–3) gives a date of 1623; however, *The Complete Handbook of Bowling* (96–101) gives a date of 1626.

9. According to Fraley, "It was more than 100 years later, in 1732, that John Chambers, Peter Bayard and Peter Jay leased for eleven years at the rental of a 'pepper-corn' the vacant space of ground immediately in front of the Battery Fort, now lower Broadway, in New York City. They enclosed this wide-open parade ground with an ornamental fence for a bowling green, and this enclosed little park at the foot of Broadway still bears that name."

10. Lemonick, Michael D. "High-Tech Rollers." *Time*, 9 Jan 2006. Some sources state that Edward III *allegedly* banned bowling, yet Wikipedia's entry on bowling claims Edward's decree was the first written reference to bowling. Wikipedia likewise credits Edward with creating nationalism, a feat no other medieval king was able to accomplish. It further states that he did this partly by manipulating public opinion during the Hundred Years' War. In any case, the skill of his archers would have occupied a high priority in his mind.

11. Taylor, *How to Talk Bowling*.

12. Ibid.

13. Fraley, *Complete Handbook*, and Dregni, Eric. "Letter From St. Louis: Bowling 101: An Unvarnished History of the Burnished Boards." *Rake* magazine, Nov 2005.

14. Weiskopf, *Perfect Game*, which further states: "Among the many references to the game that [bowling historian] Pehle found in Germany of the Middle Ages and later was one at a huge venison feast in Frankfurt in 1463. He also discovered that in 1518 the city of Breslau bestowed a valuable prize on the winner of a bowling event there: an ox."

15. Quoted in Fraley, *Complete Handbook*.

16. Casady, Donald, and Marie Liba. *Beginning Bowling*. Belmont, CA: Wadsworth Publishing Co., 1962: 5–6.

17. Steele, H. Thomas. *Bowl-O-Rama: The Visual Arts of Bowling*. New York: Abbeville Press, 1986: 8–10, 12.

18. "Bowling." Wikipedia.org.

19. According to the bowling timeline at [www.pielcanela-dancers.com], in 1961 "the number of alleys in the U.S. jumps from 6,500 to more than 10,000."

20. Dregni, "Letter From St. Louis." "According to the American Bowling Congress, more Americans bowl than vote; an estimated ninety-one million Americans bowled in 1998 compared to the paltry seventy-three million who voted in congressional elections that year." In the author's view, this number is perhaps exaggerated; a poster I viewed at Continental Lanes in Santa Rosa, California, in 2005 stated a recent annual attendance of 69 million—still enough to give the congressmen a run for their money.

21. Associated Press. "Church Remembers Duckpin Bowling." 9 Oct 2000.

22. Monsour, Theresa. "In St. Paul, Two of the Little Alleys Have Been Spared." *St. Paul Pioneer Press*, 29 Sept 2001. As of this writing, the center is still open.

23. Since bowling is an ancient and pan-cultural phenomenon, its origins are shrouded in mystery. The main challenge I faced in writing this article was to find authoritative or original sources on the evolution of the sport and its connections to religion and the law—there is a great deal of contradictory information online and in books on bowling, much erroneous attribution and dating of incidents, and thus much sloppy journalism—cribbing from unreliable sources to the point where it became obvious that the writer had slapped together a mishmash of anecdotes and ancient "urban legends." By contrast, wherever possible, I used original sources, or quotations and translations of them, so as not to perpetuate such errors, and have attributed my sources. Even then, facts can be elusive. For instance, Martin Luther is often credited with creating a rulebook for bowling—yet this is just an allegation. In several weeks of searching perhaps one hundred documents, I couldn't turn up anything to verify the existence of Luther's rulebook—nothing that might have been written by Luther on the standardization of the game, or by anyone who had actually seen such a document.

EVERYTHING YOU KNOW ABOUT GOD IS WRONG

Michael Parenti

FRIENDLY FEUDALISM

THE TIBET MYTH

THE HISTORIES OF CHRISTIANITY, Judaism, Hinduism, and Islam are heavily laced with violence. Throughout the ages, religionists have claimed a divine mandate to massacre infidels, heretics, and even other devotees within their own ranks. Some people maintain that Buddhism is different, that it stands in marked contrast to the chronic violence of other religions. To be sure, for some practitioners in the West, Buddhism is more a spiritual and psychological discipline than a theology in the usual sense. It offers meditative techniques that are said to promote enlightenment and harmony within oneself. But like any other belief system, Buddhism must be judged not only by its teachings but by the secular behavior of its proponents.

BUDDHIST EXCEPTIONALISM?

A glance at history reveals that Buddhist organizations have not been free of the violent pursuits so characteristic of many religious groups. In Tibet, from the early seventeenth century well into the eighteenth, competing Buddhist sects engaged in armed hostilities and summary executions.[1] In the twentieth century, in Thailand, Burma, Korea, Japan, and elsewhere, Buddhists clashed with each other and with non-Buddhists. In Sri Lanka, armed battles in the name of Buddhism are part of Sinhalese history.[2]

Just a few years ago in South Korea, thousands of monks of the Chogye Buddhist order fought each other with fists, rocks, fire-bombs, and clubs, in pitched battles that went on for weeks. They were vying for control of the order, the largest in South Korea, with its annual budget of $9.2 million, its additional millions of dollars in property, and the privilege of appointing 1,700 monks to various duties. The brawls partly destroyed the main Buddhist sanctuaries and left dozens of monks injured, some seriously. The Korean public appeared to disdain both factions, feeling that no matter what side took control, "it would use worshippers' donations for luxurious houses and expensive cars."[3]

A glance at history reveals that Buddhist organizations have not been free of the violent pursuits so characteristic of many religious groups.

But what of the Dalai Lama and the Tibet he presided over before the Chinese crackdown in 1959? It is widely held by many devout Buddhists that Old Tibet was a spiritually oriented kingdom free from the egotistical lifestyles, empty materialism, and corrupting vices that beset modern industrialized society. Western news media, travel

Western news media, travel books, novels, and Hollywood films have portrayed the Tibetan theocracy as a veritable Shangri-La.

books, novels, and Hollywood films have portrayed the Tibetan theocracy as a veritable Shangri-La.

The Dalai Lama himself stated that "the pervasive influence of Buddhism" in Tibet "amid the wide open spaces of an unspoiled environment resulted in a society dedicated to peace and harmony. We enjoyed freedom and contentment."[4] A reading of Tibet's history suggests a different picture.

In the sixteenth century, Mongol chieftain Altan Khan converted to Buddhism and gave the title "Dalai [Ocean] Lama" to Sonam Gyatso, an abbot at a Buddhist monastery. He was to preside over all the other lamas as might a pope over his bishops. To elevate his authority beyond worldly challenge, this Dalai Lama seized monasteries that did not belong to his sect and is believed to have destroyed Buddhist writings that conflicted with his claim to divinity.

Within 170 years, despite their recognized status as gods, five Dalai Lamas were murdered by their high priests or other courtiers.

Two centuries later, the Emperor of China sent an army to install the Seventh Dalai Lama, who was made the ruler of all Tibet. Here is quite an historical irony: A Dalai Lama was installed by a Chinese army.

The Dalai Lama who had preceded him pursued a sybaritic life, enjoying many mistresses, partying with friends, and acting in other ways deemed unfitting for an incarnate deity. For this he was done in by his priests. Within 170 years, despite their recognized status as gods, five Dalai Lamas were murdered by their high priests or other courtiers.[5]

SHANGRI-LA (FOR LORDS AND LAMAS)

Religions have had a close relationship not only with violence but with economic exploitation. Indeed, it is often the economic exploitation that necessitates the violence. Such was the case with the Tibetan theocracy. Until 1959, when the Dalai Lama last presided over Tibet, most of the arable land was still organized into manorial estates worked by serfs. Even a writer sympathetic to the old order allows that "a great deal of real estate belonged to the monasteries, and most of them amassed great riches.... In addition, individual monks and lamas were able to accumulate great wealth through active participation in trade, commerce, and money lending."[6] The Drepung monastery was one of the biggest landowners in the world, with its 185 manors, 300 great pastures, 25,000 serfs, and 16,000 herdsmen. The wealth of the monasteries went mostly to the higher-ranking lamas, many of them scions of aristocratic families.

Secular leaders also did well. A notable example was the commander-in-chief of the Tibetan army, who owned 4,000 square kilometers of land and 3,500 serfs. He also was a member of the Dalai Lama's lay Cabinet.[7] Old Tibet has been misrepresented by some of its Western admirers as "a nation that required no police force because its people voluntarily observed the laws of karma."[8] In fact, it had a professional army, albeit a small one, that served as a gendarmerie for the landlords to keep order and hunt down runaway serfs.

Young Tibetan boys were regularly taken from their families and brought into the monasteries to be trained as monks. Once there, they became bonded for life. Tashi-Tsering, a monk, reports that it was common for peasant children to be sexually mistreated in the monasteries. He himself was a victim of repeated rape, beginning at age nine.[9] The monastic estates also conscripted impoverished peasant children for lifelong servitude as domestics, dance performers, and soldiers.

In Old Tibet there were small numbers of farmers who subsisted as a kind of free peasantry, and perhaps an additional 10,000 people who composed the "middle-class" families of merchants, shopkeepers, and small traders. Thousands of others were beggars. A small minority were slaves, usually domestic servants, who owned nothing. Their offspring were born into slavery.[10] The greater part of the rural population—some 700,000 of an estimated total of 1,250,000—were serfs. Serfs and other peasants generally were little better than slaves. They went without schooling or medical care. They spent most of their time laboring for high-ranking lamas or for the secular landed aristocracy. Their masters told them what crops to grow and what animals to raise. They could not get married without the consent of their lord or lama. And they might easily be separated from their families should their owners send them to work in a distant location.[11]

One twenty-two-year-old woman, herself a runaway serf, reported in 1959: "Pretty serf girls were usually taken by the owner as house servants and used as he wished." They "were just slaves without rights."[12] Serfs needed permission to go anywhere. Landowners had legal authority to capture those who tried to flee. One twenty-four-year old runaway welcomed the Chinese intervention as a "liberation." He claimed that under serfdom he was subjected to incessant toil, hunger, and cold. After his third failed escape, he was mercilessly beaten by the landlord's men until blood gushed from his nose and mouth. They then poured alcohol and caustic soda on his wounds to increase the pain.[13]

> **"Pretty serf girls were usually taken by the owner as house servants and used as he wished."**

The serfs were under a lifetime bond to work the lord's land—or the monastery's land—without pay, to repair the lord's houses, transport his crops, and collect his firewood. They were also expected to provide carrying animals and transportation on demand.[14] They were taxed upon getting married, taxed for the birth of each child, and for every death in the family. They were taxed for planting a tree in their yard and for keeping animals. There were taxes for religious festivals, for singing, dancing, drumming, and bell-ringing. People were taxed for being sent to prison and upon being released. Those who couldn't find work were taxed for being

> **In the Dalai Lamas' Tibet, torture and mutilation—including eye-gouging, the pulling out of tongues, hamstringing, and amputation—were favored punishments inflicted upon runaway serfs and thieves.**

unemployed, and if they traveled to another village in search of work, they paid a passage tax. When people could not pay, the monasteries lent them money at 20 to 50 percent interest. Some debts were handed down from father to son to grandson. Debtors who could not meet their obligations risked being placed into slavery, sometimes for the rest of their lives.[15]

The theocracy's religious teachings buttressed its class order. The poor and afflicted were taught that they had brought their troubles upon themselves because of their wicked ways in previous lives. Hence, they had to accept the misery of their present existence as a karmic atonement and in anticipation that their lot would improve upon being reborn. The rich and powerful of course treated their good fortune as a reward for, and tangible evidence of, virtue in past and present lives.

TORTURE AND MUTILATION

In the Dalai Lamas' Tibet, torture and mutilation—including eye-gouging, the pulling out of tongues, hamstringing, and amputation—were favored punishments inflicted upon runaway serfs and thieves. Journeying through Tibet in the 1960s, Stuart and Roma Gelder interviewed a former serf, Tsereh Wang Tuei, who had stolen two sheep belonging to a monastery. For this he had both his eyes gouged out and his hand mutilated beyond use. He explains that he no longer is a Buddhist: "When a holy lama told them to blind me I thought there was no good in religion."[16] Since it was against Buddhist teachings to take human life, some offenders were severely lashed and then "left to God" in the freezing night to die. "The parallels between Tibet and medieval Europe are striking," concludes Tom Grunfeld in his book on Tibet.[17]

In 1959, Anna Louise Strong visited an exhibition of torture equipment that had been used by the Tibetan overlords. There were handcuffs of all sizes, including small ones for children, and instruments for cutting off noses and ears, gouging out eyes, and breaking off hands. There were instruments for slicing off kneecaps and heels or hamstringing legs. There were hot brands, whips, and special implements for disemboweling.[18]

The exhibition presented photographs and testimonies of victims who had been blinded or crippled or suffered amputations for thievery. There was the shepherd whose master owed him a reimbursement in yuan and wheat but refused to pay. So he took one of the master's cows; for this he had his hands severed. Another herdsman, who opposed having his wife taken from him by his lord, had his hands broken off. There were pictures of Communist activists with noses and upper lips cut off, and a woman who was raped and then had her nose sliced away.[19]

Early visitors to Tibet commented about the theocratic despotism. In 1895, an Englishman, Dr. A. L. Waddell, wrote that the populace was under the "intolerable tyranny of monks" and the devil superstitions they had fashioned to terrorize the people. In 1904, Perceval Landon described the Dalai Lama's rule as "an engine of oppression." At about that time, another English traveler, Captain W. F. T. O'Connor, observed that "the great landowners and the priests...exercise each in their own dominion a despotic power from which there is no appeal," while the people are "oppressed by the most monstrous growth of monasticism and priest-craft." Tibetan rulers "invented degrading legends and stimulated a spirit of superstition" among the common people. In 1937, another visitor, Spencer Chapman, wrote: "The Lamaist monk does not spend his time in ministering to the people or educating them.... The beggar beside the road is nothing to the monk. Knowledge is the jealously guarded prerogative of the monasteries and is used to increase their influence and wealth."[20]

OCCUPATION AND REVOLT

The Chinese Communists occupied Tibet in 1951, claiming suzerainty over that country. The 1951 treaty provided for ostensible self-government under the Dalai Lama's rule but gave China military control and the exclusive right to conduct foreign relations. The Chinese were also granted a direct role in internal administration "to promote social reforms." At first, they moved slowly, relying mostly on persuasion in an attempt to effect change. Among the earliest reforms they wrought were to reduce usurious interest rates and to build a few hospitals and roads. "Contrary to popular belief in the West," writes one observer, the Chinese "took care to show respect for Tibetan culture and religion." No aristocratic or monastic property was confiscated, and feudal lords continued to reign over their hereditarily bound peasants.[21]

The Tibetan lords and lamas had seen Chinese come and go over the centuries and had enjoyed good relations with Generalissimo Chiang Kaishek and his reactionary Kuomintang rule in China.[22] The approval of the Kuomintang government was needed to validate the choice of the Dalai Lama and Panchen Lama. When the young Dalai Lama was installed in Lhasa, it was with an armed escort of Chinese troops and an attending Chinese minister, in accordance with centuries-old tradition. What upset the Tibetan lords and lamas was that these latest Chinese were Communists. It would be only a matter of time, they feared, before the Communists started imposing their collectivist egalitarian solutions upon Tibet.

In 1956–57, armed Tibetan bands ambushed convoys of the Chinese Peoples Liberation Army (PLA). The uprising received extensive assistance from the US Central Intelligence Agency (CIA), including military training, support camps in Nepal, and numerous airlifts.[23] Meanwhile in the United States, the American Society for a Free Asia, a CIA front, energetically publicized the cause of Tibetan resistance, with the Dalai Lama's eldest brother, Thubten Norbu, playing an active role in that group. The Dalai Lama's second-eldest brother, Gyalo Thondup, established an intelligence operation with the CIA in 1951. He later upgraded it into a CIA-trained guerrilla unit whose recruits parachuted back into Tibet.[24]

Many Tibetan commandos and agents whom the CIA dropped into the country were chiefs of aristocratic clans or the sons of chiefs. Ninety percent of them were never heard from again, according to a report from the CIA itself, meaning they were most likely captured and killed.[25] "Many lamas and lay members of the elite and much of the Tibetan army joined the uprising, but in the main the populace did not, assuring its failure," writes Hugh Deane.[26] In their book on Tibet, Ginsburg and Mathos reach a similar conclusion: "As far as can be ascertained, the great bulk of the common people of Lhasa and of the adjoining countryside failed to join in the fighting against the Chinese both when it first began and as it progressed."[27] Eventually the resistance crumbled.

ENTER THE COMMUNISTS

Whatever wrongs and new oppressions were introduced by the Chinese in Tibet, after 1959 they did abolish slavery and the serfdom system of unpaid labor, and put an end to floggings, mutilations, and amputations as a form of criminal punishment. They eliminated the many crushing taxes, started work projects, and greatly reduced unemployment and beggary. They established secular education, thereby breaking the educational monopoly of the monasteries. And they constructed running water and electrical systems in Lhasa.[28]

Heinrich Harrer, later revealed to have been a sergeant in Hitler's SS, wrote a bestseller about his experiences in Tibet, *Seven Years in Tibet*, that was made into a popular Hollywood movie of the same name (starring Brad Pitt as Harrer). He reported that the Tibetans who resisted the Chinese "were predominantly nobles, semi-nobles and lamas; they were punished by being made to perform the lowliest tasks, such as laboring on roads and bridges. They were further humiliated by being made to clean up the city before the tourists arrived." They also had to live in a camp originally reserved for beggars and vagrants.[29]

By 1961, the Chinese expropriated the landed estates owned by lords and lamas, and reorganized the peasants into hundreds of communes. They distributed hundreds of thousands of acres to tenant farmers and landless peasants. Herds once owned by nobility were turned over to collectives of poor shepherds. Improvements were made in the breeding of livestock, and new varieties of vegetables and new strains of wheat and barley were introduced, along with irrigation improvements, all of which reportedly led to an increase in agrarian production.[30]

Many peasants remained as religious as ever, giving alms to the clergy. But the many monks who had been conscripted into the religious orders as children were now free to renounce the monastic life, and thousands did, especially the younger ones. The remaining clergy lived on modest government stipends and extra income earned by officiating at prayer services, weddings, and funerals.[31]

Both the Dalai Lama and his advisor and youngest brother, Tendzin Choegyal, claim that "more than 1.2 million Tibetans are dead as a result of the Chinese occupation."[32] But the official 1953 census—six years before the Chinese crackdown—recorded the entire population residing in Tibet at 1,274,000.[33] Other census counts put the ethnic Tibetan population within the country at about two million. If the Chinese had killed 1.2 million in the early 1960s, then whole cities and huge portions of the countryside, indeed almost all of Tibet, would have been depopulated, transformed into a killing field dotted with death camps and mass graves—of which we have not seen evidence. The thinly distributed Chinese military force in Tibet was not big enough to round up, hunt down, and exterminate that many people even if it had spent all of its time doing nothing else.

Chinese authorities do admit to "mistakes," particularly during the 1966–76 Cultural Revolution when religious persecution reached a high tide in both China and Tibet. After the uprising in the late 1950s, thousands of Tibetans were incarcerated. During the Great Leap Forward, forced collectivization and grain farming was imposed on the peasantry, sometimes with disastrous effect. In the late 1970s, China began relaxing controls over Tibet "and tried to undo some of the damage wrought during the previous two decades."[34]

In 1980, the Chinese government initiated reforms reportedly designed to grant Tibet a greater degree of self-rule and self-administration. Tibetans would now be allowed to cultivate private plots, sell their harvest surpluses, decide for themselves what crops to grow, and keep yaks and sheep. Communication with the outside world was again permitted, and frontier controls were eased to permit Tibetans to visit exiled relatives in India and Nepal.[35]

In the 1990s, the Han, the ethnic group comprising over 95 percent of China's immense population, began moving in substantial numbers into

Tibet and various western provinces. On the streets of Lhasa and Shigatse, signs of Han preeminence are readily visible. Chinese run the factories and many of the shops and vending stalls. Tall office buildings and large shopping centers have been built with funds that might have been better spent on water treatment plants and housing. Chinese cadres in Tibet too often view their Tibetan neighbors as backward and lazy, in need of economic development and "patriotic education." During the 1990s, Tibetan government employees suspected of harboring nationalist sympathies were purged from office, and campaigns were launched to discredit the Dalai Lama. Individual Tibetans reportedly were subjected to arrest, imprisonment, and forced labor for carrying out separatist activities and engaging in political "subversion." Some arrestees were held in administrative detention without adequate food, water, and blankets, and were subjected to threats, beatings, and other mistreatment.[36]

Chinese family-planning regulations allow a three-child limit for Tibetan families. (For years there was a one-child limit for Han families.) If a couple goes over the limit, the excess children can be denied subsidized daycare, health care, housing, and education. These penalties have been enforced irregularly and vary by district. Meanwhile, Tibetan history, culture, and religion are slighted in schools. Teaching materials, though translated into Tibetan, focus on Chinese history and culture.[37]

ELITES, ÉMIGRÉS, AND THE CIA

For the rich lamas and lords, the Communist intervention was a calamity. Most of them fled abroad, as did the Dalai Lama himself, assisted in his flight by the CIA. Some discovered to their horror that they would have to work for a living. However, throughout the 1960s, the Tibetan exile community was secretly pocketing $1.7 million a year from the CIA, according to documents released by the State Department in 1998. Once this fact was publicized, the Dalai Lama's organization itself issued a statement admitting that it had received millions of dollars from the CIA during the 1960s to send armed squads of exiles into Tibet to undermine the Maoist revolution. The Dalai Lama's annual payment from the CIA was $186,000. Indian intelligence also financed him and other Tibetan exiles. He has refused to say whether he or his brothers worked for the CIA. The Agency has also declined to comment.[38]

In 1995, the *News and Observer* of Raleigh, North Carolina, carried a front-page color photograph of the Dalai Lama being embraced by the reactionary Republican Senator Jesse Helms, under the headline "Buddhist Captivates Hero of Religious Right."[39] In April 1999, along with Margaret Thatcher, Pope John Paul II, and the first George Bush, the Dalai Lama called upon the British government to release Augusto Pinochet, the former fascist dictator of Chile and a longtime CIA client who had been apprehended while visiting England. The Dalai Lama urged that Pinochet not be forced to go to Spain, where he was wanted to stand trial for crimes against humanity.

The Dalai Lama's annual payment from the CIA was $186,000.

Today, mostly through the National Endowment for Democracy and other conduits that are more respectable-sounding than the CIA, the US Congress continues to allocate an annual $2 million to Tibetans in India, with additional millions for "democracy activities" within the Tibetan exile community. The Dalai Lama also gets money from financier George Soros, who now runs the CIA-created Radio Free Europe/Radio Liberty and other institutes.[40]

THE QUESTION OF CULTURE

We are told that when the Dalai Lamas ruled Tibet, the people lived in contented and tranquil symbiosis with their monastic and secular lords, in a social order sustained by a deeply spiritual, nonviolent culture, inspired by humane and pacific religious teachings. The Tibetan religious culture was the social glue and comforting balm that kept rich lama and poor peasant spiritually bonded together, to maintain those proselytes who embrace Old Tibet as a cultural purity, a Shangri-La.

One is reminded of the idealized imagery of feudal Europe presented by latter-day conservative Catholics such as G. K. Chesterton and Hilaire Belloc. For them, medieval Christendom was a world of contented peasants living in a deep spiritual bond with their Church, under the protection of their lords.[41] Again we are invited to accept a particular culture on its own terms, which means accepting it as presented by its favored class, by those at the top who profited most from it. The Shangri-La image of Tibet bears no more resemblance to historic reality than does the romanticized image of medieval Europe.

When seen in all its grim realities, Old Tibet confirms the view that culture is anything but neutral. Culture can operate as a legitimating cover for a host of grave injustices, benefiting some portion of a society's population at great cost to other segments. In theocratic Tibet, ruling interests manipulated the traditional culture to fortify their wealth and power. The theocracy equated rebellious thought and action with satanic influence. It propagated the general presumption of landlord superiority and peasant unworthiness. The rich were represented as deserving their good life, and the poor as deserving their mean, lowly existence, all codified in teachings about the karmic residues of virtues and vices accumulated from past lives, all presented as part of God's will.

It might be said that we denizens of the modern, secular world cannot grasp the equations of happiness and pain, contentment and custom, that characterize more traditionally spiritual societies. This is probably true, and it may explain why some of us idealize such societies. But still, a gouged eye is a gouged eye; a flogging is a flogging; and the grinding exploitation of serfs and slaves is a brutal class injustice, whatever its cultural wrapping. There is a difference between a spiritual bond and human bondage, even when both exist side by side.

Many ordinary Tibetans want the Dalai Lama back in their country, but it appears that relatively few want a return to the social order he represented. A 1999 story in the *Washington Post* notes that he continues to be revered in Tibet, but

few Tibetans would welcome a return of the corrupt aristocratic clans that fled with him in 1959 and that comprise the bulk of his advisers. Many Tibetan farmers, for example, have no interest in surrendering the land they gained during China's land reform to the clans. Tibet's former slaves say they, too, don't want their former masters to return to power.

"I've already lived that life once before," said Wangchuk, a 67-year-old former slave who was wearing his best clothes for his yearly pilgrimage to Shigatse, one of the holiest sites of Tibetan Buddhism. He said he worshipped the Dalai Lama, but added, "I may not be free under Chinese communism, but I am better off than when I was a slave."[42]

Kim Lewis, who studied healing methods with a Buddhist monk in Berkeley, California, had occasion to talk at length with more than a dozen Tibetan women who lived in the monk's building. When she asked how they felt about returning to their homeland, the sentiment was unanimously negative. At first, Lewis thought their reluctance had to do with the Chinese occupation, but they quickly informed her otherwise. They said that they were extremely grateful "not to have to marry four or five men, be pregnant almost all the time," or deal with sexually transmitted diseases contracted from a straying husband. The younger women "were delighted to be getting an education, wanted absolutely nothing to do with any religion, and wondered why Americans were so naive." They recounted stories of their grandmothers' ordeals with monks who used them as "wisdom consorts," telling them "how much merit they were gaining by providing the 'means to enlightenment'—after all, the Buddha had to be with a woman to reach enlightenment."

The women interviewed by Lewis spoke bitterly about the monastery's confiscation of their young boys in Tibet. When a boy cried for his mother, he would be told: "Why do you cry for her, she gave you up—she's just a woman." Among the other issues was "the rampant homosexuality in the Gelugpa sect. All was not well in Shangri-la," Lewis opines.[43]

The monks who were granted political asylum in California applied for Social Security. Lewis, herself a devotee for a time, assisted with the paperwork. She observes that they continue to receive Social Security checks amounting to $550 to $700 per month along with Medicare and MediCal. In addition, the monks reside rent-free in nicely furnished apartments. "They pay no utilities, have free access to the Internet on computers provided for them, along with fax machines, free cell and home phones and cable TV." In addition, they receive a monthly payment from their order. And the dharma center takes up a special collection from its members (all of whom are Americans), separate from membership dues. Some members eagerly carry out chores for the monks, including grocery-shopping and cleaning their apartments and toilets. These same holy men "have no problem criticizing Americans for their 'obsession with material things.'"[44]

To support the Chinese overthrow of the old feudal theocracy is not to applaud everything about Chinese rule in Tibet. This point is seldom understood by today's Shangri-La adherents in the West.

The converse is also true. To denounce the Chinese occupation does not mean we have to romanticize the former feudal regime. One common complaint among Buddhist followers in the West is that Tibet's religious culture is being undermined by the occupation. Indeed, this seems to be the case. Many of the monasteries are closed, and the theocracy has passed into history. What I am

questioning here is the supposedly admirable and pristinely spiritual nature of that pre-invasion culture. In short, we can advocate religious freedom and independence for Tibet without having to embrace the mythology of a Paradise Lost.

Finally, it should be noted that the criticism posed herein is not intended as a personal attack on the Dalai Lama. Whatever his past associations with the CIA and various reactionaries, he speaks often of peace, love, and nonviolence. And he himself really cannot be blamed for the abuses of the *ancien régime*, having been but fifteen years old when he fled into exile. In 1994, in an interview with Melvyn Goldstein, he went on record as favoring since his youth the building of schools, "machines," and roads in his country. He claims that he thought the *corvée* (forced, unpaid serf labor for the lord's benefit) and certain taxes imposed on the peasants were "extremely bad." And he disliked the way people were saddled with old debts sometimes passed down from generation to generation.[45] Furthermore, he now proposes democracy for Tibet, featuring a written constitution, a representative assembly, and other democratic essentials.[46]

In 1996, the Dalai Lama issued a statement that must have had an unsettling effect on the exile community. It reads in part as follows:

Of all the modern economic theories, the economic system of Marxism is founded on moral principles, while capitalism is concerned only with gain and profitability. Marxism is concerned with the distribution of wealth on an equal basis and the equitable utilization of the means of production. It is also concerned with the fate of the working classes—that is the majority—as well as with the fate of those who are underprivileged and in need, and Marxism cares about the victims of minority-imposed exploitation. For those reasons the system appeals to me, and it seems fair.... I think of myself as half-Marxist, half-Buddhist.[47]

And more recently, while visiting California in 2001, he remarked: "Tibet, materially, is very, very backward. Spiritually it is quite rich. But spirituality can't fill our stomachs."[48] Here is a message that should be heeded by the well-fed Buddhist prose-lytes in the West who wax nostalgic for Old Tibet.

What I have tried to challenge is the Tibet myth, the Paradise Lost image of a social order that actu-ally was a retrograde theocracy of serfdom and poverty, where a favored few lived high and mighty off the blood, sweat, and tears of the many. It was a long way from Shangri-La.

1. Goldstein, Melvyn C. *The Snow Lion and the Dragon: China, Tibet, and the Dalai Lama*. Berkeley: University of California Press, 1995: 6–16.

2. Juergensmeyer, Mark. *Terror in the Mind of God*. Berkeley: University of California Press, 2000: 113.

3. Seok, Kyong-Hwa. "Korean Monk Gangs Battle for Temple Turf." *San Francisco Examiner* (3 Dec 1998).

4. Dalai Lama quoted in Lopez, Donald Jr. *Prisoners of Shangri-La: Tibetan Buddhism and the West*. Chicago and London: Chicago University Press, 1998: 205.

5. Gelder, Stuart, and Roma Gelder. *The Timely Rain: Travels in New Tibet*. New York: Monthly Review Press, 1964: 119, 123.

6. Karan, Pradyumna P. *The Changing Face of Tibet: The Impact of Chinese Communist Ideology on the Landscape*. Lexington, Kentucky: University Press of Kentucky, 1976: 64.

7. Gelder and Gelder, *Timely Rain*: 62, 174.

8. As skeptically noted by Lopez, *Prisoners of Shangri-La*: 9.

9. Goldstein, Melvyn, William Siebenschuh, and Tashi-Tsering. *The Struggle for Modern Tibet: The Autobiography of Tashi-Tsering*. Armonk, NY: M.E. Sharpe, 1997.

10. Gelder and Gelder, *Timely Rain*: 110.

11. Strong, Anna Louise. *Tibetan Interviews*. Peking: New World Press, 1959: 15, 19–21, 24.

12. Quoted in Strong, *Tibetan Interviews*: 25.

13. Ibid.: 31.

14. Goldstein, Melvyn C. *A History of Modern Tibet 1913–1951*. Berkeley: University of California Press, 1989: 5.

15. Gelder and Gelder, *Timely Rain*: 175–6; Strong, *Tibetan Interviews*: 25–6.

16. Gelder and Gelder, *Timely Rain*: 113.

17. Grunfeld, A. Tom. *The Making of Modern Tibet*, rev. ed. Armonk, NY, and London: 1996: 9, and 7–33 for a general discussion of feu-dal Tibet; see also Greene, Felix. *A Curtain of Ignorance*. Garden City, NY: Doubleday, 1961: 241–9; Goldstein, *History of Modern Tibet*: 3–5; Lopez, *Prisoners of Shangri-La*: passim.

18. Strong, *Tibetan Interviews*: 91–2.

19. Ibid.: 92–6.

20. Waddell, Landon, and O'Connor are quoted in Gelder and Gelder, *Timely Rain*: 123–5.

21. Goldstein, *Snow Lion*: 52.

22. Harrer, Heinrich. *Return to Tibet*. New York: Schocken, 1985: 29.

23. See Conboy, Kenneth, and James Morrison. *The CIA's Secret War in Tibet*. Lawrence, Kansas: University of Kansas Press, 2002; and Leary, William, "Secret Mission to Tibet." *Air & Space* (Dec 1997/Jan 1998). [Editor's note: For more on the CIA and Tibet, see Laird, Thomas. *Into Tibet: The CIA's First Atomic Spy and His Secret Expedition to Lhasa*. Grove Press, 2002.]

24. On the CIA's links to the Dalai Lama and his family and entourage, see Coleman, Loren. *Tom Slick and the Search for the Yeti*. London: Faber and Faber, 1989.

25. Leary, "Secret Mission to Tibet."

26. Deane, Hugh. "The Cold War in Tibet." *CovertAction Quarterly* (Winter 1987).

27. Ginsburg, George, and Michael Mathos. *Communist China and Tibet* (1964). Quoted in Deane, "Cold War in Tibet." Deane notes that author Bina Roy reached a similar conclusion.

28. See Greene, *Curtain of Ignorance*: 248 and passim; Grunfeld, *Making of Modern Tibet*: passim.

29. Harrer, *Return to Tibet*: 54.

30. Karan, *Changing Face of Tibet*: 36–8, 41, 57–8; London *Times* (4 July 1966).

31. Gelder and Gelder, *Timely Rain*: 29, 47–8.

32. Choegyal, Tendzin. "The Truth about Tibet." *Imprimis* (publica-tion of Hillsdale College, Michigan) (Apr 1999).

33. Karan, *Changing Face of Tibet*, 52–3.

34. Kurtenbach, Elaine. Associated Press report. *San Francisco Chronicle* (12 Feb 1998).

35. Goldstein, *Snow Lion*: 47–8.

36. Report by the International Committee of Lawyers for Tibet. *A Generation in Peril*. Berkeley, 2001: passim.

37. Ibid., 66–8, 98.

38. Mann, Jim. "CIA Gave Aid to Tibetan Exiles in '60s, Files Show." *Los Angeles Times* (15 Sept 1998); *New York Times* (1 Oct 1998); Conboy and Morrison, *CIA's Secret War*.

39. *News & Observer* (Raleigh, NC) (6 Sept 1995). Cited in Lopez, *Prisoners of Shangri-La*: 3.

40. Cottin, Heather. "George Soros, Imperial Wizard." *CovertAction Quarterly* 74 (Fall 2002).

41. The Gelders draw this comparison in *Timely Rain*: 64.

42. Pomfret, John. "Tibet Caught in China's Web." *Washington Post* (23 Jul 1999).

43. Lewis, Kim. Correspondence to the author (15 Jul 2004).

44. Lewis, Kim. Additional correspondence to the author (16 Jul 2004).

45. Goldstein, *Snow Lion*: 51.

46. Choegyal, "Truth about Tibet."

47. The Dalai Lama quoted in Dresser, Marianne, ed. *Beyond Dogma: Dialogues and Discourses*. Berkeley: North Atlantic Books, 1996.

48. Quoted in *San Francisco Chronicle*, 17 May 2001.

Robert Damon Schneck

THE GOD MACHINE

BUILDING THE MECHANICAL MESSIAH

IN 1850s MASSACHUSETTS

IN OCTOBER OF 1853, on a hilltop in Lynn, Massachusetts, a group assembled to create the New Messiah. They had not come to pray to it, sing psalms, or take an otherwise passive approach to the problem; they were actually going to build Him out of metal and wood under the supervision of spirits. When the body was complete, they believed it would be infused with life to revolutionize the world and raise the human race to an exalted level of spiritual development. The spirits had given their God-building instructions through John Murray Spear, a former minister of the Universalist church and recent convert to Spiritualism. Born in Boston in 1804 and baptized by his namesake John Murray (the founder of the American branch of the Universalist church), Spear has been described as a "gentle, kindly, ingenuous" man, who possessed a beautiful simplicity and an idiosyncratic mind.[1]

With his father dead and the family poor, young John may have been apprenticed to a cobbler and worked in a cotton mill, but, at the age of twenty-four, he became a Universalist minister. By 1830, he was married and had his own church in Barnstable, Massachusetts. Universalism teaches that all souls will be saved, stresses the solidarity of mankind, and "sees the whole creation in one vast restless movement, sweeping towards the grand finality of universal holiness and universal love."[2] These ideas were to influence the course of his life.

Spear was an outspoken reformist on the subjects of slavery, women's rights, and temperance and expressed views that frequently upset his congregation. By the late 1840s, he had lost the Barnstable church and was subsequently driven from churches in New Bedford and Weymouth. In 1844, after delivering an anti-slavery speech in Portland, Maine, a mob beat him senseless, leaving him an invalid for months. When he recovered, he operated a portion of the Underground Railroad in Boston, helping runaway slaves get to Canada, and acquired a name as the "Prisoner's Friend" for his work in improving penitentiaries and abolishing the death penalty.

When the body was complete, they believed it would be infused with life to revolutionize the world and raise the human race to an exalted level of spiritual development.

While Spear crusaded in Boston, a strange series of events unfolded in rural New York State that would change his approach to reform. The Fox family—a father, mother, and two young daughters—had moved into a farmhouse in Hydesville in December 1847, where they began hearing inexplicable sounds. Before long, the Foxes found themselves in the middle of what seemed to be full-blown poltergeist phenomena.

Months of noise, especially knocking sounds, exhausted the family. On the night of March 31, 1848, eleven-year-old Kate invited the "ghost" to rap the same number of times she snapped her fingers. It did, and this display of intelligent control led to more communication. The poltergeist claimed to be the spirit of a murdered peddler, and two basic tenets of Spiritualism were established: The soul survives death, and the dead can communicate with the living.[3] The day that Kate began communicating with the ghost, Andrew Jackson Davis—a visionary writer and healer known as the "Seer of Poughkeepsie"—had a revelation that "a living demonstration is born," and the movement that was to become known as "Modern Spiritualism" (or simply "Spiritualism") began.

The Fox sisters gave public demonstrations of their mediumship, and within five years Spiritualism was everywhere. Amateurs experimented with spirit communication in home circles and attended séances and lectures by professional mediums. Hostesses were advised to introduce the "fascinating subject of spiritualism [at dinner parties] when conversation chances to flag over the walnuts and wine."[4] Reformers were especially attracted to the way it challenged social and religious orthodoxies, had neither a hierarchy nor articles of faith, and offered what seemed to be limitless possibilities wherever it was applied.

In 1851, Spear left the Universalist church and became a Spiritualist. With the encouragement of his daughter Sophronia, he developed his powers as a trance medium and accepted guidance from the spirits of Emanuel Swedenborg, Oliver Dennett (who had nursed Spear after the mob attack), and Benjamin Franklin, a very popular figure at séances. Spirits led Spear on trips to faraway towns, where he was directed to cure the sick by laying on hands or making inspired prescriptions.

That summer he received twelve messages from the late John Murray and published them as *Messages From the Superior State*. He followed this with a series of public demonstrations in which he entered a trance while spirits spoke through him on a wide variety of topics—including health and politics—and delivered a twelve-part lecture on geology, a subject about which Spear claimed to be almost wholly ignorant. The speeches, however, were not well-received, as it seemed to be the medium, rather than spirits, speaking.[5]

Spear trusted these spirit advisors without reservation. Among their "projects" was an experiment in which Spear "subjected himself to the most scathing ridicule from his contemporaries by seeking to promote the influence and control of spirits through the aid of copper and zinc batteries so arranged about the person as to form an armor from which he expected extraordinary results."[6]

Despite his efforts, Spear's reputation remained small, while the Fox sisters held sittings with leading citizens (including the First Lady, Mrs. Franklin Pierce), and Andrew Jackson Davis became a famed lecturer and author. Spear's fortunes promised to change, however, after a spirit-inspired journey to Rochester, New York, in 1853, when Spear's special mission was revealed. (Rochester is also where the Foxes made their first public appearance in 1849.)

Spear began producing automatic writing, which proclaimed him to be the earthly representative for the "Band of Electricizers." This was a fraternity of philanthropic spirits directed by Benjamin Franklin and dedicated to elevating the human race through advanced technology. Other groups that made up the "Association of Beneficence" were the "Healthfulizers," "Educationalizers," "Agriculturalizers," "Elementizers," and "Governmentizers," each of which would choose their own spokesmen to receive plans for promoting "Man-culture and integral reform with a view to the ultimate establishment of a divine social state on earth." The Electricizers began speaking through Spear, transmitting "revealments" that ranged from a warning against curling the hair on the back of the head (it's bad for the memory) to plans for electrical ships, thinking machines, and vast, circular cities.[7] These would come later, though.

The first and most important task would be the construction of the New Messiah ("Heaven's last, best gift to man"), a universal benefit that would infuse "new life and vitality into all things animate and inanimate." Spear—or the Electricizers—chose High Rock as the place to build it. High Rock is a hill rising 170 feet (52 meters) above Lynn, a town north of Boston. Lynn is now a poor city suffering from high unemployment, but it was once a center for shoe manufacturing and has a Lovecraftean history full of witchcraft, sea serpents, spontaneous human combustion, and rioting Quakers.[8] Spiritualism received an enthusiastic reception in Lynn, and some of its most devoted followers owned a cottage and observation tower on the site Spear needed.

High Rock Cottage belonged to the Hutchinson family, who were both Spiritualists and reformers. The cottage was a favorite destination for visitors, especially after 1852, when Andrew Jackson Davis witnessed a meeting of the Spiritual Congress from the tower and was introduced to the disembodied representatives of twenty-four nations.

Spear had known the Hutchinsons when he was minister in Boston and allowed them to rehearse in his church when they began singing professionally.[9] Spear was given the use of a woodshed, and work on the "Physical Saviour" began in October 1853.

Assisting Spear and the Electricizers was a small group of followers that included Rev. S.C. Hewitt, editor of the Spiritualist newspaper *New Era*; Alonzo E. Newton, editor of the *New England Spiritualist*; and a woman referred to as "the Mary of the New Dispensation." The identity of this "New Mary" has never been clear.[10]

Bringing the Messiah to life was a four-step process that began with Brother Spear entering a "superior state" and transmitting plans from the Electricizers. Building the machine required nine months for construction (gestation), and in that time he received 200 "revealments" providing detailed instructions on the materials to be used and how the different parts should be shaped and attached. The group was not given an overall plan but built it bit by bit, adding new parts "to the invention, in much the same way...that one decorates a Christmas tree."[11]

Spear's total lack of scientific and technical knowledge was considered an advantage, as he would be less inclined to alter the Electricizers' blueprints with personal interpretations or logic (what remote viewers today might call "analytical overlay"). The parts were carefully machined from copper and zinc, with the total cost reaching $2,000 at a time when a prosperous minister earned around $60 a week.[12]

No images of the New Motive Power exist, but a

Contemporary artist's conception of the "New Messiah." Credit: K.L. Keppler

description does appear in Slater Brown's *The Heyday of Spiritualism*, and it must have looked impressive sitting there on a big dining room table:

From the center of the table rose two metallic uprights connected at the top by a revolving steel shaft. The shaft supported a transverse steel arm from whose extremities were suspended two large steel spheres enclosing magnets. Beneath the spheres there appeared...a very curiously constructed fixture, a sort of oval platform, formed of a peculiar combination of magnets and metals. Directly above this were suspended a number of zinc and copper plates, alternately arranged, and said to correspond with the brain as an electric reservoir. These were supplied with lofty metallic conductors, or attractors, reaching upward to an elevated stratum of atmosphere said to draw power directly from the atmosphere. In combination with these principal parts were adjusted various metallic bars, plates, wires, magnets, insulating substances, peculiar chemical compounds, etc.... At certain points around the circumference of these structures, and connected with the center, small steel balls enclosing magnets were suspended. A metallic connection with the earth, both positive and negative, corresponding with the two lower limbs, right and left, of the body, was also provided.

In addition to the "lower limbs," the motor was equipped with an arrangement for "inhalation and respiration." A large flywheel gave the motor a professional appearance.[13] This was only a working model, though; the final version would be much bigger and cost ten times as much.

The metal body was then lightly charged with an electrical machine, resulting in a "slight pulsatory and vibratory motion...observed in the pendants around the periphery of the table."[14] Following this treatment, the engine was exposed to carefully selected individuals of both sexes, who were brought into its presence one at a time in order to raise the level of its vibrations.

Then Spear encased himself in an elaborate construction of metal plates, strips, and gemstones and was brought into gradual contact with the machine.

Then Spear encased himself in an elaborate construction of metal plates, strips, and gemstones and was brought into gradual contact with the machine. For one hour he went into a deep trance, which left him exhausted and, according to a clairvoyant who was present, created "a stream of light, a sort of umbilicum" that linked him and the machine.[15]

It was at this time that the New Mary began exhibiting symptoms of pregnancy, and the spirits instructed her to appear at High Rock on June 29, 1854, for the final stage of the experiment. On the appointed day, she arrived and lay on the floor in front of the engine for two hours, experiencing labor pains. When they ended, she rose from the floor, touched the machine and it showed signs of...something. Precisely what happened is not clear; Spear claimed that for a few seconds, the machine was animate.

The *New Era* was unrestrained. "THE THING MOVES," claimed the paper's headline, along with an announcement: "The time of deliverance has come at last, and henceforward the career of humanity is upward and onward—a mighty noble and a Godlike career."[16] Spear proclaimed the arrival of "the New Motive Power, the Physical Savior, Heaven's Last Gift to Man, New Creation, Great Spiritual Revelation of the Age, Philosopher's Stone, Art of all Arts, Science of all Sciences, the New Messiah."[17]

The machine's movements remained feeble, but this was not surprising in an "electrical infant," and the New Mary provided maternal attention while it gained strength (unfortunately, there's no mention of what this involved). Despite the headlines, visitors to High Rock were unimpressed. In a letter to the *Spiritual Telegraph*, J.H. Robinson pointed out that the New Messiah could not even turn a coffee-mill,[18] and Alonzo Newton admitted that there was never more than a slight movement detected in some of the hanging metal balls.

Andrew Jackson Davis wrote a long, carefully worded critique of the whole project. While praising Spear as a man "doing good with all his guileless heart" and a fearless defender of unpopular causes, he suggested that Spear had mistaken his own impulses for spirit directives or had been tricked by irresponsible entities into carrying out the experiment. Davis also felt that the precision and intricacy of the machine's construction was proof that higher intelligences were involved because Spear was "intellectually disqualified for the development of absolute science." He also praised the Messiah's excellent workmanship and construction; it didn't move, but it was beautifully put together.[19]

The Electricizers suggested that a change of air would provide the machine with a more nourishing environment, so the Messiah was dismantled and moved to Randolph, New York, where "it might have the advantage of that lofty electrical position." In Randolph, it was put into a shed, but a mob broke in, trampled the machine, and scattered the pieces. No part of it survived.

Spear's High Rock experiment may have been eccentric, but it was also characteristic of the period. New technologies profoundly changed nineteenth-century society, producing industrialization, urbanization, the rise of capital, and a middle class whose values came to dominate society. A conservative reaction to this might have been neo-Ludditism, but Spear was no conservative; he was on a Christ-like mission to transform humanity and believed that technology, the most powerful force of the era, could serve spiritual ends.

He spent the rest of his life working for reform and acting as spokesman for the Spiritual

If the New Messiah had not vanished, the passage of 147 years would have improved the reputation of both the object and its creator. As a medium, Spear was a failure, but he built a unique, if unintentional, example of nineteenth-century folk art. And if it had actually moved, it would be as surprising as a Papuan cargo cult making an airplane that could fly. Spear had used the vocabulary of technology, not its language, to build a statue that expressed the human urge for transcendence.

Congress. When the spirits began preaching free love, Spear fathered a child by Caroline Hinckley in 1859 and, four years later, divorced his wife to marry the mother. They went on a six-year tour of England, lecturing and holding séances, but were disappointed by the lack of interest in radical politics among British Spiritualists.[20]

The couple spent several years in California working for women's rights and socialism before settling in Philadelphia, where they lived contentedly until Spear's death in October 1887. He is buried in Mt. Moriah Cemetery.

DID AN ANGRY MOB really destroy the New Messiah? This would have been an exciting conclusion to a story that seemed headed for an anticlimax. According to Spear, the Machine was dismantled and transported hundreds of miles to the small town of Randolph. There it was housed in a temporary structure until a mob—in a scene reminiscent of peasants storming Frankenstein's castle—destroyed it. Some sources blame Baptist ministers for inflaming local opinion, and the book *An Eccentric Guide to the United States* claims the episode took place in a barn belonging to the Shelton family. Spear's account was reported in the *Lynn News*, October 27, 1854, but is he reliable? Many questioned his sanity, but no one ever seems to have doubted his integrity or suggested he was a charlatan.

The Randolph story, however, is troubling because there is no corroboration, and it seems like there should be. Randolph historian Marlynn Olson has searched through contemporary sources and found nothing. In 1854, Cattaraugus County, New York, had two newspapers—one Whig, the other Republican—and neither mentions Spear, a riot, a Mechanical Messiah, or anyone delivering anti–Mechanical Messiah sermons. No known letters or diaries mention the event. "I think," writes Olson, "the whole thing was a pipe-dream of the Rev. J.M. Spear." Perhaps, like so many other failed experiments, the machine was discreetly sunk into a pond or buried in the woods.

1. Brown, Slater. *The Heyday of Spiritualism*. New York: Hawthorn Books, 1970: 167.

2. Canney, Maurice A. *An Encyclopedia of Religions*. London: George Routledge & Sons: 370.

3. The Foxes were Methodists, a denomination founded by John Wesley, whose family also experienced poltergeist phenomena when he was a child.

4. Delgado, Alan. *Victorian Entertainment*. New York: American Heritage Press, 1971: 15.

5. Rapoza, Andrew V. "Touched by the 'Invisibles.'" In *No Race of Imitators: Lynn and Her People—An Anthology*, edited by Elizabeth Hope Cushing. Lynn, Massachusetts: Lynn Museum and Historical Society, 1992: 69.

6. Hardinge, Emma. *Modern American Spiritualism*. New Hyde Park, NY: University Books: 220.

7. Brown, *Heyday*: 170.

8. Lynn history page <genweb.net/~ebooks/ma/lynn1/lynn.shtml>. Bostonians say: "Lynn, Lynn, City of Sin, you never come out the way you went in!"

9. The Hutchinson Family Singers went on to become very popular, and their descendants still perform programs of nineteenth-century music.

10. It was probably Mrs. Newton, though Spear's wife, Betsey, and Semantha Mettler have also been mentioned. Fodor, Nandor. "John Murray Spear." In *Encyclopedia of Psychic Science*. New Hyde Park, NY: University Books, 1966.

11. Brown, *Heyday*: 171.

12. DeRoche, Celeste, and Peter Hughes. "Thomas Starr King." In *Dictionary of Unitarian and Universalist Biography* <uua.org/uuhs/duub/>.

13. Brown, *Heyday*: 172.

14. Ibid.

15. Ibid: 173.

16. Hardinge, *Modern*: 221.

17. Rapoza, "Touched": 71.

18. Hardinge, *Modern*: 223.

19. Ibid: 223–7.

20. Buescher, John. "John Murray Spear." In *Dictionary of Unitarian and Universalist Biography* <uua.org/uuhs/duub/>.

Erik Davis

THE VERGE EXTREME

CALIFORNIA'S RELIGION OF TRANSFORMATION

Adapted from The Visionary State: A Journey through California's Spiritual Landscape *(Chronicle Books, 2006).*

BETWEEN ITS EDENIC BOUNTY and multicultural mix, its wayward freedoms and hungry dreams, California remains an imaginative frontier exceptional in the history of American religion. Less a place of origins than of mutations, California long ago became a laboratory of the spirit, a sacred playground at the far margins of the West. Here, deities and practices from across space and time have been mixed and matched, refracted and refined, packaged and consumed anew. Such spiritual eclecticism is not novel, of course. But nowhere else in the modern world has such unruly creativity come as close to becoming the status quo. I call this spiritual ethos "California consciousness": an imaginative, experimental, and often hedonistic quest for human transformation by any means necessary.

Defining California's religion of transformation is no easier than defining the New Age. Though world faiths like Buddhism and Christianity have marked the West Coast's alternative *spirituality* in fundamental ways, many of the paths that cross California are, in the words of the religious scholar Robert Fuller, "spiritual, but not religious."

Even that wan word *spirituality* barely works, since many paths crisscross the realms of sacred and profane, and look more like exercise routines or art or crazy fun than sacred pursuits. But that is the point, since the quest for insight, experience, and personal growth can take you anywhere: a mountaintop, a computer, a yoga mat, a rock 'n' roll hall.

I call this spiritual ethos "California consciousness": an imaginative, experimental, and often hedonistic quest for human transformation by any means necessary.

In their quest for transformation, California seekers could be said to have taken the bait that William James dangled in his book *The Varieties of Religious Experience.* For James, personal experience was the cornerstone of the religious life, rather than dogma or institution or even belief. Because of his interest in individual experience, James accepted mysticism and "altered states" as valid points of departure. Experimenting with psychedelic compounds like peyote and nitrous oxide, James argued that such exalted states of consciousness had to be integrated into any philosophy worth its salt. Though James' approach hardly exhausts our understanding of religion, it certainly helps illuminate California consciousness, which insists that personal experience—and the psycho-spiritual practices that transform and shape that experience—are doorways into a deeper change.

One early exemplar of California consciousness is John Muir, the most articulate and prophetic poet of California's remarkable natural landscape. Fusing Emerson's joyful Transcendentalist hymns with a naturalist's gift for crisp detail, Muir's writings galvanized America's love of the outdoors. Horrified by the exploitation of the places he worshiped, Muir eventually used his public profile to achieve concrete gains, founding the Sierra Club and battling to preserve Yosemite, the Grand Canyon, and redwood groves across Northern California. Muir drank deeply of wildness, and at his most ecstatic, he seemed to melt into the earth like a pagan. In a 1869 letter, Muir wrote:

> Now we are fairly into the mountains, and they into us ... What bright seething white-fire enthusiasm is bred in us—without our help or knowledge. A perfect influx into every pore and cell of us, fusing, vaporizing by its heat until the boundary walls of our heavy flesh tabernacle seem taken down and we flow and diffuse into the very air and trees and streams and rocks, thrilling with them to the touch of the vital sunbeams.

Trippy stuff, but not as trippy as the remarkable altered state that bloomed in Muir's mind during his attempt to be the first (white) man to climb Mount Ritter in 1872. Clambering up crumbling battlements of metamorphic rock, Muir eventually found himself in an impossible spot: spread-eagled against a smooth cliff face, unable to move hand or foot. Convinced he was about to fall, Muir suddenly became "possessed of a new sense." His vision became vastly sharper, as if he saw the rock through a microscope, and an external power seemed to take control of his body,

moving it up the rock "with a positiveness and precision with which I seemed to have nothing at all to do."

This is mysticism, not as contemplative exercise, but as extreme sport. In his account, Muir scrambles about for the proper religious or scientific metaphor for this "new sense"—instinct, guardian angel, the other self. Muir had experienced what the Spanish pragmatist philosopher George Santayana described a few decades later in a lecture he gave to UC Berkeley's Philosophical Union. Speaking to the California audience about "your forests and your Sierras," Santayana noted that "in their non-human beauty and peace they stir the sub-human depths and the super-human possibilities of your own spirit." Later in the century, people would come to describe these super-human possibilities with yogic language, or the psychologist Abraham Maslow's notion of a "peak experience."

ELSEWHERE IN NINETEENTH-CENTURY California, humanity's superhuman possibilities were being explored collectively. At the time, utopian colonies were sprouting up across the United States like mushrooms, with some of the most famous, like Oneida and Brook Farm, breaking ground in the Northeast. But California, with its fruitful climate and relatively blank slate, also beckoned those who wanted to build new worlds and new communities. According to the historian Robert Hine, California wound up hosting the largest number of utopian experiments in the nation during its first century as a state.

One of the more ambitious colonies devoted to spiritual transformation opened in 1897, when Katherine Tingley lay the cornerstone for the School for the Revival of the Lost Mysteries of Antiquity on San Diego's craggy Point Loma. Robed in her trademark purple, Tingley anointed the perfectly square cornerstone with oil and wine as her followers read portions of the Bhagavad Gita, the Upanishads, and the Orphic mysteries. These readings made sense, because Tingley had recently become head of a major branch of the Theosophical Society, an organization cofounded in New York in 1875 by Colonel Henry Olcott and a cigar-smoking Russian trickster named Madame Blavatsky. Weaving together occult Neoplatonism, parapsychology, and Eastern lore, Theosophy was perhaps the most influential mystical organization of the nineteenth century, and in many ways created the template for the New Age.

Theosophy introduced thousands of Westerners to Eastern mysticism, which, unlike all but the most esoteric strains of Christianity, teaches practices that supposedly can transform the devoted practitioner into a more-than-human being. At the same time, Blavatsky's writings attempted to connect mysticism with the latest ideas in science, especially Darwin's concept of human evolution. Blavatsky believed that humanity had descended from a series of "root races," including the Lemurians and the residents of Atlantis, and that humanity was beginning to mutate into a new and superior "sixth race." In *The Secret Doctrine*, she argued that this transformation would occur in America. Annie Besant, who controlled another branch of the society headquartered in India, believed it would happen in Southern California; Besant claimed that the finest magnetic vibrations in the world were to be found in Pasadena.

Despite her mystic trappings, Tingley approached the work of human transformation as a social reformer. Tingley liked to cite a passage from Walt Whitman where the poet described an imagined community—"say in some pleasant western settlement or town"—where "in every young and old man, after his kind, and in every woman after hers, a true personality developed, exercised proportionately in body, mind, and spirit." Tingley hoped to achieve this through Raja Yoga, a training program that emphasized music, dance, and self-discipline, and that insisted on maintaining silence through much of the day. The first word that young children learned to spell in the community's schools was *attention*—the same word that the mynah bird squawks in Aldous Huxley's 1962 novel *Island*, where the bird serves to remind the inhabitants of Huxley's fictional Utopia to awaken to the moment.

By 1907, Tingley's San Diego community—nicknamed "Lomaland"—had grown to 500 people, and its gardens and Orientalist buildings were a popular draw for tourists and San Diegans alike. But Lomaland's good standing with the locals did not prevent the *Los Angeles Times* from accusing her of organizing "midnight pilgrimages" that led to "gross immoralities," although one of the pilgrimages in question consisted of little more than toga-clad Theosophists eating fruit and listening to Tingley discuss the unusual mental powers of Spot, her cocker spaniel. Following Tingley's death in 1929, the community rapidly declined.

As early as 1913, one local writer was already complaining that "No other city in the United States possesses so large a number of metaphysical charlatans in proportion to its population."

During the 1920s, a more unvarnished source for the mystical East's religion of transformation arrived in California. Paramahansa Yogananda was a charismatic swami from India who packed the halls across America with his accessible lectures about the "science of yoga." After a successful cross-country tour in 1924, Yogananda decided to settle down in Southern California, where he founded the Self-Realization Fellowship. When asked why he chose Los Angeles, Yogananda replied that he considered the city to be the most spiritual place in the country, the Benares of America—Benares being perhaps the holiest city in India, where pilgrims from across the country come to die. Though Los Angeles lacked the corpse-choked river of this ancient Indian city, the boomtown did have a surfeit of seekers. As early as 1913, one local writer was already complaining that "No other city in the United States possesses so large a number of metaphysical charlatans in proportion to its population."

Like many Hindu teachers of the time, Yogananda stressed the modernity of the mystic way, proclaiming the global unity of religions, and linking scientific invention with spiritual forces—a crucial element of California consciousness, which would try to blend ancient truths with modern ideas of biological evolution and technological progress. Yogananda taught "scientific techniques" to attain God consciousness, a practical system of energy work he called Kriya Yoga. Yogananda also compared the sound of *om* to a cosmic motor, and the third eye to a "broadcasting station." Cinema was, for him, the perfect illustration of the Vedantist claim that the material world was a passing illusion woven from waves of energy. In his book *Autobiography of a Yogi*, one of the most popular texts of the mystic counterculture to come, Yogananda emphasizes his amazing psychic experiences rather than his philosophical ideas; these cinematic descriptions of "cosmic consciousness" whetted all but the most quotidian of spiritual appetites, helping to reaffirm the central role of personal experience within California consciousness.

Though the body has usually been considered an enemy in religious mysticism, in California the healthy and happy flesh infused the emerging religion of personal transformation. California played a key role, for example, in the popularization and Westernization of hatha yoga, a holistic tantric science of kundalini awakening that today holds sway over millions of Americans. But even before Indira Devi opened America's first hatha yoga studio in Hollywood in the late 1940s, a health nut named Walt Baptiste started offering yoga stretches and pranayama at the Center for Physical Culture he founded in San Francisco in the 1930s. Baptiste had picked up the practices from his uncle, a follower of Yogananda, and they led him to reframe physical fitness as a vehicle of conscious evolution, part of a larger quest to be "infinite in every capacity." Baptiste was also a hardcore bodybuilder, one of a number of California strongmen, including Jack LaLanne, who revolutionized the American physique in the 1930s and 1940s by utilizing resistance training and by visibly transforming the body into a super-

man. In 1949, Baptiste won the Mr. America contest; a couple of decades later, he went to Swami Sivananda's yoga university in Rishikesh and was anointed Yogiraj—or "King of Yoga." Baptiste was a perfect avatar of California consciousness.

CALIFORNIA'S ETHOS OF transformation did not apply just to the body or the mind, but to the very form of spiritual pursuit—a mythos inscribed in the life of one of the state's most famous neo-Hindu avatars. In 1909, the fourteen-year-old J. Krishnamurti was discovered in India by Charles Leadbeater, a Theosophical leader and probable pederast who had already gotten in trouble for teaching young boys to masturbate. Though Krishnamurti was an indifferent student with a somewhat vacant demeanor, the middle-class Brahmin boy was recognized by Leadbeater and Annie Besant as the human vessel for the coming World Teacher—the Theosophical equivalent of the Messiah. Raised like a young raja, Krishnamurti was soon traveling the world with Besant, lecturing as head of the Order of the Star, the vehicle for Maitreya, the future Buddha.

In the early 1920s, Krishnamurti and his brother Nitya bought a small ranch house in Ojai, which they dubbed Arya Vihara. A number of prominent Theosophists had already made their home in the dry, green oasis, which today still hosts a prep school founded by Annie Besant. While in Ojai in the summer of 1922, Krishnamurti underwent an extraordinary series of convulsive pains and astral journeys that culminated in an overwhelming experience of "God-intoxication" beneath a pepper tree. After this psychospiritual crisis—whose considerable physical pain Krishnamurti could alleviate only by resting his head on the lap of his young female nurse—the Messiah became a different sort of fellow, one who often referred to himself and his body in the third person. Leadbeater believed the young man was physically evolving into an example of the sixth root race. Whatever he was, he was no longer exactly human.

Though continuing to tour as the future World Teacher, Krishnamurti began to question Theosophy, and in 1929, he left the society and publicly dissolved the Order of the Star. He rejected the whole notion of mystical schools,

Instead, he proclaimed that the spiritual search cannot be organized, that "truth is a pathless land."

magical grades, and proscribed spiritual practices—even the very notion of the guru. Instead, he proclaimed that the spiritual search cannot be organized, that "truth is a pathless land." By the time he died in 1986, Krishnamurti annually drew thousands of seekers to his spring talks, held outside at Oak Grove in Ojai. Krishnamurti's astringent message of radical freedom and "choiceless awareness" introduced a powerful existential dimension to the spirituality of the modern world and helped inspire the anarchism that lay beneath so much hippie mysticism. (The swami who appears in the 1968 Monkeys' film *Head*, for example, preaches pure Krishnamurti.) Though too depersonalized to identify with any one place, Krishnamurti nonetheless expressed a deeply Californian sense of spiritual rootlessness, a rootlessness that embraced endless process rather than specific or traditional goals. "The journey within oneself must be undertaken not for a result, not to solve conflict and sorrow; for the search itself is devotion."

A fixture on the fringes of Hollywood, Krishnamurti hobnobbed with Charlie Chaplin and Greta Garbo but also became close friends with Aldous Huxley, in many ways the true father of California consciousness. Huxley moved to Los Angeles from Britain in the late 1930s to escape the war. Once in Hollywood, Huxley wrote screenplays and lived the life of a bohemian brainiac, sharing an open marriage with his wife, who procured lovers for him while frequenting the lesbian "sewing circles" of Hollywood with the certifiably divine Garbo. But in 1942, Huxley and his wife, Maria, grew weary of the Southland's great "Metrollopis" and, in a prophetic move, headed back to the land in search of a simpler and more natural life.

Living near the ruins of a utopian colony called Llano del Rio at the edge of the Mojave Desert, Huxley plunged into the studies that made him a modern mystic devoted to the possibility of radical human transformation. In his earlier novels and essays, Huxley had cast a cold and some-

times jaundiced eye on the foibles and delusions of the human personality. As a social critic, he had concluded that people needed to change on an individual psychological level if civilization was going to avoid the disasters he glimpsed on the horizon: overpopulation, high-tech war, ecological catastrophe, and the sort of narcotized totalitarian propaganda depicted with such lasting power in *Brave New World*. Inspired by his friend and fellow pacifist Gerald Heard, who moved from England to Hollywood before him, Huxley came to suspect that only mystical experience could give people direct access to states of consciousness capable of eroding their mean and selfish egotism.

In Llano, Huxley embarked on a massive cross-cultural study of the experiential core of world religion. The resulting book, *The Perennial Philosophy*, argued that the writings of mystics across the world revealed the same ultimate reality—a oneness that transcends the muck of the ordinary personality while affirming the essential "suchness" of things as they are. Huxley's impersonal vision of Being would come to dominate the spirituality of the counterculture. But the most Californian note sounded by *The Perennial Philosophy* was its pragmatic insistence that knowledge of ultimate reality could come only through spiritual practice, rather than dogmatic belief or rote ritual. Spirituality was a matter of mind-body techniques, individual discovery, and an open-ended experimental embrace of transformation. Inspired perhaps by his friendship with the famous astronomer Edwin Hubble, Huxley compared his "empirical theology" to the technology that undergirds astronomy. While a faint smudge glimpsed with the naked eye might allow us to theorize about extragalactic nebulae, such theories can never tell us as much about the cosmos "as can direct acquaintance by means of a good telescope, camera and spectroscope." In the 1950s, Huxley would discover the perfect tool of empirical theology: psychedelics.

AT THE SAME TIME that Huxley was briefly exploring the life of a desert ascetic, the brilliant and impish Gerald Heard was building the Trabuco College of Prayer in a remote canyon in the Santa Ana Mountains. A loose-limbed spiritual training center, Trabuco College was designed to allow a crew of evolvers to creatively and collectively explore Eastern and Western mysticism without hewing to any specific tradition. Way ahead of its time, Heard's experiment lasted only a few years, after which Heard passed on the property to the Vedanta Society. But the dream of Trabuco College would be rekindled in the early 1960s by two Stanford graduate students named Michael Murphy and Richard Price, two intellectuals committed to radical psychological development. Murphy had spent sixteen months at Sri Aurobindo's ashram in Pondicherry, India, an experience that left him with a profound love of meditation—which he practiced as much as eight hours a day—but serious reservations about the guru model of spiritual training. Price was a more bohemian character, a denizen of North Beach who practiced Zen and had done time in a US Air Force mental ward undergoing past-life flashbacks and electroshock therapy in equal measure. Together, inspired by Heard's experiment, they decided to recreate Heard's "gymnasia of the mind" around a gorgeous cliffside hot springs in Big Sur. They named their center Esalen.

Esalen participants felt like they were surfing the edge of human evolution, as if a new kind of person was being birthed—or, more properly, rebirthed.

The Esalen Institute spawned and nurtured the human potential movement, an incredibly influential blend of psychological therapies and secularized spiritual practices that transformed the American image of the self into an image of total transformation. Initially, Esalen was heavily influenced by Abraham Maslow, who argued that the psychology of the day erred in its fixation on the broken or neurotic individual. Maslow spoke instead of peak experiences, those godlike flashes of joy, insight, and self-empowerment that seem to

spring from some deeper source than the mundane personalities that armor our ordinary days. (Think of Muir's experience on Ritter, or Yogananda's cinematic glimpses of cosmic consciousness.) Maslow's conception of self-actualization was crucial to the idea of human potential, but within a few years, people wanted to do the do rather than talk about it. Soon an enormous number of techniques, new and old, were piled on the Esalen table: Gestalt therapy, meditation, tai chi chuan, psychedelics, Rolphing, primal scream therapy, holotropic breathwork, hatha yoga, biofeedback, Tantra, massage. Esalen participants felt like they were surfing the edge of human evolution, as if a new kind of person was being birthed—or, more properly, rebirthed.

By the end of the 1970s, Esalen's practical therapies and holistic ideas had spread around the world, even as the institute became the butt of jokes and the flashpoint for attacks on the Me Generation. Some of the digs were deserved, as were some of the jokes: At one point in the mid-1970s, the list of staff members included "the Nine," a group of disincarnate entities channeled from the star system Sirius. But Esalen's essentially secular engagement with human transformation was, in its way, as revolutionary as anything launched in those epochal days. Esalen's leading thinkers and researchers, especially Murphy and the Aikido master George Leonard, mapped and morphed our understanding of the extraordinary capacities latent within the individual—prescient work given the radical augmentation therapies, neuropharmacological drugs, and technologies that are now transforming our definition of human being. Esalen also explored the social and psychological implications of cybernetics and ecology, developing an integral approach to mind, body and nature that would also help shape the emerging cyberculture. And they did this while largely dodging the authoritarian traps that swallowed up so many other avatars of California consciousness.

The same cannot be said of the Church of Scientology, an organization devoted to propagating a cosmic self-help "technology" invented, and brilliantly promoted, by L. Ron Hubbard. Although some of the most important Scientology centers lie outside California—in Florida and on the high seas—the institution's cultic heart beats in Los Angeles, which cradles the largest concentration of Scientology practitioners and properties in the world. Here the Church wears a Janus face: At once proselytizer and pariah, Scientology is simultaneously the most integrated and most marginalized of Los Angeles' myriad new religious movements.

In the 1940s, Hubbard dabbled in Thelemic magick with Jack Parsons, a Jet Propulsion Lab scientist and the master of an O.T.O. lodge in Pasadena. This deep brush with the occult informed Hubbard's creation of Dianetics, a do-it-yourself psychotherapy technique that made its sensational appearance in the pulp magazine *Astounding Science Fiction*. Scientology, Hubbard's subsequent religious repackaging of the secular Dianetics, offered a Gnostic approach to self-realization in a technology-informed psychobabble that would heavily influence later California self-help groups like est. According to Hubbard, buried deep within our dysfunctional personalities are immortal beings called Thetans. Long ago, according to one account, we Thetans decided to amuse ourselves by constructing the universe of space-time and then injecting ourselves into its material confines. Then we became imprisoned in the game world, falling prey to its delusions and dysfunctional programs, which Dianetics auditing and higher "Operating Thetan" teachings can help overcome. Scientology offered the transformation of the self as a sort of science-fiction programming tech, capable of producing unlimited powers.

One measure of how influential Scientology and other systems of self-programming California consciousness became in the 1970s was their presence at one of the most important research centers in the country: the Stanford Research Institute, a facility in Palo Alto that still performs high-octane research-and-development work for the government and private corporations. Stargate, one of SRI's most outlandish programs, began in 1972 and focused on remote viewing—the paranormal ability to mentally visualize and describe a distant place or object. Lead researchers Russell Targ and Harold Puthoff both specialized in laser technology but were also fascinated by the hidden powers of the mind. The two convinced the CIA—who knew that the Soviets were pursuing psi studies—to support an in-depth program of applied remote viewing. Puthoff and Targ focused on so-called "gifted individuals" like the New York artist Ingo Swann, whose astral travels to Jupiter were supposedly confirmed by the Mariner 10 spacecraft. But Puthoff was more than an expert in quantum mechanics with a sidelight interest in parapsychology. He was also an advanced Scientologist, an Operating Thetan who had supposedly cleared his mind of the reactive programs that shroud the spiritual superman within. Ingo Swann and many of SRI's psychic subjects were also Scientologists, and some of SRI's protocols were, apparently, based on Hubbard's high-level techniques. Like Scientology itself, the Stargate program reframed occult powers for a postwar, mind-ops world.

Puthoff and Targ were not the only SRI researchers tantalized by the more authoritarian wings of California mind science. Douglas Engelbart was the most visionary researcher at SRI, a pioneer of human-computer interaction whose Augmentation Research Center transformed our fundamental metaphors of computerized communication. In a famous 1968 demo at ARC, Engelbart first demonstrated much that our wired world now takes for granted: the mouse, the hyperlink, the graphical user interface, videoconferencing. Engelbart realized that the computer offered us not just a machine to program but also a space to explore—particularly when the computer in question was networked with other machines.

Indeed, ARC helped give birth to cyberspace when it and UCLA became the first nodes on the Arpanet, the predecessor of today's Internet.

Engelbart's remarkable vision was guided by a powerful belief in the cognitive possibilities opened up through the co-evolution of technology and human consciousness. Such interests may also explain all the pot smoked around ARC, not to mention Engelbart's personal devotion to the Erhard Seminars Training, that blustering juggernaut of the human potential movement better known as est. A large-group seminar devoted to the intentional reprogramming of the self, est was cobbled together by Werner Erhard out of bits and pieces of Zen, Scientology, "psycho-cybernetics," and Dale Carnegie's *How to Win Friends and Influence People*. Erhard launched the training at San Francisco's Jack Tar Hotel in late 1971, attracting scores of lost hippies who wanted to straighten out while still "getting it." The program also presented a practical and potent "technology" of human interaction and self-awareness, one that Engelbart not only embraced on a personal level but also insisted on applying to the collaborative work at ARC—a controversial move that ultimately led to the dissolution of the lab.

Parapsychology and meta-programming trainings like est encourage a quasi-scientific or technical approach to the human mind, including nonordinary states of human consciousness. Today this sort of mindtech, further repackaged into post-est regimes like the Landmark Forum, has woven itself into American business culture, especially in Silicon Valley. But perhaps the most reliable technology of altered states and temporary transformation lay in the chemistry of consciousness—in other words, in psychoactive drugs. Some of the most important psychedelics were first synthesized in Europe, but the ground zero for modern psychedelic culture lay on the West Coast, especially California. Years before Timothy Leary began dosing Harvard grad students, Aldous Huxley had penned *The Doors of Perception*, and soon Los Angeles–based psychologists and psychiatrists like Oscar Janiger, Betty Eisner, and Sidney Cohen were exploring inner space with movie stars and intellectuals in a therapeutic, spiritually informed context. When Merry Pranksters and mystic hippies started gobbling LSD in far less controlled settings, they drove such therapy underground. But to this day, the rhetoric of psychedelic proponents continues to stress the transformative possibilities of these drugs—that the experiences that they boot up can help us evolve, or at least give us glimpses of our future possible selves.

AS THE EXAMPLE of psychedelic culture shows, California's religion of transformation represents an attempt to retool the secular and even nihilistic course of Western psychology, culture, and technology and put it on a higher track. But there is a darker undertow to this grab bag of transformative tools and techniques. From some perspectives, the most striking thing about California consciousness is not its revolutionary force but its restlessness, an anxious, endless questing that Walt Whitman recognized long ago in his poem "Facing West from California's Shores." In the poem, Whitman's expansive poetic "I" broadens to encompass humanity itself, which he describes as a single being that moves westward from Asia until finally arriving at the sea:

> Facing west from California's shores,
> Inquiring, tireless, seeking what is yet unfound,
> I, a child, very old, over waves, toward the house of maternity, the land of migrations, look afar,
> Look off the shores of my Western sea, the circle almost circled.

It fundamentally rejects fundamentalism.

Here, the poet—an old child, like so many seekers—finds himself at the end of migrations. But even as he faces home again, sensing California's Pacific Rim connection to Asia and its ancient ways of mystic transformation, Whitman grows anxious. He ends the poem by asking a question that goes to the heart of California consciousness: "But where is what I started for so long ago? / And why is it yet unfound?"

In the American imagination, California's shores stage both the fulfillment and decline of the West, its final shot at paradise and its precipitous fall into the sea. That is why the California dream encompasses both Arcadian frontier and apocalyptic end zone, Eden and Babylon. As Christopher Isherwood put it, "California is a tragic land—like Palestine, like every promised land." But the Golden State is also a prophetic land, because it recognized that transformation is the name of the game.

After all, today we are in the midst of one of the most turbulent and disturbing periods of transformation humans have ever known. The biosphere we depend on is passing through a severe and possibly disastrous shuddering, while molecular engineering, brain implants, neuropharmocology, and media technology are already whipping up a posthuman human being. California has had a front seat on these transformations, not just because it is a haunt of harbingers, but because so much of the anxious science fiction we now inhabit was born or nurtured in the Golden State: freeways, fast-food chains, cinema, TV, aerospace, biotechnology, designer drugs, teenage tribes, satellites, personal computers, the Internet. In short, California has been the petri dish of posthumanity.

These transformations in matter and culture challenge our conventional ideas about who and where we are, and they demand a spiritual response. In some ways, the rise of religious fundamentalism, in the United States and abroad, makes sense. In the face of unnerving possibilities, people understandably seek fixed truths and clear definitions, which provide ballast at a time when everything threatens to both collapse and converge. But though California has minted conservative Christian leaders whose blistering attacks on liberal culture can match any in America, the Californian response to the reality of global transformation is to plunge onward and upward. The essential temperament of California consciousness is progressive and evolutionary rather than reactionary. It fundamentally rejects fundamentalism. California's unusual spiritual culture can thus be seen as a prophetic and paradoxical reflection of the crisis of our times, at once harmonizing with it and providing, or at least attempting to provide, visionary alternatives to our considerable blight.

10

GRAB BAG

H.G. Wells

JESUS OF NAZARETH DISCUSSES HIS FAILURE

Editor's Note: H.G. Wells is best-remembered as a late-Victorian pioneer of science fiction, mainly due to his 1890s novels The Time Machine, The Invisible Man, *and* The War of the Worlds. *He cranked out dozens of books in numerous genres of fiction and nonfiction, and 1945—the year before his death—saw the publication of his last two books to come out during his lifetime:* The Happy Turning: A Dream of Life *and* Mind at the End of Its Tether.

The Happy Turning *is a slim, strange work that gets even stranger as it continues. Wells sets it up by claiming that sometimes he dreams about taking his daily walk and coming across a pathway he's never noticed in real life. Taking this turn (the "Happy Turning") leads him to the utopian Dreamland (a/k/a the Beyond), where his body is perfectly fit, where society knows no war, poverty, or inequality, and where his "subliminal self" lets loose with a flood of "cryptic and oracular" symbols.*

Wells then steps back in time to relate some dreams he had when he was young, including the one that "made me an atheist." Having read about "a man being broken on the wheel over a slow fire," the preteen Wells had a nightmare. "By a mental leap which cut out all intermediaries, the dream artist made it clear that if indeed there was an all powerful God, then it was he and he alone who stood there conducting this torture." Upon awakening, he felt that he had two alternatives: go insane or stop believing in God. "God had gone out of my life. He was impossible."

Wells continues: "From that time on, I began to talk and invent blasphemy," which took the form of "a long series of drawings and writings, many of which have never seen and never will see the light of print."

Some of that blasphemy starts a couple of pages later, when Wells witnesses a procession of gods intermingled with a "swarm" of holy men. "No Carnival gone mad can compare with this leaping and tumbling procession." Wells searches in vain for a single laugh or smile among them. "Always I encounter faces of stupid earnestness. [...] They are not pretending to be such fools. They are such fools...."

Following this is Wells' Dreamland chat with Jesus, which takes up two of the longest chapters. The excerpt below is approximately the first thousand words of this encounter. The second chapter ends with Wells and Jesus deciding to invisibly spy upon schools of the author's time, presumably to observe what children are being taught (and undoubtedly to offer caustic commentary upon it). But they don't. With the close of the chapter, this entire storyline comes to an abrupt end, as if Wells forgot or didn't care to continue it.

After the Jesus part, Wells weirds out with two unrelated jeremiads. He launches into "A Hymn of Hate against Sycamores": a twelve-page rant targeting "this hoggish arborial monster" that kills entire gardens, including Wells' small one.

In the last chapter, the author waxes philosophical about beauty and literature, praising Shakespeare and spouting invective—though not nearly as bad as the anti-sycamore variety—at Romantic and Modernist poets, including Byron, Shelley, and Eliot.

His scorn and contempt for Christianity go beyond my extremest vocabulary.

THE COMPANION I FIND most congenial in the Beyond is Jesus of Nazareth. Like everything in Dreamland he fluctuates, but beyond the Happy Turning his personality is at least as distinct as my own. His scorn and contempt for Christianity go beyond my extremest vocabulary. He was, I believe, the putative son of a certain carpenter, Joseph, but Josephus says his actual father was a Roman soldier named Pantherus. If so, Jesus did not know it.

He began his career as a good illiterate patriotic Jew in indignant revolt against the Roman rule and the Quisling priests who cringed to it. He took up his self-appointed mission under the influence of John the Baptist, who was making trouble for both the Tetrarch in Galilee and the Roman Procurator in Jerusalem. John was an uncompromising Puritan, and the first thing his disciples had to do, was to get soundly baptised in Jordan. Then he seemed to run out of ideas. After their first encounter John and Jesus went their different ways. There was little discipleship in Jesus.

He played an inconspicuous role in the Salome affair, and he assures me he never baptized anybody. But he was brooding on the Jewish situation, which he felt needed more than moral denunciation and water. He decided to get together a band of followers and march on Jerusalem. Where, as the Gospel witnesses tell very convincingly, with such contradictions as are natural to men writing about it all many years later, the sacred Jewish priests did their best to obliterate him. He learnt much as he went on. He seems to have said some good things and had others imputed to him. He became a sort of Essene Joe Miller. He learnt and changed as he went on.

Gods! how he hated priests, and how he hates them now! And Paul! "Fathering all this nonsense about being 'The Christ' on *me* of all people! Christian! *He* started that at Antioch. I never had the chance of a straight talk to him. I wish I could come upon him some time. But he never seems to be here…. There are a few things I could say to him," said Jesus reflectively, and added, "Plain things…."

I regretted Paul's absence.

"One must draw the line somewhere," I said. ["]In this happy place, Paul's in the discard."

"Yes," reflected Jesus, dismissing Paul; "there were such a lot of things I didn't know, and such a lot of snares for the feet of a man who feels more strongly than he understands. I see so plainly now how incompetently I set about it."

He surveyed his shapely feet cooling in the refreshing greensward of Happyland. The stigmata were in evidence, but not obtrusively so. They were not eyesores. They have since been disgustingly irritated and made much of by the sedulous uncleanness of the saints.

"*Never* have disciples," said Jesus of Nazareth.

"*Never* have disciples," said Jesus of Nazareth. "It was my greatest mistake. I imitated the tradition of having such divisional commanders to marshal the rabble I led to Jerusalem. It has been the common mistake of all world-menders, and I fell into it in my turn as a matter of course. I had no idea what a real revolution had to be; how it had to go on from and to and fro between man and man, each one making his contribution. I was just another young man in a hurry. I thought I could carry the whole load, and I picked my dozen almost haphazard.

"What a crew they were! I am told that even these Gospels you talk about, are unflattering in their account of them.

"There is nothing flattering to be told about them. What a crew to start upon saving the world! From the first they began badgering me about their relative importance….

"And their *stupidity!* They would misunderstand the simplest metaphors. I would say, 'The Kingdom of Heaven is like so-and-so and so-and-so'.... In the simplest terms....

"They always got it wrong.

"After a time I realised I could never open my mouth and think aloud without being misunderstood. I remember trying to make our breach with all orthodox and ceremonial limitations clear beyond any chance of relapse. I made up a parable about a Good Samaritan. Not *half* a bad story."

"We have the story," I said.

"I was sloughing off my patriotism at a great rate. I was realising the Kingdom of Heaven had to be a universal thing. Or nothing. Does your version go like that?"

"It goes like that."

"But it never altered their belief that they had come into the business on the ground floor."

"You told another good story about some Labourers in the Vineyard."

"From the same point of view?"

"From the same point of view."

"Did it alter their ideas in the least?"

"Nothing seemed to alter their ideas in the least."

"It was a dismal time when our great March on Jerusalem petered out. You know when they got us in the Garden of Gethsemane I went to pieces completely.... The disciples, when they realised public opinion was against them, just dropped their weapons and dispersed. No guts in them. Simon Peter slashed off a man's ear and then threw away his sword and pretended not to know me...

"I wanted to kick myself. I derided myself. I saw all the mistakes I had made in my haste. I spoke in the bitterest irony. Nothing for it now but to know one had had good intentions. 'My peace,' I said, 'I give unto you.'

"The actual crucifixion was a small matter in comparison. I was worn out and glad to be dying [...] But being crucified upon the irreparable

things that one has done, realising that one has failed, that you have let yourself down and your poor silly disciples down and mankind down, that the God in you has deserted you—that was the ultimate torment."

John G. Bourke

HOLY SHIT

EXCREMENT AND RELIGION

Editor's Note: John Gregory Bourke (1846–1896) was a distinguished military man and a gentleman scholar who taught himself several languages, including Latin, Gaelic, and Apache. He received the Medal of Honor for his performance during the Civil War (he had joined the Fifteenth Pennsylvania Cavalry when he was sixteen). After graduating from West Point, he served in the Third United States Cavalry for the rest of his life, eventually achieving the rank of colonel.

Beginning in the 1880s, Bourke penned several books and numerous papers and articles on his military engagements and on Native American beliefs, rituals, and language. He was an active member of several academic societies devoted to science, anthropology, and folklore. Today, when he is remembered at all, it's for his 500-page Scatalogic Rites of All Nations: A Dissertation Upon the Employment of Excrementitious Remedial Agents in Religion, Therapeutics, Divination, Witchcraft, Love-Philters, etc., in All Parts of the Globe *(Washington, DC: W.H. Lowdermilk & Co., 1891). In the surprisingly large body of literature devoted to feces and urine, this dense, wandering magnum opiss has never been surpassed.*

Not that it doesn't have some drawbacks. Bourke has a tendency (actually, more of an addiction) to spiral into completely unrelated tangents lasting from a single paragraph to three consecutive chapters. Making the work even more demanding is his habit of quoting passages in foreign languages, mainly French and Latin, without any accompanying translation—no problem for the educated folk of his day, who were expected to be fluent in at least these two tongues, but not so convenient for us modern monoglots. Then there's the way Bourke often stops quoting examples and simply tells his readers to take a look at a certain book that might've been easily available in the 1890s but is now available only in the spore-filled basements of three university libraries in the world.

In assembling the excerpts below, I've plucked many of the best religion-related passages, filtering out the distractions contained within. (One exception: When Bourke directly quotes another source, I've left reference to the source's title and author.) I've resisted the temptation to litter the text with ellipses to indicate the many places where material was excised. If you want to read Scatalogic Rites *in all its glory, at least one reprint edition is still in print.*

THE URINE DANCE OF THE ZUÑIS

On the evening of November 17, 1881, during my stay in the village of Zuñi, New Mexico, the Nehue-Cue, one of the secret orders of the Zuñis, sent word to Mr. Frank H. Cushing, whose guest I was, that they would do us the unusual honor of coming to our house to give us one of their characteristic dances, which, Cushing said, was unprecedented.

The squaws of the governor's family put the long living-room to rights, sweeping the floor and sprinkling it with water to lay the dust. Soon after dark the dancers entered; they were twelve in number, two being boys. The center men were naked, with the exception of black breech-clouts of archaic style. The hair was worn naturally, with a bunch of wild-turkey feathers tied in front, and one of corn husks over each ear. White bands were painted across the face at eyes and mouth. Each wore a collar or neckcloth of black woollen stuff. Broad white bands, one inch wide, were painted around the body at the navel, around the arms, the legs at mid-thighs, and knees. Tortoise-shell rattles hung from the right knee. Blue woollen footless leggings were worn with low-cut moccasins, and in the right hand each waved a wand made of an ear of corn, trimmed with the plumage of the wild turkey and macaw. The others were arrayed in old, cast-off American Army clothing, and all wore white cotton night-caps, with corn-husks twisted into the hair at top of head and ears. Several wore, in addition to the tortoise-shell rattles, strings of brass sleigh-bells at knees. One was more grotesquely attired than the rest, in a long India-rubber gossamer "overall," and with a pair of goggles, painted white, over his eyes. His general "get-up" was a spirited take-off upon a Mexican priest. Another was a very good counterfeit of a young woman.

To the accompaniment of an oblong drum and of the rattles and bells spoken of, they shuffled into the long room, crammed with spectators of both sexes and of all sizes and ages. Their song was apparently a ludicrous reference to everything and everybody in sight, Cushing, Mindeleff, and myself receiving special attention, to the uncontrolled merriment of the red-skinned listeners. I had taken my station at one side of the room, seated upon the banquette, and having in front of me a rude bench or table, upon which was a small coal-oil lamp. I suppose that in the halo diffused by the feeble light, and in my "stained-glass attitude," I must have borne some resemblance to the pictures of saints hanging upon the walls of old Mexican churches; to such a fancied resemblance I at least attribute the performance which followed.

The dancers suddenly wheeled into line, threw themselves on their knees before my table, and with extravagant beatings of breast began an outlandish but faithful mockery of a Mexican Catholic congregation at vespers. One bawled out a parody upon the paternoster [i.e., the Lord's Prayer], another mumbled along in the manner of an old man reciting the rosary, while the fellow with the India-rubber coat jumped up and began a passionate exhortation or sermon, which for mimetic fidelity was incomparable. This kept the audience laughing with sore sides for some moments, until, at a signal from the leader, the dancers suddenly countermarched out of the room in single file as they had entered.

An interlude followed of ten minutes, during which the dusty floor was sprinkled by men who spat water forcibly from their mouths. The Nehue-Cue re-entered; this time two of their number were stark naked. Their singing was very peculiar, and sounded like a chorus of chimney-sweeps, and their dance became a stiff-legged jump, with heels kept twelve inches apart. After they had ambled around the room two or three times, Cushing announced in the Zuñi language that a "feast" was ready for them, at which they loudly roared their approbation, and advanced to strike hands with the munificent "Americanos," addressing us in a funny gibberish of broken Spanish, English, and Zuñi. They then squatted upon the ground and consumed with zest large "ollas" full of tea, and dishes of hard tack and sugar. As they were about finishing this a squaw entered, carrying an "olla" of urine, of which the filthy brutes drank heartily.

I refused to believe the evidence of my senses, and asked Cushing if that were really human urine. "Why, certainly," replied he, "and here comes more of it." This time it was a large tin pailful, not less than two gallons. I was standing by the squaw as she offered this strange and abominable refreshment. She made a motion with her hand to indicate to me that it was urine, and one of the old men repeated the Spanish word *mear* (to urinate), while my sense of smell demonstrated the truth of their statements.

The dancers swallowed great draughts, smacked their lips, and, amid the roaring merriment of the spectators, remarked that it was very, very good. The clowns were now upon their mettle, each trying to surpass his neighbors in feats of nastiness. One swallowed a fragment of corn-husk, saying he thought it very good and better than bread; his *vis-á-vis* attempted to chew and gulp down a piece of filthy rag. Another expressed regret that the dance had not been held out of doors, in one of the plazas; there they could show what they could do. There they always made it a point of honor to eat the excrement of men and dogs.

For my own part, I felt satisfied with the omission, particularly as the room, stuffed with one hundred Zuñis, had become so foul and filthy as to be almost unbearable. The dance, as good luck would have it, did not last many minutes, and we soon had a chance to run into the refreshing night air.

To this outline description of a disgusting rite, I have little to add. The Zuñis, in explanation, stated that the Nehue-Cue were a Medicine Order, which held these dances from time to time to inure the stomachs of members to any kind of food, no matter how revolting. This statement may seem plausible enough when we understand that religion and medicine, among primitive races, are almost always one and the same thing, or at least so closely intertwined, that it is a matter of difficulty to decide where one begins and the other ends.

Religion, in its dramatic ceremonial, preserves, to some extent, the history of the particular race in which it dwells. Among nations of high development, miracles, moralities, and passion plays have taught, down to our own day, in object lessons, the sacred history in which the spectators believed. Some analogous purpose may have been held in view by the first organizers of the urine dance. In their early history, the Zuñis and other Pueblos suffered from constant warfare with savage antagonists and with each other. From the position of their villages, long sieges must of necessity have been sustained, in which sieges famine and disease, no doubt, were

the allies counted upon by the investing forces. We may have in this abominable dance a tradition of the extremity to which the Zuñis of the long ago were reduced at some unknown period. A similar catastrophe in the history of the Jews is intimated in 2 Kings xviii. 27; and again in Isaiah xxxvi. 12: "But Rab-shakeh said unto them: hath my master sent me to thy master, and to thee to speak these words? hath he not sent me to the men which sit on the wall, that they may *eat their own dung and drink their own piss* with you?"

As illustrative of the tenacity with which such vile ceremonial, once adopted by a sect, will adhere to it and become ingrafted upon its life, long after the motives which have suggested or commended it have vanished in oblivion, let me quote a few lines from Max Müller's "Chips from a German Workshop," "Essay upon the Parsees [i.e., Zoroastrians in India]":

> The *nirang* is the urine of a cow, ox, or she-goat, and the rubbing of it over the face and hands is the second thing a Parsee does after getting out of bed. Either before applying the *nirang* to the face and hands, or while it remains on the hands after being applied, he should not touch anything directly with his hands; but, in order to wash out the *nirang*, he either asks somebody else to pour water on his hands, or resorts to the device of taking hold of the pot through the intervention of a piece of cloth, such as a handkerchief or his *sudra*—that is, his blouse. He first pours water on his hand, then takes the pot in that hand and washes his other hand, face, and feet. — (Quoting from Dadabhai-Nadrosi's "Description of the Parsees.")

Continuing, Max Müller says:

> Strange as this process of purification may appear, it becomes perfectly disgusting when we are told that women, after childbirth, have not only to undergo this sacred ablution, but actually to drink a little of the *nirang*, and that the same rite is imposed on children at the time of their investiture with the *Sudra* and *Koshti*—the badges of the Zoroastrian faith.

Before proceeding further it may be advisable to clinch the fact that the Urine Dance of the Zuñis was not a sporadic instance, peculiar to that pueblo, or to a particular portion of that pueblo; it was a tribal rite, recognized and commended by the whole community, and entering into the ritual of all the pueblos of the Southwest.

Upon this point a few words from the author's personal journal of Nov. 24, 1881, may well be introduced to prove its existence among the Moquis—the informant, Nana-je, being a young Moqui of the strictest integrity and veracity:

In the circle I noticed Nana-je and the young Nehue-cue boy who was with us a few nights since. During a pause in the conversation I asked the young Nehue if he had been drinking any urine lately. This occasioned some laughter among the Indians; but to my surprise Nana-je spoke up and said: "I am a Nehue also. The Nehue of Zuñi are nothing to the same order among the Moquis. There the Nehue not only drink urine, as you saw done the other night, but also eat human and animal excrement. They eat it here too; but we eat all that is set before us. We have a medicine which makes us drunk like whiskey; we drink a lot of that before we commence; it makes us drunk. We don't care what happens; and nothing of that kind that we eat or drink can ever do us any harm." The Nehue-cue are to be found in all the pueblos on the Rio Grande and close to it; only there they don't do things openly.

In addition to the above, we have the testimony of Mr. Thomas V. Keam, who has lived for many years among the Moquis, and who confirms from personal observation all that has been here said.

The extracts from personal correspondence with Professor Bandelier are of special value, that gentleman having devoted years of painstaking investigation to the history of the Pueblos, and acquired a most intimate knowledge of them, based upon constant personal observation and scholarship of the highest order.

In a personal letter, dated Santa Fé, N. M., June 7, 1888, he tells, among much other most interesting information, that he saw at the Pueblo of Cochiti, on Nov. 10, 1880, "the Koshare eating their own excrement."

Have you ever, while in New Mexico, witnessed the dance of that cluster or order called the "Ko-sha-re" among the Queres, "Ko-sa-re" among the Tehuas, and "Shu-re" among the Tiguas? I have witnessed it several times; and these gentlemen, many of whom belong to the circle of my warm personal friends, display a peculiar appetite for what the human body commonly not only rejects, but also ejects. I am sorry that I did not know of your work any sooner, as else I could have given you very full descriptions of these dances. The cluster in question have a very peculiar task, inasmuch as the ripening of all kinds of fruits is at their charge, even the fruit in the mother's womb, and their rites are therefore of sickening obscenity. The swallowing of excrements is but a mild performance in comparison with what I have been obliged to see and witness. — (Letter from Professor Bandolier.)

Major Ferry, whom the author met in the office of General Robert McFeely, Acting Secretary of War, Oct. 5, 1888, stated that he was the son of the first Protestant missionary to build a church at Mackinaw, and that the Indians of the Ojibway tribe who lived in the neighborhood of that post indulged from time to time in orgies in which the drinking of urine was a feature.

Mr. Daniel W. Lord, a gentleman who was for a time associated with Mr. Frank H. Cushing in his investigations among the Zuñis of New Mexico, makes the following statement:

In June, 1888, I was a spectator of an orgy at the Zuñi pueblo in New Mexico. The ceremonial dance of that afternoon had been finished in the small plaza generally used for dances in the northwestern part of the pueblo when this supplementary rite took place. One of the Indians brought into the plaza the excrement to be employed, and it was passed from hand to hand and eaten. Those taking part in the ceremony were few in number, certainly not more than eight or ten. They drank urine from a large shallow bowl, and meanwhile kept up a running fire of comments and exclamations among themselves, as if urging one another to drink heartily, which indeed they did. At last one of those taking part was made sick, and vomited after the ceremony was over. The inhabitants of the pueblo upon the housetops overlooking the plaza were interested spectators of the scene. Some of the sallies of the actors were received with laughter, and others with signs of disgust and repugnance, but not of disapprobation. The ceremony was not repeated, to my knowledge, during my stay at the pueblo, which continued till July, 1889. — (Personal letter to Captain Bourke.)

HUMAN ORDURE EATEN BY EAST INDIAN FANATICS

Speaking of the remnants of the Hindu sect of the Aghozis, an English writer observes:

> In proof of their indifference to worldly objects they eat and drink whatever is given to them, even ordure and carrion. They smear their bodies also with excrement, and carry it about with them in a wooden cup, or skull, either to swallow it, if by so doing they can get a few pice, or to throw it upon the persons or into the houses of those who refuse to comply with their demands. — ("Religious Sects of the Hindus," in "Asiatic Researches.")

Another writer confirms the above. The Abbé Dubois says that the Gurus, or Indian priests, sometimes, as a mark of favor, present to their disciples "the water in which they had washed their feet, which is preserved and sometimes drunk by those who receive it" (Dubois, "People of India"). This practice, he tells us, is general among the sectaries of Siva, and is not uncommon with many of the Vishnuites in regard to their vashtuma. "Neither is it the most disgusting of the practices that prevail in that sect of fanatics, as they are under the reproach of eating as a hallowed morsel the very ordure that proceeds from their Gurus, and swallowing the water with which they have rinsed their mouths or washed their faces, with many other practices equally revolting to nature" (idem, p. 71).

Again, on page 331, Dubois alludes to the Gymnosophists "or naked Samyasis of India... eating human excrement, without showing the slightest symptom of disgust."

As bearing not unremotely upon this point, the author wishes to say that in his personal notes and memoranda can be found references to one of the medicine-men of the Sioux who assured his admirers that everything about him was "medicine," even his excrement, which could be transmuted into copper cartridges.

"I was informed that vast numbers of Shordrus drank the water in which a Brahmin has dipped his foot, and abstain from food in the morning till this ceremony be over. Some persons do this every day.... Persons may be seen carrying a small quantity of water in a cup and entreating the first Brahmin they see to put his toe in it.... Some persons keep water thus sanctified in their houses." — (Ward, quoted by Southey in his "Commonplace Book.")

THE STERCORANISTES

That Christian polemics have not been entirely free from such ideas may be shown satisfactorily to any one having the leisure to examine the various phases of the discussion upon the doctrine of the Eucharist.

> **"They smear their bodies also with excrement, and carry it about with them in a wooden cup, or skull, either to swallow it, if by so doing they can get a few pice, or to throw it upon the persons or into the houses of those who refuse to comply with their demands."**

The word "stercoranistes," or "stercorarians," is not to be found in the last edition of the *Encyclopaedia Britannica*; but in the edition of 1841 the definition of the word is as follows: "Stercorarians, or Stercoranistes, formed from *stercus*, 'dung,' a name which those of the Romish church originally gave to such as held that the host was liable to digestion and all its consequences, like other food."

The dispute upon "Stercoranisme" began in 831, upon the appearance of a theological treatise by a monk named Paschasius Radbert. — (See the "Institutes of Ecclesiastical History," John Lawrence von Mosheim.)

> "The grossly sensual conception of the presence of the Lord's body in the sacrament, according to which that body is eaten, digested, and evacuated like ordinary food, is of ancient standing, though not found in Origen, nor perhaps in Rhabanus Maurus. It certainly originated with a class of false teachers contemporary with or earlier than Rhabanus Maurus, whom Paschasius Radbert condemns." He does not, however, apply the term "Stercoranistes" to his opponents. Cardinal Humbert is the first to so employ the word. This use

was in a polemic against Nicetas Pectoratus, written in support of Azymitism, etc. From this source the word was adopted into common usage. — (McClintock and Strong, Cyclop. of Biblical, Theological, and Ecclesiastical Literature.)

Brand, in his "Encyclopaedia of Science, Literature, and Art," article "Stercoranism," says: "A nickname which seems to have been applied in the Western churches in the fifth and sixth centuries to those who held the opinion that a change took place in the consecrated elements, so as to render the divine body subject to the act of digestion."

> **The inference is that the excreta of Christ were believed, as in many other instances, to have the character of a panacea, as well as generally miraculous properties.**

The same ideas obtained among the illiterate as a matter of course.

The First Gospel of the Infancy of Jesus Christ seems to have been received by the Gnostics of the second century as canonical, and accepted in the same sense by Eusebius, Athanasius, Chrysostom, and others of the Fathers and writers of the Church. Sozomen was told by travelers in Egypt that they had heard in that country of the miracles performed by the water in which the infant Jesus had been washed. According to Ahmed ben Idris, this gospel was used in parts of the East in common with the other gospels; while Ocobius de Castro asserts that in many churches of Asia and Africa it was recited exclusively. But, on the other hand, all the apocrypha were condemned by Pope Gelasius in the fifth century; and this interdict was not repealed until the time of Paul IV in the sixteenth century.

In the following extracts it will be noted that the miracles recorded were wrought either by the swaddling-clothes themselves or by the water in which they had been cleansed; and the inference is that the excreta of Christ were believed, as in many other instances, to have the character of a panacea, as well as generally miraculous properties.

The Madonna gave one of the swaddling clothes of Christ to the Wise Men of the East who visited him; they took it home, "and having, according to the custom of their country, made a fire, they worshipped it…. And casting the swaddling cloth into the fire, the fire took it and kept it" (1 Inf. iii. 6, 7).

We read of the Finnish deity Wainemoinen that "the sweat which dropped from his body was a balm for all diseases." The very same virtues were possessed by the sweat of the Egyptian god Ra ("Chaldean Magic," Lenormant).

On arrival in Egypt after the Flight—

When the Lady Saint Mary had washed the swaddling clothes of the Lord Christ and hanged them out to dry upon a post…a certain boy…possessed with the devil, took down one of them and put it upon his head. And presently the devils began to come out of his mouth and fly away in the shape of crows and serpents. And from this time the boy was healed by the power of the Lord Christ. — (1 Inf. iv. 15, 16, 17.)

On the return journey from Egypt, Christ had healed by a kiss a lady whom cursed Satan…had leaped upon…in the form of a serpent. On the morrow, the same woman brought perfumed water to wash the Lord Jesus; when she had washed him, she preserved the water. And there was a girl whose body was white with leprosy, who being sprinkled with this water was instantly cleansed from her leprosy. — (1 Inf. vi. 16, 17).

There is another example of exactly the same kind in 1 Inf. vi. 34. See, again, 1 Inf. ix. 1, 4, 5, 9; x. 2, 3; xii. 4, 5, 6. "And in Matarea the Lord Jesus caused a well to spring forth, in which Saint Mary washed his coat. And a balsam is produced or grown in that country from the sweat which ran down there from the Lord Jesus." — (Gospel of the Infancy, viii.)

An offshoot of the Khlysti, known as the "Shakouni," or Jumpers, openly professed debauchery and libertinism to excess… Others of their rites are abject and disgusting; their chief is the living Christ, and their communion consists in embracing his body—ordinary disciples may kiss his hand or foot; to those of a more fervent piety, he offers his tongue. — ("The Russian Church and the Russian Dissent," Alfred F. Heard.)

COW DUNG AND COW URINE IN RELIGION

The sacrificial value of cow dung and cow urine throughout India and Tibet is much greater than the reader might be led to infer from the brief citation already noted from Max Müller.

"Hindu merchants in Bokhara now lament loudly at the sight of a piece of cow's flesh, and at the same time mix with their food, that it may do them good, the urine of a sacred cow, kept in that place." — (Erman, "Siberia.")

Picart narrates that the Brahmins fed grain to a sacred cow, and afterward searched in the ordure for the sacred grains, which they picked out whole, drying and administering them to the sick, not merely as a medicine, but as a sacred thing.

Not only among the people of the lowlands, but among those of the foot-hills of the Himalayas as well, do these rites find place; "the very dung of the cow is eaten as an atonement for sin, and its urine is used in worship." — ("Notes on the Hill Tribes of the Neilgherries," Short.)

"The greatest, or, at any rate, the most convenient of all purifiers is the urine of a cow;... Images are sprinkled with it. No man of any pretensions to piety or cleanliness would pass a cow in the act of staling [i.e., urinating] without receiving the holy stream in his hand and sipping a few drops.... If the animal be retentive, a pious expectant will impatiently apply his finger, and by judicious tickling excite the grateful flow." — (Moor's "Hindu Pantheon.")

Speaking of the sacrifice called Poojah, Maurice says: "The Brahman prepares a place, which is purified with dried cow-dung, with which the pavement is spread, and the room is sprinkled with the urine of the same animal." — (Maurice, "Indian Antiquities.")

"As in India, so in Persia, the urine of the cow is used in ceremonies of purification, during which it is drunk." — ("Zoölogical Mythology," Angelo de Gubernatis.)

Dubois, in his chapter "Restoration to the Caste," says that a Hindu penitent "must drink the *panchakaryam*—a word which literally signifies the five things, namely, milk, butter, curd, dung, and urine, all mixed together." And he adds:

The urine of the cow is held to be the most efficacious of any for purifying all imaginable uncleanness. I have often seen the superstitious Hindu accompanying these animals when in the pasture, and watching the moment for receiving the urine as it fell, in vessels which he had brought for the purpose, to carry it home in a fresh state; or, catching it in the hollow of his hand, to bedew his face and all his body. When so used it removes all external impurity, and when taken internally, which is very common, it cleanses all within. — (Abbé Dubois, "People of India.")

Very frequently the excrement is first reduced to ashes. The monks of Chivem, called Pandarones, smear their faces, breasts, and arms with the ashes of cow dung; they run through the streets demanding alms, very much as the Zuñi actors demanded a feast, and chant the praises of Chivem, while they carry a bundle of peacock feathers in the hand, and wear the *lingam* at the neck.

"The Samaritans, in return, called the temple of Jerusalem 'the house of dung.'"

THE TRIBES HAD not many feelings in common when they came to be writers and told us what they thought of each other. As a rule, they bitterly reviled each other's gods and temples.... Judeans called the Samaritan temple, where calves and bulls were holy, in a word of Greek derivation, 'Pelethos Naos,' 'the dung-hill temple.'... The Samaritans, in return, called the temple of Jerusalem 'the house of dung.'" — ("Rivers of Life," Forlong.)

Commentators would be justified in believing that these terms preserve the fact of there having been in these places of worship the same veneration for dung that is to be found to this day among the peoples of the East Indies.

In another place Dulaure calls attention to the similar use among the Hebrews of the ashes of the dung of the red heifer as an expiatory sacrifice.[1]

In one of the Hindu fasts the devotee adopts these disgusting excreta as his food. On the fourth day, "his disgusting beverage is the urine of the cow; the fifth, the excrement of that holy animal is his allotted food." — (Maurice, "Indian Antiquities.")

"I do not think that you can lay weight on the fact that in Israel, when a victim was entirely burned, the dung was not exempted from the fire. I think this only means that the victim was not cleared of offal, as in sacrifices that were eaten." — (Personal letter from Prof. W. Robertson Smith.)

De Gubernatis speaks of "the superstitious Hindoo custom of purifying one's self by means of the excrement of a cow. The same custom passed into Persia; and the Kharda Avesta has preserved the formula to be recited by the devotee while he holds in his hand the urine of an ox or cow, preparatory to washing his face with it: 'Destroyed, destroyed, be the Demon Ahriman, whose actions and works are cursed.'" — ("Zoölogical Mythology." De Gubernatis.)

"Forty years ago, during a stay of three months in Bombay, I saw frequently cows wandering in the streets, and Hindu devotees bowing, and lifting up the tails of the cows, rubbing the wombs of the aforesaid with the right hand, and afterwards rubbing their own faces with it." — (Personal letter from Captain Henri Jouan, French Navy.)

Almost identical information was communicated by General J. J. Dana, U.S. Army, who, in the neighborhood of Calcutta, over forty years ago, had seen Hindu devotees besmeared from head to foot with human excrement.

Among the superstitious practices of the Greeks, Plutarch mentions "rolling themselves in dung-hills." ("Morals," Goodwin's trans.) Plutarch also mentions "foul expiations," "vile methods of purgation," "bemirings at the temple," and speaks of "penitents wrapped up in foul and nasty rags," or "rolling naked in the mire," "vile and abject adorations."

This veneration for the excrement of the cow is to be found among other races. The Hottentots "besmear their bodies with fat and other greasy substances over which they rub cow-dung, fat and similar substances." — (Thurnberg's "Account of the Cape of Good Hope.")

"Every idea and thought of the Dinka [a Sudanese tribe] is how to acquire and maintain cattle; a certain kind of reverence would seem to be paid them; even their offal is considered of high importance. The dung, which is burnt to ashes for sleeping in and for smearing their persons, and the urine, which is used for washing and as a substitute for salt, are their daily requisites."— (Schweinfurth, "Heart of Africa.")

> **The Romans and Egyptians went farther than this; they had gods of excrement, whose special function was the care of latrines and those who frequented them.**

EXCREMENT GODS OF THE ROMANS AND EGYPTIANS

The Romans and Egyptians went farther than this; they had gods of excrement, whose special function was the care of latrines and those who frequented them. Torquemada, a Spanish author of high repute, expresses this in very plain language:

> I assert that they used *to adore* (as St. Clement writes to St. James the Less) stinking and filthy privies and water-closets; and, what is viler and yet more abominable, and an occasion for our tears and not to be borne with or so much as mentioned by name, they adored the noise and wind of the stomach when it expels from itself any cold or flatulence; and other things of the same kind, which, according to the same saint, it would be a shame to name or describe.

In the preceding lines Torquemada refers to the Egyptians only, but his language is almost the same when speaking of the Romans. The Roman goddess was called Cloacina. She was one of the first of the Roman deities, and is believed to have been named by Romulus himself. Under her charge were the various cloacae, sewers, privies, etc., of the Eternal City.

"Colatina, alias Clocina, was goddess of the stools, the jakes, and the privy, to whom, as to every of the rest, there was a peculiar temple edified." — (Reginald Scot, "Discovery of Witchcraft.")

The devotee presented his naked posterior before the altar and relieved his entrails, making an offering to the idol of the foul emanations.

The Romans "had a god of ordure named Stercutius; one for other conveniences, Crepitus; a goddess for the common sewers, Cloacina." — (Banier, "Mythology.")

"Sterculius was one of the surnames given to Saturn because he was the first that had laid dung upon lands to make them fertile." — (Idem)

DULAURE QUOTES FROM a number of authorities to show that the Israelites and Moabites had the same ridiculous and disgusting ceremonial in their worship of Bel-phegor. The devotee presented his naked posterior before the altar and relieved his entrails, making an offering to the idol of the foul emanations.[2] Dung gods are also mentioned as having been known to the chosen people during the time of their idolatry.[3]

Mr. John Frazer, LL.D., describing the ceremony of initiation, known to the Australians as the "Bora," and which he defines to be "certain ceremonies of initiation through which a youth passes when he reaches the age of puberty to qualify him for a place among the men of the tribe and for the privileges of manhood. By these ceremonies he is made acquainted with his father's gods, the mythical lore of the tribe and the duties required of him as a man.... The whole is under the tutelage of a high spirit called 'Dharamoolun.'... But, present at these ceremonies, although having no share in them, is an evil spirit called 'Gunungdhukhya,' 'eater of excrement,' whom the blacks greatly dread." Compare this word "Gunungdhukhya," with the Sanskrit root-word "Gu," "excrement;" "Dhuk" is the Australian "to eat." — (Personal letter from John Frazer, Esq., LL.D. Continuing his remarks upon the subject of the evil spirit "Gunungdhukhya," he says: "This being is certainly supposed to eat ordure; and such is the meaning of his name.")

"BY THE MAHOMETAN [Muslim] law, the body becomes unclean after each evacuation...both greater and smaller...requires an ablution, according to circumstances.... If a drop of urine touches the clothes, they must be washed." For fear that their garments have been so defiled, "the Bokhariots frequently repeat their prayers stark naked."... The matter of cleaning the body after an evacuation of any kind is defined by religious ritual. "The law commands 'Istindjah' (removal), 'istinkah' (ablution), and 'istibra' (drying,)"—i.e., a small clod of earth is first used for the local cleansing [i.e., wiping the ass], then water at least twice, and finally a piece of linen a yard in length.... In Turkey, Arabia, and Persia all are necessary, and pious men carry several clods of earth for the purpose in their turbans. "These acts of purification are also carried on quite publicly in the bazaars, from a desire to make a parade of their consistent piety." Vambéry saw "a teacher give to his pupils, boys and girls, instruction in the handling of the clod of earth, and so forth, by way of experiment." — ("Sketches of Central Asia," Arminius Vambéry.)

Moslems urinate sitting down on their heels; "for a spray of urine would make hair and clothes ceremonially impure.... After urining, the Moslem wipes the os penis [i.e., the urethral hole] with one to three bits of stone, clay, or a handful of earth, and he must perform Wuzu before he can pray. Tournefort ("Voyage au Levant") tells a pleasant story about certain Christians at Constantinople who powdered with poivre d'Inde the stones in a wall where the Moslems were in the habit of rubbing the os penis by way of wiping." — (Burton, "Arabian Nights." Again, in footnote to p. 229, vol. iii., he says, "Scrupulous Moslems scratch the ground in front of their feet with a stick, to prevent spraying and consequent defilement.")

Marco Polo, in speaking of the Brahmins, says, "They ease themselves in the sands, and then disperse it, hither and thither, lest it should breed worms, which might die for want of food." — ("Travels," in Pinkerton.)

Speaking of the Mahometans, Tournefort says,

When they make water, they squat down like women, for fear some drops of urine should fall into their breeches. To prevent this evil, they squeeze the part very carefully, and rub the head of it against the wall; and one may see the stones worn in several places by this custom. To make themselves sport, the Christians smear the stones sometimes with Indian pepper and the root called "Calf's-Foot," or some other hot plants, which frequently causes an inflammation in such as happen to use the Stone. As the pain is very smart, the poor Turks commonly run for a cure to those very Christian surgeons who were the authors of all the mischief. They never fail to tell them it is a very dangerous case, and that they should be obliged, perhaps, to make an amputation. The Turks, on the contrary, protest and swear that they have had no communication with any sort of woman that could be suspected. In short, they wrap up the suffering part in a Linen dipped in Oxicrat tinctured with a little Bole-Armenic; and this they sell them as a great specifick for this kind of Mischief. — (Tournefort, "A Voyage to the Levant.")

"The Rabbinical Jews believed that every privy was the abode of an unclean spirit of this kind" (i.e., an excrement-eating god).

"Some of their doctors believe Circumcision was not taken from the Jews, but only for the better observing the Precept of Cleanness, by which they are forbidden to let any Urine fall upon their flesh. And it is certain that some drops are always apt to hang upon the Praeputium [i.e., foreskin], especially among the Arabians, with whom that skin is naturally much longer than in other men." — (Idem.)

"AND THOU SHALT have a paddle upon thy weapon; and it shall be, when thou wilt ease thyself abroad, thou shalt dig therewith, and shalt turn back and cover that which cometh from thee.

"For the Lord, thy God, walketh in the midst of thy camp, to deliver thee and to give up thine enemies before thee; therefore shall thy camp be holy; that he see no unclean thing in thee, and turn away from thee." — (Deuteronomy xxiii.)

Speaking of the Essenes, Josephus informs us:

On the seventh day [i.e., the Sabbath]...they will not even remove any vessel out of its place, nor perform the most pressing necessities of nature. Nay, on other days they dig a small pit, a foot deep, with a paddle (which kind of hatchet is given them when they first are admitted among them), and, covering themselves round with their garment, that they may not affront the divine rays of light, they ease themselves into that pit. After which they put the earth that was dug out again into that pit.

And even this they do only in the most lonesome places, which they choose for this purpose. And it is a rule with them to wash themselves afterwards, as if it were a defilement. — ("Wars of the Jews.")

"The Rabbinical Jews believed that every privy was the abode of an unclean spirit of this kind" (i.e., an excrement-eating god), "which could be inhaled with the breath, and descending into the lower parts of the body, lodge there, and thus like the Bhutas of India, bring suffering and disease." (Personal letter from John Frazer, Esq., LL.D.)

In descriptions of Jerusalem, we read of the "Dung Gate," by or through which, all the fecal matter of the city had to be carried. — (See Harington, "Ajax.")

ORDURE IN SMOKING

Among all the observances of the every-day life of the American aborigines, none is so distinctly complicated with the religious idea as smoking; therefore, should the use of excrement, human or animal, be detected in this connection, full play should be given to the suspicion that a hidden meaning attaches to the ceremony. This would appear to be the view entertained by the indefatigable missionary, De Smet, who records such a custom among the Flatheads and Crows in 1846: "To render the odor of the pacific incense agreeable to their gods it is necessary that the tobacco and the herb (skwiltz), the usual ingredients, should be mixed with a small quantity of buffalo dung." — (Father De Smet, "Oregon Missions.")

The Sioux, Cheyennes, Arapahoes, and others of the plains tribes, to whom the buffalo is a god, have the same or an almost similar custom.

AMONG SOME OF the Australian tribes is found a potent deity named "Pund-jel," whom Mr. Andrew Lang thinks may be the Eagle-Hawk. "As a punisher of wicked people, Pund-jel was once moved to drown the world, and this he did by a flood which he produced (as Dr. Brown says of another affair) by a familiar Gulliverian application of hydraulics [i.e., urination]." — ("Myth, Rit., and Relig.," Lang.)

Maurice cites five meritorious kinds of suicide, in the second of which the Hindu devotee is described as "covering himself with cow-dung, setting it on fire, and consuming himself therein." — (Maurice, "Indian Antiquities.")

MYTHS

"All peoples have invented myths to explain why they observed certain customs." — ("The Golden Bough.")

"Myth changes while custom remains constant; men continue to do what their fathers did before them, though the reasons on which their fathers acted have long been forgotten. The history of religion is a long attempt to reconcile old custom with new reason; to find a sound theory for an absurd practice." — (Idem.)

The Creation Myth of the Australians relates that the god Bund-jil created the ocean by urinating for many days upon the orb of the earth. The natives say that the god being angry "Bullarto Bulgo" upon the earth. Bullarto Bulgo indicates a great flow of urine.

In the cosmogonical myths of the islanders of Kadiack, it is related that the first woman, "by making water, produced seas." — (Lisiansky, "Voy. round the World.")

In the mythic lore of the Hindus, the god Utanka sets out on a journey, protected by Indras. "On his way, he meets a gigantic bull, and a horseman who bids him, if he would succeed, eat the excrement of the bull; he does so, rinsing his mouth afterwards." — ("Zoöl Mythol." De Gubernatis.)

Speaking of the god "Aidowedo," the serpent in the Rainbow as believed by the Negroes of Guinea, Father Baudin says: "He who finds the excrement of this serpent is rich forever, for with this talisman he can change grains of corn into shells which pass for money." ("Fetishism," Rev. F. Baudin.) He goes on to narrate a very amusing tale to the effect that the Negroes got the idea that a prism in his possession gave him the power to bring the Rainbow down into his room at will, and that he could obtain unlimited quantities of the precious excrement.

Another myth of the foolish [Kamtchatkan] god "Kutka" represents him as falling in love with his own excrement and wooing it as his bride; he takes it home in his sleigh, puts it in his bed, and is only restored to a sense of his absurd position by the vile smell.

The people of Kamtchatka believed that rain was the urine of Billutschi, one of their gods, and of his genii; but, after this god has urinated enough, he puts on a new dress in the form of a sack, and provided with fringes of red seal hair, and various colored strips of leather. These represent the origins of the Rainbow.

1. "They shall burn in the fire their dung." — (Levit. xvi. 27.) "Her blood with her dung shall he burn." — (Numbers xix. 5.)

2. Philo says the devotee of Baal-Peor presented to the idol all the outward orifices of the body. Another authority says that the worshipper not only presented all these to the idol, but that the emanations or excretions were also presented—tears from the eyes, wax from the ears, pus from the nose, saliva from the mouth, and urine and dejecta from the lower openings. This was the god to which the Jews joined themselves; and these, in all probability, were the ceremonies they practised in his worship. — (Robert Allen Campbell, Phallic Worship.)

Still another authority says the worshipper, presenting his bare posterior to the altar, relieved his bowels, and offered the result to the idol: *"Eo quod distendebant coram illo foramen podicis et stercus offerebaut."* — (Hargrave Jennings, Phallicism, quoting Rabbi Solomon Jarchi, in his Commentary on Numbers xxv.)

These two citations go to show that the worshipper intended making not a merely ceremonial offering of flatulence, but an actual oblation of excrement, such as has been stated, was placed upon the altars of their near neighbors, the Assyrians, in the devotions tendered their Venus.

3. "Ye have seen dung gods, wood and stone." — (Deut. xxix. 17. See Gulden's Concordance, Articles "Dung" and "Dungy," but no light is thrown upon the expression.)

"And ye have seen their abominations and their idols (detestable things), wood and stone, silver and gold, which were among them." — (Lange's Commentary on Deuteronomy. But in footnote one reads: "Margin—dungy gods from the shape of the ordure, literally thin clods or balls, or that which can be rolled about. —A. G.")

Benjamin Radford

LEGION'S LEGACY

POSSESSION AND EXORCISM

And Jesus asked him, What is thy name?
And [the demon] answered, saying,
My name is Legion; for we are many.
　　　—Mark 5:9 (KJV)

MOST RELIGIOUS DOCTRINES hold that evil lurks in the world, in the form of demons or devils who attempt to lure, tempt, and trick humans in their unholy mission. You'd think that supernatural entities would find countless opportunities for executing mayhem and evil on their own, but apparently that is not the case. For instance, if demons were really interested in causing death and destruction, all they'd have to do is appear in a busy airport's air traffic control tower. Or bring back the black plague. Or simply launch one of the many nuclear missiles that countries around the world have aimed at each other.

Nasties such as demons and devils are assumed to need (or benefit from) a human agent in this quest. For some reason, these agents of evil are too lazy to do their jobs and instead have to rely on us temptable, fallible humans. They apparently can't just ask us nicely—they have to actually take over (possess) our minds and bodies to affect the earthly realm. That's where possessions and exorcisms come into the picture, where the mythological meets the material. But of course we live in the real world, seemingly devoid of demons and devils except in our imaginations, religious texts, and fictions. Demons and devils are ambiguous, metaphorical entities. According to scriptures, we can't identify them directly (the horns, tails, and pitchforks are passé). But, like false prophets, we can know them by their fruits. And there are lots of fruits out there.

> **You'd think that supernatural entities would find countless opportunities for executing mayhem and evil on their own, but apparently that is not the case.**

Most religions claim that humans can be possessed by demonic spirits and offer remedies to address this inconvenience. The Bible recounts at least six instances of Jesus casting out demons, while Voodoo/Vodou and Catholicism prescribe elaborate rituals and cleansings to remove even stubborn spiritual stains. Christianity in particular has an odd and longstanding obsession with bodily harm and abuse. Its symbol is a medieval torture device; as the film The Passion of the Christ shows, a high point of Christian theology is the Savior's bloody abuse and torture. There are even suggestions of cannibalism in the rites of eating Christ's flesh and drinking his blood. It is little wonder, then, that Catholicism is one of the richest sources of ideas about guilt, redemption, and possession.

> **There are hundreds of Vatican-sanctioned exorcists (three to four hundred in Italy, fifteen in the United States, and a few-dozen more around the world), with more being trained every day.**

EXPLAINING EXORCISM AND POSSESSION

While many Americans likely think of exorcisms as relics of the Dark Ages, exorcisms continue to be performed, often on people who are emotionally and mentally disturbed. Whether those undergoing the exorcism are truly possessed by spirits or demons is another matter entirely. Exorcisms are done on people of strong religious faith. To the extent that exorcisms "work," it is primarily due to the power of suggestion and the placebo effect. If you believe you are possessed, and that a given ritual will cleanse you, then it just might.

There are hundreds of Vatican-sanctioned exorcists (three to four hundred in Italy, fifteen in the United States, and a few-dozen more around the world), with more being trained every day. And one does not need Rome's imprimatur to cast out evil spirits; hundreds more self-styled exorcists roam America and the world supposedly helping people cleanse themselves. In researching his book *American Exorcism: Expelling Demons in the Land of Plenty*, Michael Cuneo (a sociology professor at Fordham, a Catholic university) found no reason to think that anything supernatural occurs during exorcisms. After attending fifty exorcisms, Cuneo is unequivocal about the fact that he saw nothing supernatural—and certainly nothing remotely resembling the remarkable events depicted in *The Exorcist*. No spinning heads, levitation, or poltergeists were on display, though many involved some cursing, spitting, and vomiting for good measure. While some people claim that they have seen seemingly supernatural phenomena afoot (such as levitation, speaking in unknown languages, or climbing walls), not a single one of these instances has been documented or proven.

Some researchers, such as Canadian psychologist Barry Beyerstein, have concluded that three brain syndromes probably helped create ancient ideas about possession: epilepsy, Tourette's Syndrome, and migraine. All three can trigger mystical visions and feelings of transcendence (leaving the body) and being possessed by otherworldly forces. Epileptic seizures and Tourette's in particular can make the sufferer appear possessed (with uncontrollable seizures and unintelligible shouts), and in fact many symptoms closely match depictions in the infamous fifteenth-century witch-finding manual *Malleus Maleficarum*.

> **Epileptic seizures and Tourette's in particular can make the sufferer appear possessed (with uncontrollable seizures and unintelligible shouts), and in fact many symptoms closely match depictions in the infamous fifteenth-century witch-finding manual *Malleus Maleficarum*.**

The Vatican accepts only a small percentage of demonic possessions as "authentic," which of course suggests that there are a lot of unauthentic cases of possession out there. The Vatican issued official guidelines on exorcism in 1614, revising them in 1999. According to the Vatican, Pope John Paul II himself performed at least three exorcisms, in 1978, 1982, and 2000. And how do you know if you or a loved one is possessed? Well, according to the US Conference of Catholic Bishops, if you have an aversion to holy water or crosses, you might be possessed. If you get a rash when you enter a church, you just might need an exorcist (if you just get bored in church, you're normal). If you exhibit superhuman strength (except when lifting a small car off a trapped child), you may be drawing your powers from the demonic dark realms. And if you suddenly are able to speak in strange languages (such as Aramaic or Esperanto), that too could be a sign that a demonic polyglot has got ahold of you. This is only a partial list, and of course might include anything from spitting to depression to excessive masturbation (whatever "excessive" is for you).

If your possession is authenticated by someone claiming to be a priest or an exorcist, things might get interesting. Exorcisms take a wide variety of forms, including whipping and torture. During the Catholic exorcism ritual, you'll be sprinkled with holy water while the exorcist reads a few passages from the Bible. The priest may show you his "cross," which you may be asked to inspect or even kiss. He will say, "God please take care of this person and dismiss the demon," though that doesn't always work and more extreme measures may be called for. If you're smart (or have any doubt at all that you were in fact possessed), this is a good time to assure the exorcist that the demon is gone, everything will be fine, and he doesn't really need to go any further. If the exorcist believes you, he will stop and everyone can calm down and go home; if instead he believes that the demon inside you is trying to trick him, you may be in for a very long night.

While cases of possession were quite rare up until the 1970s, exorcisms became more common in the last three decades of the last millennium. In a 2005 interview with *People* magazine, evangelical minister Rev. Bob Larson (who claims to perform an average of one exorcism each day) rather predictably attributed the increase in exorcisms to moral decay in society. There is, however, a much more likely (and quantifiable) explanation: Exorcisms arose in the popular culture.

POSSESSION IN POP CULTURE

The public is most familiar with possession and exorcism not through personal experience, but instead through commercial entertainment. Hundreds of truly horrific films explore the battle between good and evil, usually with plenty of gore and half-baked theological twaddle.

That was how the *Amityville Horror* story came about, in fact. The story behind the film began on November 13, 1974, when six members of an Amityville, New York, family were killed. The parents, Ronald and Louise DeFeo, were shot, along with two sons and two daughters, in bed while they slept. The sole remaining family member, Ronald Jr. ("Butch"), was arrested for the crime. With the family dead (and Butch unlikely to inherit the place), the house went up for sale. The horrific nature of the massacre unnerved the otherwise quiet Long Island neighborhood, though no supernatural activity was associated with the house at 112 Ocean Avenue.

The following year, a new family, the Lutzes, moved into the house. George and Kathy Lutz, along with their three children, said that shortly after moving in, the six-bedroom abode became a hell-house. It seemed that perhaps the demons that drove Butch to slaughter his family were not in his head but in the house. The Lutzes told of many scary things happening in the house which—if true—would prompt most intelligent people to vacate, leave a nasty message with the real-estate agent, and put the place back on the market. An unseen force ripped doors from hinges and slammed cabinets closed. Noxious green slime oozed from the ceilings. A biblical-scale swarm of insects attacked the family. A demonic face with glowing red eyes peered into their house at night, leaving cloven-hoofed footprints in the morning snow. A priest called upon to bless the house was driven back with painful blisters on his hands. And so on. Still, the Lutzes stayed, long enough to collaborate with a novelist about their experiences. Several self-styled ghost-hunters, psychics, and demon experts arrived and verified the existence of the demons.

The truth behind *The Amityville Horror* was finally revealed when Butch DeFeo's lawyer, William Weber, admitted that he, along with the Lutzes, "created this horror story over many bottles of wine." The house was never really haunted; the horrific experiences were simply made up. While the Lutzes profited handsomely from the book and film rights to their story, Weber had planned to use the haunting to gain a new trial for his client, creatively suggesting that perhaps the demons and devils the Lutzes experiences had possessed Butch DeFeo and forced him to kill his family. The Lutzes also later admitted that virtually everything they had said about the haunting—and everything in *The Amityville Horror*—was pure fiction. Not only were the demons not in the house, they weren't in DeFeo's mind either.

The "demon defense" is rarely successful; indeed, the jury saw right through Weber's story, and Butch DeFeo was convicted. But it does come up occasionally, especially in cases where there is overwhelming evidence of guilt and a pouty "I didn't do it" just won't fly.

The Lutzes also later admitted that virtually everything they had said about the haunting—and everything in *The Amityville Horror*—was pure fiction.

THE EXORCIST STORY

The greatest pop-culture contribution to the public's perception of exorcism is of course *The Exorcist*. In the weeks after the film came out in 1974, a Boston Catholic center began receiving daily requests for exorcisms. The script was written by William Peter Blatty, adapted from his bestselling 1971 novel of the same name. Blatty described the inspiration for the film as an August 20, 1949, *Washington Post* article he'd read when he was at Georgetown University. The piece told of a fourteen-year-old boy from nearby Mount Rainier, Maryland, who had undergone an exorcism. Because this was before Fox News and *Inside Edition*, Blatty assumed it was an accurate account.

Many of the myths surrounding *The Exorcist* film and "real story" came about because of Blatty's breathless press releases. Blatty had a career and book to promote and was not above embellishing the story with partly (and wholly) fictional elements. Investigative journalist Mark Opsasnick investigated the case and concluded that the Mount Rainier story, as popularly held (and which Blatty used as a basis for the novel), couldn't be true. For one thing, the family that occupied the home at the time the alleged possession took place didn't have a boy there, demon-possessed or otherwise: The occupants were childless. Neighbors denied that anything horrific or supernatural had ever occurred

there. There was, however, an actual exorcism done (not in Mount Rainier but in Garden City, Maryland), though virtually all of the gory and sensational details were embellished or made up. Simple spitting became Technicolor, projectile vomiting; (normal) shaking of a bed became thunderous quaking and levitation; the boy's low growl became a gravelly, Satanic voice. And so on.

Michael Cuneo credits Blatty and *The Exorcist* with much of the modern-day interest in exorcism:

> Over the course of the twentieth century the popular cultural industry, with its endless run of movies, books, and digital delights, has gained a pervasive influence over the national consciousness. It has...attained an enormous capacity for shaping everyday beliefs and behaviors.... When Hollywood and its allies put out the Word, somebody's guaranteed to be listening.

As for historical accuracy, Cuneo characterizes Blatty's work as a massive structure of fantasy resting on a flimsy foundation of a priest's diary. *The Exorcist* story gets less and less impressive the farther away it gets from the film that made it famous.

Simple spitting became Technicolor, projectile vomiting; (normal) shaking of a bed became thunderous quaking and levitation; the boy's low growl became a gravelly, Satanic voice.

THE DEVIL MADE ME DO IT

If the best-known cases of possession and exorcism were mostly or entirely fictional, what about the real evil that is known to be done in this world? Why do some people claim to be possessed?

One answer is that most people want to be thought kindly of. We don't like to be caught doing bad things, whether it's embezzling the orphan fund, stealing a pack of gum, or banging the babysitter. We like to think of ourselves as good people who did bad, either because of a lapse of judgment ("youthful indiscretions," a favorite political excuse, is often used by presidents and other politicians to dodge questions about drug use and philandering) or, better yet, some overpowering outside influence. Like, you know—Satan and his demonic minions.

Demonic possession is a ready-made excuse paved by millennia of religious doctrine. Millions of fundamentalist Christians (and others) believe that Satan is not just some abstract symbol of evil, some storybook boogeyman, but instead a real entity actively creating evil in the world and tempting lost souls. Some even believe that all humans are basically good, and that any act of evil is therefore evidence of the influence of dark forces.

Yet even the craziest criminal has a sense of proportion; there's no use in invoking the "devil made me do it" defense unless you're dimple-deep in dookie. Speeding tickets, for example, are unlikely to be forgiven unless you can really convince the cop that your right foot had a mind of its own. No, etiquette dictates that you save the Ultimate Excuse for the big lapses in judgment—like killing a bunch of people or dismembering your child. Otherwise it just looks like you're grasping at straws and making shit up.

BELIEF AND POSSESSION

The tragic irony of possession is that in many cases evil is committed not by demons or devils but by those who believe in their reality. The only people who become "possessed" by demons or devils are those with a pre-existing belief in the reality of demons and devils. Voodoo curses hold no power over Mormons, and UFO skeptics have never been abducted or anally probed by inquisitive extraterrestrials. Tragically, there are many real-life examples of what happens when people believe in demons and devils.

• In September 2005, a man driving along the Las Vegas strip suddenly (and intentionally) steered his car onto a crowded sidewalk, killing two people and injuring twelve others. Stephen Ressa, the driver, was arrested and explained that he wanted to kill the people because they were staring at him "like they were demons."

• On January 19, 2004, Valerie Carey and her husband Christopher were found walking down an Atlanta highway in freezing temperatures. Police found their daughter Quimani at a ghastly scene in a nearby motel. Christopher Carey had stabbed his daughter with a knife until it broke as she tried to fight him off. The girl's mother then held Quimani down while her father broke both of her arms. Once the girl's limbs were limp, broken, and unable to fend off her parents' attacks, Valerie strangled Quimani to death. Blood-soaked Bible pages were torn out and tossed onto and around the eight-year-old's bleeding body.

• In 2000, when police officers in Delhi, California, found missing fifty-year-old Aurelia Lange, her teenage son David was next to her. David was naked, covered in blood, and reading a Bible; he had hacked off his mother's head with a kitchen knife and placed it next to her.

• Texas mother Andrea Yates drowned three of her children in an effort to exorcise the devil from herself in 2001, and in 2004 Dena Schlosser cut the arms off of her eleven-month-old daughter while listening to religious hymns.

• Christopher Jones, 47, a Kansas man who served for years as director of a forensics laboratory, was sentenced to life in prison in 2000 for murdering his three children, Christopher, 7; Joshua, 5; and Sarah, 2. He explained that while in a religious mystical state, he encountered a demonic spirit of overwhelming evil that possessed him and caused him to slit his children's throats with a knife.

• John Lee Malvo and John Allan Mohammed, the so-called "DC Snipers," believed that they were possessed by God when they shot over a dozen people in 2002.

Allegedly possessed people have also died at the hands of exorcists. An exorcism in 2006 at a convent in the small Romanian town of Tanacu resulted in the death of Maricica Irina Cornici, a twenty-three-year-old nun who said she heard the devil telling her she was sinful. With assistance from four nuns, priest Daniel Corogeanu bound Cornici to a cross, gagged her mouth with a towel, and left her for three days without food or water. The ritual, the priest explained, was an effort to drive devils out of the woman. Sadly, they also drove the life from her. Cornici was found dead on June 15 of that year; an autopsy found she had died of suffocation and dehydration.

In an even more tragic case closer to home, in 2003 an autistic eight-year-old boy in Milwaukee was bound in sheets and held down by church members during a prayer service held to exorcise the evil spirits they blamed for his condition. An autopsy found extensive bruising on the back of the child's neck and concluded that he died of asphyxiation. In the past ten years, there have been at least four other exorcism-related deaths in the United States, two of them children. There truly is a dark side to the belief in exorcisms, and it has nothing to do with demons or devils.

WHAT WOULD JESUS DO?

With all this death and evil going on, it's a fair question to ask just how far out in left field you have to be to believe that supernatural entities are asking you to harm others. How hard do you have to squint at the tiny type in Leviticus to make the words say that God is fine with the whole killing thing? Actually, one doesn't have to look too far to find examples. Take, for example, smashing innocent babies' heads against rocks. That certainly seems like a pretty demonic and barbaric act that would be discouraged by Dr. Phil and most parenting magazines. Yet that's exactly what God commanded villagers to do (Psalms 137:9). If the Big Guy is cool with that, asking Abraham to slaughter his innocent son Isaac (Genesis 22:2), and pious Lot offering his virgin daughters to be gang-raped (Genesis 19:8), and so on, surely a little thing like mass murder or child dismemberment can't be too far beyond the pale of what a deity might expect. And that's the good guy, the hero of the story! A person who believes he or she is possessed may be forgiven for assuming that the list of no-nos has to be even shorter when it's Satan talking.

As far as science is concerned, demons are hanging out with unicorns and Bigfoot, while possession is a mental-health issue. As long as the public remains fascinated with demons, devils, and spirits, exorcisms will appear in entertainment and demons will appear in people's minds. When the fervor of the exorcisms are over, it is not demonic bodies but instead vulnerable human ones that bear the fatal consequences of belief.

Bibliography

• Alluisi, Stanley J. "Consequences." *Free Inquiry* 22.3 (2002): 56–7.

• Almeida, Christina. "Vegas Driver Said to See 'Demons' in Crowd." Associated Press, 24 Sept 2005.

• Baker, Robert A. *Hidden Memories: Voices and Visions from Within.* Buffalo, NY: Prometheus Books, 1992.

• Beyerstein, Barry. "Neuropathology and the Legacy of Spiritual Possession." *Skeptical Inquirer* 12.3 (1988): 248–61.

• Christopher, Kevin. "Autistic Boy Killed During Exorcism." *Skeptical Inquirer* 27.6 (2003): 11.

• Cuneo, Michael. *American Exorcism: Expelling Demons in the Land of Plenty.* New York: Broadway Books, 2002.

• Eakin, Emily. "Exorcising *The Exorcist.*" *Brill's Content*, Sept 2000: 87–91, 140.

• Hansen, Suzy. "The Devil's Playthings." Salon.com, 16 Oct 2001.

• "Life Sentences in Deaths of Kids." Associated Press, 5 July 2000.

• Melley, Brian. "Woman Found Beheaded in Calif." Associated Press, 19 Sept 2000.

• "Mom Admits Killing Daughter, 8, to Rid Demon." Associated Press, 2 Nov 2005.

• Nickell, Joe. "Exorcism: Driving out the Nonsense." *Skeptical Inquirer* 25.1 (2001): 20–4.

• Nickell, Joe. *Entities: Angels, Spirits, Demons, and Other Alien Beings.* Buffalo, NY: Prometheus Books, 1995: 79–82, 119–20.

• Opsasnik, Mark. "The Haunted Boy." *Fortean Times* 123 (1998): 34.

• Radford, Benjamin. "Deadly Rituals: Nun Dies During Convent Exorcism." *Skeptical Inquirer* 29.5 (2005):7.

• Roche, Timothy. "The Yates Odyssey." *Time*, 20 Jan 2002.

• Alluisi Souter, Ericka. "Possessed!" *People*, 26 Sept 2005: 93–4.

• Van Biema, David. "If You Liked the Movie..." *Time*, 2 Oct 2000: 74.

FOUND RELIGION

Editor's Note: Let's say that, while walking to your car in a parking lot, you see on the pavement a note meant for someone else. What do you do? Leave it? How boring. Take it and show it to some friends? Better. But your best option is to send it to Found [www.foundmagazine.com], where the crew may publish it in their magazine, one of their books, or their website (or some combination).

Any given item that people around the US, and sometimes the rest of the world, send to Found was often meant to be seen only by the person who wrote it. Sometimes it was meant for one other person. As such, these notes, lists, snapshots, and other ephemera give us a tiny but unfiltered look into the life and mind of a stranger.

Want to know what religion really means to people, the roles it plays in their lives? Forget the televangelists and their multibillion-dollar media empires. Ignore the theologians and their debates about angels on pinheads. Look on the ground, under your windshield wiper, and between the pages of old books and magazines....

Darwin Sucks Jesus rules
Jesus is our god you are lost Jesus made
us darwin was just some freak that thought
he was smart
darwin sucks!
Jusus rules!

YOU ARE LOST

FOUND by Dennis Brown in Portland, Oregon

I found this note under a windshield wiper after coming out of a store. I have two plastic signs on the back of my car, a "Darwin" fish and an "Evolve" fish.

GOD HIT LIST....

ARE YOU + YOUR FAMILY ON IT. READ ROMANS 10.9 (HOLY BIBLE) TO GET TO HEAVEN

P.S. PEOPLE WHO DO NOT GO TO CHURCH

1. PEOPLE WHO DO NOT FEAR GOD
2. PEOPLE WHO HAVE SEX AND NOT MARRIED, WHOREMONGERS, MURDERERS
3. MEN HAVING SEX WITH MEN
4. WOMAN HAVING SEX WITH WOMAN
5. DEVIL WORSHIPER (IF YOU ARE NOT GOD CHILD, YOU ARE THE DEVIL'S CHILD
6. NOT GIVING YOUR LIFE TO HIS SON JESUS CHRIST (ROMANS 10:9)
7. YOU + YOUR FAMILY ARE CURSED AND GO THE THE LAKE OF FIRE FOREVER WITH THE DEVIL....

GOD HIT LIST

FOUND by Erin Shea in Los Angeles, California

Finding this piece of paper overturned INSIDE of my car (window was open) as I walked out of the gym this morning, I thought, it being my birthday, and seeing as how none of the other cars in the lot had papers stuck to their windshields, it was maybe a nice birthday wish from someone. Either that, or someone had hit me and was leaving a note. Turning it over, I did in fact see the word 'hit,' but the rest blew me away. It baffles me that people are still able to accept these beliefs as truth and virtue, and more than ever makes me wish that the liberal community can find a spiritual stronghold for people to have faith in in order to erase these pessimistic and corrupt views. Happy Birthday to me!

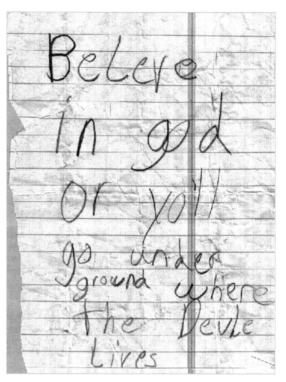

DEUT. 1:45

FOUND by Matt Durand in Northampton, Massachusetts

A year or two ago, while using the ATM, I found this beat-up-looking note over by the deposit envelopes, written on thick paper in a mixture of marker, pencil, pen, and whiteout. It seems like the kind of thing a person might carry around as a sort of inspirational message to him/herself, but if so it's a pretty bleak message, don't you think?

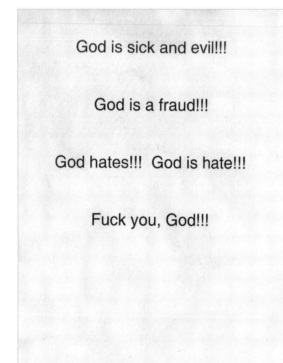

GOD IS A FRAUD

FOUND by Andrew Oberweger

On January 13 I got off the Highway 5 northbound at the Jamboree exit on my way to work. I was maybe the 3rd car in line at the light. I looked towards the curb and saw this note fluttering in the weeds. The type is so large and bold I could clearly read it from where I was sitting. I threw the car in park, jumped out and grabbed this... I call it "Someone Needs a Hug". Enjoy!

BELIEVE IN GOD OR...

FOUND by Nyck in the Northern Bible Belt

My 5 year old daughter brought this to me and asked me to read it to her. The neighbor girl had given it to her on their bus ride home from school. We're the only agnostics in our county, it would seem....

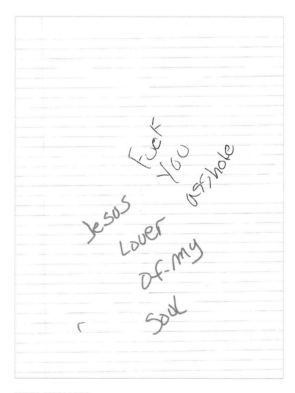

MIXED MESSAGES

FOUND by Curtis Rice

I found this note on my way to work.

EVERYTHING YOU KNOW ABOUT GOD IS WRONG

Dear Lord,
The Power
OF God
and The
Blood of Jesus, I come to the
River OF LiFe and The Waters
OF Hopes and Dreams. This Is
The Year For Me and The Man
OF My Dreams. 2004!
Lord I Pray Please Bring
me The Man OF Dreams.
Lord I Pray Please Bring
me to Him, The Man oF MY
Dreams. I Believe By Faith.
Let The Angels Come By Faith
and I Pray Please Lord Bring
Us Together. me and The Man OF
My Dreams! Forever I Come.

#1
Press
My
Faith!

August 19, 04
My Greatest
Wish oF
Desires oF The
Heart. my
God!

Dear Lord,
7 Letters
to the Lord!

The Man OF
My Dreams!

August
19, 04
#5

Lord Tears In my Eyes.
I come to The Most Beautiful
Waters. God you Have Planted
the Man OF My Dreams so
Deep Within my Heart Lord.
Just one Touch, Just one Look
Just on Tear, Just to Know In
my Heart I Love you the Man
OF My Dreams. Just to Know
Who you are, But God will Show
me who you are. By Faith God
Will Bring Us together Very Soon.
The Power OF God. and The Blood
OF Jesus
In Jesus!
Name!
I Come
Forever!
I come.
Your
Daughter
Lord.

MAN OF MY DREAMS

FOUND by Holy Smith in Oklahoma

I found several pages of this letter written to the Lord. They were floating in the water and I fished them out using a piece of long bamboo from a bridge. After I got them home I felt guilty because they were obviously put in the water as some sort of spiritual ritual. I keep them in my laundry room. I keep wondering if she found "the man of her dreams" or if by fishing them out of the water, I eliminated any hope of her ever finding him. The pages were signed and I fantasize about looking up her phone number and calling her.

CHRISTMAS: A TIME FOR REMEMBERING

Let us not forget in this season of merriement
the great traditions that have made this country
free, decent, and God-fearing. Our generous and
modest host, Ward Mehlan, often reminds me of the
importance of law and order, for example. May you
enjoy this fine piece of literature herewith enclosed and forever remember the debt we all owe to
the intrepid men in brown who tonight stand ready
to safeguard our God-given right to partake of the
proverbial grape prudently and with an ever-vigilant
eye for the sexual temptations that may arise
unwittingly.
                              Merry Christmas,
                              Peter Beck

CHRISTMAS: A TIME FOR REMEMBERING

FOUND by Andrew Berget in Minneapolis, Minnesota

A friend found this inside an old magazine my girlfriend got at work.

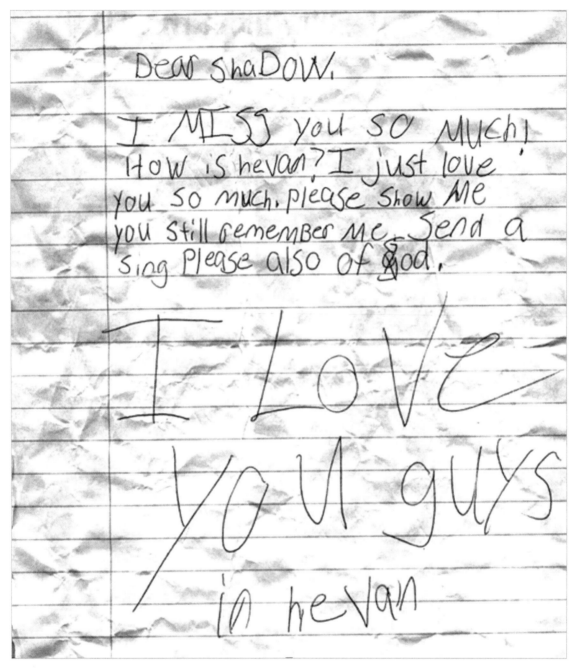

IN HEVAN

FOUND by Lisa Agostoni in Atlanta, Georgia

A friend of mine flies a Paramotor, and one day during an outing in north Georgia where he was flying, a balloon floated into the air with a note tied to the end of the string. My friend went over and grabbed the balloon and rescued the note.

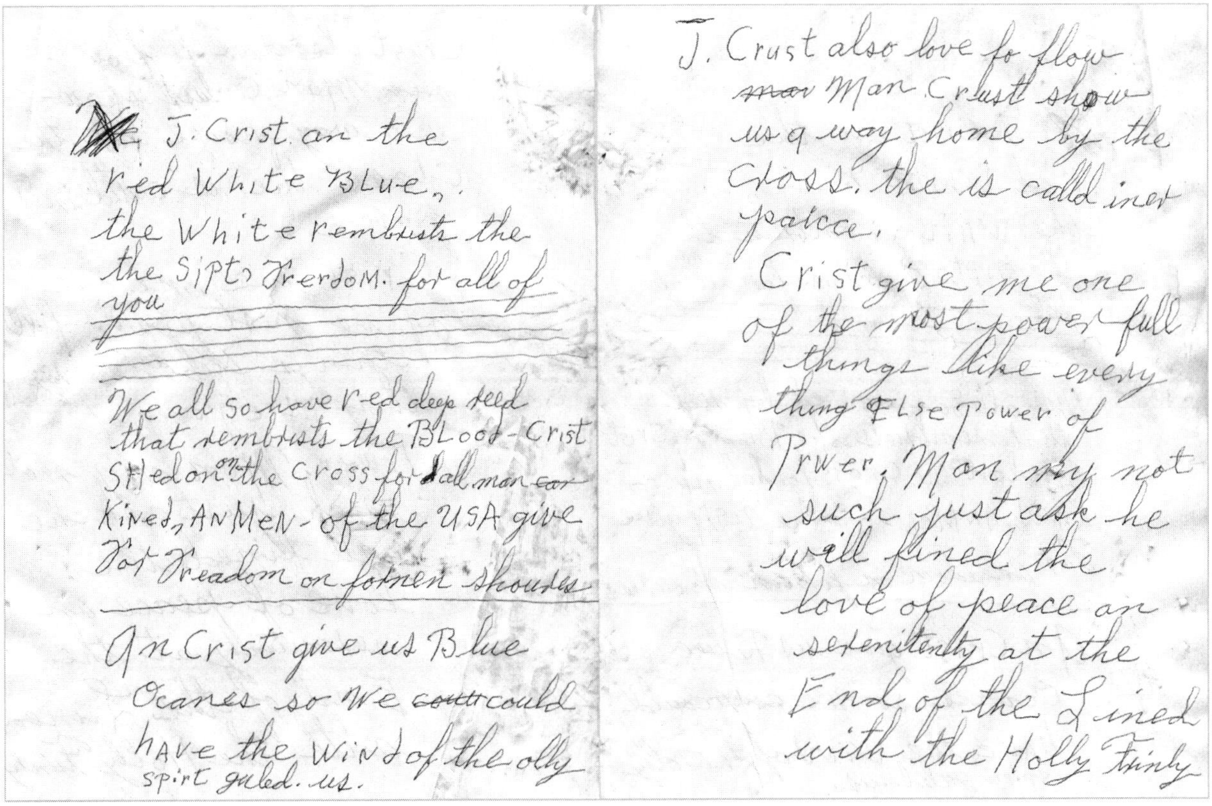

~~Me~~ J. Crist an the
red White Blue..
the White rembrsts the
the Sipt, Freedom. for all of
you

We all so have red deep seed
that rembrsts the Blood-Crist
Stled on the Cross for all man ~~cor~~
Kined, AnMen- of the USA give
Yot Freadom on fotnen shouders

An Crist give us Blue
Ocanes so We ~~coutr~~ could
have the Wind of the olly
spirt guled. us.

J. Crust also love for flow
~~mar~~ Man Crust show
us a way home by the
Cross. the is call inet
paice.
Crist give me one
of the most power full
things like every
thing Else Power of
Prwer. Man my not
such just ask he
will fined the
love of peace an
serenitenty at the
End of the Lined
with the Holly Finly

J CRUST

FOUND by Tim Mancusi in Santa Rosa, California

One evening in early November of 2005 my girlfriend, Audrey and I went for a walk near my condo and saw this piece of paper near the corner of W Steele Lane and McBride Lane. We were intrigued by the penmanship so picked it up. I have read it many times but still can't decide which side of the paper the writer started on. I think the page starting with "J. Crust" is page 2. God only knows.

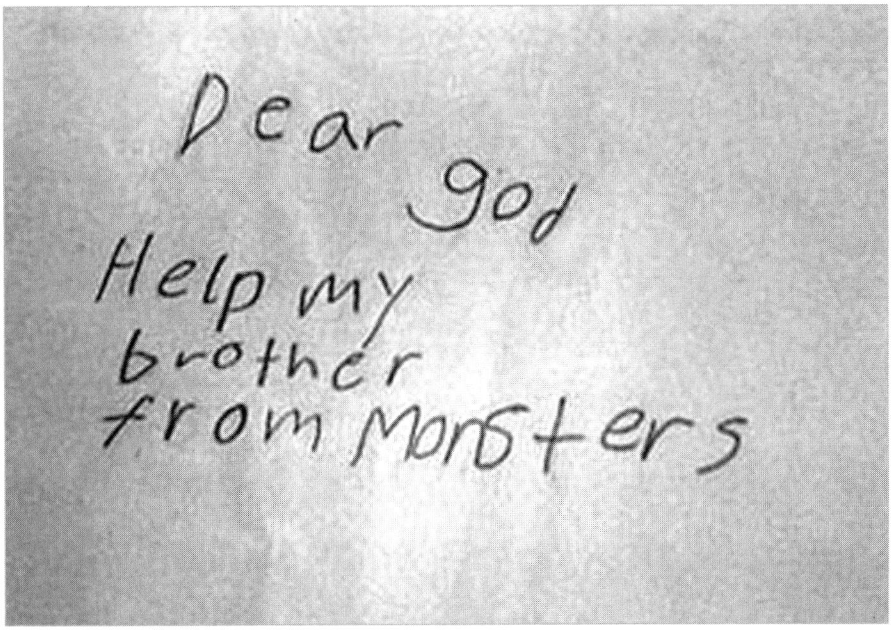

Dear god
Help my
brother
from Monsters

DEAR GOD

FOUND by Andrea Leonard in Gilmer, Texas

Found this on the ground when I was leaving a weekend camp for kids. I thought it was great that this little guy: a) thought to pray for his brother, b) that he thought to write it down, and c) monsters are still the scariest thing in his world... I'm not a hardcore believer of any kind, but this is pretty adorable. I stuck it in my journal.

BITS AND PIECES

WHO WOULD JESUS TORTURE?

If you follow a religion whose messiah and savior—the supposed Son of God—was tortured to death, you logically might have zero tolerance for such brutality. But the odds are you don't, if you're a Christian in the US.

In October 2005, the prestigious Pew Research Center polled just over 2,000 adults across the country, asking them: "Do you think the use of torture against suspected terrorists in order to gain important information can often be justified, sometimes be justified, rarely be justified, or never be justified?" They also asked for the respondents' religious affiliation (if any).

What percentages said that torture was "often" justified?

All respondents: 15%
Catholics: 21%
White Protestants: 15%
White evangelicals: 13%
"Secular": 10%

That's right: The most enthusiastic support for torture comes from Catholics. Protestants of various stripes come next, followed by those who say that they have no religion.

Then we have the other end of the spectrum, those who say that torture is "never" justified. This category is led by people without religion; 41% of them completely reject such barbarism. In comparison, only 31% of all white Protestants answered the same way, as did 26% of Catholics. Put together, 32% of the public said torture is never justified.

To frame it another way, in the US, three out of four of Catholics, two out of three Protestants, and over half of the religion-free think torture is acceptable in at least some circumstances.

While relaying these grim statistics, the *National Catholic Reporter* noted: "Carroll Doherty, associate director of the Pew center, said these results mirror those of similar surveys."

Source: Carney, Tom "Americans, Especially Catholics, Approve of Torture." *National Catholic Reporter*, 24 March 2006.

> **In the US, three out of four of Catholics, two out of three Protestants, and over half of the religion-free think torture is acceptable in at least some circumstances.**

MARY'S CONFUSED OB-GYN

One of the crucial tenets of Christianity, in all its myriad forms, is that Jesus was born of a virgin, a teenage peasant girl named Mary who was impregnated by God. It's only natural, given the extraordinary nature of this widespread belief, that over the millennia, some people have pondered exactly *how* God got Mary pregnant.

The Bible is vague. Only the Gospel of Luke (1:26-38) has much to say. The angel Gabriel appears to Mary, telling her: "And, behold, thou shalt conceive in thy womb, and bring forth a son, and shalt call his name JESUS." When Mary asks how this can happen, given her untouched state, Gabe replies: "The Holy Ghost shall come upon thee, and the power of the Highest shall overshadow thee: therefore also that holy thing which shall be born of thee shall be called the Son of God."

You might suspect that it was non-Christians who heretically pressed for answers about this seemingly impossible event, and that's partly what happened, but a surprising number of theologians, church fathers, and saints have addressed the question. And, with the apparent lack of an answer, folk beliefs have sprung up to fill the gap.

In his *Homily on Matthew*, St. John Chrysostom wondered:

> Neither the angel Gabriel nor the evangelist Matthew can say anything except that the birth of Christ was the work of the Holy Spirit, but neither of the two explains how the Spirit did this, since such a mystery is totally beyond words. Do not believe that you have understood the mystery, just because you hear the words "of the Holy Spirit." For even after we have learned this, there remain many things we do not know about.

He warned the faithful to just shut up and accept it: "[H]ow this happened we do not see. So do not pry into the mystery, but humbly accept what God has revealed, and do not be curious about what God keeps hidden."

In his towering *Summa Theologica*, St. Thomas Aquinas gave a little detail about what happened in Mary's uterus. He believed that conception normally took place because sexual intercourse draws a pure kind of blood (i.e., non-menstrual) to the woman's womb, where it mingles with the man's jism. Aquinas wrote: "This, however, did not take place in Christ's conception: because this blood was brought together in the Virgin's womb and fashioned into a child by the operation of the Holy Ghost. Therefore is Christ's body said to be 'formed of the most chaste and purest blood of the Virgin.'"

Among the earliest attempts at an explanation were those from Origen, one of the most important theologians. At one point, he invoked spontaneous generation, the mistaken notion that life can spring from nonliving matter. Marina Warner writes that he took "the strange position of likening the birth of his God to the generation of snakes from corpses, bees from oxen, wasps from horses, beetles from donkeys, or worms from almost anything, as described by Pythagoras at the end of Ovid's *Metamorphoses*."

Yet, without remarking on the apparent contradiction, Origen offered another, more long-lasting explanation: Mary conceived during the act of the angel Gabriel telling her that she was to give birth to the Son of God. To be technical, this is not a true explanation, since it doesn't address the actual mechanism by which Mary's ovum was fertilized, but it did lead to a more explicit rendering: God's semen entered Mary through her ear. This has become by far the most popular explanation for the virginal conception (technically known as the Incarnation). Warner quotes a hymn written in the sixth century and still being sung:

> The centuries marvel that the angel bore the seed [in the original Latin: *semina*, literally semen], the virgin conceived through her ear, and, believing in her heart, became fruitful.

Another biggie of the early Church—Tertullian—referenced God's semen but without saying how it arrived where it was needed: "He who had the seed of God did not need the seed of man."

St. Augustine, after noting that Mary didn't engage in "the instinct of fleshly concupiscence," wrote: "Rather she, with pious faith, merited to receive the holy seed within her."

St. John of Damascus (a/k/a John Damascene), also referring to semen, wrote: "God's wisdom and power overshadowed her, like unto a Divine seed."

And St. John Chrysostom claimed: "When God's Only-Begotten was about to enter into the Virgin, the Holy Ghost preceded Him; that by the previous entrance of the Holy Ghost, Christ might be born unto sanctification according to His body, the Godhead entering instead of the seed."

In the fourth century, St. Ephrem of Syria used an earth/plant analogy. In this case, the English word *seed* is metaphorical: "This earth is Mary's body, the temple in which a seed has been deposited. Observe the angel who comes and deposits this seed in Mary's ear."

St. Hilary of Poitiers took the same tack, claiming that Jesus was "planted like a seed in the womb of the holy Virgin, developing little by little, taking on the form of a tiny body."

Sometimes it's not God's jism but God's "breath" (specifically, the breath of the third part of the Trinity, the Holy Spirit) that enters the Virgin's ear and knocks her up. St. Ambrose wrote: "Not from human seed but by the mystical breath of the Spirit was the Word of God made flesh..." St. Proclus of Constantinople wrote an homily that said, "When the holy Virgin offered her womb, the Word rushed in through her sense of hearing." Joining this chorus were St. Augustine, Agobard, St. Ephrem of Syria, Rufinus of Aquileia, and Pope Felix I.

The history of art is filled with paintings, altarpieces, and stained-glass windows showing a white bird (often a dove), representing the Holy Spirit, at Mary's ear, subtly performing the act of impregnation. In a variation on the theme, rays of light—occasionally containing the tiny body of Fetus Jesus—shoot from the bird's mouth to Mary's ear.

Ernest Jones, one of the greatest psychoanalysts, pointed out two similar legends that predate the Christian one. Mongolia's savior, Chigemouni, is said to have impregnated the sleeping virgin Maya through her ear, so that he might be physically born nine months later. In India, legend has it that the Sun god had sex with Kunti in her ear, resulting in the birth of the hero Karna. Jones comments:

> That the danger of this form of conception is regarded by Catholics as not having entirely passed is shown by the custom with which all nuns still comply of protecting their chastity against assault by keeping their ears constantly covered... This is the acme of chastity, for it protects even against the most innocent form of conception, one reserved for the most modest women.

Some devoted poets spoke of Mary being "entered." Caelius Sedulius, some of whose work has been used as liturgies, wrote: "The grace of heaven enters in / The closed-up Mother's inmost parts." Venantius Fortunatus: "God entered her, who did not know man."

Another theory, considered heretical, says that Jesus was placed as a fully-formed fetus into Mary's uterus, where he incubated until it was time to come out. This is the implication of the Apostles' Creed, perhaps the oldest Christian creed in existence. It also shows up in many paintings that show an infant floating down to Mary's body in a beam of light.

Most theologians simply skirt the issue of exactly how the conception was achieved. In the 300s, St. Gregory of Nazianzen was a model of vagueness: "She, after having conceived in her inmost parts, illuminated by divinity, brought him to light when her time came."

The concept of a virginal conception leads to other intriguing ideas and conundrums. For example, since Jesus received no paternal DNA, he would essentially have been a clone of his mother. "Contemporary theologians still wonder what Jesus and Mary looked like," writes Warner, "and maintain that they must have resembled each other closely, as his body's substance came entirely from her."

The Birth. Little-known among laypeople is the precept that Mary remained a virgin even *while* giving birth (and, consequently, experienced no pain or even discomfort during delivery). In other words, her holy vagina was not desecrated by a baby moving through it, just as it was not desecrated by a penis nine months prior. There's nothing in the Bible to support this idea, but it was a big deal to the Church.

This belief is even more problematic than the conception. If it's tough to wrap your head around the precise way in which God could impregnate a woman, it's well-nigh impossible to grok how a baby can be delivered nonvaginally without resorting to a Caesarean section. The apocryphal book Pseudo-Ezekiel sums up the illogic pretty well when it observes: "She gave birth and did not give birth."

St. Gregory of Nyssa said that Mary didn't even *realize* she'd given birth:

> As the Son has been given to us without a father, so the Child has been born without a birth. As the Virgin herself did not know how the body that received divinity was formed in her own body, so neither did she notice the birth. Even the prophet Isaiah affirms that her giving birth was without pain, when he says: "Before the pangs of birth arrived, a male child came forth and was born." [Is 66:7]

St. Proclus of Constantinople: "For the baby has come forth, leaving the curtains of the womb intact behind him, leaving the workshop of nature as he found it and adding grace as well." St. Theodotus of Ancyra: "A woman who gives birth to mere flesh ceases to be a virgin; but the Word of God, born in the flesh, maintains her virginity, thus showing that he is the Word."

The apocryphal Protoevangelium of James contains a bizarre and explicit passage regarding the birth. Just after Mary somehow delivered Jesus, the attending midwife told a woman named Salome what had happened. Salome said—I quote directly from the book—"As the Lord my God lives, unless I insert my finger and test her condition, I will not believe that a virgin has given birth." Salome then sticks her finger into Mary's hooha, feels the holy hymen, and her hand is promptly consumed by fire. (You'll be happy to know that Salome begged forgiveness from God and was promptly healed by touching Baby Jesus.) The redoubtable St. Clement of Alexandria cited this incident as fact while defending the notion of Mary delivering virginally.

One explanation that's been proffered over the centuries is a vague notion based on the movement of light. "As a star puts forth its ray, so the virgin put forth her son, in like manner," goes a twelfth-century hymn. Psychoanalyst Ernest Jones commented that two alternate physical routes have been offered by theologians, artists, and laity: Jesus was born from between Mary's breasts, or he was delivered through her ear, which makes sense given the widespread belief that that's the route through which he was conceived.

Commenting on the birth, St. Theodotus put his foot down: "I am presenting you with a miracle; do not put forth a line of reasoning."

After the Delivery. The third aspect of Mary's virginity that has consumed history's greatest theological minds is whether she refrained from sex for the rest of her life. The consensus is that she did, with only a few dissenters, most notably Tertullian. Those who say that Mary and Joseph had conjugal relations after Jesus was born point to the fact that Matthew, Mark, John, Acts, and 1 Corinthians mention "brothers" of Jesus, and Matthew and Mark each make a brief reference to his sisters. But defenders of the sacred cherry counter that either 1) Joseph had children from a previous marriage, thus giving Jesus stepbrothers, or 2) the Greek word being translated as *brothers* can also refer to cousins and other relations.

St. Peter Chrysologus sums up: "She conceives a virgin, she gives birth as a virgin, and she remains a virgin."

Postscript: No Womb at the Inn. While reading the Church fathers pontificating about Mary and the Incarnation, one can't help but notice their fascination with, and worship of, her uterus. St. Proclus of Constantinople marvels: "Then let us admire the Virgin's womb, a womb wider than creation. For she, without difficulty, enclosed within her him who cannot be contained in anyone." He even addressed the uterus directly: "O womb wider than the heavens!... O womb, who were the bridal chamber of the clay and the potter!" In the Gospel of Bartholomew, the title character similarly cries out: "O womb larger than a city! O womb wider than the heavens! O womb that held the one whom seven heavens could never contain! Painlessly you held within your bosom him who was able to change into the smallest of things! O womb that hid the Messiah who became visible to many! O womb that became greater than the space of the entire creation!"

According to St. Theodotus, it even smells good: "[S]he received the living God, the Word, into her virginal and fragrant bridal chamber."

Some of Catholicism's finest minds have debated in excruciating detail whether any and every sexual act you can imagine is a venial sin, a mortal sin, or not sinful at all.

Sources:
• Aquinas, St. Thomas. *Summa Theologica*, part 3, chapters 28, 31.
• Boslooper, Thomas. *The Virgin Birth*. Philadelphia: Westminster Press, 1962.
• Gambero, Luigi. *Mary and the Fathers of the Church: The Blessed Virgin Mary in Patristic Thought*. San Francisco: Ignatius Press, 1999.
• Jones, Ernest, M.D. "The Madonna's Conception through the Ear." *Psycho-Myth and Psycho-History: Essays in Applied Psycho-analysis*, vol 2. New York: Hillstone, 1974.
• Warner, Marina. *Alone of All Her Sex: The Myth and the Cult of the Virgin Mary*. New York: Vintage Books, 1983. Chapter 3: "Virgin Birth."

MORE ON MARY

How Old Was Mary? The Bible is silent on this issue, although it gives some clues to those familiar with life in that place and time. Sally Cunneen—author of *In Search of Mary*—writes: "She would probably have been only twelve or thirteen."[1]

Mary in the Koran. Sally Cunneen also notes: "For Mary is deeply honored in the Qu'ran, in Islamic exegesis, and in Muslim piety. She is the only female identified by name in the Qu'ran; her name appears there (thirty-four times) far more often than in the whole New Testament."[2]

Mother's Milk. St. Bernard was said to get nourishment from sucking the breasts of statues of the Virgin Mary, which supplied him with milk.[3]

Notes:
1. Cunneen, Sally. *In Search of Mary: The Woman and the Symbol*. New York: Ballantine Books, 1996: 32.
2. Ibid: 156.
3. Coulton, G.G. *Five Centuries of Religion, Volume 1: St Bernard, His Predecessors and Successors, 1000–1200 A.D.* Cambridge University Press, 1923: 499, quoting *Cistertium Bis-Tertium* by A. Sartorius (Prague: 1700).

LET'S TALK ABOUT *CONNUBIUM*

Connubium is Latin for sex (specifically, the sex act itself), a topic that the Catholic theologians of yesteryear spent an awful lot of time contemplating. You see, in order to absolve someone of sin, the cleric hearing confession had to know exactly what constituted a sin and, more specifically, what *kind* of sin. (The two categories of sin that a person can commit are mortal—a major, knowing sin that cuts a person off from God and earns a one-way ticket to hell—and venial—a lesser or unknowing sin that doesn't cut the sinner off from God but triggers either some time in Purgatory or punishment in this life. Of course, performing certain steps—such as confession and penance—erases the need for these punishments.)

Some of Catholicism's finest minds have debated in excruciating detail whether any and every sexual act you can imagine is a venial sin, a mortal sin, or not sinful at all. The results ended up in theological works or confessors' manuals, usually written in Latin. Most of this work has never been translated into English, and the parts that have been are often embedded in extremely obscure books. Most of the passages below have been translated from the Latin especially for this volume.

The Spanish and Latin work *Llave de oro* [*The Golden Key*]—an 1860 confessors' manual by St. Antonio María Claret, then Archbishop of Cuba—has achieved legendary status as one of the most explicit of these works. In the following extract, Claret lays out some of the matters on which confessors must quiz their young female penitents:

1. Giving rise to impure orgasms, by looking and touching themselves (1) by lightly touching themselves on the vulva with the palm of the hand, (2) by lightly touching themselves with the finger inside the vulva on the clitoris, etc., (3) by inserting the finger into the vagina, (4) by inserting a piece of wood, etc. within the vulva, (5) pressing one's vulva against a table, wall, etc., sitting on a seat and pressing oneself against the seat. Sitting on the ground and pressing oneself against one's foot. Periodically crossing the legs and pressing on the actual vulva, by moving oneself gently, etc.

2. Touching oneself shamelessly with one or several girls. Acting in a sodomitic manner with girls;

from time to time with sisters, especially when lying in the same bed at night, by now pressing the vulva of one with the foot, legs, etc. of another, and so defiling themselves.

3. By mutual touching on the genitals with a boy. At times having intercourse, even though imperfectly.

4. Bestiality (1) by applying one's vulva to some animal, (2) at times by inserting the comb of a cock or a hen inside the vulva. At times placing saliva or bread in the vulva and forcing a dog to lick it. At times forcing a dog and inserting the dog's genitals into her vulva.

A few topic headings from this book were translated into English in *Centuria Librorum Absconditorum*:

Masturbation before the statue of the Virgin; If a doctor sins by spending while handling the private parts of a woman in the pursuit of his calling; Commerce with a demon under the form of a man, a woman, or an animal; Corpse-profanation; Whether copulation may be performed while the woman is with child, or during the time of menstruation.

Another work along these lines is Joannis Caspari Saettler's *In sextum Decalogi praeceptum in conjugum obligationes et quaedam matrimonium spectatntia praelectiones* (1840). Here are a few highlights from the table of contents:

How Confessors are to deal with a penitent, and Parish Priests with a female parishioner, in a case of incest.

What a holy place is; what kind of ejaculation of seed pollutes such a place, or does not do so, even though it is sacrilegious.

Whether, and in what circumstances, it is permitted to break off intercourse.

Whether it is permitted to ejaculate semen that has collected [in the body].

When an impure orgasm [that is, one not produced by normal intercourse] is to be considered voluntary in its origin, and when and how it is culpable.

Whether impure nocturnal orgasms are sins, and what sort of sins they constitute.

Whether they should be an impediment to the reception of communion.

Whether and when one should enquire about bestiality.

What should be done about intercourse with a dead woman.

What should be done about unnatural methods of intercourse.

What acting like a whore is, and what sort of sin it is. What the impediment of impotence is.

What obligation is incumbent on spouses to seek and grant what they owe their partners.

How spouses may continue to sin in the practice of their marital state.

What must be said regarding obscene touches, looks, and kisses between spouses.

Whether a married person sins, who in the absence of his partner touches him/herself immodestly, or takes pleasure in [contemplating] an act of intercourse that either has previously occurred or is to occur.

Whether the unmarried, and especially the betrothed, sin when they are delighted by the prospect of an act of intercourse, or the widowed in the case of one that has occurred.

What the Confessor should do in the case of a wife whose husband is a masturbator.

An earlier work partly in this vein is the eight-volume *Theologia moralis et dogmatica* by Petrus Dens (1690–1775). In this passage, Dens declares that it is a mortal sin for a husband to stick his penis into his wife's booty or mouth, even if he moves to her vagina (i.e., "the proper receptacle") before ejaculating:

And so a limit [to sexual activity] should be observed, or, if you will, the proper location in the body, and this principle is overturned in a two-fold manner, when the proper receptacle is not used, but intercourse takes place in the rear receptacle, or any other unnatural receptacle: this is always a mortal sin as it concerns a lesser, or imperfect, form of sodomy, and this principle must be upheld against some who would relax it, whether intercourse is completed there, or whether it is only begun there, to be completed in the natural receptacle.

Dens' contemporary, Alfonso Maria di Liguori (a/k/a St. Alphonsus), also addresses this pressing issue in his two-volume *Theologia moralis*, agreeing with Dens. But the Italian takes it a step further, looking at whether it's okay for a hubby to rub his penis against his wife's bum without actually having anal sex:

Yet is it then a mortal sin for a man to rub his genitals around the rear receptacle of his wife? Sanchez etc. deny this, because touching the rear receptacle is not a prelude to sodomy. [On the contrary:] The reason is that certainly such a touching cannot occur in a moral sense without a leaning towards sodomy.

Liguori then turns his attention to another question:

Whether and in what way spouses sin when they have intercourse in an unnatural position. The natural position is that the wife should be underneath and the husband on top; for this method is better suited to the ejaculation of male seed, and to its reception in the female receptacle for the procreation of offspring. But the position is unnatural if intercourse occurs in another manner, that is, while sitting, standing, on the side, or from the rear in the manner of cattle, or if the man is underneath and the woman on top. This form of intercourse, which is not performed in the natural position, is condemned by some in Sanchez's work as a mortal sin in all cases, whereas others say that the last two methods are mortal sin, on the grounds that nature herself shrinks from these. But others argue that in general terms none of these methods is more than a venial sin. The reason is that, although there is some irregularity, yet it is not so great as to comprise a mortal sin, since it is concerned solely with the inessentials of an act of intercourse, and on the other hand a change of position does not impede reproduction, since a man's seed is not received into a woman's womb by infusion, or by travelling downwards, but by attraction, since the womb attracts male seed naturally by itself.

Source: Quotes from these rare works are provided in Fraxi, Pisanus [Henry Ashbee]. *Centuria Librorum Absconditorum* (London: privately printed, 1879). Most passages are given only in Latin; translation into English was provided by Quintus' Latin Translation Service.

LAYING THE LAMBS (OR, FLOCKING THE FLOCK)

At what rate do men of the cloth have sexual relations with their parishioners? Not surprisingly for such a touchy subject, researchers have mostly stayed away from the topic. As I set out to see what answers may have been uncovered, I constantly came across references to two efforts: a *Christianity Today* poll and a doctoral thesis, which appear to be the only attempts to quantify the number of lamb-laying pastors.

Then I found an article issued by the Disciplinary Policy and Procedures Task Force of the Episcopal Church. While writing about making canon law tougher on touchy-feely preachers, Rev. Pamela Cooper-White, Ph.D., noted: "Research studies have estimated that up to 20% or more of clergy have violated sexual boundaries with parishioners (a higher percentage than any other professional group)."

In an endnote to this statement, the reverend neatly summarizes the two previous studies, as well as her own research, making it the definitive concise statement about what we currently know:

A range of 12–20.7% can be extrapolated from a *Christianity Today* survey, reported in "How Common is Pastoral Indiscretion?" *Leadership* (Winter 1988), 1.

A doctoral study at Fuller Seminary shows fully 38.6% of respondents having had sexual contact with a parishioner. Richard Allen Blackmon, "The Hazards of the Ministry" (unpublished Ph.D. dissertation, Fuller Seminary, 1984).

In my own most recent research among pastoral counselors and clinical social workers, respondents estimated a mean prevalence of sexual misconduct of 14.5% among pastoral counselors; and 82% had heard a client report of a clergyperson crossing a sexual boundary with him or her, with a mean of over 4 incidents told to each therapist. Cooper-White, "The Use of the Self in Psychotherapy: A Comparative Study of Pastoral Counselors and Clinical Social Workers," *American Journal of Pastoral Counseling* 4/4 (2001), 14.

Source: Cooper-White, Rev. Pamela, Ph.D. "Some Thoughts Toward Canon Revision: Canons as Gift of Grace and Dance of Love." Disciplinary Policy & Procedures Task Force, Executive Offices of the General Convention, the Episcopal Church, 2003. [www.episcopalchurch.org]. This article was also published in *Reports to the 74th General Convention* (a/k/a "The Blue Book") from the Episcopal Church.

OF BROTHELS AND ABBEYS

In his classic multivolume work, *The Mothers: A Study of the Origins of Sentiments and Institutions*, social anthropologist Robert Briffault wrote:

...pe Julius II, by a papal Bull, instituted a similar brothel in ...me, and the foundation prospered under the patronage of Leo ...and Clement VII, part of the proceeds being devoted to providing ...mfort of the Holy Sisters of the Order of St. Mary Magdalene.

Organised prostitution derives directly from the religious institutions which prevailed in the ancient Mediterranean civilizations. Brothels are still commonly spoken of on the continent as "abbeys." The term is, no doubt, used in a jocular way, but those who use it in jest are unaware that it derives from an actual historical tradition. Brothels were frequently attached to churches and religious houses. A brothel called "The Abbey" was instituted in the papal city of Avignon under the patronage of Queen Joanna of Naples. It was regulated by strict rules after the model of religious houses. None but good Christians were admitted, Jews and infidels being excluded; it was closed on Good Friday and Easter Day and, what is more notable, a system of medical inspection and of quarantine was enforced.[1] Pope Julius II, by a papal Bull, instituted a similar brothel in Rome, and the foundation prospered under the patronage of Leo X and Clement VII, part of the proceeds being devoted to providing comfort of the Holy Sisters of the Order of St. Mary Magdalene.[2] ... The Holy Virgin is, in China, the special patroness of prostitutes.[3]

1. JP Papon, *Histoire générale de Provence*, vol iii, pp. 180 sq.

2. JA Dulaure, *Les Divinités génératrices*, p. 285.

3. See above, p. 171.

Source: Briffault, Robert. *The Mothers: A Study of the Origins of Sentiments and Institutions*, vol. 3. New York: Macmillan Company, 1927: 215–6.

SAVING THE WORLD FROM FILTHY FLOWERS AND PLANT PORN

The great Swedish naturalist and physician Carolus Linnaeus (1707–1778) is best-remembered for two things: creating the binomial classification system, in which every living thing is given a two-word scientific name, and discovering that the plant kingdom is divided into two sexes and reproduces accordingly. His publications on plant reproduction triggered righteous moral outrage for decades.

In his 1737 book on botany, which was primarily an attack on Linneaus, Johann Siegesbeck wrote: "What man will ever believe that God Almighty should have introduced such confusion, or rather such shameful whoredom, for the propagation of the reign of plants? Who will instruct young people in such voluptuous system without scandal?"[1] Responding to the fact that pollen from several male plants often impregnates one female plant, Siegesbeck thundered that this kind of "loathsome harlotry as several males with one female would not be permitted in the vegetable kingdom by the Creator!" And: "Who would have thought that bluebells and lillies and onions could be up to such immorality?"[2]

Professor Londa Schiebinger, an historian of natural science, writes that in 1798: "The Rev. Richard Polwhele...asserted that the open teaching of the sexual system in botany encouraged unauthorized sexual unions."[3]

In 1808, Revered Samuel Goodenough, who later became the Bishop of Carlisle, wrote: "To tell you that nothing could equal the gross prurience of Linnaeus's mind is perfectly needless. A literal translation of the first principles of Linnaean botany is enough to shock female modesty."[4]

Notes:

1. Siegesbeck quoted in Peakman, Julie. *Mighty Lewd Books: The Development of Pornography in Eighteenth-Century England.* Palgrave Macmillan, 2003.

2. Quoted in Nickrent, Dr. Daniel L. "A Historical Look at Plant Classification." Course material for Plant Biology 304: Elements of Plant Systematics, Southern Illinois University. 20 April 1999.

3. Schiebinger, Londa. "Gender and Natural History." In *Cultures of Natural History.* N. Jardine, et al. (eds.). Cambridge University Press, 1996: 175.

4. Goodenough quoted in Blunt, Wilfrid. *Linnaeus: The Compleat Naturalist.* Princeton University Press, 2001: 248.

JOYFULLY WATCHING SINNERS ROAST IN HELL

Lest you think that eternal torment for sinners is something that you—a member of the heaven-bound elect—should feel bad about, please rest assured that it's actually a wonderful thing. The Bible says that you should "rejoice" in this everlasting torture. Tertullian, one of the greatest Church fathers, wrote that it will make him "exult" and "laugh." St. Aquinas said: "Although God rejoices not in punishments as such, He rejoices in them as being ordered by His justice."[1]

It all goes back to the touching Psalm 58:10: "The righteous shall rejoice when he seeth the vengeance: he shall wash his feet in the blood of the wicked." (Supporters of rejoicing at the inhumane fate of sinners also invoke Isaiah 66:24, although I can't grasp how that supports their cause.)

Theologians including Aquinas, Bonaventura, Vincent of Beauvais, Hugh of St. Victor, Thomas Wallensis, and Humbert de Romans have all written about the joys of watching sinners getting brutalized for eternity.[2] Tertullian waxed poetic about seeing kings, philosophers, poets, actors, and other rejecters of Christ being tortured in hell. Such a display, he declared, will be a greater joy than going to the circus, theater, or races:

But what sort of show is that near at hand? the Coming of the Lord, now confessed, now glorious, now triumphant.... And yet there remain other shows: that last and eternal Day of Judgment, the unlooked for, the scorned of the Nations, when all the ancient things of the world, and all that are rising into life, shall be consumed in one fire? what shall then be the expanse of the show? whereat shall I wonder? whereat laugh? whereat rejoice? whereat exult? beholding so many kings, who were declared to be admitted into Heaven, with Jupiter himself and all that testify of him, groaning together in the lowest darkness? those rulers too, the persecutors of the Name of the Lord, melting amid insulting fires more raging than those wherewith themselves raged against the Christians: those wise philosophers moreover reddening before their own disciples, now burning together with them, whom they persuaded that there was nothing which appertained to God, before whom they affirmed that there were either no souls, or that they should not return again to their former bodies: poets too trembling before the judgment-seat, not of Rhadamanthus, not of Minos, but of the unlooked-for Christ. Then will the tragic actors be the more to be heard, because more loud in their cries amidst real

affliction of their own: then the players to be recognized, more dissolute by far when dissolved by fire: then the charioteer to be gazed on, all red upon his fiery wheel: then the wrestlers to be viewed tossing about, not in the theatre, but in the fire—unless perchance I may even then not desire to see them, as wishing rather to fix my gaze, never to be satisfied, on those who have furiously raged against the Lord....

Such shows as these, such triumphs as these, what praetor [a type of Roman magistrate], or consul, or quaestor [a type of Roman official], or priest, shall of his own bounty bestow upon thee? and yet we have them even now in some sort present to us, through Faith, in the imagination of the spirit. But what are those things which eye hath not seen, nor ear heard, neither have entered into the heart of man? Greater joys, methinks, than the circus, and both the theatres, and any race-course.[3]

Notes:

1. Aquinas, St. Thomas. *Summa Theologica, Supplementum Tertiæ Partis*, 94, article 3.

2. Coulton, G.G. *Five Centuries of Religion, Volume 1: St Bernard, His Predecessors and Successors, 1000–1200 A.D.* Cambridge University Press, 1923: 442.

3. *Tertullian, Vol. 1. Apologetic and Practical Treatises.* (Charles Dodgson, trans.). 1842. "De Spectaculis," article XXX.

A HOST OF PROBLEMS

We're told by the New Testament that during the Last Supper, Jesus declared that the bread was his body and the wine was his blood. Some early Church fathers, such as St. Augustine, thought J.C. was speaking figuratively, but by the Middle Ages, his words were taken with absolute, concrete literalness. The Lateran Council (1255) declared in no uncertain terms the doctrine of Transubstantiation. In the mid-1500s, the Council of Trent upped the ante: Every speck, every crumb of the Consecrated Host contains the body, blood, soul, and Godhead of Christ. It *is* Jesus, and must be treated like Jesus would be treated. This led to some interesting and sometimes unfortunate outcomes.

Jews were accused of stealing and torturing Consecrated Hosts, leading to many medieval slaughters. These bloodbaths had the backing of the Church. Regarding one case in Austria, Pope Benedict XII wrote: "[I]f the Jews have committed this crime, we cannot leave it unpunished without covering our religion with shame and drawing God's wrath upon us."

People executed by hanging were often denied the Host—and, thus, absolution—at the gallows. The fear was that if the wafer were still in the condemned's mouth, then Jesus would be hanged, too.

Some people stole Hosts in order to work magic with them. Drawing on the writings of Caesarius of Heisterbach, Professor G.G. Coulton relates:

> A woman stole a Host and put it in her hive to stay a mortality among her bees; "these little insects [vermiculi], recognizing their Creator, built from their sweetest of honeycombs a tiny chapel of wondrous cunning for this sweetest of guests; wherein, erecting an altar of the same material, they laid the Most Holy Body thereon."

Another sprinkled it on her cabbages as a remedy against caterpillars; an unchaste priest, unable to seduce a woman, took the Host in his mouth to her, "hoping, if he might thus kiss her, to incline her will to his desires by the virtue of that Sacrament"; Jacques de Vitry tells of a woman who similarly stole it for a philter [i.e., a love potion]. Sprenger, in his *Malleus Maleficarum*, tells a like tale of "the detestable habit of women" in this matter, and utters a general warning:

> For this reason, all rectors and priests who give Communion unto the people are always enjoined to exercise the utmost diligence to see that the women communicate with mouths wide open, with tongues well stretched out, and with veils far removed from their faces. The more diligence is used here, the more witches are thus discovered.

But witches, sorcerers, and other Inquisition-bait weren't the only ones using the Host for off-label uses. Coulton writes: "The Host was used as a cataplasm for the eyes, with St. Augustine's approval; St. Bernard applied it to the head of a demoniac; it was buried with the holy dead; it was brought out to extinguish conflagrations, until this was forbidden by the Council of Seligenstadt. The signatures to Church Councils, for the sake of greater solemnity, were sometimes made with a pen 'dipped in the very blood of our Savior,' i.e. the consecrated Mass-wine."

Then we have this bizarre religious legend from Germany. Satan wanted to shake up the Archbishop of Cologne, so while the cleric was saying Mass, Beelzebub caused a fly to land on the Host, break off a crumb, and buzz away with it. Without batting an eye, the Archbishop prayed to God for help—*voila*, the fly landed back on the Host, dropped the crumb, and promptly keeled over. After Mass, the insect's body was burned.

What of the Consecrated Hosts that weren't eaten by churchgoers or flies? Clerics of all levels noticed—to their utter horror and dismay—that leftover Hosts eventually rotted. How could Christ's incorruptible body putrefy? St. Aquinas came to the rescue in his *Summa Theologica*, penning one of the most tortured, foggy, and incomprehensible explanations of anything ever committed to paper. It's impossible to explain, or even to understand, the finer points, but the gist is that Aquinas wants to have his Host and eat it too: Even though the bread/wafer has literally become Jesus—nay, *because* it has become Jesus—somehow everything that can happen to normal bread can still happen to it. Even though it's no longer bread. Got it?

Sources:

• Coulton, G.G. *Five Centuries of Religion, Volume 1: St Bernard, His Predecessors and Successors, 1000–1200 A.D.* Cambridge University Press, 1923.

• Aquinas, St. Thomas. *Summa Theologica*. Second and Revised Edition, 1920. Translated by Fathers of the English Dominican Province. [www.newadvent.org/summa/].

THE MOVIE THAT TRIGGERED A MAJOR TERRORIST INCIDENT IN THE US

When the history of Islamic censorship in non-Muslim countries is written, a chapter must be

Once the crisis was over, and blood had been spilled, *Mohammed: Messenger of God* quickly reopened, although it was soon given a new title: *The Message.*

devoted to the largely forgotten hostage drama involving the simultaneous takeover of *three* buildings in Washington, DC, the shooting of Marion Barry, and the murder of a reporter.

The twelve terrorists were US Hanafi Muslims. (Hanafi is one of the subdivisions within Sunni Islam, meaning that it is typically a mainstream, orthodox brand of the religion. But with the US group, things aren't so clear-cut. The American Hanafi sect was founded by a disillusioned man who left the Nation of Islam, which would seem to cast the US Hanafis as a similar, rival organization. It appears, however, that the US Hanafis have more in common with true Islam than with the NoI.)

On March 9, 1977, they seized control of the B'Nai Brith headquarters, the Islamic Center, and, most astounding, the District Building, which is Washington, DC's city hall (located a mere two blocks from the White House). During the standoffs, they brutalized many of their 149 hostages, threatened to behead them, and non-fatally shot three of them, including city councilman Marion Barry, who obviously survived and went on to become mayor, and legal intern Bob Pierce, who became paralyzed for life. The Hanafis also murdered Maurice Williams, a local radio reporter.

"It's the worst situation we've ever had," an FBI official said at the time. Muslim ambassadors from Egypt, Iran, and Pakistan talked with the terrorists, who surrendered after 38 hours. Before the year was over, all twelve Hanafis had been sentenced to prison.

So what were they so upset about? Two things. First, they wanted the government to hand over imprisoned Black Muslims who had massacred the family of the Hanafi sect's US founder in 1973. Second, they were furious about *Mohammed: Messenger of God*, an epic biopic about Islam's founder. *Time* reported that anger over the movie specifically "was thought to have triggered the attack." Naturally, the Hanafis hadn't seen the film, but they assumed that it must show the title character, which—as a number of Danish cartoonists can tell you—is considered high blasphemy by many Muslims. They didn't realize that the film's director and producer, the late Moustapha Akkad (best known for executive-producing the *Halloween* slasher flicks), had gotten creative in his efforts to work around the prohibition. Muhammad is never shown; instead, the actors, including Anthony Quinn as the Prophet's uncle, sometimes address the camera as if it were him. We never hear Muhammad's voice either, though the cast responds as if he's speaking. (Likewise, we never see any of Muhammad's wives or sons-in-law.) We do, however, get a peek at Muhammad's shadow, and even this was condemned by some.

During the standoffs, *Mohammed* was pulled out of theaters in an effort to defuse the situation. Akkad even offered to screen it for the terrorists, noting that Muslim audiences loved it. Not good enough, said the Hafanis, who threatened to execute people unless they could somehow get a guarantee that no one would *ever* see the film.

Once the crisis was over, and blood had been spilled, *Mohammed: Messenger of God* quickly reopened, although it was soon given a new title: *The Message*. Theaters were receiving phone threats for showing the flick, so the studio brass decided that a vague title with no reference to Muhammad or Islam was better for everyone's health.

As for the movie itself, it's a complete whitewash. This shouldn't come as a surprise, considering that Akkad was a Muslim, several Islamic bodies approved the film, and Muammar Qadhafi partially funded it. A reviewer on Amazon says that he's seen it air on TV in Saudi Arabia during Ramadan.

Islam spread through armed conquest, a perfect example of religious imperialism, but the movie paints it as simply having to defend its poor, abused, misunderstood self from outside aggressors. Muhammad's earliest biographies, written in Arabic by devout Muslims, contain many horrifying instances in which the Prophet asked his closest followers to butcher individuals, including an old man, who were dissing him. Somehow, these events were left out of *Mohammed*.

In a way similar to other films loosely based on historical figures, such as *Ghandi* and *Braveheart*, not to mention Bible-based celluloid, non-Muslims who watch *Mohammed* may feel that they've just gotten an accurate history lesson. This, in fact, is *exactly* what has happened as revealed by the Amazon customer reviews of the DVD; people say that they knew almost nothing about Muhammad and Islam until they were enlightened by this film. A middle-school teacher writes that she shows it to her students to teach them about the religion. Meanwhile, dozens of Muslim reviewers gush about the truthfulness of this hagiographic yarn; one says that it's essentially a documentary. Heightening the problem is the fact that this is the only English-language film to dramatize the life of Muhammad and the creation of Islam. And it's likely to remain the only one forever.

Sources:
• "25th Anniversary of Terror." *Washington Post*, 9 Mar 2002.
• "The 38 Hours: Trial by Terror." *Time*, 21 Mar 1977.
• Cole, Juan. "The Strange Death of Moustapha Akkad." Juancole.com, 15 Nov 2005.
• "Hanafi Islam." GlobalSecurity.org.
• *NBC Evening News* for Wednesday, Mar 09, 1977. Abstract of broadcast created by Vanderbilt Television News Archive [tvnews.vanderbilt.edu].

THE CHILDREN OF GOD'S BOOKS FROM BEYOND

The Children of God Sect (a/k/a The Family), though best known for originally advocating adult-child sex, had other pursuits, including channeling works "written" by famous dead people. New-religion expert William Bainbridge writes:

Many deceased celebrities wrote letters about their lives and afterlife experiences, including Marilyn Monroe, Elvis Presley, John Lennon, Albert Einstein, Richard Nixon, and Martin Luther King Jr. The Family began publishing works of literature written posthumously, such as *The Return of the Seven Keys* by C.S. Lewis, *The Greatest of These* by William Shakespeare, *Nancine* by Guy de Maupassant, and *Amaris* by Scheherazade.

Source: Bainbridge, W.S. "The Family (Children of God)." In *Concise Encyclopedia of Language and Religion*. John F.A. Sawyer and J.M.Y. Simpson (eds.). Oxford: Elsevier Science Ltd, 2001.

BE AFRAID. BE VERY AFRAID. (OR, THE ONLY THING WE HAVE TO FEAR IS GOD ITSELF.)

VERSES FROM THE OLD TESTAMENT (KING JAMES VERSION)

And the angel of the LORD called unto him out of heaven, and said, Abraham, Abraham: and he said, Here am I. And he said, Lay not thine hand upon the lad, neither do thou any thing unto him: for now I know that thou **fearest** God, seeing thou hast not withheld thy son, thine only son from me. (Genesis 22:11–12)

And Joseph said unto them the third day, This do, and live; for I **fear** God: (Genesis 42:18)

Therefore God dealt well with the midwives: and the people multiplied, and waxed very mighty. And it came to pass, because the midwives **feared** God, that he made them houses. (Exodus 1:20–21)

And Israel saw that great work which the LORD did upon the Egyptians: and the people **feared** the LORD, and believed the LORD, and his servant Moses. (Exodus 14:31)

Thou shalt not curse the deaf, nor put a stumbling-block before the blind, but shalt **fear** thy God: I am the LORD. (Leviticus 19:14)

Thou shalt rise up before the hoary head, and honour the face of the old man, and **fear** thy God: I am the LORD. (Leviticus 19:32)

Ye shall not therefore oppress one another; but thou shalt **fear** thy God: for I am the LORD your God. (Levitius 25:17)

Take thou no usury of him, or increase: but **fear** thy God; that thy brother may live with thee. (Leviticus 25:36)

[God says:] Thou shalt not rule over him with rigour; but shalt **fear** thy God. (Leviticus 25:43)

Specially the day that thou stoodest before the LORD thy God in Horeb, when the LORD said unto me, Gather me the people together, and I will make them hear my words, that they may learn to **fear** me all the days that they shall live upon the earth, and that they may teach their children. (Deuteronomy 4:10)

[God says:] O that there were such an heart in them, that they would **fear** me, and keep all my commandments always, that it might be well with them, and with their children for ever! (Deuteronomy 5:29)

Thou shalt **fear** the LORD thy God, and serve him, and shalt swear by his name. (Deuteronomy 6:13)

And the LORD commanded us to do all these statutes, to **fear** the LORD our God, for our good always, that he might preserve us alive, as it is at this day. (Deuteronomy 6:24)

Therefore thou shalt keep the commandments of the LORD thy God, to walk in his ways, and to **fear** him. (Deuteronomy 8:6)

Thou shalt **fear** the LORD thy God; him shalt thou serve, and to him shalt thou cleave, and swear by his name. (Deuteronomy 10:20)

Ye shall walk after the LORD your God, and **fear** him, and keep his commandments, and obey his voice, and ye shall serve him, and cleave unto him. (Deuteronomy 13:4)

And it shall be with him, and he shall read therein all the days of his life: that he may learn to **fear** the LORD his God, to keep all the words of this law and these statutes, to do them: (Deuteronomy 17:19)

That all the people of the earth might know the hand of the LORD, that it is mighty: that ye might **fear** the LORD your God for ever. (Joshua 4:24)

Now therefore **fear** the LORD, and serve him in sincerity and in truth: (Joshua 24:14)

Only **fear** the LORD, and serve him in truth with all your heart: for consider how great things he hath done for you. (1 Samuel 12:24)

The God of Israel said, the Rock of Israel spake to me, He that ruleth over men must be just, ruling in the **fear** of God. (2 Samuel 23:3)

And so it was at the beginning of their dwelling there [in Samaria], that they **feared** not the LORD: therefore the LORD sent lions among them, which slew some of them. (2 Kings 17:25)

Then one of the priests whom they had carried away from Samaria came and dwelt in Bethel, and taught them how they should **fear** the LORD. (2 Kings 17:28)

For great is the LORD, and greatly to be praised: he also is to be **feared** above all gods. (I Chronicles 16:25)

O LORD, I beseech thee, let now thine ear be attentive to the prayer of thy servant, and to the prayer of thy servants, who desire to **fear** thy name: (Nehemiah 1:11)

There was a man in the land of Uz, whose name was Job; and that man was perfect and upright, and one that **feared** God, and eschewed evil. (Job 1:1)

Serve the LORD with **fear**, and rejoice with trembling. Kiss the Son, lest he be angry, and ye perish from the way, when his wrath is kindled but a little. (Psalm 2:11–12)

The foolish shall not stand in thy sight: thou hatest all workers of iniquity. Thou shalt destroy them that speak leasing: the LORD will abhor the bloody and deceitful man. But as for me, I will come into thy house in the multitude of thy mercy: and in thy **fear** will I worship toward thy holy temple. (Psalm 5:5–7)

The **fear** of the LORD is clean, enduring for ever: (Psalm 19:9)

Ye that **fear** the LORD, praise him; all ye the seed of Jacob, glorify him; and **fear** him, all ye the seed of Israel. (Psalm 22:23)

What man is he that **feareth** the LORD? him shall he teach in the way that he shall choose. His soul shall dwell at ease; and his seed shall inherit the earth. The secret of the LORD is with them that **fear** him; and he will shew them his covenant. (Psalm 25:12–14)

Oh how great is thy goodness, which thou hast laid up for them that **fear** thee; which thou hast wrought for them that trust in thee before the sons of men! (Psalm 31:19)

Let all the earth **fear** the LORD: let all the inhabitants of the world stand in awe of him. (Psalm 33:8)

Behold, the eye of the LORD is upon them that **fear** him, upon them that hope in his mercy; (Psalm 33:18)

The angel of the LORD encampeth round about them that **fear** him, and delivereth them. (Psalm 34:7)

O **fear** the LORD, ye his saints: for there is no want to them that **fear** him. (Psalm 34:9)

Come, ye children, hearken unto me: I will teach you the **fear** of the LORD. (Psalm 34:11)

And he hath put a new song in my mouth, even praise unto our God: many shall see it, and **fear**, and shall trust in the LORD. (Psalm 40:3)

Thou hast given a banner to them that **fear** thee, that it may be displayed because of the truth. (Psalm 60:4)

For thou, O God, hast heard my vows: thou hast

given me the heritage of those that **fear** thy name. (Psalm 61:5)

And all men shall **fear**, and shall declare the work of God; for they shall wisely consider of his doing. (Psalm 64:9)

God shall bless us; and all the ends of the earth shall **fear** him. (Psalm 67:7)

They shall **fear** thee as long as the sun and moon endure, throughout all generations. (Psalm 72:7)

Thou, even thou, art to be **feared**: and who may stand in thy sight when once thou art angry? (Psalm 76:7)

Surely his salvation is nigh them that **fear** him; that glory may dwell in our land. (Psalm 85:9)

Teach me thy way, O LORD; I will walk in thy truth: unite my heart to **fear** thy name. (Psalm 86:11)

God is greatly to be **feared** in the assembly of the saints, and to be had in reverence of all them that are about him. (Psalm 89:7)

Who knoweth the power of thine anger? even according to thy **fear**, so is thy wrath. (Psalm 90:11)

For the LORD is great, and greatly to be praised: he is to be **feared** above all gods. (Psalm 96:4)

O worship the LORD in the beauty of holiness: **fear** before him, all the earth. (Psalm 96:9)

For as the heaven is high above the earth, so great is his mercy toward them that **fear** him.... Like as a father pitieth his children, so the LORD pitieth them that **fear** him. (Psalm 103:11, 13)

But the mercy of the LORD is from everlasting to everlasting upon them that **fear** him, and his righteousness unto children's children; (Psalm 103:17)

The **fear** of the LORD is the beginning of wisdom: (Psalm 111:10)

Praise ye the LORD. Blessed is the man that **feareth** the LORD, that delighteth greatly in his commandments. (Psalm 112:1)

Ye that **fear** the LORD, trust in the LORD: he is their help and their shield. (Psalm 115:11)

He will bless them that **fear** the LORD, both small and great. (Psalm 115:13)

Let them now that **fear** the LORD say, that his mercy endureth for ever. (Psalm 118:4)

I am a companion of all them that **fear** thee, and of them that keep thy precepts. (Psalm 119:63)

My flesh trembleth for **fear** of thee; and I am afraid of thy judgments. (Psalm 119:120)

Blessed is every one that **feareth** the LORD; that walketh in his ways. (Psalm 128:1)

Behold, that thus shall the man be blessed that **feareth** the LORD. (Psalm 128:4)

But there is forgiveness with thee, that thou mayest be **feared**. (Psalm 130:4)

He will fulfil the desire of them that **fear** him: he also will hear their cry, and will save them. (Psalm 145:19)

The LORD taketh pleasure in them that **fear** him, in those that hope in his mercy. (Psalm 147:11)

The **fear** of the LORD is the beginning of knowledge: but fools despise wisdom and instruction. (Proverbs 1:7)

Then shalt thou understand the **fear** of the LORD, and find the knowledge of God. (Proverbs 2:5)

Be not wise in thine own eyes: **fear** the LORD, and depart from evil. (Proverbs 3:7)

The **fear** of the LORD is to hate evil: pride, and arrogancy, and the evil way, and the froward mouth, do I hate. (Proverbs 8:13)

The **fear** of the LORD is the beginning of wisdom: and the knowledge of the holy is understanding. (Proverbs 9:10)

The **fear** of the LORD prolongeth days: but the years of the wicked shall be shortened. (Proverbs 10:27)

Whoso despiseth the word shall be destroyed: but he that **feareth** the commandment shall be rewarded. (Proverbs 13:13)

He that walketh in his uprightness **feareth** the LORD: (Proverbs 14:2)

In the **fear** of the LORD is strong confidence: and his children shall have a place of refuge. (Proverbs 14:26)

The **fear** of the LORD is a fountain of life, to depart from the snares of death. (Proverbs 14:27)

The **fear** of the LORD is the instruction of wisdom; and before honour is humility. (Proverbs 15:33)

By mercy and truth iniquity is purged: and by the **fear** of the LORD men depart from evil. (Proverbs 16:6)

The **fear** of the LORD tendeth to life: and he that hath it shall abide satisfied; he shall not be visited with evil. (Proverbs 19:23)

By humility and the **fear** of the LORD are riches, and honour, and life. (Proverbs 22:4)

Let not thine heart envy sinners: but be thou in the **fear** of the LORD all the day long. (Proverbs 23:17)

Favour is deceitful, and beauty is vain: but a woman that **feareth** the LORD, she shall be praised. (Proverbs 31:30)

For in the multitude of dreams and many words there are also divers vanities: but **fear** thou God. (Ecclesiastes 5:7)

... for he that **feareth** God shall come forth of them all. (Ecclesiastes 7:18)

Though a sinner do evil an hundred times, and his days be prolonged, yet surely I know that it shall be well with them that **fear** God, which **fear** before him: (Ecclesiastes 8:12)

Let us hear the conclusion of the whole matter: **Fear** God, and keep his commandments: for this is the whole duty of man. (Ecclesiastes 12:13)

Enter into the rock, and hide thee in the dust, for **fear** of the LORD, and for the glory of his majesty. (Isaiah 2:10)

Sanctify the LORD of hosts himself; and let him be your **fear**, and let him be your dread. (Isaiah 8:13)

Fear ye not me? saith the LORD: will ye not tremble at my presence... (Jeremiah 5:22)

Fear ye not me? saith the LORD: will ye not tremble at my presence? (Jeremiah 10:7)

And they shall be my people, and I will be their God: And I will give them one heart, and one way, that they may **fear** me for ever, for the good of them, and of their children after them: And I will make an everlasting covenant with them, that I will not turn away from them, to do them good; but I will put my **fear** in their hearts, that they shall not depart from me. (Jeremiah 32:38–40)

VERSES FROM THE NEW TESTAMENT (KING JAMES VERSION)

[Jesus said:] And **fear** not them which kill the body, but are not able to kill the soul: but rather **fear** him which is able to destroy both soul and body in hell. (Matthew 10:28)

[Jesus said:] But I will forewarn you whom ye shall **fear**: **Fear** him, which after he hath killed hath power to cast into hell; yea, I say unto you, **Fear** him. (Luke 12:5)

Then had the churches rest throughout all Judaea and Galilee and Samaria, and were edified; and walking in the **fear** of the Lord, and in the comfort of the Holy Ghost, were multiplied. (Acts 9:31)

There was a certain man in Caesarea called Cornelius, a centurion of the band called the Italian band, A devout man, and one that **feared** God with all his house, which gave much alms to the people, and prayed to God alway. (Acts 10:1-2)

Then Peter opened his mouth, and said, Of a truth I perceive that God is no respecter of persons: But in every nation he that **feareth** him, and worketh righteousness, is accepted with him. (Acts 10:34–35)

Then Paul stood up, and beckoning with his hand said, Men of Israel, and ye that **fear** God, give audience. (Acts 13:16)

Men and brethren, children of the stock of Abraham, and whosoever among you **feareth** God, to you is the word of this salvation sent. (Acts 13:26)

> **[Jesus said:] But I will forewarn you whom ye shall fear: Fear him, which after he hath killed hath power to cast into hell; yea, I say unto you, Fear him. (Luke 12:5)**

Having therefore these promises, dearly beloved, let us cleanse ourselves from all filthiness of the flesh and spirit, perfecting holiness in the **fear** of God. (2 Corinthians 7:1)

Giving thanks always for all things unto God and the Father in the name of our Lord Jesus Christ; Submitting yourselves one to another in the **fear** of God. (Ephesians 5:20–21)

Servants, be obedient to them that are your masters according to the flesh, with **fear** and trembling, in singleness of your heart, as unto Christ; (Ephesians 6:5)

Wherefore, my beloved, as ye have always obeyed, not as in my presence only, but now much more in my absence, work out your own salvation with **fear** and trembling. (Philippians 2:12)

It is a **fearful** thing to fall into the hands of the living God. (Hebrews 10:31)

Wherefore we receiving a kingdom which cannot be moved, let us have grace, whereby we may serve God acceptably with reverence and godly **fear**: For our God is a consuming fire. (Hebrews 12:28–29)

Honour all men. Love the brotherhood. **Fear** God. Honour the king. (1 Peter 2:17)

[An angel speaks to all the people of the world:] Saying with a loud voice, **Fear** God, and give glory to him; for the hour of his judgment is come: and worship him that made heaven, and earth, and the sea, and the fountains of waters. (Revelation 14:7)

Who shall not **fear** thee, O Lord, and glorify thy name? (Revelation 15:4)

And a voice came out of the throne, saying, Praise our God, all ye his servants, and ye that **fear** him, both small and great. (Revelation 19:5)

VERSES FROM THE KORAN (YUSUFALI TRANSLATION)

This is the Book; in it is guidance sure, without doubt, to those who **fear** Allah; (2.2)

But if ye cannot—and of a surety ye cannot—then **fear** the Fire whose fuel is men and stones,—which is prepared for those who reject Faith. (2.24)

O Children of Israel! call to mind the (special) favour which I bestowed upon you, and fulfil your covenant with Me as I fulfil My Covenant with you, and **fear** none but Me. And believe in what I reveal, confirming the revelation which is with you, and be not the first to reject Faith therein, nor sell My Signs for a small price; and **fear** Me, and Me alone. (2.40–41)

"Hold firmly to what We have given you and bring (ever) to remembrance what is therein: Perchance ye may **fear** Allah." (2.63)

So We made it an example to their own time and to their posterity, and a lesson to those who **fear** Allah. (2.66)

And who is more unjust than he who forbids that in places for the worship of Allah, Allah's name should be celebrated?—whose zeal is (in fact) to ruin them? It was not fitting that such should themselves enter them except in **fear**. For them there is nothing but disgrace in this world, and in the world to come, an exceeding torment. (2.114)

So from whencesoever Thou startest forth, turn Thy face in the direction of the sacred Mosque; and wheresoever ye are, Turn your face thither: that there be no ground of dispute against you among the people, except those of them that are bent on wickedness; so **fear** them not, but **fear** Me; and that I may complete My favours on you, and ye May (consent to) be guided; (2.150)

Such are the people of truth, the Allah-**fearing**. (2.177)

It is no virtue if ye enter your houses from the back: It is virtue if ye **fear** Allah. Enter houses through the proper doors: And **fear** Allah: That ye may prosper. (2.189)

But **fear** Allah, and know that Allah is with those who restrain themselves. (2.194)

And **fear** Allah, and know that Allah is strict in punishment. (2.196)

So **fear** Me, o ye that are wise. (2.197)

Then **fear** Allah, and know that ye will surely be gathered unto Him. (2.203)

When it is said to him, "**Fear** Allah", He is led by arrogance to (more) crime. Enough for him is Hell;—An evil bed indeed (To lie on)! (2.206)

Your wives are as a tilth unto you; so approach your tilth when or how ye will; but do some good act for your souls beforehand; and **fear** Allah. (2.223)

And **fear** Allah, and know that Allah is well acquainted with all things. (2.231)

But **fear** Allah and know that Allah sees well what ye do. (2.233)

O ye who believe! **Fear** Allah, and give up what remains of your demand for usury, if ye are indeed believers. (2.278)

And **fear** the Day when ye shall be brought back to Allah. Then shall every soul be paid what it earned, and none shall be dealt with unjustly. (2.281)

"So **fear** Allah, and obey me." (3.50)

O ye who believe! **Fear** Allah as He should be **feared**, and die not except in a state of Islam. (3.102)

O ye who believe! Devour not usury, doubled and multiplied; but **fear** Allah; that ye may (really) prosper. **Fear** the Fire, which is repaired for those who reject Faith: (3.130–131)

It is only the Evil One that suggests to you the **fear** of his votaries: Be ye not afraid of them, but **fear** Me, if ye have Faith. (3.175)

If it were His will, He could destroy you, o mankind, and create another race; for He hath power this to do. (4.133)

Help ye one another in righteousness and piety, but help ye not one another in sin and rancour: **fear** Allah: for Allah is strict in punishment. (5.2)

And **fear** Allah, for Allah knoweth well the secrets of your hearts. (5.7)

Be just: that is next to piety: and **fear** Allah. For Allah is well-acquainted with all that ye do. (5.8)

And in their footsteps We sent Jesus the son of Mary, confirming the Law that had come before him: We sent him the Gospel: therein was guidance and light, and confirmation of the Law that had come before him: a guidance and an admonition to those who **fear** Allah. (5.46)

O ye who believe! take not for friends and protectors those who take your religion for a mockery or sport,—whether among those who received the Scripture before you, or among those who reject Faith; but **fear** ye Allah, if ye have faith (indeed). (5.57)

But **fear** Allah, and listen (to His counsel): for Allah guideth not a rebellious people: (5.108)

Behold! the disciples, said: "O Jesus the son of Mary! can thy Lord send down to us a table set (with viands) from heaven?" Said Jesus: "**Fear** Allah, if ye have faith." (5.112)

> **O ye who believe! fight the unbelievers who gird you about, and let them find firmness in you: and know that Allah is with those who fear Him. (9.123)**

[Noah said:] "Do ye wonder that there hath come to you a message from your Lord, through a man of your own people, to warn you,—so that ye may **fear** Allah and haply receive His Mercy?" (7.63)

When the anger of Moses was appeased, he took up the tablets: in the writing thereon was guidance and Mercy for such as **fear** their Lord. (7.154)

O ye who believe! if ye **fear** Allah, He will grant you a criterion (to judge between right and wrong), remove from you (all) evil (that may afflict) you, and forgive you: for Allah is the Lord of grace unbounded. (8.29)

O ye who believe! fight the unbelievers who gird you about, and let them find firmness in you: and know that Allah is with those who **fear** Him. (9.123)

But when Our Clear Signs are rehearsed unto them, those who rest not their hope on their meeting with Us, Say: "Bring us a reading other than this, or change this," Say: "It is not for me, of my own accord, to change it: I follow naught but what is revealed unto me: if I were to disobey my Lord, I should myself **fear** the penalty of a Great Day (to come)." (10.15)

We sent Noah to his people (with a mission): "I have come to you with a Clear Warning: That ye serve none but Allah: Verily I do **fear** for you the penalty of a grievous day." (11.25–26)

Allah has said: "Take not (for worship) two gods: for He is just One Allah: then **fear** Me (and Me alone)." (16.51)

We have not sent down the Qur'an to thee to be (an occasion) for thy distress, But only as an admonition to those who **fear** (Allah),— (20.2–3)

O mankind! **fear** your Lord! for the convulsion of the Hour (of Judgment) will be a thing terrible! (22.1)

Behold, their brother Noah said to them: "Will ye not **fear** (Allah)? I am to you a messenger worthy of all trust: So **fear** Allah, and obey me.["] (26.106–108)

Behold, their brother Hud said to them: "Will ye not **fear** (Allah)? I am to you a messenger worthy of all trust: So **fear** Allah and obey me.["] (26.124–126)

Behold, their brother Salih said to them: "Will you not **fear** (Allah)? I am to you a messenger worthy of all trust. So **fear** Allah, and obey me." (26.142–144)

Behold, their brother Lut said to them: "Will ye not **fear** (Allah)? I am to you a messenger worthy of all trust. So **fear** Allah and obey me.["] (26.161–163)

Behold, Shu'aib said to them: "Will ye not **fear** (Allah)? I am to you a messenger worthy of all trust. So **fear** Allah and obey me." (26.177–179)

And (We also saved) Abraham: behold, he said to his people, "Serve Allah and **fear** Him: that will be best for you—If ye understand!["] (29.16)

Those truly **fear** Allah, among His Servants, who have knowledge: for Allah is Exalted in Might, Oft-Forgiving. (35.28)

Say: "I would, if I disobeyed my Lord, indeed have **fear** of the Penalty of a Mighty Day." (39.13)

They shall have Layers of Fire above them, and Layers (of Fire) below them: with this doth Allah warn off his servants: "O My Servants! then **fear** ye Me!" (39.16)

When Jesus came with Clear Signs, he said: "Now have I come to you with Wisdom, and in order to make clear to you some of the (points) on which ye dispute: therefore **fear** Allah and obey me.["] (43.63)

And **fear** Allah; for Allah is strict in Punishment. (59.7)

Had We sent down this Qur'an on a mountain, verily, thou wouldst have seen it humble itself and cleave asunder for **fear** of Allah. Such are the similitudes which We propound to men, that they may reflect. (59.21)

Allah has prepared for them a severe Punishment (in the Hereafter). Therefore **fear** Allah, O ye men of understanding—who have believed!—for Allah hath indeed sent down to you a Message,— (65.10)

As for those who **fear** their Lord unseen, for them is Forgiveness and a great Reward. (67.12)

GOOD BOOKS

CONFESSION IS GOOD FOR THE POLE

Sexuality in the Confessional: A Sacrament Profaned by Stephen Haliczer (New York & Oxford: Oxford University Press, 1996)

One of the most common themes of pornography in the 1700s and 1800s featured male Catholic clergy getting it on with parishioners and nuns, sometimes in church, even in the confessional itself. To this day, this is looked upon as a blasphemous outrage, anti-Catholicism at its most scurrilous. But the cold truth is that sexual acts between confessors and their penitents—sometimes *during* the sacrament of confession—were far from uncommon. The Catholic Church's own records prove this.

Despite the existence of this proof, scholars have studiously ignored or underplayed it. Henry Charles Lea's monumental *A History of the Spanish Inquisition*—four volumes long—has one brief chapter on the topic, and that was published over 100 years ago. That's pretty much the best coverage the topic had received. That is, until Stephen Haliczer—a Distinguished Research Professor at Northern Illinois University and one of the world's leading Inquisition experts—broke the silence. His book on the subject, *Sexuality in the Confessional*, has escaped mainstream notice,

and no wonder. It wasn't meant for the general public. Published by Oxford University Press only as a $75 hardcover (for 208 pages of text), you won't find it in your local bookstore, and it's not even likely to make an appearance at public libraries. It's aimed squarely at university libraries, where scholars and grad students are the most likely to read about these proceedings of the Inquisition.

> **You see, the Inquisition wasn't concerned solely with witches, Jews, and other heretics; it also went after priests who acted inappropriately with the people who came to them for the cleansing of their sins.**

You see, the Inquisition wasn't concerned solely with witches, Jews, and other heretics; it also went after priests who acted inappropriately with the people who came to them for the cleansing of their sins. Since confession is one of the bedrocks of the Church, the leaders rightly assumed that priests propositioning, groping, and even screwing their penitents would cause a loss of moral authority in the eyes of the people. The situation was sometimes so bad that husbands forbade their wives from going to confession in order to avoid lecherous men of the cloth.

To examine this practically unstudied phenomenon, Haliczer focused on Spain and dealt only with cases in which complete records of the proceedings still exist and were open to him. This resulted in a pool of 223 cases from 1530 to 1819, which, he admits, "represent only a fraction of the solicitation cases tried by the Spanish Inquisition." (Lea, mentioned above, gives the total figure for just 1723 to 1820 as 3,775 solicitation cases, which averages to over a case per day.) He also studied "confessors' manuals and other works written by theologians for confessors and penitents" from that time period.

Thus we find that during some acts of confession, hanky-panky really was happening. But before we get to the details, it's necessary to look at the original setting for confessions. The confessional box, made famous by Hollywood, was a later invention. Originally, there was no specific or enclosed location within the church—the priest would simply sit on a bench, a chair, or the steps to the altar or baptistry, while the penitent knelt close to him. Haliczer writes:

> Regardless of where or when it was used, the traditional penitential posture offered alluring possibilities to a confessor bent on seducing his penitent. During the twenty years between 1667 and 1687, Pedro Pons, the prior of the Augustinian convent of Nuestra Senora del Toro on the island of Menorca, took advantage of his physical proximity to his female penitents to kiss them, grasp their breasts, and attempt to set up assignations with them. On one occasion, when a thirty-five-year-old widow with whom he had a longstanding relationship came to confess with him, they first excited each other with suggestive language and then engaged in mutual masturbation.

This passage leads to an interesting point: The attention of the priest wasn't always unwelcome or brief. Some priests and women had long-term sexual liaisons that were often initiated and continued during the act of confession in the church. A woman in the Spain of old was rarely allowed to leave the house or to have contact with a man who wasn't her husband or blood relation. The big exception to these restrictions, of course, was going to confession. In fact, records show that in a small number of cases, it was the desperate housewives who made the first move.

Juan de Monseratte was able to seduce at least two kneeling penitents. "In both cases, sexual inter-

action with Monseratte kissing and caressing the women, then fondling their breasts, and finally inducing them to masturbate him…. After both women had been thoroughly aroused during confession, Monseratte had intercourse with them in the home of a woman who made extra money by renting it out for use as a rendezvous for illicit sexual interaction."

In another case, Eugenia Ordonez told a tribunal how, during confessions, she and Friar Alonso Guerrero would talk dirty to each other, she'd give him a handjob underneath his robes, then he would finger her to orgasm.

The confessional box was introduced in the latter half of the sixteenth century and was in near-universal use in Spain only by the end of the eighteenth century. But why was it created at all? As Haliczer explains: "In order to reduce the danger to morality…" You read correctly: The confessional box was created in order to curb the molestation of penitents by priests. The idea was that the screen between the two parties would prevent physical contact and shield the woman's identity. Nice in theory, but it didn't exactly work like that. Some confessionals were divided by a curtain; in others, the screen was conveniently missing. And being sealed from all outside eyes sometimes inflamed the situation.

Even with a solid divider, some priests could—and did—still verbally harass penitents. And with a willing partner, they could not only plan their trysts but talk dirty to each other while each masturbated. And then we have the case of the ingenious Francisco de las Llagas, who cut what was essentially a gloryhole in the dividing screen. Twenty or thirty times during his long-term relationship (intercourse included) with Isabel de Tena,

> he would then ask her to kiss him and put his tongue through a hole in the confessional screen so that she could take it in her mouth. Isabel willingly complied, even though she made a pretence of reluctance by asking coyly, "But Father Llagas how could you do this…and in such a holy place?"

These holy screens apparently weren't too rare, as Haliczer notes several instances, including one in which "[Vincente] Ripoll begged [Sor Catalina Angelo, a nun] to insert her fingers inside her vagina and then put them through the holes in the confessional screen."

A number of priests got into hot water for jerking off while hearing women confess their sins. Manuals for confessors stated that occasionally getting hard-ons and even ejaculating "involuntarily" while hearing confessions just go with the territory, but actually spanking it while the woman on the other side of the screen tells you her impure thoughts and actions was enough to get you arrested by the Spanish Inquisition, which no one expects.

Haliczer covers all kinds of variations on the theme: horny priests molesting sick penitents in their own homes, having penitents come to the priest's house because he's allegedly ill, one case of inserting a Host wafer into a nun's hooha during her exorcism, and treating convents as sexual playgrounds. While hearing a nun's confession in 1705, a Franciscan "proceeded to try to insert his hand in her habit, while she squirmed away from him..." He stopped only when she threatened to scream, putting her among the near-50 percent of women who rejected their confessors' advances. Very nearly 40 percent of the women completely acquiesced, with some of them having initiated the sexual activities. The remaining ten percent or so gave in to some of the priests' advances.

Notably, in the proceedings examined, adult women were almost always the target of clerical attention. Of the cases Haliczer looked at, only ten clerics were charged with engaging in sexual activities with male penitents. And only thirty-six victims (of both sexes) were under sixteen.

Specific incidents are sprinkled throughout the book, often with a lack of juicy detail, but the book's longest chapter, "Carnal Behavior and Sexual Disorders," contains a high concentration of satisfying descriptions:

> On two occasions, after he had finished hearing the confession of Sor Bernarda de San Antonio, Fray Juan de la Olmeda told her of his desire to kiss and fondle her and suggested that she think of him when she urinated. [p 156]

> Fray Juan Ibáñez repeatedly urged Sor Augustina to clean herself after menstruation by inserting her finger deep inside her vagina,... and at one point expressed a desire to see Sor Augustina and another nun engage in sex play. [p 159]

> Fray Pablo Ginard expressed a desire to shave Juana Ana Tarrasa's pubic hair and wash her clitoris. [p 159]

> When fifteen-year-old Lucía Rodríguez, who had recently married a labrador [i.e., an agricultural laborer], came to [Gaspar de Nájera] for confession, he demanded to know how big her husband's member was and if he had thrust all of it inside of her on their first night together. [p 160]

> In 1696 the Carmelite friar Alejandro Lloret came before the Valencia tribunal to confess that he had had anal intercourse with María García, the wife of a shoemaker in Játiva, on seven occasions. [p 170]

> [Pablo] Ginard ordered [Magdalena Aldover] to trace a cross on his genitals before taking them into her mouth.... Her younger sister, Margarita, accepted a dildo from Ginard and kept it in her home for two weeks since, as she told the inquisitors, she saw nothing sinful in making use of such an object. [p 171]

> [Juan] Ibanez took thirty-three-year-old Maria Angela Polop to the sacristy and had intercourse with her on the ornate cushion that was placed under the effigy of Christ during Holy Week. [p 172]

In one notably bizarre instance, a Dominican friar had a nun bring him a gorgeous silver chalice used in her convent. "[A]fter commenting briefly on its beauty and workmanship he suddenly announced that it would be ideal 'for an obscenity like the one that you would perform in a woman's hole,' thrust it under his habit, and masturbated into it."

Remember, folks, this is coming directly from the Catholic Church's Inquisition files, not the lurid imagination of some sacrilegious pornographer. The author does devote the final chapter to such anticlerical pornography, as well as mainstream novels and even exposés from former Spanish priests. While such literature may have overstated the *frequency* of priest-penitent hook-ups, there's no doubt that this kind of thing went on, not rarely.

Such cases were prosecuted until 1820, when Ferdinand VII put the brakes on the Inquisition (it was formally abolished fourteen years later). Haliczer points out that such behavior on the part of priests has almost certainly never gone away, although he cites only a single case in Spain, from 1959.

He notes: "If anything, by focusing attention on the confessional as a venue for sexual activity, the Inquisition may have eroticized confession."

HOLY PETER

The Sexuality of Christ in Renaissance Art and in Modern Oblivion (second ed.) by Leo Steinberg (Chicago: University of Chicago Press, 1995)

An image of Jesus with his penis exposed—perhaps even sporting an erection—is enough to get the Christian right, and some other people, stomping mad, howling against the sick postmodern artists who want to defile and destroy Christianity. But such shocking images aren't the brainchildren of twenty-first-century blasphemers. Such images appeared in the Renaissance and were meant to be respectful, not sacrilegious. The definitive work on the subject—the one that first gathered together this art and showed a slack-jawed world—is *The Sexuality of Christ in Renaissance Art and in Modern Oblivion* (1983) by Leo Steinberg, the Benjamin Franklin Professor Emeritus of the History of Art at the University of Pennsylvania. After discovering many more examples, and needing to respond to his critics, Steinberg brought out a greatly expanded second edition in 1995. This is the edition I'm reviewing.

Over the course of 300 images, Steinberg presents a surfeit of Renaissance works of art showing Jesus' penis, during infancy, or with him on the cross, dead on a slab (the *Stone of Unction*), being held by Mary (*Pieta*), and after the Resurrection. We see paintings, drawings, illuminations, etchings, and statues from the middle 1300s to the late 1500s by artists hailing from Germany, France, the Netherlands, and elsewhere across Western and Northern Europe. In some, Jesus is in a diaphanous cloth that either shows or clearly outlines his genitals. In many others, he is completely nude, his razzle dazzle plain to see. Most amazing are the artworks in

which Jesus has an erection. The bulk of these present the Christ child fully nude, though a few show the little tyke pitching a tent while wearing a loincloth. (Of the paintings showing adult Jesus with wood, he is always wearing a loincloth.)

In its frank depictions of Jesus' schlong, the Renaissance was unique. Both before and after this period, artists and the public were—with scattered exceptions—too squeamish to tolerate Jesus in his entirety. Thus, the book also includes many examples of the way in which artists avoided Jesus' unit, such as using a dangling cross to block the view of an otherwise naked baby Jesus. In a Byzantine illumination from the fourteenth century, we see adult Jesus being baptized while naked as the day he was born. His entire body is fully visible from the front; his groin completely lacks genitals. He looks like a Ken doll.

After the Renaissance, prudish custodians defaced the nude-Jesus artwork of the Renaissance, painting in loincloths where none had existed, or draping them over crucifixes. Unfortunately, this Puritanism still lingers—even into the late twentieth century, art critics and historians simply refused to mention what was right before them: Jesus' penis. When they did, they offered silly rationales. One claimed that Jesus' hard-on on the cross was actually a strong wind billowing his loincloth, although there is no other sign of wind in that painting—no one's hair is tousled, and robes and tunics remain unruffled. The most common excuse is that the appearance of tumescence on the adult Jesus is simply an artistic accident, an unfortunate illusion caused by the folds of his loincloth. Besides the fact that one look at the paintings themselves will expose this theory as hogwash, this is immensely insulting to the painters themselves. We're supposed to believe that these Renaissance Masters—who planned and perfectly executed even the tiniest details in their works—were so sloppy and haphazard when it came to this part of their paintings that they accidentally made it look as though Jesus has an erection? Please.

What made the artists of the Renaissance different from those of other periods was their choice to portray Jesus as *fully* human. Their emphasis was less on trumpeting the divinity of Jesus and more on portraying his humanity. To them, taking on a mortal body meant taking it on in every way, penis and all. And sometimes that penis gets hard. Steinberg explains:

> If, as Christianity teaches, God abased himself in becoming man, then his assumption of human genitals sounds the nadir of his self-abasement. And then it is the Renaissance image of Christ which reveals divine condescension, as it were, *in extremis*; God joining himself to the human condition to the point of sharing with man even that portion wherein retribution for Original Sin is most apparent, most vitiating.

To put it another way, "Christianity had once, during that Renaissance interlude, passed through a phase of exceptional daring, when the full implications of Incarnational faith were put forth in icons that recoiled not even from the God-man's assumption of sexuality."

This was the result of Renaissance artists' inclination toward naturalism (the art explanation) and of Renaissance theologians' emphasis on the humanness of Jesus (the theological explanation). Put them together, and you get reverential artwork depicting Jesus' dick.

Understand that this explanation is a general one that covers this unofficial genre of art in its entirety. Steinberg goes deep into art theory/history and even deeper into theology to explain and interpret the many interesting variations on the theme:

• Jesus and/or his mother touching his genitals in infant scenes and in postmortem scenes;

• Mary purposely exposing her child's genitals to the viewer;

• Jesus being circumcised (some theologians emphasized the fact that Jesus' circumcision when he was eight days old was the first of five times he shed blood for humanity);

• the Magi bowing before and gazing directly at the Christ Child's groin;

Holy Family with St. John the Baptist by Denys Calvaert (1540–1619). One of many Renaissance paintings showing baby Jesus with an erection. From *The Sexuality of Christ in Renaissance Art and Modern Oblivion*.

Madonna and Child with the Infant St. John by Cosimo Rosselli (1439–c.1507). No formula for baby Jesus during the Renaissance. From *The Sexuality of Christ in Renaissance Art and Modern Oblivion*.

Steinberg offers up a mountain of facts and strongly argued interpretations—presented in a style that slides from academic to lighthearted, often from one sentence to the next—but whether or not you accept his theories about why this artwork exists, you simply cannot deny that it does.

A LOAD OF *MALAKOI*

The New Testament and Homosexuality by Robin Scroggs (Minneapolis: Fortress Press, 1983)

Everyone knows that the Bible condemns homosexuality, but what does it *specifically* say about the subject?

Everyone knows that the Bible condemns homosexuality, but what does it *specifically* say about the subject? Those of us who don't believe that the Bible is a divine book dictated by Yahweh might be tempted to answer with, "Who cares?," but the question is important simply because the Bible deeply influences social and political attitudes towards gays and lesbians in the US and some other societies. Or, at the very least, the Bible gives lots of people, including politicians, a convenient justification for their pre-existing hatred of men and women who are attracted to people with the same type of genitals.

In his slim book *The New Testament and Homosexuality*, Union Theological Seminary Professor of New Testament Robin Scroggs dissects every mention or possible mention of same-sex relations in the entire Bible. The book is slim because few such references exist.

Scroggs' approach is to look at the context of the Bible's scant mentions of homosexuality—the overall cultural context in which the biblical books were written and the theological contexts in which the brief passages appear. To set up cultural context, he provides a succinct but enlightening overview of what we know about homosexuality in the Greco-Roman culture of the times, which deeply influenced the New Testament's pronouncements. The gist is that pederasty—men having sex with passive boys and adolescents—was by far the dominant form of homosexuality. (Adult men, especially

Crucifixion (1515) by Hans Schäufelein. He is risen. From *The Sexuality of Christ in Renaissance Art and Modern Oblivion.*

• the shocking woodcut *Holy Family* (1511), in which Hans Baldung Grien shows St. Anne (the Virgin Mary's mom) playing with baby Jesus' pud;

• Francesco Botticini's painting *Madonna and Child with Angels* (circa 1490), in which one of the aforementioned angels drops a stream of flowers onto baby Jesus' exposed groin;

• the subgenre of Madonna and Child images in which Mary is breastfeeding Jesus, with one mammary in full view.

without a major age gap between them, having sex with each other was practically unheard of, and women having sex with each other, while no doubt happening, was rendered invisible simply because of women's low place in society.) Several forms of pederasty existed: an essentially consensual mentor/protégé relationship, coerced prostitution in which slave boys were used, and consensual prostitution in which adolescents and young men appeared as effeminate as possible to attract clients. This last form was universally reviled.

Scroggs also looks at the attitudes of Palestinian Judaism and Hellenized Judaism, which obviously had direct effects, as well. Leviticus contains a prohibition on men of any age having sex with each other, followed two chapters later by the infamous death penalty for such behavior. "These two verses are the only legal traditions about homosexuality in the Hebrew Bible. Furthermore, no other biblical passage refers to this prohibition, nor is there any story showing the law being applied in a concrete situation."

The only other parts of the Old Testament generally thought to refer to homosexuality are the stories of Sodom and of the Levite and his concubine (Judges 19), but even if we allow that the crowds in both stories wanted to sexually violate the strangers, the tales can be seen only as condemnations of male homosexual gang rape. They have nothing to do with consensual relations.

Remaining thorough, Scroggs looks at how these passages were translated into Aramaic and Greek, and how rabbis interpreted all this.

We then arrive at the passages from the New Testament. There are only three. None come from Jesus or the Gospels, which all by itself indicates that homosexuality was a non-issue. All references are from writings traditionally assigned to Paul. Two are embedded in lists of vices. The first list (1 Corinthians 6:9–10) contains the highly ambiguous word *malakoi*, even though the Greek language contains many specific words that "Paul" could've used. *Malakoi* literally meant "soft" and had the figurative meaning of "effeminate." Used as a noun, it means an effeminate male. It is coupled with the word *arsenokotai* ("one who beds men"), and Scroggs believes that the author is specifically targeting effeminate call boys and the men who hire them. It is not a blanket condemnation of male homosexuality, much less homosexuality in general.

In the original Greek, the second list (1 Timothy 1:9–10) contains three words of varying ambiguity. When presented together, as they are, Scroggs interprets them as "male prostitutes, males who lie [with them], and slave-dealers [who procure them]." The fact that both lists contain other, non-sexual vices, Scroggs says, shows that the author wasn't too concerned about homosexuality, not even this narrow, widely hated form of pederasty.

The only sustained passage to deal with the topic (Romans 1:26–27, a mere two verses), is, in the end, ambiguous. On the surface, it seems to be a condemnation of homosexuality (with no explanation as to why). But keeping in mind the Greco-Roman milieu, Scroggs points out that the author could only have been referring to pederasty (in all its forms). It does not reference homosexuality as we know it and can't legitimately be applied to it. On top of that, "Paul" didn't write the passage as part of some ethics lesson on how (not) to behave; he was using homosexuality/pederasty to illustrate his theological point that we're living in a false, fallen world.

Scroggs concludes: "Biblical judgments against homosexuality are not relevant to today's debate." Whether or not you agree with his interpretations and ultimate assessment, he presents a fountain of facts about the culture of the time and about linguistic murkiness that show that the New Testament's pronouncements are far from clear-cut.

THE FAMILY THAT PRAYS TOGETHER, LAYS TOGETHER

Christianity and Incest by Annie Imbens and Ineke Jonker (Minneapolis: Fortress Press, 1992)

One of a tiny, all-but-nonexistent number of books to specifically address the topic, *Christianity and Incest* by Annie Imbens and Ineke Jonker was originally published in 1985 thanks to a publisher in the Netherlands; six years later it was translated into English, not by a publisher in the US, the UK, or Australia, but by a pastoral foundation in the Netherlands, funded by a grant from a nonreligious organization also in that country. If it weren't for the Dutch, the English-language version would never have seen the light of day. Even so, the US Christian publisher who dared to put it out (Fortress Press, "the Publishing House of the Evangelical Lutheran

> **"Sometimes I asked my father why he kept making me do this. Then he said, 'All women are the same as that first woman, Eve. You tempt me. In your heart, this is what you want, just like Eve.'"**

Church in America") has sadly allowed it to slide out of print.

The book is based on in-depth interviews with nineteen women who were sexually abused as girls by male relatives. All had religious mothers, and all but three had religious fathers. Of the women raised Catholic, all went to Catholic school from kindergarten through high school, and all but one went to church everyday. All the Protestant families went to services each Sunday, and most had fathers who were heavily involved in the church.

The authors—a theologian and an historian, the latter having been sexually abused by her maternal grandfather—state that their purpose isn't to determine whether abuse occurs more often in religious homes but rather "to formulate questions directed at Christian churches, so that their teachings may offer a liberating perspective to women and children as well as men."

Quote: "This study shows that religion can be a factor that is conducive to incest and compounds trauma."

Quote: "With the exception of one, all of the women interviewed have turned their backs on the church. The majority of the offenders, however, are still involved in the church. Half of them still occupy an official church position."

Quote: "We searched for answers to two questions: 1. How can the sexual abuse of girls occur in Christian families? And 2. What is the impact of the religious upbringing in the family, in school and in the church of these sexually abused girls?"

Quote: "From this study of women who have survived incest, we can conclude that, through their religious upbringing, they were made easy prey to sexual abuse in the (extended) family. Moreover, their religious upbringing caused them problems in working through their experiences."

Ellen: "In sermons, the obedience of women was illustrated by the story of Ruth, who gave her body to secure protections and to bear a son for her former husband. It was her own fault that she lived in poverty because she had left her homeland. David wasn't punished because he was spying on Bathsheba, but because she belonged to someone else. It wasn't about her, but her husband. No one asked about her feelings. I thought that story legitimated what my Grandpa [a Bible-quoting Free Evangelist] did with me. And that beautiful young girl who was made to crawl into bed with old King David when he was dying? Nobody asked her what she wanted, either."

Joan: "I come from a very strict Catholic family. My father had been in a monastery. He'd been a monk and he was terribly dogmatic....

"One month after my first period, my father took possession of me, raped my body, my emotions, and spirit. At thirteen, he made me his mother and his wife, and I didn't even realize what was happening...

"He told me so many times that he'd kill me if I didn't cooperate. Because of all his threats, his blackmail and violence—he even put a knife to my throat and threatened to kill me—I kept my resistance inside.

"A certain image of women was fostered by the church, which enabled men to treat their women that way. Adultery was forbidden when they had sexual needs. The only thing left open to a man was his daughter.

"My father often said the commandment: Honor thy father and thy mother, and: Thou shalt love thy neighbor as thyself. In the Roman Catholic Church, they say that all the time: 'Love thy neighbor.' That still makes me so furious I could almost explode. I was completely abandoned to his will because I obeyed those commandments. That Catholic morality, they always know what is good for you. Who I am, what I feel, was ruthlessly, systematically crushed out. My father was the only one who knew what was good for me."

Nell (whose family was "strict orthodox Dutch Reformed"): "I felt dirty and it made me cry, but that wasn't allowed. He called that 'defying your father.'... I deliberately wore clothes that weren't pretty, tried to blend into the background as much as possible. But nothing helped. It went on and on. Then you start feeling guilty again. 'What am I doing wrong, that God doesn't make it stop, that it keeps on happening? What is it about me that's so bad?' You don't get an answer.

"Mother kept saying that I was bad. Father said that I had asked him to do this to me....

"Sometimes I asked my father why he kept making me do this. Then he said, 'All women are the same as that first woman, Eve. You tempt me. In your heart, this is what you want, just like Eve.' I used to pray 'God let it stop.' But God didn't intervene, so I thought, either it really was God's will, or I really was as bad as they said, and this was my punishment."

Among the women, "God as a person is always seen as male, and predominantly as a father (11 times). God is seen as the ideal father (3 times), as opposed to the woman's own father. God is identified with the woman's own father (6 times); 'That was all jumbled together'; 'Father wanted to be worshipped, too'; 'Father knew how God punished, he heard that directly from God'; 'My father could have been God'; 'Father was a kind of god'; 'God resembled my father.'"

HOMESPUN BLASPHEMY

"Reflections on Religion" by Mark Twain, from *The Outrageous Mark Twain*, edited by Charles Neider (New York: Doubleday, 1987)

America's literary titan—Mark Twain (né, Samuel Clemens)—was largely unafraid to reveal and ridicule hypocrisy and stupidity with his legendary razor wit. Religion often felt the blade, but sometimes the results were so bloody that Clemens and his executors wouldn't let the results be seen. *Letters From the Earth*—in which Satan's commentary on humanity's religious customs is the vehicle for irreverent but basically good-natured criticism—wasn't published until 1962, fifty-two years after Clemens' death. It's been in print ever since.

The five short chapters on religion from his autobiography haven't fared as well. Like *Letters*, the publication of these twenty-one pages—dictated in June 1906—was blocked for decades. On the manuscript, Clemens wrote that they weren't to be published until 2406, five centuries hence. In a letter to a friend, Clemens mentioned that he didn't want them published until he'd been in the grave for 100 years. His executors complied for a long time, but his daughter Clara relented in 1960, and the five chapters were finally revealed to the world in the *Hudson Review* in 1963. Twenty-four more years would pass before they were published again, this time in *The Outrageous Mark Twain*, a collection containing other writings on religion, masturbation, and the legendary "1601," a mock-Elizabethan story about a farting contest. Sadly, the anthology didn't stay available for long, so the chapters are no longer in print. (Portions are included as an appendix in the slightly more recent *The Bible According to Mark Twain* (University of Georgia Press, 1995). Unlike most of Clemens' work, the chapters are still under copyright. I approached the law firm handling his estate about reprinting them, but the cost was *way* beyond our means.)

Unlike *Letters From the Earth*, these chapters—collectively titled "Reflections on Religion"—are harsh. No gentle mocking here; Clemens took off the gloves and opened a can of whup-ass. Since these are the raw transcriptions of what he dictated to his secretary, they're not as polished or organized as they would've been had Clemens prepared them for publication. Still, it's a joy to see one of America's most beloved writers take Christianity behind the woodshed.

He jumps right into the thick of things by attacking none other than God, accurately describing the despicable nature of the Old Testament's supreme being, who is constantly murdering, mutilating, and otherwise viciously abusing humans. "It is perhaps the most damnatory biography that exists in print anywhere. It makes Nero an angel of light and leading by contrast." He rails against the endless suffering that God continues to cause, saying that "we would detest and denounce any earthly father who should inflict upon his child a thousandth part of the pains and miseries and cruelties which God deals out to his children every day..." But as horrible as the Old Testament God is, Clemens writes, at least he's consistent and forthright, whereas Jesus spoke of mercy and love yet also threatened people with eternal punishment and damnation. He healed a few people, fed a few people, yet refused to use his God-powers to heal and feed everybody.

The next chapter mainly concerns the fact that the Bible, as well as other sacred literature, plagiarizes earlier holy books and mythologies without admitting it. "Each in turn confiscates decayed old stage-properties from the others and with naïve confidence puts them forth as fresh new inspirations from on high." Clemens mentions the ubiquitous flood stories but concentrates on gods born of virgins.

In chapter three, the old man rails against the bloody tactics of Russia, Britain, and Belgium, all having Christian governments at the time. After tangentially stating that "the Bible defiles all Protestant children," Clemens looks into his crystal ball. He sees Christianity eventually going the way of all religions—fading away and being replaced by "another God and a stupider religion."

Setting his sights once again on God in the following chapter, Clemens wonders how a supreme being can inflict such endless misery on all of his creatures. He scoffs at the notion of prayer, which he likens to begging. The originality of Clemens' inquiries goes up a notch when he dismantles the excuses that preachers make for the suffering God puts us through—namely, that it helps us, elevates us, purifies us, and makes us worthy of heaven. If that's so, he wonders, what about the suffering of animals, who experience violence, disease, hunger, and agonizing deaths in ways similar to, and often worse than, humans? No Bible-banger ever claims that "alligators [and] tigers" are being tested and strengthened so that they can earn a heavenly reward. And if God brutalizing his children is so wonderful, why don't preachers recommend that parents do the same horrible things to their own children? Sure, they often say you shouldn't spare the rod, but why not torture and starve your kids, purposely give them diseases, kill everyone they love, since these things build so much spiritual character?

Clemens uses his final chapter to ridicule the idea of heaven. "If King Leopold II, the Butcher, should proclaim that out of each hundred innocent and unoffending Congo Negroes he is going to save one from humiliation, starvation and assassination, and fetch that one home to Belgium to live with him in his palace and feed at his table, how many people would believe it?" Finally, turning his baleful gaze to the human race, Clemens unexpectedly softens:

I could say harsh things about it but I cannot bring myself to do it—it is like hitting a child. Man is not to blame for what he is.... He is flung head over heels into this world without ever a chance to decline, and straightaway he conceives and accepts the notion that he is in some mysterious way under obligations to the unknown Power that inflicted this outrage upon him...

ILLUSTRATING THE *REST* OF THE BIBLE

Illustrated Stories From the Bible (That They Won't Tell You in Sunday School) by Paul Farrell, illustrated by Kathy Demchuck (Cranford, New Jersey: American Atheist Press, 2005)

Funny thing about those books of illustrated Bible stories—they never cover certain portions of the Good Book. You know, the atrocity stories, the rape and cannibalism, the massacres and child sacrifice, all of which were performed, commanded, or, in some cases, simply allowed to happen by God.

Take one of the tales about Moses, for example. If you've read illustrated Bible stories, or condensed narratives, or if you've seen *The Ten Commandments*, you may think you know the story of Moses. God appears to him as a burning bush, tells him to go to Egypt and free the Israelites. Moses does so, then parts the Red Sea, leads the Hebrews through the wilderness and to the Promised Land (though he himself didn't quite make it). But part of the tale never makes the cut. After taking orders from aflame shrubbery, Moses rounds up his wife and two young sons, and they head for Egypt. Suddenly, with no warning or explanation, God wants to kill Moses or perhaps one of his sons. The Bible isn't clear in its use of pronouns: "And it came to pass by the way in the inn, that the LORD met him, and sought to kill him" (Exodus 4:24).

Illustrated Stories
From The Bible
(that they won't tell you in Sunday School)

Paul Farrell
Illustrated by Kathy Demchuck

Somehow, Moses' spouse, Zipporah, realizes that the Creator is in a murderous rage because one of their sons isn't circumcised. So she grabs a "sharp stone, and cut off the foreskin of her son." She then throws the foreskin at Moses' feet and says, "A bloody husband you are to me." This act of utter barbarity pleases God; as the Bible vaguely states: "So he let him go" (Exodus 4:26).

In *Illustrated Stories From the Bible*, this terrifying and crucial event in Moses' life is finally given the visual treatment. We see Kathy Demchuck's unadorned line drawing of Zipporah hacking at her son's penis with a bloody stone as the child screams in terror and agony. God looks on impassively, while Moses uncomfortably touches his own groin. Another illustration shows Zip throwing the piece of gristle at Moses' feet. In the final illo, the son continues to scream on the blood-drenched ground as God happily goes his way. As with each story, the action is accompanied by a sugary narrative text and followed by a thoughtful discussion that further explores the lunacy of the Bible.

Other simply rendered drawings show Jephthah sacrificing his young daughter, God casting a loathsome plague on David's infant son (who dies after seven days of agony), Amnon raping his sister Tamar, God slaughtering 70,000 Israelites because King David had counted the number of troops in his army (yes, that was the reason), Phinehas running two lovers through with a javelin, Israelites mass-executing little boys under Moses' orders, another Israelite running a pregnant woman through the belly with a sword, an Israelite mother who kills and eats her own son during a famine that God refused to end, and—in the only story from the New Testament—Jesus sending demons from a possessed man into a herd of swine who drown themselves. The cover illustration, rendered in gory color, depicts my "favorite" atrocity story, in which two bears sent by God tear apart a group of children who made fun of the prophet Elijah's bald head (2 Kings 2:23–24).

This is a perfect supplement to those selective, sanitized, saccharine collections of illustrated Bible stories. Buy a few copies and leave them in doctors' and dentists' offices. How can the faithful object to an illustrated edition of their own holy book?

Folktales aren't the only things to have been used as sources for biblical stories—classical Greek poetry was lifted for portions of the New Testament.

DÉJÀ VU, ALL OVER AGAIN

Does the New Testament Imitate Homer?: Four Cases From the Acts of the Apostles by Dennis R. MacDonald (New Haven, CT: Yale University Press, 2003)

Folktales aren't the only things to have been used as sources for biblical stories—classical Greek poetry was lifted for portions of the New Testament.

One specific cluster of examples has gotten a book of its own: *Does the New Testament Imitate Homer?* by Dennis R. MacDonald. MacDonald's qualifications are impeccable—Bachelor's degree from the fundamentalist Bob Jones University, where he wasn't allowed to dance or to date outside his race; a doctorate from Yale; teaching posts at numerous theological/divinity colleges, including his current position as Professor of New Testament and Christian Origins at Claremont School of Theology; and various chairman and editor positions.

He flexes his intellectual muscles by uncovering four extended "parallels" between Homer's *Iliad*, written anywhere from the eight century to the sixth century B.C.E., and the Book of Acts, written centuries later, circa 60 to 150 C.E. As a preliminary, MacDonald explains an established fact: In the Greco-Roman world that gave us the New Testament writings, imitating the classics in one's own writing was not considered plagiarism but was an expected practice called *mimesis*. Further, he shows that Homer's works, especially *The Iliad*, were by far the most popular classical literature at the time, constantly taught in schools, performed in public, and represented on coins and vases. A contemporary of Luke wrote of Homer: "In no stage of life, from boyhood to old age, do we ever cease to drink from him." To top it off, we know that the author of Acts was well-versed in classical Greek lit: "He quotes Aratus's *Phaenomena* in Acts 17:28, and Euripides' *Bacchae* in 26:14..."

Moving to the imitations themselves, we find that "the casting of lots to replace Judas among the Twelve...closely parallels the casting of lots that selected Ajax to fight Hector in *Iliad* 7." In the second example, "the corroborating visions of Cornelius and Peter...strikingly resemble two visions at the beginning of Book 2 of the *Iliad*: the famous lying dream of Zeus to Agamemnon and the vision of the serpent and the sparrows." "The third example is Peter's escape from Herod's prison," which was modeled after "Hermes' rescue of Priam from the Greek camp in *Iliad* 24." Finally, for "Paul's speech to the elders of Ephesus at Miletus...Luke rewrote Hector's farewell to Andromache in *Iliad* 6 and expected his readers to recognize that he did so."

This last, in which the Trojan hero Hector says *au revoir* to his wife before fatally returning to battle, was an extremely popular scene and was imitated (*mimesis*) by Herodotus, Sophocles, Aristophanes, Plato, Xenophon, Apollonius, Chariton, Xenophon of Ephesus, Heliodorus, Virgil, Seneca, Ovid, and Silius. And the author of Acts.

MacDonald writes: "Like Hector's farewell, Paul's consists of three parts: (1) Paul's courage in the past and present (verses 18–27), (2) the challenges facing the elders in the future (28–31), and (3) Paul's prayer for them (32–35)." Furthermore, the two farewell speeches share nine motifs:

- "the hero states that he does not know what dangers he must face"

- "the hero boasts that he never shirked his duty"

- "the hero warns of disaster"

- "the hero expresses fear concerning the captivity of his loved ones"

- "the hero invokes his gods"

- "the hero prays that his successors may be like him"

- "the hero cites a comparative quotation"

- "the hero states his willingness to face his destiny with courage"

- "the hero commands his audience to attend to their tasks"

A parallel also exists immediately after the speeches are given. *Iliad* 6.498–501: "[Andromache went home and] found there among her many maidservants; among them all she induced wailing. So they wailed for Hector in his own house while he was still alive; for they said that he would never again return from battle." Acts 20:37–38: "There was much weeping among them all. They fell on Paul's neck and kissed him, grieving especially because of what he had said, that they would never again see his face."

MacDonald wrote a similar earlier book in which he shows how Mark was patterned on Homer (*The Homeric Epics and the Gospel of Mark*). In *Does the New Testament Imitate Homer?*, he sums up this preceding volume: "I argued that the author of the earliest Gospel used the *Odyssey* as his primary literary model for chapters 1–14; he used the *Iliad*, especially the death of Hector and the ransom of his corpse, as his model for chapters 15–16." An endnote gives a more detailed summary, including the parallel characters of the Gospel of Mark and the *Odyssey* (Jesus = Odysseus/Ulysses, Jewish authorities = Penelope's suitors, Peter = Eurylochus, Judas and Barabbas = Melanthius and Irus, and so on). The encapsulation of the parallels between these two stories includes:

> "The result, then, is that between 1530 and 1780 there were almost certainly a million and quite possibly as many as a million and a quarter white, European Christians enslaved by the Muslims of the Barbary Coast."

I compare Jesus' calling of fishermen to follow him with Athena's summoning a crew; the calming of the sea transforms the tale of Aelous's bag of winds; the exorcism of the Gerasene demoniac borrows from the stories of Circe and Polyphemus; the beheading of John the Baptist resembles the murder of Agamemnon; the multiplication of loaves and fish for five thousand men and again for four thousand men and women reflects the twin feasts in *Odyssey* 3 and 4, the first of which feeds four thousand five hundred men at the edge of the sea. Jesus walks on water like Hermes and Athena.... The cleansing of the Temple imitates Odysseus's slaying of the suitors, and the agony at Gethsemane echoes Odysseus's agony during his last night with Circe before going off to Hades.

ISLAM AND SLAVERY

Christians Slaves, Muslim Masters: White Slavery in the Mediterranean, the Barbary Coast, and Italy, 1500–1800 by Robert C. Davis (New York: Palgrave Macmillan, 2003)

Servants of Allah: African Muslims Enslaved in the Americas by Sylviane A. Diouf (New York University Press, 1998)

In *Christian Slaves, Muslim Masters*, Ohio State history professor Robert C. Davis looks at the *other* slave trade—the one in which Islamic pirates seized Christian Europeans, who then became slaves. While the trans-Atlantic slave trade of black Africans to the New World is more well-known by several orders of magnitude, both slaves trades "arose and flourished—if such a term can be used—at almost exactly the same time..." In fact, Islam's slave trade was the bigger and stronger of the two for the first century and a half of their existences.

...Mediterranean slaving out-produced the trans-Atlantic trade during the sixteenth and into the seventeenth century, and this is only in terms of the Barbary Coast—without taking into account Muslim slaving activities in the Levant and eastern Europe, nor the counter-enslavement that some Christian states were practicing at the same time on their Islamic foes.... It was at just about the time when Mediterranean slaving began to falter—around the mid-1600s—that the trans-Atlantic trade really took off...

Another difference between the two slave trades was motivation. Bringing native Africans to the New World was simply a matter of economics, of money-making, while the Muslim trade in white Europeans primarily was another part of the ongoing war between Islam and Christianity. There was "an element of revenge, almost of *jihad*" in the proceedings, especially after Ferdinand and Isabella ran the Muslim occupiers out of southern Spain in 1492.

These Corsair pirates were of course most threatening to ships from and shorelines of the European countries across the Mediterranean Sea from Northern Africa—Portugal, Spain, France, and Italy—but they had the balls to occasionally sail all the way to the British Isles and even into the Thames estuary, where they seized slaves from ships and towns.

As for how many slaves were enmeshed in the Barbary Coast trade, Davis makes a valiant effort to bundle the diffuse, narrow accountings into an overall statistic. Plowing through primary and secondary sources in several languages, he takes note of many pieces: In one ten-month period, pirates based in Tunis nabbed 1,772 captives from 28 ships; over the course of seven years, Algerian brigands rustled 986 citizens of France from 80 ships; in just one year (1544), the Algerians enslaved 7,000 Italians during raids on the Bay of Naples; during 77 years in the 1600s, Spanish Trinitarians ransomed 15,573 white slaves held on the Barbary Coast. After assembling the pieces, and conjecturing about attrition, plague deaths, reproduction, and other factors, Davis surmises: "The result, then, is that between 1530 and

1780 there were almost certainly a million and quite possibly as many as a million and a quarter white, European Christians enslaved by the Muslims of the Barbary Coast."

In the following chapter, the author examines the nitty-gritty of Islam's slave trade—how ship-takeovers and raids (complete with pillaging) were executed, how the slaves were sold in markets, etc. The poet Curthio Mattei wrote about the fearful life of Europeans on the Mediterranean shores:

> Blessed was he who could flee his bed
> ...
> The mother abandoned her own child,
> The husband his wife, the son his father
> ...
> Everyone tried to flee the danger.

The bad old days are *still* echoing in the Sicilian figure of speech "taken by Turks," which basically means to be "caught by surprise."

The next two chapters look at life for the Barbary slaves (90 percent of whom were male)—their labors, their dress, their attempts to resist their captors' culture. The most common place they ended up was in a ship's galley, chained to an oar, living in absolute misery and filth, often dying of overwork. While their ships were docked at home-port, the slaves would labor in quarries from sunup to half an hour before sundown. Other slaves worked in mines, farms, and brickyards, made rope, gunpowder, or cloth, or were household servants. An unknown portion of the younger, attractive slaves ended up as concubines. A Flemish slave in Algiers in the 1640s matter-of-factly reported that his master had a harem containing "forty young Boys between nine years of age and fifteen." Slaves who made it out of captivity describe brutal punishments; thrashing with a stick seem to have been the most popular method, although whippings and beating the soles of the feet also make appearances.

In the final part of the book, "The Home Front," Davis turns his gaze to Italy, to those who had to deal with the aftermath of countrymen enslaved in Barbary: families left without husbands, fathers, sons, and brothers, and a country having to deal with huge numbers of kidnapped citizens. The situation was so bad that for well over a century Italian states leaned on their subjects to contribute—through alms and bequests—money to ransom their captive countrymen. The actual home-coming of the slaves turned into a formalized ritual. After being quarantined for a month, they were made to march in elaborate processions in front of cheering onlookers before being cleansed of any Muslim taint by a Mass. In Venice, each slave was paired with an escort from the noble class. Some repatriated slaves were required to go to Rome and march before the Pope.

Davis briefly mentions that the slave trade ran both ways, though in numbers not even close to equal. Some European powers enslaved North African Muslims during this period, mainly as galley slaves, and Spain alone pulled off some slave raids into Muslim territory, but the number of Islamic slaves in Europe pales next to the number of their Christian counterparts in Africa.

Some West Africans who had converted to Islam got enmeshed in the trans-Atlantic slave trade, ending up in the colonies in North America, South America, and the Caribbean. In *Servants of Allah: African Muslims Enslaved in the Americas*, Sylviane A. Diouf provides a rare look at this forgotten aspect of slavery in the New World.

> That Islam as brought by the African slaves has not survived does not mean that the Muslim faith did not flourish during slavery on a fairly large scale. On the contrary, systematic research throughout the Americas shows that, indeed, the Muslim were not absorbed into the cultural-religious Christian world. They chose to remain Muslims, and even enslaved, they succeeded in following most of the precepts of their religion.

Determining figures for slave trades is always a difficult, inexact endeavor, and calculating how many Muslims were enslaved is even harder since slavetraders didn't keep track of their slaves' religious beliefs. Based on the proportion of slaves taken from West Africa, and the percentage of West Africans who followed Islam, Diouf proposes "an estimate of 15 to 20 percent, or between 2.25 and 3 million Muslims over both American continents and the Caribbean Islands."

Muslim slaves were among the most rebellious, since their religion didn't allow them to accept

EVERYTHING YOU KNOW ABOUT GOD IS WRONG

being enslaved. The first slave revolt in the New World—in Hispaniola—and many thereafter were led by Muslims. Of course, slaves were routinely forced to convert to Christianity, but many—maybe most—of the Muslims only pretended to convert, secretly saying prayers five times a day. Some would pray silently, while others found secluded spots to kneel and pray aloud. On the Sea Islands of Georgia and South Carolina—home to large numbers of Muslim slaves—the Muslims prayed "very publicly in front of the other slaves, and some prayed in front of their masters."

> In Brazil, enslaved and emancipated Africans had succeeded in secretly maintaining a Muslim community large enough and sufficiently organized that the common prayer could be held in a consecrated place. The house of a free Muslim, a hut that the Africans have been allowed to build on their master's property, a room that other rented with their pooled resources—all these makeshift mosques enabled the Muslims to accomplish their devotions together, in the best way they could afford.

Many Muslims slaves also observed other Pillars of Islam, including almsgiving and fasting during Ramadan. Diouf also digs up bits of evidence that some Islamic slaves obeyed dress codes and dietary laws, such as avoiding pork.

A high percentage of West African Muslims, even women and the poor, were literate in Arabic and/or their native languages transliterated into Arabic. Documents show that slaves all over the New World owned copies of the Koran; amazingly, some were given to them by Christian missionaries, and others were purchased after much scrimping and saving. For the most part, though, we don't know how so many slaves ended up with copies. Slaves also used written Arabic for communication, writing personal letters, religious works, and autobiographies.

In the concluding chapter, Diouf looks at why the Islam of the slaves didn't take root in the New World, meaning that the religion had to be reintroduced at a later date by immigrants. It didn't disappear entirely, though: Syncretic religions, such as Santería and Macumba, incorporated bits of Islam. And the author makes a fascinating case that the blues derives directly from the music of West African Muslims, as well as their Koranic chants.

The first slave revolt in the New World—in Hispaniola— and many thereafter were led by Muslims.

RULES, RULES, RULES, AND MORE RULES

A Clarification of Questions by Ayatollah Khomeini (J. Borujerdi, trans.). (Boulder, CO: Westview Press, 1984)

When you've bought into a religion, it becomes absolutely crucial for you to know how God wants you to behave. Any slip-ups can make this all-powerful, all-knowing entity furious with you and cause you to be cast into the fiery pits of hell for eternity. Sadly for believers, holy books often contain vague and contradictory rules, and they can be silent on many important issues. This is where "holy men" come to the rescue, swooping in with their excruciatingly specific, nitpicking interpretations, guesses, and fabrications concerning how to conduct oneself in the most righteous manner.

In Islam since the 1950s, the highest-ranking clerics regularly issue books (and now websites) filled with such regulations. Among the most important of these is *Resaleh Towzih al-Masael* by Ayatollah Khomeini, the leader of the Islamic Revolution in Iran and that country's Supreme Leader after the Revolution. This work was given a full, unauthorized English-language translation by J. Borujerdi and published by the scholarly Westview Press as *A Clarification of Questions*.

Until you gaze upon the more than 3,000 precepts laid down across 414 pages, it's hard to fully grasp the overwhelmingly microscopic nature of the book. Nothing is too trivial for multiple rules. No circumstance, no hypothetical situation has been overlooked. Do you have a question of the minutiae regarding diet, prayer, sex, marriage, divorce, childbirth, handling corpses, inheritance, excretion, blood, fasting, bathing, alms, buying, selling, renting, insurance, lotteries, or hunting, among other topics? Odds are pretty good that the Ayatollah has addressed it in detail.

Simply *defining* a woman's menstrual period is a huge undertaking, covering eight pages. Because menstruation affects a woman's ability to pray, cook, divorce, touch the Koran, have sexual intercourse, be in the presence of a dying person, etc.,

etc. (the rules for which take up many additional pages), it's crucial that the faithful know when a woman is menstrual versus when she's having "undue bleeding" (non-menstrual vaginal bleeding), which invokes a whole different set of rules. Then there's the chance that she wasn't really menstruating at all: If a period doesn't last three full days (even if its lasts two days and much of the third), it doesn't count as a period (that's rule #440).

Khomeini divides menstruating women into six kinds, including those who bleed on the same day each month but not for the same amount of time, and those who start on different days during each month but who have periods of the same length. Then, to give just one of many such examples, he writes:

> #482. When a woman who possesses a regular and numerically defined period sees blood throughout her period as well as a few days before the period, all are menstrual if not exceeding ten days. When it exceeds ten days she is menstrual for a length equal to that of her periodic bleeding plus as many of the preceding days for a total equal to the length of her regular menses, thus making the initial days undue bleeding. And if she sees blood during her period as well as a few days after, with the total not exceeding ten, all are menstrual and if exceeding ten days she must reckon as menstrual the number of days totaling the days of bleeding period plus the succeeding days, up to the length of her periods, with the remainder considered undue bleeding.

Having cleared up that issue, let's turn to some further pressing questions.

Are the droppings of flies and mosquitoes unclean? No, they are clean (#83).

What do I do if I have unclean food stuck between my teeth? Rinsing your mouth with water will make the food particles clean (#172).

May I use containers made of gold and silver? No, it is unlawful (#226). May I keep them as decorations? Yes (#226). May I use containers that are just *coated* in gold or silver? Yes (#230).

What if I begin menstruating during a prayer? The prayer is void (#464).

While ritually bathing a corpse, what happens if I see its private parts? You've committed a sin, and the bath is void (#563).

In what position should a corpse be buried? On its right side, and so that it is facing Mecca (#615).

I prostrate while saying my prayers, but I have a large abscess that prevents my forehead from fully touching the ground. What should I do? Dig a hole in the ground to fit your abscess into (#1066).

While saying a prayer containing four units, I prostrated twice but couldn't remember if I had just finished the second or third unit. What should I do? Say one more unit and finish the prayer. Then say one unit of a cautionary prayer while standing or two units while sitting (#1199).

My brother died, and I know that he didn't say five prayers everyday. What can I do? You can hire someone to perform the prayers that the deceased should have performed (#1533).

What are some things that will void my fast? Copulation, masturbation, letting "dense dust" or smoke enter you throat, immersing your entire head in water (but not just half your head), using liquid enemas (suppositories for medical treatment are all right), vomiting (unless you really, really can't help it), and swallowing a fly.

I just married a woman and found out that she has elephantitis. Can I cancel the marriage? Yes. What if I find that she has "flesh or bone or a gland in her vagina, blocking intercourse"? You may cancel the marriage. (#2380)

My husband died. How long must I wait before marrying again? Four months and ten days. (#2517)

Is artificial insemination OK? Yes, but only as long as the sperm being introduced is from the recipient's husband (#2874).

Is it lawful for me to earn interest on money I've deposited in a bank? No. (#Q78)

When urinating or defecating, you must not face— or face away from—Mecca (#59). (Apparently, you must angle your body so that one of your sides is toward the city.) But having your back or front toward Mecca while wiping your ass is no problem (#61).

A man can force his wife to have any form of sex (except those forbidden by Islam) at any time (#2412), yet he cannot force her to do housework (#2414).

According to Khomeini, it's OK to have concubines. In fact, rule #2422 commands: "A husband must not abandon intercourse with his concubine for more than four months."

Not even drinking water is a foolproof activity: "#2639. Drinking too much water and drinking it after greasy food are abominations as is drinking

> **"When washing the anus with water no stool should remain in it but the persistence of the color and smell of stool is of no concern and if the anus is thoroughly cleaned of stool in the first washing it is not necessary to repeat washing it." —Ayatollah Khomeini**

water standing, at nighttime...." (The good news is that anything described as "abominable" or "loathsome" is not unlawful; rather it's "unwanted" and "is better abandoned.")

A few more of Allah's rules:

"#67. When washing the anus with water no stool should remain in it but the persistence of the color and smell of stool is of no concern and if the anus is thoroughly cleaned of stool in the first washing it is not necessary to repeat washing it."

"#72. Drainage is a recommended act that men do following urination and it is of several kinds, the best of which is as follows. First, after urination is ended, if the anus has become unclean it is cleaned. Then, using the middle finger of the left hand pressure is applied from the anus to the root of the penis three times. Then with the penis between the thumb on the top and the next finger underneath it, pressure is applied down to the circumcision site three times. Then the glans is pressed upon three times."

"#78. It is recommended that during evacuation one sits in a place that no one sees him and to use the left foot for entering the place and the right foot for coming out. And it is recommended to cover the head and lean on the left leg while evacuating."

"#107. The whole body of an infidel, even the hair, nails and its wetness, is unclean."

"#2410. If a person contracts for himself [i.e., marries] a girl who has not reached puberty and before she finishes her ninth year enters the girl he must never have intercourse with her in case he causes her path of urine and menses or that of menses and stool to become one."

"#2433. A man's look at the body of a woman who is a stranger, whether or not with the intention of pleasure, is unlawful."

"#2623. Eating a locust who has not yet grown wings and cannot fly is unlawful."

"#2827. If the Moslems fear that the foreigners have a plot to subjugate their cities, either directly or through their agents, from outside or inside, it is obligatory that they defend the Islamic countries by any means possible."

"2829. If as a result of the spread of the foreigner's political or economic and commercial influence there is fear of their domination of the cities of Moslems it is obligatory for all Moslems to defend by any means possible and to cut the hands of the foreigners, whether they are internal or external agents."

CONFUCIUS SAY ... NOTHING, REALLY

Manufacturing Confucianism: Chinese Traditions, Universal Civilization by Lionel M. Jensen (Durham, NC: Duke University Press, 1997)

Pretty much every religion, and its founder(s), has been put to the historical test, but it wasn't until 1997 that the "secular religion" synonymous with China was examined with steely-eyed clarity in *Manufacturing Confucianism* by Notre Dame Professor of History and East Asian Languages Lionel M. Jensen.

Jensen demonstrates that Confucianism was constructed by Jesuit missionaries in southern China beginning in 1579. It's always been known and admitted that the Catholics were the first to transmit these ideas and beliefs to Europe, but the full story is that they *created* the system of thought that Westerners know as Confucianism. They took some ideas from an amorphous tradition called *ru*, put a subtle Christian spin on them, bundled them as a unified whole, and—through their writings—presented the package as the very encapsulation of Chinese thought, belief, morality, and society.

On top of that, the Jesuits created Confucius himself—a wise old sage and benevolent political philosopher who was perfectly packaged for idolization by the educated of Europe and, a couple of centuries later, by the Enlightenment. They based this "fabricated" guru on an ancient Chinese sage named Kongzi—who may or may not have existed. The general view is that Kongzi was a real person who lived around 500 B.C.E. and that—once the thick layers of legends and cultural add-ons are stripped away—we know next to nothing about him. Jensen, though, goes beyond this, saying that

Kongzi is of "dubious historicity," heavily implying that the works attributed to him were written by groups of people. Sadly, the professor spends almost no time on this aspect. I realize that the book is *Manufacturing Confucianism*, not *Manufacturing Kongzi*, but I still wish he had given it more than a paragraph, some scattered sentences, and an endnote that sends the reader to a journal article by him (which states: "The name [Kongzi] is more like a mythic literary fiction and probably began, as did that of Hou Qi, as a symbolic deity that was made historical in one of its many Warring States incarnations, that one transmitted to us exclusively through the normative biographical tradition.").

In the latter part of this thick book, Jensen reveals an interesting boomerang effect: During the twentieth century, in an effort to build a national identity and history, the Chinese more or less swallowed the Western constructs of Confucius and Confucianism—mapping them onto Kongzi and *ru*, and accepting them as fact.

Quote: "The Confucius and Confucianism to which we have granted a compelling authority are conceptual products of foreign origin, made to articulate indigenous qualities of Chinese culture."

Quote: "[T]he name 'Kongzi' may recur over time, but the individual it designates is anything but consistent or continuous; the history of Kongzi, like that of Confucius, is one of differential invention and local manufacture."

Quote: "In Jesuit hands the indigenous Kongzi was resurrected from distant symbolism into life, heroically transmuted and made intelligible as 'Confucius,' a spiritual confrere who alone among the Chinese—so their version had it—had preached an ancient gospel of monotheism now forgotten."

Quote: "'Confucius,' and its attendant nomenclature, cannot be understood, even by twentieth-century Chinese scholars, as translations in the sense that they render into one language something written or spoken in another. They are, above all, interpretative constructs, rather than representations of native categories. They are representations of the seventeenth-century reading of the Jesuit missionary experience among late Ming Chinese, representations that were employed, and have been preserved, as elements within a universal system of classification by language, chronology, science, and faith."

WHEN GOD WASN'T A WOMAN

The Myth of Matriarchal Prehistory: Why an Invented Past Won't Give Woman a Future by Cynthia Eller (Boston: Beacon Press, 2000)

The idea that the human race worshipped "the Goddess" for eons before a male God supplanted her has taken up residence in mainstream consciousness to the point that it is widely thought of as an historical fact, not a theory. According to this view, all societies from the dawn of the human race were matriarchal. It was a utopian time of peace, prosperity, happiness, and attunement to nature in which neither sex was discriminated against. Women were glorified for their ability to give birth, and a Goddess of some sort was the main object of veneration. Roughly around 3000 B.C.E., for reasons that are debated by believers, men started to dominate societies, bringing about a male God, patriarchy, barbarism, warfare, and pretty much everything bad in the world. Though this Goddess/matriarchy theory was first proposed in 1861 (by a man), it didn't make inroads until the 1970s, when second-wave feminism glommed onto it and soon propelled it to its current status of unquestioned reality.

Cynthia Eller, an Associate Professor of Women's Studies and Religion Studies at Montclair State University in New Jersey, takes a close, hard look at this concept and finds it severely lacking factual support. In *The Myth of Matriarchal Prehistory*, she first defines the broad outlines of the theory and traces its rise, especially due to the publications of archaeologist Marija Gimbutas (*The Gods and Goddesses of Old Europe*, *The Language of the Goddess*, and *The Civilization of the Goddess*), then points out how it actually *reinforces* gender stereotypes. After discussing the huge inherent problems with trying to reconstruct prehistoric societies based on a relatively infinitesimal number of physical objects that have survived, Eller takes a scalpel to the evidence cited by those who make claims for a matriarchal golden age and universal Goddess worship. One of her main, most devastating points is that pretty much every prehistoric object, drawing, and marking is seen as evidence of this worship. From the literature, she compiles a list of 58 symbols that are being taken as signs of a

Goddess-driven matriarchy, including bears, lions, bulls, horses, goats, pigs, birds, snakes, turtles, bees, eyes, hands, phalli, women, trees, the moon, the sun, stones, shells, spirals, crosses, parallel lines, Xs, Vs, ovals, circles, triangles, and dots. What isn't included? Similarly, almost every old statue or carving that supposedly depicts the female form is said to represent the Goddess, the Divine Feminine, while the ones that seem to depict the male form just show some dude.

People who have attacked this book often claim that Eller denies any Goddess-worship was occurring in the time before written records, when in fact, she does admit that there's good evidence that some societies in some places did worship a goddess. Or is it goddesses, plural? After all, we know that Hindus have a whole army of goddesses, as did the ancient Greeks and Romans. As well as male gods by the dozen. Maybe the prehistoric cultures were venerating a bunch of gods and goddesses. "And whatever religions prehistoric peoples practiced, we can be fairly sure that goddess worship did not automatically yield cultures of peace and plenty led by the goddess's priestesses. This pattern has been found nowhere." Regardless, the areas and time periods that seem to have included goddesses are much too small to encompass all of human history to 3000 B.C.E.

Eller concludes that "matriarchal myth fails completely on historical grounds. Evidence from prehistoric times is comparatively sparse, and hard to interpret conclusively. However, even taking these difficulties into account, what evidence we do have does not support the thesis that prehistory was matriarchal and goddess-worshipping, or even that it was sexually egalitarian."

Quote: "There is a theory of sex and gender embedded in the myth of matriarchal prehistory, and it is neither original nor revolutionary. Women are defined quite narrowly as those who give birth and nurture, who identify themselves in terms of their relationships, and who are closely allied with the body, nature, and sex—usually for unavoidable reasons of their biological makeup."

Quote: "The enemies of feminism have long posed issues of patriarchy and sexism in pseudo-scientific and historical terms. It is not in feminist interests to join them at this game, especially when it is so (relatively) easy to undermine the ground rules.... Discovering—or more the point, inventing—prehistoric ages in which women and men lived in harmony and equality is a burden that feminists need not, and should not bear. Clinging to shopworn notions of gender and promoting a demonstrably fictional past can only hurt us over the long run as we work to create a future that helps all women, children, and men flourish."

Quote: Feminist matriarchalists "speak as though there were no relevant differences between the essential focus of religion in Siberia in 27,000 B.C.E. and Crete in 1500 B.C.E. They usually treat all of prehistoric Europe and the Near East as if it were a single cultural complex, viewing cultural variations as an epiphany of the multiplicity of the goddess rather than as evidence of distinctive religious beliefs or systems of social organization."

Quote: "Even the simplest signs can shout 'goddess.' Gimbutas, for example, relishes the fact that the stamp seals of Old Europe are 'almost all...engraved with either straight lines, wavy lines or zigzags,' which she interprets as water and rain symbolism attributable to goddess religion. Reaching even farther, Rachel Pollack claims that 'the oldest carefully marked object,' an ox rib found in France dating to 200,000 to 300,000 B.C.E., about six inches long and incised with 'a pair of curved parallel lines' (visible under a microscope), is 'precisely that image' that appears repeatedly in 'later Goddess art.'

"But if straight lines and wavy lines are both symbols of the goddess, is it possible to draw a line another way, or to use it to mean something else?"

Quote: "Feminist matriarchalists have enthusiastically embraced the interpretive scheme that sees the walls of Paleolithic caves plastered with disembodied vulvas.... Yet as some observers note, there is an undoubted resemblance between the vulvas in Paleolithic cave art (that feminist matriarchalists celebrate as the sign of the goddess) and those that 'would be right at home in any contemporary men's room.'"

Quote: "Similarly, Buffie Johnson discusses an 'amulet of the buttocks silhouette' recovered from Paleolithic Germany. Though this 1-3/4 inch sculpture has no head and no arms, Johnson asserts that wherever 'an arc and a straight line' combine to form a 'P shape,' one is viewing the 'exaggerated egg-shaped buttocks' of the goddess."

Quote: "Ethnographic analogies to contemporary groups with lifeways similar to those of prehistoric times (hunting and gathering or horticulture, practiced in small groups) show little sex egalitarianism and no matriarchy. Indeed, these societies always discriminate in some way between women and men, usually to women's detriment."

Quote: "There is also nothing in the archaeological record at odds with an image of prehistoric life an nasty, brutish, short, and male-dominated."

THE COINING OF "SCIENTOLOGY" BY ~~L. RO~~ ALLEN UPWARD

The New Word: An Open Letter Addressed to the Swedish Academy in Stockholm on the Meaning of the Word IDEALIST by Allen Upward (New York: Mitchell Kennerly, 1910)

History has forgotten Allen Upward, described by *The Dictionary of Literary Biography* as a "poet, playwright, novelist, lawyer, teacher, journalist, adventurer, anthropologist, philologist, philosopher. The role he most desired, however—that of acknowledged genius and sage—always eluded him." At least Ezra Pound thought he was wonderful, namechecking Upward five times in *The Cantos*.

Upward deserves some claim to fame, though, for his book *The New Word: An Open Letter Addressed to the Swedish Academy in Stockholm on the Meaning of the Word IDEALIST*. It was first published, perhaps self-published, in Geneva in 1908, and the well-known New York publisher Mitchell Kennerly brought out the US edition two years later. With pompous, artificially elaborate prose, Upward attempts to figure out what Alfred Nobel was getting at when he set up the Nobel Prize for Literature, which is to be awarded for "the most remarkable work of idealistic tendency." For over 300 pages, Upward tries to suss the meaning of *idealistic* and "the task of idealism." In theory this could be an interesting endeavor, but the book is an absolute yawn-fest, even though Pound gave it a great review.

But the book's mark in history has nothing to do with the word *idealistic* and everything to do with the actual "new word" it contains: *scientology*. As Jon Atack originally pointed out in his classic exposé, *A Piece of Blue Sky*, it was Upward, not L. Ron Hubbard, who really coined the word. Upward used it as a dismissive word having essentially the same meaning as *pseudoscience*. Maybe Upward was more prescient than he gets credit for being.

At one point, Hubbard said that he first used *scientology* in his alleged 1938 book *Excalibur*, which has never been published. (Hubbard claimed that Russian agents stole the original manuscript; he had a carbon copy of it, but nevertheless wouldn't allow it to be published because the knowledge it contained was too dangerous. You see, several of the chosen few who read the manuscript went insane.) Later on, in 1962, Hubbard told an audience that he and his third wife, whom he met in 1951, came up with *scientology*: "And there was the founding of that word." (But then, in the very next sentence, he says that he had been using it "to some degree before.") Depending on which version you believe, Upward invented the word *scientology* either thirty years or forty-three years before Hubbard used it.

EVERYTHING YOU KNOW ABOUT GOD IS WRONG

All this is not really science, but only scientology. It is language. It is the magic lullaby in which the shapes of things melt and reshape themselves forever. And so, when we would try to stop that wheel we call the mind, and look between the spokes, at once the All-Thing in its turn begins to spin about us, and all which it contains to slide and glide away:—as in that wondrous story of creation handed down from Finnish sorcerers of old, when the wizard Lemminkainen comes into the hall and

IV

The Going Crumb View, with its straight lines, which are curves; its crumbs which are images formed in the mind out of real crumbs and arithmetical ciphers; its Andronican elasticity, its man-faced energy of motion, and its double-faced velocity; all brought together to account for a not-quite-true law; is a fair sample, taken at haphazard, of scientological writing. It is no whit better than theological writing. And unhappily scientology is as often mistaken for science as theology is for worship.

We have now dealt with the Idealism that looks within, and the Materialism that looks without, itself. In both cases our quarrel was in words; but whereas Idealism was all words, we quarrelled with it altogether; and whereas Materialism was a mixture of facts and words, we had no quarrel with its facts. We distinguished between science and scientology.

The images above were scanned directly from the 1910 edition of The New Word; they show each occurrence of scientology (on pages 139, 149, and 156, respectively).

11

END MATTER

ARTICLE HISTORIES

• "Bits and Pieces" by Russ Kick was written especially for this volume.

• "Bridging the Leap of Faith" by Bobbie Kirkhart was written especially for this volume.

• "Broward County, Florida" by Jeff Sharlet and Peter Manseau originally appeared in *Killing the Buddha: A Heretic's Bible* (Free Press, 2004).

• "Comforting Thoughts About Death That Have Nothing to Do With God" by Greta Christina originally appeared in the *Skeptical Inquirer*, Vol. 29, No. 2 (March/April 2005).

• "Confessions of an Atheist" by Paul Krassner was written especially for this volume.

• "'End of the World Prophet Found in Error, Not Insane': A Failed Prophet's Survival Handbook" by John Gorenfeld was written especially for this volume.

• "Everyone's a Skeptic—About Other Religions" by James A. Haught is a slightly modified transcript of a talk given to the Campus Freethought Alliance, Marshall University chapter (Huntington, West Virginia), on September 10, 1997.

• "Faith = Illness: Why I've Had It With Religious Tolerance" by Douglas Rushkoff originally appeared on the author's blog [www.rushkoff.com/blog.php].

• "Faith and Curses" by Thérèse Taylor was written especially for this volume. Its genesis was the author's short article "The Sharon Death Curse" in *Fortean Times*, January 2006.

• "'Fondling the Fellows in Folly': In Which God Wonders, Why Be Gay When Straight Sex Is So Great?" by Jack Murnighan was written especially for this volume.

• "Found Religion" by *FOUND Magazine* is comprised of pieces from the magazine and from FOUND'S website [www.foundmagazine.com].

• "Friendly Feudalism: The Tibet Myth" by Michael Parenti originally appeared on the author's website [www.michaelparenti.org].

• "Gerin Oil" by Richard Dawkins originally appeared in *Free Inquiry* (December 2003).

• "The God From Galilee" by Ruth Hurmence Green originally appeared in *The Born Again Skeptic's Guide to the Bible* (Freedom From Religion Foundation, 1979).

• "God Has Left the Building: The Self-Imposed Death of Institutional Judaism" by Douglas Rushkoff originally appeared in the *New York Press*, June 11–17, 2003.

• "The God Machine: Building the Mechanical Messiah in 1850s Massachusetts" by Robert Damon Schneck originally appeared in *Fortean Times*, May 2002, and the author's book, *The President's Vampire: Strange-but-True Tales of the United States of America* (Anomalist Books, 2005).

- "Good Books" by Russ Kick was written especially for this volume.

- "Holy Blood, Holy Code" by David V. Barrett was written especially for this volume.

- "Holy Shit: Excrement and Religion" by John G. Bourke is comprised of excerpts from *Scatalogic Rites of All Nations* (W.H. Lowdermilk & Co., 1891).

- "The Honesty of Atheism" by Dianna Narciso was written especially for this volume.

- "'Incomplete Jews' and 'International Monetarists': Veiled Anti-Semitism in the *Left Behind* Series" by Michael Standaert is an expanded version of an article that originally appeared on the nthposition website [www.nthposition.com].

- "'Irish Gulags for Women': The Catholic Church's Magdalene Asylums" by Sam Jordison was written especially for this volume.

- "It Ain't Necessarily So: Music's Debt to Nonbelievers" by Dan Barker was written especially for this volume, with the exception of a few individual sections that previously appeared in *Freethought Today*.

- "Jesus of Nazareth Discusses His Failure" by H.G. Wells is an excerpt from *The Happy Turning: A Dream of Life* (W. Heinemann, 1945).

- "Journey to Bethlehem" by Neil Gaiman and Steve Gibson originally appeared in *Outrageous Tales From the Old Testament* (Knockabout Publications, 1987).

- "Jungle Drums of the Evil I" by Earl Kemp was written especially for this volume.

- "Legion's Legacy: Possession and Exorcism" by Benjamin Radford was written especially for this volume.

- "Martin Luther Goes Bowling" by Bill Brent was written especially for this volume.

- "My Weekend With Osho" by Sam Jordison was written especially for this volume.

- "Philadelphia Grand Jury Report on Abusive Priests and the Cardinals Who Enabled Them" is comprised of excerpts of "Report of the Grand Jury," Misc. No. 03-00-239, In the Court of Common Pleas, First Judicial District of Pennsylvania, Criminal Trial Division, September 17, 2003.

- "Posting the Ten Commandments" by Peter Eckstein is a greatly expanded version of an article that originally appeared on the Michigan Prospect website [www.michiganprospect.org].

- "The Private Parts on the Pope's Altar" by Kristan Lawson was written especially for this volume.

- "Reformation Hymns: Islam, Iran, and Blogs" by Nasrin Alavi is comprised of excerpts from articles and the author's book, *We Are Iran: The Persian Blogs* (Soft Skull Press, 2005).

- "Sacred Spots: Corpses, Thorns, BMW Coffins, a Hymen-Restoring Spring, and Other Religious Relics and Places" by Kristan Lawson was written especially for this volume.

- "Taking Up Serpents: A Photo Gallery of Snake-Handlers" by Robert W. Pelton is comprised of photographs from *The Persecuted Prophets: The Story of the Frenzied Serpent Handlers* (A.S. Barnes, 1976).

- "The US Is a Free Country, *Not* a Christian Nation" by Michael E. Buckner and Edward M. Buckner was written especially for this volume.

- "The Verge Extreme: California's Religion of Transformation" by Erik Davis is comprised of excerpts from the author's book *The Visionary State: A Journey Through California's Spiritual Landscape* (photographs by Michael Rauner) (Chronicle Books, 2006).

- "Voluptuous Ecstasy on the Temple: Erotic Aspects of Hindu Sculpture" by Lawrence E. Gichner is comprised of excerpts from the author's book *Erotic Aspects of Hindu Sculpture* (privately published, 1949).

- "Wanting the Topmost Peach: The Erotic Poetry of the Sixth Dalai Lama" by Coleman Barks is comprised of excerpts from the author's book *Stallion on a Frozen Lake: Love Songs of the Sixth Dalai Lama* (Maypop Books, 1992).

- "Who Wrote the Gospels?: (Hint: It Wasn't Matthew, Mark, Luke, or John)" by Gary Greenberg was written especially for this volume.

- "With the Sword: Attending a Muslim Students' Conference" by Tasha Fox was written especially for this volume.

CONTRIBUTORS

Nasrin Alavi is the author of *We Are Iran* (Soft Skull Press, 2007).

Dan Barker is co-president of the Freedom From Religion Foundation [ffrf.org] and author of *Losing Faith in Faith: From Preacher to Atheist* (FFRF, Inc., 1992). He is also a professional jazz musician and songwriter living in Madison, Wisconsin. He has produced two freethought musical CDs for FFRF: *Friendly, Neighborhood Atheist* and *Beware of Dogma*.

Born in 1937 in Chattanooga, Tennessee, and educated at the University of North Carolina and at the University California, Berkeley, **Coleman Barks** has for the last thirty-one years collaborated with various scholars of the Persian language (most notably, John Moyne) to bring over into American free verse the poetry of Jelaluddin Rumi. This work has resulted in nineteen volumes, culminating with the bestselling *Essential Rumi* in 1995, two appearances on Bill Moyers' Public Television specials, and inclusion in the prestigious *Norton Anthology of World Masterpieces*. The Rumi translations have sold over three-quarters of a million copies. It is claimed that over the last ten years Rumi has been the most-read poet in the United States. Dr. Barks taught American Literature and Creative Writing at various universities for thirty-four years, and he has published five volumes of poetry. In 2004 he received the Juliet Hollister Award for his work in the interfaith area. In March 2005 the US State Department sent him to Afghanistan as the first visiting speaker there in twenty-five years. In May 2006 he was awarded an honorary doctorate by the University of Tehran. He is now a retired Professor Emeritus at the University of Georgia in Athens. He has two grown sons and four grandchildren, all of whom live near him in Athens, Georgia.

David V. Barrett has been a schoolteacher, a programmer and intelligence analyst, and a journalist. He is now a freelance writer. His many books include *The New Believers* (2001), a 544-page study of new religious movements and their problems in society, and *Secret Societies* (1997), an investigation into the history, aims, and ideals of Rosicrucianism, Freemasonry, and other esoteric movements throughout history. His critical work has appeared in mainstream and alternative newspapers, magazines, and websites in the UK and the US. He has contributed to numerous encyclopedias on alternative beliefs, new religions, and science fiction and fantasy. His short fiction has appeared in a variety of books and magazines in several countries. He is currently researching for a Ph.D. in sociology of religion at the London School of Economics. When not researching and writing, he plays fretless bass in a rock-jazz-blues band. He lives in London.

John G. Bourke (1846-1896) was a distinguished military man and a gentleman scholar who taught himself several languages, including Latin, Gaelic, and Apache. He received the Medal of Honor for his performance during the Civil War (he had joined the Fifteenth Pennsylvania Cavalry when he was sixteen). After graduating from West Point, he served in the Third United States Cavalry for the rest of his life, eventually achieving the rank of colonel. Beginning in the 1880s, Bourke penned several books and numerous papers and articles on his military engagements and on Native American beliefs, rituals, and language.

In addition to be an avid, addicted bowler, and a collector and chronicler of the sport, **Bill Brent** founded *Black Sheets* magazine and edited all seventeen issues between 1993 and 2000. He's the author of *The Ultimate Guide to Anal Sex for Men* (Cleis Press, 2002). His fiction appears in The *Best American Erotica 1997*, *Tough Guys*, *Best Gay Erotica 2002 and 2004*, *Best S/M Erotica*, and *Rough Stuff*, plus its sequel, *Roughed Up*. He coedited the *Best Bisexual Erotica* series with Dr. Carol Queen, the second volume being a finalist in the fourteenth Lambda Literary Awards. His articles have appeared in the *San Francisco Bay*

Guardian, the *San Francisco Bay Times*, other magazines, *P.O.V.*, and at [goodvibes.com]. He has authored several chapbooks of poems and short prose, and published a number of books, including *Hot Off the Net*, edited by Russ Kick (see [www.blackbooks.com/catalog]). Want his email newsletter? Drop him a line at <verbose@comcast.net>, or check out [www.authorsden.com/billbrent] for more of his prose and other writing.

Ed Buckner, son of a low-church Episcopal clergyman, was born in Fitzgerald, Georgia, in 1946. In 1968, he married Lois Diane Bright Buckner, and they have a son, Michael E. Buckner. Buckner received his B.A. from Rice University, 1967; his M.Ed. from Georgia State University, 1975; and his Ph.D. at Georgia State University, 1983. For the Freethought Press, he has edited books by Massimo Pigliucci, Keith Parsons, Carol Faulkenberry, and Edwin Kagin. With his wife Diane, he co-edited and published freethinker and retired FBI agent Oliver G. Halle's *Taking the Harder Right* (2006). With his son, Michael, he co-edited *Quotations That Support the Separation of State and Church* (1995). Also, he wrote the concluding chapter, "Winning the 'Battle Royal,'" for Kimberly Blaker's *Fundamentals of Extremism: The Christian Right in America* (2003). He is the author or co-author of chapters or entries in two other books (besides *Everything...*) published in 2007: "Secular Schooling" in *Parenting Beyond Belief*, edited by Dale McGowan, and several entries in *The New Encyclopedia of Unbelief*, edited by Tom Flynn. From 2001 to 2003, he was Executive Director of the Council for Secular Humanism. In addition to writing hundreds of letters to the editor, Buckner has debated and spoken around the United States about freethought and secular humanism, often about the Treaty of Tripoli and "This Is a Free Country, *Not* a Christian Nation." Buckner is a member of the Advisory Board for the Secular Coalition for America and is on the Advisory Board of the Godless Americans Political Action Committee. Some of his writings and talks can be found at stephenjaygould.org, secularhumanism.org, nobeliefs.com, and infidels.org.

Michael E. Buckner, the son of Ed and Diane Buckner, was born at the Great Lakes Naval Hospital in Shields Township, Illinois, and currently lives in Decatur, Georgia. He graduated from the University of Chicago in 1992. With his father, Michael edited and compiled *Quotations That Support the Separation of State and Church* (1995), a work which has six sections: U.S. Constitution, Treaties, State Constitutions; Founding Fathers (and others of that era); Presidents and similar leaders; Supreme Court rulings; other famous Americans; and foreign sources. Also, he is the author of a widely circulated and reprinted essay about Independence Day called "The Unchristian Roots of the Fourth of July."

Greta Christina has been writing professionally since 1989. She is currently editing the new annual anthology series, *Best Erotic Comics*, scheduled to debut in November 2007. Her writing has appeared in magazines and newspapers including *Ms.*, *Penthouse*, and the *Skeptical Inquirer*, and in numerous anthologies, including two volumes of the *Best American Erotica series*. She is editor of the anthology *Paying For It: A Guide by Sex Workers for Their Clients*, and author of the erotic novella "Bending," which appeared in the three-novella collection *Three Kinds of Asking For It*, edited by Susie Bright. She is blogging obsessively about atheism, sex, politics, science, and celebrity crushes at [gretachristina.typepad.com].

Erik Davis is an award-winning writer, teacher, and performance lecturer based in San Francisco. He is the author, most recently, of *The Visionary State: A Journey through California's Spiritual Landscape* (Chronicle Books), with photographs by Michael Rauner. He also wrote *Led Zeppelin IV*, an entry in Continuum's *33 1/3* series, and *TechGnosis: Myth, Magic, and Mysticism in the Age of Information* (Harmony), a cult classic of visionary media studies that has been translated into five languages. His essays on music, media, technoculture, and spirituality have appeared in over a dozen books, including *AfterBurn: Reflections on Burning Man* (University of New Mexico Press), *Zig Zag Zen* (Chronicle Books), *The Disinformation Book of Lies* (The Disinformation Company), *010101: Art in Technological Times* (SFMOMA), and *Prefiguring Cyberculture* (MIT Press). Davis has contributed to scores of publications, including *Bookforum*, *ArtForum*, *Wired*, *Salon*, *Strange Attractor*, *Blender*, *Yeti*, *LA Weekly*, and the *Village Voice*. He has taught at UC Berkeley, UC Davis, the California Institute of Integral Studies, and Esalen. He regularly posts to www.techgnosis.com, where many of his articles and essays can be found.

Richard Dawkins FRS is the Charles Simonyi Professor of the Public Understanding of Science at Oxford University. His most recent book is *The God Delusion* (Houghton Mifflin, 2006).

Peter Eckstein is a retired economics professor and labor economist who lives in Ann Arbor, Michigan. He has a bachelor's degree in economics from the University of Michigan and a master's degree in sociology and doctorate in economics from Harvard University.

FOUND Magazine. "We collect found stuff: love letters, birthday cards, kids' homework, to-do lists, ticket stubs, poetry on napkins, doodles—anything that gives a glimpse into someone else's life. Anything goes. We certainly didn't invent the idea of found stuff being cool. Every time we visit our friends in other towns, someone's always got some kind of unbelievable discovered note or photo on their fridge. We decided to make a bunch of projects so that everyone can check out all the strange, hilarious and heartbreaking things people have picked up and passed our way."

After many years in retail, **Tasha Fox** is a homemaker in British Columbia.

Bestselling author **Neil Gaiman** has long been one of the top writers in modern comics, as well as writing books for readers of all ages. He is listed in the *Dictionary of Literary Biography* as one of the top ten living postmodern writers, and is a prolific creator of works of prose, poetry, film, journalism, comics, song lyrics, and drama. His *New York Times*–bestselling 2001 novel for adults, *American Gods*, was awarded the Hugo, Nebula, Bram Stoker, SFX, and Locus awards, was nominated for many other awards, including the World Fantasy Award and the Minnesota Book Award, and appeared on many best-of-year lists. Gaiman was the creator/writer of monthly cult DC Comics horror-weird series, *Sandman*, which won nine Will Eisner Comic Industry Awards, including the award for best writer four times, and three Harvey Awards. *Sandman* #19 took the 1991 World Fantasy Award for best short story, making it the first comic ever to be awarded a literary award. Norman Mailer said of *Sandman*: "Along with all else, *Sandman* is a comic strip for intellectuals, and I say it's about time." Gaiman's other works include *Anansi Boys*, *Good Omens* (with Terry Pratchett), *Neverwhere*, *Stardust*, and the scripts for *Mirrormask* and the upcoming *Beowulf*.

Manchester native **Steve Gibson** has written and drawn for Knockabout Comics and *Oink!*. The Lambiek Comiclopedia writes: "He has represented Great Britain since 1990 at Italy's HUMOURfest exhibition/competition, winning 2nd prize in 1996 for 'Last Tango in EuroDisney,' which the British press refused to publish. In recent years, he has produced commercial work."

Lawrence E. Gichner (1907-1992) wrote and self-published three pioneering books in the mid-twentieth century: *Erotic Aspects of Hindu Sculpture* (1949), *Erotic Aspects of Japanese Culture* (1953), and *Erotic Aspects of Chinese Culture* (1957).

John Gorenfeld is the author of a forthcoming book about Reverend Moon and his Washington adventures. He's a magazine journalist who lives in the Bay Area.

Ruth Hurmence Green (1915-1981). The Iowa native received a journalism degree from Texas Tech in 1935, married, had three children, and settled in Missouri. Ruth, a "half-hearted Methodist," first plodded through the bible when convalescing from cancer in her early sixties, calling the shock she suffered from reading the book worse than the trauma caused by her illness. "There wasn't a page of the bible that didn't offend me in some way. There is no other book between whose covers life is so cheap," Ruth discovered, prompting her to write the enduring modern freethought classic, *The Born Again Skeptic's Guide to the Bible* (1979). When terminal cancer developed in 1981, Ruth, who always insisted, "There *are* atheists in foxholes," took her own life, swallowing painkillers. In her last letter to Anne Gaylor of the Freedom From Religion Foundation on July 4, 1981, Ruth wrote: "Freedom depends upon freethinkers."

A New York City criminal defense attorney and President of the Biblical Archaeology Society of New York (BASNY), **Gary Greenberg** has long been interested in the intersection between ancient myth and ancient history, especially as it applies to Egyptian influences on the writing of the bible. The problem, he says, is figuring out how to separate the myth from the history. In 2006, he served as a consultant to National Geographic Television's *Science of the Bible* series. He has also lectured frequently on ancient history, mythology, and biblical studies and has also presented papers at several academic conferences concerned with Egyptian and/or biblical affairs. He has also written for several Egyptological journals. In 1978 he ran for Governor of New York on the Libertarian Party ticket. Greenberg is the author of *The Moses Mystery: The African Origins of the Jewish People* (Birch Lane Press, 1997); reprinted in paperback as *The Bible Myth: The African Origins of the Jewish People* (Citadel Press, 1998), *101 Myths of the Bible: How Ancient Scribes Invented Biblical*

History (Sourcebooks, 2000, paperback edition 2002), *The Sins of King David: A New History* (Sourcebooks 2002), *Manetho: A Study in Egyptian Chronology* (Shangri-La Publications, 2002), and *The Judas Brief: Who Really Killed Jesus?* (Continuum, 2007). You can read excerpts from his books along with some of his other writings on the ancient Near East and some of his academic papers at [biblemyth.com]. His blog is at [bibleandhistory.com].

James A. Haught. "I'm an old newspaper editor who has spent half a century chronicling social struggles and cultural tides. Personally, I've waged a long crusade for rational, scientific thinking as an antidote for harmful supernaturalism. I've written five books and many magazine articles against religion, astrology, mysticism, psychic claims, cults, 'New Agery,' fundamentalism, and other magical beliefs."

Sam Jordison is a writer and freelance journalist. He is the author of *The Joy of Sects*, *Crap Towns*, *Bad Dates*, and his next book will be called *Annus Horribilis*. He has written for a number of papers in the UK, most often the *Guardian*, the *Daily Telegraph*, and the *Scotsman*. He also sometimes works as a goatherd in the South of France.

Earl Kemp, a national nuisance, has been known by many (dis)guises: adventurer, explorer, lover, beloved, literary rebel, First Amendment convict savant, and numerous others, mostly all bad. He is best known as the notorious producer, during the Golden Age of Sleaze Paperbacks, of more than 5,000 novels and half again that many *Naked* people magazines. In his dotage, he dribbles memoirs at [efanzines.com/EK/index.html] and has become The (uppercase) Chronicler of the entire genre.

Bobbie Kirkhart is a former Sunday school teacher whose first national publication, an article titled "I Protest: A Santa Claus God," was in *Christianity Today*. Since discovering the bright light of reason, she has been active in many freethought groups. She is currently vice president of the Secular Coalition for America and has served as co-president of Atheists United, and as president of the Atheist Alliance International. In addition to her regular President's Messages in the *Rational Alternative* and in *Secular Nation*, her work has been printed in *Free Inquiry* and *American Atheist* magazines. She is a contributing author of *The Fundamentals of Extremism: The Christian Right in America*, published by New Boston Books. In her personal life, she is a retired teacher in Los Angeles Unified School District's Adult Division. She is married to a fellow atheist and has one adult daughter, also an atheist.

Paul Krassner is the author of *One Hand Jerking: Reports From an Investigative Satirist*. He publishes *The Disneyland Memorial Orgy* at [paulkrassner.com].

Kristan Lawson is the author or co-author of several books, including *Weird Europe*, *California Babylon*, and *Darwin and Evolution for Kids*.

Peter Manseau, the author of *Vows: The Story of a Priest, a Nun, and Their Son* (Free Press, 2005), is currently writing a novel about Yiddish in America.

Jack Murnighan has a B.A. in semiotics and a Ph.D. in medieval literature but long ago took off his mortarboard and now teaches freelance writing at the University of the Arts. For quite a few years he was editor of the online literary magazine Nerve and has written for many websites and for *Esquire*, *Glamour*, *Interiors*, and *Jockey* magazines. His fiction has appeared in seven anthologies and might even make up a book of its own one day. He edited a short-story anthology, *Full Frontal Fiction*, and has published two books on the history of sex in great books: *The Naughty Bits* and *Classic Nasty*. He lives in New York City.

Dianna Narciso is the author of *Like Rolling Uphill: Realizing the Honesty of Atheism*. She maintains the websites at atheistview.com and diannanarciso.com. She is founder and president of Space Coast Freethought Association in Florida at spacecoastfreethought.org.

Michael Parenti is an internationally known award-winning author and lecturer whose books include *The Culture Struggle*, *Superpatriotism*, *The Assassination of Julius Caesar: A People's History of Ancient Rome*, *The Terrorism Trap*, *Democracy for the Few*, *Against Empire*, and *Make-Believe Media*. He is one of the nation's leading progressive political analysts. He received his Ph.D. in political science from Yale University and has taught at a number of colleges and universities, in the United States and abroad. His website is michaelparenti.org.

Robert W. Pelton is the author of *The Persecuted Prophets: The Story of the Frenzied Serpent Handlers* (with Karen W. Carden), *Civil War Period Cookery*, *Historical Thanksgiving Cookery*, *Traitors and Treason*, and many other books.

Benjamin Radford is managing editor of two science magazines, the *Skeptical Inquirer* and the Spanish-language *Pensar*. He has written over 300 articles on various topics, including urban legends, mass hysteria, mysterious creatures, and media criticism. Radford is author of three books: *Hoaxes, Myths, and Manias: Why We Need Critical Thinking* (co-authored with Robert Bartholomew), *Media Mythmakers: How Journalists, Activists, and Advertisers Mislead Us*, and *Lake Monster Mysteries* (co-authored with Joe Nickell). The website for his books is radfordbooks.com.

Douglas Rushkoff is the author of a dozen books on media and society. His controversial text on Judaism, *Nothing Sacred*, poses that the religion was originally intended as an antidote to racism, nationalism, and superstition—even though it is being used to support them today. The *Forward* chose him as one of America's Fifty Most Influential Jews, and the Transcendental Judaism movement ordained him as a rabbi.

Robert Damon Schneck, America's Historian of the Strange, is the author of *The President's Vampire: Strange-but-True Tales of the United States of America*, as well as books for young readers, including *Detective Notebook: Are You Psychic?* He is a freelance writer who contributes to *Fate* and *Fortean Times*.

Jeff Sharlet, a contributing editor to *Harper's* and *Rolling Stone*, is the author of the forthcoming *Jesus Plus Nothing* (HarperCollins), a history of theocratic politics in America.

Michael Standaert's book examining the *Left Behind* series and Tim LaHaye's political activism, *Skipping Towards Armageddon: The Politics and Propaganda of the Left Behind Novels and the LaHaye Empire*, was published by Soft Skull Press in 2006. His satirical novel, *The Adventures of the Pisco Kid*, was released by Arriviste Press in 2007.

Thérèse Taylor is the author of a scholarly biography of a French saint, *Bernadette of Lourdes: Her Life, Visions and Death*. She has published articles on religion, folklore, and studies of life writing. She teaches history at Charles Sturt University, Australia.

H.G. Wells (1866–1946) is best-remembered as a late-Victorian pioneer of science fiction, mainly due to his 1890s novels *The Time Machine*, *The Invisible Man*, and *The War of the Worlds*. These are just a sliver of the approximately 180 books he wrote, covering topics such as politics, science, history, and the future.

ABOUT THE EDITOR

Besides the books below, Russ has written articles and a column for the *Village Voice* and several independent magazines. The Memory Hole [www.thememoryhole.org], a website devoted to rescuing knowledge and freeing information, is his labor of love. His personal website is [www.mindpollen.com]. Russ made world headlines in April 2004 when his Freedom of Information Act request/appeal resulted in the release of 288 photos of the US war dead coming home in flag-draped coffins. The previous Halloween, Russ had made the front page of the *New York Times* when he digitally uncensored a heavily redacted Justice Department report. He also runs Kick Books, whose first title was a math geek's dream: *Pi to Five Million Places*.

Books as Author

- *Outposts: A Catalogue of Rare and Disturbing Alternative Information*
- *Psychotropedia: Publications from the Periphery*
- *50 Things You're Not Supposed to Know*
- *The Disinformation Book of Lists: Subversive Facts and Hidden Information in Rapid-Fire Format*
- *50 Things You're Not Supposed to Know, vol. 2*

Books as Editor

- *Hot Off the Net: Erotica and Other Sex Writings From the Internet*
- *You Are Being Lied To: The Disinformation Guide to Media Distortion, Historical Whitewashes and Cultural Myths*
- *Everything You Know Is Wrong: The Disinformation Guide to Secrets and Lies*
- *Abuse Your Illusions: The Disinformation Guide to Media Mirages and Establishment Lies*
- *Everything You Know About Sex Is Wrong: The Disinformation Guide to the Extremes of Human Sexuality (and Everything in Between)*